Jürgen Sorgenfrei
Port Business

Jürgen Sorgenfrei

Port Business

—

2nd revised and enlarged edition

DE
G
PRESS

ISBN 978-1-5474-1702-5
e-ISBN (PDF) 978-1-5474-0087-4
e-ISBN (EPUB) 978-1-5474-0089-8

Library of Congress Control Number: 2018949268

Bibliographic information published by the Deutsche Nationalbibliothek
The Deutsche Nationalbibliothek lists this publication in the Deutsche Nationalbibliografie;
detailed bibliographic data are available on the Internet at http://dnb.dnb.de.

© 2018 Jürgen Sorgenfrei
Published by Walter de Gruyter Inc., Boston/Berlin
Printing and binding: CPI books GmbH, Leck
Typesetting: MacPS, LLC, Carmel

www.degruyter.com

for:

Anke
Alex
Gigi

About De|G PRESS

Five Stars as a Rule

De|G PRESS, the startup born out of one of the world's most venerable publishers, De Gruyter, promises to bring you an unbiased, valuable, and meticulously edited work on important topics in the fields of business, information technology, computing, engineering, and mathematics. By selecting the finest authors to present, without bias, information necessary for their chosen topic *for professionals*, in the depth you would hope for, we wish to satisfy your needs and earn our five-star ranking.

In keeping with these principles, the books you read from De|G PRESS will be practical, efficient and, if we have done our job right, yield many returns on their price.

We invite businesses to order our books in bulk in print or electronic form as a best solution to meeting the learning needs of your organization, or parts of your organization, in a most cost-effective manner.

There is no better way to learn about a subject in depth than from a book that is efficient, clear, well organized, and information rich. A great book can provide life-changing knowledge. We hope that with De|G PRESS books you will find that to be the case.

DOI 10.1515/9781547400874-203

Contents

Preface to the Second Edition

Five years ago, when the first edition of this book was published, there was widely accepted confidence in the maritime markets that in 2015, or 2016 at the latest, the global conditions for ports and shipping would be back to normal. This meant: back to the situation before the Financial Crisis, and all the problems in its aftermath. But this did not happen! Ten years later the maritime industry, and so ports, still suffer. All types of ports were directly or indirectly affected.

According to the International Chamber of Shipping around 90% of world trade is maritime trade, and ports are the gateways to the markets for the shipping industry. Everyone who eats Argentinian meat, uses an Asian manufactured mobile phone or laptop, who drives a European car or wears clothes made in South Asia indirectly participates in the advantages the efficient maritime supply chains offer. However, despite the huge economic importance, the economic framework for the maritime industry and so for the commercial ports around the world is still challenging. There have been periods of favorable market performance over the past decade for shipping, but they led to an overbuilding of new vessels, and these ships needed to be employed. The result for some ports was a gain of new services, while others lost the calls. Rate collapses followed vessel oversupply, and the pressure on all partners along the supply chain deteriorated. Nevertheless, the pressure to invest in new equipment in order to serve the vessels and to create a wider network of potential ports of call was still there.

In the past, ports often were considered as gateways to the world, growth poles, job-machines, tax generators, facilitators of trade, but the positive image has been tarnished. At the same time multiple new mega trends evolved. For instance, the Chinese government announced the huge trade and transport initiative "OBOR" One Belt, One Road. The melting ice in the Arctic already today offers new alternatives for East Asia—Europe trade, with the consequence of new routes. A series of international regulations will kick in, and the maritime industry will need to follow several new emission rules set by the International Maritime Organization, and ports will need to collect the waste. On shore power supply for vessels becomes an increasingly important topic, but as there is no standard, ports are confronted with multiple technical solutions. New emission rules will lead to revised bunker activities very soon, and ports are requested to provide the necessary infrastructure. Big ships like the 20,000+ TEU container vessel offer economy of scale savings for the ship owners, and ports need to invest in bigger cranes, larger terminals and deeper water or miss participating in the efficiency increase. The need for attractive inner-city residential areas squeezes especially old ports to vacate their attractive locations and to find new areas for their business.

DOI 10.1515/9781547400874-205

This book provides a unique study of the business of ports: what makes them work, what makes them fail, and how they might operate in the future. For this purpose, the first chapters look back into the history of ports, then provide a status quo view of ports today. Part 2 concentrates on the supply chain view and provides trade and transportation background information, explaining the role ports play along the transportation chain and focuses finally on the cargos that are transported and the problems that may occur in cargo measurement.

Part 3 explains basic port management models, discusses trends, analyzes the fundamentals of port governance and port operations and discusses the role of port lobbying. The explanations of port business end in Part 4 with a discussion of mega trends that already or may in future impact ports and terminals.

As the title "Port Business" indicates, this book is written for everybody with interests in trade and transportation and the role ports play in the global supply chain. It shall explain what ports are, which role they can play and what the restrictions are, how they are managed, what drives the business and which trends influence them.

Preface

The world economy has globalized at a tremendous pace over the past 30 years, exporting over a quarter of its merchandise output in 2010, up from 17% in 1980. Economies have become more interdependent and the digital revolution has brought buyers and sellers from around the globe closer together. While some 16% of world trade passes overland, 6.7% through pipelines, and 0.3 via air, it is estimated that world seaborne trade by volume amounts to 77% of total world trade. In 2010, this meant a total of 7.9 bn tonnes were transported by sea in the world. With the globalization of the world economy, a nation's economic competitiveness is linked increasingly to its ability to ship raw materials, intermediate goods, and final products efficiently and economically, and to receive these goods in productive, efficient and cost-effective ports. Excessive port costs on the other hand, or delays, can prompt investors to locate new production facilities in other countries or regions. Ports failing to adapt these trends and falling back in modernization could be left behind.

Throughout history, port locations have been selected to optimize access to land and navigable water, for commercial or military demand, and for shelter from wind and waves. Ports handled every kind of traffic and every kind of cargo, provided all kinds of logistics services, and have been an inherent part of historic city life. Today, in times of raising vessel sizes, ports struggle with deeper water and the pressure to be more efficient at lower costs. Medium-sized ports face new pressures of specialization and targeting selected market niches, while the very few so-called Mega-Ports have to offer the whole range of activities, yet remain specialists for all kinds of goods that are traded around the world.

Commercial databases list more than 11,000 commercial ports and terminals around the world, and port business increases in complexity every year. It is the intention of this book to put the port business into the right perspective and provide insight. For this purpose, the first part looks back into the history of ports then provides a status quo of ports today. Part two concentrates on the supply chain view and provides trade and transportation background information, explaining the role ports play along the transportation chain and focusing finally on the cargoes that are transported and the problems that may occur in cargo measurement.

Part three explains basic port management models, discusses trends and analyzes the fundamentals of port governance and port operations and discusses the role of port lobbying. The explanations of port business end in part four with a discussion of mega trends that already or may in future impact ports and terminals.

DOI 10.1515/9781547400874-206

As the title "Port Business" indicates, this book is written for everybody with interests in trade and transportation and the role ports play in the global supply chain. It shall explain what ports are, which role they can play and what the restrictions are, how they are managed, what drives the business and which trends influence them. Whilst all the information is published in good faith the author cannot accept any liability for any errors contained herein. The author can be contacted via mail: www.juergen.sorgenfrei@gmail.com and would love to receive comments and suggestions for improvements.

Part 1: **Development of Ports**

Chapter 1
History of Ports: The Ten Aims of a Port

The maritime movement of goods and people has always been the cheapest and most convenient form of transportation, and for that reason the world has built ports since at least 6,000 BC. The advancements made to ports over their historical development reveal their major functions and what drives port business. Below are the highlights of ancient port development: a brief history of the moments and motivations that led us to the harbors of today. In all, there are ten objectives that ports could be designed to accomplish. They will be introduced as we proceed through the chapter.

It is more than fifty years ago that Fritz Voigt published his famous textbook about transport science theory and global traffic development, named "Verkehr." In the first half of Part II he gave an overview about the historic development of all modes of transportation. Already in the preliminary remarks he stated: "*Der geschichtliche Teil soll ... vorzugsweise die Theorie der Verkehrswirtschaft ergänzen und die volkswirtschaftliche Gestaltungskraft des Verkehrs systems ... aufzeigen*" (Voigt 1965, page 3), loosely translated: "The historical studies should preferably complement the theory of transport science and demonstrate the economic power of the transport system." His understanding was that theory should always be measured at reality. Landing stages and ports evolved alongside the technology of the ships that they served. Initially, ports were simple wooden posts that served to tie rafts, dugout logs or curved wooden branches covered with the hides of animals.[1] As river traffic increased, simple piers were built to accommodate deeper ships that carried larger and heavier loads. The first two of the ten targets were accomplished back in Ancient Egypt.

1.1 Ancient Egypt

Egyptian history dates to about 4000 BC, when the kingdoms of Upper and Lower Egypt, already highly sophisticated, were united. The earliest known pyramids in Egypt are the pyramids of Saqqara, located approximately 20 km south of modern-day Cairo. Of huge interest from a construction point of

---

[1] For a similar kind of ship please refer to: Heyerdahl, Thor: *Kon-Tiki: Across the Pacific by Raft*, Rand McNally & Company, USA, Chicago 1950.

DOI 10.1515/9781547400874-001

view is also the so-called forgotten pyramid in Abu Rawash; built by Khufu's[2] son Djedefre, and most likely destroyed during the reign of roman emperor Octavian. The area of Giza plateau, today a tourist highlight in Egypt, is a vast burial ground, serving as the necropolis for the ancient Egyptian capital Memphis. Saqqara features numerous pyramids, including the world-famous Step Pyramid of Djoser, built during the Third Dynasty, which spans approximately from 2686 to 2613 BC.

Before, by the time of the early dynastic period of Egyptian history, approximately 3100 BC, those with sufficient means were buried in bench-like structures known as Mastabas. The first documented Egyptian pyramid is attributed to the architect Imhotep, who planned what Egyptologists believe to be a tomb for the pharaoh Djoser. Imhotep is credited with being the first to conceive the notion of stacking Mastabas on top of each other—creating an edifice composed of several "steps" that decreased in size toward its apex. The result was the Step Pyramid of Djoser that was designed to serve as a gigantic stairway by which the soul of the deceased pharaoh could ascend to the heavens. Such was the importance of Imhotep's achievement that he was deified by later Egyptians. Both Mastabas and Pyramids functioned as tombs for pharaohs. In Ancient Egypt, a pyramid was referred to as *mer*, literally "place of ascendance."

Mastabas and Pyramids continue to be some of the most impressive human buildings.[3] Although it is impossible to measure the real weight of a pyramid, calculations show that still today in the 21st century the later built Great Pyramid of Khufu on the Giza plateau is still one of the largest structures ever raised by man. And it is the only one of the Seven Wonders of the Ancient World still in existence.

Having the impressive dimensions of the ancient Egyptian buildings in mind, and bearing in mind that we talk about a historic time that is approximately 5,000 years ago, consider: how did they erect these impressive buildings? Where did the material come from? How did they organize the transport from the mines to the construction field? And finally: what role did ancient harbors and ports play in the building of the pyramids?

At construction, the Great Pyramid is estimated to have weighed 5.9 million tons. Based on this estimate, building the structure in twenty years would require installing approximately 800 metric tons (mt) of stone every day. Similarly, since it consists of an estimated 2.3 million blocks, completing the building in twenty years would involve moving an average of more than twelve of the blocks into

---

2 Also known as "Cheops"/Greek language.

3 Latest sources indicate that more than 100 pyramids have been built in ancient Egypt. Most of them have been plundered and destroyed.

place each hour, day and night.[4] Additionally, many of the casing stones and inner chamber blocks of the Great Pyramid were fit together with extremely high precision. Based on measurements taken on the north eastern casing stones, the mean opening of the joints is only 0.5 millimeters wide (1/50th of an inch). Where did the millions of limestone and granite blocks come from, and how did the Egyptians organize deliveries of twelve blocks per hour, every hour, for twenty years? In modern words: how were the logistics organized?

It is generally believed that much of the limestone was transported from nearby quarries. The Tura limestone used for the casing was quarried across the river Nile. The largest granite stones in the pyramid, found in the "King's chamber," weigh 25 to 80 mt and were transported from Aswan, more than 500 miles away. Once the blocks were cut, they were carried by boat either up or down the Nile to the pyramid site. It is estimated that 5.5 million tons of limestone, 8,000 tons of granite (imported from Aswan), and 500,000 tons of mortar were used in the construction of the Great Pyramid. A huge part of this has been carried by ship on the river and on special canals, which allowed having the material directly at the construction field. At the end of the canal there must have been a special purpose unloading facility, that is, a specialized port.

Generally speaking, a harbor is a protected area of water. A port is a harbor, plus terminal facilities: piers, wharves, docks, store buildings, and an infrastructure of roads and rivers or canals. Therefore, a harbor is just a very important part of a port. On the Giza construction field there was no natural harbor. It can thus be concluded that the ancient Egyptians were the first civilization to construct purpose-built artificial canals and harbors, equipped with specialized handling facilities, that is, the first ports in human history.

Figure 1.1, a copy taken from a relief in Hatschepsut temple in Dar el-Bahari (Eggebrecht 1984, page 374), shows the ship transport of two obelisks on the river Nile. Calculations assume that both obelisks shown in the relief have a length of 29.50 m, and each of them is fixed on its own wooden sledge. The total weight of the obelisks is expected to sum up to 650 tons. On both sides of the ship transport there must have been specialized loading and unloading facilities; the first known heavy lift port facilities.

---

4 The first precision measurements of the pyramid were made by Egyptologist Sir Flinders Petrie in 1880–1882 and published as *The Pyramids and Temples of Gise*. Almost all reports that followed are based on his measurements.

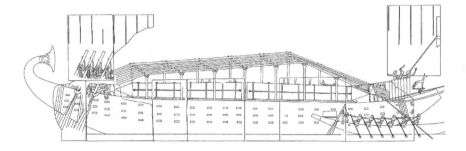

Figure 1.1: Egyptian ship carrying obelisks

It is very likely that the first ports that were built for the construction of the pyramids were the first specialized cargo handling facility for maritime trade in human history. No specialized facilities were necessary for the cargoes carried before the pyramids, also not for fishery boats. We do not know in which years the first ports were constructed, nor do we know where exactly these ports were located; but to honor the ancient Egyptians we will call these first commercial cargo ports with specialized facilities *Egyptian Pyramid Ports.*

Calculations from Egyptologists show that the capacity of a typical "Pyramid Port" like the specialized cargo port for the Great Khufu pyramid must have been able to unload on average seven vessels per day, each boat carrying ten blocks of stone (Illig 1999, page 46). It is very likely that for the great pyramid two specialized port facilities in Giza were in operation. Total annual capacities of these port facilities were:

7 vessel * 10 stones = 70 blocks of stone per day
Each block at least 2 metric tons * 70 blocks = 140 mt per day
365 days * 140 mt = 51,100 mt annual capacity

51,100 mt per year multiplied by twenty years of construction comes to a total volume of a little more than 1 mill ton. This means that only 17% of the total mass of 5.9 mill mt were carried by boat, or looked at the other way around: the majority of limestone blocks were broken near the construction field and were probably not carried by vessel.[5]

The quadrangular blocks of limestone were carved with copper chisels; copper because it was the only metal available 1,500 years before iron was discovered. The copper ore very likely arrived via the purpose-built port of Wadi al-Jarf at the west coast of the Red Sea; another example for port business elicited by the pharaohs for building their pyramids.[6] As a result, a typical Pyramid Port had an annual throughput of more than 50,000 ton per year. In today's categories, these ports were specialized general cargo handling facilities featuring heavy lift equipment. These ancient ports were part of an integral logistics chain with one final goal: to erect the pyramids as a holy tomb for the pharaoh. Even today, a capacity of 50,000 tons is a huge amount of cargo—and this was being transported at a time without specialized handling equipment and without any kind of power machines!

The core functions of all Pyramid Ports were to ensure the sovereignty of the ruler. Or in other words: ports in ancient Egypt did not fulfill any military or security function, nor were they used for large volumes of trade. The first step in historical port development came from the state's necessity to erect heavy symbols of power; and this—as always in history—combined with religion. Based on these findings two typical functions for port business in Ancient Egypt can be derived:

First target of ports = ensuring sovereignty
Second target of ports = enabling heavy lifts

1.2 Roman Empire

The Roman Empire was the post-Republican period of the ancient Roman civilization, characterized by an autocratic form of government and large territorial holdings in Europe and around the Mediterranean. The 500-year-old Roman Republic, which preceded it, had been weakened and subverted through several civil wars. Several events are commonly proposed to mark the transition from

---

5 More details about the way the granite stone blocks have been transported from Aswan port, how the boat construction with a raft in the middle between two typical sailing boats (today we would call this construction a catamaran) looked like, and how the loading and unloading in the ports was organized, can be found in the book from Illig, who considered the construction of pyramids from a historical engineering point of view (Illig 1999).

6 Tallet, Pierre and Gregory Marouard: *The Harbor of Khufu on the Red Sea Coast at Wadi al-Jarf, Egypt*, in: *Near Eastern Archaeology, American School of Oriental Research*, Vol. 77/1, pages 4–14, Boston, MA 2014.

Republic to Empire, including Julius Caesar's appointment as perpetual dicta-
tor (44 BC), the Battle of Actium (2 September 31 BC), and the Roman Senate's
granting to Octavian the honorific Augustus (16 January 27 BC). However, for our
historical overview it is sufficient to bear in mind that this historical era occurred
over 1,000 years after that of Ancient Egypt.

Roman expansion began in the days of the Republic, but the Empire reached
its greatest extent under Emperor Trajan: during his reign (98 to 117 AD) the
Roman Empire controlled approximately 6.5 million km² of land surface. Because
of the Empire's vast extent and long endurance, the institutions and culture of
Rome had a profound and lasting influence on the development of language, religion, architecture, philosophy, law, and forms of government in the territory it
governed. This influence was felt particularly in Europe, and later by means of
European expansionism, throughout the modern world.

Due to the vast size of the Empire, trade was vital for the success of Ancient
Rome—and thus, so were its ports. Trade was encouraged by many years of peace
within the Empire, and when it collapsed, trade throughout the areas that had
once made up the Roman Empire also collapsed.

The Roman Empire was crisscrossed with trade routes. There were sea routes
that covered the Mediterranean and Black seas, and the Romans built numerous
ports. Trade and transporting the Roman Army were the two principle reasons
for building ships, harbors, and roads. The most important harbor was Ostia as it
was the nearest major port to Rome itself.[7] Ostia was situated at the mouth of the
River Tiber and was only 15 miles from Rome. Many ships traveled between Ostia
and the major North African city of Carthage, a journey that took between three to
five days. Ships also arrived at Ostia from Spain and France. All their goods could
be quickly moved to Rome itself as they were taken in barges to the city up the
River Tiber after slaves had transferred the products from the merchant ships to
the barges. Ironically, the port of Ostia was to play a major part in the downfall of
Rome when Alaric the Goth captured the port in 409 AD knowing that controlling
this port would let him literally starve Rome by cutting off food shipments.

The Romans imported a variety of materials and transported them on man-
made port hinterland roads like the well-known and still today usable "Via Ostiensis" to the capital Rome: beef, corn, glassware, iron, lead, leather, marble,

---

7 Lehmann-Hartleben, Karl: *Die antiken Hafenanlagen des Mittelmeeres. Beiträge zur Geschichte des Städtebaus im Altertum. 1923.* Neudruck: Scientia-Verlag, Aalen, Germany 1963. K.
Lehmann-Hartleben published a synthesis of ancient harbors in the Mediterranean. His book
contains a catalog of 303 harbors. It mentions 184 out of at least 240 major ports in the eastern
Mediterranean, and 84 of around 180 major ports in the western Mediterranean Sea.

olive oil, perfumes, purple dye, silk, silver, spices, timber, tin, and wine were among the main imports (Figure 1.2). Rome's primary trading partners were in Spain, France, the Middle East, and North Africa. Britain exported lead, woolen products, and tin. In return, it imported wine, olive oil, pottery, and papyrus from Rome, while British traders relied on the Romans to provide security within the Empire.

Merchant ships and Roman port business reached their apogee during the Imperial period. Thanks to modern underwater excavations of ancient ship-wrecks, we know Rome had an extraordinary typological variety: from vessels used for short and medium-length coastal voyages with capacity up to 150 metric tons, to large merchant ships for longer distance like the huge amphora carriers with a capacity of up to 10,000 amphorae or 500 metric tons, or the huge grain carriers operating out of Syracuse, or Caligula's mega obelisk-carrier (1,300 t). Each year approximately 1,200 large vessels containing 50,000 modii (approx. 350 mt) reached Rome. If we consider that navigation was suspended during the four winter months (the famous mare clausum "closed sea," of the Romans), we reach an average of five large grain vessels per navigable day. This seems to be a relatively small number compared with the largest ports of today like Singapore where on average 180 cargo vessels per day have been served in 2017, but for most of the small- and medium-sized ports of today five large cargo carriers per day is still an impressive figure.

Figure 1.2: Via Ostiensis: The hinterland connection to the city of Rome

Very large ships required large ports. Their numbers were restricted—most harbors were constructed for the smaller ships. Generally speaking, the unloading of a ship of 150 mt would have taken two to four days, while a cargo of 250 mt required six to eight days. Certain cargoes required special loading and unloading facilities. Sacks of grain and lighter amphorae could be carried by dockhands. Heavier amphorae were carried by two men, using poles slipped through the handles. Mobile cranes were used for lifting heavy objects such as marble sarcophagi and wild animals in cages. For the unloading of an obelisk, weighing many tons, exceptionally strong manually operated wooden treadwheel cranes must have been built.

It is very likely that the Roman navy used warships of similar size to the merchant ships. The Roman navy not only aided in the supply and transport of the legions, but also helped in the protection of the frontiers in the rivers Rhine and Danube (in current-day Germany and Austria). During the First Punic War, the Roman navy was massively expanded and played a vital role in the Roman victory and the Roman Republic's ascension to hegemony in the Mediterranean Sea. During the imperial period, the Mediterranean became a peaceful "Roman lake"; in the absence of a maritime enemy, the navy was reduced mostly to patrol and transport duties. Another of its duties was the protection of the very important maritime trade routes against the threat of pirates. Therefore, it patrolled all the Mediterranean, parts of the North Atlantic (coasts of Hispania, Gaul, and Britannia), and had a naval presence in the Black Sea. Many of the Roman ports frequently hosted navy ships in their waters. Also, it is very likely that ports such as Ostia provided specialized handling facilities for all kinds of vessels, that is, adequate berthing facilities like stony quay walls and anchoring facilities, moles, and breakwaters, specialized warehouses, access to hinterland roads, numbers of ship chandlers, merchants, etc.[8]

The northern shore of the Mediterranean Sea is often steep, but contains many small natural harbors and landing places. The southern shore has very few natural harbors, and here artificial harbors had to be built. However, ports could be built with relative ease in the Mediterranean Sea, because of the almost complete absence of tides. Things were different outside the Strait of Gibraltar, for example, in Gades (Cádiz), at the mouth of the Guadalquivir river—this was a tidal port. Heavy weather and strong tides were a real threat for the sailing ships.

---

8 A good illustrated overview about ancient port facilities can be found under the address of the RGZM Römisch-Germanisches Zentralmuseum in Mainz, Germany. The title of the project is "The NAVIS II project": http://www2.rgzm.de/Navis2/Home/Frames.htm

What did create a problem for port access was the silt that the rivers took to the sea. The silt was carried along the coast by the Mediterranean current in a counterclockwise direction with the effect of frequently new sand banks, shallow waters, and an increased risk of stranding. Ports were therefore usually built at the opposite side of the delta. Alexandria's port, for example, was to the west of the Nile delta and therefore safe from the river silt. The Imperial ports of Ostia on the other hand suffered from their location north of the Tiber mouth: the counterclockwise current took silt to the harbors. During many centuries the coastline slowly moved seaward, and the harbors are today several kilometers inland.

The winds were another factor influencing harbor and port construction. Virtually all the best known ancient ports on the Tyrrhenian Sea shelter themselves from winds from the west and north. Often the construction of a harbor was a huge effort. The river port of Arles was, during the Republic, connected to the sea through channels, the Fossae Marianae. They made the Rhône delta navigable. The Romans sometimes used concrete that could set under water. Moles and breakwaters were constructed to provide protection against storms. Usually they were solid structures. Arched moles were built in the Bay of Naples during the early Empire. The idea behind the arches was that the water passing through them removed silt. The experiment was apparently not successful. In the second century, moles without a connection to the land were built, possibly with the same purpose.

Roman trade was the engine that drove the Roman economy of the late Republic and the early Roman Empire. Fashions and trends in archeology have tended to neglect the economic basis of the Empire in favor of the lingua franca of Latin and the exploits of the Roman legions. But the language and the legions were supported by trade while being part of its backbone. Romans were businessmen and the longevity of their Empire was due to their commercial trade, and ports played a vital role in Roman times as facilitators of trade and as home base for the navy. Based on these findings the following two targets can be added as typical ancient port functions:

Third target of ports = facilitator of river & coastal trade
Fourth target of ports = naval base

1.3 Constantinople

During its long history, the city known today as Istanbul has served as the capital of the Roman Empire (330–395 AD), the Eastern Roman (Byzantine) Empire (395–1204 and 1261–1453), the Latin Empire (1204–1261), and the Ottoman Empire (1453–1922).[9] The huge steps in maritime development and the progress in technology during the times of the Eastern Roman Empire call for taking a closer look at this era. The city of Constantinople was founded in 330 AD, at ancient Byzantium as the new capital of the Roman Empire by Constantine I, after whom it was named. The city was the largest and wealthiest European city of the Middle Ages and shared the glories of the Byzantine Empire. As successor of the first Roman Empire it was often called "The second Rome." The number of inhabitants during the late Byzantine period can be estimated between 300,000 and 400,000. The city was built on seven hills as well as on the Bosporus, and thus presented an impregnable fortress enclosing magnificent palaces, domes, and towers. The Church of Hagia Sophia, the sacred palace of the emperors, the hippodrome, and the Golden Gate were among the largest of the many churches, public edifices, and monuments lining the arcaded avenues and squares.

The Harbor of Eleutherios, later known as the Harbor of Theodosius, was one of the major ports of ancient Constantinople, located beneath the modern Yenikapi quarter of Istanbul. The harbor was located on the south side of the peninsula where the city is built, facing the Sea of Marmara. It was built in the late 4th century during the reign of Theodosius I, and was the city's major point of trade. The area was later transformed for agricultural use due to the effects of erosion and silting. In Ottoman times, the area was built over. In November 2005, workers on the Bosporus Rail and Metro Tunnel Project discovered the silted-up remains of the harbor[10] as Figure 1.3 below shows.

---

9 The internet page "LIVIUS: Articles on Ancient History" contains a short overview about the development of Constantinople: http://www.livius.org/cn-cs/constantinople/constan-tino-ple01.html

10 An interesting background story, enriched with a couple of unique pictures about the archeological work can be found at: http://www.saudiaramcoworld.com/issue/ 200901/uncovering. yenikapi.htm

"The remains of the port were discovered in 2004 when excavation began for the $4-billion Marmaray urban transit system's hub, which was then redesigned to accommodate the 10-square-block dig site. The ancient port today lies inland by about a kilometer—one of the reasons it lay undiscovered for so long."

Source: http://www.saudiaramco-world.com/issue/200901/uncovering.yenikapi.htm

Figure 1.3: Yenikapi Port excavation site

Excavations produced evidence of the 4th-century Port of Theodosius. There, archaeologists uncovered traces of the city wall of Constantine the Great, and the remains of over thirty-five Byzantine ships from the 7th to 10th centuries, including several Byzantine rowed ships (perhaps warships), remains of which had never before been found. From brick-transport vessels to round-hulled cargo boats 19 meters (60') long and small lighters used to off-load larger ships, Yenikapi is yielding the full gamut of ships that once busied one of the most active harbors of the middle ages. Some of the merchant vessels still contained their cargoes on board, preserved thanks to their burial in a thick layer of wet mud. In addition, the excavation has uncovered the oldest evidence of settlement in Istanbul, with artifacts, including amphorae, pottery fragments, shells, pieces of bone, horse skulls, and some human skulls found in a bag, dating back to 6000 BC.

The entire size of the harbor was likely an area of 10 hectares or approximately 1 mill sq ft. Graphical reconstructions of the jetties suggest that the total length of all piers in the port might have amounted to 4,000 m. Thus, the port was able to accommodate several hundred ships at a time, for example, during wintertime when the traffic nearly comes to a standstill due to weather conditions. For large ships with several hundred tons of cargo the port already provides quay walls of stone, which simplified the loading and unloading significantly over wooden gangplanks or simply wooden bridges, with the result of increased productivity. Directly behind the jetties and quay walls were large warehouses, for example, for storing the grain imports from Alexandria, and where many other goods were also up for resale or stored as buffer stocks. The whole port complex was protected by large harbor walls and breakwaters from the influences of the weather. Thus, it is demonstrated that back to the time of the Roman Empire ports were constructed as efficient protection for merchant vessels from severe weather conditions. The harbor served additionally as a naval base.

The development of the Byzantine Empire has gone hand in hand with the development of trade. Even bigger and better equipped ships, protected by a powerful navy, discovered new trade routes and new trade partners. Inner Mediterranean and Atlantic coastal trade evolved to Africa, the Middle East, India, and Asia. The number of trading partners grew constantly, and the tasks for the navy to protect the trade grew in parallel.

Constantinople was the major trade center in the eastern Mediterranean Sea from the 4th century until river silt filled the port in around 1500 AD; the harbor, its stone walls, and amazingly well-preserved remnants of the port's activities lay forgotten for centuries. The fall of Constantinople to the Turks in 1453 disrupted the traditional land trade route from Europe to Asia. Europe was forced to find alternate maritime routes. One alternative, followed by Columbus in 1492, was to sail to the west and the other alternative, followed by Vasco de Gama in 1497, was to sail to the East. Columbus stumbled upon the American continent, while Gama found a maritime route to India using the Cape of Good Hope.

As a result of investigating the port and shipping business in times of the Eastern Roman Empire the following two functions can be added as typical targets for port business:

Fifth target of ports = facilitator of international trade
Sixth target of ports = protection of the fleet

1.4 Venice and the Mediterranean Merchant Trade

After the collapse of the Roman Empire and several waves of Germanic and Hun invasions, a population of obviously former Roman inhabitants settled in the Venetian lagoon already in 5th century and founded the city of Venice in north-eastern Italy. The shallow Venetian Lagoon, an enclosed bay that lies between the mouths of the Po and the Piave rivers, was certainly not an ideal place for a new settlement, but it was a safe place. The refugees from Roman cities and from the undefended countryside finally built the so-called apostolic families, the twelve founding families of Venice who elected the first doge, who in most cases traced their lineage back to Roman families. Later, the city was historically the capital of the Republic of Venice and developed into a major financial and maritime power during the Middle Ages and Renaissance, as well as a very important center of commerce (especially silk, grain, and spice) in the 13th century up to the end of the 17th century. The City State of Venice is considered to have been the first real international financial center, which gradually emerged from the 9th century to its peak in the 14th century. This made Venice a wealthy city throughout most of its history.

The first refugees started to build houses of wattle and daub, and anchored branches with stakes to protect the foundations from currents. They started to construct boats and to obtain food by fishing. They dried seawater to extract salt and suddenly the economy of Venice was created. By the year 548 AD, Venice was already a strong power, controlling all trade on the Adriatic Sea. By the 9th century, Venice developed into a city-state and became the most famous of the so-called Mediterranean "Maritime Republics."[11] This is why Venice is the best example for the development of the Mediterranean Merchant trade during the Middle Ages.

In addition to Mediterranean trade, Venice played an important role in early Europe-Asia trade as well. Venice's goal in building an empire was not to rule over far-flung lands or to propagate religion, but to protect, expand, and encourage global trade beyond the Mediterranean; and if trade was power, then knowledge of the major trading regions in the world—the overland as well as the maritime Silk Road—was a vital part of successful trading relationships. Within this network, the port of Venice was the final destination for the ancient Chinese Maritime Silk Road. Recently, the port has again been mentioned as a potential hub

---

11 Others ancient "Maritime Republics" or city states are: Amalfi, Ancona, Gaeta, Genoa, Noli, Pisa, and Ragusa. During the Middle Ages these cities built fleets of ships both for their own protection and to support extensive trade networks across the Mediterranean.

for the New Maritime Silk Road, today better known as Chinese "One Belt, One Road" or OBOR-project (for more details, see Chapter 18.3).

Due to its location within the Venetian Lagoon, the Port of Venice always played a key role in facilitating global trade as an engine for wealth and growth. Venice was established out of trade and conflict with the East, and became immortal thanks to its merchants, who headed East, notably to Constantinople, Cairo, and Kashgar. A famous name of this time that is still today associated with the image of a traveler, adventurer, and trader is Marco Polo. The strategic position of the port, provided by the lagoon on which the city was built, in combination with the merchant spirit of its people allowed Venice to rise as a maritime power.

Seventh target of ports = facilitator of global trade

1.5 Imperial China: Early Ming Dynasty

The Ming Dynasty lasted from 1368 until 1644 AD, and after the Han and Tang dynasties, this was another high time in China's history. The greatest diplomatic highlights of the Ming Dynasty were the enormous maritime tributary missions and expeditions of Admiral Zheng He (1371–1433),[12] a favored eunuch commander of the Yongle Emperor (reign 1402–1424). Because of a report that the former emperor Hui-ti had fled overseas (and presumably for other reasons, such as promoting Chinese influence or trade opportunities), Emperor Yongle sent out expeditions overseas under Admiral Zheng He's command. In a period of twenty-eight years, from 1405 to 1433, Zheng directed seven expeditions and visited no fewer than thirty-seven countries (Figure 1.4).

---

12 Born into a family named Ma, presumably of Mongol-Arab origin, in central Yunnan Province, Zheng He was selected to be castrated by the general in charge of recruiting eunuchs for the court in 1381, when he was about ten years old. Born as Ma He as the second son of a Muslim family; later also known as Ma Sanbao.

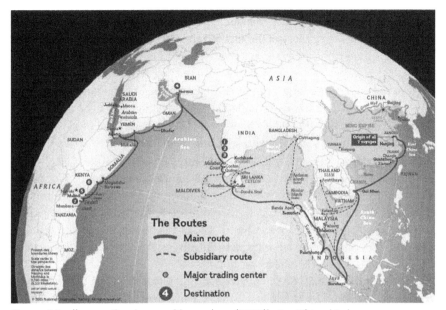

The Routes
— Main route
- - - Subsidiary route
⊙ Major trading center
④ Destination

Source: http://ngm.nationalgeographic.com/ngm/0507/feature2/map.html

Figure 1.4: Voyages of Zheng He

Zheng He's missions docked at ports throughout much of the Asian world, including those in Borneo, the Malay state of the Malacca Sultanate, Sri Lanka, India, Persia, Arabia, and East Africa. All this had taken place about half a century before the famous European sailor Columbus's voyage to America.[13] Meanwhile, the Chinese under Yongle invaded northern Vietnam in 1402, and remained there until 1428. During the Ming Dynasty, the Chinese also traded domestically by using the important fluvial transport network with several artificial canals connected to form the so-called Beijing-Hangzhou Grand Canal.[14] With a total length of 1,776 km or 1,104 miles, it is the longest canal or artificial waterway in the world. Some parts of it are still being used today. It is noticed that in 1430, Ming Emperor Xuan Zong commissioned Zheng He to deliver a message to foreign nations that

---

[13] According to the book *1421. The Year China discovered the World* by Gavin Menzies, Columbus was about seventy years behind the Chinese. Menzies collected a huge number of documents that—according to him—give good reasons to believe that China discovered America (Menzies 2003).

[14] For details of the Grand Canal, its history, the technique applied, and the Ming Dynasty restoration works at the Canal, please refer to: http://en.wikipedia.org/wiki/Grand_Canal_ (China)

he was enthroned with a new era named Xuan De. Reliable sources emphasized that this was the key purpose of the seventh and the last expedition for Zheng He.

Large tributary missions such as the ones mentioned above were halted after Zheng He, with periods of isolationism in late Ming Dynasty, coupled with the need to defend China's large eastern coastal areas against marauding Japanese pirates. Although it was severely limited by the state, trade was not overall forbidden. After 1578, it was completely liberalized. Upon their arrival in the early 16th century, the Portuguese traded with the Chinese at Tuen Mun, despite some hostilities exchanged between both sides. The Ming Chinese also traded avidly with the Spanish, sending numerous Chinese trade ships annually to the Philippines in order to sell them Chinese goods in exchange for mita-mined silver from the New World colonies of Spain. There was so much Spanish silver entering China that the Spanish minted silver currency became commonplace in Ming China. The Ming Chinese attempted to convert the silver currency back to copper currency, but the economic damage was done.

In the early days of the Ming Dynasty, China was an advanced country in the world. At the orders of Emperor Yongle, a vast fleet set sail in July 1405 from Liujia Harbor near Suzhou on a distant voyage. The purpose was to establish relations with foreign countries, to expand trade contacts, and to look for treasures to satisfy the desire of the sovereign for luxuries. Under the command of Zheng He was a vast fleet of sixty-two ships manned by more than 27,800 men, including sailors, clerks, interpreters, officers and soldiers, artisans, medical men, and meteorologists. On board the ships were large quantities of cargoes that could be broken down into over forty different categories, including silk goods, porcelain, gold and silverware, copper utensils, iron implements, cotton goods, mercury, umbrellas, and straw mats. The Emperor was very pleased with Zheng He's extraordinary feats as an envoy in making visits to various foreign countries. Between 1405 and 1433, Zheng He had been ordered eight times to act as envoy to countries lying to the west of China. Each time he had under his command a big fleet and a staff of more than 20,000 men.

On each voyage Zheng He was acting as the envoy and commercial representative of the Ming court. No matter what country he visited, he called on the ruler of the land, presenting to him valuable gifts in token of China's sincere desire to develop friendly relations and inviting the host sovereign to send emissaries to China. Wherever he was, he made a careful study of the customs and habits of local residents. Showing them due respect, he bartered or dealt with them through consultation and negotiation based on equality and mutual benefit.

In the expeditions Admiral Zheng made over three decades, China built a total of 1,622 ships. Each of the sixty-two flag ships of the expeditionary fleet were more than 400 ft long and 170 ft wide, holding a crew of up to 1,000. In 1983 a sternpost rudder 36.2 ft long and 1.25 ft in diameter was uncovered from the mud in the remains of one of the Ming naval shipyards in Nanjing. Such a rudder would have belonged to a ship at least 400 ft long. Just for comparison: Columbus's flagship, the *Santa Maria* was 75 ft by 25 ft. Ming ships were larger than any of their predecessors, and the subtle rationale for their being is quite simple: they were meant to carry huge loads and go long distances. Calculations with the sternpost rudder as reference and the collection of historical sources show that the fleet for the first expedition consists of:

- Treasure ships, used by the commander of the fleet and his deputies: nine-masted, about 127 meters (416 ft) long and 52 m (170 ft) wide. This is the size and shape of a football field.
- Equine ships, carrying horses and tribute goods and repair material for the fleet: eight-masted, about 103 m (339 ft) long and 42 m (138 ft) wide.
- Supply ships, containing staple for the crew: seven-masted, about 78 m (257 ft) long and 35 m (115 ft) wide.
- Troop transports: six-masted, about 67 m (220 ft) long and 25 m (83 ft) wide.
- Fuchuan warships: five-masted, about 50 m (165 ft) long.
- Patrol boats: eight-oared, about 37 m (120 ft) long.
- Water tankers, with one-month's supply of fresh water.

Six more expeditions took place, from 1407 to 1433, with fleets of comparable size.

If the accounts can be taken as factual, Zheng He's treasure ships were mammoth ships with nine masts, four decks, and could accommodate more than 500 passengers, as well as a massive amount of cargo. Marco Polo and Ibn Battuta both described multimasted ships carrying 500 to 1,000 passengers in their translated accounts (Needham 1971, pages 460–470). Niccoló Da Conti, a contemporary of Zheng He, was also an eyewitness of ships in Southeast Asia, claiming to have seen five-masted junks weighing about 2,000 metric tons (Needham 1971, page 452).

Many details of the early Ming Dynasty and the voyages of Admiral Zheng He are known today. What is missing in all studies, books, and reports is more detailed information on the harbors and port facilities of that time. However, it is very likely that specialized loading and unloading facilities had been in operation, particularly for the large treasure ships. Similarly, it is obvious that sufficient anchorage space and/or mooring facilities for the entire fleet had been available. It is also very likely that the ports of the Ming Dynasty, analogous to the period of the second Roman Empire, were built in protected bays or estuaries like the ones in Constantinople. Many of the jetties and mooring facilities—as well as the ships—were built of wood. Whether there was already specialized lifting equipment in use, like wooden cranes to utilize the leverage effect, is not known with certainty, though very likely. It remains that even at the time of Admiral Zheng He specialized berthing for his treasure fleet must have existed and specific port functions must have been fulfilled.

Admiral Zheng He's role in the Ming Dynasty demonstrates the eighth use for ports:

Eighth target of ports = home base for colonial missions + expeditions

1.6 Hanseatic League

The Hanseatic League (Hansa) was formed around the middle of the 12th century by German and Scandinavian seafaring merchants. At the time, the League was an economic alliance of trading cities in Northern Europe and their merchant guilds that dominated trade along the Baltic and North Sea Coast as the old undated print of the "Bibliographisches Institut Leipzig" in Figure 1.5 shows.

Source: http://en.wikipedia.org/wiki/File:Extent_of_the_Hansa.jpg#globalusage

Figure 1.5: Extent of the Hanseatic League about 1400 AD

The League itself was a commercial and defensive confederation of free cities; formed in 1241 and most influential in the 14th century when it included 180 to 200 towns (Stroob 1995, page 285). It functioned as an independent political power; the last official assembly (the so-called Hansetag) in the northern German City of Lübeck—the "Queen of Hansa"—was held in 1669.

The Port of Lübeck is a major port in northern Germany. Lying about 14 km southwest of the Baltic Sea, it rests on the Wakenitz and Trave rivers. It was the main city of the Hanseatic League and a commercial hub for northern Europe throughout the Middle Ages, and, in 1987, it was recognized by UNESCO as a World Heritage Site. Still today, the Port of Lübeck is the city's largest employer and it is Germany's biggest port on the Baltic Sea.

Count Adolf II of Holstein founded the city in 1143, but it was destroyed by a fire in 1157. Duke of Saxony Henry III rebuilt the town two years later, and it quickly became an important focal point for trade for raw materials and manufacturing for all Northern and Eastern Europe. Denmark held the Port of Lübeck in the early 13th century, but Frederick II made it his imperial city in 1226. During his reign, the city had its own constitution and laws and was self-governed for the most part. The council was dominated by merchants, and the city was oriented to trade for many centuries. Many Baltic cities later took the "Laws of Lübeck," revealing its great influence.

In Figure 1.6, an old copperplate engraving shows the typical organization of a Hanseatic city; Visby (today Sweden/Gotland): resident houses, market place, one or more churches as well as the city administration in the center, all of this protected by the town wall, and the heart of the merchants' business, the port, as central in- and outgate for the trade directly located at the waterfront and connected via roads with the city center.

Close behind the quay walls and mooring places are a huge number of warehouses; most of them typically multistoried red brick stone buildings with winches under the front roof. Several cities in the Baltic like Lübeck in Germany or Riga in Latvia still preserve today the remaining historic Hanseatic buildings as part of their own history. In the following sections, the port of Lübeck shall be considered in more depth. As Lübeck was the most important port of the whole Hanseatic League, it can be assumed that nearly all the other Hanseatic ports operated in a similar nature, and their principles of trade—manifested in the Laws—followed the same rules and regulations. Further, the techniques and developments were most advanced in Lübeck. In this sense, Lübeck can be seen as a spearhead and representative of the Hanse.

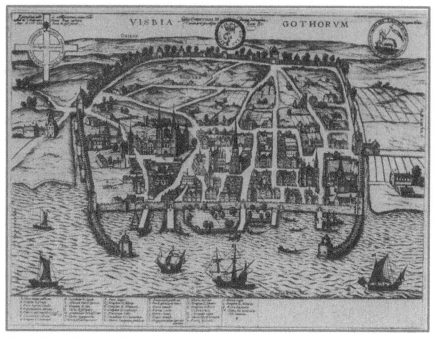

Source: Copy taken from: Stroob 1995, page 162ff. Stroob in turn took the picture from: Braun, G., F. Hogenberg, Civitates orbis terrarium, 1572–1618 (Facsimile edition) Kassel, Germany 1965, part 5, no. 39.

Figure 1.6: Hanseatic city of Visby, approximately 1598

Only very few of the Hanseatic trade documents issued in medieval Lübeck exist today. One of these is a customs document that is taken from Dollinger 1998, page 571. It shows the port's import and export statistic by regions and by goods for the year 1368/1369. As Dollinger already noticed, this statistic is probably not complete due to missing reports, and it may be that some of the trade is intentionally not shown; for the simple reason to save customs duties. In addition, it must be noticed that the a.m. statistic was made in times of war, and so the "normally" good trade relations, for example, with Norway have not been reported in this statistic (Dollinger 1998, page 277). However, it is one of the first documents that is available and it is a helpful document for getting an overview of the trade via the port of Lübeck in the 14th century. In addition to the values shown in local currency, the Luebisch Mark, Table 1.1 indicates the major trading regions in northern Europe.

Table 1.1: Port of Lubeck: Trade statistic March 18th, 1368–March 10th, 1369

Imported Goods		Origin, Destination		Exported Goods		Sum	%
150		**West**		38		188.0	34.4
44		**Livland Cities**		51		95.0	17.4
	10	i.e.	Riga		14		
	34		Reval		14.3		
	–		Pernau		22.7		
49.4		**Schonen**		32.6		82.0	15
52		**Gotland-Sweden**		29.4		81.4	14.9
19		**Prussian Cities**		29.5		48.5	8.9
	16	i.e.	Gdansk		22.8		
	3		Elbing		6.6		
		Wendish and					
17.2		**Pomeranian Cities**		25.2		42.4	7.8
	5.5	i.e.	Szczecin		7		
	4		Stralsund		7.5		
	2.2		Rostock		4.6		
	5.5		Wismar		6.1		
4.3		**Bergen**		·		4.3	0.8
3		**smaller Baltic Ports**		1.2		4.2	0.8
338.9		**Total**		**206.9**		**545.8**	**100**

All Figures in One thousand Mark luebisch.
Source: Dollinger 1998, page 571.

It is truly not possible to calculate the values of the Luebisch Mark into today's currencies. However, for getting a feeling about the importance of port trade for a Hanseatic city, some estimates are possible.

Table 1.1 shows that the value of trade the port declares for customs was 545,800 Mark Luebisch. A typical product that was traded during Hanseatic times was beer,[15] and a typical "load"—the weight unit of measurement—of beer was calculated with 7.50 Mark Prussian or 14.15 Mark Luebisch. Taking the price for a load in mind and bringing this into relation with volume and price of today, we come to an estimate of 77 mill Euros or 100 mill US-Dollar as approximate trade volume for Lübeck in 1368/1369.

---

15 Main reason for consuming beer: during the process of fermentation all germs were killed. Clear potable water was not available, and so it was healthier to drink beer instead of contaminated water.

Again, the estimation is only a very rough indication, based on only one of the typical consumer goods of ancient Hanseatic times, and it has only been made for showing the relevance of the port of Lübeck for a typical Hanseatic village with approximately 20,000 inhabitants. But what we can imagine is that a port like the one in Lübeck with this impressive trade volume was of huge importance! And just to put these figures into context, in the second half of the 14th century, a city with 20,000 inhabitants was a large city.

The two largest cities in northern Germany at this time were Cologne and Lübeck. And if we keep in mind that hinterland connections and the transport capacity via road were limited, it is even easier to understand that merchants and businessmen engaged in shipping and ports were the gateway to success! The official customs statistic for the a.m. year 1368/1369 quoted 680 seagoing vessels in the Port of Lübeck (Dollinger 1998, page 572); this means an average of two ships per day. This is also a reasonable figure for a medium-sized modern port. The structure of the cargo transported via the port of Lübeck in the year 1368/1369 is shown in Table 1.2; again, an extract from the customs declarations and to be judged with caution.

Thinking in today's categories, most of the goods are typically general cargo goods and will fall into this category. Grain, copper, and iron could be classified as typical bulk products, but the way the cargo was probably loaded and discharged (in sacks or bags, or as single pieces) will lead to a classification as general cargo.

Table 1.2 shows another important phenomenon: more and more goods coming from distant destinations were often goods that were produced in this respective area, because the craftsmen specialized themselves on these products. The result was better quality goods and lower production costs. Economist would call this the realization of comparative cost advantages. The Hanseatic merchants realized this via distinctive trade networks; they were the first traders who established specialized and committed trade offices in remote cities. These trade networks as facilitators for the realization of comparative advantages must be judged as founding principle and key success factor of the Hanseatic League. Typical products that were traded are clothes from Flanders, butter from Sweden, or linen from Westfalia.

Other products like salt from Luneburg were traded because there are only very few natural salt domes and/or caverns in Northern Europe. Luneburg had a regional monopoly as salt exporter and grew up on this business to a prosperous city.

Table 1.2 is expressed in values, but what is of interest for getting a feeling about the port performance is a statistic in volumes/tons. Unfortunately, port trade statistics in volumes from 14th century BC do not exist, and no historic source can be found that provides an accurate estimate. But the existing few sources available should provide a decent rough estimate:

- Prices for the goods that have been traded are available (Dollinger 1998, page 574), and when we take the unit price and count back the values from Mark Luebisch in metric tons, we will come to the first conclusion that the volume in Port of Lübeck in the year 1368/1369 totaled approximately 41,000 mt. This figure is to be judged as a first very rough and basic estimate.
- It is known that in the year 1368/1369 in total 680 seagoing ships called the port of Lübeck. The typical ships of that time have been the so-called Cog with a maximum cargo load up to 200 mt, and later in the second half of 14th century the so-called Hulk, a ship of new generation with a maximum load of 300 mt. It is to be supposed that both types of ships called at the Port of Lübeck that time, and that normally the ships were not "fully laden" as seaman typically say; this means: the ships were used with full tonnage capacity; this was for various reasons, like having a lot of light-weight but voluminous cargo on board. That maximum use of storage room in square meters does not automatically mean that the weight limit in mt is reached due to the specific weight of the different cargoes. It can be estimated that up to 70,000 mt of cargo could have been shipped via the port, that is, a little more than 100 mt per ship on average.

Considering that the customs trade statistic probably shows values below the reality, and that the estimations of ship capacity and utilization are also very vague, it is nonetheless possible to conclude that the trade volume has been in the range of 50,000 to 70,000 mt of cargo per year. Again, this is just an indication, but it helps to adjust the dimension we have in mind. For a port in the 14th century that trades with several partners in a network, this is certainly an impressive volume.

The final observation for the Hanseatic League ports shall concentrate on the techniques in the ports, and here especially the lifting technology, that is, the development of cranes. Back in the middle ages the crane in the Hanseatic city Gdansk was the largest port crane for cargo handling in Europe. The crane was built in the 14th century. What is unique for this crane is that it combined the functions of a city gate and a port crane, named Krantor.

Table 1.2: Port of Lubeck: Trade statistic March 18th, 1368–March 10th, 1369

Goods	Origin/Destination	Import	Export	Sum
Cloth	Flanders	120.8	39.7	160.5
Fish	Schonen	64.7	6.1	70.8
Salt	Luneburg	-	61.6	61.6
Butter	Sweden	19.2	6.8	26.0
Skins + Furs	Russia, Sweden	13.3	3.7	17.0
Grain	Prussia	13.0	0.8	13.8
Wax	Russia, Prussia	7.2	5.8	13.0
Beer	Wendish Cities	4.1	1.9	6.0
Copper	Sweden, Hungary	2.2	2.4	4.6
Iron	Sweden, Hungary	2.4	2.2	4.6
Oil	Flanders	2.7	1.5	4.2
Flax	Livland, North Germany	0.4	3.0	3.4
Other foodstuff	...	2.2	1.2	3.4
Silver	?	0.7	2.0	2.7
Wine	Rhineland	1.3	0.9	2.2
Linen	Westfalia	0.2	1.1	1.3
Miscellaneous	...	39.9	16.6	56.5
not further described	...	41.0	49.0	90.0
Total		**338.9**	**206.9**	**545.8**

Notes: All figures in one thousand Mark luebisch. Source: Dollinger 1998, page 572.

Today this crane is one of the sightseeing highlights in Gdansk and a fine specimen of historic port facilities. The reconstructed driving mechanism inside, still in working function, is an immense wooden wheel originally propelled by men literally walking in it, that is, a typical medieval treadwheel crane or Magna Rola for hoisting and lowering cargoes. The rope attached to a pulley is turned onto a spindle by the rotation of the wheel thus allowing the cargo to hoist or lower, depending on the direction the individuals walk.

Figure 1.7 shows a historical picture of the Krantor in Gdansk.

Source: Scan taken from an old postcard, approximately 1930. Postcard from J. Sorgenfrei.

Figure 1.7: The Krantor in Gdansk

Treadwheel cranes had not been invented in the Middle Ages; they already existed in Roman times. But they realized a renaissance in this time, and the ports of the Hanseatic League experienced great success by reinventing and optimizing this relatively simple technology. A lot of heavy lifts could be realized with these cranes. The real success of these cranes as facilitators of trade and supporter of the Hanseatic trade network results from their widespread dissemination.

In addition to the port functions already mentioned above, the following two can be added as result of the investigation of the Hanseatic League ports:

Ninth target of ports = development of trade networks
Tenth target of ports = realizing comparative cost advantages

1.7 Historical Drivers of Port Development

Ports fulfilled a variety of functions in history. The ports analyzed in this chapter stand proxy for typical trends that could be analyzed in parallel to the development of the human society and their techniques. The first ports just supported the requirements of the government, no matter whether it was a pharaoh, an emperor, or a king. Later, the diversified and wide-stretched needs of more and more people could be realized by using ports. But one fundamental characteristic never changed: ports have never been constructed and operated purely for their own sake. They served derivate purposes; or in other words: all kinds of port activity has never been for itself; there was always another need or desire behind their design.

Based on the historic approach, we can accumulate the ten targets as typical drivers for constructing and operating ports. The targets are listed in Table 1.3.

Table 1.3: Historical targets of ports

Historical targets of ports	Equivalent Driver Category
1. Ensuring sovereignty	Political
2. Enabling heavy lifts	Technical
3. Facilitator of river & coastal trade	Logistical
4. Naval base	Political
5. Facilitator of international trade	Logistical
6. Protection of the fleet	Technical
7. Facilitator of global trade	Logistical
8. Home base for missions & expeditions	Technical
9. Development of trade networks	Economic
10. Realizing comparative cost advantages	Economic

In history, early port activities have been for both military and business/commercial reasons. Later, with increasing specialization, the military functions as well as their equipment—the ships, terminals, warehouses, etc.—and the need for higher safety and security functions led to separate facilities. In this book we will not include the military development of ports. Rather, we will concentrate on the business or commercial functions of ports.

The targets in Table 1.3 can be grouped so that historically developed functions like the one for river and coastal trade, later international trade beyond the nearby open seas, and in more recent times the global trade between continents, are summed up as one major target: logistical facilitation of trade. The remaining historical targets of the list of ten can be grouped as well, so that the complete list can be grouped and subsumed in modern terminology under four categories of drivers for port business: economic, political, logistical, technical.

Chapter 2 will pick up these core categories of drivers and finally add an additional one, that also in history had implicitly been of huge importance: financial targets or more precisely, financial restrictions. This means that the final list of drivers for port development consists of five groups of targets:

- Economic
- Political
- Logistical
- Technical
- Financial

Although the world is more complex in the 21st century and the wording in business often covers what is behind the scenes, it will be found that the five main categories are still essential for efficient port business today.

Chapter 2
Driver of Port Business

Before going into the details of port business, it is helpful to describe the framework of factors that are influencing global trade, shipping, and maritime business. Ultimately, we are trying to answer, "What is driving the port business?" This question differs from statements often heard at maritime conferences or workshops, along the lines of, "Ports are driving economic development." This argument stresses the fact that ports are not only facilitators of trade, but also important economic institutions in and of themselves. They directly employ hundreds or in bigger ports thousands of people, they are important taxpayers for the municipalities, and via multiplier effects they are important for local economies. These effects are also called "drivers" (although the word "pusher" would better describe how ports influence the local economy). All these effects absolutely exist on the local level; however, this should not lead to the misunderstanding that ports can substantially "drive" (i.e., create or develop) trade by themselves. The only chances ports and terminal operators have are given via redirecting trade routes or influencing trade routes via better services.[1] In the following we will analyze the elements that drive a port; that is, the factors that have the power to change port business. In this understanding we can define "drivers" as follows:

> A driver of port business is a factor that influences (positively or negatively) the growth of a part of the port or the port as a whole.

A key question behind the approach of driver identification is the following: Why is there a difference in growth between two ports? Or asked differently: What factor is driving the business of one port, which the other port does not have (or, not to that extent)? What are the critical factors influencing port development (e.g., measured as cargo or passenger throughput) and port competition?

The key targets of historic port development identified in Chapter 1 already describe the main drivers of port development. Figure 2.1 below grouped the five categories of drivers around the port and shall symbolize that they all have an influence on port business, but also that there are interdependencies between the drivers. All drivers may have positive as well as negative effects. Some examples are: technical drivers may be limited by financial resources; an inefficient

---

[1] For more details, refer to Chapter 6: "Ports in Transportation Chain."

DOI 10.1515/9781547400874-002

hinterland logistic has the potential to limit port growth; a positive and high GDP (economic driver) may push imports and exports, and so the port business.

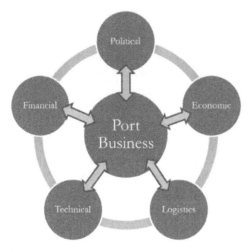

Figure 2.1: Driver of Port Business

The double-sided arrows symbolize that the factors have an effect in both directions, for example, an economic factor like global trade influenced the port business, but on the other side there is also an influence from the port on global trade. The circle around the center, connecting the driver categories with each other symbolizes that the groups are interrelated; like it is along the supply chain: all factors must reach a level to enable the port business to grow. Even if only one factor fails or underperforms, the entire chain can break, that is, the port has substantial performance problems. In transport theory, this effect could be expressed with polar diagrams (like in Figures 5.7 and 5.8). Each value per category in the diagram needs to achieve a minimum level of acceptance.

The drivers identified and described below have an influence on demand—the cargo, passenger, and traffic development—as well as on the supply side of the business, that is, on berth availability or hinterland access. Details on both sides of the market will be provided in Parts 2 and 3 below. In the following, we will describe the five categories of drivers and will identify key parameters that form each driver.

2.1 Economic Drivers

Economic Drivers:
    E1: GDP growth
    E2: World trade
    E3: ENR prices
    E4: Transportation costs
    E5: Emerging markets
    E6: Competition

E1: Economic growth, measured as an increase in the amount of goods and services produced by an economy over time, often results in increased transportation to and from markets. Economic growth is conventionally measured as the percent rate of increase in real gross domestic product (real GDP). The more an economy is growing, the more it will also increase the exchange of goods. Im- and exports will grow, and in parallel the transport volume increases.

E2: The close relation between an increase of GDP and world trade in total as well as the relation between world trade and world container port throughput shall be analyzed in more detail in Chapter 5, "Trade & Transportation." Containerized cargo often consists of consumer goods, and with increased GDP and increased income, more products will be consumed. However, this is not a linear function and discussions about "qualitative versus quantitative growth" show that the relation is not an easy one; but the discussion also shows that GDP and world trade are important drivers for trade and so too for port business.

E3: Energy & Natural Resource (ENR) prices have an influence on economies. Lower energy prices, such as shale gas in the US, have a positive effect on the economy. The low energy prices stimulate consumption of products via lower market prices as a consequence of lower production prices. Increasing prices for ENR products, such as crude oil in the years 2008 to 2014 with levels of more than 100 USD per barrel, or base chemicals that are often closely linked to crude oil price, has a diminishing effect on production as well as on consumption. Due to the high importance of several ENR products on the global economy, they must be considered as a driver as well; however, with a negative sign: increasing ENR prices tends to reduce port business. Since many ENR products are listed on commodity exchanges, they can be tracked relatively simply.

E4: Transportation costs, especially for shipping, can be taken as an indicator for port business as well. But as many shipping crises in the past have shown, the influence that transportation costs exert is not necessarily on the products being shipped; but rather on the shipping or transportation companies themselves. Due to the low unit costs of international trade and transportation (e.g., measured in metric tons or container units/twenty-foot equivalent units [TEUs]), an increase in transportation costs has very limited effects on the price of the products being shipped. This is the negative bounce back effect of the success in lowering the unit costs via optimizing global logistics. However, the effect does exist, and so it is reasonable to identify these costs as drivers for port business. With potential changes in the transportation industry, for example, via an insolvency of a shipping company, the effect transportation costs have on ports is more significant than the effects these costs have on consumer and investment products, as normally a variety of alternative routes are available for shippers.

E5: Emerging markets are an economic driver for port business because these markets are potential export markets for industries in the hinterland of a port, or these markets may offer attractive imports for new and/or cheaper and/or more competitive products. The discussion about the so-called BRIC-states Brazil, Russia, India, and China as booming markets with high real GDP growth (and thus as markets with increasing importance for ex- and imports) demonstrates how influential emerging markets are as an economic driver. With increasing trade, the port business can be influenced positively.

E6: Competition within and between economies should under market conditions lead to lower prices and increased trade via realizing absolute and comparative advantages in production. With this leverage effect, economic competition acts as a driver of port business. However, it should be additionally noted that ports as economic units are also influenced by competition within the supply chain market. A new terminal or a new port in the neighborhood can increase the competition between the port operators and authorities as well, and this has a stimulating effect on trade. To be more precise, a new port within a range could increase the competition inside the range, and with this effect increase the whole trade volume. It might be that the existing port in the range is influenced negatively and hurt by this competition, but for the regional economy it might be positive. Here we must distinguish between the effect on the economy and the effect on a single port as an economic player.

2.2 Political Drivers

Political Drivers:
  P1: Globalization
  P2: Open markets (China)
  P3: Trade policy
  P4: Internet/open access
  P5: CO_2 footprint
  P6: Security/piracy
  P7: Bureaucracy (customs, vet.)
  P8: Taxation

P1: Globalization is the politically supported trend toward increasing global economic integration. It is one of the largest forces affecting world economies and global trade and transportation at present. However, globalization is not an inevitable or irreversible phenomenon, as the example of China in Chapter 1 clearly described, or as the Great Depression in the United States in the 1930s showed, when global economic integration went into decline. Still, the current period of global economic integration is unprecedented and it is expected that the pace and extent of globalization will continue to have major ramifications for the world and for ports as facilitators of global trade. For most of the economists and politicians today, it is highly unlikely that the process of increasing global economic integration will reverse—even though at the end of the second decade in this century discussions about Brexit, more regional autonomy, new trade walls or antifree trade movements seem to have gained more influence. These developments may limit the level of an open economy, but the fact that all human beings are living in one world will be accepted finally—and this means more economic integration will be the result. Whether this is still called "globalization" or "one world economy" or something else is irrelevant for the development of trade. Bearing this in mind, globalization, defined as a trend toward increasing global economic integration, is an important political driver of port business.

P2: Open Markets and an open market policy often go parallel with globalization. But there are also national trends in some countries that push back globalization, and several political barriers have been set into force, like high import taxes, strict national regulations that must be fulfilled, etc. Both tariff and non-tariff barriers will be erected with the target to protect the national economy. For many years, Japan was a prominent example of this. A global policy with worldwide activities and active export pushing trade policy came along with a highly protected local market. Therefore, we must distinguish between globalization and a real open market policy. Both can be drivers for port business. The strong economic growth in China and the Chinese decision to become a member of the World Trade Organization (WTO) in 2001—including all the significant changes to the Chinese economy—are a clear sign that China wants to be more integrated in the world economy—mainly for exports, but also for imports as public available statistics (e.g., World Bank) show. Imports nearly tripled since China became a member of the WTO. The discussion about the British exit or in short "Brexit" with the target to leave the European Union (EU) is one of the latest examples in the discussion of open markets. Advocates for Brexit argued that by reclaiming its national sovereignty, the UK would be better able to manage immigration, free itself from onerous regulations, and spark more dynamic growth for Britain—the latter including all positive effects on employment, taxes, and public budgets. Again, the economic effects play an important role.

P3: In the same direction goes the argument of a liberal trade policy. This can support the integration of a national economy in global trade. But it has also been seen that trade policies support national means of transportation, which then may result in directed trades via political supported infrastructure. This was very often the case during the Cold War, but these same protective trade policies can be found in many countries today, though used in a less extreme way. In this sense, this factor can support or hinder port business.

P4: A truly supportive factor for global trade is the internet and the policy of open access to globally available information. These factors lead to better market transparency and can be real political drivers of business. But it is also true that still today the internet is subject to censorship in some countries, and open access to political or business data is not—or not fully—available. An extreme case of this is the dictatorship in North Korea. Here like elsewhere the limited access to information—besides all other political pressure—acts as a limiting factor for business. However, we must realize that information, and here especially open access to the internet, is a driver of trade and business. Global market platforms like Amazon are vital examples of how internet business opens access to a variety of markets elsewhere in the world.

P5: The CO_2 footprint is the most prominent argument for an environmentally friendly policy.[2] Many initiatives have shown that economic growth and environmental protection is not a contradiction, and therefore more and more politicians

---

2 Besides CO_2 there are several more greenhouse gases (GHG) that have an influence on the environment; refer to Chapter 22: "Environmental Issues."

globally support these initiatives. Especially, an alternative energy policy with a major share of renewable energies as a source is a challenge. Solar panels from China or wind turbines from India can be found all over the world today. In this sense the sensitivity for environmental issues and the CO_2 footprint are political drivers of port business (with positive and negative effect). Also, the decision of the International Maritime Organization (IMO) to reduce the current global limit for the sulfur content of ships' fuel oil of 3.50% m/m (mass by mass) down to 0.50% m/m, effective January 1, 2020, was decided by the UN states represented in IMO to reduce the global CO_2 footprint. For ports with a large share of bunker activities like Singapore, Fujairah, or Rotterdam this decision is especially important. These ports are directly affected by such political decisions, as they now must adopt or change their bunkering facilities. The new Rotterdam Gateway Terminal for LNG bunkering is a direct consequence of this policy and is intended to push Rotterdam in the forefront of environmentally friendly bunkering. On-Shore Power solutions (OPS) as installed in many ports of the world is another example of direct political influence on port business.

P6: Globalization and world trade, while often promoting port business, have also led to increased terrorism over the last decade. The answer to terrorist activity has been several initiatives to secure global trade activities and global trade routes. High levels of security helped to ensure that terrorists had little influence on a global scale. The regaining activities of pirates in some parts of the world are a threat to world trade, but the international coordinated activities for high security standards have been effective at limiting their effects. Safety and security rules and regulations are political factors for port business.

P7: Bureaucracy—in all its varieties—can be a nuisance and in many cases not a supporting factor for global trade. Nearly everybody accepts that port authorities, customs offices, or veterinary control institutions are necessary. But what should be expected is at least a little bit of service orientation. And here one can find all extremes: from very helpful, service oriented, open minded, and supportive on the one end to civil servants without any interest in the effect their work has on the development of trade and transportation. The problem with all this is that motivation can not be ordered, and when the people working inside this system of bureaucracy are not motivated and show no service orientation, this can hinder the development of ports. Nearly everybody has had personal experience with bureaucracy, and countless analyses have been made, so we shall not stress this point. All we must realize is that bureaucracy can be—and in several cases is—a negative driver for port business.

P8: Taxation as a political factor and the influence it has on port business is easy to understand: from a supply chain point of view, all taxation results in increased transportation prices. Taxes, duties, fees, charges, etc., increase logistics costs. On a high political level, all import taxes, product-related taxes, VAT, but also the port-related fees and duties have the potential to influence a port's competitive position. From a logistics suppliers' view, all these taxes, fees, duties, etc., are finally costs that need to be calculated and compared with taxes, fees, etc., on alternative routes, that is, via other transit or transshipment countries. In this sense, taxation is truly a political driver of port business and can work in both directions: as a positive incentive or negative extraordinary burden.

2.3 Logistical Drivers

Logistical Drivers:
- **L1:** Supply chain approach
- **L2:** Frequency, predictability, network, safety, etc.
- **L3:** Short berthing + quick loading/unloading/ship-to-shore-speed = speed
- **L4:** Reliability
- **L5:** Intermodality
- **L6:** Port-hinterland interface/tri-modality
- **L7:** Hub-and-spoke system

L1: The concept of the supply chain has undergone a structural reorganization in recent years. It is no longer a simple matter of "port and hinterland logistics" or "cargo delivery." Global companies recognize that optimized supply chains drive improved corporate customer service, higher margins, and increased revenue. In this sense, a customer-centric supply chain approach and the effective and coordinated use of resources—including the commercial side of the business—forms a driver of port business.

L2: Mass performance, speed, ability to network formation, predictability, frequency, safety, and convenience are the seven criteria Fritz Voigt used in 1973 when first describing both sides of the transportation market (see Section 5.4, and Voigt 1973, page 80ff). In a modern supply chain view, these characteristics for means of transportation should be subsumed under the list of logistical drivers for port business. All these factors have a direct influence on quality of the transportation chain.

L3: One factor—"speed"—is mentioned twice in the list of logistical drivers (as part of the seven criteria of Fritz Voigt as well as the separate driver L3), because the factor "time" in modern logistics becomes more and more a critical factor for success; e.g. with respect to short berthing times without delays as well as fast ship-to-shore operations. Total berthing time has a direct influence on many KPIs like berth productivity (BP)[3] or vessel turnaround time (VTT).[4] Therefore, "speed" in the sense of being faster than others is mentioned separately as a logistical driver for port business.

L4: Reliability can be defined as the "ability of a system or component to perform its required functions under stated conditions for a specified period of time." For a port, this can be seen as the ability to repeat the quality of work on the defined and expected high level. It could also be described as "repeatability." With this, it is a factor which was not explicitly mentioned by Fritz Voigt in the analytical works for transport values and affinities, but for reaching the goal of high quality logistics standards, it is definitely an important driver for port business. Reliability with the meaning of repeatability can also be described as trust in port quality; i.e. the assured reliance on the truth, ability and strength of the port or terminal in delivering the services as agreed and confirmed.

L5: Intermodal transport as a logistical driver for port business can then be understood as the *movement of goods whereby at least two different modes are used in a supply chain.* Some definitions restrict intermodal transport to unitized transport with containers or swap bodies, or they include that a part of the transport must be on the road, but these are a very narrow definitions. If we understand intermodality in the above mentioned more wider definition as "transport without handling of the goods themselves in changing modes," we must nominate this a logistical driver. The ability to handle multiple modes of transport qualifies ports and has the potential to strengthen their competitive edge.

L6: Another driver to consider is the degree to which a port is dependent on its hinterland, which is closely related to the trade and economic power of the port's respective region. The port-hinterland interface is of huge importance for efficiently loading and unloading goods. Parts of this interface can include on-dock-railway terminals, remote terminals, highway connections, efficient

---

3 For example, a container terminal defined and measured in two ways: as ship arrival and departure process time—consisting of the time between berthing and first move and between last move and departure—and operating productivity, defined as the number of moves between the first and last container lift divided by time.

4 For more details on KPIs, refer to Chapter 16: "Increased Economic Efficiency."

barge service, etc. The change between modes of transport is often the real problem when applying intermodality. In some ports, this is the direct responsibility of the terminal operator. In other ports, this is an act of coordination between several transport operators, like private terminal operators, national railway companies, and foreign barge operators. This might already sound like it could be a difficult chain to manage, and in some ports it is. However, using more than one mode of transport—for example, road and rail—offers a logistical advantage as it provides alternatives. Thus, a multimodal option is an important driver of port business. Ports with access to inland waterways offer a third option besides road and rail and often promote this as "trimodality." Especially for low value bulk products, this additional option creates a competitive edge. The transport value "convenience" as described by Fritz Voigt already in 1973 highlights this importance (Voigt 1973, page 91).

L7: The concept of hub-and-spoke systems is explained in Chapter 4.5 below, and due to the power of rerouting cargo from one port to another, being a hub port and having the potential of realize scale effects is undoubtedly a key logistical driver of port business.

2.4 Technical Drivers

Technical Drivers:
 T1: Port performance
 T2: Port infrastructure
 T3: Port access
 T4: Hinterland connections
 T5: Vessel fleet/size
 T6: Containerization
 T7: Easy to use systems/port community systems
 T8: Innovations (AGVs, double twin-lifts, ...)

T1: Port performance can be measured with a set of indicators, often referred to as key performance indicators (KPI) (see also Chapter 16). They should provide insight for the port management into operational details of the key areas of port business. They can be used, first, to compare performance levels with targets and second, to observe industry trends in performance levels. For example, the productivity for handling containers per hour (so-called moves per hour) may vary month to month. If successive monthly figures showed a decline (or increase) in moves per hour, action can be taken to determine the reason for the decline (resp. the increase). With a KPI set, performance levels can be measured and used to improve performance, creating a competitive advantage. In this sense, the intention to increase technical efficiency and port performance is a technical driver of port business.

T2: Port infrastructure must be identified as an enabler or as a prerequisite for port business. It is also a KPI in the way it can support the business by providing smooth and efficient operations, for example, at the quay wall by providing sufficient berths or a Vessel Traffic Management System (VTMS) that allows navigation and berthing even during the night or in bad weather conditions. The reality is that port infrastructure is a limiting factor in many ports. This is because ports are often fully—or at least partly—publicly financed, and the public budgets for maintenance and repair or for further extensions are often limited. An inherent negative factor in this context is the fact that planning and construction periods for ports are long. It takes a long time before success is seen following infrastructure construction on a port, and there is nothing that shows immediate and fast success. As a result, port infrastructure planning is often not on the top of the agenda of politicians who decide about budgets. In most cases, port infrastructure is a hindering factor, that is, it does not push the business forward, but can limit the business if not sufficiently available. However, it is a driver of port business.

T3 + 4: As part of a supply chain, ports are enabling trade at the interface of waterborne and landside traffic. Due to this, it is obvious that an effective—and at best, multimodal—port access from or to the open sea and also into or out of the hinterlands is essential in driving port business. Therefore, we list port access as well as hinterland connections as important drivers.

T5: The size of vessels calling a port is of importance for the volumes handled. Larger vessels must attract more cargo per call, which then has a direct impact on the volumes handled per call. Within a hub-and-spoke system, the ports may increase the number of trans-shipment cargo, which also increases the volume (multiplier effect). And when a port is so attractive for shipping lines that many of them call the port with larger vessels and larger volumes, the vessel fleet composition pushes throughput and business. That's why we list "vessel size and fleet" as a technical driver for port business.[5]

---

5 The huge impact even bigger vessels have on ports is also discussed in Chapter 17: "Tendency to Oligopolize."

T6: Containerization describes the trend of using a mode of standardized transport, which uses a common size of steel container to transport the cargo—often in 20 ft or 40 ft units. These containers can easily be transferred between different modes of transport, for example, from container vessels to trucks and trains. This makes transport and trade of goods cheaper and more efficient,[6] and the low unit costs due to standardized transport and handling result in low logistic costs for the products that are transported in containers. From a market share of zero when first invented in 1956, the success of containerization resulted in approximately 90 per cent market share in 2016—just sixty years later. Here only an approximate figure can be calculated, because over the last two decades the "trend into the box" and the invention of highly specialized containers led to the effect that cargoes that in the past have been classified as bulk products are transported more and more in containers. Here we just mention all the different types of tank containers for liquid cargoes. At conferences it can often be heard that experts believe that containerization will come to an end. What this means is that the trend in the direction that typically general cargo and/or bulk products will be transported more and more (that is, with increasing share) in containers will stop. This is correct for developed countries and sophisticated supply chains, but should not be misunderstood to mean that all container transport will come to an end. In many emerging countries there is still a need for more efficient and cheaper transport, and containerization can be the answer. Bearing all this in mind, it is easy to understand why containerization is classified as a technical driver.

T7: Booking cargo on a commercial vessel is not as easy as ordering a book on Amazon.com; still today booking procedures require special knowledge and often the assistance of professionals. Shipping lines realized this and started several initiatives with the target to ease booking and administrative procedures. The systems should be easy to use, as Fritz Voigt stated when defining the values and affinities for conveyance. He named this "convenience" and expressed that systems that are more transparent and less time-consuming will attract business. In this sense we must take them into consideration as drivers.

---

6 More details about "containerization" can be found in Section 3.2: "Container Ports."

For larger ports initiatives to ease communication have already been in place for a few decades and resulted in the creation of so-called Port Community Systems (PCSs).[7] A PCS is an electronic platform that connects the multiple systems operated by a variety of companies and organizations that make up a seaport community. Key drivers for the establishment of PCSs were the need for a standardized and easy-to-use communication platform in order to improve individual systems in terms of punctuality, reliability, or costs, as well as the need to secure a competitive position among ports. Simplification and reduction of procedures and documents made PCS necessary, especially in growing markets. An oft-heard argument is that of a "Single Window" solution; the idea behind this is illustrated in Figure 2.2.

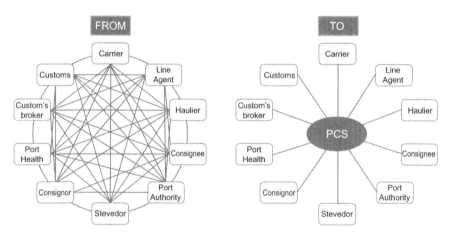

Figure 2.2: Conceptual idea behind a Port Community System

T8: All kinds of technical innovations can have an effect on productivity of port and/or terminal operations. Driverless systems like automatic guided vessels (AGVs) or twin-lift-moves with a gantry crane on container terminals or high-speed-pumping systems on liquid bulk terminals will reduce the average costs for moving the cargoes. In this sense innovations are also important technical drivers for port business.

---

7 For more details, see Chapter 21: "Port Community Systems."

2.5 Financial Drivers

Financial Drivers:
- **F1:** Interest rates
- **F2:** Monetary policy
- **F3:** Financial market conditions
- **F4:** Public-private partnerships
- **F5:** Fund policy

F1: Investments in port and terminal infra- and superstructure are often very high, with costs for a new terminal easily reaching one billion USD. Port business is a capital-intensive business, with investments depending greatly on the conditions of the financial markets. Here especially, interest rates act as key cost components for loans. Lower interest rates on the interbanking market, for example, the LIBOR or London Inter-Bank Offering Rate, (should) lead to lower interest rates on the capital markets. Commercial banks can offer more attractive rates for financing port infra- and superstructure when interest rates are low.

F2: The target of the monetary policy of the central state, or to be more precise, the central bank, is in the same direction. The most influential economics tool a central bank has under its control is the ability to increase or decrease discount rates: the rate commercial banks must pay for borrowing money from the central bank. Shifts in this crucial interest rate have a drastic effect on the building blocks of macroeconomics, such as consumer spending and borrowing. The leverage effect works via interest rates. Quantitative tenders of a central bank are having comparative effects to interest rate fixings. Due to the importance of these measures, the monetary policy of the central bank is listed here as a financial driver for port business, although we all know that central banks focus on the whole macroeconomics for all sectors of a country or region, and not a single sector like ports, shipping, or logistics. But the monetary policy has an impact and is therefore of importance.

F3: Financial market conditions show the reactions of the markets in response to the central bank's initiatives. For many years these reactions have been considered as relatively stable and foreseeable, but the financial crisis of 2008 and onward has shown that reactions of the market, and thus the conditions for their customer are not as stable as previously assumed. The fact is, ports need the financial institutions for financing infra- and superstructure investments. Unse-

cure risks in financing due to unstable financial market conditions hinder investments. In this sense, financial market conditions are drivers for port business.

F4: Public-private partnerships (PPPs) are joint initiatives for typically big projects, resulting in effects that are of interest for private businesses (e.g., via profitable business) as well as for the public (via job creation, reducing unemployment,
increasing taxes, etc.). PPP initiatives can help realize projects that are too large
for one party only; in this sense they enable business and drive port development.
Port and terminal development can be organized as PPP.

F5: In several countries the system for retirement pensions is based on private
funds, often called pensions funds, schemes, or plans. These funds collect money
from their members or shareholders over a long period of time, often forty years
or more, and based on this they guarantee a retirement pension. To secure the
pensions, the fund manager invests the money collected in relatively safe investments. By nature, these funds have a long-term perspective. Therefore, pension
funds are often invested in infrastructure like ports and airports. Unlike typical
investments funds that collect money (equity) for high rentable short-term investments (three to seven years), pensions funds are not interested in "cherry picking"
and "slicing" assets. Therefore, pension funds are ideal partners for port investments. Changes in fund policy (i.e., investing in airports instead of ports) can
have an impact on port development and port business. Therefore, "fund-policy"
is listed as a financial driver for port business.

In total we identified thirty-four drivers of port business over the last few pages.
They are categorized in five groups. This list of thirty-four drivers is not exhaustive: certain ports may have other drivers of importance that were not listed above,
but ultimately the following points are important:
1.   There are specific forces that have a huge impact on port business, such as
     the growth of the world trade.
2.   There are many additional drivers with the potential to influence a specific
     port; positively or negatively.

2.6 The "Port Model"

As we have seen, there are many factors influencing port development, and it
is the task of port or terminal development managers to consider these drivers
when justifying investments. Port development managers should understand
the complexity of the factors affecting their port business and have a vision for

the development of their business. Because ports are built and maintained with huge sums of taxpayer money, there is often a competent audience interested in seeing the funds used competently. Public controlling needs this kind of control and feedback.

A systematic and scientific approach could help to justify port and terminal investments by modeling the future, that is, depicting future scenarios for a specific port or terminal. Economists in these cases would try to build an econometric model to analyze the impact of each factor on the port. The reason for doing this is to secure investments, as the majority of expensive port infra- and superstructure investments will be in operation for decades. This "port model" takes into account the most influencing drivers, looks at how they develop and influence the port, and builds a "scenario model" out of these factors. Thus, the model can be used to open up discussions about the most effective way of structuring the port, and has the potential to change the course of its development. "Interpersonal reexamination" is important in this process: transparency regarding how the facts and figures concerning the port are related to each other. Here the mathematical calculations are less important than the discussion of drivers and their possible influence. Identifying the important drivers and implementing these into the calculations and model building is the most critical part of port modeling. The resulting product should be a forecast for the port or terminal, which illuminates the key areas for investment.

Before examining a port model, keep in mind that although every single driver has an influence on port business:
1. Not all drivers have an effect in the same direction (positive or negative).
2. Not all drivers are of equal importance (stronger or lesser influence).
3. The port/terminal management can not directly influence all drivers.

However, it is still possible to estimate the influence of each driver as well as its tangibility. Some drivers are easy to measure on a scale and can be classified as "tangible," like GDP growth or degree of containerization or interest rates. Factors that are soft and difficult to measure are classified as "intangible." The port model impact graphic (see Figure 2.3) is a rough classification, based on the experience of the author.

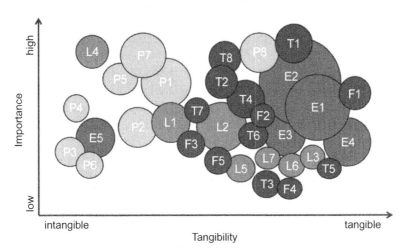

Impact on Port Model expressed by size of the bubble

Driver Set:

E1: GDP growth	**L4:** Reliability
E2: World trade	**L5:** Intermodality
E3: ENR prices	**L6:** Port-hinterland interface/tri-modality
E4: Transportation costs	**L7:** Hub-and-spoke system
E5: Emerging markets	**T1:** Port performance
E6: Competition	**T2:** Port infrastructure
P1: Globalization	**T3:** Port access
P2: Open markets (China)	**T4:** Hinterland connections
P3: Trade policy	**T5:** Vessel fleet/size
P4: Internet/open access	**T6:** Containerization
P5: CO_2 footprint	**T7:** Easy to use systems/port community systems
P6: Security/piracy	**T8:** Innovations (AGV's, double twin-lifts, ..)
P7: Bureaucracy (customs, vet.)	**F1:** Interest rates
P8: Taxation	**F2:** Monetary policy
L1: Supply chain approach	**F3:** Financial market conditions
L2: Frequency, predictability, network, safety, etc.	**F4:** Public-private partnerships
L3: Short berthing + quick loading/unloading/ ship-to-shore-speed = speed	**F5:** Fund policy

---

Figure 2.3: Driver Impact on Port Model

Port models can be used to identify and validate the most important drivers in history, but more important is the insights they lend for the future: based on historic evidence, forecasts of cargo volumes, throughput figures, terminal utilization, business models (i.e., investment plans), and infrastructure needs can be developed.

It is easy to identify in Figure 2.3 that the economic drivers (labeled E) are of huge importance and are probably having the largest impact on port business and thus on the port model. Such a model can now be constructed by combining the driver and modeling their influence. For medium- and long-term forecasting, causal models like regressions and econometric models are best for accuracy and identification in turning points, although they require a lot of data. Such an econometric model specifies the statistical relationship between the various drivers. The model explains the relations pertaining to the outcome.

A simple linear example of an econometric port model is one that assumes that the throughput T within period t (e.g., last months) depends on world trade (WT) volume of last period t-1 as well as local GDP of last period. Then the model will consist of the equation:

$$T_t = \alpha + \beta^*\mathbf{WT}_{t\text{-}1} + \gamma^*\mathbf{GDP}_{t\text{-}1} + \delta$$

The objective of the analysis team will then be to obtain estimates of the parameters α, β, and γ as well as the error term δ. These estimated parameter values, when used in the model's equation, enable predictions for future values of port throughput contingent on the prior month's trade and GDP development.

This simple model only considers two drivers as indicators, not all thirty-four discussed above, or even another set of additional relevant drivers. And the model itself is a simple linear model for two periods. With the help of econometric computer processed models, much more complex relations between variables can be identified, and methodological errors that may occur can be eliminated. The final target of such a port model is an accuracy rate that provides the best available forecasts. There is no shortage of literature on econometric modeling, and therefore we will not go into more detail.[8]

Forecasting is an important and difficult task, and economic forecasting should not be compared with weather forecasts where analysts predict the weather. Economic forecasting is *not* a prediction; it is a statistical method to

8 See, for example, Reiss, Peter C. and Frank A. Wolak (Stanford University): *Structural Econometric Modeling: Rationales and Examples from Industrial Organization, Handbook of Econometrics,* Vol. 6A, pages 4280–4412, Elsevier, Oxford, UK 2007.

model the future by taking the relevant drivers into consideration and calculating scenarios of the future. The aim is to give empirical estimations concerning economic, political, logistical, technical, and financial relations. Port managers often use port models to justify their actions regarding investments.

2.7 Impact on "Port Master Planning" Process

Port master plans help clarify and communicate the port vision, including an outlook on future cargo and passenger traffic. They also provide a strategic framework for port authorities to consider a range of internal and external factors that may impact current and/or future operations. Many of the described thirty-four drivers in this chapter have an impact on trade and traffic, and therefore a more or less direct impact of driver's effect on port master planning exists. Judgments need to be made based on the contextualization of each port.

As will be explained later in Chapter 13, port masterplans should, among other things:
- Clarify the port's mid- and long-term "vision" to a wide range of stakeholders.
- Outline a plan for attracting investments and creating jobs.
- Assist in overall supply chain management through:
  o Integrating the port into broader network considerations (by promoting greater understanding of the port needs within regional and local planning agencies).
  o Ensuring that vital seaport (and logistic chain) infrastructure is delivered when and where it is needed (via well-considered staging options).
- Maximize economic and productivity improvements through efficient management of critical infrastructure delivery and protection.
- Provide increased environmental protection by identifying environmental values early in the design process.
- Strategize how to sustainably develop port infrastructure in order to handle the forecast growth in maritime trade.
- Create additional economic value through increased industry and investment confidence.
- Address interface issues (social and environmental) in and around port areas (i.e., help to inform port users, employees, and local communities as to how they can expect to see the port develop over the coming years).
- Set out the approximate timeline for development.

Chapter 3
Major Commercial Ports

3.1 Classification of Ports

Professional port databases like the IHS Sea-web[1] port database contain information of more than 10,000 ports and terminals around the globe. Today ports are the facilitator of globalization and they handle more than 90% of the world trade. But not all ports are of equal importance for the global economy. Some ports handle massive amounts of cargo, measured in millions of tons, whereas other ports are comparably small in tonnage, but important for the country, for example, by connecting islands to the mainland, as cruise or passenger ports, or as river ports, functioning as a link from a landlocked country to an overseas hub port. Figure 3.1 classifies all ports.

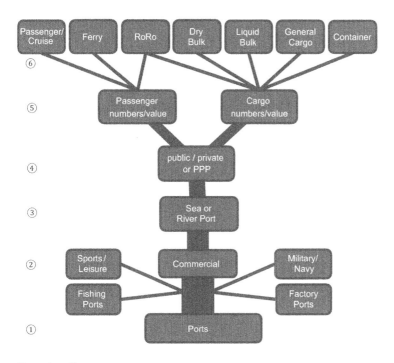

Figure 3.1: The port tree

---

1 Refer to http://www.ihs.com/products/maritime-information/port/

DOI 10.1515/9781547400874-003

Level ① of the port tree in Figure 3.1 considers all kinds of ports. Based on the findings in Chapter 1, this is the best way to get a holistic picture of port utilization and port opportunities. In this book we will not study all ports, but will focus on commercial ports. On level ② we see what will and what will not be discussed here. The following four groups of ports will not be examined:

- **Sport and leisure ports**: Sometimes called marinas, these ports are often used for sailing boats and yachts; they are typically without warehouses, cranes or terminals; in most cases with very restricted draught conditions; and usually not used for commercial cargo business.
- **Fishing ports**: Here we refer to typically small anchorage places in protected waters, where fishermen moor their boats. These facilities are also called ports, and for many fishermen this is the place where they pursue their profession. But just like in marinas, there are usually no terminals, no cargo handling equipment is available, and the draught is also limited. Very often these ports are part of the natural shore. From a technical perspective these ports are not more than anchorage places, but colloquially called "ports" as well. These small "fishing ports" should not be confused with commercial ports that are used for the fishing industry with their trawlers. The industrial fishing ports are categorized under "general cargo ports."
- **Military or navy ports**: Ports used for military function have existed since the Roman Empire demonstrated its naval power. Still today, many countries have their own navy, and the naval infra- and superstructure together forms an essential part of the public safety and security system. Due to its importance and unique safety standards, navy facilities today are usually separate from commercial facilities. Even when in the same location, the military part of a port is often isolated from the commercial area.
- **Factory ports**: Huge companies sometimes have their own ports. The typical characteristic of such a factory or plant port is its isolation from any other port business. It could often be seen that bulk products like coal, iron ore, or crude oil are delivered by ship as part of an industrial supply chain. The ports themselves can be equipped like any other commercial port; but since these facilities are not open for other users, pure factory ports will also not be further discussed.

The interest of this book concentrates instead on **commercial ports**. These ports can be sea ports like Los Angeles or Sydney, located directly at the open sea, or river ports like Duisburg or Chongquing, located a few hundred or—like Chongquing, one of the largest Chinese inland ports—approximately 1,000 miles away from the open sea, deep in the hinterland (level ③ of the port tree; especially in chapters 5 and 6 we will consider the transportation chain aspect and the role of hinterland destinations in more depth).

Commercial ports can be operated under many different forms of management, often described as "The Port System" (level ④ of the port tree; refer to Chapters 8ff in Part III). In today's ports, all management systems can be found: the completely public operated port, the purely private operated port, as well as mixed forms between public and private functions and interests. The mixed forms between public and private functions—often referred to as the public-private partnerships (PPP)—are the most common ones. Typical examples for this are "landlord ports" or "tool ports" (explanations in Chapter 10).

On level ⑤ of the port tree we must distinguish between passenger and cargo ports. The facilities installed are different, the functions these ports fulfill are different, and the drivers behind the port business differ as well. Passenger and cruise ports often count their business in numbers of port calls, passengers, shipping lines, etc., and the result of the business is then expressed in value terms like nominal or real USD. Cargo ports on the other hand count their business often in tons and like to use these ton-figures for rankings and comparisons in statistics. Business success is equally expressed in value terms.

Ports on levels ③, ④, and ⑤ in the port tree can come along in any combination: it can be a public river port for cargo business, a private sea port for cruise, a public-private venture for cargo business in a sea port, etc. All combinations are possible and will be discussed below. On level ⑥ in Figure 3.1 we find typical expressions for all the combinations possible. In the following sections 3.2 ff these ports will be analyzed in more detail.

Ports must specialize and concentrate the operations to handle the respective goods as appropriate and effectively as possible. The results are specialized ports and/or terminals with specialized handling equipment. Table 3.1 explains the relation between goods,[2] the normal units in which it shows up, and the ordinary handling method.

---

2 It is unusual to classify passengers as "goods," but following the example of the airline industry that named its guests "pax" or "self-moving cargo," it should be allowed. The main target of Table 3.1 is to demonstrate that different modes of operations due to the nature of goods or needs of passengers lead to specialized ports.

Table 3.1: Ports and related goods

Gr.	Type of Port	Method of Cargo Handling	Units	Example
1.	Passenger/cruise	self-moving	single	Passenger
2.	Ferry	rolling, self mov.	small	Cars, trucks, passenger
3.	RoRo	rolling	small	Cars, trucks, flats
4.	Dry bulk	grab	bulk	Coal, ore
5.	Dry bulk/grain	sucking/hoisting	bulk	Corn, wheat, oats
6.	Liquid bulk	pumping	bulk	Crude oil, chemicals
7.	General cargo	with cranes	small	Machinery, all "high & heavy"
8.	Container	with cranes	box	Consumer goods, minor bulk prod.

In the following sections the most important ports per category will be described. Importance is hereby measured in terms of throughput, because the amount of cargo handled by a port mirrors its economic relevance. Regarding the terms that are normally used to describe ports, it must clearly be stated that a pure "container port" or 100% "dry bulk port" rarely exist in reality. Many ports of the world would call themselves a "universal port"; that is, a port that can handle most of the different kinds of goods—if not all of them. But it is also true that many ports—due to a variety of reasons like the industry related to the port, the limitation of draught in port access channels, or the number of consumers in an area—have specialized themselves in one way or another. In the following the economically most relevant ports per category will be listed.

Before going into further detail, the world's largest ports in terms of tonnage throughput shall be identified. Table 3.2 shows the top twenty largest ports in the world and their development between 2005 and 2015.

The dominance of China in the global port business is obvious. Fourteen out of the twenty biggest ports in the world in terms of cargo throughput, measured in metric tons, are in China. Also remarkable is the speed of Chinese port development during the last years. The total throughput of Ningbo & Zhoushan for example (including river trade) grew more than 610 million tons between 2005 and 2015. This increase alone is far more than the total amount of throughput of all other ports in the world; except Shanghai, the number two port in the world, which reached a level of throughput of 717.4 mt in 2015.

Table 3.2: Top twenty world ports, 2005–2015 in mill mt*

Rank	Port	Country	2015	2014	2013	2012	2011	2010	2009	2008	2007	2006	2005
1	Ningbo & Zhoushan[1]	China	889.0	873.0	809.8	744.0	691.0	627.0	570.0	520.1	473.4	309.7	272.4
2	Shanghai[2]	China	717.4	755.3	776.0	736.0	727.6	650.0	590.0	582.0	560.0	537.5	443.2
3	Singapore[4]	Singapore	574.9	581.3	560.8	538.0	531.2	502.5	472.3	515.4	483.6	448.5	423.2
4	Tianjin	China	541.0	540.0	500.6	476.0	451.0	408.0	380.0	355.9	309.6	257.6	240.7
5	Sushou[3]	China	540.0	480.0	454.0	428.0	380.0	328.8	246.3	203.5	183.8	-	-
6	Guangzhou	China	519.9	500.4	454.7	434.0	429.0	400.0	375.0	344.3	343.3	302.8	241.7
7	Quingdao	China	500.0	480.0	450.0	402.0	375.0	350.1	315.5	300.3	265.0	224.2	186.8
8	Tangshan	China	490.0	500.8	446.2	364.6	308.0	250.6	175.6	108.5	67.6	-	-
9	Rotterdam	Netherlands	466.4	444.7	440.5	441.5	434.6	430.2	387.0	421.1	409.1	381.8	370.3
10	Port Hedland	Australia	452.9	421.8	326.0	246.7	224.3	178.6	159.4	130.7	130.6	110.1	84.2
11	Dalian	China	415.0	420.0	408.4	373.0	338.0	300.8	203.7	185.2	165.4	145.2	176.8
12	Rizhao	China	361.0	353.0	309.2	281.0	252.6	221.0	181.3	151.0	111.8	110.1	84.2
13	Busan[4]	South Korea	347.7	335.4	313.3	298.7	281.5	262.1	226.2	241.7	229.9	217.9	217.2
14	Yingkou	China	338.5	330.7	309.2	301.1	261.0	225.0	176.0	150.9	122.1	94.8	75.4
15	South Louisiana[5]	USA	265.6	264.7	241.5	253.0	248.8	223.3	205.7	212.0	234.1	238.5	220.3
16	Hong Kong[2]	China	256.6	297.7	276.1	269.3	277.4	267.8	243.0	259.4	245.4	238.2	230.1
17	Quinhuangdao	China	253.1	274.0	272.6	271.5	287.0	257.0	243.8	252.2	245.7	204.9	169.0
18	Yantai	China	251.7	237.7	221.6	203.0	180.3	150.3	123.5	111.9	101.3	60.8	45.1
19	Port Klang[4]	Malaysia	219.8	217.3	200.3	197.9	194.2	171.0	137.7	152.3	135.5	122.0	109.7
20	Shenzhen	China	217.1	223.3	234.0	228.1	223.0	221.0	194.0	211.2	199.9	176.0	153.9

* Without Ras Tanura port, Saudi Arabia; throughput 2014 = 349.2 mio mt; no data rows available
[1] Ports merged in 2006
[2] Including river trade
[3] Integration of Changshu, Zhangjiagang and Taicang ports
[4] Converted from freight tons (= 0.920 mt) to metric tons
[5] Converted from short ton (= 0.907 mt)
Sources: China Statistical Yearbook; www.portofrotterdam.com/several years of port statistics; selected port web pages.

Before Ningbo and Zhoushan merged, Shanghai was the largest port in the world. Shanghai's volume is also much more than the remaining 9,980 of the 10,000 ports of the world will ever achieve within the foreseeable future as total annual volume. Few fast-growing major ports in economic growth areas, combined with hub and spoke concepts and increasing concentration are the result of this development. It is a matter of fact that today only a handful of ports are dominating the commercial port business.

The combined port of Ningbo and Zhoushan, the largest port in the world since 2012, more than tripled its throughput between 2005 and 2015. And according to the port management it is very likely that Ningbo-Zhoushan will be the first port ever to achieve a throughput volume of more than a billion of metric tons per year—a historic benchmark and another example of the fast-growing port business in China.

3.2 Container Ports

The enforcement of a standard box as unitized cargo box and the beginning of the so-called containerization started in April 1956, when the first full container vessel was loaded in the Port of Newark, NJ. The vessel was a 524-foot long tanker with a metal platform installed above the pumps and piping that cluttered the vessels main deck. At that time, it was a strange looking ship. The *Potrero Hills*, as the ship was formally called, had been launched near the end of World War II. For the experiment of coastwise trailer ship business, it was renamed *Ideal X*. The trailer had been removed from their wheels, and the sea container with the typical 20 and 40 ft measurement was born.

Since 1956, container shipping and container port business grew over proportional and the penetration of containers into the world transport system has increased gradually. The container shipping and the container port story is a real story of mutual success.[3] At the beginning of the "containerization" mostly standardized consumer and investment products with low requirements to the physical handling have been transported in a sea container, that, is, textiles, shoes, and a lot of other consumer goods; but the process of containerization made it possible for more and more specialized container and supporting stuffing devices offered the possibility that goods with highly demanding critical requirements could be transported in containers.

Containerization led to the invention of specialized containers, such as the reefer container with cooling aggregates, high cube containers for low weight and oversized cargo, open top containers, open side containers, tank containers, etc. These inventions made it possible for goods, which at the beginning of containerization were considered inappropriate for a container transport—like coffee—to be today nearly 100% containerized. Many ports adopted the new way of transporting cargo overseas and specialized themselves in all the new requirements combined with the container; for example, we can mention the specialized cranes for container handling, the sophisticated and demanding requirements

---

3 For further information about the development of container shipping, refer to Donovan (2006) and Levinson (2006).

for handling dangerous cargo, or the necessity to apply sufficient power plugs for reefer containers, etc.

Typical for the container business and for container statistics is the way of packing the cargo which is the center of interest. This is different from most of the other transport statistics like for bulk or conventional general cargo (e.g., steel); here the requirements of the product are the focus of interest. The sea container as a standardized box with defined technical specifications for the corner fittings can take a huge variety of products. For many statistics in foreign trade or for customs, this frequently leads to misinterpretations because a container statistic is not a cargo statistic. However, container statistics are important just because of the huge amount of container trade, but everybody in port business must be aware of the differences.

Table 3.3: Top twenty container ports, 2015

Rank	Port	Country	TEU in thousand	Throughput total mill tons	Container in mill tons	Share of cont. in %
1	Shanghai	China	36,537	717.4	...	...
2	Singapore	Singapore	30,922	574.9	331.7	58%
3	Shenzhen	China	24,204	217.1	214.3	...
4	Ningbo-Zhoushan	China	20,620	889.0	...	...
5	Hong Kong	China	20,114	256.6	177.5	69%
6	Busan	South Korea	19,469	347.7	333.3	96%
7	Guangzhou	China	17,625	519.9	...	...
8	Quingdao	China	17,510	500.0	...	...
9	Dubai	UAE	15,592	170.2	115.9	68%
10	Tianjin	China	14,100	541.0	...	...
11	Rotterdam	Netherlands	12,235	466.4	126.2	27%
12	Port Klang	Malaysia	11,890	219.8	189.0	86%
13	Kaohsiung	Taiwan	10,264	110.9	37.1	33%
14	Antwerp	Belgium	9,654	208.4	113.3	54%
15	Dalian	China	9,450	415.0	...	...
16	Xiamen	China	9,182	210.0	...	...
17	Tanjung Pelepas	Malaysia	9,120	136.3	...	...
18	Hamburg	Germany	8,821	137.8	90.6	66%
19	Los Angeles	USA	8,160	176.7	38.8	22%
20	Long Beach	USA	7,192	162.8	35.6	22%

Sources: IAPH, World Container Port Stat.; AAPA World Ports Rankings 2015, ISL, Shipping Statistics MR.

Today several large ports have specialized themselves in the container business, and for many ports the container volumes represent a huge share of their total throughput, in some cases up to nearly 100%. In the last two decades especially, the container business was very often the fastest growing business for these ports and today represents a considerable share of their cargo volume.

Table 3.3 shows the throughput of the top twenty container ports in 2015 in container units TEU (twenty-foot equivalent unit), the total cargo throughput in million tons as well as the share of container; in million tons and in percent. Unfortunately, Chinese ports do not sufficiently report their ports data, but it is obvious that for several ports like Hong Kong, Busan, Dubai, Port Klang, and Hamburg, the container business builds an essential part of their throughput. For example, the European Port of Rotterdam held the position of the world's largest port for several years and was also the biggest container port of the world. Rotterdam is still the biggest port in Europe today, but as Table 3.3 shows, Rotterdam is not even in the top ten container ports globally. The container business, driven by the typical consumer and investment products that are transported in these boxes, is a fast-growing business, and the top ports of today may disappear from global lists very soon. In fast-growing markets, container ports have a good chance for growth in throughput as well; or in other words, ports are dependent on trade.

Table 3.4 shows which ports were the global top container ports between 1970 and 2015. The emergence of China as an economic powerhouse and production center for many goods can be identified easily within this ranking.

Table 3.4: Top container ports, 1970–2015

Year	Port	Country	TEU in million
1970	Oakland	USA	0.3
1975	Rotterdam	Netherlands	1.1
1980	New York	USA	1.9
1985	Rotterdam	Netherlands	2.7
1990	Singapore	Singapore	5.2
1995	Hong Kong	Hong Kong	12.6
2000	Hong Kong	Hong Kong	18.1
2005	Singapore	Singapore	23.2
2010	Shanghai	China	29.1
2015	Shanghai	China	36.5

Source: Several years of container statistics.

The left side of Figure 3.2 illustrates the data of Table 3.4; the increase of maximum handled container volumes every five years. It is easy to see the sharp increase in container volumes beginning in the 1990s. It is also evident that the five-year increase stagnates beginning in the 2000s; the gain varied around 5 to 6 mill TEU.

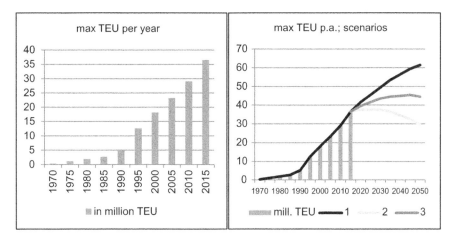

Figure 3.2: Container increase, 1970–2015 and potential scenarios

Interesting question for every port planner in this respect is: what about the future development of container trade? Three potential scenarios are illustrated on the right side of Figure 3.2. Scenario 1 is very optimistic with further strong increases in container traffic. Scenario 2 estimates the contrary, a decrease of container volumes that falls back to the level before the financial crisis happened, and finally a moderate middle scenario is presented like in scenario 3.

These questions about future trade evolution and thus the future throughput volumes are of interest for everybody involved in port development, as ports and terminals are built for future trade. Therefore, the best available information is needed to justify the huge investments (often many millions of dollars). This is not a simple mathematical problem that can be solved, for example, by extracting a regression curve based on historic data. Trade development models are needed that include at best all drivers mentioned in Chapter 2. In Chapter 13 we will come back to this.

Figure 3.3 shows a long-term graph of total throughput and container development in Rotterdam as an example. What can be identified is that the container cargo in Rotterdam has not displaced other commodities, or in other words, the container cargo has been developed without losing other commodities. The management of the port was able to grow both the container as well as the rest of the cargo, mainly liquid and dry bulk. In 1975 Rotterdam handled 260 mill mt of noncontainerized cargo, and in 2016 a total of 334 mill tons of noncontainerized cargo; an increase of 74 mill tons of mainly bulk cargo (total cargo in 2016 = 461.2 mill tons).

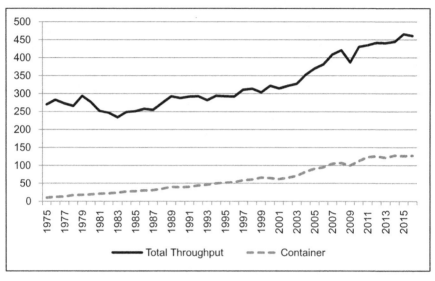

Figure 3.3: Port of Rotterdam, 1975–2016; in mill metric tons

This independent growth of containerized and noncontainerized cargo has not been the case in all container ports. The Port of Hamburg in Northern Germany, a competing port to Rotterdam and ranking on position number 18 in Table 3.3, shows a different development when analyzing the data. The noncontainerized cargo in 1975 amounted to 45.2 mill tons, and in 2016 this part of the business is more or less exactly on this level: 46.3 mill tons. That is a relative stagnation over a forty-year period, with few variations over time, as Figure 3.4 illustrates.[4] In other words, all additional throughput that has been achieved in this port stems from the container, and the trade behind the container business; plus a stagnation in noncontainerized trade.

A specialization of ports can be identified on this very high level of data by interpreting the throughput figures. Often structural changes take place behind these figures; but this mainly occurs inside the categories; i.e. inside the conventional general cargo or inside the container business.

---

4 Noncontainerized cargo is expressed as the difference between the two lines.

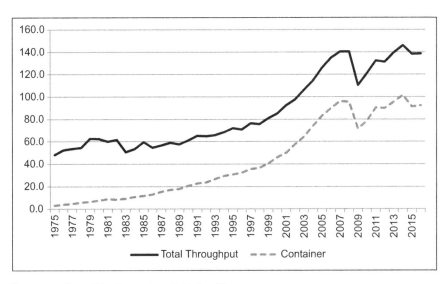

Figure 3.4: Port of Hamburg, 1975–2016; in mill mt

High-level figures are not sufficient for a final judgment, but provide a reasonable categorization. Data for most ports contain the same potential of information. For specialized younger Chinese ports like Yantian, today part of the Shenzhen port group in the hinterland of Hong Kong, it is even easier to interpret the data: the port was opened in July 1994, is still operated by Yantian Container Terminals Ltd. and majority owned by Hong Kong-Chinese Hutchinson Port Holdings, and is more or less 100% a container port.[5] Nearly all business grew with the container. Today Yantian, in addition to Da Chan Bay and Shekou, is still a key contributor to Shenzhen container volume; refer to Table 3.3: Shenzhen in 2015 was container port number 3 in the world, handling 24.2 mill TEU of container.

3.3 General Cargo Ports

Before describing the most important general cargo ports here in Chapter 3.3 or the liquid and dry bulk ports in the following two chapters, it is necessary to understand how cargoes are clustered in maritime business. The term "general cargo" is not a generally accepted defined term. Very often "general cargo" describes cargo consisting of various kinds of goods, not one single type of good. It is essentially a

---

5 With the exception of heavy lift cargo that could be classified as general cargo.

generic term and not a cargo classification. Having this in mind, "general cargo" describes the residuum of cargo that is not handled as bulk cargo. There are several ways to differentiate total cargo. In statistics, this ambiguity raises problems when comparing port cargo statistics that do not clearly draw a dividing line between the groupings. Stated below are two of the most common ways to distinguish and classify:

A

Total Cargo			
General Cargo		Bulk Cargo	
Conventional	Container	Dry Bulk	Liquid Bulk

B

Total Cargo			
General Cargo	Container	Bulk Cargo	
		Dry Bulk	Liquid Bulk

Historically, all cargo that was not handled as a typical bulk product—for example, with a grab or suction pump—was classified as general cargo; consequently, *definition A* divided the total amount of cargo in two groups: general cargo and bulk cargo. The introduction of the container and the huge success of the box led to the further distinction between "conventional general cargo" and "containerized general cargo," or in short "container." The conventional general cargo hereby was everything that was not in a container. Thus, the method of handling the cargo affected how the statistics were categorized. With the introduction of the container, cargo was no longer the only category measured with statistics.

Iron and steel, for example, can be handled in a conventional way with a crane under a hook or with forklift trucks, or if the cargo allows, inside a container. A product like a steel coil is a good example: it can be handled "conventionally," but it is also possible to transport steel coils inside a box. The same is true for many other products.

The success of the container led consequently to an effect that port people described as "the cargo went into the box," that is, more and more typical conventional general cargo. Also, more and more bulk products have been containerized, that is, the process of "containerization." The reaction of wide parts of the industry was and still is that from the very beginning of export and import procedures, the planner and organizer have the typical measurements of 20 and 40 ft-sized sea-containers in mind. With the integration in supply chains for reasons of cost savings and efficient transportation, it is automatically implied that the dimensions of logistics are considered as technical restrictions.

As a second effect of containerization, the way trade is measured has changed. Historically, statistics counted volumes (i.e., in tons) or values, that is, in money terms (e.g., Pound, Sterling, or USD). With the ubiquity of the container, trade began being counted in units: twenty-foot equivalent unit (TEU) or forty-foot equivalent unit (FEU); TEU being the most common way of counting.

Concept B takes this into consideration; it distinguishes between bulk, container, and general cargo. It is important to understand that this is a typical way a "cargo handling statistic" is constructed. This is not a "cargo statistic"! Without further information and taking only the figures of the "cargo handling statistic," it is not possible to get a clear picture of the cargo handled in these ports. For this way of classifying "goods" the term "conventional handled general cargo" usually does not appear.

Today it is acceptable to describe "general cargo" as the residuum of cargo that is not handled as bulk on typical bulk terminals or as containers handled on typical container terminals. This character of being the not- or not-yet-containerized cargo marked the image of general cargo as being a little old fashioned or outdated. But this is a wrong image! Especially for the municipalities around these types of ports it is essential to have a reasonable amount of conventional general cargo, because the number of port jobs combined with this kind of transport is absolutely the highest (measured per unit; e.g., per tons of throughput). Due to the nature of cargo handling much more port workers are needed, e.g., 1 mill ton of general cargo compared with 1 mill ton of containerized cargo. Additionally, qualified cargo handling specialists with certified knowledge of the different cargoes are needed for general cargo handling activities.[6] Handling specialists for high-value products such as windmill blades, off shore equipment, or huge machineries are more expensive to employ. This is a cost variable that operators must include in their calculations.

Statistics following concept A often measure cargo in volumes, for example, tons, and provide additional TEU-information for the container trade. Here container trade data are often available in tons. Statistics following the classification of concept B are often counting containers only in TEU, that is, container data measured in tons are not or only rarely available —also refer to Table 3.3 above and the missing values for container cargo in tons; this is a direct effect of different cargo measurement.

Unfortunately, Chinese ports typically follow concept B, and thus do not provide additional cargo volume information (container cargo in mt). This may

---

6 For further details on this effect, refer to Chapter 16, here: Table 16.5: Generalized value added creator.

lead to the top twenty general cargo ports seen below in Table 3.5 being incomplete, as there is missing information about conventional cargo volumes in ports.

Table 3.5: Top twenty general cargo ports, 2015; in mill tons

Rank	Port	Country	Unit	2015
1	Los Angeles	USA	MT	126.3
2	Nagoya	Japan	RT	97.1
3	Long Beach	USA	RT	89.1
4	Kitakyushu	Japan	RT	71.0
5	Osaka	Japan	RT	44.7
6	Kobe	Japan	RT	44.3
7	Yokohama	Japan	RT	37.0
8	Singapore	Singapore	MT	29.9
9	Inchon	South Korea	RT	28.9
10	Rotterdam	Netherlands	MT	27.7
11	Ningbo-Zhoushan	China	MT	25.0
12	Mumbai	India	MT	19.8
13	Vancouver	Canada	MT	16.8
14	St. Petersburg	Russia	MT	16.2
15	Port Klang	Malaysia	MT	15.7
16	Taichung	Taiwan	MT	15.5
17	Zeebrugge	Belgium	MT	15.2
18	Antwerp	Belgium	MT	14.7
19	Amsterdam	Netherlands	MT	12.3
20	Hong Kong	China	MT	11.5

Sources: Port websites; ISL Shipping Statistics Dec. 2016; own calculations.

Singapore, the second largest container port in the world, handled a container volume of 331.7 mill tons[7] in 2015, whereas the largest general cargo port, Los Angeles, CA, handled roughly 126.3 mill tons of cargo,[8] or approximately one-third of the volume. The containerized cargo has outpaced the general cargo; but for a universal port it is of importance to offer handling facilities for typical conventional general cargo.

---

7 Container volume of first ranking container port Shanghai is not available.

8 This number for Los Angeles looks very high, but the reliable ISL Shipping Statistics (Dec. 2016 volume) stated that total cargo volume was 176.7 mt, share of general cargo = 93.4%, container volume in mt = 30.75 mt. This results in 126.3 mt conventional general cargo. US AAPA statistics on the other side quotes only 54.6 mt as total volume.

The most important goods handled as general cargo today are:
- Iron and steel products (e.g., rail tracks)
- Industrial components (e.g., machinery, such as a boiler)
- "Oversized" machinery (e.g., locomotives and railcars)
- Timber
- Offshore equipment

3.4 Liquid Bulk Ports

Table 3.6: Top twenty liquid bulk ports, 2015; in mill tons

Rank	Port	Country	Unit	2015
1	Ras Tanura*	Saudi Arabia	MT	349.2
2	Rotterdam	Netherlands	MT	224.6
3	Houston	USA	ST	199.2
4	Singapore	Singapore	MT	195.8
5	South Louisiana	USA	MT	150.3
6	Gwangyang	South Korea	RT	128.2
7	Ulsan	South Korea	RT	123.5
8	Chiba	Japan	MT	104.0
9	Al Basrah*	Iraq	MT	100.8
10	Mina al Ahmadi*	Kuwait	MT	93.0
11	Corpus Christi	USA	ST	81.6
12	Jebel Dhanna*	UAE	MT	68.7
13	Botas	Turkey	MT	67.2
14	Antwerp	Belgium	MT	66.7
15	New York/New Jersey	USA	ST	66.6
16	Yanbu	Saudi Arabia	RT	60.3
17	Novorossisk	Russia	MT	59.8
18	Primorsk	Russia	MT	59.6
19	Ningbo-Zhoushan	China	MT	58.0
20	Daesan	South Korea	MT	55.8

* 2014 data
Sources: US DoT; ISL; port websites; own calculations.

Viewing the terminal layout of a liquid bulk facility from a birds-eye perspective it is easily visible that terminals differ from container, general cargo, or dry bulk ports, because they normally do not need to have many harbor cranes at the quay wall, there is only a limited operational area available, and instead of sheds and warehouses tanks, pipes and huge valves are located in the yard. The connection to the vessels is operated via jetties with loading arms or transfer hoses that are connected between the valve header on the dock and the manifold header on the vessel. The several loading arms will normally interact with the tanker's ballast system to control the loading operation.

In addition, the quay wall itself is not the typical several hundred-meter-long concrete wall found in most ports, but instead a smaller wall for support vessels plus a mooring facility or jetty for the tanker with a lot of different pumping stations that are connected via pipelines with the terminal tank facilities. A huge variety of tanks for all the different products is also a typical characteristic of liquid bulk facilities. Some liquid terminals are built for export, others for import of liquid cargo. It is not obvious that terminals provide bidirectional trade. Table 3.6 listed the top twenty liquid bulk ports in 2015.

The no. 1 ranking port is Ras Tanura, located close to Jubail on the Arabian Gulf coast. This port is often not listed in statistics for mainly two reasons: first, because the Saudi Ports Authority (SPA) is not supervising the port—this is the task of oil giant Saudi Aramco—and this means statistical data is rarely made public. The second reason Ras Tanura is not often seen in lists is because the port is considered a factory port, not a commercial port. This second argument is not easy to judge. While it is true that the port is operated exclusively as an export facility for one company, it is also an open port called by several tanker lines, and so by many customers. With this fact the port in our understanding does not fulfill the criteria of a factory port, and consequently the port is listed here.

A key topic for liquid bulk ports is the question of operational safety since many liquids are hazardous to the environment and often flammable. Therefore, in 1978 the first edition of The International Safety Guide for Oil Tankers & Terminals (ISGOTT) was issued.[9] In the meantime the fifth edition is available, and the ISGOTT standard is the main global standard for oil tanker operation. Over the last decades, the standard has become very detailed and provided comprehensive information for a safe operation. Most of the world's ship-to-shore operations must follow ISGOTT standards.

Typical liquid cargoes that are im- and exported:
- Crude oil
- Oil products/petrochemical products
- Chemical products
- Pharmaceuticals

---

9 Published by the International Chamber of Shipping: ISGOTT International Safety Guide for Oil Tankers and Terminals, fifth edition, Witherby & Co., London 2006.

3.5 Dry Bulk Ports

Table 3.7: Top twenty dry bulk ports, 2015; in mill tons

Rank	Port	Country	Unit	2015
1	Port Hedland	Australia	MT	444.7
2	Quinhuangdao	China	MT	233.0
3	Tianjin	China	MT	223.5
4	Dampier	Australia	MT	172.0
5	Newcastle*	Australia	MT	165.2
6	South Louisiana	USA	ST	153.2
7	Itaqui	Brazil	MT	138.8
8	Tubaro	Brazil	MT	121.5
9	Hay Point*	Australia	MT	115.0
10	Ningbo	China	MT	112.0
11	Sepetiba	Brazil	MT	104.3
12	Richards Bay	South Africa	MT	98.6
13	Gladstone	Australia	MT	98.6
14	Saldanha Bay	South Africa	MT	70.8
15	New Orleans	USA	ST	48.1
16	Plaquemines	USA	ST	40.5
17	Brisbane	Australia	MT	40.2
18	Cincinnati	USA	ST	40.2
19	Paradip	India	MT	38.0
20	Vancouver	Canada	MT	35.7

* fiscal year ending June 30
Sources: Port web pages; ISL Shipping Statistics; own calculations.

Dry bulk is cargo that is transported unpacked and in huge quantities. A dry bulk terminal typically has deep water in front of heavy quay walls where the bulker can lay at the berth. The cargo is often loaded and unloaded with grabs (e.g., for coal and ore) or with suction pumps (grain). The yard of a dry bulk terminal is used for storing the cargo, and depending on the requirement of the cargo, the yard is covered (often necessary for fertilizer) or used for uncovered storage (e.g., for ore piles).

Table 3.7 reveals that dry bulk ports are achieving the largest amounts of cargo throughput, measured in tons. The top twenty liquid bulk ports together achieved a combined cargo volume of 2.3 bn tons, the top twenty dry bulk ports 2.5 bn tons. When only considering the top ten, the concentration is slightly higher: top ten liquid bulk ports achieved a result of 1.7 bn tons, the dry bulk ports 1.9 bn tons, or nearly 300 million tons more. This demonstrates that dry bulk ports are the ports with the highest cargo volumes.

Port Hedland, Dampier, Newcastle, and Hay Point in Australia are coal and iron ore export facilities, serving the Chinese market for energy and steel production, and accordingly the Chinese ports of Quinhuangdao, Tianjin, and Ningbo are the corresponding coal and iron ore import facilities. Typical dry bulk products for most of the ports in the top twenty lists are iron ore, coal, agribulk, scrap, and fertilizer. Some products can be stored in open storage areas (stock piles), other products like fertilizer require covered storage facilities, for example, sheds with specialized loading and/or unloading facilities. Most of the dry bulk ports also offer value added services such as screening, blending, crushing, and packing.

Yet another important factor is the nearby availability of information about every conceivable aspect related to dry bulk, including financial services, cargo inspection, and control and logistics services. As a result, historically many commodity exchanges are located in port cities.

3.6 RoRo Ports

Roll-on/roll-off (RoRo or ro-ro) ships are vessels designed to carry wheeled cargo such as automobiles, trucks, semitrailer trucks, trailers, trailer-flats, or railroad cars that are driven on and off the ship on their own wheels. This is in comparison to lo-lo (lift-on/lift-off) vessels, which use a crane to load and unload cargo. RoRo ports and terminals must provide the corresponding infrastructure to serve these vessels and to prestore and store the often-huge amount of rolling cargo. The biggest challenge for these ports is the fact that this kind of cargo can not be stacked. All rolling stock takes up ground level yard space.

The difference between cargo RoRo vessels and Ro-Pax ferries is that the latter can accommodate more than twelve passengers on board. For a larger number of passengers, the ports are obliged to provide the necessary infrastructure; therefore, we distinguish between cargo RoRo and (Ro-Pax and other) ferry ports. RoRo ports as described here concentrate on cargo operations.

RoRo vessels often have built-in ramps, which allow the cargo to be efficiently "rolled on" and "rolled off" the vessel when in port. The term "RoRo" is generally reserved for larger ocean-going vessels, not for smaller ferries. The ramps and doors may be stern-only, bow, and stern or quarter ramps for quick loading and unloading. The ports must provide the RoRo-ramp connections to allow the cargo to roll onboard. For some vessels, the ports must also be able to level out the tide via lifting the rolling platform. These facilities are very special and can only be used for RoRo vessels with stern or bow loading ramps. Compared with LoLo, the operating costs are often higher per unit and the utilization rates are lower. The big advantage of RoRo is the possibility of fast unloading and loading with huge teams of qualified drivers.

The requirement for special RoRo-terminals led to the development of stern and/or bow quarter ramps, which offer considerable advantages in cargo access. The main benefit of these is that they allow the vessel to berth in the normal manner alongside a quay wall without the need for dedicated terminal facilities. Ports are no longer obliged to provide ramps belonging to special RoRo vessels. This flexibility and independency from specialized port equipment is the main reason why modern ships are often equipped with quarter ramps. Another advantage of such vessels is that they require minimum port infrastructure, and so they can operate in poorly equipped environments.

Global port statistics for RoRo ports are not available, and public rankings like the one that can be found in the various literature for container ports do not exist. However, it is possible to at least get an impression about the most active RoRo ports in Europe. European statistics allow to extract different kind of RoRo cargo trades. It is possible to differentiate between the so-called pure car carrier (PCC) or RoRo vehicle ships facilitated vehicle trade (Table 3.8) and the rest; the so-called RoRo carrier (Table 3.10) trade. For European exports, the trade of vehicles such as personal cars, busses, and trucks is of huge importance. Therefore, the vehicle trade shall be described separately as shown in Table 3.8.

PCCs, as the name already indicates, are specialized carriers for only one type of cargo: vehicles. The word "car" in PCC stems from most private cars that make up the majority of trade. General RoRo carriers are not specialized for selected cargoes; they carry all types of rolling cargo. The number of calls of typical PCC as well as the dwt, that is, approximately the carrying capacity, indicates that the vehicle carrier segment is smaller than the RoRo carrier segment. However, for many ports the vehicle trade forms an important part of their business.

Table 3.8: Top twenty RoRo vehicle ports in Europe, 2015; unit = number of vehicles

Rank	Port	Country	imports	exports	total
1	Zeebrugge	Belgium	1,005,659	1,422,291	2,427,950
2	Bremerhaven	Germany	578,000	1,685,000	2,263,000
3	Emden	Germany	272,529	1,135,041	1,407,570
4	Grimsby1	UK	839,163	215,684	1,054,847
5	Antwerp	Belgium	481,661	488,045	969,706
6	Southampton	UK	393,450	521,550	915,000
7	Barcelona	Spain	265,501	616,189	881,690
8	Vlissingen	Netherlands	376,000	363,000	739,000
9	Bristol	UK	507,341	130,277	637,618
10	London2	UK	523,000	96,150	619,150
11	Valencia	Spain	174,471	433,076	607,547
12	Koper	Slovenia	208,888	398,438	607,326
13	Tyne	UK	211,515	369,700	581,215
14	Livorno	Italy	376,784	98,234	475,018
15	Santander	Spain	161,631	292,631	454,262
16	Vigo	Spain	54,315	371,994	426,309
17	Cuxhaven	Germany	80,000	340,000	420,000
18	Derince	Turkey	183,700	229,000	412,700
19	Salerno	Italy	83,842	314,159	398,001
20	Copenhagen/Malmö	Denmark/Sweden	220,000	140,000	360,000
		Total	**8,791,225**	**11,717,318**	**20,508,543**

[1] Combined Humber ports of: Grimsby, Immingham, & Killingholme
[2] Not all London terminals provided data, therefore estimates in line with average rise
Source: Automotive Logistics: 2015 European ports survey.

In Europe there are two very large and important vehicle ports, as shown in Table 3.8: Zeebrugge and Bremerhaven, both handling more than 2 million units per year. The Top 20 European RoRo Vehicle Ports represent approximately 80% or 16.7 mill. units out of the 20.5 reported as total. Of those ports surveyed by Automotive Logistics, import rose most significantly in reporting year 2015, climbing 14.1 % to 8.79 mill units, supported by the growth in sales across many European markets. Exports, which had been the dominant growth and volume driver for many ports, especially in northern Europe and Spain, were still strong over the last few years, reaching a level of 11.7 mill units in 2015. All top three ports in Belgium and Germany are mainly driven by exports, whereas most of the UK ports are dominated by imports. This reflects the consistently strong position of Germany's car manufacturers. In total the vehicle market was driven by internal demand within Europe and exports to North America; exports to China, on the other hand, saw broad declines. This is a clear sign that Chinese car manufacturers—some of them with European and American shareholders—are gaining increasing markets shares. Table 3.9 shows the most important customers of the top ten vehicle ports.

Table 3.9: Key customers of European vehicle ports, 2015

Rank	Port	Country	top carmakers
1	Zeebrugge	Belgium	Mercedes-Benz, Opel/Vauxhall, Toyota
2	Bremerhaven	Germany	BMW, Daimler, Volkswagen-Group
3	Emden	Germany	VW Group: Audi, Porsche, Skoda, VW
4	Grimsby*	UK	Kia, PSA, Mercedes-Benz, VW Group
5	Antwerp	Belgium	FCA, Ford, Mazda
6	Southampton	UK	BMW, Ford, Jaguar Land Rover
7	Barcelona	Spain	Renault, Nissan, Seat
8	Vlissingen	Netherlands	Ford, Jaguar Land Rover
9	Bristol	UK	FCA, GM (Vauxhall), Toyota
10	London*	UK	Ford, GM, Mercedes-Benz

* Port group: Grimsby, Immingham, & Killingholme
Source: Automotive Logistics: 2015 European ports survey.

Table 3.10 provides an overview of the top twenty RoRo carrier ports in Europe. Bremerhaven and Emden are top vehicle ports, but are not listed under top twenty RoRo carrier ports. This indicates a high level of specialization in these two ports on vehicle business, whereas Zeebrugge, the no. 1 vehicle port, is also highly engaged in other RoRo business, handling in total 13.9 mill tons of rolling cargo.

Finally, Table 3.10 also shows that some ports that are listed in the general cargo, container, or bulk lists are also active in handling the RoRo carriers for cargo. A good example of this type of universal port is Rotterdam. This also indicates that ports that are active at a high level in many segments, that is, the typical "universal ports" are rare. Most ports are specialized in trades that are predominantly set by the industrial pattern in port hinterland.

Table 3.10: Top twenty RoRo carrier ports in Europe, 2015

Rank	Port	Country	Cargo in mill tons
1	Dover	UK	27.1
2	Calais	France	19.5
3	Immingham	UK	16.1
4	Zeebrugge	Belgium	13.9
5	Lübeck/Travemünde	Germany	12.8
6	Dublin	Ireland	11.7
7	Rotterdam	Netherlands	11.7
8	Trelleborg	Sweden	10.9
9	Livorno	Italy	9.5
10	Gothenburg	Sweden	8.7
11	Palma de Mallorca	Spain	8.0
12	Genova	Italy	8.0
13	Rostock	Germany	7.8
14	London	UK	7.8
15	Liverpool	UK	7.4
16	Dunkirk	France	7.3
17	Messina	Italy	7.1
18	Helsinki	Finland	7.0
19	Puttgarden	Germany	6.7
20	Rodby	Denmark	6.7
	Total		**215.7**

Source: RoRo & Ferry Atlas 2016/2017, page 7.

3.7 Ferry Ports

Like for RoRo ports, there is no global list or ranking of the top ferry ports. There-fore, we again concentrate on European ports only, and because of missing actual data, Table 3.11 ranks the ports based on 2014 data. However, the table shows the most important ferry ports. Typical "overnight ferries" are generally also Ro-Pax ferries but with night cabins. As the name says, these vessels also carry rolling cargo. Ro-Pax and overnight ferries are generally much larger than pas-senger-only ferries. Typical and high frequency ferry connections like the link between the UK and France Dover-Calais can be identified. Table 3.11 includes all kinds of ferries.

Table 3.11: Top twenty ferry ports in Europe, 2014

Rank	Port	Country	Passenger in mill
1	Dover	UK	13.4
2	Helsinki	Finland	10.9
3	Calais	France	10.7
4	Stockholm	Sweden	9.9
5	Tallinn	Estonia	9.1
6	Piraeus	Greece	8.1
7	Helsingborg	Sweden	7.7
8	Naples	Italy	7.7
9	Helsingor	Denmark	7.6
10	Messina	Italy	7
11	Villa San Giovanni1	Italy	6.2
12	Capri	Italy	6.1
13	Puttgarden	Germany	6
14	Rodby	Denmark	6
15	Algeciras	Spain	5.4
16	Palma de Mallorca	Spain	4.9
17	Piombino	Italy	3.4
18	Turku	Finland	3.2
19	Mariehamn	Finland	3
20	Portoferraio	Italy	2.9
	Total		**139.2**

[1] Mentioned also as Reggio di Calabria
Source: RoRo & Ferry Atlas 2016/2017, page 10.

3.8 Passenger Ports

Pure passenger ports are normally relatively small facilities with few quay walls, road access, and passenger waiting facilities. Passenger ships transport the guests on board usually between few points only, for example, by connecting an island with few mainland ports. Due to the small size of the vessels—often with low draught—the small size of the ports, and the limited economic importance, they will not be discussed in detail. Due to the absence of global statistics the top twenty European passenger ports are listed in Table 3.12.

Table 3.12: Top twenty passenger ports in Europe

Rank	Port	Country	in 1,000
1	Piraeus	Greece	15,814
2	Dover	UK	13,082
3	Helsinki	Finland	11,214
4	Stockholm	Sweden	9,887
5	Calais	France	9,757
6	Tallinn	Estonia	9,299
7	Helsingborg	Sweden	7,670
8	Helsingor	Denmark	7,644
9	Paloukia Salaminas	Greece	7,050
10	Perama	Greece	7,050
11	Messina	Italy	7,021
12	Napoli	Italy	6,484
13	Puttgarden	Germany	6,141
14	Rodby (Faergeh.)	Denmark	6,139
15	Reggio Di Calabria	Italy	6,053
16	Palma Mallorca	Spain	5,496
17	Algeciras	Spain	5,473
18	Cirkewwa	Malta	4,740
19	Mgarr, Gozo	Malta	4,740
20	Capri	Italy	4,355

Source: Eurostat; Port web pages; own calculations.

Well-known port connections and port-pairs can easily be identified, like Dover—Calais (with Dover having additional lines and more passengers), Perama—Paloukia Salaminas (connecting the Salamina island with Athens, the capital of Greece), Messina—Reggio Di Calabria (connecting mainland Italy with Sicilia), Helsingborg—Helsingor (connecting Sweden and Denmark), Rodby—Puttgarden (connecting Denmark with Germany), or Cirkewwa—Mgarr (connecting Malta with Gozo island). Other port connections like Algeciras—Ceuta or Algeciras—Tangier are binding Spain and Morocco in North Africa.

A typical characteristic of all these passenger port connections is that they "extend" the highways over the waters and connect families and businesses. The EU-concept of "Motorways of the Sea" expresses the idea behind this concept very well. In many cases passengers use their own cars to board the vessel and the journey itself is fairly short.

3.9 Cruise Ports

For cruise ships and by extension cruise ports, transportation of cargo, or a short connection over a waterway is not the primary goal of the voyage. The journey itself, the ships' amenities, and the various stopover locations for tourists are the primary focuses of the cruise. The layout of cruise ports therefore is completely different from cargo ports. No spacious warehouses are necessary, many cranes are also not necessary, and other heavy cargo handling equipment like Van Carriers, Transtainers, or Reach Stackers are also not needed; nor are storage facilities for cargoes/products.

The cruise business is nevertheless a growing business with a strong economic impact. Cruise vessels are often much larger than passenger ships, the draught is comparable with mid- to large-sized cargo vessels, they have the capacity for several thousand passengers, and the power such a vessel needs is comparable to that of a small town.[10] They operate on routes that return to their originating port, so the ports of call are usually also the ports of destination. During the voyage, the cruise vessel stops at different destinations, and it is the intention of the cruise line industry to keep most of the passengers on board in one port only. This will limit the staff needed in the ports en route. Though this is not always possible, that is typically the cruise's intention. We can distinguish between the following three categories of cruise ports:

1. Home ports: the starting and (or) ending point for a cruise
2. Ports of call: ports visited by a cruise vessel during the cruise
3. Hybrid ports: a mixture of the previous two categories

Hybrid ports are the starting and ending point for some cruise itineraries but also act as intermediate points for other cruises. From a port's point of view, it is most attractive to act as the home port, as this generates the highest revenues for the port as well as for the tourist industry and other facilities, like airports, hotels, and restaurants. In home ports, there are very often branch offices from cruise operators, and the check in/check out facilities are located here as well.

---

10 Medium-sized cruise ships like the one calling the Port of Copenhagen in Denmark typically have an energy consumption of 7 to 11 MW while they are in port. This is equal to the average electricity consumption of 27,000 to 42,000 Copenhagen households as a study issued by the Port of Copenhagen reports (Cruise Ships Copenhagen, 2015, page 11). Other studies came to similar results: a typical medium-sized cruise vessel consumes the electric power of a small city like Portsmouth in Virginia, Nancy in France, or Bolzano in Italy with 30,000 to 40,000 households or approximately 100,000 inhabitants.

Many cruise ports also feature huge parking lots, bus stops, taxi stands, etc., and hotels offer attractive packages for cruise passengers; the intention here is to lengthen the passengers' vacation for a couple of days. Cruise lines calculate that a typical cruise passenger spends six to seven times more money in a home port than in a port of call. This is a huge incentive for the tourist industry to concentrate the cruise passengers in their preferred ports.

Typically, cruise ports are located in attractive touristic areas, which offer a wide variety of highlights and in most cases feature comfortable climate conditions. Table 3.13 lists the most appealing destinations to cruise according to the CLIA Cruise Liners International Association.[11]

Table 3.13: Most appealing destinations to cruise

Caribbean/Bahamas	33.7%
Mediterranean/Greek Islands/Turkey	18.7%
Europe without Mediterranean	11.7%
Asia	9.2%
Australia/New Zealand	6.1%
Alaska	4.1%
South America	2.7%
Other	13.8%

Source: FCCA Florida-Caribbean Cruise Assn., Industry Overview 2017.

The international cruise industry as it is known today is only about forty years old, but the concept of cruise vessels dates back to the late 19th century. After World War II, the operators of underemployed passenger ships sought new destinations and new cruise voyages were introduced, however, pure cruise operations remained far less popular than passenger transportation.

The modern cruise industry started in the Caribbean, which is still the main market for mass cruises. The pioneering company became Norwegian Caribbean Lines (NCL). NCL later started up a cooperation with Ted Arison, who later broke out and bought his own ship, which became the start of Carnival Cruises (1972). Another Norwegian company, Royal Caribbean Cruise Lines (RCCL), started with the vessel *Song of Norway* in 1970. These three companies have dominated the modern cruise industry in the last four decades and remain dominating players today (mainly Carnival and RCCL).

---

11 Quoted after: FCCA Florida-Caribbean Cruise Association, Cruise Industry Overview – 2011, Pembroke Pines, Florida, USA 2012, page 8. See www.f-cca.com.

Since the beginning of modern mass cruises, the main source market is North America; followed in the last two decades by Europe (mainly UK), as Table 3.14 indicates. But with more than 50% of cruise passengers, North American tourists are still the key customers of cruise liners and cruise ports.

Table 3.14: Worldwide cruise revenue by source, 2015

Source Region	
North America	58.6%
Europe	25.9%
Asia	8.5%
South America	2.5%
Australia/New Zealand	4.3%
Middle East/Africa	0.2%
Grand Total	100%

Source: www.cruisemarketwatch.com

Table 3.15: Top twenty cruise ports, 2015

Rank	Port	Country	Passenger
1	Miami	USA	4,980,490
2	Port Canaveral	USA	4,248,296
3	Port Everglades	USA	3,826,415
4	Cozumel	Mexico	3,636,649
5	Nassau/Paradise Island	Bahamas	3,521,178
6	Shanghai	China	2,847,000
7	Barcelona	Spain	2,683,594
8	The Out Islands	Bahamas	2,549,803
9	Civitavecchia	Italy	2,339,676
10	Galveston	USA	1,730,289
11	Georgetown	Cayman Islands	1,711,853
12	Palma de Mallorca	Spain	1,720,000
13	Southampton	UK	1,700,000
14	St. Thomas/St. John	US Virgin Islands	1,694,008
15	Pointe Blanche	Sint Maarten	1,668,863
16	Venice	Italy	1,605,660
17	Marseille	France	1,597,213
18	New York/New Jersey	USA	1,537,695
19	San Juan	Puerto Rico	1,379,367
20	Sydney	Australia	1,309,000

Sources: CLIA; FCCA; Cruise Med; Cruise Europe; own calculations.

Taking the touristic destinations in mind, it is a natural consequence that the most active home ports as well as ports of call are in these areas, too. Table 3.15 shows the ranking of the top twenty cruise ports. The busiest cruise port in the world is Miami, Florida, and it has been for many years. Together with Port Canaveral and the Everglades, it is easy to identify the "Sunshine State" of Florida as the global center of cruise business. The big cruise lines are also located in this area.

The fact that a home port generates higher revenues than a pure port of call has led many ports to offer attractive tourist packages in their area to become a home port. Although this is not in favor of the cruise lines, they support this trend, because it opens new markets for tourists that are interested to board a vessel close to their preferred airport or city. As a result, it is no longer possible to clearly distinguish between these two kinds of ports. Therefore, Table 3.15 only lists total passengers.

Part 2: **Ports in Maritime Supply Chain**

Chapter 4
The Role of Ports in Supply Chains

4.1 Definition "Ports"

In a very general way, the globally recognized maritime expert and lecturer Professor Gerhardt Muller[1] defines the term "port" as: "a harbor or haven where ships may anchor, or a harbor area with marine terminal facilities for transferring cargo/passengers between ships and land transportation." In this definition the word "marine" may imply that a port is a territorial unit established on a coastline, that is, located more or less directly at the open sea. This definition from Muller does not explicitly consider the existence of many river ports, which, in some cases, handle considerable international traffic although they may be dozens of miles away from the open sea (e.g., Chongquing in China, Duisburg in Germany or Asuncion in Paraguay). For all these locations the word "marine" is normally not used.

In a report prepared for the Commission of the European Communities, the term "port" is more widely defined as: "an area of land and water made up of such improvement works and equipment as to permit, principally, the reception of ships, their loading and unloading, the storage of goods, the receipt and delivery of these goods by inland transport and can also include the activities of businesses linked to sea transport."[2]

The official UN and EU Transport Statistics Glossary defines the term "port" as: "A place having facilities for merchant ships to moor and to load or unload cargo or to disembark or embark passengers to or from vessels, usually directly to a pier."[3] These more comprehensive definitions include the fact that ports are not only transferring cargo or passengers between (ocean going) vessels and land transportation, but could also be involved in hinterland activities; and this for all modes of transportation. For many of the world's big river systems like the Mississippi, St. Lawrence, Yangtze, Nile, Danube, or Volga this kind of traffic represents

---

1 Muller, Gerhardt. *Intermodal Freight Transportation*, Washington 1999, page 471.
2 Commission of the European Communities, *The Main Seaports of the Community*, Brussels 1986, page 5.
3 United Nations, *Glossary for Transport Statistics, 3rd Edition,* Document prepared by the Intersecretariat Working Group on Transport Statistics, Office for Official Publications of the European Communities, Luxemburg 2003, page 79 (UN Transport Glossary).

DOI 10.1515/9781547400874-004

most traffic, that is, we need to include this traffic in our understanding and will thus use the UN-definition.

From a holistic supply chain point of view, the above mentioned operational definitions of ports are not sufficient. We must include the view along the supply chain and put the port functions into the right perspective. In this view, ports, ships, and all other modes of transportation are partnered within logistics processes from seller to buyer, from factory to consumer/investor. Ports are the transfer points (nodal points) within a transportation flow. They move cargo or passengers from one mode of transportation to another, for example, from a land transport mode like rail or truck to a waterborne mode like ships or barges. Figure 4.1 outlines the position of ports within supply chain flows.

Especially for river ports with sometimes very low waters on the river, the function as transfer point between two modes of land transportation may be as important as its waterborne role. What remains from a holistic supply chain point of view is the core function as *location for changing the mode of transportation;* or as Park and Medda called it as a "bridge between shipping activity and inland transport network."[4] In our understanding, this function must be offered for all conveyance (ship, inland vessel, rail, truck, pipelines), although we know that ships are the dominant and most visible ones. With this definition, ports represent "immobile" knots within a highly mobile and flexible transportation network. They are not a means for themselves but have to fulfill a transportation task along the supply chain. This is the core function of ports, and this is the commercial authorization of their existence.

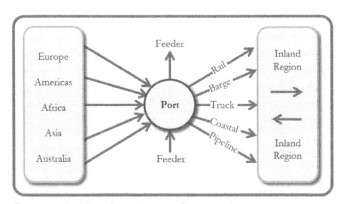

Figure 4.1: Position of ports in networks

---

4 Park, Yong-An and Francesca Medda, *Classification of Container Ports on the Basis of Networks,* 12th WCTR July 11–15, Lisbon, Portugal 2010, page 2.

4.2 Port Functions

Additional tasks may support the *core function* of ports and by nature they are relatively close to the core business, that is, bunkering for vessels or veterinary services. These tasks are not essential or—in other words—are not a "must" for a port to fulfill its core function; but having them available 24/7 close to the ships and terminals is a real advantage and may—as the word says—support the core business. Therefore, we will name them "supportive functions."

Other tasks that can be found in ports may be complementary to the core and to the supportive business, although they are more distant than the supportive functions. These tasks do not directly support the core business; therefore, we call them "complementary functions"; like forwarding services in the hinterland or empty container storage. All these tasks may ease the transport or may (i.e., for reaching critical masses) increase the throughput to be economically efficient, but they remain supportive or complementary to the core business.

The long list of tasks ports may offer could be:
- Storage of cargo (buffer stock function)
- Collecting cargo for long haul trades (prestorage)
- Empty container storage and supply
- Bunkering for ocean vessel
- Ship supply (ship chandler services)
- Ship maintenance + repair
- Ship assistance/pilots, VTMS, etc.
- Customs services/free trade areas
- Veterinary services
- Services for passenger and cargo: cooling, packaging, container repair, etc.
- Infra- and superstructure supply, like dredging
- Hinterland operations, like forwarding services
- Port Traffic Management Systems
- Home for supporting industries

The list above is not exhaustive, but it shows that the variety of additional port services and functions is huge. The border between core functions, supportive functions, and complementary functions as delineated in Figure 4.2 is not sharp and clearly defined. We will thus not group them; however, it is necessary to understand that not all tasks a port fulfills are of the same importance for the core business.

Different ports provide different functions, and larger ports provide a wide variety of services. Especially for terminal operators, it could be of economic interest to enlarge their business and create new and additional offerings within the area of supportive and complementary functions. With all this, many ports represent important players within their regional economy. This is with no doubt true and shall not be questioned. But considering this in all its bearings, it should not be forgotten that the core function of a port within a supply chain is its function as a nodal point in transferring passengers and cargo from one mode of transportation to another.

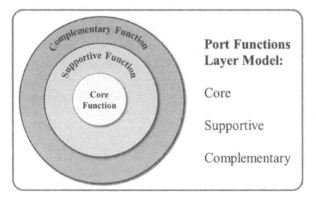

Figure 4.2: Port functions

From a supply chain point of view, the core function as "location for changing the mode of transportation" is in the center of interest. In our understanding trade is the key driver for transportation, and port business is derivative business, that is, the foundation of the business is built on trade. Therefore, the supply chain view is important!

4.3 Port Customer Groups

Ports and port customers are partners within a supply chain, and such a chain can be described as a system of companies, institutions, people, activities, and information that moves products and services from supplier to final customer. Maritime supply chains include waterborne transportation, which requires ports as nodal points for modal shifts, for example, from oceangoing vessel to road and rail hinterland transportation devices. Also, any supportive or complementary function can help to increase the attractiveness of a maritime supply chain. A port in such a system deals with many partners, which from a business point of view, should be seen and treated as business customers.

In commercial ports, partners (customers) are not final consumers. In other words, port business or port activities are nearly exclusively business-to-business (B2B) arrangements, and not business-to-consumer (B2C) sales of goods and services to public customers. Port activities as part of maritime supply chains are B2B arrangements.

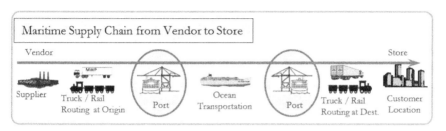

Figure 4.3: Ports in supply chains

The sketch in Figure 4.3 highlights that the shipping industry as well as all kinds of hinterland transportation are the key partners of ports. Figure 2.2 in Chapter 2 already showed in more detail that behind these industries are several companies that help to facilitate the trade, like shipping companies and their agents, hauler/forwarding companies, stevedores, customs brokers, public institutions like police, port authorities, port health, veterinary control, ship maintenance companies, ship chandlers, industry associations, warehousing companies, etc. Key targets for all these partners include the smooth flow of cargoes and the easy and efficient in-time delivery of services and goods. A Port Community System as briefly described in Chapter 2.1, can help to increase efficiency of the supply chain via optimizing information flow.

While the abovementioned partners are important in the supply chain, the key customer groups of ports are the shipping lines and their agents, as well as the road and rail industry and their agents. For ports with access to inland navigation, organizers of this mode of transportation are also important business partners. In the container business, such transports organized by the transportation industry including the land transports to and from the ports are defined as "carrier's haulage." The "International Commercial Terms" or "INCOTERMS" (see Chapter 5.5) clearly describe the rights and duties along the supply chain, but for the identification of key customer groups it is sufficient to cluster them or their agents as "carriers." These carriers can be shipping lines, forwarders, or even railways. If larger parts of a container trade are not organized by carriers but rather via traders or the industry directly, this type of trade is known as "merchant haulage."

In the bulk shipping business, "carriers haulage" does not exist. Throughout history and still today, cargo like crude oil and iron ore was traded with more direct business relations between seller and buyer. Based on these contacts and the contracts signed between vendor and customer, the transport of bulk cargo is organized by this industry. INCOTERMS are also of relevance during these trades; specialized bulk shipping companies are working within this close and specialized environment.

4.4 Port Cluster

A port cluster can be defined as a geographic concentration of interconnected supply chain businesses at the sea-land interface. There is no need for the ports to be in one state only. It is more important that they are considered as potential competitors within the same relevant market. Port clusters can be important in terms of strategic port development in geographical economics.

In the past, ports in many countries have usually been developed as part of local port development programs. Such programs normally do not take into consideration the corresponding plans of other ports within the country or the adjacent region, a factor that could have resulted in better coordination for increased national benefit. In many cases, instead of attempting to achieve mutual aims, undue competition tends to develop between ports within the same country or region. In government-owned ports, this situation can result in uneconomical investment of national capital in competing projects, and moreover, in loss of opportunities to attract a portion of international maritime traffic.

Figure 4.4 identifies ports in regions that could potentially cooperate to increase mutual success. A key element of port clustering is the potential to realize competitive advantages of each port within the cluster. Specialization is the ultimate result of strategic port clustering; one or few ports concentrate on selected group(s) of cargoes or passengers, while the other ports focus on different customers. This will lead to specialized liquid bulk ports, dry bulk ports, RoRo ports, cruise ports, container ports, military ports, etc., within the region of the cluster.

From a single ports perspective, this is exactly the opposite of a universal port concept. And this is exactly the weakest point in this concept: a single port will lose part of its autonomy for the sake of the overall cluster concept. Unfortunately, this is the reality today, and therefore the good idea of clustering and division of labor within a region will not be successful in the future if market economies and local competition exists.

Cluster	Container ports	Distance*
Pearl River Delta	Hongkong, Shenzhen, Guangzhou, Zhongzhan, Jiuzhou	130
Malacca Strait	Singapore, Port Klang, Tanjung Pelepas	340
Yangtze River Delta	Shanghai, Ningbo	180
Rhine-Scheldt Delta	Rotterdam, Antwerp, Zeebrugge, Amsterdam	105
Bohai Bay	Dalian, Quingdao, Tianjin,	350
San Pedro Bay	Los Angeles, Long Beach	10
Korean Twin Hub	Busan, Gwangjang	135
Helgoland Bay	Hamburg, Bremerhaven, Wilhelmshaven	95
Tokyo Bay	Tokyo, Yokohama, Shimizu	50

* Largest distance in km between competing ports in the cluster
Source: Time to move beyond competition, Peter W. de Langen, in: *Ports & Harbors*, March 2008, pages 34–35.

Figure 4.4: World port cluster: major ports in proximity

4.5 "Port" Terms in Common Use

The word "port" is often used with an explanatory second word carried in front that should give an indication of what kind the port is, like "hub port" or "bulk port." However, the supplementary word in combination with "port" is not sufficient to explain the full content of the meaning. Therefore, we will explore frequently used terms below, but first let's clarify the difference between the terms "port" and "terminal."

Port versus Terminal

The UN Glossary describes a port as an area with facilities for vessels to moor and load or unload cargo or to disembark or embark passengers. This definition, like most others available, highlights the geographic dimension, which is used when speaking about ports. The "port" or "port area" is a precisely defined geographical area. In the special case of a "free port" this area must be fenced, and this visible fence (in other cases, the boundary) shows the special limits of the port area.

Port areas commonly underlie special laws, often called "port development laws." In this sense, a port also has a juristic dimension as its own legal entity. Inside the port area there can be roads, railways, waterways, industrial estates, green fields, and terminals. Port areas have underlying special rules and regulations and may be protected; but in most ports the infrastructure is at least partly open for the public (i.e., access roads). In addition, special public or semipublic institutions are often responsible for port governance and port administration—the so-called port authorities.

A "terminal" is an area inside the port, a facility where cargoes are trans-shipped between different transport vehicles for onward transportation, or where passengers embark or disembark. Key elements of terminals include berths, a yard for operations, buildings like warehouses, sheds or offices, and (very often) cranes; this is the physical place where the operations between ships and land take place. Terminals can be operated by public authorities or by private entities. For security reasons, terminals are normally protected and can only be entered with special permission. Terminals are often specialized for cargoes, like container terminals, dry bulk terminals, tank terminals, RoRo terminals, ferry terminals, cruise terminals, off shore terminals, etc. A port can have any number of terminals.

The activities of the port administration and the terminals are interdependent. The port authorities prepare the frame (e.g., the physical and regulatory infrastructure) for the (public or private) terminal operator(s). Conflicts of interest are inherent and system-related and need to be moderated for mutual success. The way a port is governed is described below in Chapters 8ff.

Figure 4.5 shows the Haifa Port in Israel. The figure key reflects the many different terminals that constitute the port.

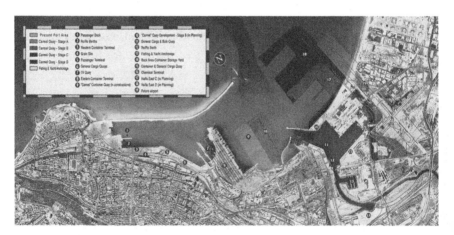

Figure 4.5: Port + terminals in Haifa, Israel

The various shades stand for roads, bridges, rail tracks, a tank storage farm, anchorage areas, warehouse complexes, berths, water basins, a breakwater, several terminals, and a development area for future port expansion. The whole complex forms "the port." What can not be seen in this figure is the borderline; but this line does exist. In Figure 4.5 we can see several terminals for passenger, container, general cargo, dry bulk, and liquid bulk. Terminals normally consist of a berth and the coherent area behind this berth. The size of a single terminal is fixed in a contract between the port authority and the single terminal operator.

Container Port

A "container port" is a port where sea containers and containerized cargo represent most of the cargo that is handled. The container can be moved as a full container that is not opened in the port, a so-called full container load (FCL). Alternatively, the container (the "box") can be stuffed or unstuffed inside the port, a so-called less container load (LCL). The container handling activities between ship and shore take place on container terminals. A container port can consist of several container terminals. Container terminals usually provide storage facilities for both loaded and empty containers. Loaded containers are stored for relatively short periods, while waiting for onward transportation; unloaded containers may be stored for longer periods awaiting their next use. The distinguishing characteristics of a container port include having lots of container gantry cranes and providing many services around sea containers.

There is no precise threshold that defines what "a container port" is, but in our understanding a port receives the "container port" classification when at least 50% of its cargo handling volume is containerized cargo. Ports with less than this 50% are ports that handle containers but should not be named "container port." For further details and a container port statistic, refer to Chapter 3.2. The container handling activities inside the port can take place on a single terminal, like it is usual for many smaller ports with limited throughput, or even across several terminals (up to eleven, like in Shanghai; or nine, like in Hong Kong or in Ho Chi Minh City) with competing operators.

The Port of Busan in South Korea had a throughput of 347.7 mt in 2015, and out of this 333.3 mill t was containerized cargo, as reported in Figure 3.3. The degree of containerized cargo in relation to total throughput was 96%. With this, the Port of Busan can be called a container port. The same is true for Port Klang in Malaysia, a port with nearly 12 mill TEU in throughput and a share of 86% in container trade.

General Cargo Port

The term "general cargo port" concentrates on the cargo that is handled as major cargo in such a port. As explained in Chapter 3.3, there are different understandings of what "general cargo" is. Some definitions include containerized cargo, others do not. However, to be classified a "general cargo port" the respective port should handle more than 50% of the throughput as cargo in this category. For further details, see Chapter 3.3.

Bulk Port

The term "bulk port" puts the focus on the type of products that are handled as major cargo in such a port. When the majority is bulk cargo like coal, ores (dry bulk), crude oil, oil products, or chemicals (liquid bulk), then these ports are often classified as bulk ports. If one product dominates the trade, such a port could also be named after the product, for example, oil port. Specialized ports often have a share of close to 100% of the respective cargo, for example, like Port Hedland and Dampier in Australia, or Ras Tanura in Saudi Arabia, some of the largest bulk ports in the world. For further details, see Chapter 3.4 for liquid bulk and 3.5 for dry bulk.

RoRo Port

The term "RoRo port" concentrates on the kind of traffic in such a port. A RoRo port is a port where RoRo traffic dominates the trade in the port. Also, we should have a threshold of 50% in mind; ports with RoRo traffic below 50% should not be classified as RoRo ports, but as ports with RoRo traffic. For further details, see Chapter 3.6.

Ferry Port

The term "ferry port" also concentrates on the kind of traffic in such a port. A ferry port is a port where ferry traffic dominates the trade in the port. Also, we should have a threshold of 50% in mind; ports with ferry traffic below 50% should not be classified as ferry ports, but as a port with ferry traffic. For further details, see Chapter 3.7.

Passenger Port

The term "passenger port" highlights the fact that most of the traffic in such a port is passenger traffic; this is often the case when islands need to be connected. As proposed above, a threshold of 50% of total traffic should be from passengers to classify a port as a passenger port. Passenger ports often provide small RoRo ramps for light vehicles, bicycles, and pedestrians. For further details, see Chapter 3.8.

Cruise Port

A "cruise port" is a port that concentrates on tourism. When most of the business in such a port is cruise business, these ports should be classified as "cruise ports." As proposed above, a threshold of 50% of total traffic should be used to classify a port as a cruise port. In addition to the typical touristic facilities with waiting halls, check-in and check-out gates, customs procedures, etc., these ports often provide small cranes for ships' supply, like food and beverage for the passenger, or spare parts and equipment for the ship. For further details, see Chapter 3.9.

Universal Port

A port that handles most of the typical cargoes is called a "universal port." It is the opposite of a specialized port that concentrates specifically on one or a few typical products. The word "universal" hereby reflects a variety of products. A typical universal port handles containers, conventional general cargo, liquid bulk, dry bulk, RoRo traffic, cruise business, etc.

Universal ports do not fall in one of the categories mentioned above; these ports provide a little bit of everything. Universal ports can be small ports in remote areas that have to provide a wide range due to missing alternatives in the vicinity, but a universal port can also be a huge port like Rotterdam, that grows due to the dominant location inside Europe in more or less all cargo categories.

Dedicated Port/Terminal

The term "dedicated port" describes a port that is working for just one group of companies and is dedicated to the shipping line(s) belonging to these companies. Some bulk ports fall into this category. More frequently used is the term "dedicated terminal." This describes a terminal—often a container terminal—that is operated by a single shipping company, or by a group of shipping companies. Shipping lines like Maersk (Denmark), CMA CGM (France), or Evergreen (Taiwan) operate their own container terminals, and these facilities are open for vessels of the group or—in some cases—also for partners of the shipping line. As a tool for corporate identity, the facilities of these terminals like gantry cranes or buildings are usually painted in the colors of the shipping line, that is, in dark blue for CMA CGM, in green for Evergreen, or in light blue with a white star for Maersk.

The main reason for shipping lines to build or to have a stake in dedicated terminals was (and in some parts of the world still is) the fear of not having enough capacity for future growth available. Especially in the early 2000s, shipping lines often used the argument of ensuring land side handling and growth capacity. Building a new port or terminal can take a long time, and this lengthy duration was the reason for considering container terminal capacity as a limiting factor along the supply chain. Building a ship can be realized in two or three years; having a new greenfield container terminal with all hinterland connection established often takes more than a decade. Container Shipping Lines envisaged a bottleneck in container terminals and reacted with the strategy of enlarging their activities along the logistics chain and being engaged in terminal operations.

It is complicated if not impossible to find out exactly which facilities are more efficient and economical: universal terminals, which are open for many users, or dedicated facilities, which are bound to one company (or one group of companies). No terminal will fully open their books to provide economic details about their port. But from an operational point of view, if we only consider port activities, dedicated terminals are not as efficient as universal terminals. Berth utilization is often higher at universal terminals; however, this argument ignores the fact that a dedicated terminal is more than just a single terminal. These terminals are part of a supply chain, and so the isolated port argument is often lacking in substance. In other words, universal ports are often considered as profit centers, whereas dedicated terminals are cost centers.

The A.P. Møller-Maersk group, which owns the world's largest container shipping line "Maersk Line," has founded its own subsidiary for dedicated terminals: APMT or APM Terminals. Maersk is large enough to create its own terminal company for ensuring terminal capacity for the Maersk Line vessel, and with this, Maersk realized additional growth potential by enlarging the business along the supply chain. In its 2016 Annual Group Report Maersk reported that the network contains "73 operating ports in 69 countries,"[5] and the ports in total handled a

---

[5] A.P. Møller-Maersk A/S Group Annual Report 2016, Copenhagen, Denmark 2017, pages 15–16.

volume of 37.3 mill TEU in 2016. With this business, APMT contributes 11.2% to the group's revenue; profit in 2016 was 438 m USD. The unit costs in 2016 could be reduced and turned out at an average of 172 USD per move. In such a concept, dedicated terminals should not be analyzed and assessed as a single terminal; they are cost centers and part of a production chain.

Main Port

The term "main port" is often used as a regional economic argument. Within a region or cluster there are several ports and it is often heard that one port claims to be the main port. The argument of being "main" is often used in relation to the total cargo throughput volume. In this context, "main port" means the largest in volume, busiest, and therefore most important port. But having the greatest cargo volume is not necessary for being classified as the main port. The classification of "main port" can also relate to the port's relationship with the hinterland. If a port is of huge importance for the hinterland, that is, due to its dominant position at the mouth of a river, it is often heard that these ports call themselves main port. If in the neighborhood of such a main port, for example, a huge bulk facility exists, it could be that the volume of the bulk terminal is larger; although this bulk terminal is not considered the main port. The third criteria for being considered the main port is the character of being a universal port, and not bound to few commodities only. Another argument for claiming main port status is the large variety of shipping lines calling this port, and so the integration of this specific port in transportation networks.

There is an overlapping of the definitions, but the four arguments "volume, hinterland, universality, and net-integration" are typical characteristics for main ports. Typical indicators for the definition of "Main Port" do not exist. This is negative for quantitative oriented scientists but offers flexibility in praxis.

Major Port

Regarding the regional economic functions, the term "major port" is very similar to "main port," but in some countries, for example, in India, the term has an additional important implication. A major port belongs to the central government; in the case of India, the major ports are part of the administration of the central government in New Delhi. They are part of the nation-wide transport policy and belong to the Ministry of Transport and report to New Delhi. All major ports are seaports like Mumbai, JNPT, Chennai, or Tuticorin.

The number of major ports under the administration of the central government in India has changed during the last years, but swings around ten to twelve ports, only. The local port authority of a major port does not report to the municipal or state government, but to the central government. And the central government often is far away from the ports; both in terms of kilometric distance as well as in questions of daily management. Inflexibility is often the consequence of this set up.

Minor Port

A "minor port" is the pendant to the above-mentioned major port. Minor ports are administered from lower governmental levels, that is, from state levels, like in India. This gives more flexibility, and regarding the economic importance, some minor ports today are even more a "main port" than other major ports. The terms major and minor just reflect the governmental level of port administration.

Hub Port + Feeder Port

The concept lying behind "hub ports" is the so-called hub-and-spoke-model, a concept named after a bicycle wheel, which has a strong central hub with a series of connecting spokes. A hub port is a huge port to which many shipping lines direct their cargo from a remote port to the hub port. The shipping lines in this context are serving as the "spokes" that connect the remote small ports with the hub, as outlined in Figure 4.6, left part of the graphic.

The hub-and-spoke system may appear like the map on the right side of Figure 4.6: along the coastline of a continent there are several ports, and for various reasons one port has developed itself as hub port with international and intercontinental hub connections, plus additional spoke connections on the same continent. Smaller ports are "feeding" the major port, and therefore these ports are called "feeder ports." The services connecting the hub port with the number of smaller ports are accordingly called "feeder services"; the lines traveling between these ports are called "feeder lines."

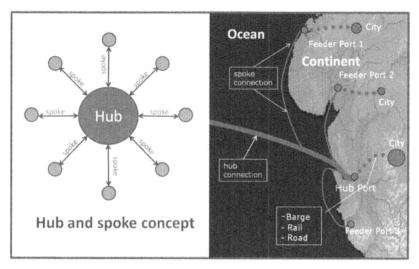

Figure 4.6: Outline of hub-and-spoke concept

Key factors for a port to become a hub port are:
- Location (proximity to major world routes)
- Fast turnaround time for vessels
- High quality and efficient port services
- Well-connected hinterland; access to rail, inland navigation, and road distribution networks
- Excellent feeder network covering neighboring feeder ports
- High local market potential (loco-potential = local commodities potential)
- Efficient port administration and terminal operation
- Reasonable tariffs and costs
- Ability to accommodate appropriate vessels/sufficient water depth
- Existence of logistic cluster supporting value-added services

A hub-and-spoke system has the big advantage of reducing the number of long haul trades without reducing the connectivity of smaller ports. The hub port serves as concentrator and opens the advantages for economies of scale for the shipping lines that can employ bigger vessels with reduced slot costs. This is of advantage for smaller ports, too, because they are connected to a wide network. But the concentration on the hub does not come for free. Additional (transhipment) moves in the hub port must be calculated.

With increasing feeder moves in a feeder port it could be of interest to frequently (re)calculate the possibility of switching from feeder connections to direct calls. The break-even volumes depend on many variables, but it has been seen quite often that smaller ports grow with volume and develop to port of calls, and some even develop into hub ports. But the other way is true as well, that ports can lose their hub functions and revert to a port with regional importance only.

A real drawback of this model is the fact that it is highly centralized, and day-to-day operations may be relatively inflexible. Even small changes at the hub, or in a single route, could have unexpected consequences throughout the network. It may be difficult or impossible to handle occasional periods of high demand between two spokes, for example, between Feeder Port 1 and Feeder Port 3 in Figure 4.6.

Route scheduling is complicated for the hub port network coordinator. Scarce resources must be used carefully to avoid starving the hub. Careful traffic analysis and precise timing are required to keep the hub operating efficiently. The hub may constitute a bottleneck or single point of failure in the network. Total cargo capacity of the network is limited by the hub's capacity. Delays at the hub (caused, e.g., by bad weather conditions) can result in delays throughout the network. Delays at a spoke can also affect the network.

All cargo from feeder ports must pass through the hub before reaching its destination, requiring longer journeys than direct point-to-point trips. This trade-off may be desirable for freight which can benefit from sorting and consolidating operations at the hub, but not for time-critical cargo and passengers.

The hub-and-spoke concept was first developed by the American airline industry after deregulation at the beginning of the 1980s in the last century. From there it spread throughout the whole transportation industry. Today many ports name themselves "hub port" and use this term intensively for marketing purposes.

Gateway Port

The term "gateway port" is often used for a port with high regional importance, for example, for the main or even only port of an island. This port serves as "gateway to the world" for its dedicated hinterland. If the local market is large and the gateway port collects the cargo from neighboring ports—in other words, serves as hub port—then the function as gateway or enabler of trade for the hinterland is obvious.

The relatively new port in London named itself "London Gateway." This should express that this port is the main port in this area, that is, at least for the greater London area, if not for whole southern UK. In this case the term "gateway" is used for marketing and should express the port's high importance, without using a superlative in the name. In this sense the adjective "gateway" has a positive meaning.

Way Port/Zero-Deviation Port

"Way port" unlike gateway port, is not a positive classification. A way port is often considered to be a second-class port, although in fact this is not true. This negative touch derives from the reality that a way port is the junior partner between two (often bigger) established markets or ports.

A "way port" is a port that lies on the way between two destinations, and this port can be called by vessels with more or less zero deviation from the main route; this is why this type of port is also named "zero-deviation port." If this port has an attractive hinterland, it can establish its own business, using the way port function as a start.

There are several ports functioning as way ports: a good example is the Port of Cuxhaven in the north of Germany, located on the southern banks of the river Elbe, not far away from the entrance to the Kiel Canal, the world's busiest artificial waterway. In close proximity to the Port of Cuxhaven there are two big ports: Bremerhaven and Hamburg; this limits the Cuxhaven port's hinterland potential, and Cuxhaven itself is a small city with little industry. Fortunately, the trade lane between Scandinavia and UK passes the Port of Cuxhaven directly. Though there is no cargo potential for direct calls between UK and Cuxhaven or Scandinavia and Cuxhaven, a stop in Cuxhaven to load or discharge relatively small cargo volumes on the way from Scandinavia to the UK or vice versa makes sense and is economically feasible. The shipping lines get additional business for little cost. This is a win-win situation for all participants.

Other way ports working under similar conditions are the ports of Panama, lying on the way from Asia to the US, the port of Port Said in Egypt, directly located at the Suez Canal, and the Malaysian ports at the Strait of Malacca.

Transhipment Port + Transit Port

In spelling "tranship" is a variant of "trans-ship"; both words have the same meaning and are used synonymously, that is, we can say transhipment (with one "s") or trans-shipment ("ss"). To tranship means to transfer cargo from one ship or conveyance to another. From a ports perspective, it is the shipment of goods via an intermediate port. Figure 4.7 illustrates how transhipment traffic could happen.

The sketch in Figure 4.7 shows trade and traffic between the open sea and two countries: Land A and Land B. In both lands there is one port: Port A and Port B. The quay walls of the ports are the interface between sea and land. The number of movements over the quay walls are performance indicators of ports.

This is easy to understand because the loading and unloading of vessels is the core business of terminal operators and so of ports. But the quay wall KPI doesn't say much about a country's trade. Trade and traffic statistics are different sources and not easy to compare. One reason for this is the existence of transhipment (trade via sea) and transit (im- and export via a green border).

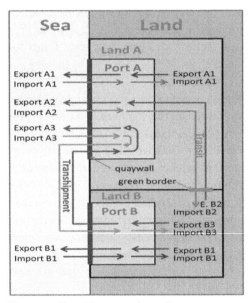

Figure 4.7: Transhipment and transit

Let's suppose each single trade equals 100; then the example in Figure 4.7 shows the following:
- Land A: import A1 and export A1 of land A sums up to 200 (each trade 100). Foreign trade of land A is 200.
- Land B: import and export of land B sums up to 600 (direct export + import B1, transitsB2 and transshipments B3). Foreign trade of land B is 600.
- Port A handles a throughput of 800; 200 the foreign trade of land A, 200 the transits B2 for Land B via port A as im- and export A2, and 400 transhipment (im- and export A3 in and out).
- Port B handles a volume of 400; 200 the im- and export B1 of land B, and 200 the im- and export B3, which is transshipment volume A3 for port A.

If Port A is a hub port, and Port B a feeder port, then Figure 4.7 describes a situation that can be found in many parts of the world; and here mostly for container trades. A good example of this is Singapore: this port functions as a hub port for many smaller feeder ports in surrounding countries. What we can easily learn from Figure 4.7 is that transhipment volumes push the port throughput figures up because of the double counting of quay wall moves (the so-called amplifier or multiplier effect); but it says less of the importance of the port for the country itself. Figure 4.7 shows that the foreign trade volume of land A is 200, but the port handling volume 800. Land B is a stronger trading country (and probably has a stronger economy), but it only has a port throughput of 400 and a foreign trade volume of 600.

This means for transhipment ports there needs to be a decoupling of port growth and economic growth. Transhipment is often a result of location, and not automatically tied up with economic growth. More details of the relation need to be analyzed within an econometric port model, and this must be calculated for every single port. Singapore, for example, has a transhipment share in container business that is higher than 90%, that is, the majority of containers are coming and leaving the port on the same way as waterborne transport. In this sense a transhipment port can be an important business unit *inside* the country; but is not necessarily an important business unit *for* the country. Huge ports in small countries often have high transhipment shares in their business.

The word "transit" as it is also assumed in Figure 4.7 means "to go across; to pass over"; in port business transit cargo is cargo that comes in via the open sea, leaves the port with a conveyance like road, rail, or pipeline, crosses the port country, and is carried into another third country, like the incoming trade A2 in Figure 4.7, which after crossing the border to another country (here: land B), converts into import B2 (vice versa for the export). For land A this cargo is transit cargo; for land B import cargo (resp. export when leaving land B). For port A the exact classification (import/export or transit) depends on various factors; most important are the main cargo documents (bill of lading [B/L]) and the local customs regulations. It could be that the import B2 starts as transport from oversea to port A with a B/L that says that the destination is port A/country A; and during the journey of the cargo, the wholesaler sells the cargo to somebody in land B. This could then be declared as transit. The more we go into detail, the more we need to analyze the local cargo declaration and customs rules. This unfortunately varies a lot, and still today is a big source for misdeclarations and errors in statistics.

Transit volumes instead of transhipment volumes are only counted once in port statistics. Transit cargo is often welcomed by ports because these volumes are considered an enlargement of the hinterland, that is, an enlargement of business opportunities and thus of economic importance.

Excursus: Problem Inland Navigation

How to consider inland navigation cargo volumes: as transit or transhipment cargo? In many seaports, the cargo that came in from overseas is carried on with inland navigation. If this, for example, happens in a port like New Orleans in the southern part of the United States, and the onward transportation on the Mississippi river is inland transportation, then this cargo volume should be considered in the same way as national road or rail traffic. The question remains: how is this volume counted? Is it double-counted because it moves two times over a quay wall? (Is this traffic counted like "transhipment," although it does not leave the country of the port?) Here no common regulations exist. Some ports distinguish between seaborne cargo (ocean cargo moving into foreign countries), and inland navigation cargo—no matter where it's going (inland, foreign country, etc.). Others do not and just count port volumes, that is, counting both trades as port volume.

This is more complicated when it comes to inland navigation trade that moves to foreign countries, like on the river Rhine in West Europe as hinterland trade from Port of Rotterdam/Netherlands, to Germany and Switzerland. Inland navigation is not (ocean) sea trade, and so this cargo is not comparable with feeder trades. It should be considered as "transit on waterways." The quay wall counting should distinguish between seaborne trade and inland navigation; but this is not always the case.

Regional Port

A "regional port" is a port with a comparably small hinterland, which in most cases handles small volumes compared with the top ten ports of similar structure. Regional ports also have limited importance for the national country. In container business, feeder ports are typical "regional ports." The economic importance of regional ports is limited and they lack additional strategic functions, for example, as an important im- and export facility for the national industry. However, the port is very important for the local industry and/or in case of passenger transportation for the people living in that region; these ports can even be essential when serving an island. A regional port is a kind of geopolitical classification. The typical Indian distinction between major ports and minor ports shows this way of thinking: being a regional port is like being classified as a minor port.

Sea Port

A "sea port" is a port that is located at international waters and that mainly serves ocean-going vessels. In addition, many sea ports are located directly at the open sea, or at least close to it. There are, however, also examples of ports that are more than 100 km away from the open sea, like the Port of Hamburg in Germany, that are still considered sea ports. From the geographical location, these ports could be considered as inland or river ports. But the real distinctive feature of a sea port is that the entrance to said port is via open waters, that is, the access river or channel is not a national waterway; they are open for international trade without any customs procedures. A port that is located at the open sea and has access to international waters but does not service a reasonable numbers of ocean vessels should not be classified as a sea port. Typically, fishing ports fall into this category. Another distinctive criterion and a huge problem for many ports is necessary water depth. Sea ports usually have the minimum water depth (e.g., 10 m minimum; at best 15 to 20 m) to serve the most common ocean-going vessels.

Deep Water Port

A "deep water port" is a subcategory of a sea port, and you may have guessed from its nomenclature that this port stands out from other sea ports due to its depth of water. Deep water ports are typically used by very large and heavily loaded ships. The depth of water helps these ships get access to the terminals of the deep water ports. The deeper a port's water, the deeper vessel draughts it can handle. Although the relationship between "depth of the water" and "draught of the vessel" sounds relatively simple, it is not always as straightforward as you might think. The draught depends of the condition and temperature of the water and the direction the vessel sails: upstream is different from downstream. Here the Plimsoll line helps, also called Plimsoll mark or international load line, which is a mark on the side of vessels to indicate the maximum permissible loading depth. It was introduced in Great Britain through the Merchant Shipping Act of 1875 and soon found worldwide acceptance. It is named after Samuel Plimsoll, a merchant and shipping reformer who campaigned for its introduction. Application of the law to foreign ships leaving British ports led to general adoption of load-line rules by maritime countries. The maximum safe loading depth varies with ocean regions and seasons. In the tropics the water is warmer and therefore less dense than in temperate regions, so ships will float higher in cold regions than in the tropics. Summer and winter cause similar changes. The Plimsoll line therefore contains several lines, with letters to indicate cargo, season, and location (differentiated based on local salt content of the water). Inland navigation vessels have so-called draught marks instead of Plimsoll lines on the hull, for the same reason, to measure the max. draught.

The relation between depth of the water and the maximum draught of a vessel is often mixed up in political discussions, for example, about funding a necessary dredging. An additional confusing factor is the fact that not all access channels need the same exact depth over the whole length of the channel. In some ports with high tides, the combined effect (tide + depth) can assure sufficient draught for a vessel. So, there is not always a simple measurement used to classify deep water ports. The Plimsoll line marks how deep a vessel dips into the water, but this is only the maximum draught of the vessel. For ports that due to location are usually not the first ports of call and often not the last ports within the range, it is a matter of fact that most of the vessel never come with maximum draught into such a port.

Another question is what "deep water" means compared with other ports? The latest generation of container vessels with 22,000 TEU have a maximum draught—that is, with full loading, or as seamen say: fully laden—of 14.5 m or 47.5 ft. These vessels require a depth of minimum 16 m. Bulker and Tanker have draughts of up to 24.5 m or 80 ft.[6] These vessels require special terminals. Ultimately there is no common criteria for distinguishing a "deep water" port. Very often the qualification as deep water port is used in container business, but here one can easily see that ports with sufficient depth also for the biggest container vessels do not name themselves deep water port, whereas other ports with less depth use this characterization.

Deep water port is a marketing attribute, with no set minimum depth for the classification. The use of the term "deep water port" should qualify the respective port as an important facility in global trade, capable of receiving the largest container vessels. Deep water ports should be an "elite-club" of the most important container ports; however, this is only true in publicity.

River Port

A "river port" is a port that is located on a river; usually not in the mouth or estuary region, but more remote from the open sea. This term just describes the location of the port and includes the fact that the river port is part of the national waterway

---

6 Like the double-hull tanker "TI Asia" from Tanker International LLC: 380 m long, 68 m beam and a maximum draught of 24.5 m. Loading capacity 513684 qm of oil.

system. In other words, river ports usually have no direct ocean access and are not called by sea-going vessels. For customs procedures this is very important. Normal vessels in river ports are inland navigation vessel, barges, push boats, tugs, etc.

Inland Port

The term "inland port" has two different meanings. The first is very similar to river port and describes the port's location as being away from the coast somewhere in the inland. In this sense, the terms could be used synonymously. The second meaning of the term "inland port" concentrates on the core function of a port, that is, as a location for changing the mode of transportation. But with one exception: these inland ports only serve rail and road—and in some case the airfreight industry; not inland navigation. This classification tries to transfer the high efficiency and, in some ports, huge volumes to a complete "dry" port. From an operational point of view, these "inland ports" would be better named logistics centers, cargo centers, distribution centers, etc. But the term "port" conveys internationality and efficiency. In this sense it is also a marketing attribute.

Dry Port

A "dry port" is a cargo and distribution center without access to waterborne traffic, that is, for trucks, trains, and airplanes. The term dry port is like the second meaning of inland port: an analogy that should convey the attributes of a "wet" port to a land based dry port.

Free Port

The term "free port" concentrates on tax regulations or tax exemptions that may exist for the whole port or for a part of this port: the free port area. In some countries a turnover tax does not have to be paid while inside the free port area. In other countries, additional tax exemptions exist; the variety of regulations is huge. In addition to taxes there are also areas where other rules and regulations do not appear, that is, free production areas, where the labor can be paid in foreign currency. With enlarging political areas like the European Union or free trade areas like NAFTA, the importance and number of free ports are shrinking.

State Port/Service Port/Public Port

The following five terms all concentrate on the port system, that is, the port administration model and the ownership of the port, that is, the port authority and the terminal operator. The terms "state port" and "service port" are used synonymously. Usually infrastructure and superstructure planning and operation are in the hands of the state; state ports are managed like a public department. Reasonable private port operation did not take place in such a port. These ports are usually smaller ports with regional importance only. More details can be found in chapter 8ff.

Autonomous Port

An "autonomous port" is a port administration model where an independent public body (the "autonomous institution") is responsible for the port; independent here means independent from other ministries. This administration model is a mix of state and municipal management, and so a special type of a state port. This model has existed for a long time in the southern ports of Europe, and the ports, for example, in France called themselves "port automone du ... " (name of the city). Private participation in port business is very much limited. Smaller ports typically used these models. Today several autonomous ports are on the way to becoming a landlord port. More details can be found in chapter 8ff.

Tool Port

A "tool port" is a port administration model where the port authority owns, develops, and maintains the port infrastructure as well as the superstructure; including cargo handling equipment such as cranes, van carriers, transtainers and forklift trucks. Port authority staff usually operates all equipment. Private companies carry out additional operations, often vessel related, and rent the equipment and staff from the port authority. More details can be found in chapter 8ff.

Landlord Port

A "landlord port" is a mixed public-private operation of port management. The port authority acts as landlord, owning the infrastructure up to the pavement including the quay walls, and the private terminal operator leases the terminals on long-term based contracts from the port authority. The private companies build the necessary terminal infra- and superstructure and carry out the port operations. In bigger ports, the private companies often act as competitors for the same group of customers. More details can be found in chapter 8ff.

Private Port

Fully "private ports" are few and can only be found in the United Kingdom and New Zealand. A full privatization of port ownership, administration, and management is an extreme model of port reform. In this model, a port is considered like other factories or industrial plants and is reduced to the transportation and logistics function. Often these ports are not really open for all operators or im- and exporters. More details can be found in chapter 8ff.

Industrial Port/Factory Port

An "industrial port" is a port that belongs to one kind of industry. These ports are part of the production plan and are usually not open for other operators. Many coal and ore export facilities fall into this category. They are part of the industrial production, are often 100% in private hands, and can be considered factories, which is why the synonym "factory port" is often used for these ports as well.

Home Port (Cruise)

There are two meanings of the term "home port"; the first is a port where a specific vessel is registered or permanently based. Some vessels have a close relation to their home port and build a close relationship to their port and city. This is especially true for many traditional ships like the two sailing vessels *Gorch Fock* with the port and city of Kiel and the *Kruzhenstern* with the port and city of Kaliningrad. "Home" in this sense has a meaning close to homestead or homeland. In the cruise business, home port means the starting and (or) ending port for a cruise, regardless of the registry of the ship.

Commercial Port/Noncommercial Port

According to our port tree in Chapter 2, "commercial ports" are all ports that are used for commercial purposes. The "noncommercial ports" are the ones for sports and leisure, (nonindustrial) fishing ports, factory ports (they are often not open for third business, although they are part of a commercial production, which is why we do not consider them), and military ports.

Statistical Port

A "statistical port" consists of one or more ports. Statistical ports are normally controlled by a single port authority that can record ship and cargo movements. In statistics, the single units are combined as one port, although there may be huge distances between the locations. Zhenzhen Port Authority in China's Pearl River Delta is a good example of this. The terminals of Da Chan Bay, Shekou, Chiwan, Yantian, etc., are single terminals with more than 70 km between them, but they are unified under the umbrella of Shenzhen Port Authority; in this sense Zhenzhen is a statistical port. This term is used in traffic statistics like UNCTAD, Eurostat, ITF, etc. (e.g., Glossary EU 2003, page 79).

★ ★ ★

Big Port

Or: Size Matters! The "big ports" we saw in the top ten or top twenty world ranking lists are often not purely "dry bulk ports" or "container ports." Instead they are best characterized as universal ports. The problem of size: a small port with 100.000 TEU per year is, due to its traffic, considered a "container port." A huge port like Rotterdam on the other hand, with 100 times more containers per year, but also handling more than 200 mill t of bulk cargo, would not fall into the container port category. Although this might be correct in theory, in day-to-day reality, such a port, which has a substantial amount of one type of cargo is also named a "dry bulk port," "liquid bulk port," or "container port." Big ports are those that fall into this kind of category, that is, being identified as global players with global importance. Big ports are ports with huge amounts of cargoes, although they will not fall into one of the above-mentioned categories as container or bulk port. Due to the variety of cargo, they are best classified as "universal ports" with relevant amount of cargo, that is, a volume that will put them on the list of the top 100 ports globally in terms of throughput measured in tons.

Chapter 5
Trade & Transportation

5.1 Macroeconomic Relations

Trade plays a key role in an increasingly interconnected and interdependent world, and it makes up a large part of the global economy. It is not the task of a book about ports to dive into fundamental discussions about the key drivers of economic growth: is traffic demand primarily derived from the needs of the consumers and the industry, or is it rather the supply, which creates its own demand? We can not solve this hen-and-egg problem, but what remains true is that we must consider transportation and logistics as its own market. World trade is what drives this market. Figure 5.1 below shows the close relationship between the growth of world gross domestic product (GDP) and global trade. GDP over the years moves on a higher level, but the fluctuations in growth are visible for both graphs.

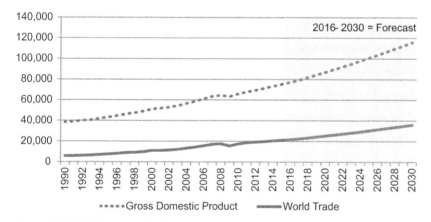

Source: UNCTAD, IHS, own calculations

Figure 5.1: World GDP and world trade in real 2005 US dollar

Figure 5.2 also shows that the annual growth rates of world trade have been above the growth of GDP for many years. In other words, world trade is growing faster than world GDP. This is a clear sign that the world gets more and more interconnected and that more and more people are willing and, in a position, to purchase foreign goods. This is the source of steadily increasing transportation, and ports are acting as facilitators along this supply chain.

DOI 10.1515/9781547400874-005

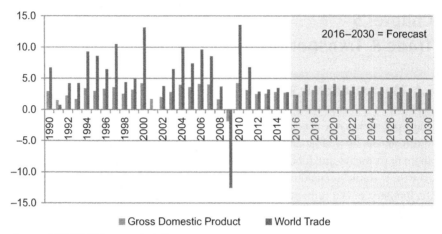

Source: UNCTAD, IHS, own calculations

Figure 5.2: World GDP and world trade; real annual growth rates in %

What we identify when analyzing the data is an effect, which could at best be described as "trade-amplifier" or "trade-multiplier." Over the twenty-five-year period from 1990 to 2015 we can see that a positive growth rate of real GDP leads to a stronger positive growth rate of trade (at least for the first twenty years until 2010). During the period 1986–1992 the multiplier reached an average of 2.03, between 1994 and 2000 a slightly higher multiplier of 2.46 had been achieved for the ratio of real world trade to real world GPD, and for the period 2002 to 2008 the multiplier reached a level of 2.17. During 2009, when the effects of the global financial crisis hit the economy, we can see in the figure that a negative rate of GDP leads to an even stronger negative effect of world trade. For the twenty-five-year period 1990 to 2015 this trade-amplifier effect leads to an average value of 2.0. This means—on average—that a growth of 1% of GDP results in a growth rate of world trade of 2.0%; or another example, 2.6 % of GDP will push the trade growth rate 5.2 % upward. The ratio of 2:1 "trade-GDP" was also a ratio that many people in shipping business learned during their first years in business, and what they had as a rule of thumb in mind when leading the business, that is, ordering new vessels.

But after 2011 this multiplier lowered drastically: between 2011 and 2016 the ratio resulted at 1.37, and forecasts for 2017 to 2025 show the ratio further down at a level of 1.2. This means that growth in world trade will, in the long run, be growing with a smaller multiplier. Why is this so? The reduction in containerization seems to be one argument for this, while miniaturization of products and growing use of 3D-printers are others. There is also the statistical effect that a higher base of traded volume mathematically results in smaller growth rates (e.g., an increase of ten units—this can be millions of dollars or millions of metric tons—with a base of 100 results in a growth rate of 10%; the same increase of ten units on a base of 200 is just 5%, and when the base volume is 500, the same increase will result in a growth rate of just 2%). The reduced multiplier should not be misinterpreted as shrinking trade; growth will continue, but the percentage will be lower. What makes trade analysts nervous is the speed at which the multiplier is shrinking, and the many misinterpretations that still hit the shipping industry with oversupply nearly ten years after the financial crisis.

Overlapping (geo-)political effects, time lags, and natural disasters have an influence on trade as well. The integration of China into the global economy is a good positive example of this; the negative effect of the terrorist attack in New York in September 2001 with the hampering effect due to increased uncertainty is a negative one. The many politically driven economic sanctions that happened over the last decades are also influencing global trade. Such effects overlap the relatively stable GDP-trade relation. An example of such a year was 2001. The burst of the "dot.com-bubble" in combination with a weak Asian (or more specifically, Japanese) economy in combination with the terrorist attack led to the result of an under proportional growth of world trade. In the next twenty years, it can be seen that trade grows faster, and is expected to do so in the coming decades as well, that is, the trade-amplifier effect will last; on a lower level for the foreseeable future, but still with positive effect.

World trade in Figure 5.2 contains all kind of goods: liquid bulk and dry bulk, which are mainly for industry and agriculture production, as well as various consumer goods; the latter being transported more and more via container. It is no wonder that there is a close relation between world GDP and world container trade as well.

Figure 5.3 shows this relation with the two more or less parallel graphs (*Note*: left scale for GDP spans from 10,000 to 80,000, whereas the right scale for the containers in TEU spans from 0 to 160). World GDP approximately doubles in this period from 40,000 to 80,000, and the container trade quintuples from 25 to 130 on the scale. What we see is another expression of the trade-amplifier effect.

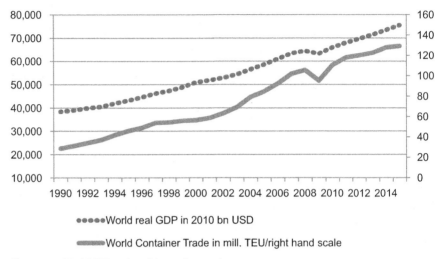

Figure 5.3: World GDP and world container trade

As world trade in total and world container trade are both influenced by the amplifier effect, it would certainly be expected that a relatively stable relationship exists between these two indicators. The effective relationship between global trade (all goods) and container trade is expressed in Figure 5.4.

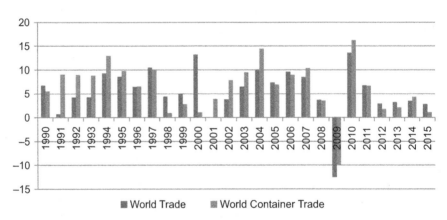

Figure 5.4: World trade and world container trade

During the 1990s, the growth rate of container trade was higher than world trade in total. This is the result of containerization: more and more products could be stored and transported in containers, and more and more specialized containers were invented.[1] Since the middle of the 2000s, this effect slowed down. As Chapter 3 shows, there is not that much cargo (i.e., general cargo) left that could be containerized. It can be assumed that this effect will not lead to over proportional growth rates in the future. On the contrary, a slightly higher growth rate of container trade in relation to world trade can be expected realistically, that is, a slow increase of containerization due to technical innovations (also for bulk products) and due to a better adaption of industrial products to logistical requirements. Transportation by containers is normally cheaper than sending oversized or over-weighted pieces of cargo on board specialized vessels around the world. If it is technically possible, industrial production takes the dimensions of containers as orientation and maximum dimension for products that shall be shipped with containers. This adaption of container dimensions by industrial designers drives containerization as well; in other words, the logistical requirements and implied logistics costs will already be respected in the very early product planning processes.

Another interesting trade relation exists between world container trade and the world container port throughput. Technically this is easy to understand; the first is the sum of all products that are traded globally via container: world container trade. The second is the amount of all containers that have been moved over a quay wall in ports: the world container port throughput. This is the sum of all container movements that have been counted in ports.

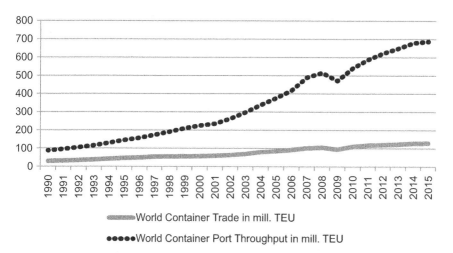

Figure 5.5: World container trade and world container port throughput

---

1 For more details on specialized container, refer to Appendix D: Definition: "Container."

It is obvious that there is a relation between container trade and container handling at ports, but it is not the same! Sometimes these two indicators are mixed up in public discussions and articles, which causes false interpretations. Figure 5.5 shows the relation and the huge difference in quantity, and Table 5.1 expresses these numbers in five-year steps.

Table 5.1: World container trade and port throughput for selected years

	World Container Trade	W. Cont. Port Throughput
1985	18.9	55.9
1990	28.7	88.0
1995	46.0	145.0
2000	56.5	225.0
2005	84.8	376.0
2010	110.5	542.0
2015	129.2	687.0

Source: Own calculations.

Container port throughput in 1985 was three times higher than container trade. Fifteen years later, in 2000, port throughput was already four times higher than trade. Again, fifteen years after that in 2015, the relation was 5.3:1; port throughput was more than five times higher than trade. This effect was a result of increased transhipment via hub-and-spoke style port callings, which were themselves a result of increasing vessel size (driven by the need to reduce costs per TEU). To explain this, take as an example a container (20 ft = 1 TEU) with shoes from Chongquing in inland China, located at Yangtze River, heading to the Baltic seaport of Helsinki in Finland; this is the trade of 1 container that is counted several times:

1. The full container is loaded in Chongquing on board of an inland vessel. Then there is the first move (first move[2] = first count): the container goes over the Chongquing quay wall and on the Yangtze River to Shanghai Port.

---

2 Port people often count "moves" over the quay wall. One "move" is one movement by crane, for example, from a lashing platform into the vessel and back with one or more containers under the spreader. Therefore, the statistic is often called move-statistic or the "quay wall counting." The problem is that one move with one 20 ft container represents one TEU, one move with a 40 ft container two TEU, and with twin lift spreaders this figure goes up to four TEU per move. Throughput or move statistics are expressed in "moves"; this is not equivalent with a TEU-statistic.

2. Unloading the container from the barge to the Shanghai container terminal is the second move. Here a problem can occur: some ports include the river transportation and the handling of river cargo in their total ports statistic, other ports distinguish between sea-going cargo and river cargo/river throughput. Be aware that this is a possible source for mistakes in statistics and a source of misinterpretations.
3. The first seaport move is loading the container in Shanghai onboard an ocean vessel headed to Europe.
4. Unloading the container in Rotterdam from the ocean vessel on the Rotterdam container terminal is the second seaport move. The box is then stored in the yard.
5. The third seaport move is loading the container in Rotterdam on board a Baltic feeder vessel.
6. Finally, the fourth seaport move is loading the container in the Helsinki Port from the feeder vessel on the Helsinki Container Terminal. Then there is Hinterland transportation, for example, via truck.

We just followed one container from China to Finland. The trade statistic will count this as one container; in this case, 1 TEU. Due to the way the container went from Chongqing via the hub ports of Shanghai and Rotterdam to Helsinki, the same container experienced four seaport moves over the quay walls of a terminal. The world container (sea) port throughput statistic will count four moves! The same example with one 40 ft container from Chongqing to Helsinki would result in trade statistics as "2 TEU from China to Finland," four moves of a container in seaports over the quay walls, and 8 TEU in port throughput statistic.

The question may come up: why are the ports counting this way? Ports are service providers, and a key service is to load and unload ships. Therefore, ports count "moves" or throughput data. This is also the base for the accounting system and for invoicing, so these performance indicators are necessary and important for terminal operators.

A remaining question might be: Why are so many containers often loaded and unloaded in hub ports? Isn't it easier and cheaper to have direct transportation? There is no straightforward answer to this question. Yes, if there are direct links between two ports, this is in most cases the best and cheapest way to ship goods, because there is no cost and time-consuming "extra" transportation in between ports. However, there are not that many ports in the world with such dense shipping networks that all potential markets can be served. Returning to our shoe container example: there is no direct shipping connection between Chongqing and Helsinki, nor between Shanghai and Helsinki. So, the utilization of hub ports is (economically) not only the second-best alternative, but often the only feasible one.

The amplifier between container trade and port throughput data according to Figure 5.5 and Table 5.1 is between three and five, due to the existence of hub ports and the necessary reloading activities. So-called hub-and-spoke concepts have the disadvantage that they increase the number of moves and "blow up" the throughput statistic, but the advantages of connecting smaller ports and additional markets via the "spokes" outweigh these additional moves. The access to global markets via a link to a hub port offers a huge trade network at competitive prices for regions with smaller ports.

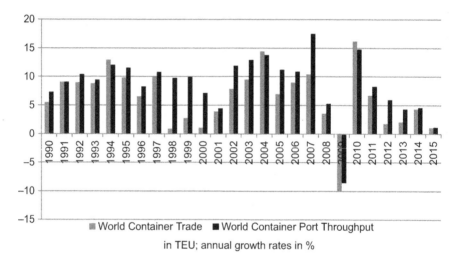

Figure 5.6: World container trade and world container port throughput

The comparison of growth rates of world container trade and world container port throughput as expressed in Figure 5.6 shows that we have a second reinforcing effect, here called "container-multiplier." This effect is a combined amplifier of the two trends mentioned above: containerization and hub-port concept. Over the twenty-five-year period in Figure 5.6, the multiplier has a value of 1.4, that is, when the container trade grows 1%, the port throughput statistic grows on average with 1.4%.

As explained above and what is true here as well: in a short-term view, the amplifier effect is overlapped with political and other factors, meaning the multiplier fluctuates over the years. It is not recommended to use the amplifier for forecasting, but ex post they are delivering explanations and insight. The long-term results (1990–2015) of the amplifier are shown in Table 5.2.

Both amplifier effects—trade and container—are cumulative. As a result, we see that a 1% GDP growth rate has a cumulative increase of around 3% in container port throughput. For the top twenty container ports in 2015, the average amplifier effect was 2.4%. As the figures above show, the amplifier takes effect in both directions: positive and negative amplification.

Table 5.2: Top twenty container ports; long-term amplifier effect

Rank	Port	Country	Amplifier Effect	Top 3 hi/low
1	Shanghai	China	2.0	
2	Singapore	Singapore	2.2	
3	Shenzhen	China	3.3	
4	Ningbo-Zhoushan	China	2.7	
5	Hong Kong	China	1.6	
6	Busan	South Korea	1.5	low
7	Guangzhou	China	2.0	
8	Quingdao	China	2.1	
9	Dubai	UAE	3.6	high
10	Tianjin	China	1.8	
11	Rotterdam	Netherlands	3.1	
12	Port Klang	Malaysia	2.2	
13	Kaohsiung	Taiwan	0.7	low
14	Antwerp	Belgium	4.0	high
15	Dalian	China	1.9	
16	Xiamen	China	1.1	low
17	Tanjung Pelepas	Malaysia	1.6	
18	Hamburg	Germany	4.1	high
19	Los Angeles	USA	3.0	
20	Long Beach	USA	2.7	

Sources: Port websites; IMF; own calculations.

There is a close relationship between trade and transportation, impacting ports with reinforcing effects. Sources of these effects are globalization and increasing world trade. This effect we call "trade-multiplier." Especially for the fast-growing segment of container trade, there is a second reinforcing effect that we call the "container-multiplier." Drivers for this are mainly containerization and the increase of hub-port concepts.

5.2 Drivers of Global Trade

Global trade is the backbone of the port and shipping industry. Producers as well as consumers in various nations try to profit from expanded markets. There are many reasons that trade across national borders occurs, and the identification of these drivers helps us identify and understand key influencing forces. The following key drivers can be identified:

1. Political alliances and free trade agreements
2. Deregulation and privatization of public services
3. Distribution of natural resources
4. Globalization of sourcing and production
5. Spreading out of buyer markets
6. Environmental awareness
7. Innovations
8. Integrated supply chain logistics

It is easy to understand that not all drivers create the same momentum for all segments of port business. Distribution of natural resources is of huge importance for bulk products but may be of no interest in cruise business. In the following, we want to identify drivers without evaluating their relevance for product groups or various ports. However, keep in mind that evaluating driver relevance is necessary for further detailed analysis, for example, for the preparation of a specific port master plan.

Political Alliances and Free Trade Agreements

A political alliance is an agreement between two or more states for mutual support and for cooperation between the countries. The economic cooperation that often follows the political alliances is of interest to global trade and port businesses. This cooperation can include free trade agreements, which eliminate tariffs, import quotas, and preferences on most (if not all) goods and services traded between the countries of the alliance. Countries use free trade agreements as tools for economic integration if their economic structures are complementary. If their economic structures are competitive, they are more likely to form a customs union rather than an agreement.

The economic aim of political alliances and free trade agreements is to reduce exchange barriers so that trade can grow as a result of specialization, division of labor, and via comparative advantage. For all types of overseas trade, ports are then the natural partner along the supply chains and will benefit from increased trade. The theory of comparative advantage argues that in an unrestricted marketplace (in equilibrium), each source of production will tend to specialize in that activity where it has comparative (rather than absolute) advantage,[3] that is, that there is a mutual benefit from trade even if one party is more productive in every possible area than its trading counterpart (provided each party or country concentrates on the activities where it has a relative advantage). The theory argues that the net result will be an increase in income and trade. Ports benefit from this kind of specialization and increased global trade. In this case, political alliances and free trade agreements are drivers for port business.

Deregulation and Privatization of Public Services

Deregulation is an act by which the government regulation of businesses, consumers, and market activity is reduced or eliminated to create and foster a more efficient economy. The stated rationale for deregulation is often that fewer and simpler regulations will raise levels of competitiveness, increasing productivity and efficiency, creating more jobs, and lowering prices. In addition, the expectation is that it creates an economic environment favorable to upstart companies that were unable to enter the industry prior to deregulation. Deregulation should also serve as a catalyst for increased innovation and mergers among weaker competitors. Opposition to deregulation usually centers on fears of environmental pollution, quality standards (such as the removal of regulations on hazardous materials), the increase of fraud and unfair practices (like insider trading in the banking system), and general economic and financial uncertainty. The most noted period of deregulation occurred globally during the 1970s and 1980s in response to criticisms that economic regulation inhibited rather than promoted competition. During this period, industries were deregulated, including the port systems, communications, and banking industries.

Privatization is often the natural consequence of deregulation. Privatization occurs when state-owned service providers are moved to the private sector. Many public port authorities faced this trend and have deregulated their services with the result that typical state functions like port police, fire protection, or customs have been concentrated into new public bodies, and many other services that do not necessarily need to be public have been privatized, like stevedoring, warehousing, lashing, bunkering, mooring, etc. Privatization often leads to terminals

---

3 The "law of comparative advantage" was first analyzed and described by David Ricardo (1772–1823), one of the most influential classical economists (Ricardo 1979).

and terminal-related services like warehousing, mooring, or tugboat services being transferred to private operators. As expected, in many cases productivity is increased, more jobs are created and the economic success, including tax payments for the public-sector increase. Therefore, we can see deregulation and privatization as drivers for port business. There are still many ports in the world that can be deregulated. However, ports need to reach a minimum flow of traffic to be deregulated. It normally does not make any sense to replace one public body by a private one. Competition is a necessary prerequisite for success in privatization, that is, at least two operators for a specific service are needed.

Distribution of Natural Resources

Natural resources are distributed unevenly across the globe. Therefore, countries may not have the resources that are important for their local industry, but trade and transportation enable them to acquire those resources from places that do. Economic activities in a country or region relate to the resources within that region. Economic activities that are directly related to resources include farming, fishing, ranching, timber processing, oil and gas production, mining, and tourism. In the past, these natural resources often led to human migration and new settlements. The gold rush in the United States or the oil boom in the Middle East and Africa are causes of historical migrations, but the development of the Hanseatic League (Chapter 1.6) was also the cause of a migration.

The process of industrialization has changed this trend of humans moving to areas with resources. With the invention of steam and gas-powered vessels, the transportation of large amounts of bulk products became more and more economical. Industrialized countries now had the ability to import huge quantities of energy products like coal, oil, and gas. Ports as im- and export facilities adopted these trends and built new terminals and storage facilities.

Today the trend with natural resources has changed again, steadily and slowly, but consistently. Developing countries are now participating more along the value-added process from the raw material to the final product. A good example of this is the oil industry. In the past, crude oil was often extracted in developing countries, and huge carriers (the so-called very large crude oil carrier [VLCC]) transported the raw material to industrialized countries. The carrying capacity of these vessels exceeded 500,000 t dwt in the 1970s. Transportation of crude oil as well as the liquid bulk imports are still of huge importance today, representing a major share of business for many ports.

Traditionally, refineries in industrialized countries cracked the crude oil into a large variety of products. These products have been and still are essen-

tial inputs for many industries. A huge added value is combined with these processes. Refineries and processing industries are now being erected directly in the
oil producing countries. This trend will likely grow in the coming decades. From
many points of view building refineries and processing plants in the oil-produc-
ing country makes a lot of sense; however, this will lead to serious consequences
for the shipping and port industry. VLCCs and other crude oil carriers will no
longer be needed as in the past; demand for crude oil carriers will decrease while
demand for product tankers will increase. Less demand for oil carriers will surely
lead to lower charter as well as freight rates. For the ports, the consequence is that
they must expect decreasing crude oil imports and increasing volumes of refined
products. The whole infrastructure like pipelines, tanks, pumping stations, etc.,
must be adjusted.

A major part of port business today is bulk business, primarily oil and oil
products, coal and iron ore.[4] All these products are natural resources, and so it is
important to identify the current and future distribution of natural resources as
an important driver for port business.

Globalization of Sourcing and Production

Global sourcing in manufacturing has evolved from being an administrative pur-
chase-function to a strategic business function with global outreach—causing
dramatic shifts in how and where product components and capabilities are
sourced, and where work gets done. In recent years, manufacturing companies
have faced mounting business pressures on basic R&D and product development
operations, due to increasing consumer demand for innovative, feature-rich products accompanied by shrinking product lifecycles, and declining margins. Global
sourcing can help enhance revenue by accelerating new product development,
reducing time to market, enabling expanded business analytics, freeing up time
and resources for deeper customer interaction, and opening new global markets.

Global production started as "outsourcing" in the early 1960s as a revolution-
ary phenomenon of sending unskilled work from developed countries to developing countries. American and European companies started outsourcing their
back-office work to Mexico and India and their manufacturing work to Southern
Europe, Japan and China, as these countries offered cheap labor. As the economy
of these countries started growing, the process of outsourcing and global production moved toward new emerging countries, like Vietnam and Indonesia. The

---

4 For quantities, refer to Chapter 3.

key motivation for outsourcing and global production was a cheap labor source, low working condition standards, and very limited or nonexistent environmental standards. The result was cheap products on the global market.

The trend of outsourcing and intensive global production for lower prices has been changing since the early 2000s. Products that require higher standards of manufacturing, such as mechanical and plant engineering started coming back to America and Europe. In addition, the governments of emerging countries are less and less willing to be considered labor-cheap and environmentally unhealthy production places. Increased GDP levels and higher living standards enable these countries to refuse the outsourced work. All this again has an influence on global sourcing, global production and finally on trade. Therefore, we consider this as driver for trade and transportation.

Spreading Out of Buyer Markets

A "buyer market" is an old economic term, but in the last decades it has been used only in niche markets such as real estate. A buyer market is a market that has more sellers than buyers; or in other words, an excess of supply over demand. Competition is usually high in these markets, and the quality level of these products is also very high. This is an ideal situation for consumers because they usually get what they want. Most of these markets are present in the industrial countries. After World War II, more and more markets for products and services in these countries came into play. Industrialized countries are worlds of abundance—at least according to Maslow's hierarchy of needs.[5]

The opposite of a buyer's market is a seller's market. In history, seasonal changes led to limited buyer markets: in times of harvest there was a huge supply of foodstuff, in winter there was a low supply and high demand. Both situations of over-supply and over-demand had and still have influence on prices.

Buyer's markets and seller's markets usually do not last forever. It is hard to predict what the market will do with any accuracy. But it is true that in the developed world, with numerous buyer markets, many products from other parts of the world are demanded and can be sold. This then leads to cost efficient long-dis-

---

5 Refer to: http://en.wikipedia.org/wiki/Abraham_Maslow. Abraham Maslow was an American professor of psychology who created the first pyramid or hierarchy of needs: Basic or physiological needs like food and water are at the bottom; then, safety needs; love and belonging on level 3; fourth level is the esteem-level; and the top level is the need for self-actualization. References can be found on the website.

tance transportation, that is, for agricultural products or for products from countries with comparative advantages in production. All this leads to increased trade and transportation; therefore, we consider the trend of more and more competitive buyer markets as a driver of global trade.

Environmental Awareness

Environmental awareness focuses on increasing understanding and consciousness toward the health of the environment and its problems, including the human influence on the planet. Ecological awareness has grown more common, especially in affluent industrial countries. Here the population has enough time and money to spend on environmental protection and to fight for a more sustainable world. But ecological thinking, sustainability, and environmental protection is not a "luxury playground" of developed societies. Globalization has transferred this into a global task, and there are many serious scientists around the globe pointing out that environmental problems and the pollution in many parts of the world are the most serious problems we are facing today. The real problem is that most of the world's population is not aware of our finite resources and how quickly they are being used up. To address the limitations of resources, increases in pollution, and its effects like global warming, an environmental awareness is needed. This awareness and consciousness for the environment is increasing.

At its crux, environmental protection is an attempt to balance relations between humanity and the planet. Environmentalism and environmental concerns are often represented by the color green, and many initiatives include the prefix "green," like green ports, green shipping, etc. The line between serious projects that wish to help the environment and projects that are just for marketing purposes (or "greenwashing" projects) can often become blurred. However, we must realize that environmental questions are growing increasingly important and that there are many ways, environmentalists and environmental organizations seek to give the natural world a stronger voice.

Because of environmental protection activities, the way foodstuffs, consumer products, and industry products are produced and the way the service industry performs will change. For example, we see more and more calculations being made regarding CO_2 emissions (these calculations indicate how environmentally friendly a product [like a refrigerator] or service [like a trip with an airplane] is). Trade is impacted by the new products and services created in response to environmental change; therefore, the environment and environmental awareness is a driver for trade.

Innovations

There are many definitions of "innovation" out there, and how innovation differs from ideas, concepts to realize ideas, improvements, inventions, and imitations. Inventions are often the basis for innovations; an innovation in this sense is the commercialization of an invention. Imitations are often copies of innovations, and in science it is discussed whether imitations are "real innovations" as well, or if they are more of the character of an improvement. These are theoretical discussions; in practice new products and services are called innovations.

Inventions themselves can be realized in universities, laboratories, R&D departments, etc., but innovations need a market. Only when new products emerge on the market they are called innovations. These differ from improvements in that "innovation" refers to doing something different rather than doing the same thing better. Innovation is the creation of better or more effective products, processes, services, technologies, or ideas that are readily available to markets, governments, and society. Chief among the technological innovations are inventions that have improved the speed of transportation and communications and lowered their costs. These include the development of the jet engine, containerization in international shipping, and the revolution in information and communications technology. Equally notable are changes in production methods, which have created new tradable products, expanded global production in food, and made manufacturing more efficient.

In this sense innovations create new markets, and new markets create trade. Therefore, we identify innovations as a further driver for global trade.

Integrated Supply Chain Logistics

A supply chain is a system of organizations, people, technology, activities, information, and resources involved in moving a product or service from supplier to customer. Starting with unprocessed raw materials and ending with the final customer using finished goods, a supply chain may link many companies together. Supply chain activities transform natural resources, raw materials and components into a finished product that is delivered to the end customer. In sophisticated supply chain systems, used products may reenter the supply chain at any point where residual value is recyclable.

The Council of Supply Chain Management Professionals (CSCMP) defines supply chain management as follows:[6]

> Supply Chain Management encompasses the planning and management of all activities involved in sourcing and procurement, conversion, and all logistics management activities. Importantly, it also includes coordination and collaboration with channel partners, which can be suppliers, intermediaries, third-party service providers, and customers. In essence, supply chain management integrates supply and demand management within and across companies. Supply chain management is an integrating function with primary responsibility for linking major business functions and business processes within and across companies into a cohesive and high-performing business model. It includes all of the logistics management activities noted above, as well as manufacturing operations, and it drives coordination of processes and activities with and across marketing, sales, product design, finance, and information technology.

A typical supply chain starts with checking all necessary regulations of natural resources, followed by the human extraction of raw material, and includes several production links (e.g., component construction, assembly, and merging) before moving on to several layers of storage facilities of ever-decreasing size and ever more remote geographical locations, until finally reaching the consumer.

Many of the exchanges encountered in the supply chain will therefore be between different companies that will seek to maximize their revenue within their sphere of interest but may have little or no knowledge or interest in the remaining players along the supply chain. The supply chain management team must coordinate the interests and partners along the chain. This may lead to new routes, new shipping lines, new ports, and new hinterland transportation; all this for the target to improve supply chain efficiency. In this sense integrated supply chains drive global trade.

5.3 Antitrade Movements/Protectionism

In economic science, free trade between free economies with minimal barriers is optimal and has the largest potential for creating economic welfare for the inhabitants of all countries. Free trade in this sense is defined as a policy of nondiscrimination against imports from and exports to foreign countries. Buyers and sellers

---

6 Supply chain Management Terms and Glossary, Updated February 2010, Council of Supply Chain Management Professionals (CSCMP), http://cscmp.org/digital/glossary/glossary.asp, Lombard, IL, page 180.

from separate economies may voluntarily trade without the domestic government applying tariffs, quotas, subsidies or prohibitions on their goods and services. Together with technical innovation, free trade is one of the key drivers of rising productivity and resource efficiency, helping to increase living standards. Free trade as a guiding economic principle has been responsible for a large proportion of the dramatic drop in poverty rates across the world in the last fifty years. Free trade as a rational welfare-optimizing concept is the opposite of trade protectionism or economic isolationism.

But, a basket of negative side effects can accompany free trade, for example, the fear of losing control, risk of uncontrolled influence of multinational organizations, loss of work places to foreign countries, "importing" unfavorable work conditions and compensation standards, retrogression of ethical and environmental standards, completely deregulated markets with standards set by foreign countries, lower safety standards of products, etc. People opposing free trade believe that international agreements and global or supranational organizations, such as the World Trade Organization (WTO) or the European Commission, undermine local decision making and ignore regional interests.

Though free trade's positive effects are accepted in theory, many individuals find these positives outweighed by their own negative experience. The result is a strong antitrade attitude that—when organized—can best be described as an antitrade movement. Such attitudes and organized movements have existed since free trade evolved, but their strength and the size of their influence fluctuates. The winners of free trade, for example, the a.m. multinational corporations, sometimes dismiss the proponents of antitrade movements as loser; such emotional disputes are not helpful at all, but as some experience managers sometimes quote correctly: "Emotions are the hardest facts in business!"; they can not be ignored, because the economic decision makers are human beings. It is a matter of fact that after a long period of supported free trade following World War II, the financial crisis occurred, sparking antifree trade sentiment, particularly in highly developed countries.

Antitrade movements are based on individual attitudes, whereas protectionism is any governmental action and policy that restricts or restrains free trade. Protectionism is the politically organized expression of antitrade sentiment. The arguments against globalization and free trade are often the same as for protectionism: protecting local businesses and workers from the negative impacts of foreign governments, companies, institutions, etc. Typical methods of protectionism are tariffs and quotas on imports and subsidies or tax cuts granted to local businesses. The primary objective of protectionism is to limit what they call "unfair competition" from foreign industries and make local businesses or industries more competitive by increasing the price or restricting the quantity of imports entering the country. It is a politically motivated defensive measure that—in the short run—can work. However, most economists and experts in political science agree that antitrade action is destructive in the long term. It makes the country and its industries less competitive in international business.

The remaining question then is: what explains the rebirth of protectionism in America and Europe in the second decade of the 21st century? There are likely many factors behind it, but arguably the most prominent are the protracted weakness of the economies after the financial crisis; ongoing deindustrialization across much of Europe and the United States; the strong and ever-increasing position of China in global and local markets; slower wage growth than the 20th-century trend; heightened perceptions of income and wealth inequality within countries; and anxiety over technological and economic change at an ever faster pace.

Without the beneficial force of free trade and open markets, the task of growing prosperity for everyone—particularly the world's poorest—will be made more difficult. Antifree trade movements and protectionism together result in negative effects on trade, and thus on ports as facilitators of trade.

5.4 Transport Value and Affinity

The pure economic theory of Adam Smith, David Ricardo, and other followers is free of regional or special dimensions. As a first approach to include the special dimension into the overall economic theory, some regional theories have been developed but have at the beginning been very static, that is, by just adding costs per mile or km on a microeconomic level as an add on to the production function. Another approach was the locational (or institutional) competition approach; in this approach, transport infrastructure facilities like ports and transport markets are considered locational factors and policy instruments in the competition between regions to attract highly mobile capital.

The role of transport on spatial patterns of economic activity has been shaped by Fritz Voigt's theory "transport as a space-shaping factor" (Voigt 1973). Voigt saw the effects of internal developments within the transport system (comprising transport infrastructure, market formation, technology, economic policy) on the economic and spatial evolutionary process within a region and the observable long-term impact on economic structures that could be attributed to these intra-transport developments. In his approach, Voigt combined elements of different general growth theories within a development model that stressed the crucial role of the condition of the transport system on regional economic growth and the pattern of economic activities. Improvements as well as deficiencies in different parts of the transport system (i.e., ports) may induce wide-ranging processes of spatial differentiation, which are often irreversible and influence economic growth and production structures of regions for a long time.

Voigt considered both sides of the transportation market—supply and demand—and introduced two new categories to measure how they fit together for specific transportation needs: "Verkehrswertigkeit," best translated as "transport value" (sometimes also "transport efficiency") and "Verkehrsaffinität" or "transport affinity" (affinity descended from Latin for "relationship").

Transport value in this context is a merged index that describes the different dimensions of a single means of transport or the quality of transport services. In other words, this describes the supply side of transportation. Transport affinity, on the other hand, is an index describing demand criteria, using the same characteristics as the transport value. In his first studies, Voigt used both indicators in a qualitative way and measured their expression on a scale between 0 and 1. Later, more and more quantitative approaches were developed with the aim of better describing supply and demand, but these were adjustments and improvements to Voigt's original approach.

Seven characteristics per mode of transport or conveyance can be distinguished according to Voigt. As a combined index, these characteristics describe an early form of a logistics performance indicator for both sides of the market:
1. Mass performance (= Mass perf.)
2. Speed
3. Ability to network formation (= Network)
4. Predictability (= Predict.)
5. Frequency of transport services (= Freq.)
6. Safety
7. Convenience (= Conven.)

Mass performance: This indicator expresses the ability to transport massive quantities in volume, that is, bulk shipments with large quantities of each good. This could include crude oil with tankers or iron ore and coal with bulkers. Mass performance could be measured as maximal carrying capacity (dwt per vessel) or ton per kilometer or hour. The units used to measure mass performance do not particularly matter, these will vary depending on the mode of transportation (rail, vessel, etc.). What is important is that the transport value and the transport affinity are expressed in the same units so that both categories (transport value and affinity) are expressed by the same indicator.

Speed: Speed refers to a means of transport's ability to relocate passengers or cargo from one destination to another under the constraint of time. The speed of a specific transport is calculated based on average velocity (with waiting times taken into account). This indicator is *not* related to the maximum speed that is possible for the respective means of transport. For example, the speed of a railway transport from a coastal port to an inland capital will be calculated with all waiting times in front of signals. The average time between source and destination is what counts.

Ability to network formation: Network-forming ability is the ability of a conveyance to switch within a nodal point from one connection to another, and so on to create networks. An example of this is commuter planes that are coordinated with departures of intercontinental lines, or feeder vessels coordinated with oceangoing mother vessel. A network in this sense is more than just having several smaller planes feedering a hub, that is, it is not just the number of smaller and larger planes that counts. The logistical connection between the commuter and the intercontinental line creates the real net. This may in specific cases mean that a plane, ready for departure, is still waiting for the last commuter and the final passengers to board the big plane. Interconnectivity is an essential part of a network. All this sounds very simple, but in reality the characteristic of network ability is highly vulnerable and it takes a huge effort to operate networks. The term "logistics" and most of the logistics efforts concentrate on this characteristic.

Predictability: This is the ability and reliability of a conveyance to stick to the proposed times of departure and arrival—for a single transportation from A to B, or within a network—for example, from A via B and C to D. Predictability and reliability plays a significant and ever-increasing role when assessing transport requirements. Modern production concepts request that transportation is reliable and deliveries be on time, that is, trucks delivering supplier parts for the automotive industry just-in-time around the clock. Predictability in practice is often confused with speed; here we must draw a clear distinction. Just-in-time does not mean "as quickly as possible"; the transport must arrive at a given time, and not before, but also not later. To fall in the appropriate time window is the most important criteria.

Frequency of transport services: This is the ability of the transport system to provide the demanded services at the time and in the frequency when needed. Supply of transport should always be able to fulfill the needs of demand so that there are no shortages, extraordinary waiting times, lack of capacity, etc. Feeder vessels and their cargo would, in an ideal world, always find a mother vessel to the final destination in an acceptable amount of time. If the feeder vessel is delayed and the mother vessel could not wait any longer, then the frequency of transport services become relevant. If there are daily intercontinental services, the problem is normally not that serious. But when there is a low frequency and long additional waiting times, huge problems can occur.

Safety: Safety refers to the ability of a means of transport to carry out its transport without damages, loss of cargo, or risk to the health of its passengers. This includes any loading and unloading processes or handling operations en route. To measure safety, the frequency of accidents involving personal injury and property damage as well as the value of quality degradation can be used. Safety is provided by a variety of factors, such as the traffic density on the roads, the reliability of air traffic control for planes, or the absence of piracy for ships in international waters. Safety should be an indivisible value! Risks to passengers are unacceptable. So too are risks to cargo and any problems the cargo load may cause (e.g., in case of an oil spill with tankers). Accidents happen, but it should be a main goal to increase safety wherever and whenever possible.

Convenience: The characteristic "convenience" expresses the extent to which a conveyance is easy or difficult to use. The more complicated regulations and bureaucracy needed, the less convenient the transportation is. And very often regulated and inconvenient transportations are more cost intensive and therefore unattractive. Convenience is a soft factor and not easy to measure. Initiatives like "Daily Maersk" or "INTTRA" are targeting exactly this factor.[7] Their intention is to ease the way container bookings are made.

The seven characteristics for transport value and transport affinity can be expressed in statistics or in network diagrams; also called polar diagrams. The latter provides a fast-visual depiction of transport values and transport affinities. Figure 5.7 shows transport values of an airplane and an ultra large crude carrier/tanker (ULCC), and it is easy to compare the different expressions per characteristic.

The value of each characteristic can be expressed on a scale, for example, between 0 and 10. A very low value of 1 for mass performance of an airplane is exactly the opposite of the mass performance ability of an ULCC; here expressed by a value of 10.

---

7 More details can be found on following webpages: www.dailymaersk.com, www.inttra.com, www.changingthewaywethinkaboutshipping.com. The companies want to introduce a "one-click-shipping" and make it as easy as ordering a book online. These approaches are welcome initiatives to shippers who are used to inconvenient and in-transparent procedures.

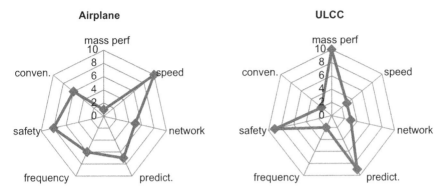

Figure 5.7: Transport values: Example airplane and ULCC

With this tool of Fritz Voigt, different modes of transportation can be character-ized and qualified. For products like crude oil, coal, or iron ore it is easy to under-stand that they have a high affinity for mass performance, safety, and predict-ability, whereas passengers of air transportation have an affinity for speed and convenience and the highest safety.

Voigt did not use these diagrams for transport infrastructure. But it seems to be logical to use the same characteristics to classify ports by using the same seven indicators. For a benchmarking of ports these are appropriate indicators. Table 5.3 contains an estimation of how the expression of transport values for typical ports will look. Figure 5.8 shows the corresponding set of polar diagrams.

Table 5.3: Transport values of typical ports

	Container	General Cargo	Liquid Bulk	Dry Bulk	RoRo	Ferry	Pass. + Cruise
Mass Performance	7	5	10	10	5	3	1
Speed	5	5	3	3	7	7	9
Network	7	4	2	1	6	7	7
Predictability	7	6	7	6	7	9	10
Frequency	5	3	2	2	6	7	8
Safety	9	8	9	7	9	9	10
Convenience	4	4	2	2	5	7	9

* Measured on a scale between 0 and 10; 0 being the lowest and 10 the highest fulfillment; own estimation.

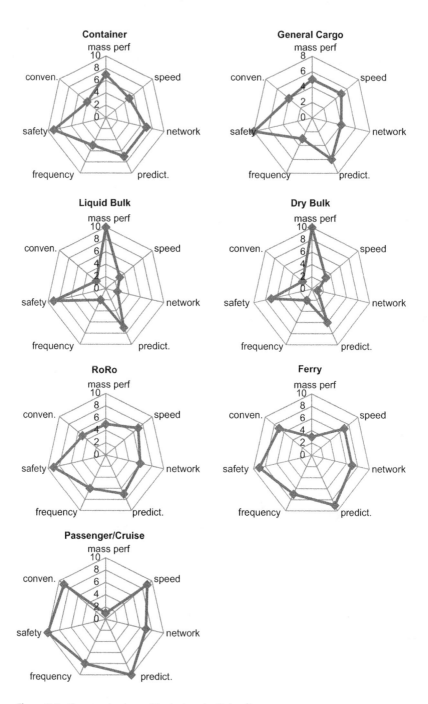

Figure 5.8: Transport values of typical ports: Polar diagrams

The different character of each type of port can be easily identified by just comparing these polar diagrams. Another exercise would be to compare specific ports per category. For this we need more specific indicators to measure the characteristics. These indicators are normally described as key performance indicators (KPIs); for further details refer to Chapter 16, section 2.

5.5 International Commercial Terms

Rights and duties along the supply chain must be clearly regulated and precisely defined. The different languages spoken along a supply chain makes it necessary to ensure common understanding in global trade and transportation. As in any complex and sophisticated business, small changes in wording can have a major impact on all aspects of a business agreement. Word definitions often differ from industry to industry. This is especially true for global trade and transportation. Fundamental phrases like "delivery" can have a far different meaning in the business than in the rest of the world.

For global business terminology to be effective, phrases must mean the same thing throughout the industry. A key goal is to remove or at least reduce uncertainties along the supply chain. Confusion over meanings can result in lost sales or bad deals. Thus, it is essential that the parties involved have a clear understanding of the terms they are agreeing to before finalizing a contract. That is why the International Chamber of Commerce created "International Commercial Terms" or "Incoterms." They are designed to create a bridge between different members of the industry by acting as a uniform language they can use. Incoterms are not an international law; they are rules on which the contracting parties can agree on voluntarily. "The Incoterms rules are an internationally recognized standard and are used worldwide in international and domestic contracts for the sale of goods. First published in 1936, Incoterms rules provide internationally accepted definitions and rules of interpretation for most common commercial terms."[8] "Incoterms" is a registered trademark of the International Chamber of Commerce. The Incoterms rules have been periodically updated, with the eighth version—*Incoterms 2010*—having been published on January 1, 2011.

The Incoterms rules are intended primarily to clearly communicate the tasks, costs, and risks associated with the transportation and delivery of goods. The

---

8 Website of International Chamber of Commerce. The world business organization. Visited on July 2, 2012, page 1: http://www.iccwbo.org/products-and-services/trade-facilitation/ incoterms-2010/

Incoterms rules are accepted by governments, legal authorities, and practitioners worldwide for the interpretation of most commonly used terms in international trade.

The eleven predefined terms of *Incoterms 2010* are subdivided into two categories based only on the method of delivery. The larger group of seven rules applies regardless of the method of transport, with the smaller group of four being applicable only to sales that solely involve transportation over water. Each Incoterm refers to a type of agreement for the purchase and shipping of goods internationally. For example, the term FCA is often used with shipments involving Ro/Ro or container transport.

Incoterms are most frequently listed by category. Terms in the following[9] beginning with *F* refer to shipments where the primary cost of shipping is not paid for by the seller. Terms beginning with *C* deal with shipments where the seller pays for shipping. The *E*-term occurs when a seller's responsibilities are fulfilled when the goods are ready to depart from their facilities. *D* terms cover shipments where the shipper/seller's responsibility ends when the goods arrive at some specific point. Because each shipment is moving into a country, *D* terms usually involve the services of a customs broker and a freight forwarder. In addition, *D* terms also deal with the pier or docking charges found at virtually all ports and determining who is responsible for the charge.

EXW (EX-Works) (named place of delivery)

One of the simplest and most basic shipment arrangements places the minimum responsibility on the seller with greater responsibility on the buyer. In an EX-Works transaction, goods are basically made available for pickup at the shipper/seller's factory or warehouse and "delivery" is accomplished when the merchandise is released to the consignee's freight forwarder. The buyer is responsible for making arrangements with their forwarder regarding insurance, export clearance, and handling all other paperwork.

FOB (free on board) (named port of shipment)

The seller must load the goods on board the vessel nominated by the buyer. Cost and risk are divided when the goods are on board of the vessel. The seller must clear the goods for export, and the buyer must provide the seller with details about the vessel and the port where the goods are to be loaded. FOB specifically refers to ocean or inland waterway transportation of goods. The term is appli-

---

9 The Incoterms listed here can only give a short overview. For more details, refer to the ICC and the official definition of *Incoterms 2010*.

cable for maritime and inland waterway transport only but not for multimodal sea transport in containers. "Delivery" is accomplished when the shipper/seller releases the goods to the buyer's forwarder. The buyer's responsibility for insurance and transportation begin at the same moment.

FCA (free carrier) (named place of delivery)
In this type of transaction, the seller is responsible for arranging transportation, but he is acting at the risk and the expense of the buyer. Where in FOB the freight forwarder or carrier is the choice of the buyer, in FCA the seller chooses and works with the freight forwarder or the carrier. "Delivery" is accomplished at a predetermined port or destination point and the buyer is responsible for insurance.

FAS (free alongside ship) (named place of delivery)
In these transactions, the buyer bears all the transportation costs and the risk of loss of goods. FAS requires the shipper/seller to clear goods for export, which is a reversal from past practices. Companies selling on these terms will ordinarily use their freight forwarder to clear the goods for export. "Delivery" is accomplished when the goods are turned over to the buyer's forwarder for insurance and transportation. The term FAS is suitable only for maritime transport, but not for multimodal sea transport in containers. FAS is typically used for heavy-lift or bulk cargo.

CFR (cost and freight) (named port of destination)
This term defines two distinct and separate responsibilities—one is dealing with the actual cost of merchandise "C," and the other "F" refers to the freight charges to a predetermined destination point. It is the shipper/seller's responsibility to get goods from their door to the port of destination. "Delivery" is accomplished at this time, that is, risk is transferred to the buyer once the goods are loaded on the vessel. It is the buyer's responsibility to cover insurance from the port of origin or port of shipment to the buyer's door. Given that the shipper is responsible for transportation, the shipper also chooses the forwarder.

CIF (cost, insurance, and freight) (named port of destination)
This arrangement is like CFR, but instead of the buyer insuring the goods for the maritime phase of the voyage, the shipper/seller will insure the merchandise. In this arrangement, the seller usually chooses the forwarder. "Delivery" as above, is accomplished at the port of destination. This Incoterm is for maritime transport only.

CPT (carriage paid to) (named place of delivery)
In CPT transactions the shipper/seller has the same obligations found with CIF, with the addition that the seller must buy cargo insurance, naming the buyer as the insured while the goods are in transit.

CIP (carriage and insurance paid to) (named place of delivery)
This term is primarily used for multimodal transport. Because it relies on the carrier's insurance, the shipper/seller is only required to purchase minimum coverage. When this agreement is in force, freight forwarders often act in effect, as carriers. The buyer's insurance is effective when the goods are turned over to the forwarder.

DAT (delivered at terminal) (named place of delivery)
This term is used for any type of shipment. The shipper/seller pays for carriage to the terminal, except for costs related to import clearance, and assumes all risks up to the point that the goods are unloaded at the terminal.

DAP (delivered at place) (named place of delivery)
DAP is used for any type of shipment. The shipper/seller pays for carriage to the named place, except for costs related to import clearance, and assumes all risks prior to the point that the goods are ready for unloading by the buyer.

DDP (delivered duty paid) (named place of delivery)
DDP tends to be used in intermodal or courier-type shipments. Whereby, the shipper/seller is responsible for dealing with all the tasks involved in moving goods from the manufacturing plant to the buyer/consignee's door. It is the shipper/seller's responsibility to insure the goods and absorb all costs and risks including the payment of duty and fees.

It is essential for shippers to know the exact status of their shipments in terms of ownership and responsibility. It is also vital for sellers and buyers to arrange insurance on their goods while the goods are in their "legal" possession. Lack of insurance can result in wasted time, lawsuits, and broken relationships. Figure 5.9 gives a quick overview of the responsibilities of sellers and buyers for the aforementioned Incoterms. Starting on the left side when the seller made the goods available for the buyer's forwarder at the outgate of the factory (EXW), going along the supply chain via export declaration procedure, inland dray, loading in seaport for export, maritime transportation, unloading in the port of arrival, inland carriage, and finally the customs declaration and taxes to be paid:

	EXW	FCA	FAS	FOB	CFR	CIF	DAT	DAP	CPT	CIP	DDP
Loading on truck (carrier)	B	S	S	S	S	S	S	S	S	S	S
Export-Customs declaration	B	S	S	S	S	S	S	S	S	S	S
Carriage to port of export	B	S	S	S	S	S	S	S	S	S	S
Unloading of truck in port of export	B	B	S	S	S	S	S	S	S	S	S
Loading charges in port of export	B	B	B	S	S	S	S	S	S	S	S
Carriage to port of import	B	B	B	B	S	S	S	S	S	S	S
Unloading charges in port of import	B	B	B	B	B	B	S	S	S	S	S
Loading on truck/carrier in port of import	B	B	B	B	B	B	B	S	S	S	S
Carriage to place of destination	B	B	B	B	B	B	B	S	S	S	S
Import customs clearance	B	B	B	B	B	B	B	B	B	B	S
Import taxes	B	B	B	B	B	B	B	B	B	B	S
Insurance	n/a	n/a	n/a	n/a	n/a	S	n/a	n/a	n/a	S	n/a

n/a = not applicable   S = Duty of Seller   B = Duty of Buyer

Figure 5.9: Duties of Seller and Buyer according to *Incoterms 2010*

Chapter 6
Ports in Transportation Chain

6.1 The Role of Ports in Supply Chain

A "supply chain" is a sequence of business processes and information that provides and accompanies a product or service from suppliers through manufacturing and distribution to the ultimate consumer. "Maritime supply chains" use the sea for transportation, with ships being the means of transportation and ports as important connection points. Inside a network and from a global perspective, the shipping routes represent the lines, and ports the nodal points. From a regional economic point of view, parts of the maritime supply chain are often described as hub-and-spoke-systems, having a (large and important) hub port in the center that is served by several small ports via the spokes. Larger spokes connect the hub ports.[1]

Further definitions of "maritime supply chain" highlight the use of the ocean for gathering natural resources like oil, gas, or wind energy. In this case the maritime supply chain can start at open sea, for example, at oil and gas offshore rigs or at FSOs or FPSOs,[2] or even end there, in the case of erecting new windmills or rigs.

In the following figure, we will concentrate on the first definition and consider "maritime supply chains" from the transportation point of view. Such a chain begins with the sourcing of raw material and ends with the sale of the finished product or service. Pre- and intermediate products are all considered "products," as they are sold on the market like other products.

The maritime supply chain is an integrated group of processes to "source," "make," "deliver," and "sell" products and services. From a process-oriented point of view, a larger number of participants act together along the chain: supplier, manufacturer, transporter, storage facilities, ports, shipping lines, wholesaler, distributor, and retailer.

A typical maritime supply chain, including ocean transportation, a transhipment hub, and a feeder transportation is illustrated in Figure 6.1.

---

1 For further details about hub-and-spoke systems please refer to Chapter 4.4; Figure 4.5.

2 FSO = Floating Storage and Offloading vessel; FPSO = Floating Production and Offloading vessel

DOI 10.1515/9781547400874-006

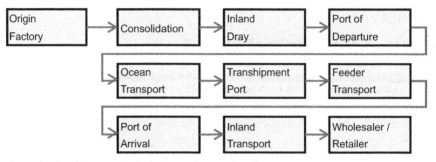

Figure 6.1: Maritime supply chain illustration: Product flow

A single supply chain describes the transport from point A to B; from the origin factory to the retailer. If we look to the typical cargo load of a vessel, for example, one container, then we can assume that the box is packed in the factory and moved as a fully loaded full container load (FCL) box from the factory to the wholesaler. Here the box will be discharged. If we now consider that the factory in country A is producing for more than one wholesaler and for more than one country, then we must consider many supply chains. A vessel with 14,000 TEU, which is equivalent to 10,000 containers on board, may be involved in up to 10,000 different supply chains. The number of engagements should be and usually are much lower because most containers are not booked one by one. Management companies try to consolidate and usually book complete "packages," that is, larger quantities of containers as a single bloc. But this only changes the scale, not the principle of how it works.

In addition to the physical product flow above, supply chain management (SCM) must manage two additional flows: information and finance. That means that an SCM consists of the following three flows:
–   Product flow
–   Information flow
–   Finances flow

The product flow includes the movement of goods from a supplier or the origin factory to a wholesaler or retailer, and finally to the customer. The information flow involves transmitting orders and updating the status of delivery. The finances flow consists of credit terms, payment schedules, and consignment and title ownership arrangements.

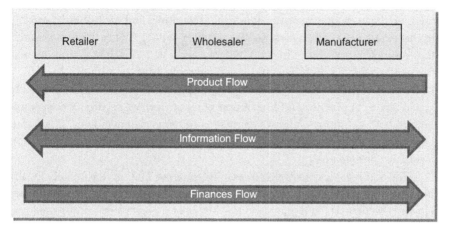

Figure 6.2: SCM flows

SCM as an operating business is comprised of sourcing, planning, designing, demand forecasting, transportation, storage, and distribution. In most definitions, manufacturing, marketing, and sales are also components of SCM. At its core, SCM is managing the flow of products, information, and finances through the supply chain to attain the level of synchronization that will make it more responsive to customer needs while lowering costs. Key elements of effective SCM are:

- Information
- Communication
- Cooperation

The terms "supply chain management" and "logistics" are sometimes used synonymously, and from a broad perspective the content of the concepts is similar. Both definitions concentrate on the design of object flows (goods, information, values) along the processing stages from supplier to final customer, targeting an increase of the (end) customer benefits (effectiveness) as well as an improvement of the overall cost-benefit ratio (efficiency). Most definitions of "logistics" concentrate on the object flows, often independently of institutional issues. Logistics focuses on aspects of transportation, inventory, warehousing, material handling, packaging, security, etc. In this view, logistics is more a technical or engineering science with concentration on product and information flows. SCM as used in the definition above explicitly include all business functions of coordination and structuring of corporate entities. The SCM therefore emphasizes, in contrast to the inter-organizational logistics, the typical logistics management tasks. In this sense, SCM highlights the business management tasks. SCM includes not only logistics, but all other fields of business administration such as marketing, production, business management, financial accounting, and controlling. Logistics in this perspective can be classified as a subset of SCM. It is easy to understand that staunch supporters of logistics will not agree with this SCM definition, and frequently come up with new and more comprehensive definitions of logistics. Ultimately, it is a question of the definition that is used. Because of this, as already stated above, in practice and from a port point of view, we see frequent overlapping of both definitions, and we can use both terms synonymously. If supportive functions like marketing are important, the relevant content of the definition used must be explained.

SCM and logistics are highly interactive systems, and—unfortunately for the industry—the system contains an accelerator or amplifier effect, the "bullwhip effect." Fluctuations in demand on the customer markets can lead upstream to serious fluctuation in the industry.

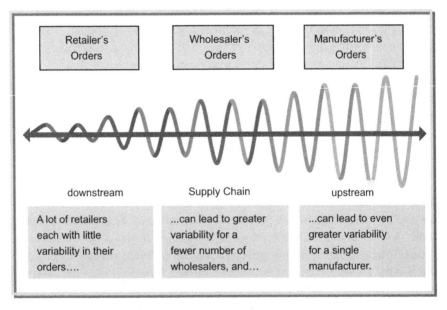

Figure 6.3: The "bullwhip effect"

Uncertainties in the supply chain cause a lot of problems and require interference. Having the right information at the right time and in the right quality is essential for managing the supply chain. One problem managers face are unexpected costs combined with uncertainties. Typical uncertainties that may disturb the SCM and create serious problems are:

- Wrong forecasts
- Late deliveries
- Poor quality
- Machine breakdowns
- Canceled orders
- Erroneous information, that is, due to ambiguous wording

It sounds trivial, but all uncertainties and disruptions along the chain are important issues, because a supply chain is only as strong as its weakest link.

Traditional drivers of SCM are factors like:
- Price
- Globalization
- Origin and factory requirements
- Last mile delivery requirements
- Bundled contract options
- Reduced costs for IT
- Pick and pack transload options
- Unit costs per revenue dollar
- Increased transportation network
- Inventory carrying costs

It is very likely that with increased globalization, over proportional growth of world trade (in relation to GDP growth), and increased competition the set and composition of future driver will change. Future SCM models will in addition to the already identified drivers in chapters above take (infrastructure) bottlenecks of the transportation system into consideration. Due to the long periods it takes to build a new port or terminal or to upgrade an existing one, it is very likely that an efficient port can become a positive driver of logistics, or a negative one by increasing bottlenecks and problems in port management and operation.

To compare maritime supply chains, it is necessary to define an indicator that measures performance. In 2007, the World Bank initiated the so-called Logistics Performance Index. "The Logistics Performance Index (LPI) and its indicators are a joint venture of the World Bank, logistics providers, and academic partners. The LPI is a comprehensive index created to help countries identify the challenges and opportunities they face in trade logistics performance. The World Bank conducts the LPI survey every two years" (WB 2010, page III).

The index itself is a multidimensional assessment of supply chain performance, rated on a scale from one (worst) to five (best). Based on a worldwide survey, it uses more than 5,000 individual country assessments made by nearly

1,000 international freight forwarders and express carriers to compare the trade logistics profiles of 155 countries. With this, the LPI has the character of a benchmarking tool for global supply chain performance, based on questionnaires and individual judgments.

The LPI summarizes the performance of all countries in six areas that capture the most important aspects of the current supply chain environment:
- Efficiency of the customs clearance process
- Quality of trade and transport-related infrastructure
- Ease of arranging competitively priced shipments
- Competence and quality of logistics services
- Ability to track and trace consignments
- Frequency with which shipments reach the consignee within the scheduled or expected time

The LPI report criteria range from traditional issues (customs procedures and infrastructure quality) to new concerns (tracking and tracing shipments, timeliness in reaching a destination, and the competence of the domestic logistics industry). Having a closer look at these six areas, we can see that they are nearly identical and can be summarized more generally under Fritz Voigt's seven characteristics outlined in Chapter 5.4: Efficiency of customs clearance and quality of infrastructure are subsets of predictability; ease of shipments is identical to convenience; ability to track and trace is part of the network formation; and frequency is used identically in both lists. Not explicitly mentioned in the LPI are speed (this may partly be included in quality), mass performance and safety. Mass performance measures how the logistics' ability to handle the cargo; in this sense it is likely a part of quality. Safety can be classified as ubiquitous; everybody assumes that a satisfactory level of safety is ensured. With increasing numbers of pirate attacks in recent years, it could be a good suggestion to include this characteristic in one of the next editions of the LPI.

The importance of efficient SCM and logistics for global trade and economic growth is widely acknowledged. Analysis based on the LPI has shown that better logistics performance is strongly associated with trade expansion, diversification of exports, ability to attract foreign direct investments, and economic growth. In other words, trade logistics matters.

It is an important finding of the LPI that—except for high-income countries— the availability and quality of trade-related infrastructure (like ports) is a major constraint to economic performance and growth. The ranking of constraints tends to vary across countries. Information technology infrastructure is widely available and widely used for trade processing, even in low-income countries, whereas countries in the intermediate range of logistics performance tend to be relatively more impacted by the quality and availability of physical infrastructure (like ports). Sadly, rail services still receive very low scores in almost every category.

Determining where the weakest links of supply chain performance are and addressing them through targeted development interventions has become a major element of the trade facilitation and logistics agenda. Until the World Bank's LPI has been developed, policymakers and private sector stakeholders have not had the data needed to identify trade constraints or create constituencies for reform. The LPI fills that gap and is a good indicator of global port performance.

6.2 Port Hinterland

"Hinterland" (in German, literally "the land behind") is the area where traffic demand originates. The term port hinterland is applied to the inland region lying behind a port. The port hinterland is connected to a port by lines of communication or transport routes: roads, railways, pipelines, and rivers/canals. It is the area from which export products are delivered to a port for shipping elsewhere, or where import products are demanded. In some literature, this area is also called market area; however, this term does not take the transport geography into consideration. Other sources call the area over which a port sells its services and interacts with its clients the hinterland. This is a good definition in that it highlights the interactions with the client. In most definitions, the term hinterland describes the geographical catchment area and has only little relation to national boundaries. Border crossings are only important for the port hinterland when they cause hindrances and have negative impact on trade flows.

In the English language, the term hinterland was first used in 1888 by George G. Chisholm in his work "Handbook of Commercial Geography.[3] The corresponding German word to hinterland is "Vorland" or "Foreland"; this term is used to describe the opposite direction of the supply chain and is made up of the seas accessed from the ports. The term is not widely used, and so we will in the following concentrate on Hinterland as the economic geographically catchment area behind a port.

The size of a hinterland depends on a combination of economic structures, quantity and size of industry, population and geography, but also on the ease,

---

[3] Refer to the *Encyclopaedia Britannica*: http://www.britannica.com/EBchecked/ topic/113260/ George-G-Chisholm.

speed, and cost of transportation between the port and the hinterland destinations, also known as transport affinity.

The various kinds of hinterland and the varying size of cargo volumes that need to be shipped in or out of these areas led to different sized ports. In this sense, the trade intensity of the hinterland is an essential driver for port business. The hinterland creates the trade for the port.

Figure 6.4 explains which factors determine size and shape of a port hinterland.

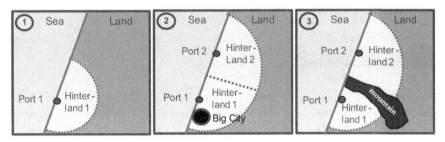

Figure 6.4: Hinterland 1–3

Picture 1 shows an ideal situation with only one port on a coastline, no traffic infrastructure restriction in the hinterland and no competition. This is the picture people have in mind when telling "our hinterland spans xxx kilometers."

Picture 2 shows a similar situation with no traffic restrictions in the hinterland, but with a second port, that is, competition. If ports 1 and 2 are identical in cargo structure and there are no other factors that may give a preference for port 1 or 2 (e.g. the shipping lines calling the ports), then the relevant market for port 1 is hinterland 1 and the market for port 2 is hinterland 2. The pure distance to the ports determines the shape and size of the hinterland. But this says very little about the economic potential of the hinterland. In Picture 2, we have included a big city in hinterland 1. This makes the area much more interesting for business than hinterland 2. But with such a big city, the precondition of unrestricted traffic in the area becomes unrealistic.

Picture 3 shows that all types of traffic obstacles can have an influence on the port hinterland. This may be a natural barrier like a mountain, or a river or an area without good rail and road access. Ultimately, the costs for trade in the hinterland are defining the relevant market. In Picture 3 the hinterland area of port 1 is smaller in size, but if there is a huge economic potential, that is, big cities and/ or industrial complexes, then this may be of higher interest than the larger hinterland 2. The economic potential and "cost distance" into a hinterland shapes the hinterland area. So-called iso-cost-lines are describing best the relevant hinterland markets for a port.

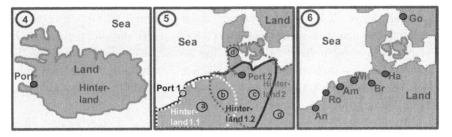

Figure 6.5: Hinterland 4–6

In Picture 4 in Figure 6.5 we come closer to reality. If there is a situation of an island with only one port (or better, one major port), then the whole island represents the hinterland area of this port, despite the traffic infrastructure, natural barriers, or the location of big cities in this area. This is the situation of Iceland with the Port of Reykjavik.

Picture 5 now includes competition under real circumstances. We assume that port 1 handles two different groups of commodities, like container and liquid bulk. Port 2 only handles containers. This leads to the situation that port 1 claims hinterland 1.1 for container business (the light dotted line) and hinterland 1.2 (solid line) for liquid bulk. The fact that port 2 does not handle liquid bulk leads to the hinterland of port 1 being used for liquid bulk. The solid line includes port 2 and huge parts of hinterland 2. This overlapping for different products and the missing clear border is the real *hinterland dilemma*. Port 2 is certainly not interested in promoting its hinterland for liquid bulk products, and so port 2 will always announce that its hinterland is hinterland 2, surrounded by the dark dotted line. It is even more complicated when considering the huge variety of cargoes big ports can have.

Picture 6 shows the real situation in northern Europe with the ports of Gothenburg (Go), Hamburg (Ha), Bremen (Br), Wilhelmshaven (Wi), Amsterdam (Am), Rotterdam (Ro), and Antwerp (An). These are only the big ports in that range, but considering only these ports, it is still easy to understand that a clear differentiation of hinterlands is nearly impossible. Most of the ports in the hinterland spend a reasonable amount of money for sales and marketing activities in this area to claim markets as relevant for their own hinterland.

The areas b for container and c for liquid bulk in the example of Picture 5 in Figure 6.5 are marking overlapping areas, that is, the areas with highest competition, or a "contestable" hinterland. Why does this overlapping happen? If only costs count, and we exclude personal preferences for one or the other port, then the decision making for ports 1 or 2 should not lead to an overlapping. This is true if we only consider the road or rail costs, for example, from area b to the ports.

But as explained above, a port is part of a long supply chain, and if port 1 does not offer the shipping service a customer needs for a specific day and time in area b, he may swing over to the other port. For the isolated distance from area b to the port, this may be suboptimal, but for the whole supply chain it is the best solution. Therefore, some port managers include the foreland in their thinking (i.e., the shipping side), as mentioned above.[4]

We must bear in mind that the hinterland dilemma occurs because information about cost components of the respective supply chain is incomplete and interest groups (i.e., port lobbying or port sales staff) only concentrate on parts of the supply chain, that is, by intention promote a possibly suboptimal solution. This problem becomes even larger when these interest groups try to optimize their small part of the supply chain, for example, from one of the ports in Figure 6.5, Picture 6, to an industrial complex like the Rhine-Ruhr-valley in Germany. This may lead to a distorted and highly contestable hinterland situation. An analysis of a specific port's hinterland situation must bear this in mind.

The term "hinterland" in transport economics is the logistics synonym for what economists in competition theory call the "relevant market": the market in which one or more goods competes. The term "market" in this definition of "hinterland" concentrates on the geographical dimension and combines the goods market and the geographic market. The "hinterland" or "relevant market" defines whether two or more goods (i.e., products and services) can be considered substitute or interchangeable goods and whether they constitute a particular and separate market for competition analysis, here often called the "hinterland analysis." This background clearly pointed out that hinterland analysis is not just a geographical description of a region, it is a competition analysis.

One question remains: how does one measure this geographical distance? There are at least four different approaches:
– Aeronautical distance in km or miles
– Traffic distance (per mode of traffic)
– Time
– Cost

Aeronautical distance is simply the distance between a port and a location in the hinterland; this is measured without taking natural barriers like mountains

---

4 The literature about port hinterland is huge, and many authors have introduced additional groupings and classifications for hinterland regions (for example, Rodrigue Notteboom Hinterlands 2006, UN Hinterland 2010, Park Medda 2010; Notteboom 2009).

or rivers or the traffic infrastructure into consideration. Figure 6.4 Picture 1 shows this approach. The hinterland is defined per km or miles and circled in. As a first rough approach at measuring the hinterland, this approach is acceptable; however, it is far from sufficient for an analysis of the hinterland's competitive situation.

Traffic distance includes the road, rail, inland waterway, or pipeline infrastructures in its measurement, and the distance is measured in units such as road km. This is a relatively simple and good approach that leads to reasonable results, but here it is necessary to distinguish between modes of transport. A rail connection, for example, via a tunnel may be shorter than a road connection that crosses a mountain.

The time approach takes into consideration that driving 100 km on a highway does not take the same amount of time as driving 100 km in the inner city or on suburban roads. In this approach, time matters more than pure distance. But here measuring becomes quite tricky; as the time approach needs to consider the type of vehicle being used. Congestion is another matter.

Ultimately, time is money, so the best approach is to calculate the cost-distance from the port by factoring in geographical infrastructure and the time it takes to reach a specific location; e.g. where can I go for 500 US Dollar per truck load? If we then connect all destinations with the same cost level, we can draw so-called iso-cost-lines; i.e. lines that show all combinations of the same cost level. These iso-cost-lines show the best results for hinterland dimensions, but they need clear definitions of conditions, including cargo load (20 ft or 40 ft, what weight, is there hazardous material or not, etc.), transport equipment (which locomotive, how many railcars, etc.), infrastructure (use of highways with toll, urban roads, congestion or not, etc.), and so on. The amount of conditions makes this approach unwieldy and rarely used in practice, although it is the most accurate one.

Loco-Potential

A term often used in port business is the loco-potential, or "local commodities potential." This is the cargo potential that in daily port practice is described as "100% bound to the port," or the "captive" hinterland. This means that (the majority of) the cargo out of this area will most likely go via this port. In this sense, the loco-potential describes the cargo potential in a specific hinterland region. Due to the definition of the term, this hinterland area describes a region very close to the port; often the city area around or adjacent to the port. But in some port marketing materials there is an inflationary use of the term "loco potential" and "loco area," and so the term could be used for something like a hinterland, although this is inaccurate. The loco-area is the area adjacent to the port, and the loco-potential is the cargo potential in this area. In competition theory, this should be the area where the port has a regional monopoly. The loco-area is a subset of the hinterland.

6.3 Ports and Shipping Networks

The topic of port and shipping networks has two different dimensions. The first is the question of how ports can be integrated as partners (i.e., as port of call) in existing, rearranged, or newly created shipping networks, for example, after a merger occurred or after route adjustments (these adjustments often reflect the changes in market conditions). The second dimension asks if—besides shipping networks—real port networks exist, that is, connections between ports that belong to same terminal operator. We will start with the first question.

Shipping Networks

Ships are often engaged in networks, and shipping networks are constructed to cover large areas of relevant markets so that vessels can easily be filled with cargo. For bulker and tankers, the networks are usually not that large. Very often these vessels are engaged in pendulum services from the source of the cargo, for example, an oil field or a mine, to the port of discharge, which is at best close to the place where the cargo is needed, for example, a refinery or a power plant. Due to the nature of this business, the bulker and tanker are often traveling back empty.

Counter to bulker and tanker services, the container shipping industry uses highly detailed and frequently optimized networks. Here we can find services that call twenty or more ports per round-trip, like the following NYK PAX Pacific Atlantic Express Service,[5] which calls twenty-five ports on a round-trip.

---

5 For detailed information, refer to: http://www2.nykline.com/liner/service_network

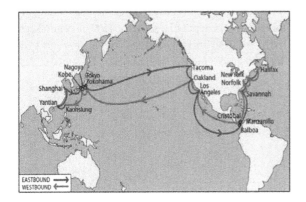

Port Rotation

Origin	ETA/ETD
Kaohsiung	TUE/TUE
Yantian	WED/THU
Shanghai	SAT/SUN
Kobe	TUE/TUE
Nagoya	WED/WED
Tokyo	THU/THU
Tacoma	SAT/SUN
Oakland	TUE/WED
Los Angeles	THU/THU
Balboa	THU/THU
Manzanillo (Panama)	THU/FRI
Savannah	TUE/TUE
Norfolk	THU/THU
New York	FRI/SAT
Halifax	MON/TUE
To/Fm Europe	
Halifax	MON/MON
New York	WED/THU
Norfolk	FRI/FRI
Savannah	SAT/SUN
Manzanillo (Panama)	WED/THU
Cristobal	THU/THU
Los Angeles	THU/FRI
Oakland	SAT/SUN
Yokohama	THU/FRI
Kobe	SAT/SAT
Kaohsiung	TUE/TUE

Turnaround days 98
Weekly/Fixed Day Service

Figure 6.6: NYK PAX Service

With "PAX," NYK of Japan is providing a service from the Asian east coast to North and Central America, that is, a transpacific service, with an additional link to the United States and Canadian east coast via the Panama Canal. Although it is called "express," the time it takes between cities like Kaohsiung to Halifax is relatively long.

The whole turnaround time for this service is ninety-eight days, as the port rotation schedule shows. It is a weekly service, meaning fourteen vessels are employed (98/7=14). Having a fixed weekly service is very convenient for the customer, which is why many of the trunk services try to arrange this for their customers. For hub ports within the rotation, like Shanghai or Los Angeles, the fixed schedule makes it easier for the feeder as well as for the hinterland modes of transportation to provide ongoing services to smaller ports that are not included in such rotation schedules.

Other transpacific services like the TP1 from Maersk Line,[6] connecting Los Angeles with Shanghai and Ningbo, only take thirty-five days per round-trip. But here there are only three ports connected, and this seems to be the minimum time for crossing the Pacific Ocean. Shanghai to Los Angeles takes twelve days, and Los Angeles to Ningbo takes sixteen days. Crossing the Pacific efficiently takes about two weeks.

---

6 For detailed information about all Maerk Line services, refer to: http://www.maerskline.com/link/?page=brochure&path=/routemaps

Services that do not concentrate on hub ports like Shanghai and Los Angeles often include several smaller ports. Transpacific service TP7 of Maersk, for instance, has fourteen ports in the rotation and takes seventy days per round-trip. This service employs ten vessels in a fixed day weekly service.

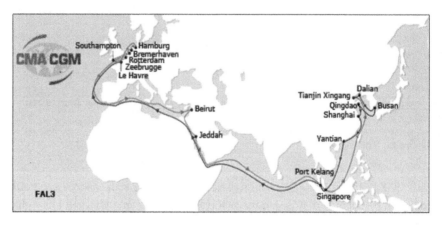

Figure 6.7: CMA CGM FAL3

CMA CGM's French Asia Line service No. 3 (FAL3)[7] is an example of a so-called Asia-Europe or Far East-Europe-Service, connecting the East Asian coastline with North-European ports. These services pass the Strait of Malacca between Indonesia and Malaysia, and many services then pass the horn of Africa and sail via the Suez Canal and Strait of Gibraltar to the European north continent, like the FAL3 in Figure 6.7. In times of vessel oversupply, like in the years 2010 to 2017 (and probably ongoing for few more years), combined with low demand in the market and increasing pirate activities at the horn of Africa, it becomes more and more attractive to go further south and sail via South Africa and along the west African coast toward North Europe. This saves money for the expensive Suez passage, and ships are employed. Shipping lines are always interested in offering competitive services, and so these calculations on network design are frequently made; it is a constant task for a shipping line.

---

7 For more information about CMA CGM services, refer to: http://www.cma-cgm com/eBusiness/ Schedules/LineServices

For many years, Asia-Europe has employed the largest container vessels on the market, and vessels as well as port calls are regularly adjusted according to market needs. FAL3, for example, had a turnaround time of seventy-seven days in the summer of 2017, and employs eleven CMA CGM vessels with capacities between 12,917 TEU (CMA CGM Nevada and Alaska) and 13,892 (like the APL Merlion, LionCity, Raffles, etc.).[8] All vessels were built between 2009 and 2013. This composition of similar-sized very young and big vessels is typical for this service, and comparable facts and figures can be found from other services. FAL1 East Asia-Europe service employed twelve vessels between 13,830 and 17,859 TEU in 2017, with most of the vessels built in the last four years.

Other services may have fewer ports of call and fewer vessels employed but follow the same pattern, like the Asia-Europe Loop 3 (LP3) from NYK with thirteen ports in the rotation and seventy-seven days turnaround time, or the LP4 with only nine ports and a turnaround time of seventy days. As a reasonable benchmark for an Asia-Europe service we can keep approximately four to five weeks for one way in mind. The latest generation of so-called triple-E vessels from Maersk with 18,000 TEU are also being employed on the Asia-Europe trade lane. In fact, the East Asia-Europe-services today employ the largest ships globally.

Transpacific and Asia-Europe are the most important intercontinental trade routes with the highest volumes; the transatlantic route—the link between Europe and North America—has much lower volumes and consequently fewer services. The highest volumes worldwide can be found in the inner-continental routes of the so-called Intra-Asian-Services.

Finally, it should be mentioned that beyond container liner shipping, other services provide liner schedules, like the RoRo service from Wallenius Wilhelmsen[9] in Figure 6.8.

---

8 APL has been integrated into CMA CGM in 2016.
9 For more information, refer to: https://www.2wglobal.com/global-network/route-maps/route-maps-list/

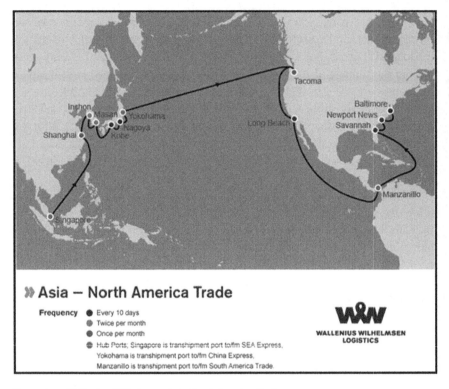

Figure 6.8: Wallenius-Wilhelmsen Asia-North America Trade

Container, General Cargo, RoRo, and Ferry shipping lines serve widespread consumer and investment goods markets; therefore, it is essential for these services to cover a relevant share of the market potentials. The ability to network formation according to Fritz Vogt in Chapter 5.4 clearly describes the necessity of doing so. Because of this, the examples above of shipping networks could not be examined as standalone services. We always must bear in mind that each single service like the NYK PAX, Maersk TP7, or CMA CGM FAL3 is part of an overall network. This is for targeting an attractive share of the relevant market, or in other words, with the aim to serve as many customers as possible. And in case a single shipping line is not large enough to provide the service alone, consortia, alliances, or slot sharing agreements are common tools to expand into the market. Also, mergers and takeovers are common strategies for ensuring the companies own market share. The risk of oligopolization or (regional) monopolization is always present.

If we now shift the view from these very flexible global shipping networks to the ports within these networks, then we shift from highly flexible assets to immobile assets. The view is no longer from a global perspective into local markets, but the other way around: from a local market with a given hinterland situation to global markets that are worth relating to. For ports, it is of huge importance and high interest to attract global shipping services and to relate to other ports. A prerequisite for this is a cargo volume in the port that makes it worth calling. The cargo can come directly out of the loco area, the direct hinterland, or the extended hinterland via a hub function.

Shipping lines add ports into their rotation when the amount of cargo within its hinterland is of interest and transport volumes can be increased. Bearing this in mind, it is easy to understand why many ports and terminals try to attract additional shipping lines, because this pushes the volumes of the port and the business for the terminal operator. Ports with a strategically good position and high volumes may find it much easier to attract additional services. Smaller ports in a region of less interest because of limited cargo volume find it often very difficult to get the attention of the shipping market. Feedering is often the second-best solution.

Shipping, from a transportation science point of view, represents the "foreland" and in this sense is similar to judge like the ("dry") hinterland, but with one exception: on the "waterside," ports deal with only one mode of transportation, and not with a variety of modes. On the other—more emotional—side in day-to-day business shipping is often associated with a flavor of internationality, huge cargo volumes that represent huge importance, and a touch of freedom. It can be assumed that the "monopolistic feeling" (expressed in statements like: we are the one and only important mode of transport you serve), in combination with the image of importance and freedom, is a key driver for many port sales managers to concentrate on this side of the business. Therefore, the content on many port and terminal websites about hinterland and foreland business is not balanced, and neither are the marketing and sales activities.

The relationship between transhipment cargo versus local cargo can be a major problem for some ports. If most cargo in a port is coming from the local industry or will go to local markets, then it represents no great risk. But when the share of transhipment cargo is very high, so is the competitive risk of being replaced by another port. Many ports with high transhipment shares faced this problem in the past. Reasons for this could be an overcapacity of existing ports and terminals, as was the case in the Mediterranean in the 1990s, or purpose-built new ports near already successful huge ports. Singapore and the neighboring ports in Malaysia are good examples of this.

Getting integrated in shipping networks is important for ports, but the growth of the port should be substantial and not artificially bubbled up. A "port bubble" can cost millions in taxpayer money. Substantial port business growth originates from the local catchment area of the port, that is, the loco potential, or alternatively out of a prominent and favorable location close to a main shipping route.

Port Networks
The second part in this chapter discusses what types of port networks exist and what are their functions. There are four different types of port network activities, and two of these fall under the category vertical integration while the remaining two fall under the category horizontal integration. The terms vertical and horizontal in the enumeration below refer to the start position within the supply chain (see Figure 6.1: Maritime supply chain). A vertical integration expands the activities along the supply chain, that is, upstream or downstream, whereas a horizontal integration intends to build the network on the same stage within the supply chain:
1. Vertical integration:
   a. Extended gateway partnerships
   b. "Dedicated" liner terminals
2. Horizontal integration:
   a. Port authority partnerships
   b. Global port operator

1a Extended Gateway Partnership
The extended gateway partnership is a concept where bigger ports (hub ports) extend their network into the hinterland and build cooperations with ports that are less integrated in global liner services or huge bulk trades. This may be the case along a river when the big port at the mouth of the river cooperates with inland ports (e.g., along the Mississippi, along the Yangtze, or the Amazon), or when a big port at a favorite location cooperates with smaller ports in less central seas, for example, the North Sea ports with Baltic ports, Canadian ports with ports in the Great Lakes area, Central Med ports with Adriatic or Black Sea ports, or a Caribbean hub port with other ports in the Gulf and Caribbean area. The ports in these extended gateway partnerships are independent and can decide for themselves the value of such a partnership. In most cases one big port (the "gateway") cooperates with several smaller ports, which is, from an operational point of view, a typical hub and spoke situation. These networks are built either as partnerships between port authorities or as business networks of port operators/stevedores. The lower the "natural ties" are, the higher the wish to establish a close cooperation. The targets are to secure market share from the hub ports point of view, and to secure market access from the smaller ports point of view. It can be a win-win situation, but gateway partnerships cost money. This means it is necessary from time to time to reevaluate the real value of such a partnership.

1b Dedicated Liner Terminals

Dedicated liner terminals—here we typically discuss terminal(s) inside a port, as opposed to the whole port—are terminals that are in the hands of one or more liner shipping companies. A good example of this is APMT,[10] the A.P. Moller Terminals Group belonging to the A.P. Moller Maersk Group. In mid-2017, APMT operated a network of sixty-one ports, plus an additional 189 port and inland facilities. This is a dense network for the Maersk Line and their alliance partner, established to enlarge shipping business and to integrate more and more stages along the supply chain into the business. Another example of this are the CMA Terminals and the "Terminal Link" group (as subsidiary of the French CMA CGM Shipping Line), operating more than twenty terminals together. The Euromax Terminal Rotterdam[11] is a good example of a dedicated terminal. This terminal was originally operated by four shipping lines—COSCO, K-Line, YangMing, and Hanjin[12]—plus Rotterdam stevedore ECT as a joint venture. As a group they share the terminal and are able to operate a facility that is large enough to gain economies of scale. Several smaller terminals would not be as efficient as this dedicated liner terminal. Although nobody would say this too loudly, all dedicated facilities give preference to their owners and their own shipping lines; this is how "dedicated" needs to be understood. This is very good from a company's point of view, because it secures terminal access even in busy times, when other lines may face increased congestion due to terminal shortages in combination with increasing prices. CMA CGM's new CEO Rodolphe Saade ("Terminal Link" and "CMA Terminals" belong to the group) formulated this principle at a 2017 conference in Long Beach[13] in this way: "Terminal investments are not a strategic decision"; their key target is to support CMA CGM core liner shipping business.

Adding dedicated terminals to existing shipping networks was driven by the fear of a shortage of terminal capacity. The early 2000s were characterized by double digit growth rates in shipping, that is, fast growth in the number and size of container vessels, without corresponding terminal expansion in most parts of the world. Staying in business and operating vessels with profit was the motivation for establishing dedicated terminals.

---

10 For more details, visit the website: www.apmterminals.com

11 For more details, visit the ect website: http://www.ect.nl

12 Hanjin shares will be sold after Hanjin went bankrupt.

13 Rodolphe Saade was keynote speaker at 2017 TPM Trans-Pacific Maritime Conference in Long Beach, CA, Feb. 26–March 1, with more than 2,000 attendees, making it one of the largest maritime conferences in the world.

Ports and terminals are at least partly publicly financed and the public decision making includes the public opinion building, and these processes including the realization of the projects later are very much time consuming. The infrastructure used to access terminals, for example, roads, railway lines, customs offices, water channels, or the dredging in front of the berths is in most cases 100% publicly financed; and this infrastructure is essential for port activities. While these public-private processes will continue for years to come, ultimately, the hope of many politicians and port managers is to establish dedicated (private) facilities, as this will probably lead to faster development.

Dedicated terminals like the A.P. Moller Terminals "APMT" or CMA CGM's Terminal Link facilities are not independent, they belong to a company or a group of companies. Organization and ownership is the big difference between dedicated terminals and gateway concepts. From an operational point of view, the logic of expanding the business along the transport chain is similar.

2a Port Partnerships

Port partnerships or more precisely, port authority partnerships, are completely different from the two aforementioned partnerships. These partnerships are not driven by operational business and the wish to gain market shares or to increase profitability. Port authority partnerships are politically driven. A port authority partnership between two ports is often not more than a declaration of friendship and friendliness. The authorities know that they only provide the infra- and/or superstructure, and are not the decision makers of the business. Some ports have only a few partnerships and they try to live them, that is, to be engaged in the activities of the partner-port at exhibitions or in workshops or congresses. Other ports collect the partnership declarations as a kind of trophy and soon after hanging the declaration on the wall there is essentially no more activity. A typical declaration for a port authority partnership could look like the one in Figure 6.9. Such a declaration could be entitled "Sisterport Agreement," "Port Partnership Declaration," "Memorandum of Understanding," etc. Here it is not the name that is important, but the content.

Typical activities as outlined in a partnership declaration are (extracted from another type of declaration with more details):

1. Exchange of Information and Expertise
Marketing and Market Research
Share market data helpful in forecasting future trade flows, developing marketing strategies and obtain additional market knowledge. This will include, but will not be limited to transit information, commodity types, cargo tonnage, future plans, and ocean carrier services.

Marketing Communications
Both parties agree to assist one another in the area of marketing communications specific to the Republic of ... and the Republic of ... These efforts will include, but will not be limited to a review of market specific ads, web-based products, and other market specific collateral for effectiveness, grammar and market/cultural issues, translation assistance, media recommendations related to ad placement, wherever possible assist with leveraging publications for the benefit of each party taking advantage of media frequency levels enjoyed by the other port while remaining contractually and financially responsible for contractual obligations under separate and independent insertion orders, the building of editorial relationships within each market corresponding to both trade and general business publications, joint press conferences and editorial round tables, encourage visits by journalists in both the print media and television, monitoring the publication of news releases in conjunction with each port's own efforts, monitoring the advertising activities of port competitors in each respective market, the sharing of media resource tools and expertise, trade show/conference recommendations, joint sponsorship of trade show/conferences when necessary, the building of relationships with key shipper and other transportation related associations, the exchange of direct mail lists applicable to each market, and other communications materials or activities of mutual interest.

Information Exchange Related to Organization, Management, and Operations
Exchange information concerning organizational and management systems, port construction and engineering techniques, strategic planning, modern technology applications, security procedures, cargo handling expertise, port operating procedures, and the evaluation of equipment and/or technology efficiency prior to the purchasing phase.

The Agreement
On
Establishing Sister-Port-Ties
Between
The Port of..........
In the Republic of..........
And
The Port of..........
In the Republic of..........

The Port of..... and the Port of..... have built up a friendly relationship and now intend to foster the development of trade, traffic and economic cooperation between the two ports.

Each of these two ports is the foremost port in its region. They have at their disposal efficient and productive facilities for all types of cargo handling as well as other port operations. They also see tremendous potential for growth in trade and for stepping up economic contacts.

The Port of..... and the Port of..... intend to promote their mutual commercial interests through close cooperation as well as exchange programs. Both of them will cooperate on drawing up the program and nominate an executive to be responsible for implementing this.

The Port of..... and the Port of..... hereby declare that they shall be partner ports with effect from Month day, year. The partnership shall serve to improving international understanding and promote economic relations between their respective region.

CITY 1 and CITY 2
month day, year

....	....
CEO Port of ...	*- signature -*
....	....
CEO Port of ...	*- signature -*

Figure 6.9: Port partnership declaration

Management and Employee Training and Employee Exchange Program

Share information surrounding training programs at both the management and hourly employee level. Both sides agree to further discuss joint management of professional training programs and cooperation in the areas of professional port management, operations, marketing, finance, external affairs, strategic planning, engineering and maintenance, customer service, and trade development. Both sides agree to further discuss the exchange of port professionals for a limited and specified period in order to share ideas and knowledge, as well as to expand a mutual interest in increasing productivity and cargo activity between the two ports.

Safety Programs, Safety Training, Emergency Response, Hazardous Materials Handling, and the Environment

Share information surrounding safety programs and training. This may include the development of joint training seminars, as well as cross-training activities to promote safety in the workplace. Both sides agree to encourage visits between those responsible in each port for fire service, ambulance service, and other emergency and disaster services. These encounters may be used to explore opportunities for the provision and exchange of training, technology, equipment and management, and coordination systems. Both parties agree to exchange ideas surrounding the handling of hazardous materials and environmental issues facing the modern port.

2. Expanding International Trade, Service Developments, and Education

Work cooperatively to expand international trade and the development of services that will encourage increased levels of trade and investment between the respective regions to strengthen business, social, and cultural ties in the interest of mutually rewarding economic prosperity. This shall include such items as recommendations and assistance with trade missions in each port's immediate hinterland, as well as both sides agreeing to encourage business missions from both countries to explore the possibility of investment projects.

Both parties agree to identify areas of possible cooperation between the two ports, possibly including some coordination of seminars and/or courses offered by institutions in each country. Both sides will also encourage the exchange of students within each of the universities and areas mentioned with counterpart universities.

3. "Port Model A" and the "Port Model B"

Both parties agree to exchange ideas surrounding the success of both port models for the future expansion of trade between the ports. The port authority of … agrees to discuss the strategy of consolidation centers in the port of … working in tangent with retail import distribution centers in the port area of port …The port authority of … agrees to discuss strategies for promoting the channeling of that cargo through the port of …

4. Proposed Conference

Consideration will be given to the possibility of convening, in alternating locations, a conference of senior representatives of the port … and port … every two years, or as needed. The purpose of the conference will be to identify additional areas of possible cooperation between the two ports. Segments of the conference could possibly include meeting with common service providers, customers, and prospects.

5. Designated Liaisons

Both the port authority of ... and the port authority of ... will designate a "liaison," or a single point of contact, at their respective corporate headquarters whose responsibility shall be to ensure effective communication between the parties in pursuit of the objectives previously stated.

Most of the five paragraphs above deal with questions of port marketing, promotion, information exchange, training of staff, and the intention to learn from each other. Business development is also a topic, but as stated before: it can only be achieved indirectly. Port authority partnerships are efficient tools to level the information in horizontal networks; in this sense they can be effective marketing instruments.

2b Global Port Operaors

Global port operators as well as "global terminal operators"[14] are the last group of port networks, consisting of several terminals owned by one company. It is typically a huge holding that has one branch dealing only with terminals and/or ports. The largest global port operator in the world is Hutchinson Ports Holding (HPH). HPH traces its history back to 1866 when Hong Kong & Whampoa Dock Company was established. Today, HPH is a subsidiary of Hong Kong-based conglomerate Hutchison Whampoa Ltd. (HWL), a highly diversified group, with telecommunication companies, retail businesses, hotels, financial services, energy, and other businesses in its portfolio. HPH oversees HWL's ports and related services. It is a Fortune 500 company and one of the listed companies under Cheung Kong Group.

Other Global Operators, which will be analyzed in more detail in Chapter 11, are Dubai-based DP World and Singaporean PSA. Their business is like the one of dedicated liner terminals: they operate terminals, in most cases container terminals. They also have partner terminals and/or ports in other parts of the world, belonging to the same group. But the main difference between global operators and dedicated liner terminals is ownership and their function within the supply chain, and therefore their commercial expectations.

The ports and terminals of global port operators are business units; their operation costs a lot of money, and they must earn money by offering this business. This is not—or at least, not always—the case with dedicated liner businesses. These terminals are extension units of the shipping business and must function

---

14 For further details of the terms "port operator" and "terminal operator," refer to Chapter 11: "Port Operator."

in this way. Global port operators must be neutral to their customers, or in other words, they are trusted to be neutral. They are open to the market and serve the whole industry, whereas the dedicated terminals are liner-dependent facilities.

The descriptions above are written from a top management view and represent the vision and mission for the business. Managers at the lower levels, particularly sales representatives of dedicated facilities, would deny that their terminal will give preference for the owners and would stress that they have tough commercial targets and therefore open to the whole community. And this is true! But reality shows that preferences and priorities for the mother company (the terminal owning shipping line) exist. This is demonstrated in situations when problems occur, for example, after a storm when there are long queues of ships that want to berth at the same time, or when the port is short on handling equipment, like gantry cranes, AGVs or straddle carriers.

Global port operators stress these points regularly, underlining neutrality and trying to build their USP out of this.

6.4 Port Costs in Transportation Chains

As already explained, ports are partners along a transportation chain from A to B. Ports get paid for their services, but what builds port revenue? And what, from a supply chain perspective, generates costs; the costs for port charges, duties, fees, etc. How relevant are ports regarding the costs? Are ports cost-critical elements of a logistics chain? If so, what can port managers do to better position their facilities?

Table 6.1 shows the approximate costs of a 20 ft standard container (= 1 TEU) from China's Guangzhou hinterland to Munich, Germany. The Guangzhou region has been chosen because it is an important region to produce toys. Statistics show that more than 75% of all globally sold toys are coming out of this region. Therefore, it is a region with high global relevance. The fact that a majority of toy export companies are headquartered in Hongkong supports this; however, for this transport Shenzhen shall act as port of loading, and Rotterdam as port of discharge. The city of Munich has been chosen because it is a big city in central Europe; not very close to the coast, but also not that far away like other cities. Mode of transport to/from the port is a truck.

Table 6.1: Logistics costs 20 ft container Guangzhou–Munich

approx. costs in US Dollar	USD	%	km	km %
road transport Guangzhou - Shenzhen port	80	3.7%	120	1.0%
storage, handling, loading Shenzhen port (Yantian)	100	4.7%	0	0.0%
sea transport Shenzhen - Rotterdam	900	41.9%	11,160	91.9%
unloading, handling, storage Rotterdam port	120	5.6%	0	0.0%
road transport Rotterdam - Munich	950	44.2%	870	7.2%
Total transportation costs	**2,150**	**100%**	**12,150**	**100%**

Source: Own calculations.

All cost components that partly must be paid in local currency, for example, very often the security or ISPS (International Ship and Port Facility Security) fees, or other local fees, have been converted into USD. Total price for the transport is 2,150 USD. The two major components of total costs are ocean transport with 41.9% and truck hinterland transport with 44.2%. In this calculation, it should not be forgotten that the price for ocean transport (since the financial crisis happened) is on a very low level. Before 2009 the price was more than double compared with recent levels. For a sensitivity analysis, as well as for traffic forecasts including route analysis, this could be of interest.

Here the way the contracts are made between shippers, shipping lines, and terminals are of huge importance. Typically, in container business, shipping lines negotiate a volume per service with terminals along the route. The shipping line knows how many containers are transported between all the ports of call during a round-trip. This process of route analysis is a permanent task for shipping lines. And the shipping lines are paying the terminals for their service: in Table 6.1 an amount of 100 USD is paid in Shenzhen for gate services, export storage, loading, and all other terminal-related fees, and 120 USD in Rotterdam for unloading, stowage, and import services. This is the price the shipping lines pay to terminals; sometimes called terminal fees, service fees, handling charges, or stevedoring fees.[15]

These fees should not be confused with terminal handling charges (THC)! THCs are charges that the shippers pay to the shipping lines, not to the terminals. Shipping lines use THCs to give preferences to ports. In our example, it could be that the THCs for Shenzhen on the invoice are calculated with 150 USD, and the THCs for Rotterdam with 130 USD. With this, the shipping line discriminates

---

15 For further details, refer to Chapter 12: "Port Cost Analysis."

Shenzhen via high THC. Reasons for this might be that the line intends to concentrate volumes in Hong Kong. In such a scenario, Hong Kong might have a THC of 100 USD. Shipping lines use THC as a strategic instrument to give ports of interest a preferential position (e.g., to bundle cargo volumes). Ports and terminal operators should be aware of this.

Although the sea component of the transport covers more than 90% of the distance, its share of the transportation cost is much lower. The shares for the two ports Shenzhen and Rotterdam are around 5% each regarding total costs. Because both ports are independent and don't belong to the same group as the shipping line, the single port position with regard to total supply chain cost relevance is low. Figure 6.10 visualizes the shares. All black boxes are no-port-costs. The approximate 5% of Shenzhen are highlighted by five gray boxes, while Rotterdam's approximately 6% share is highlighted in white.

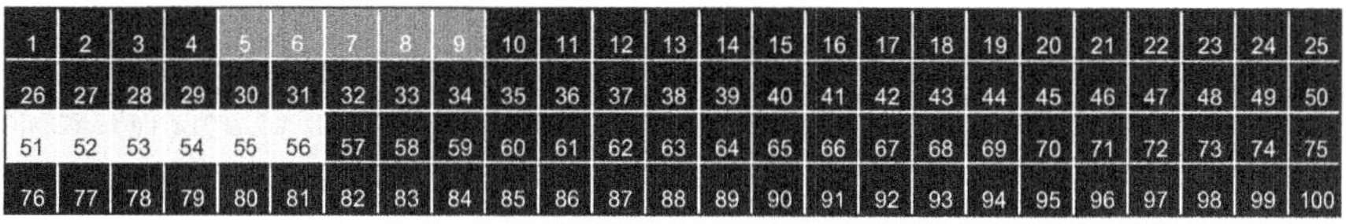

1	2	3	4	5	6	7	8	9	10	11	12	13	14	15	16	17	18	19	20	21	22	23	24	25
26	27	28	29	30	31	32	33	34	35	36	37	38	39	40	41	42	43	44	45	46	47	48	49	50
51	52	53	54	55	56	57	58	59	60	61	62	63	64	65	66	67	68	69	70	71	72	73	74	75
76	77	78	79	80	81	82	83	84	85	86	87	88	89	90	91	92	93	94	95	96	97	98	99	100

Figure 6.10: Share of ports in logistics chains

As a ballpark figure, 5% of total supply chain costs for a single port business is a realistic figure. Total port costs for a transport with two ports rarely exceeds 10% to 12%. Also, for supply chains with three or four ports along the chain (transshipment and feeder), the total share will not increase because the costs for all other components increase as well.

For destinations further from ports, the share of hinterland transport can increase and reach a level of more than 50%. In the future, when the shipping market is more balanced, the share for ocean transport can increase. Bearing all of this in mind, the 5% share becomes a maximum figure for port-related costs. Calculations for other routes (e.g., South Africa–North Europe) as well as for other products like dry and liquid bulk show comparable amounts of port cost shares for total supply chains.[16]

With an average share of max. 5%, the monetary influence of a single port is limited. Via costs, ports, and terminals have very little influence on a shipper's

---

16 This has also been confirmed in several industry meetings, see, for example, Durban Transport Forum: Port costs as a component of total supply chain Cost, Durban, September 3, 2015. Parts of the conference documents are available via the internet, see slideshare.net.

decision making. Other nonmonetary factors like reliability, flexibility, frequency, or safety count much more than cost.

In this context, it is important to distinguish between independent "universal ports" that are open to the general public, and "dedicated terminals," operated by a shipping line.[17] Often the shipping lines consider the terminal business as a logical add-on to their core business of shipping, and so the commercial view is often more cost-centered instead of an independent profit center. Of course, a goal is to operate the terminal(s) as efficiently as possible, but ultimately the terminals are part of a global group, like CMA CGM, and their core function is to support the shipping business. Therefore, it is more adequate to consider these terminals as supply chain cost centers.

In smaller ports, independent terminal operators (often with shareholdings in local public bodies), are intended to act as facilitators of trade and as independent business units that should reach a minimum level of profit. They are treated as (public) companies with the goal of being profitable and supporting the regional economy, for example, by creating jobs. Being profitable is even more important when the terminals belong to an owner with commercial interests. This seems to be the case with some global port operators; here a higher level of profitability is often requested, and profitability is the key guiding principle in day-to-day work. Regional economic growth and offering employment are also part of global port operator mission, but it is not at the top of the agenda. This creates a different business behavior.

---

17 For more background on dedicated ports and terminals, refer to Chapter 4.4: "Port Cluster."

Chapter 7
Cargoes

Ports move passengers or cargoes between conveyances, which is the core function of ports. We will now take a closer look at the cargo business, leaving out the pure passenger and cruise ports in this chapter.

Port performance needs to be measured, and the ports accounting departments need a base for calculation and invoicing. In most cases type and weight of cargo are used for these measurements. This makes it necessary to take a closer look at the cargoes. Port cargo statistics are often not very precise when using the terms "goods" and "cargoes." Therefore, it is necessary to define the content of both terms.

According to the OECD Glossary of Statistical Terms,[1] "Goods are physical objects for which a demand exists, over which ownership rights can be established and whose ownership can be transferred from one institutional unit to another by engaging in transactions on markets; they are in demand because they may be used to satisfy the needs or wants of households or the community or used to produce other goods or services." In economic theory, "goods" is the generic term for the two subcategories: merchandise or (hard-)wares and services. Because "services" are not transported, the terms "goods" and "merchandise or wares" are consequently used synonymously.

To provide comparable statistical coverage of transported goods in all concerned modes of transport, the United Nations Economic Commission for Europe (UNECE) introduced (effective January 1, 2008) a new compulsory goods classification, the so-called NST 2007[2] (French: Nomenclature uniforme des marchandises pour les statistiques de transport, English: Standard Goods Nomenclature for Transport Statistics). NST 2007 is the transport classification system of the European Union but has the potential to be identified as the global standard for transport statistics.

The NST 2007 was prepared with extraordinary diligence to guarantee greatest possible extent with comparable standards; their advantage lies in better coordination with other classifications, like the classification of products by activity (CPA), which is the classification of goods and services at the level of the European Community. CPA is a macroclassification of products, which comprises the European version of the central product classification (CPC) prepared and rec-

---

1 Glossary OECD 2007, page 336ff.
2 See, Government Documents in Bibliography: NST 2007.

DOI 10.1515/9781547400874-007

ommended by the UN. The CPA is legally binding in the European Community. The CPA-2008 version has been adopted as a national product classification. CPA product categories are related to activities as defined by the Statistical classification of economic activities in the European Community (NACE; French abbreviation: Nomenclature statistique des activités économiques dans la Communauté Européenne).

Each CPA product—whether a transportable or nontransportable good or a service—is assigned to one single NACE activity. This linkage to NACE activities gives the CPA a structure parallel to that of NACE at all levels. The CPA is part of an integrated system of statistical classifications, developed mainly under the auspices of the United Nations Statistical Division. This system makes it possible to compare statistics across countries and in different statistical domains. The CPA, apart from having a greater level of detail, differs from the CPC in its structuring criteria. The classification criteria in the CPC is the nature of products: products are grouped according to their physical and composition properties. The CPA, on the other hand, follows the production origin criterion, in other words, products are grouped in compliance with their economic activity of origin.

The NST 2007 is more comparable to the so-called harmonized system (HS) or harmonized tariff system of the World Customs Organization (WCO). The WCO maintains the international Harmonized System goods nomenclature and administers the technical aspects of the WTO Agreements on Customs Valuation and Rules of Origin. Although HS is also not fully comparable with NST 2007, the new transport statistics of goods is a step forward to better statistical integration.

The most important innovation of the NST 2007 is that the external form of goods is no longer considered; rather it is based on the economic activities from which these cargoes have emerged. Some so-called divisions that are primarily of traffic statistical significance have been added.

The NST 2007 contains two levels of classifications (twenty divisions and eighty-one groups) and provides the opportunity to include an additional third level for further differentiation. The first level includes information about the division, which the member states of UNECE must report mandatory to Eurostat. On the second level further information should be provided to allocate the data into one of the eighty-one groups of cargoes. Table 7.1 names the twenty divisions and their description.

Table 7.1: NST 2007

Division	Description
01	Products of agriculture, hunting, and forestry; fish and other fishing products
02	Coal and lignite; crude petroleum and natural gas
03	Metal ores and other mining and quarrying products; peat; uranium and thorium ores
04	Food products, beverages, and tobacco
05	Textiles and textile products; leather and leather products
06	Wood and products of wood and cork (except furniture); articles of straw and plaiting materials; pulp, paper, and paper products; printed matter and recorded media
07	Coke and refined petroleum products
08	Chemicals, chemical products, and man-made fibers; rubber and plastic products; nuclear fuel
09	Other nonmetallic mineral products
10	Basic metals; fabricated metal products, except machinery and equipment
11	Machinery and equipment n.e.c.; office machinery and computers; electrical machinery and apparatus n.e.c.; radio, television, and communication equipment and apparatus n.e.c.; medical, precision, and optical instruments; watches and clocks
12	Transport equipment
13	Furniture; other manufactured goods n.e.c.
14	Secondary raw materials; municipal wastes and other wastes
15	Mail, parcels
16	Equipment and material utilized in the transport of goods
17	Goods moved in the course of household and office removals; baggage and articles accompanying travellers; motor vehicles being moved for repair; other nonmarket goods n.e.c.
18	Grouped goods: a mixture of types of goods which are transported together
19	Unidentifiable goods: goods which for any reason can not be identified and therefore can not be assigned to groups 01–16
20	Other goods n.e.c.

Source: NST 2007

The term "cargo" is used for merchandised goods carried by a means of transportation. Cargo is used for freight loaded into a ship or carried by another means of transportation. So "cargoes" are goods subject of a shipment, or in other words, materials/goods/(hard-)ware being carried. Another characteristic of cargo is "movement." Ports, as part of a supply chain, handle (or, move) the goods via ships, railways, trucks, etc. Bearing this in mind, it is understandable that most of the worldwide port statistics count "cargoes" instead of "goods."

Regarding the reporting standards, the NST 2007 would be a much better statistic with regard to the goods transported; but in the port business, it is traditional and logical to count cargoes, and this very often on high level (e.g., "liquid bulk"). Although this difference in statistics sounds marginal, the differences that are used to measure im- and export flow cause huge problems because they are not easy to compare.

Ports move cargoes from one means of transportation to another, for example, a container from onboard the vessel on the yard to a railway wagon. The ports get paid for this business and the handling equipment is specialized for this. If there are no special requirements like containers with reefer or hazardous goods inside, the port operator is not very much interested in whether they are moving textiles, furniture or electronics from A to B. The container business does not focus on the type of goods transported, but rather the way the goods are packed and transported. Therefore, port statistics are not pure transport goods statistics and cargo statistics, according to the NST 2007, HS, or other classification systems. Port statistics are often a mix and refer to their own classification.

Main categories for (trans-)port cargo classification are:
– Bulk cargo (liquid and solid)
– General cargo
– Container
– RoRo cargo

Special consideration will be given to dangerous or hazardous goods and to the quality of seaworthy packaging (essential for safe transportation) in Chapter 7, section 1.

7.1 Port Cargo Categories

The category of bulk products puts the cargo itself in the center of interest (coal or iron ore as major dry bulk products, or crude oil or petroleum products as important liquid bulk products). Containerized cargo puts the size of the transport units in the center of interest (e.g., 20 ft container/1 TEU), and not the cargo itself. If there is no special cargo inside the container, like hazardous cargo, and if the weight is correctly declared, it is of no interest what is inside the container. Whether there are shoes, textiles, machinery parts, or toys inside, or even nothing at all (e.g., empty container redisposition); for terminal operation this is one unit, one TEU.

This is different from bulk. Characteristics of bulk cargo include:
1. Volume that is transported by vessels and loaded and unloaded in ports are high, often more than 100,000 tons per vessel.
2. Terminals are dedicated to the product or to a small range of products.
3. A vessel often carries one product only (coal, ore, crude oil, etc.).
4. The price per unit (barrel, ton) is comparatively low.

Table 7.2: Assignment of NST, 2007 Cargo Divisions: Bulk Cargo

NST 2007 Divisions*	L = Liquid Bulk** D = Dry Bulk**
01 Agriculture + fishing	
02 Coal, oil, gas	D, L
03 Ores + mining products; peat	D
04 Food products	
05 Textiles and leather	
06 Wood; pulp & paper; printings	
07 Coke + refined petroleum products	D, L
08 Chemicals, fibers, plastics, nuclear	L
09 Other nonmetallic mineral products	D
10 Basic metals + metal products	
11 Machinery + equipment; electronics	
12 Transport equipment	
13 Furniture + other manufacturing goods	
14 Secondary materials & wastes	
15 Mail, parcels	
16 Equipment + material for transport	
17 Removals, baggages, vehicles, etc.	
18 Grouped goods	
19 Unidentifiable goods	
20 Other goods	

* according to Table 7.1: NST 2007
** Assignment of main divisions; a classification without overlapping is not possible

Table 7.2 shows that most of the NST 2007 cargo divisions for bulk fall into the category of "natural resources," like division 2 for coal as dry bulk and oil as liquid bulk. In total, only five divisions of NST 2007 are representing bulk cargoes. This relatively small number stands contrary to the relevance of bulk product trade, measured in metric tons.

Figure 7.1 shows that bulk cargoes represent the majority of world seaborne trade. In 2000, approximately 85% of global seaborne trade was bulk trade, and at that time dominated by liquid bulk. In 2010, the shares of liquid and dry bulk have nearly balanced out, while the total share of bulk decreased slightly to 83% of the total trade. For the next several years, it is very likely that the share of bulk will further decrease, or in other words, the share of general cargo/container cargoes will increase.

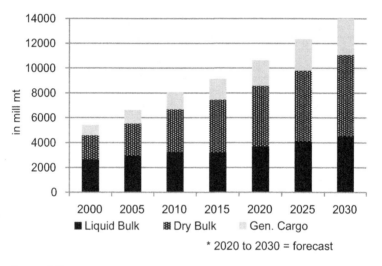

Source: IHS

Figure 7.1: World seaborne cargo trade

Here it is important to realize that Figure 7.1 shows cargo distribution based on metric tons. A similar statistic based on cargo values would look different, because the value of one metric ton of bulk products like coal or iron ore is—depending on quality, location, and exact type of product—in most cases below 100 USD. Even in historic peak times the unit price did not exceed the level of 200 USD. On the other hand, a laptop computer (a typical containerized product) has a weight of 1.0 to 3.5 kg, including package material. Let's assume that three laptops weigh 10 kg together, then a metric ton represents 300 laptops, each calculated with 500 USD only. This means that such a ton of laptops has a value of easily 150,000 USD; a full container load not infrequently exceeds the value of 1 mill USD. This simplified example shows how huge the value span between bulk and containerized cargo per unit might be. But not all bulk products are as low as coal and ore, and not all containers carry computers. Although it's a matter of fact that bulk products are of a lower value per unit than containerized cargo, in the shipping industry one metric ton is one metric ton.

Liquid Bulk

Liquid bulk cargoes are free-flowing liquids that are not boxed, bagged, or hand stowed but poured into and sucked out of large tank spaces for transport by ship. Liquid bulk materials can be classified into five groups:
- Oil products (such as crude oil, gasoline, naphtha, diesel, and fuel oil)
- Chemicals (such as methanol, xylene, MEG, and styrene)
- Biofuels and vegetable oils
- Liquefied natural gas (LNG)
- Liquefied petroleum gas (LPG) (propane, butane)

Because most of the liquid bulk materials trans-shipped are classified as "dangerous goods," special safety requirements are set up for handling, storing, and transporting these materials. The characteristics of liquid products can be split up in physical properties, chemical properties, flammability, materials of construction, toxicity, and cargo handling. All these characteristics must be known if they are proposed for ocean transport. According to this classification, the liquid products are assigned to property groups. These property groups define how the liquid will react if a spill occurs. This implies that the supply chain of different liquid bulk products varies due to material specific characteristics.

Oil products: Crude oil is transported from the well to the refinery in large batches (ULCC up to 300,000 dwt), but the oil products are transported in smaller quantities from the refinery to the user, often in specialized product tankers with up to sixty single tanks on board. Terminals must be fitted to serve these vessels. The tank farms in ports are often similar in size to vessels; aboveground crude oil tanks are often the largest tanks with single storage capacity of up to 660,000 barrels per unit. Cushing is a large tank in Oklahoma, armed with dozens of tanks that can store up to 82 mill barrels of oil. Tanks for liquid bulk products like naphtha or kerosene are much smaller (e.g., 5,000 to 20,000 cbm).

Chemicals: Chemical transport is characterized by isochronal transport of various grades of petrochemical products in so-called small parcels that are carried on ships with several specialized tanks on board. These parcels are shipped together on "product tankers" because they often must travel long distances, and this is more economical with larger carriers. The supply chain of petrochemicals is linked to the supply of oil products. For ports and terminals, these supply chains require specialized equipment able to load and/or unload and store the various products.

Biofuels and vegetable oils: The supply chain of biofuel starts at feedstock production, because the fundamental source of biofuel is biomass feedstock. The harvested biomass is collected (regionally) and transported to biorefineries. At the biorefinery ethanol is produced, which is transported to blending facilities where the ethanol is mixed with gasoline. The biofuel is ready to be distributed after blending.

Palm oil is the most widely used vegetable oil in the world; it can be used for food production, in cooking, and as feedstock for biofuel. The production of vegetable oils is achieved by using an oil mill or by chemical extraction using a solvent. Next it is transported to a refinery/fractionation plant; here the oil is refined and by-products are extracted. These by-products can be used for other purposes, such as margarine production.

LNG: Natural gas is produced in subsurface gas reservoirs and reached through drilling. After extraction, the gas is cleaned of impurities and liquefied by cooling it to a temperature of approximately −160° centigrade at a processing plant (liquefaction factory); this can also take place on board a vessel (FPSO) for offshore fields. The liquefied gas only has one six hundredth of its original volume and is therefore easier to store in a tank and much more economical for the transport. At the receiving terminal or plant the LNG can be regasified. After regasification, the gas is transported via pipelines for distribution to residential, commercial, or industrial end-users. Due to the very low temperature for loading and unloading the terminals, special equipment is required, and the personnel must be trained accordingly. LNG handling requires sound information of the product for everybody engaged in handling and transportation.

LPG: Petroleum hydrocarbon products such as propane and butane, and mixtures of both, have been categorized by the oil industry as LPG. It can be produced as a by-product at oil and gas wells, as well as a by-product of the crude oil refining process. From the refinery or processing plant, the LPGs are transported to downstream storage terminals just like other oil products. LPG is widely used for domestic and industrial purposes today. The most important property of LPG is that it is suitable for being pressurized into liquid form and transported. But there are conditions related to pressure and temperature that need to be maintained for this to be carried out without posing a threat to life, environment, and cargo. At least one of the following conditions needs to be complied with, for transportation of LPG:

– The gas should be pressurized at ambient temperature.
– The gas should be fully refrigerated at its boiling point. Boiling point of LPG rangers from –30°C to –48°C. This condition is called the fully-refrigerated condition.
– The gas must be semirefrigerated to a reduced temperature and pressurized.

Other gases such as ammonia, ethylene, and propylene are also transported in liquefied form in LPG carriers. Ethylene and Ethane, however, have lower boiling points than other LPGs. Hence it must be carried in semirefrigerated or fully-refrigerated conditions. Over the last decade, specialized vessels have been developed for the individual products.

The same holds true for terminal operations. Specialized insulated tanks, pipes, and loading arms are required, as well as highly specialized port workers.

Dry Bulk

Dry bulk is loose, mostly uniform cargo, such as agribulk products like sugar or cocoa, coal, fertilizer, and ores, which are stored and handled at specialized dry bulk terminals, for example, coal terminals with huge areas of stock piles for coal, or fertilizer terminals, all with appropriate handling and storage facilities. Figure 7.1 shows that today dry bulk trades dominate global shipping, measured in tons, and as forecasts indicate, this process will continue into the foreseeable future.

Dry bulk cargoes cover a range of produced and raw materials (see Table 7.2) that have two features in common: they are unpacked and homogeneous. These two properties make it easier for dry bulk cargoes to be dropped or poured into the hold of a bulk carrier. Most dry bulk terminals use grabs for these operations. Coal and iron ore are the two dominant single product groups in bulk shipping and bulk handling. Figure 7.2 demonstrates this, and it is expected exports of iron ore (global exports in particular) will increase until 2020.

As the name suggests, several dry bulk cargoes need to be kept dry, any moisture that finds its way into the cargo could ruin the entire load at considerable cost to the ship owner. Cement is a good example of this. Cement not only needs special ground handling, but also vessels equipped with special cargo treatment facilities. During the construction phase of the new Panama Canal locks, these vessels showed their qualifications.

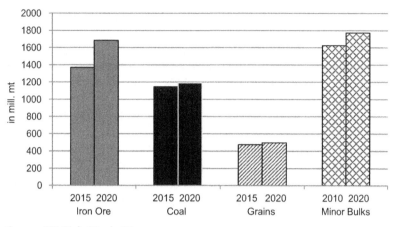

Source: GTA Global Trade Atlas

Figure 7.2: Dry bulk exports, 2015 and forecast 2020

General Cargo, Break Bulk, Heavy Lift, Oversized

As already mentioned in Chapter 3.3, the term "general cargo" is not clearly defined. The term often describes the way the cargo is handled within the port. When a group of products is not classified as bulk cargo, it is either described as a group of all other cargoes like in definition A the light gray box (general cargo). This group can further be divided in "conventional general cargo" and "containerized general cargo"—in short "container." A second way of classification is shown in definition B: everything that is not bulk cargo is either classified as "container" or "general cargo."

This does not only sound confusing, it is really confusing and causes frequent misunderstandings and misinterpretations of statistics. Until today no global standard exists, so we must live with this.

	Total Cargo			
A	General Cargo		Bulk Cargo	
	Conventional	Container	Dry Bulk	Liquid Bulk

	Total Cargo			
B	General Cargo	Container	Bulk Cargo	
			Dry Bulk	Liquid Bulk

Definition A divided the total amount of cargo into two groups: general cargo and bulk cargo. The introduction of the container led to the further distinction between "conventional general cargo" and "containerized general cargo," or in short "container." Conventional general cargo is everything that was not transported in a container. The way of handling the cargo drove the way the statistics were made. Containers require different handling equipment.

Iron and steel, for example, can be handled in a conventional way with a crane under a hook or with forklift trucks, or—if the cargo allows—inside a container. A product like a steel coil can be handled "conventionally," but it is also possible to transport steel coils inside a box. The same is true for many other products. Therefore, the same product can be categorized as "conventional general cargo" or as "container."

Concept B distinguishes between bulk, container, and general cargo. It is important to understand that these port statistics are "cargo handling statistics." Concept B is not a "cargo statistic"! RoRo in both definitions are a subcategory of conventional general cargo.

Today "general cargo" can be used to describe the residuum of cargo that is not handled as bulk on typical bulk terminals or as a container, handled on typical container terminals. Statistics using concept A often measure cargo in volumes, for example, tons, and provide additional TEU-information for the container trade. Here container trade data are often available in tons. Statistics following the classification of concept B are often counting containers only in TEU, that is, container data measured in tons are not available.

More and more products are containerized. Raw coffee is a good example for this. In the early 1990s, the degree of containerization was nearly zero. The cargo requires a special humidity, and air-conditioned containers could not offer this at that time. Less than fifteen years later, more than 90% of raw coffee in many European ports is containerized, using specialized air-conditioned containers. Other typical general cargoes are wood products like timber, wood chips, or other biopower products like pellets, as well as pulp and paper on big rolls, and cellulose. For further details, refer to the NST 2007 groups.

Table 7.3 assigns typical NST 2007 divisions that are transported as general cargo. Food products like grain mill products, tobacco, or raw coffee are still handled in single sacks, and due to the relatively high value and the high requirements the cargo has with regard to the storage conditions, it is economically efficient to stow and handle these products as general cargo.

Table 7.3: Table 7.3: Assignment of NST 2007 Cargo Divisions: general cargo

NST 2007 Divisions*	G = General Cargo**
01 Agriculture + fishing	
02 Coal, oil, gas	
03 Ores + mining products; peat	
04 Food products	G
05 Textiles and leather	
06 Wood; pulp & paper; printings	G
07 Coke + refined petroleum products	
08 Chemicals, fibers, plastics, nuclear	G
09 Other nonmetallic mineral products	G
10 Basic metals + metal products	G
11 Machinery + equipment; electronics	G
12 Transport equipment	
13 Furniture + other manufacturing goods	
14 Secondary materials & wastes	G
15 Mail, parcels	
16 Equipment + material for transport	G
17 Removals, baggages, vehicles, etc.	
18 Grouped goods	
19 Unidentifiable goods	
20 Other goods	

* According to Table 7.1: NST 2007
** Assignment of main divisions; a classification without overlapping is not possible

A typical shipping term for handling general cargo is break bulk or breakbulk. It is used for any loose material that must be loaded individually and in huge quantities, and not in containers nor in bulk as with oil or grain. In other words, break-bulk is general cargo of the same size, style, and quality that is handled in huge (or, bulk) quantities. Good examples of this are the goods in NST 2007 division 10, like basic iron, steel, or ferro-alloys, and products like tubes, pipes hollow profiles, and related fittings. These goods are all the same size (length, weight per unit) and style (e.g., as pipe, tube, or structural steel), and often ports charge or discharge full ship loads of them. In this sense, these products are "bulk"-products, but handled conventionally, that is, break bulk. Break bulk is a subcategory of general cargo. Not all general cargo is break bulk, but all break bulk is general cargo.

Another subcategory of general cargo is project cargo. Here we do not have the character of "bulk" cargo like we do with breakbulk. Project cargo is often unique; in many cases, it consists of single pieces of heavy, oversized or outsized goods. There is no precise definition for "project cargo." This is due to the multiplicity of forms in which this cargo can come, including heavy lifts, overwide, over-high units and cargo, which exceeds axle load. Their parameters differ from each other, which affects the multiplicity of means of transport engaged in the oversized transport. Sometimes specially designed equipment is needed to transport a particular type of oversized cargo. In most ports, there are special handling installations (terminals, road and rail access, cranes, etc.) for oversized transport. So-called heavy lifts are those measured from tens to hundreds of meters and weighing hundreds or even thousands of tons. Some extra-large oversized units are being transported on special, unique ships, built for this purpose. It could be said that in all cases, "oversized" determinants for project cargo are:

1. Dimensions of the cargo
2. Weight of the cargo
3. Available cargo space on the vehicle (ocean vessel, river barge, rail, etc.)
4. Permissible pressure and stress on the loading surface (terminal + quay wall)
5. Permissible stress on surface of road/rails

Another important element is the shape of the cargo, because its irregular geometry could negatively affect static and dynamic stability of the vehicle. In every case, handling, stowage, and securing of such cargo must be done under the supervision of specially qualified surveyors. Proper calculations should be made prior to the transport, and necessary permits and certificates should be obtained. All appropriate rules, issued by regulators like the International Maritime Organization, the Road Administration or Rail Administration, should be strictly respected. Regarding size, there are no permit procedures for transport of oversized cargo in maritime transport. This makes maritime transport attractive for all kinds of project cargo.

Container

In some statistics, containers are a subcategory of the whole "general cargo"; often described as "containerized general cargo." The advantage of most of these statistics of "type A" is that they describe the cargoes in weight (e.g., in tons) as well as in load units like "one container equals 1 TEU," or Twenty-Foot Equivalent Unit. This is the standard container; further details can be found in annex D. A 40 ft container in this way of counting equals two TEU or—in some countries and statistics—one FEU, or Forty-Foot Equivalent Unit. Two TEU require equal space on board a vessel or in a container yard like 1 FEU.

The process of containerization as explained in Chapter 3.2 led to the effect that specialized containers have been invented, like reefer containers with cooling aggregates, high cube containers for low weight and (slightly) oversized cargo, open top containers, open side containers, tank containers, etc. The containerization process made it possible for goods, which had been considered impossible for container transport—like coffee mentioned above—now to be widely shipped via a container. Many ports adopted to this new way of transporting cargo overseas and specialized themselves for all the new calls being made due to specialized containers.

Table 7.4: Assignment of NST 2007 Cargo Divisions: Container

NST 2007 Divisions*	C = Container**
01 Agriculture + fishing	C
02 Coal, oil, gas	
03 Ores + mining products; peat	
04 Food products	C
05 Textiles and leather	C
06 Wood; pulp & paper; printings	C
07 Coke + refined petroleum products	(C)
08 Chemicals, fibers, plastics, nuclear	(C)
09 Other nonmetallic mineral products	C
10 Basic metals + metal products	C
11 Machinery + equipment; electronics	C
12 Transport equipment	C
13 Furniture + other manufacturing goods	C
14 Secondary materials & wastes	C
15 Mail, parcels	C
16 Equipment + material for transport	C
17 Removals, baggages, vehicles, etc.	C
18 Grouped goods	C
19 Unidentifiable goods	C
20 Other goods	C

* According to Table 7.1: NST 2007
** Assignment of main divisions; a classification without overlapping is not possible

At the center of the container business' interest is the way of packing cargo and the logistics requirements that come along with this. Packing therefore determines the way port and transport statistics count the cargoes. This is different from most of the other transports like the conventional general cargoes mentioned above;

here the focus is on products. In a container, the focus is on TEU, and it is even one TEU that is handled when the box is empty (e.g., for redispositioning).

Table 7.4 assigns typical NST 2007 cargo divisions to container transportation. Many agriculture, fishing, and food products today are transported in containers; often in reefer containers when the cargo requires it, like meat or meat products from South America to Europe. Also, most of the textiles and leather products (division 5) like wearing apparel from Asian countries to North America are transported in container; this in cases and cardboard boxes, but also hanging on coat hangers in specialized containers.

Cargoes of divisions 7 and 8 can rarely also be found in containers; due to the often-low value of the cargo per ton, it is in most cases more economical to use bulk transports. But especially fibers, plastics, rubbers, and pharmaceuticals are more and more often packed in smaller units and then are containerized.

For the remaining cargo divisions like metal products, machinery, electronics, furniture, and other cargoes in smaller lots with relatively high values per unit, it is easy to understand why the containerization process nearly finished: already since years these products have been transported in containers. Containerization also offers a security feature. The container itself is an ideal cargo protector, as numerous boxes make it difficult for thieves to target and find specific goods.

RoRo Cargo

The category of RoRo cargo is slightly like container cargo: here the way the cargoes are moved is counted in port and transport statistics, and it is not the product that appears in RoRo statistics. Like container cargo, here we find smaller volumes that are capable of being transported on roads or moved on flats with trailers. Heavy paper rolls for the newspaper industry are typical products that are transported on rolling flats onboard of RoRo vessels (division 6 in Table 7.5). Transport equipment like automobiles, or agricultural machines like grain harvesters, are typical rolling cargo in division 12 in Table 7.5.

Because the cargo units are rolling, they can not be stowed. This leads to the effect that RoRo ports often require relatively high terminal space compared with other terminals; this is also an important cost factor.

Table 7.5: Assignment of NST 2007 Cargo Divisions to RoRo cargo

NST 2007 Divisions*	R = RoRo Cargo**
01 Agriculture + fishing	
02 Coal, oil, gas	
03 Ores + mining products; peat	
04 Food products	
05 Textiles and leather	
06 Wood; pulp & paper; printings	R
07 Coke + refined petroleum products	
08 Chemicals, fibers, plastics, nuclear	
09 Other nonmetallic mineral products	
10 Basic metals + metal products	
11 Machinery + equipment; electronics	
12 Transport equipment	R
13 Furniture + other manufacturing goods	
14 Secondary materials & wastes	
15 Mail, parcels	
16 Equipment + material for transport	R
17 Removals, baggages, vehicles, etc.	R
18 Grouped goods	R
19 Unidentifiable goods	R
20 Other goods	

* According to Table 7.1: NST 2007
** Assignment of main divisions; a classification without overlapping is not possible

All Cargoes

Table 7.6 provides an overview of typical cargo divisions that are assigned to port and transport statistics. The still growing dominance of container cargo is easy to identify in this chart. But this classification and split into NST cargo divisions is just regarding the way the NST 2007 is constructed. It should not be forgotten that the few categories of bulk products represent huge amounts of port cargo throughputs and cargo loads for the shipping industry.

Table 7.6: Assignment of NST 2007 Cargo Divisions: all cargo

NST 2007 Divisions*	All Cargo**
01 Agriculture + fishing	C
02 Coal, oil, gas	D, L
03 Ores + mining products; peat	D
04 Food products	G, C
05 Textiles and leather	C
06 Wood; pulp & paper; printings	G, C, R
07 Coke + refined petroleum products	D, L, (C)
08 Chemicals, fibers, plastics, nuclear	G, (C)
09 Other nonmetallic mineral products	G, D, C
10 Basic metals + metal products	G, C
11 Machinery + equipment; electronics	G, C
12 Transport equipment	C, R
13 Furniture + other manufacturing goods	C
14 Secondary materials & wastes	G, C
15 Mail, parcels	C
16 Equipment + material for transport	G, C, R
17 Removals, baggages, vehicles, etc.	C, R
18 Grouped goods	C, R
19 Unidentifiable goods	C, R
20 Other goods	C

* According to Table 7.1: NST 2007
** Assignment of main divisions; a classification without overlapping is not possible
G = general cargo; D = dry bulk; L = liquid bulk; C = container; R = RoRo

Dangerous/Hazardous Goods

Dangerous and hazardous goods are classified according to different criteria. Most of these goods are categorized in NST divisions 2, 7, and 8. *Dangerous goods* are classified based on immediate physical or chemical effects such as fire, explosion, corrosion, and poisoning that may affect property, people, or the environment (e.g., petrol, pool chlorine). *Hazardous substances* are classified only based on human health effects—both medium and long term. Dangerous goods and hazardous substances are covered by separate legislation. The classifications of dangerous goods are those defined by Chapter VII of the International Convention for the Safety of Life at Sea (SOLAS, 1974), as amended and as detailed in the International Maritime Dangerous Goods (IMDG) code.

The classes of dangerous goods are those defined by the seventeenth revised edition of the UN Recommendations on the Transport of Dangerous Goods;

Amendment 38-16 to the IMDG code. The code itself is a working document that frequently is adjusted to actual needs and changes. Ports often receive dangerous goods and must handle them according to the IMDG code. Classes of the code are:

Class 1: Explosives

Class 2: Gases

Class 3: Flammable liquids

Class 4: Flammable solids; substances liable to spontaneous combustion; substances which, on contact with water, emit flammable gases

Class 5: Oxidizing substances and organic peroxides

Class 6: Toxic and infectious substances

Class 7: Radioactive material

Class 8: Corrosive substances

Class 9: Miscellaneous dangerous substances and articles and environmentally hazardous substances

Class 10: Marine pollutants

Due to the high risks for people, property, and the environment when handling dangerous and/or hazardous goods, an adequate seaworthy packing of all cargoes handled in ports is of utmost importance.

Seaworthy Packaging

Ordinary commercial packaging merely refers to certain practices, which are customary in the consignor's country: the conditions the product will be expected to withstand during transport, which are determined by the route, duration of transport, destination, duration of storage as well as possible onward transport must be considered. Seaworthy packaging indicates that the packaging must withstand the conditions of maritime transport and thus more severe stresses. However, this often disregards the fact that the most severe stresses do not occur during maritime transport itself, but instead during cargo handling (due to impact, pushing, overturning, etc.) in ports and at terminals.

It is thus advisable to stipulate the exact nature of the packaging when making contractual agreements. This may be achieved by specifying the following seaworthy packaging parameters:

– Packaging material
– Packaging container
– Packaging aid
– Mandatory standards and legislation
– Package design
– Strength requirements

To guarantee that the standards for seaworthy packaging are met, many consignors issue packaging directives that clearly describe how to pack and how to handle the cargo. For a safe and secure transport and for not losing insurance, it is of utmost importance that logistics companies, stevedores, and the respective authorities cooperate quite closely.

Seaworthy packaging is a supportive port function and secures a lot of well-paid jobs in and around ports.

7.2 Cargo Measurement

For all business transactions, it is necessary to measure accurately and on comparable scales, because these measurements are the basis for business decisions, calculations, invoices, statistics, etc. In many global businesses, it is normal to calculate in different currencies or scales and to switch from the USD to the Japanese Yen or from kilometers to miles, cubic feet to cubic meters, millibar to hecto Pascal, or from degrees in Celsius to degrees in Fahrenheit. Exchange rate conversions add a somewhat complicated factor because they fluctuate. This problem does not occur when using different scales with fixed conversion tables.

The matter gets complicated when things should be compared that are incomparable, for example, when a weight in tons is compared with a volume measure like cubic meters. Objectively, this is not possible without further information. However, since both can be expressed in currencies, it is partially possible when using a common (re-)conversion table to calculate backward in weight or volume. The different units used in Tables 3.5, 3.6, and 3.7 already expressed this problem. In fact, the different measurement of port throughput has already led to the "the world's biggest port" title being given to a port that was not the world's biggest. Different units of measuring cargo (e.g., expressed in metric tons vs. freight tons) led to this wrong classification.[3] A comparable standard of measurement is needed for day-to-day business; otherwise we are comparing apples to pears. Therefore, the different ways of measuring cargo will be explored in detail below.

---

3 Sorgenfrei, Jürgen: Hong-Mi-Sing-Sha, *The Journal of Commerce*, New Jersey, USA, April 18, 2005, page 49.

Linear Measure or Unit of Length: Two-Dimensional

Units of measurement are generally defined on a scientific basis, overseen by governmental or supra-governmental agencies, and established in international treaties. One such treaty is the preeminent General Conference on Weights and Measures (CGPM), established in 1875 by the Treaty of the meter (British: metre). The meter, as a unit of length, was redefined in 1983 by the CGPM as the distance traveled by light in free space in 1/299,792,458 of a second, while in 1960 the international yard was defined by the governments of the United States, United Kingdom, Australia, and South Africa as being exactly 0.9144 m.

Historically, before standard units were widely adopted around the world, the British systems of English units and later imperial units were used in Britain, the Commonwealth, and the United States. The system came to be known as United States customary units and is still in use in the United States and in a few Caribbean countries.

The metric system is the dominant measurement system globally. It is a decimal system of measurement based on meter units for length, and kilogram units for mass. Multiples and fractions of the units are expressed as powers of 10 for each unit. Unit conversions are always simple because they are in the ratio of ten, one hundred, one thousand, etc. Convenient magnitudes for measurements are thus achieved by simply moving the decimal place. Since the 1960s, the International System of Units (French: Système International d'Unités, or: SI) is the internationally recognized metric system. All lengths and distances are measured in meters (m), or thousandths of a meter (mm), or thousands of meters (km). There is no profusion of different units with different conversion factors as in the imperial system, which uses, inches, feet, yards, fathoms, rods, etc. For switching between metric and imperial units, fixed relations are in use and make length measurements easy and definite. In Table 7.7 the upper block describes the conversion of length measure from metric to imperial or vice versa. The middle block converts volumes, the lower imperial to metric weight.

Table 7.7: Conversion table metric—imperial

metric	imperial	imperial	metric
1 cm	0.3937 Inches	1 Inch	2.54 cm
1 m	3.281 Feet	1 Feet	0.305 m
1 m	1.094 Yards	1 Yard	0.914 m
1 km	0.621373 Miles	1 Mile	1.60934 km
1 cm3	0.061 Cu-Inches	1 Cu-Inch	16.3873 cm3
1m3	35.3134 Cu-Feet	1 Cu-Feet	0.0283 m3
1m3	1.3079 Cu-Yards	1 Cu-Yard	0.765 m3
1 g	0.0353 Ounces	1 Ounce	28.35 g
1 kg	2.205 Pounds	1 Pound	0.4536 kg
1000 kg	1.102 Short tons	1 Short ton	908 kg

Solid Measure or Cubic Measure: Three-Dimensional

Fortunately, including the third dimension does not change the metric scale; the new third dimension is simply added, and one continues using the metric scale for convenient magnitudes by simply moving the decimal place. Conversion between metric and imperial scale is also easy as the conversion relations are fixed.

CBM, cbm, or m³ stands for cubic meter. This is the most common unit used for the measurement of volumetric cargo. To calculate the cbm, at first all measurements must be converted into meters. Normally dimensions are in length x width x height. For example, the dimensions of a high cube 20 ft containers are 6.1 x 2.44 x 2.59 m; the volume in cbm are simply 6.1 x 2.44 x 2.59 = 38.55 cbm (or, 1.360 cu ft)

Weight Measure/Ton Definitions

Weight measurements for port cargo are a little more complicated and confusing than length and cubic measurements. In general, weight refers to the downward force produced when a mass is in a gravitational field. The word "mass" refers to the intrinsic property of all objects to resist changes in their momentum. In free fall (no net gravitational forces), objects lack weight but retain their mass. The imperial units of mass include the ounce, pound, and ton. The metric units' gram and kilogram are units of mass, which, for purposes of port cargo measurements are considered as units of weight. Devices for measuring weight or mass are called "weighing scales," "weight measures," or simply "scale." The block in the bottom of Table 7.7 shows the most common metric and imperial units. A very old and often used term in context of the port and shipping business is the "ton." Down below are some of the most common definitions of what the term "ton" may stand for:

1: Ton, metric ton or tonne (mt)

Tonne: a metric unit of weight, equal to 1000 kilograms, or approximately 2204.623 British Pounds avoirdupois. The metric ton is known officially as the tonne. The symbol "t" is recommended for this unit.

$$1 \text{ metric ton} = 1 \text{ tonne} = 1 \text{ t or } 1 \text{ mt}$$

The big advantage of the metric system is that it is a decimal system. The next larger unit is always 10 times as large, the next smaller always 1/10 as large. To convert, one simply must move the decimal point.

2: Ton (tn or T or LT or ST)

Ton: a traditional unit of weight equal to 20 hundredweight. In the United States and Canada, there are 100 pounds in the hundredweight and exactly 2,000 pounds (907.185 kilograms) in the ton. In Britain, there are 112 pounds in the hundredweight and 2,240 pounds (1016.047 kilograms) in the ton. To distinguish between the two units, the British ton is called the *long ton* (LT) and the American one is the *short ton* (ST). Some statistics called the short ton "net ton" (NT), but this term is not widely used today. To convert between LT, ST, and t calculate:

$$
\begin{aligned}
1 \text{ long tong} &= 2{,}240 \text{ pounds} = 1016.047 \text{ kg} \\
1 \text{ short ton} &= 2{,}000 \text{ pounds} = 907.185 \text{ kg} \\
1 \text{ metric ton} &= 2205 \text{ pounds} = 1000 \text{ kg}
\end{aligned}
$$

In Roman times and still in the Latin language, a "tunna" was a large cask used to store wine. Because these "tunnas" or "tuns" were of standard size, more or less, the tun came to represent both a volume unit, indicating the capacity of a cask, and also a weight unit, indicating the weight of a cask when it was full. The best symbol to use for this unit is tn. In the U.S. mining industry, *T* is used to distinguish the traditional ton from the metric ton, but T is the SI symbol for the tesla. The symbol *t*, traditionally used for the long or short ton, is now reserved for the metric ton. For conversion between metric, long and short ton, the following table can be used. For example, if we have a cargo load measured in long ton and would like to know how many metric tons this is (line 2 in the table), then we must multiply the long ton value by 1.016. The result is the weight in metric tons or *t*.

Table 7.8: Conversion table tons

to convert	into	multiply
Long Tons	Short Tons	1.12
Long Tons	Metric Tons	1.016
Metric Tons	Long Tons	0.9844
Metric Tons	Short Tons	1.1025
Short Tons	Metric Tons	0.907185
Short Tons	Long Tons	0.89287

Source: NIST Handbook 2017, Appendix C.

3: Avoirdupois Pound (avdp)

Avardupois pound: the avoirdupois system is a historic system of weights (or precisely: mass) based on a pound of 16 ounces. It is still used as the everyday system in the United States and to varying degrees in the United Kingdom, Canada, and some former British colonies; despite the official adoption of the metric system. A statute of Henry VIII of England (AD 1491–1547) made avoirdupois weights mandatory, but details of the system changed over time.

In the avoirdupois system, all units are multiples or fractions of the pound: a dram or drachm is 1/256 of a pound or 1/16 of an ounce, an ounce is 1/16 of a pound, a stone has 14 pounds, a quarter 28 pounds, and a hundredweight 112 pounds. Based on the international yard and pound agreement of 1959, an avoirdupois pound is now defined as 0.45359237 kg exactly; an ounce accordingly 28.35 g, a drachm 1.772 g, a stone 6.35 kg, a quarter 12.7 kg, and a hundredweight 50.8 kg. The word "avardupois" stems from old French "aveir de peis," later expressed as "avoir de pois" or "goods of weight."

Billing Systems: Weight + Volume

Mixed measurement systems take either the volume or the weight of the cargo as basis for billing. This makes sense particularly for light weighted cargo with high volumes because this kind of cargo occupies over proportional transport space, which is cost intensive and must be paid. From a transport economic point of view, these billing systems are correct, but for statistical reasons we clearly have to point out that the following definitions of "tons" are neither a weight nor a volume measurement and should not be compared with metric tons, short tons or long tons. Due to missing alternatives this is wishful thinking. Metric, short, and long ton declarations are frequently mixed with revenue and freight tons. To understand this, let's continue with our list of definitions of "tons":

4: Ton (RT)

Revenue Ton: a ton on which the shipment is freighted; a billing unit in the shipping industry. One revenue ton is the weight in metric tons or the volume in cubic meters; whichever is higher in terms of freight. Weights are usually based on metric tons and volume measures are based on cubic meters.

To continue with the example mentioned above under "cubic measure": if the rate is quoted as 15.00 Euros per cbm and 20.00 Euros per metric ton and the weight of the package is 2856 kgs = 2.856 tons, then the freight rate for this will be

$$5.712 \text{ cbm} \times € 15 = 85.68 \text{ Euro or}$$
$$2.856 \text{ tons} \times € 20 = 57.12 \text{ Euro}$$

Since the cbm rate is higher, the freight rate of 85.68 Euro will apply. Ideally the revenue ton (RT) should apply the cbm measurement for volumetric cargo and the weight measure for high density cargo.

There is an additional billing standard for rail and truck business in the hinterland of ports. This distance is included as an additional billing standard, which leads to the RT/m or revenue-ton-mile: a metric used in the logistics industry. It accounts for the revenue brought in for the movement of one ton of goods over the distance of one mile. Which ton (metric, short, or long) applies differs from country to country and must be investigated from case to case. The Revenue ton mile is often used to determine profitability in the logistics business.

5: Ton (FT)

Freight Ton "A": a unit of weight or mass measurement equal to one metric ton = 1 t or 1000 kilograms of freight of any volume. The symbol FT is used for this unit.

Freight Ton "B": a traditional unit of volume used for measuring the cargo of a ship, truck, train, or other freight carrier. This freight ton is exactly 40 cubic feet, or approximately 1.1326 cbm. However, the term "freight ton" is also being used to mean a metric ton of freight, volume not specified. Perhaps because of this confusion, the 40 cubic foot unit is often called the "measurement ton" (MTON). This confusion seems impossible to dispel; some shippers are using "measurement ton" to mean a metric ton of freight. To further complicate the situation, the freight ton is also called the U.S. shipping ton; the British shipping ton is 5% larger at 42 cubic feet (1.1893 cbm).

It must be stated that the term freight ton is not a generally valid statistical term, if widely used. The most distinctive characteristic of a freight ton is that it is a mix of volume and weight measurement. Confusingly, both symbols FT and MTON are used for this unit. Some statistics alternatively call a freight ton a cargo ton.

Arabesque: Additional "Ton" Definitions

There are several more "ton" definitions in use, and in order to precisely differentiate between the alternative meanings of "ton" and to clearly distinguish between the alternative abbreviations, the following definitions shall be added, although they are not cargo measuring terms.

6: Register Ton (RT or rT)

Register Ton: a unit traditionally used to measure the cargo capacity of a merchant ship. During the Middle Ages, merchant ships were rated by the number of tons of wine they could carry. Today the merchant marine ton is defined to be exactly 100 cubic feet, or approximately 2.8316 cbm. This (volume measuring) unit is often called the register ton, since it is recorded in official registers of ships. The symbol RT, which is also used for the revenue ton, seems to be in wide use for this unit especially in the shipping business. In addition, the symbol RT is also used for the refrigeration ton (see definition 8).

7: Displacement Ton (DT or dT)

Displacement Ton: a unit of volume used traditionally to measure the "displacement" of ships, especially warships. One way to describe the size of a ship is to state the volume of sea water it displaces when it is afloat; in other words, the volume of that part of the ship below the waterline. The actual weight of sea water varies somewhat according to its temperature and how salty it is, but for this purpose it has been agreed that a long ton of sea water occupies about 35 cubic feet. Accordingly, the displacement ton is defined to be exactly 35 cubic feet, or approximately 0.9911 cbm.

Since this is a much smaller unit than the register ton, warships have a higher "tonnage" than merchant ships of approximately the same dimensions. For port tariffs the distinction between DT and RT (register ton) is important. The symbol DT is recommended for this unit.

8: Refrigeration Ton (RT)

Refrigeration Ton: a unit of power used in refrigeration engineering. One ton of refrigeration is intended to be the power required to freeze one short ton of water at 0°C in 24 hours. This is assumed to be exactly 12 000 Btu per hour (Btu/h or "Btuh"), which is equivalent to 200 Btu/min, 3.516 853 kilowatts, 4.7162 horsepower, or 0.8396 (kilogram) calories per second (Cal/s). The symbol RT is in use for this unit, but it is also used for the "revenue ton" and the "register ton." This unit is sometimes used for refrigerated cargo either in refrigerated ships or in reefer containers.

9: Ton (tn or T)

Ton: confusingly, the term "ton" is also used as a unit of energy. Tons measure the energy of an explosion, especially a nuclear explosion. In this usage, one ton is supposed to be the amount of energy released by the explosion of one short ton of TNT. This is defined in the United States to equal exactly 4.184 gigajoules (GJ) or roughly 4 million Btu (British thermal unit = unit of energy).

10: Ton

Ton: The word "ton" is finally British slang for 100, especially the sum of 100 pounds, a speed of 100 miles per hour, or a score of 100 in darts or cricket. The origin of this usage is not clear.

In addition to all the weight and volume measures above, two shipping "tons" are often used in port business, for example, as basis for port tariffs:

11: Deadweight Ton (DWT or dwt)

The deadweight of a ship is the difference in tonnes between the displacement of a ship on summer load-line in water with a specific gravity of 1,025 and the total weight of the ship, that is, the displacement in tonnes of a ship without cargo, fuel, lubricating oil, ballast water, fresh water and drinking water in the tanks, usable supplies as well as passengers, crew and their possessions. DWT is a measure of how much weight a ship can safely carry.

12: Gross tonnage (GT or gt)

Gross tonnage is a measure of the size of a ship determined in accordance with the provisions of the International Convention on Tonnage Measurement of Ships, 1969.

Unit Measure

Huge quantities of port cargo are measured in or on standard units, like containers, measured in TEU "Twenty-Foot Equivalent Units," or for RoRo cargo in car equivalent units (CEU). Typical flats for oversized and heavy cargo often also use the standard 20 ft or 40 ft container size. Therefore, TEU, CEU, and other widely used units shall be explained below.

Twenty-Foot Equivalent Unit (TEU)

TEU is a standard linear measurement used in quantifying vessel loading capacities, container traffic flows, and container yard space (ground slots) on terminals. As examples, one twenty-foot long container equals one TEU while one forty-foot container equals two TEUs. The normal standard TEU is 20 ft long, 8 ft high, and 8 ft wide.[4]

The unit is useful for measuring port and shipping capacity at all levels of the cargo industry including a terminal, a port, a port range, a single ship, a train, an entire fleet of ships, a shipping company, or an entire supply chain. It should be noted that the number's derivation relative to cargo volume is inexact for two primary reasons:

1. The volume of the containers, in practice, does not typically correlate to the amount of cargo that can be shipped, as many objects may necessitate an entire container but come far from filling it to capacity. For example, one could likely fit two steel coils into a single TEU, but they would hardly occupy the entire volume of the container.
2. The height of the containers is highly variable (from 4 ft to 9 ft). Ultimately, the height of the container used is dependent more upon the shipping needs than any standard practices.

Further, shipping containers come in a wide range of sizes and lengths to facilitate large and odd-sized cargo. For example, a ship may need to utilize container 45 ft long to transport a particularly large piece of cargo. This container would be classified as 2 or 2.25 TEUs (depending on the exactitude of the measurement).

The metric is used primarily in the port and shipping industry to measure and compare capacities, that is, terminal and whole port throughput capacity. Round

---

4 Further details about ISO freight container and the most common codes in use can be found in Appendix D.

numbers giving approximations of scale (rather than exact numbers of minutia) are typically preferred as; again, the metric is nonexact but gives a reasonable indication about the port's potential.

The number of TEU throughput per terminal and/or port is an indicator of port performance. Many port statistics count the number of TEU's handled per month, per quarter, or per year. As port operators get paid for this, it is understandable that the number of boxes is counted instead of the cargo inside. But for many forecasts this causes problems—as already explained above—, because trade and transportation statistics are widely incomparable.

The TEU as a container size was invented in the United States; and this is why the standard size is 20 ft long by 8 ft high by 8 ft wide, which is 6.095 m * 2.438 m * 2.438 m in metric units. The maximum size inside a 20 ft standard container is 5.71 m * 2.352 m * 2.352 m. Many pallets around the world do not measure in ft. The European Standard Pallet for sea transportation has a size of 1.0 m * 1.2 m (ISO), and the so-called Euro-pallet 0.8 m * 1.2 m (CEN). With this size, only 9 or 10 standard pallets fit into one TEU, and only 11 Euro-pallets. The space inside the container is suboptimal due to units based on different measurement standards.

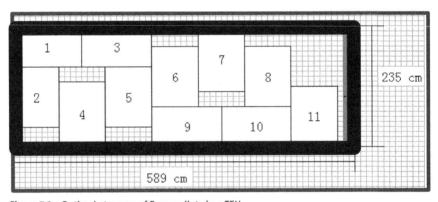

Figure 7.3: Optimal stowage of Euro-pallets in a TEU

Clearly the use of Euro-pallets or European Standard pallets in a 20 ft container is not optimal, but this is the price the industry has to pay due to different standards in measuring, or, due to a lack of global standardization. In addition, the size of 2.352 m wide is not compatible with European truck widths of 2.45 m. In 2.45 m, 3 Euro-pallets can sit parallel to one another (0.8 +0.8 +0.8 = 2.4 m). But in a container this is not possible. There are huge saving potentials via standardization, but this is a difficult task politically.

Intermodal Transport Unit (ITU)

ITUs can be defined as a container, swap body, or semitrailer/goods road motor vehicle suitable for intermodal transport. ITUs are freight-carrying units optimized to road vehicle dimensions and fitted with handling devices for transfer between modes, usually road and rail. These units often come to logistics centers and/or port warehouses, but they are not usable for maritime transport. Due to the popularity and ubiquity of sea containers, many ITUs have the same measurements as a container, that is, 20 ft in length, and with the same measure of the four corner fittings to lock the units on trucks and trailers. Most of the ITUs are not designed to be stacked when full or top-lifted. An ITU would need UIC approval to be used on rail. Some swap bodies are equipped with folding legs on which the unit stands when not on the vehicle.

Flat or Flat Rack

A flat or flat rack is a loadable platform having no superstructure whatsoever but having the same length and width as the base of a container and equipped with top and bottom corner fittings. "Flat rack container" is an alternative term used for certain types of specific purpose sea containers—namely platform containers and platform-based containers with incomplete structures. Flat rack containers are frequently used instead of general intermodal cargo containers where freight is bulky, heavy or can not be loaded through open top or side doors. Building materials, logs and machinery are often transported or exported on a flat rack container; sometimes also called "flat bed container." Flat racks are normally in 20 ft, 40 ft, and 45 ft lengths.

RoRo Unit or RoRo Flat

RoRo units are wheeled equipment for carrying goods, like rolls of newspaper and magazine paper for the printing industry, which can be driven or towed onto a vessel. The size and dimensions of these flats are often like flats and sea containers, but additional sets of wheels at one end of the unit make them easy to handle for special gooseneck-trailers.

Car Equivalent Unit (CEU)

RoRo cargo is often measured in units of "lanes in meters" (LIMs) or "lane meters." This is calculated by multiplying cargo length (in meters) by the number of decks, and then by its width (in lanes) (lane width differs from vessel to vessel and there are several industry standards). This is a clear standard, as a metric meter is a meter, and when a cargo load requires 5.00 lane meters, then there should be no misunderstanding.

Car carriers are typical RoRo vessels, whose capacity if often measured in CEU units. These units are based on a 1966 Toyota Corona RT43; this standard is the car equivalent unit (CEU). The lane meters in this case are represented by car equivalents. This standard gives an overview of how many cars of a defined size can be stored aboard a vessel. The dimension of this equivalent CEU RT43 is: 4125 mm x 1550 mm x 1400 mm. The ground space required for a CEU RT43 is approx. 6.4 sqm, and the ground slot with the necessary distance between the cars is 7.40 sqm. Thus, a vessel with a capacity of 1,000 CEU can store 1000 cars of the 1966 Toyota Corona size. Cars that are bigger may require 1.2 or 1.3 CEU RT43. This standard is widely used and measuring car carrying capacity in CEU RT43 is close to a global standard.

Unfortunately, there are other CEU-standards that are also in use. Another definition of one CEU equals 10 sqm,[5] which is approx. the size of a standard American 4-door sedan. One CEU RT43 in this case equals 0.74, or in short: 1 RT43 = 0.74 CEU. Having these two different standards make it necessary to always distinguish which standard is being used when shipping.

The situation becomes even more confusing when talking about a vehicle equivalent unit (VEU) instead of CEU. The same is true for the passenger car equivalent (PCE) as standard: these are not precisely defined nor widely used. VEUs and PCEs are company standards. The most common and accepted units you will see are CEU RT43, as described above.[6]

---

5 Information gathered from following presentation: U.S. Department of Transportation: 2010 National Census of Ferry Operators, presentation held from: RITA Research and Innovative Technology Administration, Bureau of Transportation Statistics, Definitions and Clarifications, page 4, Washington, 2010.

6 It should only be mentioned as additional information that the abbreviation CEU in the shipping industry also exists for: cost equivalent unit. This is a unit for containers, used to make them comparable with regard to the costs. A typical 20 ft container equals 1 CEU. A standard 40 ft container with regard to rentals and costs equals approximately 1.6 TEU. As this is not a unit for measuring, it shall only be mentioned as additional information.

Verified Gross Mass (VGM)

Misdeclared container weights have been a long-standing problem for the transportation industry and for governments, as they present safety hazards for ships, their crews, the other cargo on board, workers in the port facilities, and on roads. Misdeclaration of container weights also gives rise to customs concerns.

The International Maritime Organization (IMO) has amended the Safety of Life at Sea Convention (SOLAS) to require, as a condition for loading a packed container onto a ship for export, that the container have a verified weight. Since July 1, 2016, the shipper is responsible for the verification of the packed container's weight. It is a violation of SOLAS for a terminal to load a packed container onto a vessel if the vessel operator and marine terminal operator do not have a verified container weight. Shippers are required to provide a signed document declaring the VGM of a container to be loaded onto a ship.

The VGM of a container to be shipped can be measured by one of two methods: Method 1) weighing the container after it has been packed using "calibrated and certified equipment"; or Method 2) adding the weight of the cargo (contents, packaging, etc.) to the tare weight of the empty container. The VGM requirement applies globally. Shippers, freight forwarders, vessel operators, and terminal operators have been requested to establish policies and procedures to ensure the implementation of the regulatory change.

7.3 Errors in Port Cargo Measurement

To avoid problems and to reduce errors with maritime cargo on board of vessels and during port and inland operations, the shipper has two key obligations in maritime trade.[7] According to SOLAS the first is to provide 'appropriate information on the cargo sufficiently in advance of loading to enable... proper loading' of the ship. The second is to ensure that the gross mass presented to the ship is as declared and verified via a VGM declaration.

Many shippers understand the importance of the current requirements in relation to safety at sea as well as inland legs of the supply chain and take steps to comply. The requirements are generally consistent with the "Advanced Cargo Information" systems implemented by a growing number of countries and at least partially aligned with domestic legislation in many countries with regard to regulations of the weight of containers carried on land by road or rail. But the

---

7 Safety of Life at Sea Convention (SOLAS), Chapter VI, Part A, Regulation 2.

regulatory scheme is only one side of the coin; on the other side is the fact that errors and misdeclarations occur during daily practice. Some examples of such problems are below.

Workflow Difficulties

Clearly, the logical place to ensure that the gross mass of a consignment packed in a container is correctly declared is prior to the commencement of its transport—the point when packing is complete and doors will be closed/according to method 1 for the VGM declaration. Apart from the fact that this not always happens, the reality of trade is that the consignment weight is generally estimated at the time of booking the container according to VGM method 2.

Ineffective Enforcement

The regime covering any inland transport prior to loading on board a ship will inevitably be governed by domestic legislation. Indeed, for some landmasses around the globe, there could be a series of differing regulations applicable before the container reaches the seaside. There is, however, no simple international legal mechanism by which to achieve consistent regulation on land. In view of the fact that the vast majority of containers packed, and sealed inland will arrive at their foreign destination without being opened in transit, it could be argued that validation of the correct declaration of gross mass for the maritime mode will equate to correct declaration for every other mode. Even the new 2016 SOLAS VGM regulation is only as good as the regime that enforces it.

Perception that Weight Is Peripheral

In some parts of the market there is a perception that weight of cargo inside a container or another unit is not of paramount importance. However, a wrong declared container weight will lead to severe incidents, from property damage to loss of human life, for example:
−   Damage to the containers
−   Damage to the terminals
−   Damage to the vessels
−   Accidents leading to injury or casualty
−   Legal weight restriction

- Negative impact on vessel planning
- Rolling of containers and loss of income

Since the introduction of the SOLAS VGM rules, it is the obligation of the shipper to stow the cargo correctly and to accurately declare the exact weight of the unit. If the cargo and weight declaration is incorrect, all pertaining charges incurred and consequences are normally to the account of the shipper or the customers.

Using Different Standards to Measure

When a container is loaded in a port, different types of cargoes can be stowed inside, for example, on different pallets, with each pallet possibly having several cartons on it, secured in shrinking plastic wrap. In such a situation, the dock workers may not have time to check all the cargo. And here it happens that a pallet measured in metric tons stands beside a pallet measured in freight or revenue tons. The question then is how to calculate the exact weight? If the weight is not correctly declared, you might end up with a situation like the one seen in Figure 7.4.

Source: World Cargo News, May 2008, page 78.
Figure 7.4: Damaged container

In addition to potential risks for the terminal staff, the cargo, and the container, the added risks for the vessel operator can be even more serious: lost lives or lost ships. Even today, after the introduction of VGM rules, shippers still declare incorrect weights per container. When a heavy container is declared as light, this container will be stowed in the upper tiers. This is done to ensure that the center of gravity of the container stack and the overall center of gravity are kept as low as possible. If the center of gravity of a ship becomes erratic due to the inaccurately declared container masses, this may cause instability or even a negative stability and could cause the vessel to capsize. Investigations of vessel disasters have proven this to be a really serious problem. In the past, up to 20% of cargoes were incorrectly declared. The vessel MSC Napoli was seriously damaged in 2007 in a storm and beached off the Devon coast in the UK due to a wrongly declared weight. An investigation showed that hundreds of tons of cargoes inside containers had not been declared, and consequently these boxes were stowed wrongly on deck. This at least supported the instability that ended in a tragedy.

Statistical Consequences

Finally, applying different measuring standards for cargo also results in inaccurate statistics. In Chapter 3, the three top twenty lists for general cargo, liquid bulk, and dry bulk ports were listed. Most international ports display rankings in this way, that is, using FT, RT, ST, and MT or freight, revenue short and metric tons in one way or the other.

The three tables 7.9–7.11 show a recalculation of these rankings. For making the incomparable FT and RT amounts comparable, it's assumed that one freight ton (respectively, one revenue ton) equals an amount of 0.75 metric tons. This relation between RT/FT and MT is just used for demonstration. It is very likely that the relation is very different from this, depending on the cargo. The fact is that the amount is bigger than 0 (because cargo is transported) and less than 1,000 kg, because for loads weighing above 1,000, the real weight would have been taken. Realistic estimations differ based on the port and the structure of the cargo being transported.

The ranking of the top twenty general cargo ports in Table 7.9 changed the rankings in 25% of the cases. This recalculation was made only for the top twenty general cargo ports. A second calculation with the assumption that a freight ton equals only 0.5 metric tons or 500 kg results in fifteen of the top twenty ports changing in ranking. It is very likely that some of these ports would no longer rank in the top twenty group if the top 100 list were recalculated. But this exercise is only to show that there are inaccuracies in the statistics.

Table 7.10 also shows that a simple recalculation would change the rankings for the top liquid bulk ports. Here it must be considered that some US-American ports report figures in ST = short tons. The figures in short tons have been correctly transferred into metric tons according to the conversion factor as mentioned above in Table 7.8. This results in Houston slipping from position 3 to position 4. Due to the fact that other top-ranking ports use RT as standards leads to twelve out of the twenty ports changing their position in the ranking list. The two major liquid bulk ports of Ras Tanura and Rotterdam with huge amounts of crude oil and refined products stayed unchanged.

Table 7.9: Top 20 General Cargo Ports, 2015 in mill. t; 1 RT/FT equals 0.75 MT

Rank new	old	Port	Country	Unit	2015
1	1	Los Angeles	USA	MT	126.3
2	2	Nagoya	Japan	MT	72.8
3	3	Long Beach	USA	MT	66.8
4	4	Kitakyushu	Japan	MT	53.3
5	5	Osaka	Japan	MT	33.5
6	6	Kobe	Japan	MT	33.2
7	**8**	Singapore	Singapore	MT	29.9
8	7	Yokohama	Japan	MT	27.8
9	**10**	Rotterdam	Netherlands	MT	27.7
10	**11**	Ningbo-Zhoushan	China	MT	25.0
11	9	Inchon	South Korea	MT	21.7
12	12	Mumbai	India	MT	19.8
13	13	Vancouver	Canada	MT	16.8
14	14	St. Petersburg	Russia	MT	16.2
15	15	Port Klang	Malaysia	MT	15.7
16	16	Taichung	Taiwan	MT	15.5
17	17	Zeebrugge	Belgium	MT	15.2
18	18	Antwerp	Belgium	MT	14.7
19	19	Amsterdam	Netherlands	MT	12.3
20	20	Hong Kong	China	MT	11.5

bold: higher ranking; gray: lower ranking
Source: Port Websites, ISL Shipping Statistics; own calculations.

Table 7.10: Top 20 Liquid Bulk Ports, 2015 in mill. t; 1 RT/FT equals 0.75 MT

Rank new	old	Port	Country	Unit	2015
1	1	Ras Tanura*	Saudi Arabia	MT	349.2
2	2	Rotterdam	Netherlands	MT	224.6
3	4	Singapore	Singapore	MT	195.8
4	3	Houston	USA	MT	180.7
5	5	South Louisiana	USA	MT	150.3
6	8	Chiba	Japan	MT	104.0
7	9	Al Basrah*	Iraq	MT	100.8
8	6	Gwangyang	South Korea	MT	96.2
9	10	Mina al Ahmadi*	Kuwait	MT	93.0
10	7	Ulsan	South Korea	MT	92.6
11	11	Corpus Christi	USA	MT	74.0
12	12	Jebel Dhanna*	UAE	MT	68.7
13	13	Botas	Turkey	MT	67.2
14	14	Antwerp	Belgium	MT	66.7
15	15	New York / New Jersey	USA	MT	60.4
16	17	Novorossisk	Russia	MT	59.8
17	18	Primorsk	Russia	MT	59.6
18	19	Ningbo-Zhoushan	China	MT	58.0
19	20	Daesan	South Korea	MT	55.8
20	16	Yanbu	Saudi Arabia	MT	45.2

* 2014 data   bold: higher ranking; gray: lower ranking
Source: Port websites; ISL Shipping Statistic; US DoT; own calculations.

Table 7.11 and the listing of the top twenty dry bulk ports also changed in 4 positions, simply by converting the exact measured short tons with 0.907185 mt into a comparable scale of metric tons. Other than the estimation of freight and revenue tons this is an exact measurement. The position of South Louisiana is interesting in this list. In short tons, it was clearly ranked between Newcastle and Itaqui. When converted into metric tons, it looks different: South Louisiana in fact handles nearly the same amount as Itaqui.

Taking all three top twenty rankings in mind, we must accept that using different standards in port throughput statistics is not a minor problem—it is a problem that leads to several changes in the lists of top twenty ports. If everybody knows what the abbreviations RT, FT, ST, LT, or MT mean, it is ok to report this way. But very often "one ton" was recorded as "one ton"; without knowing what was behind this "ton." This oversimplification leads to wrong interpretations of port throughput statistics.

Table 7.11: Top 20 Dry Bulk Ports, 2015 in mill. t; 1 ST = 0.907029 MT

Rank					
new	old	Port	Country	Unit	2015
1	1	Port Hedland	Australia	MT	444.7
2	2	Quinhuangdao	China	MT	233.0
3	3	Tianjin	China	MT	223.5
4	4	Dampier	Australia	MT	172.0
5	5	Newcastle*	Australia	MT	165.2
6	6	South Louisiana	USA	MT	139.0
7	7	Itaqui	Brazil	MT	138.8
8	8	Tubaro	Brazil	MT	121.5
9	9	Hay Point*	Australia	MT	115.0
10	10	Ningbo	China	MT	112.0
11	11	Sepetiba	Brazil	MT	104.3
12	12	Richards Bay	South Africa	MT	98.6
13	13	Gladstone	Australia	MT	98.6
14	14	Saldanha Bay	South Africa	MT	70.8
15	15	New Orleans	USA	MT	43.6
16	**17**	Brisbane	Australia	MT	40.2
17	**19**	Paradip	India	MT	38.0
18	16	Plaquemines	USA	MT	36.7
19	18	Cincinnati	USA	MT	36.5
20	20	Vancouver	Canada	MT	35.7

* Fiscal year ending June 30
bold: higher ranking; gray lower ranking
Source: Port Webpages; ISL; own calculations.

Part 3: **Port Management**

Chapter 8
Frame Conditions

8.1 Port Business Environment

A port is not an entity producing an isolated service. Besides the "external" effect where ports are partners along a supply chain, a variety of "internal" activities take place within the boundaries of a port. Thus, it is important to consider the diverse characteristics of each service that may lead to different regulatory schemes, as some present natural monopoly properties while others could be better produced under competition. By the same token, and given that all services must be produced within a limited area, it is important to analyze the ways and means of inducing public and private interests in ports and to identify the role of port authorities as institutions in charge of regulation within a port.

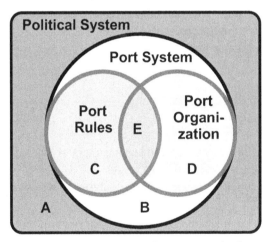

Figure 8.1: Port system—port rules—port organization

The term "port system" describes part of a political system:
1. The general rules and framework parameters (e.g., laws) set by the political system
2. Impact and extent of competition and state aid
3. The division of labor between public and private tasks in ports
4. Shared responsibilities between public/government and private/business

DOI 10.1515/9781547400874-008

Figure 8.1 symbolizes that ports are part of the political system, that is, the political and socioeconomic framework (area "A") of a country. A few processes take place on this level: the debate on port and maritime infrastructure efficiency, the imposition of competition rules and state aid regulation, the integration of ports into the transport policy of the country, and further fundamental discussions and decision-making processes. The political system of a country in this case defines the frame for ports. The port system "B" describes the fundamental port regulations, like the share of public and private engagements; the level of federal, regional, and municipal responsibilities, etc. Some literature puts technical port rules (C) on the same level as the Port System, but this is imprecise. The term port rules contains basic rules on how to behave in or with a port.

Typical technical and navigational port rules contain, among other additional port specific regulations, the following topics:
- General
  - o Technical characteristics of the port
  - o Business hours and duration of the navigation season
  - o Vessel traffic management in the port territory
  - o Tidiness and safety on port territory
  - o Security requirements
  - o Agency services
  - o Scheduling coordination
- Vessels entering and leaving the port
  - o Pilotage management
  - o Notification procedure for the entering and leaving intent of a vessel
  - o Registration of the entering and leaving of a vessel
  - o Requirements of state supervisory bodies for the entering and leaving of the vessels
- Vessel traffic in the port waters
  - o Vessel mooring
  - o Vessel relocation
  - o Special conditions
  - o Vessel towing
  - o Vessel traffic under special weather conditions
- Vessel stay in port
  - o Requirements to moored vessels
  - o Special conditions
  - o Deck operations on moored vessels
  - o Communications organization
  - o Vessel connection to onshore supply systems
  - o Dredging and diving operations

- Handling of dangerous cargo; handling of petroleum products
  - o Tanker loading/discharging
  - o Bunkering
- Reception of ship-generated waste and cargo residues
- Fire safety requirements in the port and management of rescue operations
- Passenger service regulations within the port boundaries, etc.

The list shows that port rules target a specific port, whereas the regulations of the port system are normally more general for most or all ports in a country.

The circle "D" in Figure 8.1 symbolizes the port organization. This term describes the internal organization of a specific port, for example, the organizational set up of the port authority, its hierarchical structure, the number, correct name (in some charts also the telephone number and/or email) of the leader of the departments, etc. The port organization could also display and describe the organization of the port authority and its relation to the terminals as well as other organizations, like customs, police, veterinary control, etc. Like the port rules, the organization is oriented to a specific port. The overlapping area "E" in Figure 8.1 symbolizes the area where port rules influence the port organization or vice versa. Rules and regulations concerning fires, for example, must be fixed in the port rules but must also be integrated in the port organization.

Figure 8.1 also shows that the port system has an influence on the port organization; this influential direction from the overall system to the subordinate organization is given. The other way around it is not automatically true that the rules and regulations or the organization of a terminal or subordinary administration (like veterinary control, pilotage, or bunkering) has an influence on the overall port system; at least not on short notice. The port system—as mentioned above—describes the more general rules that are intended to provide a stable framework. These frame conditions provide the principal guiding rules that should allow for attracting long-term oriented business. This does not mean that these rules are "carved in stone" and unchangeable, but normally good arguments and sound discussions are needed for change.

An allowed question is: why does a state have a port system? Either as a written law or regulation or just by matter of fact? The answers in most of the states around the world would be:

- Because a port as facilitator of trade is more than just a private business; it is a critical infrastructure for the whole economy
- Because we have "market failure"
- Because we have "state failure"

We already came across the first argument in Chapter 1 when looking back at history. It is of interest for the rulers to be integrated in global markets, and for the physical movement of cargo. This historic strategic argument is still relevant, and it will be supported by the following two arguments.

Total free markets are not perfect. Economic theory already shows that markets fail (e.g., via the tendency of monopoly behavior, not only in total free markets, but also in real market economies), and due to this it is advisable to have public interests installed in ports, too. It is also common economic knowledge that 100% state-owned organizations also often fail. This is not only due to a lack of efficiency, it is also very often the huge and time-consuming bureaucracy, which leads state-owned entities to fail. Because of both market and state failure, most of the port systems today prefer a mixed system that balances out public and private interests.

8.2 Basic Management Concepts

The question "how a port is positioned" within the sphere of public and private interests often has a symbolic range, as displayed in Figure 8.2. Where exactly is a specific port located between public and private interests? How big is the influence of the state; how big is the influence of the private business? Because many ports have been close to the state in the past, relevant questions deal with port privatization, commercialization, and corporatization. Commercialization in this sense is the introduction of (private) business rules under state ownership, whereby the "state" can be represented by the federal government or a local municipality. Corporatization goes one step further into privatization and includes institution building.

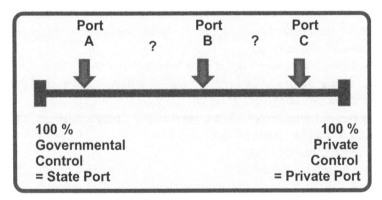

Figure 8.2: State vs. private port

A variety of factors influence the way ports are organized, structured, and managed, including the political system and the socioeconomic framework, historical structures like the ones analyzed in Chapter 1, the cargoes handled (bulk or general cargo/container), the competitive situation, as well as size and access to hinterland markets.

Four main categories of ports have emerged over time, and they can be classified into four main models: the public service port, the tool port, the landlord port, and the fully privatized port or private service port. These models are distinguished by how they differ with respect to such characteristics as:

- Public, private, or mixed provision of service
- Local, regional, or global orientation
- Ownership of infrastructure (including port land)
- Ownership of superstructure and equipment (particularly ship-to-shore handling equipment, sheds, and warehouses)
- Status of dock labor and management

So-called public service ports and tool ports mainly focus on the realization of public interests. Landlord ports have a mixed character and aim to strike a balance between public (port authority) and private (port industry) interests. Fully privatized ports focus on private (shareholder) interests.[1]

According to Figure 8.2, service and tool ports with their dominating public character are very close to the extreme left side of the axis, representing huge governmental influence and control. Landlord ports, which are a mix of public and private interests, could be placed in the middle, and private ports with huge private industry influence are located on the right side of the axis. Table 8.1 provides an overview of the four basic port management models.

Table 8.1: Basic port management models

Type	Infrastructure	Superstructure	Port Labor	Other functions
Public Service Port	public	public	public	majority public
Tool Port	public	public	private	public/private
Landlord Port	public	private	private	public/private
Private Service Port	private	private	private	majority private

Source: Port Reform Toolkit 2007, page 85; revised by author.

---

1 Port Reform Toolkit, page 81.

Government-controlled public service ports are as rare as fully privatized ports. The two extremes are not the preferred models. But keeping history in mind, we must realize that in the past there were many more public-controlled ports than there are today. It was, and in a few countries still is, a 100% public task to build and operate ports and terminals. The main reason behind this seems to be the interests of governments having control of im- and exports. Countries with public ports often also have public shipping and public rail and road transport.

During the 1970s and 1980s there was a strong commercialization trend on all continents to privatize the public port business and to transform the public dominated port system into a hybrid public/private system. Commercialization has often been the first step in utilizing public resources through private tools for increased economic activity.[2]

The UK and New Zealand fully privatized several ports in the recent past, but most countries have considered this method of privatization extreme. The privatization is considered extreme because in many cases the governmental bodies lost complete control of the ports. The privatization had a negative effect on small- and medium-sized enterprises (SMEs), whose foreign trade activities were extinguished by the change in port ownership; alternative options for im- and exports at competitive prices rarely exist. Private ports are often not open to the public, but SMEs rely on open ports and terminals for their business. Extreme cases of privatization are often in favor of large and in many cases multinational, global enterprises; and their interests in local, regional or national interests are limited. Smaller countries (i.e., their government as well as local SMEs), such as New Zealand, take the risks to be over-ruled by global business interests.

Before going into more detail about the privatization process, the four different management models shall be characterized in general.

---

2 For further details, refer to Chapter 9: "Port Commercialization and Privatization."

Table 8.2: Port management models' characteristics[3]

Public Service Ports	
Ports like:	Nampho/N. Korea, Puerto Cabello/Venezuela, Nouakchott/Mauret.
Criterion:	– Infrastructure and superstructure planning and operation is in the hand of the state – Managed like a public department – No private port operation – Normally smaller ports
Tool Ports	
Ports like:	Chittagong/Bangladesh, Dakar/Senegal, Ravenna/Italy
Criterion:	– An independent public body is responsible for the port – Independent from other ministries – Small private operators – Often a mix between state and municipal management – Many ports "in transition"
Landlord Ports	
Ports like:	Rotterdam/Netherlands, New York/USA, Singapore
Criterion:	– Infrastructure in the hand of the municipal government – Superstructure private (planning and financing) – Public port authority + private terminal operators – Public and private power is balanced – Main organizational structure in North Europe
Private Ports	
Ports like:	Felixstowe/UK, Nordenham/Germany, Tauranga/New Zealand
Criterion:	– Both infra- and superstructure is in the hand of private companies – No (or limited) public influence (e.g., for planning, financing) – Normally not universal ports – Often work ports with concentration on one product (e.g., coal import for a power plant)

Model 1—Public service port: Public service ports have a predominantly public character. The port authority of a public service port performs the entire range of

---

3 For details on Table 8.2 and for further information on models 1–4 mentioned below, also refer to "Port Reform Toolkit 2007," pages 81 ff.

port-related services required for the functioning of the seaport system, as well as that of owning the entire infrastructure. This means that the port authority owns, maintains, and operates every available asset (fixed and mobile) and cargo handling activities are executed by labor employed directly by the port authority. Some ancillary services can be left to private companies. Public service ports are usually controlled by (or partly controlled by) the Ministry of Transport, and the chairman (or director general) is a civil servant appointed by, and/or directly reporting to, the relevant minister. The port authority is commonly a branch of a ministry and most of the employees are civil servants.

The main function of a public service port authority is cargo handling activities. In some public service ports, the cargo handling activities are carried out by a separate public entity often referred to as the "cargo handling company." Such public companies usually report to the same ministry as the port authority.

To have public entities with different and sometimes conflicting interests reporting to the same ministry, and which are forced to cooperate in the same operational environment, represents a challenge. For this reason, the port authorities and cargo handling companies of some ports were merged into one single entity.

Public service ports are generally seen as less efficient than private ports. Therefore, the number of public service ports in Europe and in the United Sates is limited. Many ports in developing countries (approximately 70%) are public service ports. Most of the public service ports are smaller ports and are not represented in the top ten lists seen in Chapter 3.

Model 2—Tool port: Such ports are similar in many aspects to a public service port, but a tool port differs in the private handling of its cargo operations, although the terminal equipment itself is still owned by the port authority. In the tool port model, the port authority owns, develops, and maintains the port infrastructure as well as the superstructure, including cargo handling equipment such as quay cranes and forklift trucks. Port authority staff usually operate all port authority-owned equipment.

However, other cargo handling onboard vessels as well as on the apron and the quay is usually carried out by private cargo handling firms contracted by the shipping agents or other principals licensed by the port authority. In the past, these companies tended to be small, with few capital assets and fragmented activities. Their costs were almost entirely variable. The cost of underutilization of port facilities was usually absorbed by the port authority, which minimized the risk for the cargo handling companies. The lack of capitalization of the cargo handling companies constituted a significant obstacle to the development of strong companies that could function efficiently in the port and be able to compete on an international level.

The above-mentioned division of tasks within the tool port system clearly identifies the essential problem with this type of port management model, namely the split of operational responsibilities that leads to operational inefficiency. Whereas the port authority owns and operates the cargo handling equipment, the private cargo handling firm usually signs the cargo handling contract with the ship owner or cargo owner. However, the cargo handling firm is not able to fully control all cargo handling operations itself. To prevent conflicts between cargo handling firms, some port authorities allow operators to use their own equipment (at which point it is no longer a true tool port). In several cases, a tool port is a transitional stage between a public service port and a landlord port. This is also the case for the autonomous ports or "Port Autonome" in France, which a few years ago were converted into "grand ports maritimes," or landlord ports.

Model 3—Landlord port: The landlord port is characterized by its mixed public-private orientation. Under this model the port authority is the owner of the basic seaport infrastructure and acts as both the regulatory body and landlord. Private companies supply port operations (especially cargo handling) as services for clients. A key role for many port authorities is that of the landlord, with the responsibility of managing the real estate as well as the public infrastructure within the port area. This management includes the ownership, the economic exploitation and long-term development of the land, and the upkeep of basic port infrastructure such as fairways, berths, access roads, bridges, and tunnels. However, other infrastructure, particularly terminals, is leased to private operating companies and/or to industries such as refineries, tank terminals, and chemical plants. The most common form of lease is a concession agreement where a private company is granted a long-term lease in exchange for a rent based on the size of the facility, plus an investment required for building, renovating, or expanding (e.g., land reclamation and quay wall construction).

The private port operators provide and maintain their own superstructure, including buildings (e.g., offices, sheds, warehouses, and workshops). They also purchase and install their own equipment on the terminal grounds (e.g., quay cranes, pumping stations, and conveyor belts) as required by their business, while maintaining operating standards. Dock labor is employed by private terminal operators, although in some ports part of the labor may be provided through a port-wide labor pool system.

The biggest advantage of the landlord model is that the decision-making power in and for the port is balanced. Public and private stakeholders share responsibilities and commitments for the success of the port. At present, the landlord port is the dominant port model in large- and medium-sized ports in Europe and North America. Clear examples of landlord ports are Antwerp and Rotterdam in Europe, Los Angeles and New York in the United States, and the Port of Singapore in Asia.

Model 4—Private port: Full privatization means that the state no longer has any meaningful involvement or public policy interest in the port sector. In fully privatized ports (which often take the form of a private service port), the port authority is entirely privatized with almost all the port functions being under private control, with the public sector retaining a standard regulatory oversight. Despite this, public entities can be shareholders and gear the port toward strategies that are deemed to be of public interest. In these ports, the real estate of the port is privately owned (contrary to the situation in other port management models). This requires the transfer of ownership of such land from the public to the private sector.

The risk in this type of arrangement is that land can be sold for carrying out activities that are neither related to the port nor to maritime transport. Therefore, port land is usually sold to private parties with a mandate that the facilities retain their maritime role. In addition, along with the sale of port land to private interests, some governments may simultaneously transfer the regulatory functions to private companies. For example, in the United Kingdom, in the absence of a port regulator, privatized ports are essentially self-regulating.

Fully privatized ports are few and can be found mainly in the United Kingdom (e.g., Southampton) and in New Zealand. The decision to move to full privatization in the United Kingdom was taken in the 1980s for three main reasons:
-   To modernize institutions and installations, both of which often dated back to the early years of the industrial revolution, making them more responsive to the needs and wishes of the users.
-   To achieve financial stability and hit financial targets, with an increasing proportion of the financing coming from private sources.
-   To achieve labor stability and a degree of rationalization, followed by more labor participation in the new port enterprises.

The level of change from public service ports and tool ports (like the so-called autonomous ports in Southern Europe) to the landlord model has been significant. In many countries, port authorities are no longer permitted to carry out terminal handling services, either directly or indirectly via holding shares in stevedoring companies. In Figure 8.2 this is indicated as a general trend from left to right—from higher levels of governmental control toward more private control.

Each of the four mentioned models has strengths and weaknesses. Table 8.3 provides an overview of each port management model.

Table 8.3: Strengths and weaknesses of port management models

	Strengths	Weaknesses
Public Service Ports	– Superstructure development and cargo handling operations are the responsibility of the same organization (unity of command). – Port Cluster with specialized ports, for example, for liquid bulk, for RoRo, or for container, could be realized.	– There is either no role or only a limited role for the private sector in cargo handling operations (lack of internal competition), which leads to inefficiency. – There is less problem-solving capability and flexibility in cases of labor problems, which is because the port administration is also the major employer of port labor. – Wasteful use of resources and under-investment because of government interference and dependence on government budget. – Operations are less user-oriented and less market-oriented. – Political tariffs instead of cost-based prices for services. – Tendency to over-rate the port labor interests in port development.
Tool Ports	– Investments in port infrastructure and equipment (ship/shore equipment) are decided and provided by the public sector, thus avoiding duplication of facilities. – Low barriers to entry for new private market participants, for example, shipping lines, forwarder, etc. ("protective" competition).	– The port administration and private enterprise jointly share the cargo handling services (split operation), which can lead to conflicting situations. – As the private operators do not own major equipment, they tend to function as labor pools and do not develop into firms with strong balance sheets. This causes instability and in turn limits the future expansion of their companies. – Risk of underinvestment. – Lack of innovation.

Table 8.3 (continued)

Landlord Ports	– A clear distinction between the management of infrastructure and the provision of services. – Private terminal handling companies generally are better able to cope with market requirements. – Close interrelation of port authority and private terminal operator with regard to port development (realistic needs). – Innovative pushes from private service companies	– Endemic risk of overcapacity because of pressure from various private operators. – Risk of misjudging the proper timing of capacity additions. – Limited public budgets may hinder private business expansion (obstructive port authorities).
Private Ports	– No direct government interference. – Ownership of port land enables market-oriented port development and tariff policies. – • Maximum flexibility regarding investments and port operations.	– Possible absence of a port regulator. – There is a serious risk of underinvestment in port infrastructure. – The government loses its ability to execute a long-term economic development policy with respect to the port business. – • There is a serious risk of speculation with port land by private owners.

Source: World Bank Port Reform Toolkit; supplementations from author.

The historically dominating public ports could not match their corresponding growing market economies. The following enumeration summarizes most of the arguments that led to more commercialization and privatization. Public service and tool ports were not able:

– To provide services, which are efficient and cost-effective from the port user's perspective.
– To respond to changes in cargo handling technologies.
– To respond to the changing requirements of the port users.
– To provide choices of services and foster competition.
– To make timely capital investments to improve efficiency and expand capacity.
– To generate the funds needed to finance investments.
– To enforce labor discipline in the face of strong trade unions.

A trend toward more private sector integration via commercialization and privatization was the logical consequence of this.

8.3 Port Labor Organization

Once a sector relying on mostly occasional and low-skilled labor, port work today requires highly skilled port workers[4] and is an important factor of port management and success. To cope with the irregularity of port traffic and the ensuing fluctuations in labor demand, the port labor market has in many places been subject to specific laws, regulations, and collective agreements.[5] In most cases, these rules entail the reservation of temporary labor for a steadily available pool of registered workers who enjoy unemployment benefits or similar pay when there is no work available. Even if these arrangements take on very different shapes around the globe, access to the port labor market is often restricted under rules that differ from general labor laws. In addition to general questions regarding formal qualifications and training as well as labor health and safety, the port-specific question of the port labor regime–that is, the port labor organization–is of key interest here. The way port labor is organized has direct impact on port management.

Shipping business, and therefore port work, is not comparable to a typical 9 to 5, Monday through Friday industrial job. Ships arrive irregularly, and still today (e.g., due to weather conditions) are often not arriving on time. Delays of several hours are not untypical. Port work, and especially the work closely or directly related to the ship, must be very flexible and quick responding. In addition, since tight schedules of capital-intensive shipping often require 24/7 availability of port

---

4 The words "port worker" and "docker" are often used interchangeably. Here "port worker" is preferred as it is a more neutral and general term. In fact, experts argue that the word "docker," which came into use with the opening of closed dock and warehouse areas in the first half of the 19th century, has a pejorative or at least outmoded ring and that it should be replaced by port worker, as the latter term acknowledges that the profession now requires special skills, formal qualifications, and frequent training and relies on the use of sophisticated technology. However, workers' organizations continue to call their members dockers, and the famous antiliberalization slogan used by European unions was "proud to be a docker." In some European countries the English word "docker" still serves as the official, legal title of the port worker. The International Labor Organization (ILO) named port workers "dock workers" and discussed "dock work conventions."

5 For global rules and standards, visit the web pages of the ILO: http://www.ilo.org/global/standards/subjects-covered-by-international-labour-standards/dock-workers/lang--en/index.htm

work, port management has to offer adequate port services 24 hours a day, seven days a week.

Port workers, though, are human beings; they are not an undefined work force. This means that port workers require similar conditions to workers in other industries, and for this they organized themselves into unions. Labor unions, such as the International Longshore and Warehouse Union (ILWU) in the United States, are associations of workers who pursue common objectives and help protect the rights of workers. The port workers use this platform to bargain collectively on behalf of most workers. To be a part of the labor union, workers typically apply for membership and pay dues. Automation, fewer mass-production jobs, and increasing competition in labor markets have contributed to the decline in labor union membership in the 21st century in general, but typical port worker unions like the ILWU are still strong. All unions fight for fair payment, good working conditions, and the rights of the workers.

A solution to overcome the huge fluctuations in port worker employment is the creation of labor pools, with staff that can be shifted around as the need arises. These pools can smooth out variations in demand for labor among different employers and help prevent the build-up of labor, which could result in redundancy when the demand shifts. An example of such a pool is the company Gesamthafenbetriebs-Gesellschaft m.b.H. (GHBG) in the Port of Hamburg that works as a pool personnel service provider and labor lessor.[6] It is a company founded by employer associations and is not focused on profit, but on qualified labor supply. Approximately 1,100 of Hamburg's 5,000 port workers are employed by this pool. The terminals and port companies pay only for work that is needed, which is a great advantage for them. The fact that the costs per hour are higher compared with their own staff is the negative side of this solution, but due to the high fluctuations in workload, it is ultimately a win-win situation for both the port companies and the labor pool.

An additional advantage is that with more than 1,100 permanent pool workers (plus up to 250 part-time workers that can be hired), nearly all qualifications and certified skills are available for port companies. Setting up such labor-leasing companies sometimes requires special laws or regulations, but this is not always the case. The model of port labor pools is a widely accepted form of organization that supports the needs of port management to flexibly serve clients, but saves costs at the same time to stay profitable and survive competition. This system also serves the needs of the port worker to create sustainable, safe, and attractive work places in ports. Some pools not only serve one local port (like the Hamburg

---

6 For more details, refer to: www.gesamthafen.de

GHBG for the Port of Hamburg), but spread out to several other ports in the range, for example, when several smaller ports along a river or a coastline exist. In some cases, port worker pools are also working internationally; this is then the step from a special and often nonprofit local service provider to an international personnel service. However, the ideas behind these are comparable.

Guaranteeing fair and sustainable incomes for dockworkers is a major task for unions as well as for pools. Even though cargo handling activities in ports are currently increasingly capital-intensive, to the detriment of labor, it is still true that dockworkers' wages account for a major part of port operating costs. In any case, the wage rates fixed for dockworkers should at least be comparable with those in other jobs requiring a comparable level of effort, skill, and responsibility.

The question of dockworkers' remuneration may be subject to specific regulations or a collective agreement. It might also be fixed by the enterprise, or it may be covered by legislation applicable to other workers. The issue may also be addressed by a combination of these methods. In most countries, dockworkers are paid essentially on an hourly basis. Modern ports for productivity reasons, or due to competition from neighboring ports, often operate 24 hours a day, 7 days a week. In such cases, dock work is usually organized in shifts and therefore must be performed on the weekend or outside normal hours. A premium may be paid to workers for this inconvenience, although such working conditions are like many other workers such as policemen, medical doctors, nurses, taxi drivers, waiters, etc.

In some parts of the world—especially in the United States—the relationship between port management and the port worker (or port union) is unbalanced. It is natural that in a changing world disputes happen, including disputes between port unions and employers. Often work stoppages are the result of such conflicts. The right to strike is an essential means for defending workers' interests, even if certain conditions relating to the procedures of a strike need to be accepted and followed. The possible consequences of such work stoppages are well known: ships are delayed, inland transport held up, perishable goods damaged and rendered unusable, or exports hindered. If the work stoppage is prolonged, the impact on the national economy itself may be serious.

It is therefore of the utmost importance for both workers and employers that acceptable rules and circumstances should exist for the rapid settlement of conflicts and disputes. Necessary measures should be taken to prevent disputes from spreading and, where possible, to allow work to continue, pending their settlement. The often-complex procedures for settlement adopted in most countries vary according to the specific characteristics of each country. Some states leave dispute settlements to collective bargaining. Conciliation procedures are sometimes available to the parties concerned. In some cases, arbitration is provided where conciliation fails. However, it should be accepted by both sides that ports, as part of complex supply chains, should not be misused for individual group interests, as happens again and again in U.S. ports. The interests of port workers and port management should be balanced out, and political tools like laws and regulations should be used to find a balance. The best management model to support these processes is the landlord model.

According to ILWU sources,[7] or via U.S.-sources investigating the port labor market (McEachern, 2009, pages 289–290), all statements accept that ILWU port workers are paid well, or very well (the question is whether they earn 1.5 times the U.S. average, or up to 2.5 or 3.0 times of comparable industrial workers). McEachern named port workers the "highest blue-collar worker in the nation."

Without evaluating the level of the wages, it seems to be acceptable for port management and the public that the payments are high. Still, huge conflicts result from the way unions like ILWU push their interests. Many ports of the globally active logistics industry can not accept frequent strikes and cost-intensive frictions of supply chains. Therefore, bypassing the U.S. west coast and serving Central and West-American markets via other ports is at least after the widening of the Panama Canal a logical consequence. ILWU is a negative example of how particular interests destroy transportation chains and ultimately work places; this is a result that is obviously not in the interest of today's port worker and unionists.

8.4 Cultural and Religious Influence

In some parts of the world, port management is influenced by typical cultural or religious traditions and patterns. Some work interferences occur due to varying religious traditions, like praying five times a day, even when continuous work needs to be provided at the berth, or to visit a church or mosque during working hours. It is relatively easy to organize work activities around these religious obligations, unless bigger investments are needed. In some ports, mosques are built on port real estate, that is, port management is confronted with this topic. Overall, adequately accommodating the religious and cultural needs of port workers seems to be an easy task for most ports.

---

7 For a statement by Dean McGreath, president of ILWU Local 23 (Tacoma), refer to: https://www.seattletimes.com/business/local-business/seattle-tacoma-dockworkers-earn-less-than-reported-average/

Many ports have statements like the following in their code of conduct to ensure that people are treated equally:

- The Port of xxx is dedicated to maintaining and improving a work environment that extends equal opportunity to all individuals, regardless of their race, color, sex, religion, or national origin. Employment decisions shall be made in such a manner as to further the principle of equal employment opportunity.
- We affirm through this policy statement our continuing commitment to the principles of nondiscrimination and affirmative action.
- Through written programs of specific result-oriented goals, each member of port management is charged with the responsibility to take effective action to achieve the objective of equal opportunity for all.
- This policy applies to all employment practices, including recruiting, hiring, benefits, social and recreational programs, compensation, promotions, transfers, port-sponsored training and educational programs, downgrade, layoff, recall, and any other terms and conditions of employment.
- The Port will ensure that promotion decisions are in accordance with the principles of equal employment opportunity by imposing only valid requirements for promotional opportunities. Port policy prohibits racial, ethnic, religious, and sexual harassment. The port intends to continue to recognize the worth of individuals based solely upon their performance and contribution to the success of the port.

The religious or cultural tradition of only consuming fresh meat has some influence on trade and transportation. In some parts of the world, live animals are transported over long distances, what in and of itself is a usual procedure. It is a matter of fact that this only happens in some parts of the world, not globally. Livestock carrier and terminals for livestock are the result of this. Some of these terminals are huge, and handle thousands of live animals per day, and often there is nothing to criticize. But some of these terminals have come under criticism for their treatment of the livestock. For example, "Animals International"[8] frequently uncovers new forms of cruelty to transported animals. The unloading of cows, for example, from vessels with a gangway more than 3 m above the ground causes the first animals leaving the vessel to fall and die. The livestock behind them then breaks their bones when tripping over the bodies in front of them. This is a sad ordeal for dozens of lives. The brutal scenes of port workers "cleaning up" the berth with forklifts of dead and half-dead animals are hard to forget. All

---

8 For more details, refer to: https://www.animalsinternational.org

this for what is understood as "fresh meat"! It seems to be a fact that the wish for fresh meat does not seem to be in line with the treatment of these animals, which deserve respect and protection. However, the port manager allows procedures like this to happen.

The same criticism around these issues arose internationally concerning Norway, Iceland, and Japan, the last three countries in the world still hunting whales (and bringing said whales to port). The International Whaling Commission banned commercial whaling in 1986, but these three countries are arguing they are hunting whales for scientific purposes. Ports that allow such vessels to berth are ultimately part of the whale-hunting system and must live with criticism. Ports often say, "our business simply serves ships"; but in reality, port managers are responsible for the activities in their ports, even when these activities lead to critical questions.

Chapter 9
Port Commercialization and Privatization

9.1 Background for Port Reform

In many cases, changes in port systems toward commercialization or privatization are undertaken to improve efficiency and productivity and to reduce the role of government in port activity and/or port ownership. Privatization is often understood as a transfer of government services to the private sector. At this high level of understanding, it is important to have a clear definition of "commercialization" and "privatization." In line with the old, but still relevant UNCTAD paper "Guidelines for Port Authorities and Governments on Privatization of Port Facilities," we take the following definition:[1]

> Privatization is the transfer of ownership of assets from the public to the private sector or the application of private capital to fund investments in port facilities, equipment and systems.

In this definition, privatization implies that assets are completely transferred from the public sphere to private holders. This is not one smooth, comprehensive transition. Ports deciding to move toward privatization sometimes call the interim steps before full privatization "partly privatized," or even "commercialized." Commercialization, in this understanding, is the introduction of private management tools and methods to emphasize the profitable or commercial aspects of port business, but without a full transfer of ownership. The word commercialization describes an aspect of devolution and is sometimes described as a pure devolutionary process: the delegation of administrative power from a higher administrative level to a lower one. Devolution is a form of administrative decentralization, but does not highlight what the key target is: to create an inspiring commercial-minded environment for port management!

Because of the often-missing inspiring commercial environment in pure devolution processes, the term commercialization better describes what is intended. The same goes for the term corporatization. This word denotes the process of transforming state assets, government agencies, or municipal organizations into corporations. It does not imply that the transfer is combined with a new focus

---

1 UNCTAD, Gustaaf DeMonie: *Guidelines for Port Authorities and Governments on Privatization of Port Facilities*, Belgium, Antwerp 1998, page 1.

DOI 10.1515/9781547400874-009

on efficiency, productivity, and commercial success. Thus, we will stick to using "commercialization" in the meaning.

The goals of commercialization, in addition to reducing government ownership are to facilitate and stimulate economic growth and to help meet national development policy targets. The commercialization process often needs to be broken down into several steps, as most private companies are often specialized and therefore unable or unwilling to undertake all the functions of an entire port. Deciding to reorganize a port is never easy because numerous parties with vested interests are involved in the process. This explains the long time it takes from first initiatives toward a new port system. Before initial steps are taken toward privatization, public bodies in charge must ask: can a private company produce the goods and services that the public desires at a cheaper cost to the society than the public company, that is, would commercializing and privatizing increase efficiency? If the answer is yes, reorganization could bring benefits.

There are in fact many reasons for commercializing or privatizing a public-owned enterprise and to increase private sector involvement:

1. Desire to raise money (hard currency) by the sale of state assets
2. Reduction of external debt and/or drain of subsidies to state firms
3. Relieve government of high investment burdens
4. Increase private sector participation
5. Shift implementation and operating risks to private sector
6. Facilitate fast-track implementation
7. Widen capital ownership
8. Invigorate capital markets
9. Introduction of higher standards of efficiency of the economy generally, and/or of specific utilities and other services in particular
10. Attract foreign investment
11. Increase investment in utilities
12. Improve the efficiency of a service by opening it up to the private markets
13. Improve managerial expertise of international financial institutions
14. Compliance with the wishes of international financial institutions
15. Increase national prestige by implementing a fashionable policy
16. Gain electoral support by implementing a popular policy

Transferring ownership of a public institution like a service port or a tool port is one component of port commercialization and privatization. Additional fundamental requirements for the transfer are a clear legal and regulatory framework, a stable macroeconomic environment, and a viable business rationale. In many cases, experienced legal and consulting companies will assist the public institu-

tions on their way to increasing private sector involvement. This helps minimize the many risks on the way to privatization. The transfer itself can be organized in different ways:
- Sale of the existing unit as a whole
- Sale of the existing unit after breaking it down into several parts
- Sale of parts of the existing unit after dismantling it
- Sale of peripheral parts of an existing enterprise

9.2 Commercialization

The general objective of port commercialization is to make port management market oriented—that is, cost and revenue focused—and thus enable it to satisfy client needs. This objective is important for the success of any port reform. The notion of the market is an extremely important factor in port analysis and the restructuring process. Throughout the world, there are both successful and unsuccessful ports with varying structures and management styles. However, big or small, public or private, successful ports have one thing in common: they all are highly market oriented, while unsuccessful ports are not.

Profit and loss (or in short P/L) statements, which report costs and revenues, are a standard document for many working in the business sector. Public institutions, on the other hand, very often do not work with P/L statements. Traditionally an administration like a port authority receives a budget from the central planning ministry and must work with this budget over the year. The level of the budget depends on the budget requests from the years before. In other words, the amount of money a port receives for its annual budget depends on the planning and the budgeted volume from previous years. This means that administrations make sure to use every penny in their budget, otherwise their budget might shrink the next year. This is the reason why at the end of fiscal years money often must be spent "in time." A double-entry bookkeeping does not exist, and there are no incentives for port managers to cut costs or increase revenues. This is the traditional way of state planning and budgeting, but following the principle of subsidiarity, this is no longer acceptable for ports on the way to commercialization.

If public sector ports are not profitable, it may not be possible to privatize them until action has been taken to remove the causes for their losses. Thus, it may be necessary to first deregulate and commercialize ports. In this sense, commercialization can be seen as a step toward privatization. If ports are profitable over the long term, it is not simply because they have been commercialized, but because they have satisfied the market. In other words, if ports cannot make money for their development it is often because they have failed to adapt their organization and management to the market's requirements. Commercialization may pave the way toward market success, and it redefines the port authority's role by disengaging the public sector from the port activities, which are best done by the private sector. Port commercialization is foremost a political decision, although it must be carried out as an economic exercise. Commercialization is contingent on government policy rather than on the wishes of port managers.

A clear understanding of what the government intends to accomplish through its commercialization programs is essential. Some possible government objectives of private sector participation and commercialization are:

–   Improving efficiency and productivity of operations by harnessing the strengths of the private sector in minimizing costs and improving services.
–   Reducing the financial and administrative burden of the public sector by employing private sector resources to replace those of the public sector.
–   Generating increased revenue and reducing public investment.
–   Reducing government risk in terms of revenue expectation by divorcing private operator payments from the amount of cargo handled. In addition, the private sector is increasingly being invited to fund, build and operate port projects, or buy the right to operate existing facilities, which can release funds for the government to invest in other sectors.
–   Social objectives, for example, commercialization being used as tool of broader social policies aimed at redistributing wealth or moving marginal communities closer to the middle of the economic mainstream.
–   Promoting private sector involvement in the economy to supplement government spending, which in some Asian economies has been the primary driving force of the economy.
–   Attracting new or additional business and trade by inviting private sector participants that are already involved in trade or transport services (e.g., shipping lines) with the aim of a port user becoming an investor who will funnel additional traffic through the port.

There is sufficient worldwide experience in commercialization to illustrate the numerous approaches, which, under the right circumstances, can be successful in the achievement of national objectives. The optimal approach will reflect the economic and social setting and unique characteristics of specific projects. Whether the process will be realized via organizational restructuring, corporatization, management contracts, service contracts or via leasing, ultimately implementing commercial or market driven principles in management is what counts.

The introduction of double-entry bookkeeping and a focus on both costs and revenues is an essential tool on this way. The landlord model below is a guideline for port reorganization. This model allows several opportunities for commercialization, for example, for selected terminals that will be made profitable to keep the business and hold the work places and tax payers locally, or even for a general division between public tasks in administration and commercialized tasks for services. Building joint ventures for selected units like a terminal is also a way of introducing commercial principles.

9.3 Privatization

The theoretical underpinning for privatization is the same as for commercialization: compared to publicly owned enterprises, private companies can take advantage of market conditions to operate efficiently. Further, unlike private-sector companies, publicly owned and operated enterprises are not exposed to full competition in the product and capital markets. Another factor to consider is that unlike private companies, public sector enterprises cannot go bankrupt. Finally, compared to private companies, public-sector enterprises are much more likely to experience both direct political interference in operating decisions and potential conflicts between the government's role as an owner and operator of an enterprise as well as its regulator. Consequently, the link between revenues (or rewards) and cost control (efficiency) is often weak or absent altogether in public-sector enterprises. In such an environment, double-entry bookkeeping principles are not relevant.

Several studies and surveys provide evidence that privatization (in the sense of transfer of ownership of assets from the public to the private sector or the application of private capital to fund investments in port facilities, equipment and systems) generally leads to improved performance over public-sector operations. Studies in the early 1990s examining divestitures of state-owned enterprises provide persuasive empirical evidence of the benefits of privatization. The net welfare changes in terms of gains and losses to government, buyers, consumers, workers, and others, have been identified to be positive; the magnitudes of the gains were substantial. Still today, privatization processes for ports from Greece to Canada expect similar gains both for the ports and the national transport sector.

Whether it is full or partial (less than 100% of the shares transferred to a private firm), privatization has the potential to generate efficiency improvements. It enables an enterprise to take advantage of the stronger incentives associated with private ownership, reduces the potential for political interference, and exposes the enterprise to the full range of capital market disciplines and financing alternatives. Full privatization of a complete terminal has the potential to yield substantially greater benefits than partial privatization. The emergence of Global Port Operators like PSA of Singapore or DP World of Dubai is thus a logical development.[2] These companies take full advantage of the fact that experienced niche operators—here for container terminals—with sound financial backgrounds, huge international client contacts, and experienced staff are needed to fill the gap in port operations. Privatization paves the way for them.

The French Example

One of the latest and most comprehensive examples of port reform occurred in France recently. The main reasons for the reform were:
- Poor efficiency
- Little incentive for the private sector to invest
- A harmful confrontation between the state and a heavily unionized workforce[3]

A long wave of port reforms started in France in 1992 (LOI n° 92-496 du 9 juin 1992 modifiant le régime du travail dans les ports maritimes) and was aimed at transferring the port workforce and handling equipment to private operators. The process was completed with the passing of major laws in 2004 and 2008. Those laws modernized the ports code, and their enforcement began in 2010, reforming the French port system "réforme portuaire." Some of the main aims of the reform were to include the local authorities, representatives of the private sector and workers' unions more extensively within the ports' steering committees, and to create a better environment for collective bargaining. The port reforms changed the management and gradually permitted the shift from the tool port to the landlord port model.

Regarding industrial relations, the 2008 port reform (in force since 2010) helped to bring the uncompleted 1992 reform to full completion. Cargo handling equipment was transferred to private operators. The 1992 reform allowed the signature of concession schemes, creating privately operated terminals. The 2008 reform made a clear distinction between "sovereign tasks" (police, security), and handling operations: infrastructure, accesses, maintenance works, and planning duties, which the ports now must follow. The port reform in France thus created a landlord port system, whereby integrated operators are responsible for owning,

---

2 Also refer to Chapter 11 for further details on global port operators.
3 Compare the French arguments with Table 8.3.

investing, and maintaining handling equipment, operated by a directly employed and controlled workforce. The reforms have had a direct impact on port structure and management:

- The transfer of handling equipment to private operators signaled the end of the tool port model.
- Whereas some of the workforce was already on the private handling company's payroll, crane operators were still employed by the ports themselves. Now that restructured handling and stevedoring companies employ and control the entire workforce, productivity should rise.

Those two aspects of the reforms in France have been completed in 2011 and have a direct impact on port management. Finally, the former seven metropolitan ports, before named "Port Autonome de ...", renamed themselves as Grand Port Maritime/Large Maritime Port (GPM).[4] The reform simultaneously has transferred the cargo handling activity to private cargo handling companies to strengthen the competitiveness to compete more efficiently with other European ports.

The French example indicates that there are several objectives when commercializing ports. One of the most obvious is to relieve a financially strapped government by turning to the private sector for an infusion of capital required to modernize and sustain port operations, or to bolster the national treasury. Another is to reap economic benefits from competition by cutting labor costs, eliminating publicly sanctioned monopolies, reducing port labor forces, and removing other institutional barriers that discourage innovation and isolate port management from the exigencies of global competition. The French example proves this list of objectives can be transformed into real organizational changes. French ports today are more competitive than ever before.

9.4 Ways to Privatize

Privatizing comes in many forms, and the government can undertake one method or a mix of approaches (this applies to the privatizing of any public enterprise):
1. **Contracting out:** A government/public authority contracts part(s) of its operations, such as the handling and storing of goods, to a private company.

---

4 See, for example, Port of Marseille. The old tool port name was "Port Autonome de Marseille"; today the official name after transformation is Grand Port Maritime de Marseille (GPMM).

2. **Management buy-out:** The public authority transfers the shares or the ownership to former management stuff. The argument for this mainly is continuity; the former management knows best how to survive in the market.
3. **Franchising:** Handing over the exclusive rights to market a product or provide specific services, often in a specific area such as the provision of the right to carry passengers on certain routes.
4. **Joint venture:** Forming a joint enterprise between the government and a private company, where the responsibilities and duties of both partners are specified.
5. **Leasing:** Government owned assets/facilities are leased out to conduct private business. The terms and conditions of leasing must be agreed upon.
6. **Management contracts:** Via contracts the provision of management services by private companies to a public enterprise, with certain controls being retained by the government.
7. **Public offering of shares:** The government undertakes the sale of a large block of shares or all its shares to the public.

Commercialization and privatization can inspire strong emotions in people and often there is opposition to privatization from various parties, like dock workers and/or unions. This pushback must be identified and overcome if privatization is to be successful. Such opposition can be grouped under three basic categories:
1. **Financial:** The overall performance and conditions of country/company/market, etc.
2. **Attitude:** The bureaucratic resistance stemming from the loss of kickbacks (bribes) for officials of the public organization and the loss of job security/power. This is highly likely in countries where there is no welfare system and hence no guarantee of any unemployment benefits.
3. **Political:** The problems associated with nationalism, tribalism, and the distribution of gains from privatization.

Former state enterprises, with a high number of employees, fear commercialization and privatization activities. Opposition can also come from politicians and influential civil servants who fear that privatization will put their position and influence at risk.

If we summarize all potential opposition, we will come to the following list of arguments against commercialization, which should be taken very seriously:
1. **Reduction in employment:** Quite often, state-owned enterprises (SOEs) are created to provide employment, and therefore an excess number of people are employed by these organizations. Thus, to these employees, privatization

automatically means job losses. Looking back at the last decades, this has been the case in Argentina, India, and the countries of the commonwealth of independent states (CIS) (e.g., USSR), the three Baltic states, and former eastern bloc countries like Poland, the Czech, Republic and Eastern Germany.

2. **Fear of closure:** Again, a very realistic fear, especially felt in Africa and in Eastern Germany after the opening of the iron curtain, where there was no justification for the existence of these SOEs. Closure of the SOE does not necessarily mean closure of all units, as often parts of it can be salvaged.

3. **Loss of control:** This is the fear that the control of these enterprises will be gained by foreigners or unpopular ethnic groups and being at their mercy. (Often the SOEs that are privatized are the most profitable ones as they are the ones likely to appeal to private companies, be that local or foreign), for example, in Chile, Venezuela, and Mexico.

4. **Reduction of control:** Over the economy/society and loss of patronage opportunities, for example, in Brazil, and—again—in East Germany where the most vociferous opposition came from within the organizations, that is, those in control of them.

5. **Fear of dismissal:** Once privatization is completed, many employees fear the risk of being fired because of increased productivity; others than the "reduction of employment" (no. 1) that often happens soon after the transfer, this is a long-term risk employees fear, for example, in Ecuador, where vested interests from within the SOEs resisted privatization.

6. **Reduction in national prestige:** That foreigners can dictate is also a strong argument against commercialization and privatization; this happened in Nigeria after oil had been discovered in the 1960s of last century, and when the export of huge quantities of oil via tanker started in the 1970s; all important port and export facilities have been controlled by multinational companies.

7. **Increase of social imbalances:** Further concentration of wealth and widening class distinctions.

8. **Increase in corruption:** Chances for bribes, etc., for (senior) officials of the SOEs being privatized.

It is not unusual for transport sector privatization to take 10–15 years to be completed. But, daunting as this may sound, if the benefits are sound and the private sector can provide them, it is far more efficient and profitable in the long run to commercialize and privatize. As past processes have shown, almost all port services (safe customs, safety at work, port health, and other such matters of national government policy), can be commercialized or privatized and be performed in a more efficient manner. Services eligible for commercialization and privatization are displayed in the table below.

Table 9.1: Services eligible for commercialization and privatization

stevedoring, aboard and ashore	vessel supply
cargo handling	provisions
loading	water
discharging	fuel
tallying	consumables
weighing	vessel service
marking	towing
drying	docking/berthing
cleaning	mooring
sorting	cleaning
consolidation/deconsolidation	painting
storing	port services
distributing	supplying
surveying	cleaning/waste removal
lashing/delashing	maintenance and repair
repairing	etc.

Depending on the nature of a port, its location, specialization, and other criteria, there are several additional services that could and should be considered for commercialization. The rule is that anything other than territorial and sovereignty functions may be commercialized or privatized, if the quality of services improves, prices decrease, and the state monopoly is not being replaced by private monopolies.

Chapter 10
Port Governance

10.1 Port Authorities

The World Bank Port Reform Toolkit states that, "Ports usually have a governing body referred to as the port authority, port management, or port administration. Port authority is used widely to indicate any of these three terms. The term port authority has been defined in various ways. In 1977, a commission of the European Union (EU) defined a port authority as a 'State, Municipal, public, or private body, which is largely responsible for the tasks of construction, administration and sometimes the operation of port facilities and, in certain circumstances, for security.' This definition is sufficiently broad to accommodate the various port management models existing within the EU and elsewhere."[1] The term "authority" implies a specific form of public management, often associated with characteristics like "bureaucratic" or "ineffective." But "authority" in our understanding is the generic term for the body with statutory responsibilities in managing the whole port, whether public or private.

Ports authorities are established at all levels of government: national, regional, provincial, or local/municipal. The most common form is a local port authority, which is an authority overseeing only one port area. However, national port authorities still exist in various countries such as Tanzania and South Africa.

In a 2011 report by the European Sea Port Organisation (ESPO),[2] the author summarized four basic functions that port authorities may have:
1. Landlord
2. Regulator
3. Operator
4. Community Manager

The landlord function can be considered the principal function in this context. Although many port authorities are not the owner of the land within their jurisdiction, most of them have been given the legal rights to lease or rent real estate and/ or specific infrastructure like quay walls and terminals to interested parties. The other three functions have changed considerably in recent times, with increased

---

1 Port Reform Toolkit 2007, page 77.
2 Verhoeven 2011, page 16ff.

DOI 10.1515/9781547400874-010

private interests in port business (refer to Chapter 8 for details). Most notably, the function of operator has ceased to exist.

In addition to the functions mentioned above, ESPO identifies three basic types of port authorities, according to their self-image and business behavior:
1. Conservator
2. Facilitator
3. Entrepreneur

For the overall performance of ports, ESPO differentiates between four essential factors in total, two of them (1 and 2) being formal factors and two (3 and 4) informal factors:[3]
1. Legal and statutory framework
2. Financial capability
3. Balance of power with government
4. Management culture

All four factors are highly inter-related, but Table 10.1 shows the space between these for different functions and activities. The characterization of the three types of business behaviors clearly indicates that there is much room for port authorities to facilitate trade and port business, as well as to be engaged in own business development. The bottom line in Table 10.1 "geographical dimension" expresses the fact that the more pro-active authorities are, the more likely they enlarge their business beyond their own borders and are active on regional, national or global levels. Successful authorities have shown that the following is no contradiction: to be active globally and to fulfill a role as community partners; although it must be said that global activities of port authorities are rare exceptions (only very few authorities are active globally) and are concentrated on core functions.

Which of the four different functions a specific port authority will play depends on the shareholders, be it a ministry, a municipal administration, another institutional body, or a mix of these. The board of shareholders is the port's principal steering body. The ownership in all these cases is a public one. In addition to the shareholders or owners, port authorities often include additional stakeholder groups as members of their steering and/or supervising committees. They do this to include the interests of these various groups into the regional port business. This group is often referred to as the port community.

---

3 Verhoeven 2011, page 18ff.

Table 10.1: ESPO typology of port authorities

Type Function	Conservator	Facilitator	Entrepreneur
Landlord	Passive real estate "manager": – continuity and maintenance – dev. mainly left to others (go-vernmental /priv. sector) – financial revenue from real estate on "tariff" basis	Active real estate "broker": – continuity, maintenance, and improvement – development broker and coinvestor – includes urban and environ-mental real estate brokerage – financial revenue from real estate on commercial basis Mediator in commercial B2B rela-tions between service providers and port customers Strategic partnerships with inland ports, dry ports, and other seaports	Active real estate "developer" – continuity, maintenance, and improvement – direct investor – includes urban and environ-mental real estate development – financial revenue from real estate on commercial basis – financial revenue from non-core activities Direct commercial B2B negotiations with port customers – ctive pursuit of market niches Direct investments in inland ports, dry ports and other seaports
Regulator	Passive application and enforce-ment of rules and regulations mainly set by other agencies Financial revenue from regulator role on "tariff" basis	Active application and enforcement of rules and regulations through cooperation with local, regional, and national regulatory agencies + setting of own rules and regulations Provide assistance to port com-munity to comply with rules and regulations Financial revenue from regulator role on "tariff" basis with differential charging options for sustainability	Idem facilitator Idem facilitator + selling expertise and tools outside the port Financial revenue from regulator role on commercial basis
Operator	Mechanistic application of concession policy (license-issuing window)	Dynamic use of concession policy, in combination with real estate broker role "Leader in dissatisfaction" about performance of private port ser-vices providers Provide services of general economic interest and specialized commercial services	Dynamic use of concession policy, in combination with real estate develop-ment role Shareholder in private port service providers Provide services of general economic interest as well as commercial services Provide services in other ports
Community Manager	Not actively developed	Economic dimension: – solve hinterland bottlenecks – provide training and education – provide IT services – promotion and marketing – lobbying	Idem facilitator type but economic dimension with more direct commercial involvement
Geogr. Dimen.*	Local	Local + Regional	Local + Regional + Global

Source: Verhoeven 2011, page 17.   * = Geographical Dimension

In most port authorities, the shareholders appoint a kind of supervisory unit consisting of shareholders and/or stakeholders, which guides the authority in its general and strategic tasks. The supervisory unit decides about the organization and regulates the balance of power with the government. This means that this supervising body sets the framework for potential activities and agrees or disagrees about the basic function the authority should have, that is, it decides how far and to what extent possible facilitating and entrepreneurial responsibilities shall be or can be fulfilled by the authority. Regarding Table 10.1, the supervisory unit decides about the type and intensity of the port authority's activities.

Figure 10.1 describes a typical organizational structure of a port authority. The steering and supervisory body on top of the decision-making hierarchy is a "supervisory unit." These units have different names, like:
- Board of directors
- Commissioners
- Supervisory board
- Board of trustees, etc.

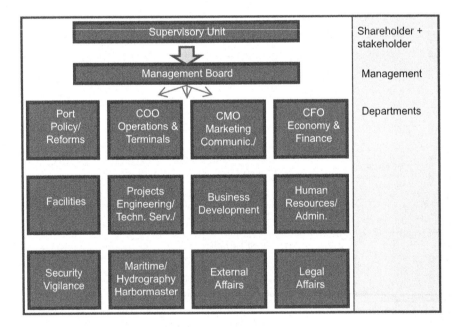

Figure 10.1: Organizational structure of a port authority

When the supervisory body is organized as a unit close to public authorities, then directors of other public bodies (e.g., ministries) are often members of the board, and consequently the institution is named "board of directors." The stakeholders in this set up are experts from other ministries. This set up can often be found in smaller ports. If board members are selected based on their individual skills and expertise, the supervisory body is called a "board of commissioners." Here the institutional aspect ranks second. This kind of supervision is typical in the United States. When mixed groups of interests are included, the resulting board is often called a "supervisory board." The seats in these boards are linked to institutions, like unions, and these institutions decide who gets nominated to be a board member. This form is typical for the bigger European landlord ports. In some countries, like India, ports are set up as trusts. Consequently, the members of the steering group are called Trustees, and the board is the "Board of Trustees." This form is very similar to the board of directors (though with a different legal and tax status).

In most of the ports worldwide, the supervisory board appoints the management of the ports. For a large port, this includes the chief executive officer (CEO), the chief operating officer (COO), the chief financial officer (CFO) and in some ports also a chief marketing officer (CMO). These titles describe the port's core functions. The position titles often vary. Especially in small- and medium-sized ports, the CEO is often called the "port director." This is an old-style title, descended from the public history of the respective port; but often this title is used with pride and honor. Here in this section we will try to accurately describe the different titles and the functions the title-holders perform.

Figure 10.1 shows twelve typical departments, which can often be found in the organization charts of ports. It goes without saying that smaller ports have fewer departments as they have fewer functions to fulfill and/or they are more specialized. Marketing, sales, communications, and external affairs are often combined into one department in smaller ports. The same is true for financial, human resources, administration, and legal affairs departments; these tasks can also be bundled into one office. Larger ports on the other hand need to have "more" and also "more detailed" departments. In this sense, Figure 10.1 should be considered as a typical overview of large ports. For the few mega ports around the globe, some authorities go into even more detail. For example, the COO might have specific departments for all modes of transport as well as for the port infrastructure. In this case the operations department could be structured this way:
- Port infrastructure (mainly roads and open sea access)
- Port railway
- Port inland waterway (access and specialized facilities)

Finally, it is the nature of the port that dictates its organizational structure. A huge liquid bulk port must be prepared to deal with all questions of pipelines, pumping stations, tank farms, jetties, dangerous and hazardous goods regulations, etc. Consequently, individual departments focusing specifically on these tasks might be created.

In case the authority is not fully public, there is an important point affecting authorities established as joint stock companies. Generally, port authorities are responsible for operating the entire port. In the event of a landlord port situation, a corporatized or privatized port authority must ensure a level playing field among many terminal operators and other service providers (regulatory function). To avoid conflicts of interest, a legal act should explicitly regulate the powers and duties of the port authority in relation to private operators with respect to investments and share participation. Such special port laws can be found in many ports; they set the legal frame for port activities.

10.2 Sphere of Activity: The PA-Paradox

Port authorities are confronted with the system-inherent problem that they are considered local business development creators, which facilitate and develop businesses, create jobs, and enable tax revenues (and, in the case of tool ports, carry out port services). Due to the nature of ports, this in most cases means "developing maritime trade," that is, shipping business. Port authorities shall facilitate the local business and support the local community by attracting (global) maritime trade. This exactly is the port authority, or PA-Paradox: The expectation is inconsistent with the performance potential!

The following are statements published on the websites of major ports, expressing what the port authority should do (the "expectations"):
1. Develop the port as a global hub and intermodal maritime center
2. The port powers global trade and goods movement
3. The port stimulates the economy and attracts business
4. The main issue in port policy is a swift, safe, and environmentally sound implementation of goods traffic, both over water, road, and rail
5. The port plays a crucial role in the development of international trade as well as the land and national economy
6. Our port secures 1 million jobs throughout the country
7. Our port has always been a key factor in economic development, etc.

These expectations are very high, but—unfortunately—unrealistic for the PAs to achieve. The real sphere of PA activity and the targets they can realistically achieve differ very much from their stated goals; this is the PA-Paradox:

Table 10.2: The PA-Paradox

PA targets - expressed in PA mission statements	Expect.* "we want to do.."	Possib.* "we can do…"	Key Business Driver - who else can do
increase port throughput/goods movement	+	-	Im- and Export-Industry
attract shipping lines	+	(-)	Terminal Operator
create jobs	+	(+)	Terminals, Port Industry
create tax income	+	(-)	Terminals, Port Industry
attract port industry / industrial cluster	+	-	regional economic environment/business climate
connect the country with the world	+	+/-	Shipping Lines
create a global hub	+	-	Shipping Lines, Forwarder, Hinterland Logistics Ind.
stimulate economic development	+	(-)	Business climate (PA neg. influence)
increase global trade	+	-	Im- and Export-Industry

* Expect.=Expectations; Possib.=Possibilities; **with:** + = yes   (+) = partly yes   +/- = indifferent   (-) = nearly no   - = no

Many PA mission statements list similar aims, but are their aims even attainable? Let's check. Key goals commonly outlined are:

1.   The PA shall increase the port throughput

This is not possible for an authority that provides and/or operates infrastructure. Ports in global networks are providing the necessary infrastructure to change between modes of transportation, for example, to unload cargo from trains and load onto vessels. Besides this core function, ports and PAs can take over supportive or complimentary functions, like ship assistance or traffic management, but the infrastructure provider has no direct influence on the cargo, the amount shipped, and on its route. All this lies in the hand of the im- and export industry and their partners. Therefore, in Table 10.2 the possibility to achieve this mission statement target is marked with a negative sign.

2.   PAs shall attract shipping lines

Most PAs are not active in port operations, and so they can not offer any service to shipping lines. The lines are looking for partners that (as core business) can load and unload their vessels. This is a service offered by terminal operators, because they have the necessary facilities like cranes and yard operation equipment. Most of the authorities do not offer this service. Only smaller PAs offer this service, but in this case they fulfill terminal operator tasks, not typical PA tasks. Therefore, in Table 10.2 the function to attract shipping lines is marked as "nearly no."

3. PAs shall create jobs

Port authorities are often seen as local job machines: they shall create business and secure jobs. This is only possible on a lower level, which is very close to public business. PAs can create jobs inside the ports and they can take over a lot of supportive and complementary functions; but all these PA-created jobs are ultimately financed by taxpayers, and all these jobs are inside the public sphere. Private business jobs can not be created by the PA directly; this lies in the hands of terminal and service operators and port industry. However, it is possible for PAs to create public sphere jobs; therefore, the possibility is marked as "partly possible."

4. PAs shall increase tax income

Ports are, without a doubt, important local businesses. But compared with stevedoring companies, warehouse and logistics providers, forwarders, railway companies, or other port-related companies like refineries or factories, the potential of PAs to raise tax income for local communities is very limited. To increase or decrease business is not in the hand of the port authorities; therefore, in Table 10.2 the paradox marked the possibility to achieve this target with "nearly no."

Other arguments like the creation of a global hub port status or port industry cluster are of the same nature: nearly impossible for a public authority to achieve. Why do port authority mission statements veer so far from what they can accomplish?

A few answers are possible:
1. PAs are not aware what a mission statement is.
2. PAs over-rate and overemphasize incentives.
3. PAs consider themselves "the port."

Ad 1: The literature of business economics provides several definitions of what mission and vision are. Here we will agree that a mission is what an authority is and why it exists, while the essence of a vision is a forward-looking view of what the authority wishes to become. In this sense, mission statements like the ones listed above are statements that define the role a specific port authority plays in the community. The mission statement refers to a need of the (local) community and reflects the PAs scope of business activities. Broader definitions include the wider scope (i.e., the development of the whole port), but most of them realistically refer to the tasks an organization can achieve. In strategic management literature, mission statements are clearly understood.

Mission statements should be:
- Feasible
- Precise
- Clear
- Motivating
- Distinctive
- Indicate major components of strategy
- Indicate how objectives are to be accomplished

Mission statements of port authorities can and do vary in length, content, format, and specialization, and they are a clearly visible and public part of the strategic port management. Members of the steering boards take this strategic part of the business very seriously. It is thus very unlikely that the authorities are not aware of the content and importance of these statements, nor that they mixed it up with their long-term vision.

Ad 2: Infrastructure providers depend on the business of their users. Port authorities provide infrastructure and can only anticipate how their business might grow. Infrastructure provision is an incentive for business development, and sometimes the economy and trade grow as predicted. However, there are also examples of port infrastructure investments producing little to no economic effect—despite millions and millions of Euros or dollars being invested. There is no automatism in trade economics! It is very likely that port authorities underestimate risks by just providing infrastructure incentives like yards, basins, or hinterland connections, or—in other words—over-rate and overemphasize the possible benefits of creating infrastructure incentives.

Based on the author's nearly three decades of experience with port authorities, it can be said with confidence that this has to do with the personal behavior of port authority leaders and their intention to set themselves up as monuments; this very often to stimulate future memory of their outstanding achievements. Many terminals, quay walls, roads, or famous places in port areas are named after important PA leaders; and it is not rarely the case that these infrastructures are built because an ambitious leader had a personal vision of what the port's function should be. Sometimes these local heroes over-rate what realistically can be achieved. Associations of taxpayers in several countries frequently publish cases of wasted tax funds, and ports (port authorities) are unfortunately on this list. In Germany, the tax payers association annually publishes a "Schwarzbuch" (black book) where extreme cases of wasted taxes are listed. Projects in a port like Hamburg are in these lists.[4]

Ad 3: Port authorities often have the whole scope of port activities in mind when talking about a mission and objectives. Also, it is true that activities like fixing contracts for port operators have an influence on this business. But it should realistically be stated that many of these contracts have an extremely long time horizon, as in thirty years or more. Further, often these contracts are so-called rolling contracts, for example, when the remaining time for a terminal operator is less than ten years and the operator wants to invest in new equipment having a depreciation period of twenty years, the terminal contract will be renewed for another thirty-year period. This example demonstrates that port authorities have an influence beyond their core activities, but it is limited. However, the authorities often consider themselves as "the port," and since no other institution is taking over this part, it is very likely that port authorities are not clear in their scope.

Arguments 2 and 3 lead to the PA-Paradox, that is, the inconsistency between what the port authority wants to achieve and what it realistically can achieve. An increased negative role in this context stems from port marketing. Very often, marketing people simplify the context and interdependencies, which then leads to inaccurate statements about what the PA can achieve. Over the years these simplifications, combined with the intention to rule the whole port, result in mission statements like the ones mentioned above. For many ports, it is time to reformulate the PA vision, mission, and objectives.

Within a transportation chain, port authorities have a clearly defined role as infrastructure provider. This should be the core business expressed in a PA's mission and objectives. The vision may go beyond and could include statements about trade, shipping, forwarding, and other businesses, but should always be based on the core tasks. Especially internationalization or globalization targets (i.e., the "global dimension" in Table 10.1) should be considered with extreme caution.

---

4 Bund der Steuerzahler e.V.: Das Schwarzbuch. Die öffentliche Verschwendung 2016/2017: Kreislaufbaggerung im Hafen. The Case of Dredging in Port of Hamburg. Berlin, Germany 2017. See also: www.steuerzahler.de

10.3 Objectives of a Port Authority

The core objective of a port authority is to exercise jurisdiction over a port territory and provide and develop the necessary infrastructure of this economic and functional unit. The legal basis for this unit's existence is often a special port law that provides the legal status for the authority. Typical technical and navigational port tasks have already been mentioned in Chapters 8.2 and 9.1. In nearly all ports (with the exception of private ports), the objectives are aligned with the macroeconomic goals of the nation and the business needs of the region, such as strengthening the local economy, creating jobs, etc.; although the authority itself has only limited possibilities to achieve these goals. What needs to be worked out is a more precise set of objectives for a typical port authority that is necessary to provide and develop the infrastructure; and this without stepping into the trap of the PA-Paradox.

A port authority's powers and duties regarding land management are regulated according to port law. Special attention should be paid to the laws governing ownership and use of port land. A port authority may own the land or have a perpetual or time-specific right to use the land. Powers to act as a landlord may need to be specifically elaborated, as well as the limitations of such powers, such as the interdiction of the sale of port land. While the authority is engaged in, or provides for, construction of operational infrastructure like quay walls and waterways, the maintenance of such infrastructure constitutes a duty for the authority. The port's law should specify the exact responsibilities of the port authority and those of the state with respect to investments in basic and operational infrastructure, port road access, maritime accesses, and rail and waterway infrastructure as well as hinterland connections.

The fundamentals for setting the port authority's task frame have already been listed in the UNCTAD Handbook for Port Planners in Developing Countries:[5]

- **Investment:** Port authorities should have the power to approve proposals for port investment.
- **Financial policy:** Power to set common financial objectives for infrastructure investments (e.g., required return on investment defined on a common basis), with a common policy on what infrastructure will be funded.
- **Tariff policy:** Power to regulate rates and charges as required for protecting public interests.

---

5 UNCTAD Handbook for Port Planners, page 5ff.

- **Labor policy:** Power to set common recruitment standards, a common wage structure, and common qualifications for promotion for public port staff; and the power to approve common labor union procedures.
- **Licensing:** Power to establish guidelines for licensing.
- **Information and research:** Power to collect, collate, analyze, and disseminate statistical information on port activity for general use, and to sponsor research into port matters as required.
- **Legal:** Power to act as legal advisor.

All these fundamentals are still relevant framework parameters for port authorities and set the frame for specific objectives. In addition, the following two fundamentals should be added to meet today's requirements:
- **Environment:** Port authorities should have the power to set standards for environmental protection and sustainable development inside the port area; including the water areas. The sustainable development of the port should also be part of the authority's constitution.
- **Security:** Power to set safety and security standards according to national and international law or agreements (e.g., CTPAT).

Based on these fundamentals, the scope of objectives for a port authority could be outlined as below. Here it must clearly be stated that the authority is responsible to achieve the objectives; this does not automatically mean that all tasks must be carried out by the authority itself. Via outsourcing with licenses or subcontracting, the authority can transfer some of the tasks for reaching the objectives to other companies or institutions.

Typical *objectives for a port authority* that should also be considered in the port law are:
- **Administrator:** Administration, management, maintenance, rehabilitation, and renovation of operational infrastructure and the port area.
- **Contractor:** Establishment of contractual (concession or lease) and other conditions (public license) for private operators to provide port services and to guarantee intraport competition.
- **Regulator:** The authority sets and/or supervises the regulations of marine safety and security, and ensures public order inside the port area.
- **Planner:** The port authority is responsible for planning the physical development for future operations and capital investments.
- **Harbormaster:** The port authority must secure the nautical services and facilities inside the port and/or on the fairways, including coordination of berthing and unberthing of vessels.

- **Safeguard:** The port authority is responsibly safeguarding the port environment.
- **Marketer:** The port authority must secure that the tasks of economic development as well as port marketing and promotion are assigned.
- **Logistics partner:** Especially in smaller ports, the authority may take over cargo handling, storing, and other logistics functions (if not possible to be fulfilled by others).
- **Proxy:** The port authority is the responsible body for ancillary activities as well as the contact point for port-related topics (in case new topics came up).

In Figure 10.2, all bubbles are the same size; this indicates that all the objectives are of equal importance. This is not the case in reality; some objectives are more important than others because the nature of trade determines the real structure of the respective authority. Port authorities in an area with huge crude oil export and only very few additional trades need to highlight other objectives than ones that are in huge international competition, for example, like for container trades in East Asia.

Figure 10.2: Objectives of a typical port authority

Figure 10.2 illustrates the PA from an organizational point of view. In addition to its core function, authorities may provide supportive or complementary functions. But here we should come back to the basic typology and ask, are the share and stakeholders looking for a "conservator" as described in Table 10.1, are they looking for a "facilitator," or do they expect the authority to act as an "entrepreneur"? These basic questions needed to be answered first, before creating a hierarchy of objectives.

A key role for many port authorities is as administrator or "passive manager," with the responsibility of managing the real estate within the port area. This management includes economic exploitation, long-term development, and the upkeep of basic port infrastructure, such as fairways, berths, access roads, and tunnels.

Regarding the regulatory powers, the authority is responsible for applying conventions, laws, rules, and regulations. As a public organ, it is responsible for observance of conventions and laws regarding public safety and security, environment, navigation, and health care. Port authorities also issue port bylaws, comprising many rules and regulations with respect to the behavior of vessels in port, use of port areas, and other issues. Often, extensive police powers are also assigned to the port authority.

Serving as port planner in coordination and close cooperation with the regional and local government is a complicated affair, especially for large ports located within or near a city. The port planner must consider:
– The consistency of plans with the general terms of land use that have been set by the competent authority.
– The total set of interconnected port-city relations that exist; ports are often important parts of city and regional development plans.
– The impact of port development proposals on the immediate surroundings (environment, traffic, facilities, and roads).
– The appropriateness of port development proposals in the context of international, national, and regional port competition.

Oversight of nautical operations should be within a port authority's mandate and is often referred to as the harbormaster's function. This position generally comprises all legal and operational tasks related to the safety and efficiency of vessel management within the boundaries of the port area. The harbormaster's office allocates berths and coordinates all services necessary to berth and unberth a vessel. These services include pilotage, towage, mooring and unmooring, and vessel traffic services (VTS). Often, the harbormaster is also charged with a leading role in management of shipping and port-related crises (e.g., collisions, explosions, natural disasters, or discharge of pollutants). In view of its general safety aspects, the harbormaster's function has a public character.

A variety of ancillary functions such as pilotage, towage and ship chandlering, fire protection services, linesmen services, port information services, and liner and shipping agencies exist within the port community. Large port authorities usually do not provide these services, except for pilotage and towage. In several smaller ports, however, these are part of the port authority operations because of the limited traffic base.[6] In addition, new tasks for a port may arise due to changed political circumstances, new needs for port safety and security, or due to environmental legislation. There needs to be a body that "takes care" of these issues; this is what we called the "proxy" objective. Before it is finally decided who or which institution or company is responsible for a new task, the port authority must do this by proxy. Later on, it might be delegated or outsourced.

The objectives mentioned above, and the explanations provided by the Port Reform Toolkit are describing the "full basket," that is, the maximum set of tasks an authority can fulfill. In practice, the real set of tasks is defined according to specific local needs. Structure follows strategy. When the strategy of the port is limited, for example, because it is a specialized port for bulk export, not all tasks are provided extensively. Figure 10.1 above shows how the set of tasks could be transferred into an organizational chart.

"Going international" is a relatively new objective for large port authorities, like Rotterdam Port. The idea behind this strategy is to extend business and to build networks. "Meet your customer twice" is one of the slogans often heard in discussions about "going international," and this means that a port will in its international strategy be engaged in that port that is called by many of the already existing shipping lines, for example, a container that is stowed on board of a vessel in Europe can be discharged in South America for the same customer. This slogan, however, is not accurate. Port authorities are providers of infrastructure and supportive and/or complementary tasks. In most cases huge landlord ports are not in direct touch with shipping lines regarding business. Thus, it is not possible for these PAs to "meet customers twice," because the authorities are not in direct business relations. This is a strategy that could be enforced by stevedores.

Still, for huge authorities with detailed experiences in several of the fields, it could be of commercial interest to be engaged with other (foreign) port authorities. The spillover-effects due to specialized know-how could make for a commercially attractive business solution. But this should not be interpreted as integration along the supply chain; it is more of a consulting mission with the goal of procuring new information. And when the providing authority, in return for their engagement, gets a stake in the receiving authority, this is indeed an interesting

---

6 For more details, refer to: Port Reform Toolkit 2007, pages 80 and 81.

economic opportunity. Still, such activity is far from being a PA core task. From a macroeconomic point of view, such market concentration has no advantage. This new form of international engagement seems to be possible only for a few very large authorities.

10.4 PA Task Overview

Port authority objectives, as described in Chapter 10.3, are the end points envisioned for proposed tasks or projects, for example, the objective to build a new access road. In this chapter we are concentrating on the planning and construction tasks a PA might oversee. Objectives are achieved, or they are not. They are not performed or carried out. They do not yield results or data. These descriptions apply to the domain of "tasks." Tasks in a port authority's work (or research) plan are steps taken to achieve the stated objectives. They are, for example, a sequence of analyses, actions for projects, field works, maintenance activities, etc., that together lead to attainment of the objectives.

The list of tasks that port authorities fulfill is long and varies with the specific niches the ports are operating in. This means that not all ports are concentrated on all tasks. The list of key bullet points below is a collection of tasks that has been developed by visiting several web pages of ports. It is structured by main activities per department and shall provide a comprehensive overview:

Executive Management:

- Managing the operations, work, activities and affairs, and properties and facilities of the port authority.
- Employing, supervising, and discharging employees, establishing positions and salaries for employees, and authorizing other persons to act on its behalf.
- Collecting the revenues and moneys due to the port authority and depositing them into the accounts of the port authority.
- Making purchases and entering into contracts.
- Administering the port authority's relations with public and private bodies, agencies, and associations, and serving such entities in capacities as directed by the supervisory unit or required in connection with discharging the duties.
- Reporting to the supervisory board and other authorities as the supervisory board directs, or as required in connection with the discharge of the duties.

- Keeping and maintaining records, accounts, books, files, and papers of the port authority, except those pertaining to the duties and functions of third parties, like auditors.
- Signing and delivering on behalf of the port authority, agreements, deeds, leases, rental agreements, licenses, franchises, permits, minutes, notices, accounts, receipts, invoices, warrants, requisitions, vouchers, checks, records, and other instruments, as required in the lawful and proper discharge of the duties, as may be approved or as directed by the supervisory board, or otherwise pursuant to applicable law.
- Performing all other duties of the CEO, executive director, and general manager of the port.
- To initiate and perform all tasks of an authority as directed by the supervisory board and required by law.

Strategic Planning:

- Coordinating with departments and divisions of the port authority in developing strategic initiatives presented to the supervisory board and/or to stakeholder associations.
- Providing advice to executive management on strategic planning issues and possible implications for the port authority.
- Assisting with analyzing and evaluating internal business plans.
- Aligning the strategic initiative projects with the port authority's budget.
- Managing the application of cost-benefit analysis throughout the port authority to prioritize capital projects, ensuring that capital resources are linked to strategic initiatives and used to maximize port authority performance and the regional benefits of capital expenditures.
- Developing financial models and additional decision support tools to assist in the port authority's strategic planning, business planning, capital planning, and performance measurement, to advance its strategic vision and guide investment and policy choices.
- Creating new processes and systems to evaluate and analyze the port authority's capital projects and optimize the approval process.
- Coordinating federal and port authority requirements for the access channels and waterways, tributary channels, and adjacent berthing areas at port authority facilities, which includes: receiving and coordinating the resolution of reports of draft restrictions in the federal channels or at port authority berths; analyzing quarterly surveys of port authority berth depths; and

assuring dredging is accomplished to enable efficient and effective use of port authority facilities.

- Managing the port authority's land used for placement of dredged material, which includes: contracting for ditching of disposal sites to regain capacity (volume), mowing, levee repairs, and pest control; coordinating private company use of port authority-owned disposal sites; and coordinating port authority-contracted construction of drainage ditches and spill box repairs.
- Managing and recommending actions on licenses for pipelines over, under, along, and across port authority property.
- Reviewing, coordinating, and preparing proposed actions on applications for construction of permanent facilities constructed in or along navigable waters, along access channel and tributary channels, as those facilities relate to or affect navigation or commerce.
- Reviewing and preparing of recommendations for actions on leases of submerged lands owned by the port authority.
- Managing access channel and other channel projects (widening, deepening, realignment, federal coordination).
- Coordinating authorization to access port authority-owned property for conducting seismic surveys.
- Participating in federal and regional safety organizations and sponsoring federal navigation safety programs.
- Participating and coordinating programs such as regional heavy weather (storm), disaster as well as education programs, port authority association programs, and regional and local industry group activities.
- Participating in, as well as actively supporting regional Navigation Safety Advisory Committees, which often addresses the full spectrum of maritime safety issues in close cooperation with other regional institutions.
- Collecting data about all relevant aspects of port operation, management, and traffic.
- Tracking federal legislation regarding vessel discharge and providing senior management with information that might be relevant to port operations.
- Conducting special studies to ensure future trade and traffic and to benchmark the port authority against other ports.
- Assisting with structured information to support federal and other requests.
- Facilitating annual environmental compliance and providing general awareness to employees, tenants, users, and contractors.
- Assisting with the reduction of emissions in the goods movement fleet through accelerated engine turnover using various grant-funding programs.

–   Overseeing noise monitoring, particulate matter, air emissions, storm water runoff, and wetlands to minimize the impacts of construction on the surrounding communities.
–   Developing a sustainability strategy that aligns with port authority strategic initiatives.

Engineering and Real Estate:

–   Designing new facilities, renovations, and major repairs (by civil, structural, and electrical professional engineers).
–   Preparing plans and specifications to receive bids/proposals and/or contracts, using in-house engineering with support from outside consultants.
–   Producing construction details, real estate documents, and project plan set design drawings, as well as perform redline corrections to as-built construction plan sets (using computer aided drafting "CAD").
–   Executing project construction-phase operations.
–   Managing construction projects per the requirements of the contract requirements, materials testing schedules, and technical specifications.
–   Performing hydrographic surveys to establish draft conditions at port authority quays.
–   Providing instrument surveys as requested by various port authority departments.
–   Providing procurement assistance.
–   Providing technical and professional assistance to engineering, construction, security, information technology, material testing, and field surveying services.
–   Maintaining analytical reports of existing port authority facilities and assisting with future planning.
–   Assisting in inspection programs for maintenance of port authority infrastructure.
–   Providing program management for major contracts.
–   Controlling engineering projects from inception to completion.
–   Verifying costs and obtaining approval of baseline cost estimates.
–   Controlling costs and schedule changes.
–   Evaluating and recommending firms for professional services for architectural, civil, structural, and electrical projects.
–   Obtaining auxiliary professional services, for example, geotechnical, underwater and quay inspection, and surveying, for engineering projects.

- Providing analysis and geographical and infrastructural data through the geographical information system (GIS) section.
- Administering geodatabase design, updates, maintenance, and documentation.
- Identifying GIS-user applications for the port authority and development of required applications.
- Managing and analyzing land use for the real estate portfolio; both for developed and undeveloped property, including rail, road, and utility infrastructure.
- Marketing and leasing of real estate.
- Performing financial modeling for real estate proposals and valuations.
- Negotiating real estate transactions including sales, leases, purchases, lease assignments, and right-of-entry agreements.
- Preparing real estate transaction documents.
- Collecting rents and other amounts due from port authority tenants and others.
- Coordinating tenant meetings related to matters of security, environmental, construction, and other related issues.
- Managing special conservation tracts and work with other port authority divisions regarding habitat protection measures.
- Overseeing the port authority buildings, including office support and related services.

Access Channel and Turning Basins:

- Coordinating and partnering with industry and customers to generate a strategic plan to foster and promote efficient and economical cargo movements along the access channel(s) and within the port area.
- Ensuring that facilities including quay walls, lighting, fenders, pile moorings, anchorage areas, and dredging are maintained in optimal operating conditions; then initiating capital and expense projects to accomplish this objective.
- Scheduling vessels into public-use channels, waterways, anchorage areas, basins, and terminals, and coordinating arrival and departure traffic to maximize utilization (often explained as harbormaster function).
- Ensuring that facilities are in compliance with tariff rules, regulations, agreements, and freight handling assignments.
- Recommending stevedore licenses to permit stevedores to perform vessel loading and unloading services at port authority quays.

- Tracking tonnage performance for conformance on assignments and lease agreements with users and tenants.
- Monitoring the use of port authority facilities including free time, utilization, condition, damages, construction, and environmental compliance.
- Safeguarding access to restricted areas.

Finance and Administration:

1. Financial Accounting
Accounting
- Recording and processing of financial activities including recording and tracking of port authority assets, monthly/quarterly/annual financial adjustments, recording of revenues and expenses, and maintenance of enterprise funds.

Financial Reporting
- Preparing periodic financial statements for use by the supervisory unit, management, and others.
- Preparing the annual Comprehensive Annual Financial Report including blended component unit financial statements, related footnotes, and supplemental analytical reports.
- Preparing annual financial statements and related footnotes, for example, for pension and retirement plan audits.
- Preparing annual single audit reports in accordance with national, regional, or local regulations, for example, for municipal environmental actions

Cash Management
- Recording and reporting of debt activity including borrowings and repayments of bonds, commercial paper and related transactions.
- Recording and reporting of ad valorem tax collections and related transactions.
- Monitoring and execution of wire transfers in coordination with financial partners and banks.
- Daily recording and tracking of cash receipt and disbursement activity.
- Preparing period cash position reports to management.

Financial Analysis/Budget/Forecast Reporting
- Preparing reports with an analysis comparing actual to budgeted/forecasted financial results.
- Assisting cost-center managers regarding revenue and expense trends and analysis of results.

Internal Control

-   Maintaining the corporate financial control systems, including documenting and monitoring the financial control structure to mitigate potential financial risks.

2. Revenue
Customer Billing

-   Recording and processing of revenue billings and related cash receipts in a timely manner.
-   Generating revenue reports including detailed operational statistical data.

Customer Credit

-   Reviewing and approving of new customers.
-   Monitoring, identifying, and addressing credit issues as they occur.

3. Disbursements
Accounts Payable

-   Overseeing and administering the port authority's vendor disbursement processes, including invoices, check requests, and employee expense reimbursements.
-   Resolving payment disputes and/or other discrepancies.
-   Periodic reporting of transactions to management and in response to open records data requests.

Payroll

-   Overseeing and administering the port authority's employee compensation processes, including wage and salary computation and distribution, regulatory compliance and reporting (e.g., payroll tax filings, annual payroll reporting, etc.), and garnishment processing.

4. Treasury and Corporate Finance

-   Managing relationships with commercial and investment banks and rating agencies.
-   Leading the process for selection and implementation of depository banking services.
-   Acting as an organizational resource, that is, aiding with financial aspects in RFP's, answering questions relating to foreign currency payments, etc.
-   Providing liquidity status reports and cash flow forecasts.

- Assisting with merger, acquisition, and divestiture transactions, including negotiating agreements with financial advisors and counterparties as directed by management and/or the supervisory unit.

5. Debt Management
- Soliciting, recommending, and negotiating short-term and long-term debt facilities as may be approved by management and supervisory units.
- Ensuring compliance with any financial covenants in PA's indentures or other debt agreements.

6. Investment Management
- Investing excess funds prudently, in line with goals of safety of principal, liquidity to meet capital and other cash requirements, diversification of assets, and yield.
- Ensuring compliance with port authorities investment policy and any relevant public funds investment acts.
- Providing regular investment reports to the supervisory board.

7. Pension and Benefits
- Participating in reviews of pension, deferred compensation, other post-employment benefit, and other related plans.
- Monitoring investment performance, including review of trustee statements.
- Acting as central contact point for trustees and other service providers.
- Providing recommendations to management and the pension department regarding changes to pension and benefits plans.

8. Financial Planning and Analysis
Operating Plan
- Preparing, analyzing, and maintaining multiannual (e.g., five-year) plans, regular forecasts, and the budgeting model.
- Developing corporate-wide assumptions used in the multiannual plan.
- Acting as a resource to the divisions and provide adequate training on the IT-system to complete the operating budgets and forecasts on a timely basis.
- Providing assistance to accounting to ensure the proper recording of transactions.

- Creating the annual budget presentation for the supervisory board and for the public.

Capital Plan
- Aggregating and maintaining the capital plan for all departments.
- Updating capital schedules as necessary to reflect changes relating to project estimates, award, and completion dates.
- Working with accounting to establish appropriate depreciation.
- Collaborating with accounting and engineering to develop overhead allocation estimates for capital projects.
- Creating reports on liquidity and available cash based on the capital and operating plans.

9. Grants Program
- Managing all aspects of the security grants process, filing reports as necessary, and requesting reimbursements.
- Providing guidance on other grants and direct grant requests.
- Ensuring receipt of grant monies and the proper recording by accounting.

10. Information Technology
- The Information Technology (IT) department provides technology solutions and support for the port authority.
- IT plans, implements, manages, and maintains all port authority's IT assets, including all physical security hardware and software.
- Provides end-user support through a service desk and maintains the phone systems.

11. Purchasing
- The purchasing department is responsible for procuring all goods and services necessary to maintain the port authority's operations and facilities.
- The purchasing department follows the national rules and regulations, as well as internal procurement statutes and policies.

12. Risk Management
- Developing programs to protect employees and third parties from injury and/or exposure to harmful elements.

- Identifying operational risk exposures and implementation of risk management techniques to address anticipated risks.
- Maintaining information on losses, property values, and operational changes for insurance carriers.
- Preparing applications and obtaining proposals for various insurance coverage plans.
- Coordinating and managing liability, workers' compensation and property claims.
- Reviewing claims history to identify adverse trends and loss prevention opportunities.
- Reviewing contracts, leases, rights of entry, and pipeline licenses for insurance and liability issues.
- Administering internal subrogation activities.
- Managing third party liability disputes.
- Administering port authority claims.

Legal:

- Providing legal assistance to the supervisory board, management, and staff on business transactions, compliance, and regulatory matters, including preparing and reviewing required legal documents.
- Selecting and overseeing outside counsel: The port authority makes use of outside law firms or special counsel, typically only when the matter requires expertise outside that of the legal division, or the project requires resources beyond those of the legal division.
- Researching legal, statutory, and related administrative and business matters, and providing opinions, advice, and memoranda regarding such matters.
- Collecting legal information to assist management decision making.
- Evaluating and advising on the practical consequences of legal strategies.
- Analyzing the possible prosecution and defense of lawsuits.
- Reviewing port authority materials, such as memoranda, reports, publications, advertisements, etc., for legal concerns.
- Reviewing requests for proposals (RFPs), requests for qualifications (RFQs), competitive sealed proposals (CSPs), competitive sealed bids (CSBs), and other procurement documentation for compliance with national laws and regulations as well as internal requirements.
- Supervising preparation of the regular supervisory board agenda and minutes and assisting for matters of compliance.

- Drafting, reviewing, and advising on operational matters, including leasing and terminal operations matters.
- Advising on international and national maritime security law and regulatory compliance.
- Assisting with environmental compliance matters.
- Drafting proposed legislation on matters affecting the port authority and assisting with government relations.
- Assisting with financial and risk management matters.
- Assisting with human resource matters, including providing advice and direction on disciplinary actions.
- Responding to requests for information based on national or regional laws.
- Periodically updating and revising form leases, freight handling agreements, licenses, amendments, and other legal documents.
- Researching and maintaining familiarity with legislation, court decisions, and regulatory matters.
- Handling routine litigation tasks such as responding to writs of garnishment, filing bankruptcy proof of claims, etc.
- Providing preventive counseling, that is, providing timely and effective legal advice before legal problems arise to prevent or minimize legal liability.
- Participating in the definition and development of internal and external policies, procedures, and programs.
- Developing and conducting staff training sessions and workshops.
- Providing other assistance and information to port authority constituents.
- Representing the port authority as an industry leader by speaking locally and nationally on port specific topics such as international maritime security laws and regulations.
- Providing voluntary pro bono legal services to disadvantaged clients.
- Developing training to keep port authority employees informed about record retention.
- Working with the IT department to assist with compliance of electronic records.
- Maintaining an on-site central repository for hard copy records.
- Creating and maintaining an electronic records system, maintaining files on microfilm, and maintaining some "nonrecord" materials.
- Assisting with location of port authority records stored outside of central files and offsite (i.e., in other departments).
- Managing the centralized file numbering system by assigning file numbers, setting up new files, and managing a database of file numbers.
- Managing files stored offsite.

Human Resources:

- Administering salaries and performance reviews for all employees.
- Administering benefits for all active, retired, and disabled employees.
- Developing and training staff to enhance employee knowledge, skills, and abilities.
- Developing and administering policies and procedures to comply with national regulations pertaining to employment law.
- Managing staffing requirements necessary to meet department and agency needs, including tracking of employee sick days, vacation, etc.
- Processing all personnel actions including, but not limited to, new hires, retirements, salary changes, promotions, transfers, resignations, terminations, title changes, etc.
- Coordinating employee and retiree special events.

Origination/Business Development:

- Devising, directing, and steering the port authority trade development business plan, targeting commodities, vessels, and potential cargo flows.
- Tracking the competitiveness of the inland carriers serving the area to maximize the port's hinterland, forging cooperative efforts that bring various entities together.
- Responsibility for the introduction of important stakeholders and executive staff to port authority key accounts.
- Conducting executive trade development visits to major existing and potential port authority customers.
- Participation in the work of trade development organizations.
- Developing and bringing new business opportunities to the port authority, following through to completion, whether by tariff or contract.
- Keeping the customer relationship management system useful and current.
- Defining focal segments (industries, trade zones, customer types, etc.) and ensuring clarity and proper coverage of all desired port authority customers through appropriate account assignments.
- Participating in periodic trips to visit customers throughout the world, including planning of itineraries and subsequent follow-up.
- Organizing various port authority-sponsored receptions, luncheons, etc.
- Managing international and local representatives' offices.
- Hosting various commercial clients and visitors.

- Managing resources to properly acquire economic data, market, and statistical information for originating new business and trade.
- Interpreting and analyzing statistical information and market data.
- Prioritizing the port authority's market research needs, including economic trend forecasting for the regional port-related industry.
- Distributing and preparing annual foreign trade statistics.
- Monitoring trade patterns and trends in the maritime industry.
- Acting as the port authority's liaison with local, national, and international trade and commercial organizations and governmental bodies.
- Achieving proper coverage of all desired port authority customers through appropriate canvassing efforts and promotional activity.
- Participating in periodic industry events worldwide, including planning of itineraries and subsequent follow-up.

Public Affairs and Economic Analysis:

- Overseeing analysis and forecasts of the regional maritime economy, as well as monitoring national and global trends, which may influence the performance of port authority business.
- Providing regular and timely advice to the management on economic issues and their possible implications for the port authority.
- Managing the application of cost-benefit analysis throughout the port authority to prioritize capital projects and ensure that capital resources are used to maximize port authority performance and the regional benefit of capital expenditures.
- Developing and using additional decision support tools to assist in the port authority's strategic planning, business planning, capital planning, and performance measurement, to advance its strategic vision and guide investment and policy choices.
- Managing the provision of guidance and assistance to line businesses on forecasting issues, business planning, and long-term trends in the economy affecting their respective businesses.
- Preparing and providing reports and presentations on the regional maritime economy for the region's stakeholders.
- Overseeing economic impact analyses.
- Developing and maintaining collaborative working relationships with economists at public, private, academic, and not-for-profit organizations in the region.
- Serving as the liaison and spokesperson with the news media.

- Informing and educating internal and external stakeholders about the purpose, activities, services, and accomplishments of the port, as well as the impact as an economic engine for the region, state and nation.
- Responsibility for the branding and messaging of the port authority.
- The annual publishing of port magazines, monthly port reports, e-newsletters, annual reports, employee newsletters, educational and trade brochures and fact sheets, year-in-reviews, as well as preparation and publication of speeches and PowerPoint presentations for staff who appear at public functions on behalf of the port authority.
- Maintaining the port authority website.
- Developing and maintaining positive relationships with local governments and organizations, such as community advisory panels and local chambers of commerce in communities within or adjacent to port authority operations.
- Providing support for the coordination of special events for the port authority.
- Acting as ambassadors and the public face of the port authority with community, civic, nonprofit, business, and international organizations.
- Identifying, developing, and organizing appropriate sponsorship opportunities, special events, programs, and activities.
- Overseeing the employee volunteer program to drive and motivate employee engagement.
- Conducting and arranging briefings and tours of port authority facilities for community and educational groups, as well as for local elected officials.
- Overseeing reservations and bookings for the port authority's public tours and special tours, including trips for dignitaries
- Providing analysis of legislative issues and developing response strategies.
- Advising on changes and proposed changes in local, state, and federal laws.
- Promoting and facilitating cooperative intergovernmental initiatives.
- Serving as the liaison to the staff of other local governments, state and federal government elected officials and agencies.
- Developing and implementing strategies educating and updating elected and appointed officials and governmental agencies on policy priorities and the importance of the port as a local business unit, job machine, and tax generator.

Port Security and Emergency Operations:

- Port security and emergency operations (including port police and marine fire departments) role is to implement the port authority's security commitment to work with public and private partners to provide secure facilities for the community, for our customers, businesses, and employees, and for the others who work and visit the port.

- Preventing loss or harm from threats to health, welfare, and assets.
- Monitoring, evaluating, and implementing programs for continued security improvement.
- Providing proactive emergency response planning to ensure operational recovery.
- Maximizing port security while expediting the flow of commerce.

Terminal Operations (Optional; Often for Smaller Ports):

- Providing and managing port labor for all terminal activities including vessel, yard, and gate operations.
- Facilitating mandated inspections (e.g., coast guard, customs, department of agriculture, etc.).
- Interchanging trucks and railways delivering/receiving import and export cargo.
- Scheduling vessel arrival and departures in cooperation with shipping lines and corresponding agencies.
- Managing yard layout to generate the highest possible utilization while maintaining high levels of productivity for vessel operators.
- Developing new processes by utilizing advanced technologies to increase terminal efficiencies.
- Planning and assisting in the development of future terminal expansion.
- Providing preventative maintenance and repairs to all terminal equipment including quay cranes, yard handling equipment (like rubber-tired gantry cranes [RTGs]), and all supporting equipment with a staff of skilled technicians.

The above list is not exhaustive, although it is already a very long list; it just describes the huge variety of tasks a typical landlord authority oversees. This list is also good supporting evidence of the PA-Paradox as described in Chapter 10.2 above. Some port authorities believe that they really can attract new business or substantially influence trade flows, although this task falls under the "business development" sections. Activities like delegation trips to port customers (precise: in most cases customer of the stevedores) around the world or hosting client events at home are not having negative impetus. But positive effects like the attraction of new shipping lines or warehouse customers have rarely been disclosed. It is more likely that the private operators (mis-)use the public activities and budgets for their own purposes. This is the classic case of the economic "free rider problem." Port authorities must be aware that activities like organizing a delegation trip is a walk on the edge between (well-intended, but inefficient) port marketing and a waste of taxpayer money.

10.5 Port Policy and Regulation

Port authorities are active on a local level, but a competitive and cost-effective port business is also of huge interest for all governmental levels. This is because ports are the facilitator of trade for their hinterland, and the im- and export policy, or foreign trade policy, is important for nations as well as for international organizations, like the United Nations (UN). High port costs due to ineffectiveness have an economic impact like a generalized import duty, increasing the cost of all imported goods and reducing the competitiveness for exports. Decreasing port costs, on the other hand, increase trade and competitiveness. Therefore, the public is interested in having ports working at reasonable and competitive costs, operating transportation and cargo equipment safely, and with minimal environmental impact.

In nearly all countries around the globe there is a strong public interest in ensuring that ports operate efficiently and safely, that fair and competitive services are provided, monopolistic or oligopolistic tendencies in pricing with unjustified "economic rents" are prevented, and that ports support and foster economic development (i.e., trade) locally and nationally. Public interest in ports stems from their vital role as gateways to economic trade and commerce. In a democratic system, the Ministry of Transport typically performs a variety of port policy and regulation functions at a national level to ensure the port system supports economic interests. With respect to coastline, waterway, and port issues, the main tasks and responsibilities of a typical Ministry can be summarized as follows:

Policy making. The ministry develops transport and port policies related to:
- Planning and development of a basic maritime infrastructure including coastline defenses (shore protection), port entrances, waterways, lighthouses and aids to navigation, navigable sea routes and canals
- Planning and development of ports (location, function, type of management)
- Planning and development of port hinterland connections (roads, railways, waterways, pipelines)

Legislation. The Ministry drafts and implements transport and port laws, national regulations and decrees. It is responsible for incorporating relevant elements of international conventions (e.g., SOLAS, Law of the Sea, MARPOL) into national legislation.

International relations. Specialized departments of the Ministry represent the country in bilateral and multilateral port and shipping forums. The Ministry may also negotiate agreements with neighboring countries relating to waterborne or intermodal transit privileges.

Financial and economic affairs. A Ministerial department is usually responsible for planning and financing national projects. It should be able to carry out financial and economic analyses and assess the socioeconomic and financial feasibility of projects in the context of national policies and priorities.

Auditing. Auditing functions should be performed independently from the affected line organization and are usually included in a staff office. The auditors should report directly to the Minister.

Ensuring the efficient and competitive functioning of a port is the purpose of economic regulation. This typically involves setting or controlling tariffs, revenues, or profits; controlling market entry or exit; and overseeing that fair and competitive behavior and practices are maintained within the sector. Determining when economic regulation is necessary and how to tailor it to a port is the main focus of ministerial port and transport policy. In many countries, transport directorates are established as independent bodies within a Ministry and perform this executive function. They are usually responsible for one of the modes of transport, for example, the maritime and ports directorate (maritime administration) or the directorate for railways.

Principal elements of a typical maritime and ports directorate are:
- Ship inspections and register of shipping (oversight of ship safety and manning conditions)
- Traffic and environment safety (safe movement of shipping and protection of the marine environment)
- Maritime education and training (maritime academies, merchant officer's exams, licensing of seafarers)
- Port policy (execution of national ports policy)
- Hydro-technical construction (construction of protective works, sea locks, port entrances, etc.)

- Vessel traffic systems and aids to navigation (construction and maintenance)
- Search and rescue

The increasing introduction of private participation in port activities generates a general need for regulation in the provision of port services to prevent inefficiencies due to local monopoly power. Such a case is more likely to occur in small ports with captive traffic because of the inadequacy of competition within the port and the difficulty of competition between ports. Thus, regulation of port activities is a key aspect of port policy and a key task for maritime and port directorates in close cooperation with port authorities.

A usual way to introduce private participation in ports is through contracts between the private and the public entities. Thus, the contract is a tool for the regulator. Its form will depend on the initial conditions prevailing at the port, on its size, and on the specific activity under consideration. Contracts come in a wide variety, ranking from concessions (Building, Operation and Transfer, BOT, etc.; refer to chapters 9.4 and 14.3), where the private firm is temporarily given the port site for constructions and operations, to licenses for the provision of a given type of service. The choice of the most adequate form of contract will depend on the objectives of the regulator and the restrictions faced. An important element to consider is the condition of asymmetric information of the parties involved, as firms usually know their costs and demand conditions better than the regulator.

On the other hand, the most usual regulatory systems to prevent abuse from a dominant monopolist are the application of maximum prices (price cap) and the limitation of firm profits through the rate of return. Hybrid regulatory systems contain pricing elements as well as profit limits. Price caps act as an incentive towards efficiency, as cost reduction makes profit grow under given prices. The disadvantage is that captivity of demand combined with price limits provokes an incentive to diminish quality and to increase environmental damage as part of a pseudo cost reduction strategy. The rate of return regulation diminishes capital risk and its cost because of a guaranteed profit rate but has no incentives toward efficiency. Thus, contract design and price regulations have proved to be the most appropriate tools to introduce private participation in port activities, preserving quality while inducing efficiency.

There are cases in which regulation might not be needed or only plays a minor role. For example, when port competition is feasible, as it has agreed advantages as an instrument to induce discipline on economic agents intervening in a given market. Whether competition is both feasible and desirable will depend on the traffic volume moved within a port. Even when no competition is feasible within the port, the need to regulate prices would be subject to possible competition between ports inside a country or a political union like the EU. It is a matter of fact that, in general, competition has increased within the port industry, but this does not have equal impact on all ports or all activities. It depends on many aspects, such as location, type, level structure of traffic served, and so on.

Within the EU, an open debate is still going on regarding public subsidies to ports, as they could limit competition. This is a typical case demonstrating the conflict between the central or intergovernmental desire to regulate on a high level and the local interests to continue to operate, administer, and regulate their own ports in their individual way. This is not a port specific issue, but a basic democratic one that relates to how much influence should be given to lower regional bodies; the so called "subsidiarity principle." Port policy and regulation ultimately must follow the way how the political instances structure this principle.

10.6 Intraport Competition

Port-related competition can be identified as interport competition (macroeconomic view) and as intraport competition (microeconomic view); Figure 10.3 below illustrates the two types. Interport competition arises when two or more ports or their terminals are competing for the same customers and the same cargo, like Hong Kong and Shanghai for the Far East-Europe and Transpacific containerized transhipment cargo, or Antwerp, Rotterdam, Wilhelmshaven, Bremerhaven, and Hamburg for the central European hinterland trades, or Long Beach, Los Angeles, and Oakland as US-ingates for transpacific trade routes. Of highest interest for interport competition are transit and transhipment cargoes, because they are only loosely connected to a specific port.

Intraport competition refers to a situation where two or more different port service operators within a single port are vying for the same markets, like in Los Angeles, where there have been nine container terminals, with container terminal operators APMT, APL Terminal, Ports America Terminals, China Shipping Container Terminal, Yang Ming Container Terminal, etc.; or in Rotterdam with Tank Storage operators Koninklijke Vopak, Argos Terminals, Standic, LBC Rotterdam, Maasvlakte Olie Terminal or Odfjell Terminals, etc.

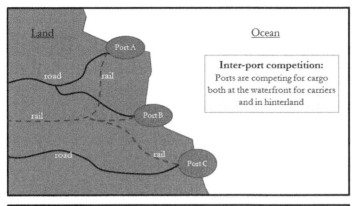

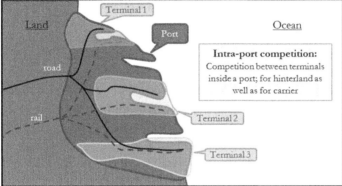

Figure 10.3: Inter- and intraport competition

Typically, intraport competition happens in container terminal business as well as in container related services, more rarely in RoRo, general cargo, or bulk business. Intraport competition for bulk exists, but these examples are rare exceptions.

In the following, we will concentrate on intraport competition, because here port authorities (and so the port governance) has a substantial influence.

According to De Langen, et al.,[7] intraport competition has at least two positive effects:

1. Intraport competition prevents market power of port service providers.
2. Intraport competition leads to specialization, flexible adaptation, and innovation.

---

7 De Langen Intraport competition, pages 4ff.

For economists, it is widely accepted that all types of competition will prevent monopoly pricing and support realistic market pricing without abnormal tariff or price levels and rigid operational conditions. No unjustified "economic rents" will occur. The incentive to reach out for unjustified economic rents is especially high in port areas with huge loco potentials and less interport competition. As a result, it is of huge importance that the port authorities are aware of this basic structure economic framework parameter and are actively supporting intraport competition via their regulatory power. National port policy provides the frame for these activities, and the port authorities must use their contractual power to support and realize this.

In daily business, the importance of this topic often seems to be a little beclouded. Authorities must negotiate several long-term contracts, and so it is often not clear which contract supports which trend. A frequently asked question is: is the actual contract supporting the general port policy or not? Here a clear vision and mission statement for the authority is helpful and can provide guidance. All new contracts should be measured by the self-set goals. Only then can a stringent and continuous contract design support the objectives of the authority. It can not be stressed enough that with these contractual and regulatory tasks, the authorities fulfill a substantial economic objective, which goes far beyond a simple contract.

New long-term trends of contracting business partners for the stevedores (e.g., shipping lines as shareholding partner for a terminal) need to be taken into consideration when fixing new contract terms. "Meeting customers twice" (a goal of global stevedores; in economic terms the vertical integration along the supply chain) as trend of shipping lines and their stevedoring subsidiaries are important trends that may have an influence of a single port. For each terminal contract, all types of new economical or logistical trends need to be scrutinized, to prevent hidden terms that may lower port competition. The principle of equal treatment must also be considered.

The second argument that intraport competition leads to specialization, flexible adaption and innovation can be seen as a direct reaction to the competitive situation inside the port. Competitors face similar regulations and try for example via specialization to achieve an additional competitive advantage; a better selling position; highly specialized handling equipment for example has the potential to build such a competitive advantage. With this specialization, they enhance port performance and become more competitive, be it regarding pricing or with regard to quality and innovation.

Because of intraport competition, the organizational structures incorporated by port authorities are based on "both economies of scale and economies of variety. The competition and/or interaction between several providers of port products/services/facilities promotes the prospect of autonomy, entrepreneurship, creativity, and decentralized management. This variety ensures innovations are introduced (and copied) and competing firms constantly aim to improve services to their customers. This dynamic process keeps ports competitive."[8]

Intraport competition helps ensure that the private sector passes savings on to users and reduces opportunities for monopolistic abuses. A private terminal operator can be presumed to be more tempted than a public port authority to exploit any market power that it may have. But experience has shown that public sector monopolies are often stronger, more authoritarian, and noncompromising than private sector monopolies. Moreover, they are often more difficult to fight as their directors deny the existence of a monopoly or justify such a monopoly as for the public good.

If a market is competitive, private operators can not price much above their long-run marginal costs; they may be able to do so in the short run if demand temporarily outstrips supply, but only for as long as it takes to provide additional capacity. If the markets are noncompetitive, however, public port or terminal operators are often able to sustain prices well more than marginal costs whether they are in developed or developing countries. In practice, governments consider such ports as "cash cows" and are often reluctant to limit or lower port tariffs and terminal handling charges. Private terminal operators will also be tempted to raise their tariffs above the economically reasonable level. In such a case, tariff regulation by port authorities (acting as regulator and contracting partner at the local level) is an efficient solution to the problem of noncompetitive pricing.

When effective intraport competition can be established and maintained in the relevant markets and activity sectors, privatization has proven to have great potential for reducing costs and improving service quality. Without competition, privatization can still bring some improvements, but the gains are relatively limited. Therefore, it is so important that port authorities identify intraport competition.

10.7 Case Studies

In the following, the governance bodies of three major ports will be described. The information presented comes primarily from the public port websites and annual port reports; both media are important tools for identifying a port's mission, vision, objectives, tasks, news, etc.

---

8 De Langen Intraport competition, page 8.

These case studies follow the same structure for all three authorities: company profile, mission, vision, core values, strategy, structure of the organization, and organigram/organization chart. The information for each port has been collected from different sources. Most of the statements are directly copied in from official websites or from annual reports to guarantee authenticity. The following ports will be analyzed:

- Rotterdam
- Singapore
- Los Angeles

Port of Rotterdam Authority, The Netherlands[9]

Company Profile:

The Port of Rotterdam Authority is manager, operator, and developer of Rotterdam's port and industrial area. The Port Authority is a public limited company (N.V.) with two shareholders: The Municipality of Rotterdam and the Dutch State. As is apparent from the objects stated in the articles of association, it operates in two domains: the shipping and port area.

The objectives under the articles of association are:

- The development, construction, management, and operation of the port and industrial area in Rotterdam.
- Promoting the effective, safe, and efficient handling of shipping in the Port of Rotterdam and the offshore approaches to the port.

The Port of Rotterdam Authority rents out—on long-term leases—port sites to businesses, particularly to storage firms, cargo terminals, and the chemical and petrochemical industry, including energy producers. The main sources of income are rent and harbor dues.

The Port of Rotterdam Authority invests in the development of new port sites, Maasvlakte 2, in public infrastructure such as roads in the port area, and in customer-specific infrastructure such as quay walls and jetties. To handle shipping as effectively as possible, the Port of Rotterdam Authority is investing heavily in a traffic management system, traffic control centers, and patrol vessels.

---

9 Refer to the website: www.portofrotterdam.com; Port of Rotterdam Annual Report 2016: Building a sustainable future. Make it happen.

A total of 1,100 people were employed by the Port of Rotterdam Authority in 2016.

Although, the Port of Rotterdam Authority is not listed as a public limited company, it does comply with the all legislative requirements imposed on 'large' companies. Since July 21, 2008, the Port of Rotterdam Authority has operated under a more future-oriented two-tier board system. This means that the general meeting of shareholders are authorized to assign and dismiss executive board members. The executive board conducts the day-to-day management of the company. The independent supervisory board supervises the executive board and oversees the state of affairs in the company. Shareholders, the municipality of Rotterdam (approximately 70%), and the Dutch State (approximately 30%) exercise influence on the company through the General Meeting of Shareholders. The powers of the supervisory board and the general meeting of shareholders are laid down by law and in the articles of association.

Mission:

In line with its objectives under the articles of association, the Port of Rotterdam Authority has formulated the following mission statement:

> *The Port of Rotterdam Authority creates economic and social value by working with customers and stakeholders to achieve sustainable growth in the world-class port.*

To fulfill this mission, the authority has formulated a "Port Vision 2030." According to the port's official website, "the Port Vision 2030 sets out the ambitions for the future of the Port of Rotterdam. The port vision is like a compass: ambitions are a spot on the horizon, even when circumstances change. Flexibility is the key trait needed here. Industry and logistics have been the pillars of the Port of Rotterdam for decades, thanks to its favorable location and an entrepreneurial spirit: daring to act with a clear vision. The port is of great value to the region, the Netherlands and Europe. This goes far beyond euros and employment."[10] The port authority follows the targets outlined in the vision statement and regularly checks the progress of work.

---

10 For further information, refer to: https://www.portofrotterdam.com/en/the-port/port-vision-2030

Vision 2016:

The Rotterdam Port Authority formulated the following vision as guideline for the next decade ahead as follows:

> *We continually improve the Port of Rotterdam to make it the safest, most efficient and most sustainable port in the world. We create value for our customers by developing logistics chains, networks and clusters, in both Europe and growth markets worldwide. As an enterprising port developer, the Port Authority is the partner for world-class clients. In this way, we are also strengthening the competitive position of the Netherlands.*

Vision 2011:

Just five years earlier, the port authority formulated a slightly different vision. This is a good example showing that neither mission nor vision statements are carved in stone for any time; they are living guidelines. But as guidelines, they show the way ahead; and this means that there must be continuity. This is what both vision statements express in a very good way. Here is the Port of Rotterdam Authority's 2011–2015 vision:

> *The Port of Rotterdam Authority is fully committed to the continued development of Rotterdam's port and industrial complex so it can become the most efficient, safe and sustainable in the world. The Port of Rotterdam is creating value for customers by developing chains, networks and clusters, both in Europe and in growth markets worldwide. As an enterprising port developer, the Port of Rotterdam is the partner for customers of world stature in petro-chemicals, energy, transport & logistics. In this way the Port of Rotterdam is enhancing the competitiveness of the Netherlands.*

Core Values:

The core values are the most important values within the Rotterdam Port Authority. They stimulate cooperation and work to realize the port's business plan. The values guide how the authority wants to be perceived by the outside world. Here are the Rotterdam port's core values (original text):

Passion	Passion for the port and our profession
Together	Working jointly with our colleagues, but also with our customers, our shareholders, and people living and working around the port area, to achieve our collective ambitions

Continuous improvement	Keen to learn, evaluate, develop, and set new frontiers
Reliable	Reliable for our stakeholders, a careful and trustworthy partner, building on our solid basis of decades of experience as Europe's leading port

These core values and other standards are described in the business code of the Port of Rotterdam Authority. This code sets out who the "Port of Rotterdam" is, what it stands for, and what the authority feels is important in business and public life; both internally and externally. The code contains guidelines that state clearly what is and is not permitted.

Strategy:
The Port of Rotterdam Authority is very much involved with the port and industrial area in Rotterdam and fully committed to the continued development of Rotterdam's port and industrial complex. The target is to become the most efficient, sustainable, and safest port in the world. To realize this development, the authority wants to be proactive in contracting partnerships with international players. They also want to contribute actively to the quality of chains and networks. For this reason, the Port of Rotterdam has explicitly opted for the following strategy components:

- Put extra effort into developing new growth markets, such as biobased and offshore.
- Invest in overarching infrastructure (energy, transport, utilities, data) for a sustainable and competitive industrial cluster.
- Invest in further improving the efficiency of maritime, interterminal and hinterland transport and connectivity of hinterland connections.
- Play an active role in the development of data and data applications in the logistics chain.
- Develop space by restructuring and modernizing, including actively directing environmental space and accessibility.
- Increase the service level of the port for the customers (ease of doing business), among other things nautical services, targeted investment and pricing policy, and in the field of obtaining permits, procedures, enforcement, and supervision.
- Create an excellent climate for innovation.

To achieve their targets and strategic priorities, the port authority adopts the position of enterprising developer, focusing on the customer and working toward a flexible, efficient organization and excellent quality from its personnel.

To achieve the targets set out by the mission and vision statements, the Port of Rotterdam organized the authority as explained in the Figure 10.4.

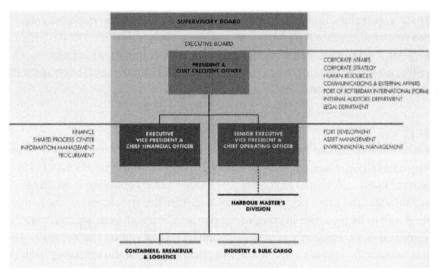

Figure 10.4: Organigram Port of Rotterdam Authority

The Maritime and Port Authority of Singapore, Singapore[11]

Company Profile:

The Maritime and Port Authority of Singapore (MPA) was established on February 2, 1996, with the mission to develop Singapore as a premier global hub port and international maritime center (IMC), and to advance and safeguard Singapore's strategic maritime interests. MPA is the driving force behind Singapore's port and maritime development, taking on—according to the port itself—the roles of port authority, port regulator, port planner, IMC champion, and national maritime representative. MPA partners with the industry and other agencies to enhance safety, security, and environmental protection in our port waters, facilitate port opera-

---

11 Refer to the website: www.mpa.gov.sg; Port of Singapore Annual Report 2016: Strength in Unity. Towards A Future-Ready Maritime Singapore.

tions and growth, grow the cluster of maritime ancillary services, and promote maritime R&D and manpower development.

In 2016 the MPA employed approximately 680 people.

The Port of Singapore is comprised of several facilities and terminals that handle a wide range of cargo transported in different forms, including containers and conventional and bulk cargo. The Maritime and Port Authority of Singapore (MPA) is responsible for the overall development and growth of the Port of Singapore, which includes terminal operators, such as the PSA Corporation and Jurong Port Pte Ltd. The MPA recently planned and started construction of the new Tuas port at the western border of the city. This port will have a final handling capacity of 100 mill TEU, making it the largest container terminal project in the world.[12]

Below are the MPA's mission, vision, and core value statements, which have remained unchanged for years. In 2016 the MPA celebrated its twenty-year anniversary, and these key statements will guide the MPA into the future.

Mission:

To develop and promote Singapore as a premier global hub port and an international maritime center, and to advance and safeguard Singapore's strategic maritime interests.

Vision:

A leading maritime agency driving Singapore's global maritime aspirations.

Core Values:

The core values are the most important values within the MPA. They stimulate cooperation and work to realize the port's business plan. The values guide how the authority wants to be perceived by the outside world. Here are MPA's core values:

Forward thinking: To be proactive and innovative. We will harness the best technologies and practices to stay relevant, efficient, and competitive.

Integrity: To act responsibly, honestly, and to be morally courageous in carrying out our duties. We will be fair and above board in all our business dealings and relationships.

---

12 For example, refer to: Tuas mega port: First phase of works crosses halfway mark: The Straits Times, 25.9.2017; also available at: http://www.straitstimes.com/singapore/tuas-mega-port-first-phase-of-works-crosses-halfway-mark

Respect: To respect the feelings of the individual and to appreciate his dignity and self-worth, his time and effort, and his need to balance work and family life.

Service excellence: To strive to serve our customers competently, courteously, and efficiently. We shall persevere to excel in all areas of our work through continual learning and a positive work attitude.

Teamwork: To value teamwork, harmony, and unity in our working relationships. We shall do our work with steadfastness and consideration for our colleagues and customers.

Strategy:

MPA's strategy is in line with the "whole-of-government strategic outcomes" that are grouped into six broad categories:

-   Sustainable economic growth
-   Robust social security
-   World-class environment and infrastructure
-   Secure and influential Singapore
-   Strong families, cohesive society
-   Effective government

MPA works to achieve its vision through its "5 Ps"-strategy:

Nurturing competent and committed people: MPA recognizes you as our most important asset and hence wants to nurture you to bring out your best.

Building strong partnership: MPA believes that building strong partnerships with others will bring about deeper relationships and help attract and entrench our partners in Singapore.

Developing a probusiness environment: MPA believes that a probusiness environment would determine whether the industry flourishes and thrives. Hence as regulator and promoter, MPA has an important role in facilitating the growth of the industry.

Improving operational processes: MPA understands that we need to constantly review our processes and ensure that they remain flexible and nimble so that we can react quickly to our external environment.

Achieving international prominence: MPA believes that achieving international prominence as a maritime nation is vital to MPA's success in driving Singapore's global maritime aspirations.

To achieve the targets set out by the mission and vision statements, the MPA organized the authority as explained in the Figure 10.5.

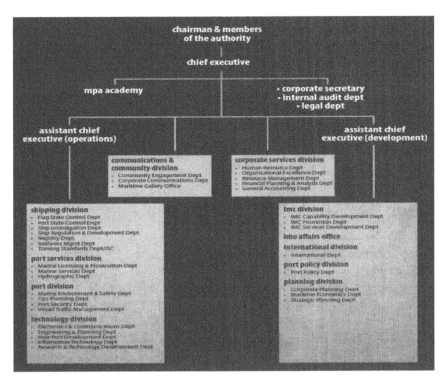

Figure 10.5: Organigram MPA Singapore

Port of Los Angeles, USA[13]

Company Profile:

The city of Los Angeles and its harbor area experienced unparalleled population growth in the early 20th century. City leaders recognized the port's growth opportunities and created the Board of Harbor Commissioners on December 9, 1907, thus marking the official founding of the Port of Los Angeles. The cities of San Pedro and Wilmington were annexed to the city of Los Angeles on August 28,

---

13 Refer to the website: www.portoflosangeles.org; Comprehensive Annual Financial Report 2010/2011; Port of Los Angeles Strategic Plan 2010/2011.

1909, making the Port of Los Angeles an official department of the city of Los Angeles.

Today, the Port of Los Angeles is one of the world's largest trade gateways and the scope of its economic contributions to the regional economy is far-reaching. The port is connected directly and indirectly with tens of billions of dollars in industry sales each year in the Southern California region. Those sales translate into hundreds of thousands of local jobs and billions of dollars in wages, salaries, and state and local taxes.

The Port of Los Angeles generates:
- 144,000 jobs in Los Angeles
- 517,000 jobs in Southern California
- 1.6 million jobs throughout the United States
- $89.2 billion in California trade value
- $223 billion in U.S. trade value
- $5.1 billion in state tax revenue
- $21.5 billion in federal tax revenue

Approximately 70% of the regional direct, indirect, and induced benefits connected to the port occur within Los Angeles county. A total of 999 people are employed directly by the Port of Los Angeles.

The port is a proprietary department of the City of Los Angeles and was created by the City Charter to promote and develop a deep-water port facility. It is governed by a five-member Board of Harbor Commissioners, which has the duty to provide for the needs of commerce, navigation, and fishery for the citizens of California. It operates similarly to a private business and is substantially autonomous from the city.

The port operates primarily as a landlord. Its docks, wharves, transit sheds, and terminals are leased to shipping or terminal companies, agents, and to other private firms. Although the port owns these facilities, it has no direct hand in managing the daily movement of cargoes. The port is also a landlord for various fish markets, boat repair yards, railroads, restaurants, a shipyard, and other similar activities.

The major sources of income for the port are from shipping services (wharfage, dockage, pilotage, assignment charges, etc.), land rentals, and fees, concessions, and royalties.

Mission:
We deliver value to our customers by providing superior infrastructure and promoting efficient operations that grow our port as North America's preferred gateway.

Vision:
We are America's port—the nation's #1 container port and the global model for sustainability, security, and social responsibility.

Core Values:
Sustainable green growth: To achieve sustainable green growth, the port will maximize its social, economic, and environmental objectives to find mutually reinforcing solutions, recognizing their interdependencies. Likewise, the social, economic, and environmental impacts of port actions are considered when assessing organizational performance.

Strategy:
Growing competition from U.S. West Coast ports —coupled with the creation of new shipping line alliances and other major operational changes—means that the Port of Los Angeles must be ready to meet the opportunities and challenges of a dynamic and changing trade landscape. Considering these profound changes in the cargo industry, an updated strategic plan was developed in 2014 as an update to the 2012–2017 strategic plan. An updated plan with four core strategic objectives and in total twelve initiatives is the result of that process.[14]

Objective 1: World-Class Infrastructure that Promotes Growth

Initiative 1: Develop a capital improvement program (CIP) that improves the port's operational strength and financial sustainability.
Initiative 2: Deliver terminal and infrastructure projects on time and within budget.
Initiative 3: Optimize maintenance to extend infrastructure life and utility.

---

14 For further details, refer to: City of Los Angeles Harbor Department, 2012–2017 Strategic Plan; 2014 Update; Port of Los Angeles, CA, Los Angeles 2014.

Objective 2: An Efficient, Secure and Environmentally Sustainable Supply Chain

Initiative 1: Facilitate supply chain efficiencies and terminal velocity with supply chain partners.
Initiative 2: Implement security and public safety strategies that support goods movement and mitigate risk.
Initiative 3: Continue environmental stewardship through implementation of programs with clear and measurable standards.

Objective 3: Improved Financial Performance of Port Assets

Initiative 1: Increase cargo revenue by attracting new volumes and establishing long-term volume commitments.
Initiative 2: Increase the utilization of port facilities.
Initiative 3: Ensure that port properties are revenue efficient and reflect current land values and market-based compensation.

Objective 4: Strong Relationships with Stakeholders

Initiative 1: Enhance a world-class customer service delivery product.
Initiative 2: Attract visitors to the LA waterfront of Wilmington and and San Pedro.
Initiative 3: Make the harbor department the employer of choice by by providing opportunities for professional development and promoting excellence.

To achieve the targets set out by the mission and vision statements, the Port of Los Angeles organized the authority as explained in the Figure 10.6.

Conclusion:

1. **Company profile—organization:** Rotterdam Port Authority is a public limited company with two major shareholders. MPA belongs to Singapore's state administration. Los Angeles Port is 100% owned by the municipality. Three slightly different set ups, but all with a direct reporting line to public administration. All three ports are operating as landlord ports. No dominating port governance model with these three case studies, and not when comparing with other Top 100 ports.

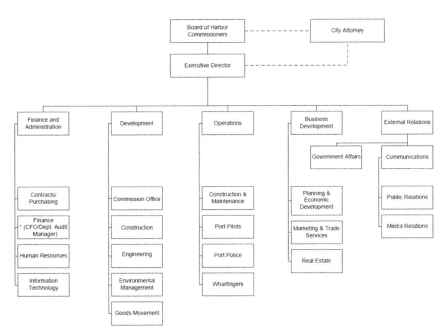

Figure 10.6: Organigram Port of Los Angeles

2. **Company profile—employees:** The ports of Rotterdam and Singapore both handle huge amounts of cargo[15] and can therefore be compared directly for this survey: Singapore, the bigger port, employs approximately half the staff of Rotterdam. This is an indicator that the Rotterdam Port Authority fulfills tasks inside the authority that are outsourced or not seen in Singapore; or even temporarily not necessary, like specialized development departments. Los Angeles is in the middle of these two ports in terms of staff size.

3. **Mission and vision statements:** All ports intend to be the leading port in their respective region. For the last couple of years, Los Angeles as frontrunner, and Rotterdam as an earlier follower, has been highlighting sustainable and green growth. In Singapore (and so in many other Asian ports) this aspect came later, but with huge power on top of the agenda. The three ports in this case study are very realistic in defining their mission and vision, that is, the PA-Paradox does not occur.

4. **Core values:** These values describe the way these authorities intend to work internally and with their customers and partners. Rotterdam's ranking of the

---

15 Refer to Table 3.2: World top twenty ports.

value "Together" is a bit strange: "Working jointly with our colleagues, but also with our customers" does not sound like the typical "Customers First"— philosophy that can be found in most other businesses. It sounds more like "We first, customers second," but this is likely an inaccuracy in translation.[16] Rotterdam port is very much customer oriented and close to the market. Los Angeles does not publish a list of its specific values, but it can be assumed that similar values apply to the port.

5. **Strategy:** The three ports explain briefly how to achieve their objectives. Additional documents from the port—not included here—go very much into detail and explain how to achieve each step year by year. The wording and structure may vary, but all three ports in the case study have precise plans for the near future. Unfortunately, such is not the case with other large ports in the world.

6. **Organigram:** The three organization charts, taken from the port websites and annual reports, look different but in one way or the other cover the objectives described in Chapter 10.3, and the set of functions and departments mentioned in Figure 10.1. An atypical task is featured in "Maasvlakte 2" in Rotterdam's scheme. The Port of Rotterdam is preparing itself for the future, and Maasvlakte 2 is a huge development and construction program. This is probably one of the reasons Rotterdam has a larger staff than MPA. Instead of sourcing all tasks out, the Port of Rotterdam Authority employs its own staff. Singapore's project for the new Tuas mega port has a dimension comparable to Maasvlakte 2, but as mentioned above: MPA outsourced many tasks and works with external experts and other city departments.

These three case studies show how port governance via port authorities is realized in Europe, Asia, and North America. The main objectives are fulfilled in all three ports, but the organizational structure in each port is slightly different, the framework parameters for the authorities are different, laws are different, and the self-image and business behavior (e.g., conservator, facilitator, or entrepreneur) of the authority is different. Still, the ports' customers from the shipping side are often the same calling with the same vessels. Therefore, ports around the world fulfill similar tasks under different circumstances and in different ways.

---

16 The original Dutch version can be found on the website www.portofrotterdam.com sounds: "Samen Wij werken onderling samen, maar ook met onze stakeholders, klanten en aandeelhouders, om zo onze gezamenlijke ambities te realiseren."

Chapter 11
Port Operator

In a typical landlord model, a port operator oversees all operational activities above the pavement, including planning and construction of all necessary buildings (the "superstructure"), and the port authorities are responsible for the port infrastructure, including fairways. Figure 11.1 illustrates this very general principle of sharing costs and responsibilities. In practice, there is a lot of overlapping, which is why negotiating contracts with clear definitions about areas of responsibility is a huge topic for both operators and authorities.

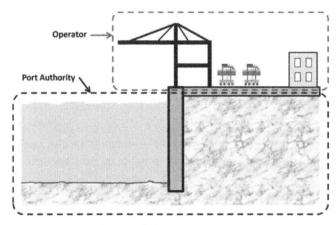

Figure 11.1: Areas of responsibility

Terminal operator and port authorities are key players when it comes to the supply side of port business, but additional partners are necessary to fulfill the tasks. The shipper and the beneficial cargo owner (BCO) behind the shipper are delivering the cargoes and must pay the bills for handling and transportation. The carrier, or ocean transport company, is performing the physical maritime shipment and is the natural partner of the port operator and authorities. Additional service providers like tug boat operators or line handlers are also necessary to perform the business. These services could also be part of the terminal operator or port authority's activities, but as the services are highly specialized, they are often outsourced. Still, port operators work quite closely with the authorities, carriers, and service providers.

Figure 11.2 indicates key services that are provided in this network as well as typical fees and charges that are paid for these services.

DOI 10.1515/9781547400874-011

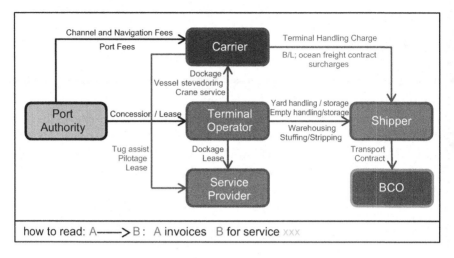

Figure 11.2: Port operator's business framework

11.1 Classification

In general, ports move passenger and/or cargoes between modes of transportation; this is the core function of ports, or to be more precise: the core business of port or terminal operators. Before going into detail, the terms "terminal operator" and "port operator" need to be defined:

A "terminal operator" is a company or institution that operates a single terminal.

A "port operator" is a company that operates several terminals within a single port.

In addition to terminal and port operators, a lot of service providers are active in most of the ports around the globe. They are not directly involved in terminal operations (i.e., ship-to-shore operations), but are essential for supporting the operators in fulfilling their tasks. They can be defined as facilities operator and service operator.

A "port facilities operator" is a company or institution that operates facilities that are complementary to terminal operations, for example, warehouse companies, tank storage companies, tallying services, consolidation/deconsolidation companies, etc.

A "port service operator" is a company or institution that can support both the terminals as well as the facilities operator and/or provides additional port services, for example, pilots, tug boats, mooring services, equipment maintenance and repair, etc.

The term "terminal operator" in some literature is also used for a single company that operates the same kind of terminals in several ports, for example, DP World or HPH, running container terminals in many ports around the world. More accurately, those companies are also called global terminal operators; just to distinguish them from a single terminal operator. Sometimes a company is active in several businesses (e.g., cruise and conventional general cargo businesses) in more than one port. These companies could be described as global or multiple port operators. The terminal business is very complex in structure and with high diversity regarding the activities that need to be performed, and it doesn't always use precise and accurate titles. In the following sections, these titles (illustrated in Table 11.1) will be defined.

Table 11.1: Definitions: Operator

active in:	one Port	several Ports
one business line (e.g., container)	Terminal Operator	Global Terminal Operator
several business lines	Port Operator	Multiple Port Operator

The term "multiple terminals operator" is used for a company that operates the same kind of terminals (e.g., container terminals) in one port only. Here we consider this as a subgroup of "terminal operator." To further describe operators we identified six criteria:

1. Criterion: Ownership

A port operator in this sense can be a 100% public-owned institution or company, a semi public-private company, or a fully private company. All ownership models exist, but it is matter of fact that the pure public company model is becoming less and less common as more activities are being given to private owners. Together with the public authorities, this system forms a well-balanced landlord model. The operators themselves can be independent private companies, for example, owned by investment funds or family trusts, can be daughter companies of shipping lines, outlets from other state businesses, etc. The variety is huge. Ownership is an important criterion when analyzing an operator.

2. Criterion: Cargo Segments

Specialized terminals are needed for all types of cargoes. A liquid bulk terminal is, from an operational point of view, something completely different than a container or cruise terminal. Some operators concentrate themselves on cargo segments, whereas others are offering a wider range of activities. However this is organized in practice, it is of huge importance that ports have a clear picture of the operator's specialization and in which segments the operator is active.

3. Criterion: Number of Terminals

An operator can be active in different terminals. The terminals themselves can be of the same type (e.g., container terminals), but it is also possible that the operator is active in different segments of different terminals, for example, in conventional general cargo business, in dry bulk business, and on cruise terminals. When analyzing an operator, it is important to know in how many terminals they are working and what type of terminals these are.

4. Criterion: Market Share in Cargo Market

When analyzing the position of port operator, it is also crucial to know how big the market share per operator is within a specific port and/or port range. For example, knowing a general cargo terminal operator handles a throughput of 3 mill tons of cargo is important. But even more important, from an economic point of view, is the question: how relevant is this? If the whole port operates 30 mill tons of comparable cargo per year, and the relevant market share is just 10%, we can assume that the 3 mill-share is under high competitive pressure. But when the whole general cargo throughput of the respective port is just 3 mill tons, and the terminal operator is the only one within the port range, the market behavior might be different. The market share, in context of the correlating cargo market, is an important criterion when analyzing port operators.

5. Criterion: Port Market Share

The fact that terminal operators could be active in different cargo segments leads to the fact that in some ports we find dominant operators. They may be active in several cargo businesses, for example, dry bulk: coal import, dry bulk: fertilizer export, conventional general cargo, container business, and cruise/passenger terminals. They don't necessarily have to be the key terminal operator in all segments, but being active in so many segments gives them a dominant position. Especially for smaller ports with just a single (and often: public) operator this often happens. It is a natural effect on the path of growth, that is, having a single operator is common when a port is growing.

6. Criterion: Number and Size of Global Activities

Port operators can be active in their local market, but in the last few decades the port business has become more global, and there are several companies operating on global scale. Therefore, it is important to know details about worldwide activities to fully describe and analyze an operator.

The six criteria above describe the information needed to evaluate port operators and to get an overview about their market position and competitive situation. Additional basic business information like balance sheets, profit & loss accounts, or annual reports are also critical materials in an evaluation. The combined set of market and company information provides a good tool set to examine, check, and rank port operators.

In addition to the typical terminal operator's tasks further services that will be described in more detail down below are performed at the terminals; however, final task is to serve the trading industry and to enable cargo flows at competitive conditions. Figure 11.3 below illustrates the cargo flow of a terminal:
–   A ship is berthing at the quay wall
–   The cargo is moved to the yard
–   On the yard or outside the terminal, but within the port area the cargo is manipulated
–   At the outgate the cargo leaves the terminal and/or the port

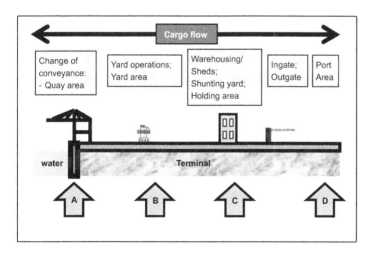

Figure 11.3: Fields of activities for port service and facilities operators

Export procedures follow this chart, but in the opposite direction: from land to sea. The change of conveyance within a port is typically between ships and modes of land transportation, but it can also be between these land transportation modes themselves, for example, between rail and road. This is common for inland terminals, for instance. The often-used term "trimodal center" for an inland terminal highlights the fact that all three modes of transportation are of equal relevance.

Figure 11.3 also illustrates at which stages of the cargo flow the port service operator and port facility operators are active: at position "A," within the quay wall area (e.g., line handling or mooring services), at position "B," within the yard (e.g., terminal operations support), at position "C," in the back areas on the terminals or outside the terminals, but within the port (e.g., by operating warehouses), and at position "D," outside the terminals, but still within the port.

Port facilities as well as port service operators are not directly involved in terminal operations, like ship-to-shore operations with cranes, but they are essential via supporting the terminal operators in fulfilling the tasks illustrated in Figure 11.3. Therefore, after analyzing the terminal operators we shall have a closer look to both the facilities as well as the service operators.

11.2 Terminal Operator

By general definition, a terminal is a point or part forming a limit, boundary, extremity, or end. A terminal inside a port is a purpose-built reception and departure structure at the terminus of land and sea transport routes; a site where cargoes (or passengers) are unloaded, stored, in some cases reprocessed, and reloaded for further transportation. Figures 11.1 and 11.3 illustrate the interfaces between sea and land transport by showing the quay wall as a physical interface between the two modes of transport and the crane as physical equipment to move cargoes from sea to shore or vice versa.

A terminal operator is an institution or company that operates and controls the quay wall as well as the area behind the quay wall (often referred to as "terminal," "terminal area," or "quay hinterland"). Here the cargo is loaded and unloaded from ships, and sometimes between land modes of transportation (e.g., from road to rail). Other types of supportive and complementary services, like mooring, towing and ship supply, also take place at the quay wall.

Companies active in the business of loading and unloading vessels are also called stevedores. The terms "terminal operator" and "stevedore" have different etymological roots. "Terminal operator" describes the company that operates the respective port facility; the term "stevedore" originates from the Portuguese word "estivador" or the Spanish word "estibador," which means "docker," "dock-worker," or "longshoreman"; in the original meaning "men who load ships." A stevedoring company is a company that employs stevedores and that is active in ship loading and unloading. In different countries, both terms are used with slightly different meanings. To be precise, we will use the term "terminal operator" for the institutions or companies that operate the quay and quay hinterland area, that is, the "terminal."

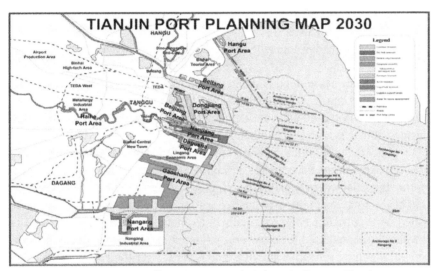

Source: Wikepedia website http://en.wikipedia.org/wiki/File:Tianjin_Port_Planning_Map_2030.svg, visited on December 1, 2017.

Figure 11.4: Port and terminals: Tianjin case

Figure 11.4 shows an example of a port (in this case: Tianjin in China) with several different terminals; all of them displayed in different colors. This is a very typical situation for many ports around the world: at the interface between sea and land transportation are the quay walls and the basins for the ships in front of the walls. At the waterfront side, there are several anchorage areas in front of the basins, and access channels are connecting the terminals with the open sea or the fairways. The areas directly behind the quay walls are the terminals or terminal areas (here displayed in different shades), and behind the terminals are areas for additional port facilities and services, all of them being inside the port area. Together this complex of water areas, access channels, quay walls, terminal areas, and additional port areas forms "the port."

The legend of Figure 11.4 shows the following areas:
- Container terminals
- Dry bulk Terminals
- General cargo terminals
- Equipment assembly
- Administration and support areas
- Passenger terminals
- RoRo terminals
- Liquid bulk terminals
- Logistics support areas
- Areas for future development

In addition, railways and roads are displayed, and the bold chain line shows the port area limits on the waterside of the port. With all these functions, Tianjin is a true universal port that offers a wide range of port services, not including cruise business. There is no cruise terminal in this example.

It is not the task of this overview to delineate all facets of a technical port or of terminal planning. Nevertheless, it should be mentioned that a great deal of literature is available that explains the principles of port layouts and port planning. One of the first comprehensive handbooks for port planners was a study published by UNCTAD in 1985.[1] Originally only intended for developing countries, the handbook was used for many port planning tasks. The handbook provided general planning principles for all types of ports. Over the years, many technical details of ports have been discussed, and national, international, and global associations and port lobby groups (such as the three IAPH Technical Committees for "port planning and development," "port operations and logistics," and "trade facilitation"[2]) assembled an excellent collection of port knowhow. Many terminal operators meet with port development engineers to increase their understanding of terminal planning and development.

The IHS Ports & Terminals Guide provides a very good overview of more than 11,000 ports and terminals. This service is updated daily and access can be accessed via the internet, in addition, an annual CD-version is available.[3] The

---

[1] UNCTAD: Port Development. A handbook for planners in developing countries, second edition; revised and expanded, United Nations, New York 1985.

[2] For further details, refer to the IAPH International Association of Ports and Harbors website and their technical committees: http://www.iaphworldports.org/AboutIAPH/TechnicalCommitttee.aspx

[3] Refer to the IHS website for further information: http://www.ihs.com/products/maritime-information/port/ports-terminals-guide.aspx

"port details" overview, as displayed in Figure 11.5, provides a general overview of a specific port; here Tianjin in China is again taken as an example.

Figure 11.5: IHS Ports & Terminals Guide: Port Details example Tianjin

The "Port Details" button provides an overview about the facilities of the port. Information that is not available for Tianjin as selected port is information about multipurpose facilities, LPG[4] facilities and LNG[5] facilities. Also, the port is at the beginning of 2018 still not CSI[6] compliant. However, all other facilities are available, and this information is in line with Figure 11.4, the port map of Tianjin.

The button "Berths and Cargo" provides a detailed overview of all berths inside the selected port as well as details on the loading and unloading facilities. Figure 11.6 displays an extract of this subsection. Additional information about the terminal operators can be found under the button "Addresses."

---

4 LPG = liquefied petroleum gas
5 LNG = liquefied natural gas
6 CSI = container security initiative. CSI is a program intended to help increase security for maritime containerized cargo shipped to the United States from around the world. A list of CSI ports as well as additional information can be found here: https://www.cbp.gov

The Ports & Terminals Guide provides comprehensive information about the most important terminals around the globe and is a helpful tool to get an overview about terminal equipment, the facilities, as well as many additional details about the infra- and superstructure that is available for business.

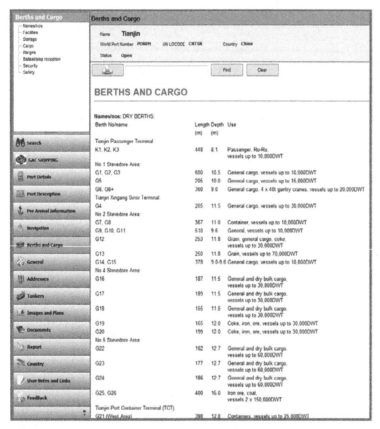

Figure 11.6: IHS Ports & Terminals Guide: Tianjin Berths & Cargo; extract

11.3 Port Facilities Operator

As described above as well as ranged in Chapter 4.2, a "port facilities operator" is a company or institution that operates facilities that are complementary to terminal operations, for example, warehouse companies, tank storage companies, tallying services, consolidation/deconsolidation companies, etc. In some parts of the world (e.g., Australia), the term port facility operator is used more broadly and includes terminal operators as well. Here we will distinguish between terminal and facility operators as explained above.

The existence of a terminal often creates businesses for companies directly related to the terminals. Very often that business did not exist before. Typical activities that take place behind the quay wall area inside a port are:
- Warehouse operations
- Tank storage
- Tallying services
- Bunkering and lubricant
- Logistics companies
- Freight forwarding
- Cleaning services
- Container storage
- LCL container services
- Container maintenance
- Manufacturing and repair

Example: LCL Container Services

We will explore LCL services in further detail, as an example of one of these port areas. Port facility operators like LCL service companies often work very closely with a specific terminal or with a small number of terminals, and they are located adjacent to container terminals inside the port area, but there is no need to operate along the quay wall. These companies normally are not crane operators. An LCL[7] container service company receives full container load (FCL) boxes from a terminal (or, from different terminals) and opens the container and inspects the cargo. On behalf of the vendor or buyer, these companies also provide commodity inspections including pest control, veterinary inspections, etc. Seaworthy packaging of export material is another important task, that is, packaging that must additionally strengthen and withstand the conditions of maritime transport and then resist to more severe stresses.[8] Container storage is another service, and the list of possible activities for LCL services can also include:
- Container packing station for im- and export
- Storage of all kind of cargoes; including reefer cargo

---

7 LCL = less than container load; a shipment that is not large enough to fill a standard container. Often quantities of material from different shippers or for delivery to different destinations carried in a single box. LCL container services are loading and unloading standard containers, so that the terminal can handle FCL only.

8 Refer to Chapter 7.1, All Cargoes; here: seaworthy packaging.

- Handling of heavy lifts and oversized cargo
- Commissioning and distribution services
- Warehousing/bonded warehouse
- Sorting
- Confection services
- Re- and new packing of cargo
- Lists of contents
- Expertise service weight and tare service
- Labels, marks, and numbers
- Samples distribution
- Palletizing
- Stretching
- Cargo lashing
- Fumigation
- Safety and security services
- Customs seals
- Customs clearing and customs transit

This list is already long, but behind these listed tasks are many more tasks. For example, for specialized cargoes, these companies provide a variety of specialized and cargo-related services. For import cars that are stored in containers, for instance, a lot of additional services are provided, like dewaxing, predelivery inspections (PDI), defleeting, refurbishments or enhancements like security alarm fit, air conditioning, badge fit, step bars, in-car entertainment, satellite navigation systems, etc. These examples are intended to illustrate that many hidden tasks and businesses lying behind the listings above. The spectrum for port facility operators is huge, and the specific service in each port is normally in close relation to the im- and export structure of the trade that goes via this port.

11.4 Port Service Operator

According to the description above as well as in Chapter 4.2, a port service operator is a company or institution that can support both the terminals as well as the facilities operator and/or provide additional port services. Port service operators can have their offices or workshops inside the port, but it is not necessary for all services. The nature of service is not that closely linked to the terminals, as is the case for facility operators. The services located inside a port are listed as port service operator. The scope of service is as huge as the scope for facility operators. A rough overview would list the following:

- Port development contractors
- Landscaping
- Haulage/trucking
- Forwarding agents
- Vehicle storage
- Ship chandelling
- Pilots
- Tug boat services
- Parts distribution hub
- Lashing contractors
- Prime mover contractor
- Waste collection
- Duty-free shop
- Convenience stores
- Canteen operators
- Insurance services
- Pest control
- Cleaning services
- Mooring services

Economic impact studies of terminal activities concluded that it is highly likely that several hundred companies and different services will follow terminal business, depending on the type of terminal. The economic effect is a multiplier of public investment, spent in inter-related private business: in port facility operations and—less closely linked—port service operations. The multiplier effects can also be called value-added services (VAS).

These economic multiplier effects have been used by many port authorities to justify direct public sector investments; but the relationship between public investment and accompanying private business is very complex—not an easy one—and a source of frequent misunderstanding. Chapter 13 will discuss these relations in more detail.

An illustration of how terminal business can increase the port facility operations (PFO) and port service operations (PSO) is outlined in Figure 11.7. The container business is clearly the business that creates the highest potential for add-on services.

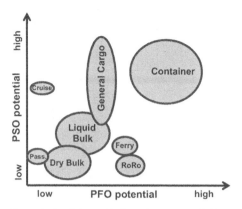

Figure 11.7: Value-added services—potential in ports

11.5 Global Container Terminal Operator

The container business has grown significantly within the past six decades, from ground zero to the dominant unit in general cargo trade, and in addition with slightly increasing volumes in selected segments of bulk trade.[9] With this impressive growth, a new group of terminal operators arose: the globally acting container terminal operators. The unitization of terminal handling procedures and management methods—including the advantages of global procurement—created this profitable business. In combination with the intention to meet the customers twice on both sides of the ocean many profitable business opportunities emerged. Therefore, this new group of operators came to be.

Consulting companies like Dewry define "global container terminal operators" (GCTO) as companies that operate one or more international container terminal facilities and related handling and storage facilities, generally under concessions awarded from port owners for long time periods. Typical characteristics of these are:

- Ownership and/or operations in more than one world region
- Strong investment partners as shareholder
- Very few truly global operators, like HPH, DPW, APMT, PSA
- Most are international container terminal operators
- Some companies are active in selected markets only, like Eurogate
- Some are large single region operators like Bollore T&L in Africa
- Others are large single country operators, like Transnet in South Africa

---

9 See, for example, "Figure 3.2: Container Increase 1970–2015" in Chapter 3.2.

The fact that the GCTO business is a fast growing one attracted the interest of pension and equity funds as investors, who pursue companies with EBITDA margins between 20% and 45%.[10] The natural consequence in the logic of this financial engagement is that typical commercial ratings of the container terminal industry evolved, and along with this interest of rating agencies came up, like e.g. DBRS.[11] Ratings represent a marking system that is designed to inform interested parties.

Rating companies are private-sector firms that assign credit ratings for issuers of debt. A credit rating considers the debt issuer's ability to pay back its loan. The ratings are given to large-scale borrowers, whether companies, private investors, or governments, and are an indication to buyers of this debt how likely they are to be paid back. The score card can also affect the amount that companies or governments are charged to borrow money, that is, the rating may affect the costs for future terminal expansion and investment. If a terminal is deemed to have suffered a downturn in fortunes and its rating is lowered, investors may demand higher returns to lend to it, as it is judged a riskier bet.

A key question in scoring and rating is "how to measure GCTO's activities." Two methods exist to accomplish this, which are not comparable; mixing figures of both methods frequently leads to wrong interpretations.

1. **Total TEU method:** The total number of terminal TEU throughput is the criteria for measurement; no account taken of shareholding percentage. This is a simple approach with a tendency to double countings and unrealistically high figures.

2. **Equity TEU method:** The TEU volumes are adjusted according to shareholding. This is a more realistic measurement but does not cover the "operators owning operators" problem, nor the "owners owning owners" problem. Still this measurement is a much more realistic one.

Here is an example measurement (an extreme case to explain the problem):

---

10 Refer to: The World's Top 5 Terminal Operators, Port Technology website, 4.12.2014, London, UK 2014.
11 See, for example, Rating Container Terminal Operators. Methodology, August 2017, DBRS, Ontario, Canada 2017. DBRS (originally known as Dominion Bond Rating Service) is a full-service credit rating agency established in 1976. Spanning North America, Europe, and Asia, DBRS is respected for its independent, third-party evaluations of corporate and government issues.

Table 11.2: GCTO throughput measurement: Total vs. equity method

	method	calculation	result
1	Total TEU method	engaged in 10 terminals * 10 mill TEU =	100 mill TEU
2	Equity TEU method	10 terminals * 10 mill TEU * 5% share =	5 mill TEU

GCTO "A" is engaged as shareholder in 10 terminals, each terminal handling 10 mill TEU. GCTO "A" has a share of 5% in each operating company.

This simple and extreme example in Table 11.2 clearly shows that the measurement by the first method "total TEU" leads to much higher figures. The total throughput of the ten terminals is 100 mill TEU, and, given the case twenty shareholders have all 5% shares in each of the terminals, the result in an overall statistic will show that all the twenty companies report having a throughput of 100 mill TEU, that is, in total 2 bn TEU. This is unrealistic. The second "equity TEU method" in this case will report that twenty companies in total report a shareholding of 20 * 5 mill TEU = 100 mill TEU. Again, an extreme and unrealistic case, but it illustrates the problem.

In a more realistic case for the equity TEU method, for instance, two terminal operators may have respective stakes in their terminal of 60% and 40%. If that terminal handles 100,000 TEU per year, then 60,000 TEU will be attributed to one terminal operator and 40,000 TEU to the other.

Table 11.3 illustrates the real case of Chinese COSCO Shipping Ports Limited (CSPL), the port branch and pure terminal operator of the group. CSPL completed its reorganization in March 2016, becoming a pure terminals operator (mainly container, but also bulk). This involved the acquisition of China Shipping Ports Development Co., Limited and the disposal of Florens Container Holdings Limited, the container leasing, management, and sale business. In 2016 the company also changed its name; this not only reflects the company's strategic goals and more focused business, but also highlights the group's synergies with its parent company and largest shareholder COSCO Shipping Holdings Co., Ltd., whose ultimate parent company, China COSCO Shipping Corporation Limited, is one of the largest integrated shipping companies in the world. CSPL benefits from the competitive advantages brought by its parent company and the synergies among COSCO shipping group companies. CSPL is shareholder in forty-eight terminals, but only in one single case the company holds 100% of the shares. In most of the cases it is a minor shareholding. This underlines how important it is to compare global container terminal operators on equity shareholding.

Table 11.3: COSCO Shipping Ports Ltd. shareholdings

Bohai Rim	Yangtze River Delta	Southeast Coast & others
24.0% Dalian Automobile Terminal	30.4% Jiangsu Petrochemical	80.0% Jianjiang Pacific Terminal
35.0% Dalian Dagang Terminal	55.0% Lianyungang New Oriental Terminal	20.0% Kao Ming Terminal
40.0% Dalian International Terminal	16.1% Nanjing Longtan Terminal	82.4% Quan Zhou Pacific Terminal
20.0% Dalian Port Terminal	20.0% Ningbo Meishan Terminal	70.0% Xiamen Ocean Gate Terminal
25.0% Dongjiakou Ore Terminal	20.0% Ningbo Yuan Dong Terminal	70.0% Xiamen Tongda Terminal
51.0% Jinzhou New Age Terminal	20.0% Shanghai Mingdong Terminal	
16.0% Quingdao New Qianwan Terminal	30.0% Shanghai Pudong Terminal	
31.2% Quingdao Qianwan Intelligent Terminal	39.0% Taicang Terminal	
20.0% Quingdao Qianwan Terminal	55.6% Yangzhou Yuanyang Terminal	
5.6% Quingdao Qianwan United Advance T.	51.0% Zhangjiagang Terminal	
8.0% Quingdao Qianwan United Terminal	**Pearl River Delta**	**Southwest Coast**
30.0% Quinhuangdao New Harbour Terminal	60.0% Asia Container Terminal	40.0% Quinzhou International Terminal
30.0% Tianjin Euroasia Terminal	50.0% COSCO-HIT Terminal	
28.0% Tianjin Five Continents Term.	40.0% Guangzhou Nansha Stevedoring Term.	
40.0% Yingkou New Century Terminal	39.0% Guangzhou South China Oceangate T.	
50.0% Yingkaou Terminal	14.6% Yantian Terminal Phase i & II	
	13.4% Yantian Terminal Phase III	

Overseas

20.0% Antwerp Terminal	26.0% Kumport Terminal
49.0% COSCO-PSA Terminal	100% Piraeus Terminal
5.5% Busan Terminal	13.3% Seattle Terminal
35.0% Euromax Terminal	20.0% Suez Canal Terminal
90.0% Khalifa Terminal Phase II	24.0% Zeebrugge Terminal

Source: COSCO Shipping Ports LTD., 2016 Annual Report, Hong Kong 2017, page 25.

In the past, global operators purchased more and more shares in terminals resulting in the number of competitors in some regional markets being drastically reduced. In short, it increased concentration of the business in few hands. In the beginning of the 1990s the concentration process sped up. The share of "others," that is, the operators that did not belong to global conglomerates, was in the range of two-thirds in 1991, as shown in Figure 11.8.

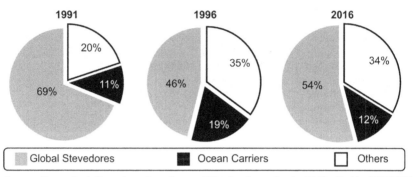

Source: Own calculations, based on: Drewry Shipping Consultants, 2001; cited in: UNESCAP–Korean Maritime Institute, Free Trade Zone and Port Hinterland Development, Thailand 2005, page 37, and: Yilport presentation, TOC Americas, Sept. 18, 2017, Lima, Peru 2017 (Drewry cited by Yilport).

Figure 11.8: Terminal ownership structure in %, 1991–2016

The share of global container terminal operators (here: stevedores and ocean carriers) increased in 1991 with a share of 31% up to a total share of 46% in 2016. On a global level, this is not a serious problem of concentration, but—as mentioned above—in some regional markets the reduction of competition via increased concentration is a real threat.

The top ten global container terminals in 2001 are listed in Table 11.4, with Hutchinson Port Holdings (HPH), Hong Kong, being the absolute number one with a market share of 11.8% of global container throughput. HPH is a subsidiary of today's multinational conglomerate Hutchinson Whampoa Limited (HWL). The history of HPH began in 1866 when the Hong Kong and Whampoa Dock Company was established. For over 100 years, it provided ship construction and repair services before diversifying into cargo and container handling operations in 1969 when its flagship operation, "Hong Kong international terminals" (HIT), was established. In 1994, HPH was founded to manage its growing international port network.

Table 11.4: Global container terminal operators, 2001

Ranking 2001	Operator	mill. TEU 2001	share 2001
1	Hutchinson Port Holdings (HPH)	29.3	11.8%
2	PSA Singapore	19.5	7.9%
3	APM Terminals	13.5	5.5%
4	P&O Ports	10.0	4.0%
5	Eurogate	8.6	3.5%
6	DPA Dubai Ports Authority	4.7	1.9%
7	Evergreen	4.5	1.8%
8	COSCO Pacific	4.4	1.8%
9	Hanjin	4.2	1.7%
10	SSA Marine	4.0	1.6%

Source: Drewry; cited in: Notteboom + Rodrigues, Corporate Geography of GCTO 2012, page 28.

Ranking number two in 2001 and still a major player today is "PSA Singapore," the former Port of Singapore Authority that was formed in 1964 to take over the functions, assets, and liabilities of the Singapore Harbor Board. In 1997, a parliamentary bill was passed to corporatize the authority, and so PSA Corporation Ltd. was built. In 2003, PSA restricted the shareholding, with PSA International Pte Ltd becoming the main holding company for the PSA Group of companies. Since 1997, PSA is no longer the Port Authority of Singapore, even if the abbreviation of the name originally stems from here. The port authority in Singapore is MPA (refer to Chapter 10.7). PSA as global active operator concentrates on international container business with Singapore being the major base and flagship terminals.

"APM terminals" or APMT ranked as the third largest container terminal operator in the world in 2001 as well as in 2005 as Table 11.5 indicates. This company is different from HPH and PSA because it is like the world's largest container shipping line Maersk a subsidiary of the A.P. Moller-Maersk Group in Denmark. HPH and PSA have no direct relation to specific shipping lines, which is why they—like others that are ownership independent from shipping lines—are called universal terminals. They are open to all shipping lines without having any preference. This is what APMT and other terminal operators in the hands of shipping lines claim for themselves as well: that they treated all customers in the same way, but reality and experience show that terminals belonging to shipping lines give preference to their shareholding company. At least via the supervisory boards, the owners of shipping line terminals are informed about the details of the terminal business; and so, they can get first-hand confidential information about their competitors.

Table 11.5: Global container terminal operators, 2005

Ranking 2005	Operator	mill. TEU 2005	share 2005
1	Hutchinson Port Holdings (HPH)	33.2	8.3%
2	PSA Singapore	32.4	8.1%
3	APM Terminals	24.1	6.0%
4	P&O Ports	21.9	3.3%
5	DP World	13.3	2.5%
6	Evergreen	11.5	1.7%
7	Eurogate	11.4	1.6%
8	COSCO	8.1	1.5%
9	SSA Marine	6.7	1.4%
10	HHLA	5.7	1.3%

Source: Drewry; cited in: Port Reform Toolkit 2007, page 87.

Originating as Maersk Line's terminal operating arm, APM Terminals was established as an independent division within the A.P. Moller-Maersk Group in 2001, moving its corporate offices from Copenhagen to The Hague in the Netherlands in 2004, and reporting results as a separate business entity within the group as of 2008. The company's history in terminal operations began more than half a century ago with a general cargo facility at the Port of New York in 1958.

The company P&O Ports, ranking at position four in 2001 and 2005, disappeared from the list in 2010 (Table 11.6). P&O Ports, The Peninsular, and Oriental Steam Navigation Company's port operations has been a terminal operating company that operates terminal facilities worldwide, including several terminals in the United States. In March 2006, DP World acquired P&O Ports for 3.9 billion British pounds or approximately 7 billion USD, making DP World one of the top marine terminal operators in the world, with the widest common user terminal network of any operator.

"DP World" was founded in 2005 by merging Dubai Ports Authority (DPA) and Dubai Ports International.[12] Today DP World (sometimes also referred to as DPW) is one of the few independent GCTOs.

---

12 In 2005 DPI Dubai Ports International (founded in 1999 for international port investments, including the acquisition of CSX World Terminals in January 2005) officially merged with the Dubai Ports Authority (DPA) to form DP World, with "Dubai Ports" (DP).

Table 11.6: Global container terminal operators, 2010

Ranking 2010	Operator	mill. TEU 2010	share 2010
1	PSA Singapore	51.3	9.4%
2	Hutchinson Port Holdings (HPH)	36.0	6.6%
3	DP World	32.6	6.0%
4	APM Terminals	31.6	5.8%
	SIPG Shanghai Internat. *	19.5	3.6%
	China Merchants Holding Int. *	17.3	3.2%
5	COSCO	13.6	2.5%
6	MSC	9.9	1.8%
7	SSA Marine	8.6	1.6%
8	Ports America	8.1	1.5%
9	Evergreen	7.0	1.3%
10	Eurogate	6.2	1.1%

* In 2010 not engaged in global markets
Source: Drewry 2011, page 4.

DP World acquired the whole portfolio of P&O Ports, but after an extended discussion about port security, DP World decided not to take over the former P&O Ports terminals in the United States. Still, with this deal DP World jumped from the sixth position in 2001 and the fifth position in 2005 to the third position in 2010. DP World still ranked third in 2016, behind PSA and HPH.

To get a broader overview of the ranking of GCTOs, Table 11.7 listed the global top fifteen in 2016. Several shipping lines are listed with throughput figures below 10 mill TEU annually. These facilities are dedicated terminals for the shipping lines, in many cases solely used for purposes of the line, respectively the alliance.

When comparing the four figures for 2001 to 2016, one can see that there are no big changes in names and rankings. Only a handful of operators, such as PSA, HPH, DP World, and APMT have dominated the business for years. The new companies entering the market are subsidiaries or former subsidiaries of huge shipping lines, like "China COSCO Shipping Ports Ltd.," or TIL, a company that was founded in 2000 to secure berths and terminal capacity in the major ports used by the Mediterranean Shipping Company (MSC).

The only real new independent operator is "Yilport" from Turkey, ranked no. 13 in 2016. Yilport Holding started activities in 2004 by acquiring Sedef Port, a former shipyard from STFA Holding. In 2005, the group acquired Alemdar Holding, Inc. and subsequently merged the two operations to create Yilport Container Terminal and Port Operators. Yilport Holding Inc. was established in

August 2011 to consolidate port and container terminal operations of Yildirim Group under one roof.

Table 11.7: Global container terminal operators, 2016

Ranking 2016	Operator	mill. TEU 2016	share 2016
1	PSA International	52.4	7.5%
2	Hutchinson Ports	45.6	6.5%
3	DP World	40.0	5.7%
4	APM Terminals	37.3	5.3%
5	China COSCO Shipping Ports	29.1	4.2%
6	China Merchants Port Holdings	27.9	4.0%
7	Terminal Investment Limited	19.3	2.8%
8	ICTSI	7.9	1.1%
9	Evergreen	7.6	1.1%
10	Eurogate	7.4	1.1%
11	SSA Marine / Carrix	6.5	0.9%
12	Hanjin	5.7	0.8%
13	Yilport	5.2	0.7%
14	CMA CGM	5.1	0.7%
15	NYK	3.4	0.5%
Total	Global Container Terminal Op.	320.5	45.8%

Source: Drewry; presented by Yilport at TOC Americas, Lima, Peru, Sept. 18, 2017.

"Eurogate," first on the list in 2001 to rank no. 5, and in 2016 at position 10, is Europe's leading container terminal and logistics group. Jointly with Contship Italia, they operate sea terminals on the North Sea, in the Mediterranean region and on the Atlantic, with excellent connections to the hinterland of Europe. Along with container handling, they offer a full range of "box"-related operations, from cargo-modal services, to container-depot services, container servicing, and container repair.

In September 1999, the family-owned Hamburg-based company Eurokai joined with BLG Logistics Group of Bremerhaven to form Eurogate. The company's head office was established in Bremen. Since then, Eurogate has developed into Europe's largest terminal operator. Contrary to HPH, PSA and DP World, Eurogate operates as a shipping line-independent container terminal group on Europe mainly. With this concentration, Eurogate is a typical "Regional Operator"; not a real global one. This makes Eurogate different from the other top three players. The fact that the market grew mainly in Asia during the last two decades led to the effect that the rank of Eurogate declined from rank no. 5, representing a share of 3.5% of global container port throughput in 2001, down to rank no. 10 with just 1.1% market share in 2016. Another typical "Regional port operator" is the Russian company "Global Ports," the major container operator that is active in Russia and Finland only.[13]

Significantly worse is the position of the second German terminal operator, the state-owned "HHLA" Hamburg Port and Logistics Corp., a company that developed a good economic base after the reunification of Germany, ranking at position no. 10 in 2005. But with the change of the company's management board, a strong vision for the HHLA was lost. In 2010, the company barely made position 15, and in 2016 HHLA was no longer listed as a global terminal operator. HHLA's mission to privatize a large share of the company was scaled back, and the share price after an IPO of approx. Thirty percent of the shares dropped from approximately 60 Euros at the end of 2007 down to less than 15 Euros in 2016, and only slightly recovered since then. Realistically, HHLA is no longer a major player in this segment and—at least until early 2018—does not have the potential to come back nor the ambition to be engaged in the global market; a sad fate for a promising company. All this was caused by poor management that limited HHLA within a fast-growing market.

Exactly the opposite happened with "SIPG" the Shanghai International Port Group, a state-owned company like HHLA. Shanghai International Port (Group) Co., Ltd. is the exclusive operator of all the public terminals in the Port of Shanghai in China. Incorporated in January 2003 by reorganizing the former Shanghai Port Authority, SIPG is a large-scale business conglomerate specialized in the operation of ports and related businesses. In June 2005, SIPG was turned into a shareholding limited company. In October 2006, SIPG listed in the Shanghai Stock Exchange and became the first whole-listed company of China's port industry. The city of Shanghai, and the state of China, is still the largest shareholder of SIPG. The Hong Kong-based CMG China Merchants Group of companies is the second largest shareholder with 24.49%.

In 2016, SIPG realized a total port throughput of 37.1 mill TEU in the port of Shanghai, and in 2017 SIPG surpassed the 40 mill TEU barrier. In addition to the operations in Shanghai, as well as in few other Chinese ports, SIPG is engaged in the Bayport Terminal in Haifa, Israel. In 2015 they won the bid for a twenty-

---

13 Russian company Global Ports is Russia's leading container terminal operator in terms of throughput and capacity. But Global Ports is also a good example of the "operators owning operators"-problem as mentioned above when explaining the advantage of equity TEU measurement. Global Ports is 30.75% owned by operator APMT.

five-year concession. Bayport terminal is expected to be in full operation in 2021. SIPG will be responsible for the construction of the facilities at the back terminal, deployment and installation of the equipment, and the daily running and operation of the terminal. Measuring 1,500 meters in quay length, with a 78 ha surface and a 17.3 m draft, Bayport's new terminal will handle the designed annual container throughput of 1.86 mill TEU.

China Merchants Group (CMG), founded in the self-strengthening movement[14] in 1872, is a leading state-owned conglomerate based in Hong Kong, and "China Merchants Port Holdings" (CMPH) is part of this group. CMPH is the largest public port operator in China with investments in Mainland China, Hong Kong, and overseas. Its nationwide port network expands across the Bohai Economic Zone, the Yangtze River Delta, the Xiamen Bay Economic Zone, the Pearl River Delta, and the Southwest region. This includes the coastal hub ports in Hong Kong, Shenzhen, Ningbo, Shanghai, Qingdao, Tianjin, Xiamen Bay, and Zhanjiang. Internationally, the group has been engaged with the Tin-Can Island Container Terminal in Nigeria, the Djibouti Doraleh Multi-Purpose Port, the Colombo International Containers Terminal Ltd., as well as with the Hambantota port project in Sri Lanka as part of the Chinese belt-and-road-initiative (BRI). The company has also worked in the Lome Container Terminal in Togo, in the Kumport (Istanbul) in Turkey, and has a 90% stake of the Port of Paranagua in Brazil. "Going international" is a relatively young initiative of CMG, but has been pursued intently.

Table 11.8: Key changes, 2000–2015

	2000	2015	% chang
Global container port throughput (mill TEU)	224.8	687.7	305.9%
Chinese ports share of world TEU	18%	28%	155.5%
Global/International terminal operators share of world Throughput (Equity TEU basis)	54%	46%	−14.8%
Largest container ship (in TEU)	8,000	19,000	237.5%

Source: MWP Hamburg

---

14 The so-called Self-Strengthening Movement in China (1861–1895), was a period of institutional reforms initiated during the late Qing dynasty following a series of military defeats and concessions to foreign powers. China Merchants received such a concession.

Table 11.8 highlights select key changes in the port industry between 2000 and 2015. Global container throughput has more than tripled, and the share of Chinese ports after the opening of the Chinese market to the world has further increased from 18% to 28%. (Today, more than a quarter of global port throughput is concentrated on one country only!) Meanwhile, in terms of equity TEU, the global and international terminal operators account for over 46% of world throughput, compared with 54% fifteen years before; a slight decrease of share within a strong growing market, but still impressive when bearing in mind that only a few companies have reached this level. In parallel to container throughput, the vessel size grew up to a size of 21,000 TEU; and the order book shows that 24,000 TEU vessels will enter the market very soon. Combined with increased vessel size, this will result in a completely new organization of the terminals.

The major key players are:
– Hutchinson Port Holding (HPH)
– PSA Singapore
– DP World
– APM Terminals

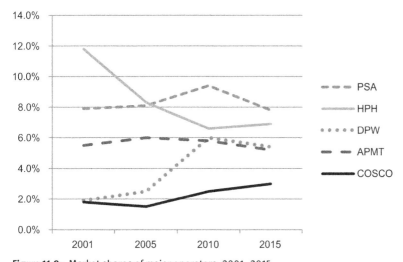

Figure 11.9: Market shares of major operators, 2001–2015

Figure 11.9 illustrates the development of market shares between 2001 and 2015. The decline of HPH is visible, and the increase of DP World's shares after the acquisition of P&O Ports and the upcoming development of COSCO Shipping Ports Ltd. after the merger of COSCO with China Shipping.

In 2016, each of these four major groups handled more than 35 mill TEU. At position five and six are the two Chinese groups CSPL and CMPH, which together handle 57 mill TEU—more than PSA. Today nobody knows if they will ever merge, but if they did, they would become the new no.1 operator. It can be expected that within the next few years a reorganized Chinese group will join the "former top 4 operators" club. All other operators are handling substantially less cargo.

The speed at which some of the operators developed is impressive. And all these operators are very profitable, earning EBITDA margins more than 40%, with the exception of APMT (here the margin increased steadily over the years, already being beyond 20%, with an upward trend). Global port operation is a lucrative business.

A final distinction of operators can be made when analyzing their ownership. In principal, there are three different types of ownership, all having different interests and different methods for driving expansion in business.

- Stevedores
- Shipping companies
- Investment funds or financial holdings

Table 11.9 provides a good overview of the different business models and shows under which operation style certain terminal operator types work.

Table 11.9: Types of global terminal operators

	Stevedores	Companies	Financial Holdings
Business model	**Horizontal integration**	**Vertical integration**	**Portfolio diversification**
Position of terminal operations w.r.t. core business	Port Operation is the core business; Investment in container terminals for expansion and diversification	Maritime shipping is the main business; Investment in container terminals as a support function	Financial assets management is the main business; Investment in container terminals for valuation and revenue generation
Dominant expansion strategy	Expansion through direct investment	Expansion through direct investment or through parent companies	Expansion through acquisitions, mergers and reorganization of assets
Examples	PSA (public), HHLA (public), Eurogate (private), HPH (private), ICTSI (private), SSA (private)	MSC (private), APL (private), CMA CGM (private), Evergreen (private)	DPW (Sovereign Wealth Fund), Ports America (AIG; Fund), RREEF (Deutsche Bank; Fund), Macquarie Infrastructure (Fund), Morgan Stanley Infrastructure (Fund), SSA Marine (Goldman Sachs)

Source: Notteboom + Rodrigues, Corporate Geography of GCTO 2012, page 29.

Stevedores follow a horizontal integration strategy, that is, they are looking for the same kind of business at the same stage within the supply chain. Maritime shipping companies on the other hand follow a primarily vertical integration strategy. This means their core business is shipping, and to enlarge the activities along the supply chain, they are starting activities in terminal operation. Investment funds with financial interests ranging from investment banks and retirement funds to sovereign wealth funds have no such strategy; they are just looking for interesting—that is, profitable—investments in new market segments as an asset class for generating revenue.

The figures and statistics above are all global figures on a worldwide scale; but the activities of the global and international terminal operators are not spread equally around the world. In 2018, DP World operated seventy-seven terminals on all continents, with container handling generating around 80% of its revenue. Still, DP World is weak in the Americas as well as in west and east Africa. APM Terminals operates nearly the same number of port and terminal facilities (75) in forty-one countries, but has no operation in Australia or east Africa.

The two operators are concentrating themselves on different regional markets, as Figures 11.10 and 11.11 exemplify. However, in a few years from now it is very likely that most of the global operators will be spread equally around the world to best serve their customers.

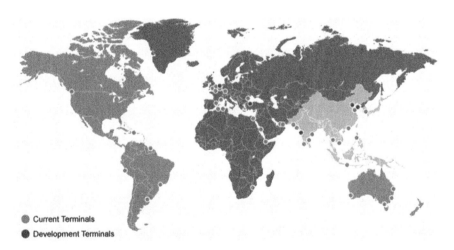

● Current Terminals
● Development Terminals

Source: http://www.dpworld.com :Media Centre

Figure 11.10: DP World network

Figure 11.11: APM Terminals network

11.6 Terminal Operators Growth Path

Ports and terminals in most cases start as small business units, and very often this business starts as a public operation to ensure that trade to or from a region finds its best possible way to market. Private (industrial) ports also often start as small units with few berths and limited operations, but these business units typically stay close to one or very few business locations and are not open for the public or for other clients. Small public ports on the contrary are normally open to the market and intend to grow; because this is the easiest way to cover best the fixed costs of the investments.

In developing ports, it is often identified that with growing volumes and diversified activities in several segments, the intention to privatize the terminal business arises. The pressure to do so comes from the market—that is, local businessmen or companies that want to incorporate private business—as well as from the customers (from the shipping business as well as from the hinterland operator who puts pressure on efficient terminal operations). Sooner or later parts of the operations will be commercialized and private terminal activities will follow. This first split between administration and terminal operation within the second development phase opens the door for additional new businesses. With further growing private activities, the consequence is often a clear wish to clearly distinguish between public administration tasks that cannot be privatized, like security, harbor police or fire brigade, and private tasks; realized, for example, via port laws. A typical landlord model is often the best operational model for accomplishing this. Figure 11.12 includes this as step three.

Small public port > with growth: Authority + Operator > with growing private business: Landlord Model > specialized terminal operator > Going international: GTO

Figure 11.12: Terminal operator development path

As, the terminal business grows, it tends to specialize more and more. For example, in container business, dedicated facilities are established; while in liquid bulk business, highly specialized product terminals are installed, like LPG or LNG terminals. In conventional general cargo, growing volumes lead to product specific terminals, like timber terminals or coffee terminals with specialized warehouses in the back. The process described above takes years, if not decades, but the patterns lead to specialization in terminal operations.

The last step very often is an internationalization strategy with a trend to global terminal operators (GTOs). Specialized operators often have limited market potential, but on the contrary, their knowledge and skills are very high. As a result, a "going international"-strategy is a chance to gain further market shares and grow the terminal business. For GTOs with maritime shipping companies as shareholders or owners, this also supports vertical integration. For terminal operators, an internationalization strategy is the normal method for enhancing business opportunities.

Chapter 12
Port Cost Analysis

Port pricing strategies are often influenced by the cost of production, market structure, supply and demand balance, competitive situation, and institutional factors. These factors are more complex for ports (i.e., authorities and terminals) for various reasons.

1. Today, most ports operate as providers of infrastructure, including navigational, whose operations are interdependent. Therefore, splitting production costs for pricing purposes, for example, between the typical public function as port police and the mixed function as infrastructure provider can be very difficult if not impossible. In addition, since investments in ports are largely "irreversible" and therefore "sunk" costs, operational or variable costs play an important role especially in short-term pricing.

2. The port governance system and the self-image of the authority[1] are reflected in pricing strategy. State owned ports charge their customers for public services; often tariff-based. Typical landlord ports charge via the authorities for public services (e.g., dredging of access channels), plus also invoice the customer for private services offered by the terminal operator. Total port costs in such cases consist of various components, and these modules are not easy to compare as they may include various service components.

3. The basis for pricing varies a lot. There is no standard, and with the different strategies of the authorities and service operator, the tariff structure and the pricing scale can be quite diverse. Recently, authorities have worked to reduce their carbon footprint; therefore, various rebate and price deduction schemes have been included in port pricing. Other ports want to attract huge vessels to better utilize the infrastructure. Some ports charge higher prices for work on weekends, others offer rebates when a vessel comes more frequently, etc.

4. As port authorities are regarded as both public assets and businesses, a port's pricing strategy can vary substantially depending on the role on which it wants to focus. Costs for typical public functions for the whole port community, such as port safety and security tasks, need to be mixed with specific costs that are undoubtedly caused by a specific user.

5. Pricing for the services of the authority are often subject to strong regulations via other public authorities as well as via the supervisory board. Changes

---

[1] For details of self-image, refer to Table 10.1.

DOI 10.1515/9781547400874-012

to port tariffs, dues and charges require careful planning and justification. As public bodies, port authorities are under public scrutiny, for instance, via local newspapers and journalists. Because of this, transparency of pricing is necessary.

6. Because ports are logistics nodes and partners along the transportation chain, pricing should consider both competition between ports and cooperation along the supply chain. This implies the equilibrium price can even be outside the competitive-monopoly price range. Pricing of supply chain partners can be a component of port pricing. A good example of a port authority pricing strategy is the influence of shipping lines THC fixing for ports. Especially within an area of high competition, the influence of THCs is at least considered; and with this has an influence on port pricing.

Shipping lines are major customers of port authorities, terminal operators, and supportive or complementary service, as well as all types of hinterland transportation providers. For ports acting as nodal points in a supply chain, the following four major categories build the basis for their pricing. For port customers as clients of the authority and the operators, these services form the group of port costs.

7. Services to the ship for safe navigation (= NAV)
    a. Infrastructure provision
    b. Aids to navigation
    c. Pilotage
    d. Towage
8. Services to ship at berth (= BERTH)
    a. Berthing/mooring
    b. Berth infrastructure
    c. Stevedoring
    d. Wharf handling
9. Hinterland services (= HL)
    a. Gate services
    b. Storage
    c. Customs surveillance/attendance
    d. Rail, truck, barge, and pipeline operations
10. Services to the cargo (= CARGO)
    a. Storage
    b. Cargo processing
    c. Equipment/short-term rental
    d. Consolidation/deconsolidation
    e. Warehousing

Table 12.1: Port services classification

Service Group	Type of Service	Mainly Charged by
1. = NAV		Port Authority
2. = BERTH	cargo flow resp. traffic related	Terminal Operator
3. = HL		Supporting Service Op.
4. = CARGO	cargo/product service related	Terminal Operator, Supporting Service Op.

The first three of the four different services are for cargo flow or traffic related services, for example, for vessels entering the port, for services along the berth or for services for hinterland modes of transport, like loading or unloading trucks. These services are charged by port authorities (e.g., for dredging the access channel and the basins in front of the berths), by terminal operator (for stevedoring or yard handling services), or by supporting/complementary service provider (e.g., for navigational aids or mooring services). All three services enable the cargo to "flow," that is, for export purposes to move the cargo on board of the vessel and allow the vessel to leave the port or vice versa, for import services to move the cargo from the ship via the terminal to the hinterland and then to the final customer. No manipulation of the cargo itself happens.

Service group four is different from this. Here the terminal operator or service partner works with the cargo itself. This can be a blending of a liquid bulk cargo, it can be a service to RoRo cargo like dewaxing of cars, or it can be LCL cargo consolidation for the container business. Cargo or product related services are not normally offered by authorities; they are considered private services.

Port authorities, terminal operators, and service providers charge port customers for all the services. When analyzing bills that port customers receive, the first thing that became obvious is that there is no standard; not for the names of the services nor for their base of calculation. Similar services can be designated on a bill differently, depending on the port. In port A, a service may have the same name as in port B, but if the ports use different bases for pricing, the "port due" can vary greatly. This makes it complicated to compare and benchmark port costs. However, detailed studies of consulting firms that analyzed port costs and port pricing structures concluded that port cost components in most cases fall into three different categories:

- Port dues (charges for the utilization of port and terminals)
- Cargo fees (cargo-related fees)
- Miscellaneous

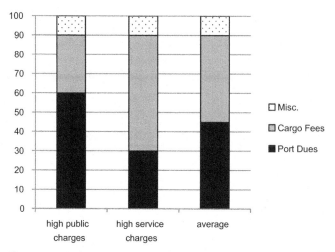

Figure 12.1: Typical composition of port costs

As a general ballpark figure, the three major components of port costs as indicated in Figure 12.1 are often in the following percentage range (part of total port costs):

Port dues: often 30%–60% of total costs
Cargo fees: often 30%–60% of total costs
Miscellaneous: often 5%–20% of total costs

12.1 Port Dues

The term "port dues" is not commonly defined. In our understanding, this is the *generic term for all charges and fees that users like vessels must pay for the use of a port*. Regarding Table 12.1, the dues must be paid for most of service group 1: navigational aids, as well as for parts of groups 2 and 3: berth and hinterland services. Port authorities charge such dues for the utilization of port infrastructure. Railway and pipeline operators must pay for the utilization as well, but in the following we will concentrate on vessel traffic. Typically, these charges are levied against a ship owner, ship manager/agent or ship operator, either by the port authority, or by the terminal or service operator. Terminal operators that lease the terminal often call the infrastructure charge a "berthing fee" to differentiate this payment from the public port authority charge. The major shares of costs are for the authority, and therefore we will at first have a look at the public port dues.

Port authorities call their charges and fees for vessels port due, port charge, port tariff, harbor due, channel due, marine charge, tonnage due, or something like this. Very often the dues depend on ship type; then the due may be called tanker due, bulker due, cruise ship due, RoRo fee, etc. In addition, the dues vary with respect to the amount of cargo discharged or loaded. Port dues are usually paid to a port authority by a vessel for each harbor entry, usually on a per gross tonnage (GT) or dwt basis, to cover the costs of basic port infrastructure and marine facilities such as buoys, beacons, and vessel traffic management system.

This due is the first one the vessel owner or his representative must pay, often regardless of how much cargo the vessel intends to discharge or load. The dues are mostly a multiple of a vessel characteristic like GT, multiplied with a fee. In some ports, a fix block is added to lift the basic amount and reduce the rate of ascent. Other ports add a factor that is related to the percentage of max. cargo load, for example, "GT * % of cargo loaded." Normally this is done to give a rebate for full loadings. Port dues are typically a fee with a structure as follows:

$$\text{Port Dues} = \text{GT} * \text{fee, or:}$$
$$\text{Port Dues} = \text{DWT} * \text{fee} + \text{fixed charges}$$

Typical vessel design, volume or load indicators like dwt, NRT, GRT, GT, and NT are frequently mixed up and are not consequently applied.

Another important factor is how often a specific vessel calls the port. Rebates are often provided for frequent and regular services like liner calls. This means that the costs that a vessel operator must pay for a specific vessel with the same amount and type of cargo varies depending on the number of calls the vessel or the company made to this specific port. Figure 12.2 illustrates the case for agribulk vessels calling the Port of Rotterdam.

In this real example, the vessel operator must pay 100% of the port dues for a single call, and for the same vessel with the same amount of cargo he may get a discount of up to 25% when calling the port regularly. The logic behind this is very simple: frequent customers who are familiar with the port and that are used to operating inside the port boundaries get a rebate, that is, a typical customer loyalty program.

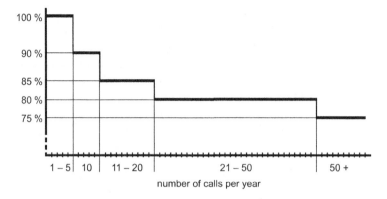

Source: Port of Rotterdam: General Terms and Conditions including Port Tariffs 2018, page 21.
Figure 12.2: Rotterdam port due discounts for frequent calls

Due to these huge rebates (in the Rotterdam case, up to 25%, in other ports like Zeeland Ports in the Netherlands, up to 50%), it is not possible to say what a single call of a specific vessel really costs. Comparable discounts like in Rotterdam and Zeeland can be found in many ports for various types of vessels, depending on the strategy of the port authority. Therefore, it is always necessary to clearly define the base parameter for port benchmarking. There are also additional discounts and surcharges on the market that influence total cost, such as:
– Discounts for double-hull tanker
– Environmental discount incentive (ESI, env. awards, "Blue Angel")
– Environmental discount incentive (LNG powered)
– "No cargo handled" discount (e.g., for ship repair)
– Penalties for wrong data submission
– Transhipment rebates

Port authorities have long-established pricing and tariff structures. These are contained in published schedules, which vary in length from a few pages to more than one hundred. Some tariffs are extremely complex while others are relatively simple. There is, however, an increasing desire on the part of port users for greater transparency in the billing of port services. This highlights the need for more easily understandable and comparable tariff structures.

Clearly comparing the dues of one port with another is not possible just by looking to the quantity of cargo loaded, the size of the vessel or the number of port visits per year. There are many exemptions possible, as well as many surcharges that are combined with cargo loading that make it difficult, if not unrealistic, to simply compare one charge with another. This is due to many reasons that are often tied up with national, regional, or company-specific historical rules.

Two short examples of tankers in Arabian Gulf ports demonstrate the complexity of benchmarking. For the comparison, we will look at the charging rules of the two national port authorities of Bahrain and Fujairah and calculate the cost of calls for two different vessels (a VLCC and an Aframax tanker) in each of the ports and will assume that the same amount of oil is loaded (= 100,000 tons).

The two ports are quite close to each other, so there are no huge political or cultural differences that need to be considered. The vessels are the same and so is the cargo: there is no difference in quality between the crude oil, so one might assume that the difference in port dues is small. But that is not the case as the examples will show.

Example 1

In Bahrain, port dues are calculated by taking the vessel size plus the amount of cargo load into consideration as Table 12.2 shows. This means that the dues are calculated based on vessel and cargo load, as the tariff of the Ministry of Transport indicates.

Table 12.2: Bahrain liquid tanker dues[2]

% of dwt	BHD per GT
up to 20%	0.014
21–30%	0.021
31–40%	0.028
41–50%	0.035
51–60%	0.041
61–70%	0.048
71–80%	0.055
81–90%	0.062
91–100%	0.069

– Bulk liquid dues are charged based on the proportion of cargo tonnage to dwt
– 1, – BHD Bahrain Dinar = 2,65 US Dollar
– Charges apply on import and export cargo
Source: Bahrain MoT Port Tariff

---

2 It shall just be remembered that gross tons (GT) is a measurement of volume, whereas dwt is a weight measurement. It is mixed up here as well as in other Arabian Gulf ports, but fact is—as the explanation by the Bahrain Ministry of Transport on their web page expressed—that the proportion of cargo is relevant.

A typical VLCC tanker like most of the Bahri crude oil tankers is of the following size: nearly 320,000 dwt, 160,000 GT with a length of 330 m. If our example tanker loads 100,000 t of oil products in Bahrain's Sitra port (thus is 31.3% laden), it will pay the following as liquid tanker due (LTD):

0.028 BHD per GT, or in total = *4,480 BHD* or 11,872 USD

A second Aframax crude oil tanker like Frontline's "Sea Bay" of approx. 60,200 GT, a length of 240 m and with a capacity of 108.760 t, loading the same 100,000 t of oil products in Sitra port shall pay the following:

0.069 BHD per GT, or in total *4,154 BHD* or 11,008 USD

It is only a minor difference in price, although the size of the vessels varies substantially. With this tariff structure, the Ministry of Transport in Bahrain gives preference to larger vessels; or—other way round—charges smaller tankers with nearly the same amount of LTD the way they charge the big ones; a strategy that is expressed in this tariff. Preference is for larger vessels that at best should load maximum cargo. We can only speculate the reasons behind this strategy, but arguments like "better infrastructure utilization" or general "economies of scale" are probably not wrong.

Example 2:

The Port of Fujairah charges port dues for the first 48-hour period, which commences at the time of first line on the jetty. The total visit time ends when the last line is let go. This is in line with the general assumption above. But, if on completion of 48 hours, the vessel opts to remain in the port to continue operations, charges "GT * 0.20 Dhs" will apply at a rate of a 6-hour period and part thereof. For our example, we will assume that the vessels are in the port for less than 48 hours.

The general underlying marine charge for any tanker that enters and berths at a jetty or berth is as follows,

a) GT 0–2000 = Dhs. 3,165
b) GT 2001 and above = Dhs. 1.60 per GT

This is a mix of a minimum base block rate (3165 Dhs) plus an additional linear increasing rate per GT and a surcharge factor for only one of the two factors (here: factor "b," the linear costs). There is no relation of tanker dues to any kind of cargo load; in other words, the port does not charge based on cargo load, and the additional loading charge of 0.75 Dhs up to 5 mill tons, 0.70 Dhs between 5 and 10 mill tons and 0.65 Dhs over 10 mill t on the other hand has no relation to vessel size.

For the same two crude oil tankers used in example 1 above, the port dues in Fujairah amount to:

160,000 GT= 3165+(160000-2000)*1,6 = 255,965 Dhs or 69,900 USD
60,200 GT= 3165+(60200-2000)*1,6 = *96,285 Dhs* or 26,300 USD

Conclusion: In Bahrain the port charges nearly the same amount of due for the two tankers, because the Ministry intends to support the call of large vessels. In Fujairah there is no relation to cargo load; the only factor for pricing is vessel size; with the effect that the larger vessel will be charged more than double the price the smaller Aframax tanker must pay.

★ ★ ★

What the two examples show is that it is not possible to simply compare the port dues for one vessel with another and just calculate the cost per single call. In the Bahrain example above—like in many other ports—dues are linked to a variety of parameters, like cargo load, environmental friendliness, or number of annual calls. It is also not possible to calculate exactly what it will cost to bring a specific amount of cargo to a specific port, as the Bahrain example shows. It depends on vessel size. The same amount of cargo can lead to different costs just based on the size of the vessel.

Port authorities also use the port tariff structure to express their development strategy regarding the ship types most welcomed in their port. Bahrain, as explained, seems to prioritize larger vessels. The Irish port of Dublin,[3] as another example, has an easy to read "tonnage due" that is only based on vessels GT. For what they called a solid Bulker (e.g., coal or ore carrier), the rate is fixed at 1.17 € per GT. For a LoLo carrier, for example, a more cleanly conventional general cargo carrier, the rate is fixed at 0.578 € per GT. With this, a bulker of same size as a general cargo vessel is more than twice as expensive. This describes a clear strategy for selected vessels; in this case obvious for ships with clean cargoes on board. "Dirty"

---

3 For more details, refer to: Dublin Port Company, Port Charges on Vessels (Tonnage Dues), Dublin, Ireland, April 2017.

bulkers are more expensive. The same is true in Dublin for the two comparable types of RoRo carriers. A RoRo car carrier will be charged with 0.337 € per GT, and a RoRo freighter with 0.079 € per GT. With this tariff, the car carriers are charged more than four times more than the freighter; a clear priority is thus expressed.

Finally, beside the public infrastructure charge described so far there are additional dues ship owners or their representatives must pay for services like berthing or pilotage. All these costs occur for the vessel (and not to forget: as well as for all other modes of transport) for the utilization of infrastructure. An overview of the major dues public and private entities charge for the utilization of infrastructure is very long, and—as already mentioned—the terminology can vary from port to port. Below are the key charges that can often be found on invoices for port services:

- Light dues, both national and local
- Buoy dues
- Anchorage fees
- Way-leave charge
- Hose handling fees
- Pilotage, in and out
- Towage, in and out
- Terminal fees/charges
- Mooring and unmooring expenses
- Stand-by tugs and/or stand-by launches, when compulsory
- Watchmen
- Conservancy dues
- Harbor dues
- Port dues
- Quay dues
- Berth hire
- Warping charge
- Fender charge
- Tonnage dues
- Wharfage/dockage/berthage
- Launches
- Port clearance
- Quarantine/free pratique fees
- Skimmer charge
- Customs surveillance/attendance
- Customs overtime
- Sundries and petties
- Agency
- ISPS costs

12.2 Cargo Fees

A second main block of fees, which most ports charge are cargo related fees, or in short, cargo fees. These can be divided into two main groups:
1. Cargo handling fees
2. Cargo processing fees

Cargo handling fees will be charged for all kinds of cargo movements. Most prominent here are the fees for loading and unloading vessels, but also charges for train or barge loading activities can be charged, as well as yard movements for rolling cargoes or pumping activities for liquid products. Every cargo that "flows" and that (depending on the port management concept) is handled by a stevedoring company, for example, can be charged. For standardized products like container or dry bulks, as well as for all other kind of products, there are often unit prices that will be multiplied by the amount of cargo handled.

Not all ports name these fees "cargo handling fees"; sometimes they are confusingly entitled "port charge," "stevedoring tariff," or "wharfage." In passenger transport, the "units" that are the base for the charge are the people using the ports and terminals. Such fees are often called "embarkation fees." Most of the fees are calculated as a multiplier of the volume of cargo or the unit loaded or discharged, multiplied by the unit price:

$$\text{Cargo Fee} = \text{mt} * \text{fee, or more general:}$$
$$\text{Cargo Fee} = \text{unit} * \text{fee (unit like TEU, lane meter, etc.)}$$

Table 12.3 demonstrates an example for dry bulk handling in Sri Lanka. Here the port authority also offers cargo handling activities and publishes tariffs for this kind of services. In landlord ports, cargo handling activities are offered by private companies, and they are not that open in publishing tariffs. Additionally, these tariffs are open for negotiations. Therefore, we took the example of a public operator like SLPA that regularly published the handling fees.

Table 12.3 shows that as volumes increase, unit prices decrease. The first 999 mt will be charged with 5.00 USD per mt. With increasing volumes, the unit price per category, and so the average unit price, decreases. Every mt above 7000 mt will only be charged with 1.25 USD. Another specialty here is the fact that the unit prices are charged based on daily average outputs. With this, the SLPA expressed that they want a quick turnaround with high volumes. This is the most attractive option for a ship owner.

Table 12.3: SLPA Sri Lanka port tariff, 2015 dry bulk

Cargo Operations; payable by Ship/Cargo Owner Dry Bulk Cargo	Rate per mt (in USD)
1. Dry Bulk Cargo (Manual Handling) - Irritant/Non Irritant	5.00
2. Totally mechanized handling of bulk cargo / daily average output	
7000 mt and above	1.25
6000 mt to 6999 mt	1.50
5000 mt to 5999 mt	2.00
4000 mt to 4999 mt	2.50
3000 mt to 3999 mt	2.80
2000 mt to 2999 mt	3.00
1000 mt to 1999 mt	3.50
below 1000 mt	5.00
3. Handling of Cement in Bags	5.70

Source: http://portcom.slpa.lk/Tariff/Tariff%20-%202015.pdf

In case the cargo requires special handling equipment, it is also common practice to charge for the utilization of such equipment. Fees are named based on the tools used in the service being charge, like "forklift fee," or more general still "usage fees." Such fees will be charged, for example, for:
– Forklifts (by size: e.g., up to 2, 2-5, 6-12, 13-25 and over 25 tons)
– Bobcats
– Loading-arms
– Pay-loaders
– Hoppers
– Handling of hatch covers
– Terminal trailers
– Nylon/rope slings, nets
– Wire or chain slings (by size)
– Pallet bars
– Drum hooks
– Shackles
– Chain hook
– Spreaders
– Reefer pads and electricity supply
– Entrepot services
– Interterminal trucking

Plus, all types of typical port labor, like lashing or cleaning gangs, container storage workers, safety officers, cargo inspectors, tally services, security, as well as all other specialized port workers. These fees are charged for work at regular port working times, for overtime, as well as for night shifts, weekend work, etc. Some ports also add general "administrations fees" on top of this.

The variety of fees for cargo handling is huge, and it is very hard to compare a special fee of one port with a fee of a similar name but a different base for calculation at another port.

Cargo processing fees will be charged for all types of activities that change or manipulate the cargo itself. This can, for example, be the blending or commingling of liquid bulk products to achieve a cargo with a new product designation, or the blending of coffee to create a new mix for a designated market, or, as another example, the adjustment of cars in order to meet regulatory or seasonable requirements, like colored lights and specialized mirrors for some markets or even canopy tops in the summer. Such activities are often not core activities of port operators, but performing such services is necessary to be awarded with a handling contract. Specialized port service companies often are subcontracted for such activities. In line with Figure 4.2 above, these services can be classified as supportive or complementary port services.

The term "cargo processing fee" is also often used by customs authorities; sometimes also named "merchandise processing fee." When they handle the products they often call this "processing," but the meaning of the word here is more in the sense of checking, handling, dispatching, finally getting clearance and putting a fee on it. The cargo itself will not be manipulated, processed, converted or worked on.

12.3 Miscellaneous

The port dues and cargo fees listed above are often the key cost components when analyzing the total cost of calling a port. However, there are many additional costs that will be charged for a port call as well, as the following list explains. These costs are neither typical port dues nor cargo fees; therefore, we cluster them as "miscellaneous."

- Communication charges (when not using standards)
- Translation charges
- Ballast water charge
- Cancellation fees
- Extended lay-time charge
- Convoy surcharges
- Heavy weather surcharges/storm surcharge, etc.

The list of additional cost components to standard port dues is not exhaustive; there are more arguments and positions to vary the charges.

12.4 Port Costs Benchmarking

After analyzing the confusingly long list of port dues and cargo fees that are obviously not easy to compare, the question comes up: what is the best way to compare and benchmark port costs? The bottom-up analysis that studies all the various cost components and tries to match them on a lower or higher level is very complicated or—due to the different cost pricing strategies—not possible. So, the best way is a top-down analysis: after a vessel calls a port, all bills for all services will come in and can be added up. With this we will have the total costs of a port call. And at least the total costs can be analyzed and compared precisely. But also, here comparable preconditions should be set:
-   Compare total costs of a typical call
-   Define what a typical call is, for example, a frequent liner call that calls the port x times per year
-   Select one (or few) typical vessels as reference vessel
-   Vessel parameter need to be comparable, for example, LNG engine, emissions
-   All rebates and discounts should be disclosed
-   Define the exact time in port (weekend or holidays can be more expensive)
-   Define a specific cargo load; measured in tons, TEU, or units

A benchmarking of ports based on these parameters should provide a good base for comparison, but it should also not be forgotten that there is the additional problem of diverse currencies. A comparison is only possible on a joint scale, for example, based on USD. But in many cases, port dues and other fees must be paid in local currency. Thus, a problem of using the accurate exchange rate occurs. On top of this, around the globe the cost of living is not the same, the exchange rate fluctuates sometimes abruptly, and the purchase power of one USD varies from country to country. Therefore, economists in such cases prefer to take the purchase power parity (PPP) as a benchmarking standard. The idea behind PPP is that the actual purchasing power of any currency is the quantity of that currency needed to buy a specified unit of a good or a basket of common goods and services; PPP is determined in each country based on its relative cost of living and inflation rates. With this, the PPP is a more realistic measure for all types of international benchmarking. Every three years, the World Bank constructs and releases a report that compares various countries in terms of PPP and USD. This data can be used for benchmarking.

The Korean Maritime Institute (KMI) in cooperation with ESCAP, the United Nations Economic and Social Commission for Asia and the Pacific, prepared a "Comparative Analysis of Port Tariffs in the ESCAP Region" in 2002, and saw very interesting results when comparing twenty-one Asian ports as Table 12.4 shows:

Table 12.4: KMI study: Comparison of port tariff levels (3,000 TEU class ship)

Country	Port	Nominal exchange rate		Purchasing power parity	
		Tariff (US$)	Manila=100 (Rank)	Tariff (US$)	Osaka=100 (Rank)
Australia	Sydney	181,991	351 (18)	201,282	198 (9)
China	Shanghai	84,033	162 (8)	366,129	361 (15)
	Tianjin	75,706	146 (5)	329,848	325 (13)
Hong Kong	Hong Kong	205,000	395 (20)	189,221	187 (6)
India	Mumbai	92,429	178 (9)	450,857	444 (16)
	Madras	93,663	181 (12)	456,877	450 (17)
Indonesia	Jakarta	77,819	150 (6)	703,060	693 (20)
Japan	Osaka	144,746	279 (16)	101,435	100 (1)
	Yokohama	359,882	694 (21)	252,198	249 (12)
Malaysia	Port Klang	68,928	133 (4)	163,703	161 (2)
Myanmar	Yangon	189,935	366 (19)	855,384	843 (21)
New Zealand	Auckland	132,250	255 (15)	164,625	162 (4)
Pakistan	Karachi	92,883	179 (11)	356,052	351 (14)
Philippines	Manila	51,848	100 (1)	213,145	210 (10)
South Korea	Busan	92,535	178 (10)	163,809	161 (3)
Singapore	Singapore	157,459	304 (17)	167,497	165 (5)
Sri Lanka	Colombo	132,149	255 (14)	478,948	472 (18)
Taiwan	Kaohsiung	123,926	239 (13)	228,896	226 (11)
Thailand	Bangkok	63,424	122 (2)	199,961	197 (7)
	Laem Chabang	63,769	123 (3)	201,049	198 (8)
Viet Nam	Saigon Port	81,836	158 (7)	482,562	476 (19)

Source: KMI, Comparison of Port Tariffs, page 40.

1. The costs for a vessel with 3,000 TEU vary greatly based on nominal exchange rates from approximately 52 kUSD up to nearly 360 kUSD as expressed also in Figure 12.3 below. The most expensive port is nearly seven times as expensive as the cheapest one. A surprisingly huge spread.
2. Recalculating the tariffs under PPP-consideration changes the ranking substantially. Taking nominal exchange rates puts several less developed (in 2002) countries in front. The PPP approach turns this around, and the developed countries Japan, South Korea, New Zealand Singapore, and Australia are now under the top ten.
3. The "mega"-container ports[4] of Singapore, Hong Kong and Shanghai are ranking in the middle; under the nominal ranking as well as the PPP ranking. This means their success is not a result of their low costs; there are other reasons for success.[5]
4. The great difference between Japan's Osaka and Yokohama ports is a clear sign that in Japan there is no National Port Authority that regulates the ports and levels the costs. Japan has autonomous landlord ports that led to this huge difference. Thailand shows the opposite: Bangkok and Laem Chabang are on nearly same level; both ports were under the national "Port Authority of Thailand" (PAT) in 2002.

Total port costs are composed of at least three groups of charges: port dues, cargo fees, and miscellaneous costs. Due to the different port management systems that exist, it is not always clear what fees are public or private. Because of this, it is only under strict adherence of compatibility possible to compare and benchmark single costs. The approach of comparing total costs is more realistic, but also here it is necessary to make sure that there is comparability. Factors like discounts for frequent calls may deform the comparison of a single call of a defined vessel with defined cargo load and lead to distorted benchmarking.

---

4 Refer to Tables 3.3 and 3.4 for the dominant position of Singapore and Hong Kong.
5 For a better understanding of the whole set of drivers for port competition, refer to Chapter 2: "Driver of Port Business."

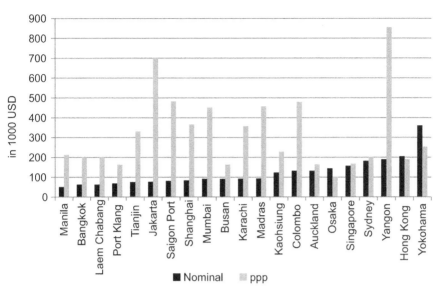

Figure 12.3: KMI study: Comparison of port tariff levels (3000 TEU ship)—ranked

Chapter 13
Cargo Demand Forecasting

Because ports are primarily service providers for global maritime trade, they must provide infra- and superstructure for expected future services. All historic and modern port development was/is based on future demand expectations. This sounds trivial but means that port infra- and superstructure is based on cargo demand forecasts and expectations about future trade flows. Forecasting is the process of making predictions of the future based on past and present data, most commonly by analyzing trends.

A port's physical infrastructure must exist before ships can be serviced, business can start, and revenues can be earned. Again, a simple time lag relation, but since decision making, design, planning, and construction can take years, it is important to work with accurate information before spending millions of dollars on a port.

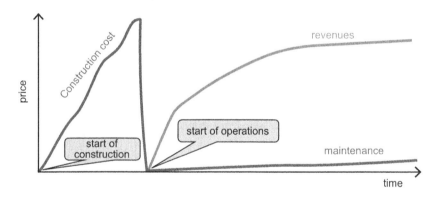

Figure 13.1: Port construction and revenue over time

Because of the time gap between port construction and the expected revenue stream, it is necessary to get a substantiated understanding of future demand. Forecasting customer demand for cargoes and services is a proactive process of determining what products are needed where, when, and in what quantities, that is, demand forecasting is a customer-focused activity. Cargo demand forecasting is also the foundation of a port's or terminal's entire operational process. It supports other planning activities such as capacity planning, human resource planning, and even overall business planning.

DOI 10.1515/9781547400874-013

The following facts are important for all types of port businesses:
- Port development and construction is highly time consuming
- Predictions about future trade flows are essential
- Port competition plays an important role
- Supply chain relations may lead to new routings
- Global trends may have substantial impact on local business
- Trends in trade and logistics imply changes for port service offerings
- External factors may substantially influence port business

A key document for port development and future port and terminal business is the so-called master plan. The master plan should take all arguments into consideration and clarify the port's own strategic planning for the medium and long term. It shall assist regional and local planning bodies as well as the transport network providers in preparing and revising their own development strategies, and shall inform port users, employees, and local communities as to how they can expect to see the port develop over the coming years.

13.1 Port Master Plan

A port master plan presents a vision for future operations at the port and critically examines how the existing land can be optimized for merchandise trade purposes. A typical master plan consists of at least two main parts:
1. An "economic part," which contains a market analysis and based on this a cargo demand forecast. The result is a projection of expected volumes for the next two or three decades per group of commodities (e.g., for bulk) or per transport units, like container. The competitive frameworks as well as global trends must be considered.
2. An "engineering part," which describes how expected volumes can be handled, and what is needed to upgrade the facilities to realize forecasted volumes and optimize land use. This includes all components of a port, starting from the access channel via navigational aids to the required berth, the necessary terminal infra- and superstructure, and ending at the port outgates like roads, inland waterways, pipelines, or rail tracks.

Engineers often call the economic part of the master plan the "soft" or "weak" part because it does not contain hard facts like the second part, where square meters, dredging volumes, cranes, or road lengths can be calculated precisely. And, yes, this is true. Part one deals with markets, market trends, global innovations, and competitive behavior. In this sense, the information does not have the concreteness of an engineer's calculations.[1] But this does not mean that information in part one is less important. Quite the opposite! An engineer's exact calculations for a million-dollar berth extension won't help the port if there are no customers and the investment is unprofitable.

Cargo demand forecasts are essential for successful long-term port planning and operation. Therefore, its part within the port master planning process should attract the same attention as all other parts of the plan. In general, the planning process follows this procedure (see Figure 13.2):

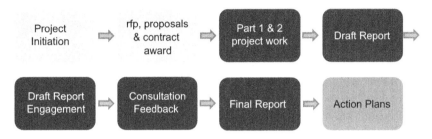

Figure 13.2: Port master planning process

Stakeholders in port development realize that for securing the port's future it is necessary to take action; in this phase, the port development project is initiated. Based on a port's needs, a request for proposals (RFP) is issued to qualified project partners like specialized engineering companies. If the company feels they are qualified and are interested, they must prepare a proposal. Such proposals usually consist of two major parts that must be submitted in two separate sealed envelopes: a technical proposal and a financial proposal. If the technical proposal meets the requirements of the RFP, the financial proposal of the qualified bidders will be opened. The process of proposal evaluation varies, but in most cases the proposals will be assessed and a team of evaluators (e.g., own staff, assisted by external experts) will create a ranking based on qualification points (QPs) they are willing to grant per task. There is also often a ranking between technical and financial proposals, for example, 70% of all QPs go for the technical, plus 30% for

---

1 The fact that civil engineers also fail dramatically can be followed up in Hamburg, Germany, where a new opera house was built. Construction costs have been calculated with 77 mill Euro, and it finally ended up with an additional seven years of construction and total costs of 866 mill Euros; more than ten times of calculated costs; and this for just one house! Other examples in Germany are the new airport in Berlin or the Stuttgart rail station. Similar projects can be found around the globe, what relativized engineering accuracy.

the financial proposal. This may lead to a first ranking technical proposal ending up as the second-best candidate when the technical second-best bidder is much cheaper and gains substantially more points for the financial proposal.

Such processes allow various manipulations if not handled seriously. The best way to reduce such manipulations is via transparency. This is the way how it is handled, for example, by most of the global development banks, like World Bank, Asian Development Bank (ADB), or African Development Bank (AfDB). The evaluation criteria are published during the submission of the RFP. This is a fair and reasonable process. For RFPs issued by port authorities directly, this is a good way of handling proposals.

Based on the evaluation criteria, the winner of the bidding will be awarded with a contract. Usually after a short commencement period, the project work for both the economic and engineering parts begins. This is now the time when cargo demand forecasts must be developed. Since port infra- and superstructure will be built for decades, the forecasting period usually spans between fifteen and thirty years; in some cases, like in Singapore, up to fifty years. This is the challenge for economists: to provide reasonable information of trade flows and routings as well as information about ship sizes and hinterland modes. The best information available needs to be considered to gain insight into future port development. The results of the forecast will be used by the engineers.

Creating the master plan often takes several months, and the results are presented in a draft report. This report will be discussed with stakeholders, and they must provide their input to adjust the vision for the port's future. Sometimes several additional consultations are necessary to align the market potential with the ideas of the relevant stakeholders. This means adjustment, not manipulation. For example, there might be a larger market potential for dry bulk, and a smaller potential for container business for a specific port. Given the fact that the port is limited in space and has the wish to develop in clean operations (maybe the location is close to residential areas), then the report needs to be focused on container trade instead of dusty dry bulk.

Based on the feedback, the final report of the master plan will be prepared. Often these reports will be published. This is for two reasons: first because they are paid with taxpayer money, and so the public has a right to be informed, and second because the authority wants to inform all stakeholders about the development plan and potentially upcoming investments. Finally, it must be stated that a master plan is not a business plan or legally binding land-use plan. These action plans will come later but should be aligned with the master plan.

The master plans can:
- Help clarify and communicate the port vision—they form a critical part in a ports' "license to grow."
- Provide a strategic framework for port authorities to consider a range of internal and external factors that may impact on current and/or future operations.
- Articulate the medium- and long-term "port vision" to a wide range of stakeholders.
- Create additional economic value through increased industry and investment confidence.
- Assist in overall supply chain management by:
    - integrating the port into broader network consideration (by promoting greater understanding of the port needs within regional and local planning agencies).
    - ensuring that vital seaport (and logistic chain) infrastructure is delivered when and where it is needed (via well-considered staging options).
- Maximize significant economic and productivity improvements through efficient management of critical infrastructure delivery and protection.
- Provide increased environmental protection by identification of critical environmental values early in the design process.
- Address interface issues (social and environmental) in and around seaport areas (i.e., help to inform port users, employees, and local communities as to how they can expect to see the port develop over the coming years).

Each port will ultimately need to determine the nature and content of their master plans based on their own historical, economic, environmental and "interface" planning considerations. Cargo demand forecasts form a substantial part of this process as they set the frame for development options.

13.2 Demand Forecasting Models

Cargo demand forecasting is a crucial activity for planning business development and building logistics infrastructures and therefore, an understanding of forecasting models is of the utmost importance. Seaports are required to carefully monitor market changes and estimate industry trends before undertaking huge investments in new facilities that commit resources in the long term. Hence, the realization of port infrastructures needs a great amount of public and private financial resources and an endowment of technical and organizational capabilities. Port planning consists in a complex analytical work that should be able to match cargo flow projection and future demand estimation with the setting of a suitable supply of infra- and superstructures. The forecasting models create the base for all these activities.

Typically, business planning periods are clustered as follows:
- **Short term:** Three to six months, operating decisions, production and service planning
- **Medium term:** Six months to two years, tactical decisions, for example, employment or equipment changes
- **Long term:** Two years and on, strategic decisions, for example, new markets, new products (e.g., hinterland rail)

Demand forecasting is typically long-term planning that is necessary for adequate port and terminal capacity utilization for the existing business, and at times in assessing future capacity requirements when entering new markets, for example, cruise or RoRo business. Cargo demand forecasting involves techniques including both informal methods, such as educated guesses, and quantitative methods, such as the use of historical sales data and statistical techniques or current data from test markets. The three main categories and major tools are:

11. Qualitative Techniques
    a. Market research
    b. Delphi method
    c. Panel consensus
    d. Collective opinions method
    e. Visionary forecast
    f. Historical analogy
12. Time Series Analysis and Projection
    a. Moving average
    b. Exponential smoothing
    c. Trend projections
    d. Box-Jenkins method
    e. X-11 method
13. Causal Methods
    a. Regression model
    b. Econometric model
    c. Input-output model
    d. Anticipation surveys
    e. Simulation models

The first group uses qualitative data (e.g., expert opinion) and information about special events and trends and may or may not take the past into consideration. The second, on the other hand, focuses entirely on patterns and pattern changes, and thus relies entirely on historical data. The third uses highly refined and specific information about relationships between system elements and is powerful enough to take special events formally into account. As with time series analysis and projection techniques, the past is important to causal models. More details about general forecasting models can be found in nearly all basic economic literature as well as in specialized working papers, like "Portopia: Port Traffic Forecasting Tools."[2]

In general, a holistic model includes and combines several tools to achieve the best results. A key problem for all models is data availability. Especially for time series and causal tools, massive data sets are required to rebuild and explain historic trends and identify key drivers. At a high level, the model approach consists of three stages:

1. Analysis of Historic Trade and Port Behavior

The first step is to understand the historic relationship between the typical drivers of global port business as analyzed in Chapter 2, for example, economic growth and global trade flows that need to be broken down into country and regional trade flows at the lowest regional level possible (i.e., NUTS 3 in Europe) and port-level trade flows. The port throughput development needs to be compared with global figures. Because all kinds of local factors may have an influence on local port business, it is important to include these in the master plan as well. Examples of such factors can be good weather, which attracts tourists, or port location, like the Panama Canal directly on a major trade route. The target is to explain historic activities at the port level. Figure 13.3 illustrates how to achieve historic data at port level.

---

2 For example, refer to: Portopia, EC 7th Framework Programme: Deliverable 1.3 Port Traffic Forecasting Tool, Document ID Portopia/D/1.3/DT/201506.15, Brussels, Belgium 2015.

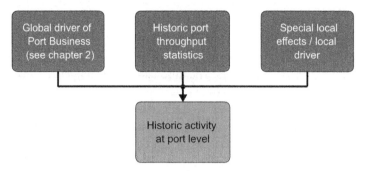

Figure 13.3: Analysis of historic trade and port behavior

2. Analysis of Port Level Trade Potential

The second step as illustrated in Figure 13.4 is to build port- and commodity-specific trade forecasts through the end of the forecast period. These forecasts detail the overall level, as well as the mix and origin, of all commodities entering each of the ports under consideration. At this level, the forecast identifies a trade potential, that is, the potential amount that in an optimal case may travel via this port.

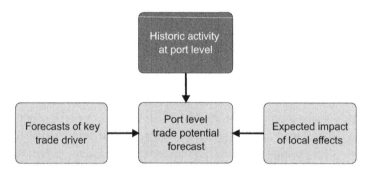

Figure 13.4: Forecast of port level trade potential

3. Port Level Cargo Forecast

The third and final step is to extract the realistically achievable amount of cargo throughput out of the max. cargo potential. External competitor behaviors as well as internal restrictions both result in limited throughput. The model must be able to recalculate results and work with scenarios. In effect, this demonstrates how the port will handle changes based on the level, origin, and mix of commodities flowing through the port; please see Figure 13.5 below.

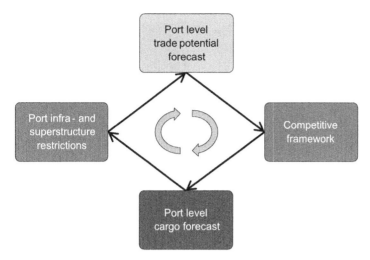

Figure 13.5: Port level cargo forecast

Each subsequent stage carries forward the results from the previous stage and incorporates additional data assets for analysis. The following graphic in Figure 13.6 provides a high-level overview of the entire process, including the relationships between the various data assets that were brought together.

Historic port-level activity from the first stage was carried forward via a trade potential forecast to the final stage, the port level cargo forecast. The application of trade forecasts based on HS-level data allows for changes in absolute commodity levels through time, but also in the relative flows transiting through a given port as a function of the relative commodity mix each port handles. Because of variations in the types of commodities and types of vessels that each port is equipped to handle, changes in commodity mix through time on a country-to-country basis—that is, the trade—has the potential to change a shipping lines port selection. This finally has the potential to change port volume over time—positive as well as negative. This allows for the understanding of differentiated changes through time by port, both in absolute levels and in commodity structure.

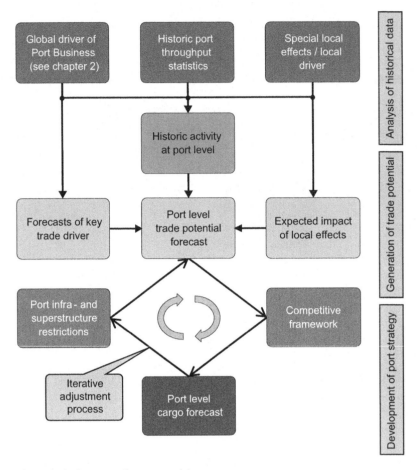

Figure 13.6: Port cargo forecast model

This dynamic assessment, instead of merely scaling topline results, is crucial to accurately understand the nuanced changes that each port in the analysis will experience over the forecast period. The result of this process is a port-level cargo forecast that is based on granular commodity data and forecasts (for this the causal methods and time series can be implemented). The results can be adjusted by iterative adaption processes to include qualitative parameter like trends and behaviors, incorporated via tools like Delphi method or panel consensus. The results of the iterative adjustments can be two additional forecast scenarios: a more optimistic and positive one, and a second more pessimistic one that gain weight on some of the negative factors. Important hereby is that the spread stays within a small corridor, for example, max. $+/-$ 10% deviance from the basic scenario. Including qualitative parameter in scenario building is necessary to include nonquantitative factors that have substantial impact, like political decisions.

The outcome of such demand forecasting models is a set of potential development scenarios for port cargo throughput. The demand forecasting models establish the maximum achievable amount of throughput for the port. This figure helps civil engineers establish some of the main frame conditions for the master plan. These include the technical and operational options for port investments. Port planners will get a feeling about expected future commodities and volumes; and the decision-making bodies, such as port management and the supervisory boards will have a framework for port extension planning, business plans, and financial analytics.

13.3 Case Studies

In this chapter we will have a look at some publicly available master plans and identify the impact of demand forecasting. In all master plans, there is a section entitled "market assessment," "forecast," or "factors affecting demand," etc. In some cases, a master plan has two different sections: an economic part that includes demand scenarios, and a second engineering section. And even when the only part that is published is the engineering one—there must be an indication about expected trade and throughput volumes somewhere.

The following tables of content show how demand forecasting is implemented in real master plans. Plans of the following ports have been analyzed; more can be found on the internet (in italics: demand sections):

- Port Manatee, Florida
- Dublin Port, Ireland
- Aktau Port, Kazakhstan
- Hong Kong Port, Hong Kong/China
- Port of Los Angeles

Port Manatee Master Plan 2009
Mission Statement
Table of Contents
Executive Summary
I   Introduction
II Existing Conditions
   A. Waterside Facilities
   B. Upland Infrastructure

The *right* turn on Tampa Bay

DUBLIN PORT COMPANY
MASTERPLAN
2012-2040

Aktau Port Masterplan

1. EXECUTIVE SUMMARY
2. EXISTING PORT TRAFFIC
3. *THE ECONOMY*
4. *TRAFFIC FORECASTS*
5. PORT FACILITIES
6. EXISTING PORT EQUIPMENT
7. EXISTING PORT OPERATIONS
8. CARGO HANDLING OPTIMISATION
9. PORT CAPACITY & IDENTIFICATION OF POTENTIAL OPERATIONAL CONSTRAINTS
10. PORT SAFETY
11. CAPACITY OF RAIL, PIPELINES AND TANK FARMS
12. SBM OPTIONS
13. DEVELOPMENT OPTIONS AND COST ESTIMATES
14. ECONOMIC EVALUATION
15. FINANCIAL EVALUATION
16. CONCLUSIONS
17. RECOMMENDATIONS

Hong Kong Port 2030

1. Introduction
2. *Demand and Supply of HKP*
3. *Competitiveness of Hong Kong Port*
4. *Contribution to Hong Kong's Economy and*
5. *Forecast Throughput at Hong Kong Port*
6. Capacity of HKP
7. Issues Affecting HKP
8. Recommended Development Plan
9. Summary & Conclusion

Los Angeles Port Master Plan 2014

1. INTRODUCTION
2. BACKGROUND
3. DEVELOPMENT GOALS
4. *FACTORS AFFECTING DEMAND FOR PORT DEVELOPMENT*
    4.1 *Demand for Cargo Handling Facilities*
    4.2 *Demand for Commercial Fishing Facilities*
    4.3 *Demand for Recreational Boating Facilities*

Chapter 14
Financing Port Development

Port business is a capital-intensive business that requires a huge amount of up-front money before revenue can be expected. Capital expenditures for terminal investments or access channels are major purchases that port authorities and terminal operators make to maintain or expand their business. Because such purchases involve acquiring assets that provide value and use for a period of several years, the authorities and operators recover the cost of these acquisitions gradually by depreciating the assets over time. Ordinarily, businesses are not allowed to deduct the full costs of capital expenditures in the year the costs are incurred.

Therefore, the substantial outlays of capital required for such investments must be carefully planned out, usually years in advance. These investments are often based on master plan recommendations, so that authorities and operators can avoid overextending themselves financially and creating cash flow problems. For capital-intensive port investments, good management of capital expenditures is crucial for survival and growth. It requires striking a proper balance between a port's needs for equipment and their ability to generate revenues or obtain financing. The general investment plans for such investments are based on the master plan, more detailed feasibility studies, and a business and financing plan.

The responsibility for investments and financing is directly linked to the basic port management concept.[1] For a 100% state-owned port, all financing naturally has a priority for public funds or taxes, whereas in private ports or within a landlord model, private terminal operators will most likely get back to the capital market; although public grants are welcome. The range of financial solutions for ports is very broad, and to make the best use of scarce funding sources, it is important for authorities and operators to understand the full range of potential financial structures, and not be linked to just one potential solution, that is, tax financing.

Before 1980, public service ports and tool ports were mainly financed by the government.[2] The general infrastructure of landlord ports was typically financed jointly by the government and the port authority, and the terminal superstructure and equipment by private operators. In the event a government had no funds for expensive port infrastructure, either port development was halted or money was

---

1 Refer to Chapter 8.2 for further details on basic management concepts.
2 For details of port management concepts, refer to Chapter 8.2: "Basic Management Concepts."

DOI 10.1515/9781547400874-014

acquired at preferential rates from an international finance institution, such as the World Bank, EBRD, or ADB.

Whether governments are willing to finance basic port infrastructure depends on the government's political and economic policies as a matter of principle. For example, if ports are considered part of the general transport infrastructure of the country, then investments in them may be considered to promote national interest. Research shows that in approximately *two-thirds* of the top container ports, the public sector was responsible for creating and maintaining basic port infrastructure. An often-occurring problem with public (thus political) investment decisions is that the decision to invest does not necessarily originate at the same level of government as that of the financing sources and responsibilities. Because of this disconnect, the interest of public officials to increase efficiency and profitability of port assets is usually limited because they are not held accountable for the success or failure of their investment decisions.

Besides sourcing, the scale of the project is a major decision-making criterion. Larger ports tend to have large-scale projects and capital improvement programs, along with sophisticated capital structures necessitated by such extensive capital needs. Smaller ports with fewer or smaller projects may rely more on governmental and operating funding sources for ongoing financing requirements.

Over the last decades, the governmental view of ports has evolved. Increasingly, ports are considered separate economic entities, although still beholden to national regional and local planning goals. As such, they should operate on a commercial basis. By the same token, subsidies for operational port infrastructure construction, such as port land, quay walls, common areas, and inner channels, should be avoided. There still is, however, a category of port infrastructure for which it will be hard to find private investors: expensive and enduring infrastructure (e.g., breakwaters and locks, entrance channels and fairways, and coastal protection works). The main stumbling block for private financing of such projects is their life span, which often exceeds 100 years, and the sunken investment aspect of these projects. Cost recovery of such works often can not be achieved in twenty to thirty years, which is a normal repayment period for long-term loans for infrastructure works by international financing institutions. However, for all investments, the financing partner needs substantiated investment plans including economic calculations, considerations of nonfinancial benefits, project chances and risks, cash flow statements, etc.

Such an investment plan outlines the need for the project as well as the expected revenue and/or increase in productivity because of the project. From a financial point of view, this forms the project's creditworthiness, and thus its financial viability. Port authorities and terminal operators must develop a thorough understanding of their creditworthiness. Understanding the credit rating process and potential impacts related to any specific project under consideration for capital investment is necessary to assess the attractiveness of the project for investment partners or traditional finance institutions like banks. Also, to determine the impact, if any, on the port's existing credit ratings.

To further clarify financing approaches, it is important to distinguish among investments in basic port infrastructure, operational port infrastructure, port superstructure, and port equipment. Understanding these distinctions will help in deciding which investments should be paid for by the port and which should be paid for by the local or regional community, the central government, and private investors. Table 14.1 lists various types of port assets under these four categories.

Table 14.1: Categories of port assets

Basic Port Infrastructure:	Port Superstructure:
– Maritime access channels	– Paving and surfacing
– Port entrance /road, rail & waterway	– Terminal lighting
– Protective works, including breakwaters and shore protection	– Parking areas
– Sea locks	– Sheds, warehouses, and stacking areas
– Bridges	– Tank farms and silos
– Safety & custom fences	– Offices
– traffic infrastructure / corridors	– Repair shops
– Inland waterways within the port area and connecting port areas with their hinterland	– Other buildings required for terminal operations
Operational Port Infrastructure:	**Port Equipment:**
– Inner port channels and turning basins	– Cranes
– Revetments and slopes	– Straddle carrier, Reach stacker
– Quay walls, jetties, and finger piers	– RTGs / Rubber Tired Gantries
– Aids to navigation, buoys, and beacons	– RMGs / Rail Mounted Gantries
– Hydro and meteorological systems	– terminal tractors & forklifts
– Specific mooring buoys	– Dredging equipment
– Patrol and fire-fighting vessels	– Ship and shore handling equipment
– Rail connection to general rail infrastructure, and marshalling yards	– Tugs & barges
– Dry docks for ship repair	– Line handling vessels
– Communication infrastructure / WLAN	– other cargo handling equipment

Of highest interest for private investors are investments in port equipment and port superstructure. Here the expected return on investment shall be realized within a comparably short period. Funding large basic or operational port infrastructure investments is considered riskier because of certain complicating factors, including:

- The large proportion of necessary equity contributions (e.g., a minimum proportion of 60 percent) due to the high risk associated with long construction and payback periods
- The difficulty of projecting future trade demand and traffic volumes
- The capital-intensive nature of the investments
- The continuing risks associated with operations, such as a refusal of requests for tariff adjustments, changes in tax policy, or introduction of new handling techniques that make existing facilities obsolete

14.1 Financial Planning

Port authorities must rely on operating revenues and private market lenders for their financing, as they are often barred from most federal sources of revenue. Key sources of revenue generation are port dues and—depending on the management concept—cargo and miscellaneous fees. The way ports are established makes it difficult for them to acquire financing for investments that would allow substantial investments to maintain or enhance port competitiveness:

- Access to federal funds for capital investment is limited.
- Payments to government out of operating revenues (the gross revenue charge and payments in lieu of taxes) reduce funds available for investment.
- Additional revenue-generating opportunities beside the core assignation are reduced.
- Private borrowing is capped for many ports, which effectively restricts the size of projects that could be financed by private lenders.
- Ports (others than private real estate owner) may not use their property as security on borrowed funds; instead, they must rely on future cash flow to build investor confidence.

Since future operating revenues must be used as the primary basis for generating investment funds, port authorities would be unlikely to obtain significant amounts of capital investment even if the cap on borrowing were lifted. Bearing this in mind, it is easy to understand why public budget financing—although alternatives are available—is the usual way of financing development projects for port authorities as well as operations for state-owned ports.

Port authorities are faced with the ever-present dilemma of efficiently and effectively utilizing the limited financial and natural resources to fulfill the economic and social obligations of the primary shareholder, usually the Government. Ports face limited financial resources due to restricted budgets, the resistance of the government to guarantee financing obligations, and often a local community full of expectations. How can port authorities know which projects to undertake, how to prioritize the needs of the industry, and which capital acquisitions to make at which time for exactly which projects? In short, how do ports get access to public money for investments?

The answer can be found in the general business economics literature, and here under the headline "project management tools." Everybody who scans the internet under this topic will find a long list of tools and a broad range of supporting software that is available. All these tools help structure projects, slice it into pieces along the timeline, calculate costs and revenues, evaluate benefits, build scenarios for various demand expectations, group pieces into logical phases and finally come to cost figures, and—since not all benefits have a market price (e.g., environment or safety)—to cost/benefit or benefit/cost ratios. Based on such ratios a ranking of projects can be included in public budget planning and decision making.

In general, the evaluation of options for a port investment should:
- Examine the economic benefits
- Examine the costs
- Examine the nonfinancial benefits
- Identify the risks and their impact on the investment
- Account for other qualitative supporting information

The approach for such an evaluation of a port investment project to be (fully or partly) financed by public funds can be structured as follows:
1. Identify and categorize the benefits
2. Identify and categorize the costs
3. Information gathering
4. Develop a basis for the estimation of costs and benefits
5. Estimation of costs and benefits
6. Cash flow analysis
7. Financing mechanism
8. Risk analysis
9. Assembling the analysis in a business case

The first step "categorization of benefits" is often dominated by the intention of the project, for example, the creation of a new berth or a completely new greenfield terminal. From a financial and project management point of view, the driver for such an investment may come from inside the port, for example, the wish to have deeper water in front of a new quay wall to optimize yard utilization, or from the outside world: the chance to increase traffic, enable trade facilitation, increase tax income, or create new jobs. The project management must identify and cluster all these benefits; typically, into four categories:

- **External economic benefits:** Trade facilitation, municipal tax generation, job creation, agency and partner savings and revenue, indirect savings and revenue, etc.
- **Internal economic benefits:** Increased revenue, economies of scale, employee productivity savings, other utilization savings, etc.
- **Value score:** Increased social/service delivery, better environmental score, enhanced governance (transparency), etc.
- **Qualitative factors:** Stakeholder support, strategic alignment, attractiveness of comparable projects (e.g. a rail station), etc.

The second step "cost categorization" involves more than examining the capital costs but also the operating costs associated with the acquisition or project; operating costs like administration and management costs for insurance, legal fees, consultants, or contractors; personnel/staff expenses like salaries, overtime payments, and training; facilities expenses, for example, maintenance and repair as well as all other expenses. Typical capital costs occur for market planning, assets, assembly and training, procurement charges, contractor's fees, consultancy fees, and financing charges.

The third step, "information gathering" should commence as soon as possible to ensure that the most reliable data available is collected and collated to facilitate estimates and projections of costs and benefits. During the project management phase, the availability and quality of data increases, but it should be a key target to frequently evaluate existing data and gather more granularity as soon as possible to best steer the project. Some of the challenges that may be encountered during the process are:

- Inability to locate data
- Collection of unreliable data
- Changes in project requirements
- Changes in alternative options for analysis

Step four "estimating costs and benefits" identifies and categorizes future costs and economic benefits. The first part of this step—estimation of future costs—is often the easier part as cost components are mostly visible and can be estimated. But it is a matter of fact and should not be underestimated that, especially for long term forecasts of twenty years and more, not all cost components are already known today. For example, ten years ago it was not clear that the IMO would introduce new emission limits for maximum sulfur content of bunker fuel. All ships need to comply with this, and ports must be able to provide low sulfur bunker fuel as well as new waste reception facilities in case exhaust gas cleaning technology is installed and/or they must invest in alternative bunker fuel options, such as LNG. This shows that in long-term forecasts cost components have an element of uncertainty. But even more complicated is the economic evaluation of intangible benefits. These often don't have a price, like clean air or increased security, and so it is necessary to adjust an adequate price for all components to measure costs and benefits on a comparable scale. Tools that help to estimate an adequate price for a specific benefit are sometimes considered arbitrary. But what is the alternative? To rank options (i.e., investments), it is necessary to find a comparable scale, and prices are acceptable means—but only if transparency about cost and benefit calculation is guaranteed.

In step five "estimation" all cost and all benefit components will be summarized and benefit cost ratios (BCRs) will be calculated to achieve a comparable scale for the projects. When all benefits of investment alternative ① together reach a level of 100, and all costs also 100, the BCR is 1. For the larger investment alternative ② the costs are higher at 130, but the expected and transparently calculated benefits sum up to 150, then the BCR stands at 1.15. This means, that alternative ②—although it is more expensive—has a better ratio. Step five will make the calculations transparent and comparable.

Step 6 assesses the timing of the "cash flows." It is necessary to get information about cost and benefit streams over time to calculate accurately year by year. A key measurement of finance calculations hereby is the net present value (NPV) of the investment, a discounted value. Time affects the value of cash flows. One million dollars today has another (higher) value than one million dollars in ten or twenty years. Step 6 compares the values over time. In practice, the most intensive discussions are often around the "adequate" interest rate.

Step seven provides an overview and recommends alternatives for the best "financing mechanism," such as:
- Internal sources
- Government funding
- Asset-backed financing
- Capital markets (loans, bonds)
- Pooled investments
- Public private partnerships

The best mix of sources for investment financing according to options, merits, or demerits and level of applicability must be found for each single investment. Proposals for this should come from the finance department. Government funding is often the preferred alternative, but options need to be checked and evaluated.

Step eight "risk analysis" is about developing an understanding of the risk. Some of the major risk factors for port projects are:
-   They require major political involvement
-   The project budget is overrun
-   The project completion time is overrun
-   There is a failure to achieve anticipated benefits
-   Cruise ship boycott
-   Natural disasters

The main risk factors in investment analysis are consequence and likelihood. The final risk rating is a multiplication of consequence and likelihood.

The ninth and final step "assembling the analysis in a business case" is a kind of summary and recommendation. The alternatives for the project and the corresponding financing alternatives will be evaluated, and the recommended project financing amounts can be implemented in public multiannual budget plans.

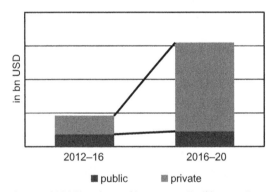

Source: AAPA Planning and Investment Toolkit, page I–1

Figure 14.1: Public and private capital expenditures in U.S. ports

Figure 14.1 illustrates the situation of port financing in the United States. The data is based on historic figures for 2012 to 2016 and a survey issued by the American Association of Port Authorities (AAPA) for 2016 to 2020. The fact that huge amounts of money will be spent for future investments up to 2020 indicates the need for more modern ports, but what is of much more interest is the fact that the structure is expected to change substantially. In the past, the share between public (port authority) and private (terminal) investments have approximately been balanced. This is expected to change in the future as a much larger share will be financed by private sources. The total amount of public investments is expected to increase from 18.3 bn USD to 22.6 bn USD. This is a moderate gain of 24% in five years' time for public expenditures. Complementary private investment is expected to increase from 27.6 bn USD to 132.2 bn USD; a boost of 379%, or more than ten times the public increase.

Although the situation of U.S. port financing is unique and can not be transferred to other countries and ports; the argument that more private capital expenditures in port business are highly appreciated can be found frequently in literature, workshops, conferences, etc. Therefore, the joint model of public-private financing becomes more attractive.

14.2 Public-Private Partnerships

Public-private partnerships are mainly driven by limitations in public funds for investments but also by efforts to increase efficiency of spending and the quality of public services. The ultimate purpose of the collaboration between public and private sectors is added value; a qualitatively better product for less cost, better accountability, and promotion of private sector innovation.

According to the widely accepted definition of the World Bank, public-private partnerships (PPPs) are a mechanism for government to procure and implement public infrastructure and/or services using the resources and expertise of the private sector. Where governments are facing ageing or lack of infrastructure and require more efficient services, a partnership with the private sector can help foster new solutions and bring finance.[3]

For port development, PPPs can be an attractive alternative for financing, but not all investors access the same investment routes. For example, the lack of liquidity in some infrastructure instruments implies that the group of possible interested investors is only a subset of the more general group of investors in debt and equity markets. In the case of listed equity and market-traded debt, investors can build exposure through allocations to traditional investment in stocks and bonds. Given the higher liquidity of such investments, mutual funds and exchange-traded funds have included these instruments in the portfolios of retail investors, high net worth individuals, and institutional investors. Unlisted equity or private debt, however, do not benefit from an active liquid secondary

---

3 For more details, visit the website of the World Bank: WorldBank PPP 2017.

market. For this reason, they are typical "buy and hold" asset classes, suited to long-term investors with a clear preference for long-dated cash flows and diversification benefits.

Different competencies are required to assess the risk and return of port investments. Direct investment requires significant expertise and resources on the part of the investor. An investor in public port infrastructure must be able to assess the risk/return profile of the investment throughout its economic life including its construction phase (greenfield investments) and during the operational phase (brownfield investments) as described within the nine steps for a typical investment project in the chapter above. The assessment is even more important if the investment is made directly in the equity of the project or if the investor lends directly to the project. However, the need for additional, more sophisticated valuation skills also remains in the case of the indirect investment (i.e., private equity infrastructure funds or debt/credit funds).

There is a wide range of financing channels for PPP infrastructure investment, both direct and market-based—each with its own set of characteristics and implications for lending or investment portfolios. Capital markets can be an efficient way to allocate risks to those investors that are most willing to bear them at an agreeable rate of compensation. The taxonomy serves to clarify the role of market-based financing for infrastructure across the spectrum of investors and instruments. The private sector evaluates its participation in port equipment and superstructure projects (Table 14.1) based on the following elements:

- Expected yield
- Adequate debt/equity financing structure (e.g., 60/30, 70/30, 75/25)
- Strong sponsorship
- Realistic demand scenarios
- Consistent investment plan
- Solid legal contracts
- Transparent legal framework
- Fair and open bidding procedures

Principles of Port Investment Finance

The top-tier funding provided by lenders or capital market investors, usually referred to as "senior debt," typically forms the largest but not the sole source of funding for the investment. The rest of the required financing is provided by the port authority or the terminal operator in the form of equity or junior debt. Grants, in effect, often in the form of public sector unremunerated equity for private investors, may also contribute to the financing package.

Since senior lenders do not have access to authorities' or operators' financial resources, they need to ensure that the investment project will produce sufficient cash flow to service the debt. They also need to ensure that the legal structuring of the project is such that senior lenders have priority over more junior creditors in access to this cash. In limited recourse financings, lenders will seek additional credit support from the investors and/or third parties to hedge against downside scenarios and the risk of the project's failing to generate sufficient cash flow. Finally, lenders will want to ensure that when an investment project suffers shortfalls in cash because of poor performance by one or more of the engaged subcontractors, these shortfalls flow through to the subcontractor, leaving the ability of the investor to service the debt unimpaired.

Financing Structure

The financing of a PPP project consists principally of senior debt and equity, but the financing structure may also include other forms of junior debt (such as "mezzanine" debt, which ranks between senior debt and pure equity) and in some cases grant funding. The investors need to seek to achieve optimum (as opposed to maximum) risk transfer between the public and private sector. But the allocation of risks among the private sector parties is also crucial. Financial structuring of the project relies on a careful assessment of construction, operating, and revenue risks and seeks to achieve optimum risk allocation between the private partners to the transaction. In practice, this means limiting risks as far as possible to senior lenders and allocating this to equity investors, subcontractors, guarantors, and other parties through contractual arrangements of one kind or another.

As a general principle, the higher the gearing of a project, the more affordable it is likely to be to the public sector. This is because senior debt is less expensive than other forms of financing (except grants). Other things being equal, project gearing (i.e., the level of debt senior lenders will provide relative to the level of equity) will be determined by the variability of a project's cash flow. The greater the degree of risk in the cash flows, the greater the "cushion" lenders will need in the forecast of available cash flow beyond what will be needed for debt service. This is necessary to reassure lenders that the debt can be repaid even in a worst-case scenario. Lenders will specify their requirement in terms of forward-looking (i.e., predicted) annual debt service cover ratio (ADSCR) above a specified minimum level. The value of required ADSCR will depend in large part on project risk, and therefore variability of cash flows. One of the fundamental trade-offs in designing an optimized finance structure for a port development investment is to strive for the right balance between senior debt and equity.

Debt

Senior debt enjoys priority in terms of repayment over all other forms of finance. Mezzanine debt is subordinated in terms of repayment to senior debt but ranks above equity both for distributions of free cash in the so-called cash waterfall (i.e., priority of each cash inflow and outflow in a project) and in the event of liquidation of the company. Since mezzanine debt's repayment can be affected by poor performance of the investment authority or company, and bearing in mind the priority in repayment of senior debt, mezzanine debt typically commands higher returns than senior debt.

Debt to an investment is typically priced based on the underlying cost of funds to the lender plus a fixed component (or "margin") expressed as several basis points to cover default risk and the lender's other costs (e.g., operating costs, the opportunity cost of capital allocations, profit).

Bear in mind that the underlying cost of funds is typically determined based on floating interest rates (i.e., rates that fluctuate with market movements). These are normally based on interbank lending rates such as EURIBOR (European Interbank Offered Rate) in the euro market or LIBOR (London Interbank Offered Rate) in many English-speaking markets. In contrast to these floating rate funds, the revenues received by the authority or terminal operator do not generally change along with the interest rates. This mismatch is typically remedied using an interest rate swap, through which the investor ends up paying a fixed interest rate (this is referred to as the "hedging").

Debt for major investments may be provided by either commercial banks, international financial institutions (such as the European Investment Bank), or directly from the capital markets. In this last case, project companies issue bonds that are taken up by financial institutions such as pension funds or insurance companies that are looking for long-term investments.

Financial advisers will be able to advise on the likely sources of funding for a given project. They would also be expected to assess the anticipated costs and benefits of funding options. This will include an assessment of the debt tenors (the length of time to maturity, or repayment, of debt) likely to be available from various sources. This is particularly important if long-term funding is not or not yet available for the project and where the public sector may be drawn into risks associated with the need to refinance short-term loans (so-called mini-perm structures). In other words, the investor will use this type of financing prior to being able to access long-term financing or permanent financing solutions.

Equity

Equity is usually provided by the project sponsors, that is, the port authority or the terminal operator, but may also be provided by the contractors who will build and operate the project as well as by financial institutions. A large part of the equity (often referred to as "quasi-equity") may be in the form of shareholder subordinated debt, for tax and accounting benefits. Since equity holders bear primary risks under such an investment project, they will seek a higher return on the funding they provide.

14.3 Alternative Port Financing and Management Schemes

The increasing role of private enterprise in the port sector exerts a direct influence both on port management and operations, as well as on the way port investments are financed. The private sector has become interested in financing port equipment and parts of the superstructure, like office buildings, and increasingly, also the construction of entire terminals, including quay walls, land reclamation, sheds and warehouses and dredging of basins and access channels. This has given rise to a large variety of project financing and management schemes such as BOT (build-operate-transfer), BOO (built-own-operate), and BOOT (build-own-operate-transfer).[4] Each is designed to mobilize private capital while balancing public and private interests. Legal experts often classify them as a kind of concession, but whether it is a contract or a concession is a question of the exact legal definition. These new financing modes are a typical type of privatization via management contracts as described in Chapter 9.4: "Ways to Privatize."

BOT: This arrangement acknowledges the fact that the grantee never has ownership of the facilities, but that he has been granted the right to build and operate the facility for a specified (long) period. After expiration, the grantor can lease out the facilities or, if the facilities must be completely rehabilitated, can possibly grant another concession (but with a different "object"). As the grantee is not the owner he can not expect at the end of the BOT arrangement to receive compensation for the transfer of the facilities.

---

4 Other, not too popular concepts are: BLT: build-lease-transfer, DBFO: design-build-finance-operate, DBOT: design-build-operate-transfer, DCMF: design-construct-manage-finance, etc.

BOO: The assumption in this type of scheme is that the concession granted gives the grantee two exceptional advantages: first, he is explicitly granted ownership of the facilities that he will build, and second, there is no specified duration, which implies that the facilities will not have to be transferred back at a specified time against an agreed level of compensation.

BOOT: This scheme is like the previous one, but provides for the return of the facilities, possibly against payment of a mutually agreed indemnification for the residual asset value.

Some or even all the following different parties could be involved in any of the three schemes:
- The "host" of the port development project/that is, the port authority or a ministry: Normally, the host is the initiator of the project and decides if the model is appropriate to meet its needs. In addition, the political and economic circumstances are the main factors for this decision. The host normally provides support for the project.
- The "concessionaire": The project sponsors who act as concessionaire create a special purpose entity (often called: SPV special purpose vehicle), which is capitalized through their financial contributions.
- "Lending banks": Most projects are funded by commercial debt. The bank will be expected to finance the project on a "nonrecourse" basis meaning that it has recourse to the SPV and all its assets for the repayment of the debt.
- "Other lenders": The SPV might have other lenders such as national or regional development banks.
- "Parties to the project contracts": Because the SPV has a limited workforce, it will subcontract a third party to perform its obligations under the concession agreement. Additionally, it must assure that it has adequate supply contracts in place for the supply of all kind of resources necessary for the project, including all kind of supportive services.

Concessions under any of these three schemes BOT, BOO, and BOOT have intrinsic shortcomings, such as:
- A dominant position of the grantor (e.g., the port authority).
- The risk that the grantee is mainly interested in special tax advantages or in real estate development, that is, there are concealed interests.
- The risk of inconsistent legal interpretations since the SPV and/or the grantee are of foreign nationality.
- The likelihood that if the concession scheme operates at a deficit the grantee will be reluctant to finance new investments or properly maintain facilities.

– The danger that the grantee will reduce maintenance and investments to a minimum in the final years of the concession and leave behind a nonoperational facility.

These shortcomings can, however, be tackled head on when negotiating the concession agreement and drafting the concession terms. They will require adapted clauses and careful wording, that is, they should not constitute a major legal or operational obstacle.

A concession like BOT is a contract by which the grantor (e.g., the port authority) permits the grantee the right to: finance, build, and operate a facility or equipment for public use, for a stated period, after which the facility or the equipment will be transferred to the grantor. As such, the concession—exactly like a lease—is not a permanent transfer of the asset, but only a temporary one. Legally, it is a technique for creating, delivering and operating a public service. Although the concessionaire may be a public or mixed company, most BOT schemes and their variants have a private concessionaire.

BOO and BOOT stipulate that ownership of the facilities belongs to the grantee (because of the "own" term) and that it is transferred to the grantor at the end of the concession period, but this is not legally correct. Ownership of the facilities by the public grantor takes effect the day construction starts. Thus, the grantee is never the owner; this has serious implications regarding bank guarantees and mortgages as it restricts the grantee's capacity to work out a financing plan. This problem is mostly settled by the government's giving its guarantee to any loan contracted by the grantee (a good solution and possibly better for bankers than a mortgage because the security on immovable port facilities is at best mediocre). Another solution is to stipulate in the concession contract that the "buildings and port facilities built on public property shall be considered the concessionaire's property during the effective terms of the concession"; a frequently used legal definition that also heals the term "own" in the abbreviations.

The payments by the grantee to the grantor may be, as in the case of leases, either fixed or on a revenue-sharing basis. It is also possible for both parties to agree on a fixed amount, covering fixed costs, and then when the facility is well established, to increase the concession fee with a share in the profits in the form of a royalty or a percentage on the net income from the concession.

Tariffs of the concessionaire should be established during the bidding phase, as bidders should make proposals for the tariffs to be applied if they are awarded the concession (these tariff figures will then also form an input in the development of the investment plan). As for the risk of giving the grantee a monopoly, this can not be ruled out. The solution is then to control the tariff and establish maximum or ceiling rates. But the risk is limited and should not be exaggerated.

Finally, the advantages of applying BOT, BOO, and BOOT financing and management schemes can be summarized as follows:

– Use of private sector financing to provide new sources of capital, which reduces public borrowing and direct spending, and which may improve the host government's credit rating.
– Ability to accelerate the development of projects that would otherwise have to wait for, and compete, for sovereign resources.
– Use of private sector capital, initiative, and know-how to reduce project construction costs, shorten schedules, and improve operating efficiency.
– Allocation to the private sector of project risk and burden that would otherwise have to be borne by the public sector.
– The involvement of private sponsors and experienced commercial lenders, which ensures an in-depth review and is an additional sign of project feasibility.
– Technology transfer, the training of local personnel, and the development of national capital markets.
– In contrast to full privatization, government retention of strategic control over the project, which is transferred to the public at the end of the contract period.
– The opportunity to establish a private benchmark against which the efficiency of similar public-sector projects can be measured and the associated opportunity to enhance public management of infrastructure facilities.

Chapter 15
Lobbying

We define "lobbying" as the attempt to influence business and government leaders to conduct an activity or create legislation that will help the port industry. The target is to influence the thinking of decision makers and public officials for or against a specific cause. Lobbying involves the advocacy of an interest that is affected, or potentially, by the decisions of business and government leaders. Unlike voters, who each get one vote, lobbyists vary in their degree of influence. The level of influence a lobbyist has over the respective decision-making process is often proportional to the resources—time and money—the lobbyist can spend to achieve its goal.

The reason why many stakeholders have a negative perception on lobbying is usually for monetary reasons. Lobbyists spring into action when their interests are directly threatened; this is "reactive" lobbying. That defensive way of protecting interest is often seen by the media as being destructive, hampering necessary changes in society and giving lobbyist their bad image. The opposite type of "proactive" lobbying is much more quiet and invisible. It is the successful sum of all activities that guide into the intended direction before interests are threatened.

The term "lobbyist" has been traced to the mid-seventeenth century, when citizens would gather in a large lobby near the English House of Commons to express their views to members of parliament. By the early nineteenth century, the term "lobby agent" had come to the United States, where it was applied to citizens seeking legislative favors in the New York Capitol lobby, in Albany. By 1832 it had been shortened to lobbyist and has been widely used since then.

Today lobbyists practice business trade not only in the halls of the U.S. Capitol and the corridors of state legislatures and parliament buildings across the world, but also on playgrounds, in boardrooms, in manufacturing plants, at cocktail parties, in workshops, at trade and transportation fairs and in chambers of industry and commerce. Contemporary lobbying methods include political action committees, high-tech communication techniques, coalitions among groups and industries sharing the same political goals, and campaigns to mobilize constituents at the grassroots level. But since the early days of the nineteenth century, there has been a continuing debate over the proper role of lobbyists in a democratic society. Lobbyists contend they offer a valuable service to decision makers and government officials, providing information and raising questions about pending legislation or executive action. Critics argue that many lobbyists are nothing more than influence peddlers seeking political favors for their clients.

DOI 10.1515/9781547400874-015

Despite the noncorrupt success of many lobbyists within the port and maritime industry, lobbyists are often regarded as ethically questionable individuals. This reputation was enhanced whenever lobbyists abused their position with improper practices such as bribing. Although lobbying today is widely accepted and specifically protected in most of the democratic nations, numerous attempts have been made to regulate it—attempts that, not surprisingly, lobbyists have historically resisted.

In most countries, several lobbying statutes and decrees have been enacted to regulate special situations—such as lobbying by the agents of foreign governments or employees of holding companies. Most of the business lobbying we are referring to in this chapter is not very strictly regulated, and so the freedom of decision making in port lobbying is relatively high—although it is still frequently confronted with a negative image.

15.1 Mission of Port Lobbying

Mission Statement:

Port lobbying protects and advances the common interests of the port industry and its diverse players as they connect their communities with the global trade and transportation system.

For realizing this mission within a specific local, regional, national or international context, port lobbying needs an institutional set up and a clear description of targets. The lobbying institution will attain its mission through several goals that are important for all ports; the key goals are as follows:

1. **Advocacy:** Advocate port and transport related policies that strengthen and expand opportunities for the specific port community. Port lobbying will influence public policy on all levels to achieve a safe, efficient, and environmentally sustainable port sector, operating as a key element of trade and transport industry. It also involves a high degree of outreach to important governmental and industry stakeholders.

2. **Public awareness:** Achieve better understanding of the important role and economic value of the port business. Ports are commercially viable, self-sufficient business enterprises acting as "gateways to trade" for the communities and regions they serve. Ports provide a relevant number of jobs, enable trade and create tax income. They are important partners of essential supply chains.

3. **Business development:** A business-oriented objective of port lobbying is to encourage and stimulate the development of the port industry and to

advance the vested interests of the port community. The mission is accomplished through the development of programs that enhance and promote the business climate within the port industry.

4. **Representation and relationship-building:** Another key objective is to effectively represent the interests of the port community in building solid bridges to key government and port authority officials (at all levels), and valued business partners in trade and transport industry. This is done to ensure that issues do not become problems, and that problems that do occur find quick solutions inside the network of interests.

To achieve these four objectives outlined in the mission statement, the stakeholders of port lobbying must appoint qualified staff, build organizational structures, create organizations and equip them with necessary resources, that is, people, money, and access to data. In addition, the port lobbying institutions must have access to relevant information and need a high level of governance to be an accepted partner. The lobbying institutions or set-ups need to carry out following main tasks:

1. **Outreach to stakeholders:** Build and sustain strategic partnerships with government, industry, and groups interested in port business to achieve key priorities and to ensure that the economic importance of the port industry is recognized.
2. **Leadership and culture:** Create a culture of leadership and involvement to create awareness that ports can play a role as proactive partners in business and transport policy, and that safety and security standards are as important as being proactive in protecting the environment.
3. **Engagement and involvement:** Create acceptance and involvement among the port community with appropriate communications tools and relevant education and/or information.
4. **Internal organization:** Enhance efficient practices and processes to enable effective execution of the strategic direction.
5. **Financial resources:** Ensure sufficient financial resources to attain the priorities set out for the special lobby group.

15.2 Players and Target Groups

Historically, port lobbying was a public task executed by the authorities administrating and operating the ports. Still today, the port authorities play an important role, but with new models of port management and increasing private business in ports, several activities have been taken over from private operators and their institutions. In some cases, public-private partnership (PPP) models also occur. Figure 15.1 provides an overview of all relevant players.

institution / goals	Single Port Authority	Nat./Reg. Port Auth. group	Global Port Auth. Assn.	Single Terminal Operator	Nat./Reg. Terminal Operator	Global Term. Op. Assn.	Local Port Marketing	Nat./Reg. Port Marketing	Global Port Marketing	Local Employers Assn.	Nat./Reg. Employers Assn.
Advocacy	L	N, I	I, G	L	N, I	./.	./.	N, I	./.	L	N, I
Public Awareness	L, N	N, I	I, G	L, N	N, I	./.	L, N	N, I	./.	L, N	N, I
Business Dev.	L, N	./.	./.	L, N, I	L, N, I	./.	L, N, I	N, I	./.	./.	./.
Represent. + Relationsh. B.	L, N, I	I, G	I, G	L, N, I	L, N, I	./.	L, N, I	N, I, G	./.	L, N	N, I, G
example:	Sydney Ports, Australia	ESPO Europ. Sea Ports Org	IAPH Intern. Ass. Ports+H.	GTK Gdansk, Poland	Patrick, Australia		Seaports of Nieders., Ger.	AAPA Amer. Assn. Port A.		Long Beach Harb. Empl. A.	MEA Marit. E. A., Canada
with:	**L** = concentration on Local market; **N** =... on National market; **I** = ... on International market; **G** = ... on Global market; ./. = non-existing									
in gray colour = fields of major activity										

Figure 15.1: Port lobbying matrix

The key types of institutions in Figure 15.1 are as follows (for each institution few examples will be mentioned in bottom line of the table. The list shows only a small selection and is neither comprehensive nor exhaustive):

- **Single port authorities,** such as "Sydney Ports Corp." in Australia, or the Port Authority of New York & New Jersey (PANYNJ), or many other port authorities.
- **National and/or regional port authority groups or institutions,** such as the European Sea Ports Organisation (ESPO), Baltic Ports Organization (BPO), Association of Canadian Port Authorities (ACPA), the Finnish Ports Association (Finnports), China Ports & Harbors Association (CPHA), the Japan Ports & Harbors Association (JPHA), or Ports Australia as peak body or umbrella organization representing the interests of port and maritime authorities in Australia. The lobbying groups with multiple members should clearly be distinguished from a national port authority like the Administracion Nacional de Puertos (ANP) in Uruguay. A national port authority is a single body; not a lobbying group (although they do their own lobbying with similar targets). In Figure 15.1 ANP would be listed as single port authority.
- **Global port authority association(s),** such as the International Association of Ports and Harbors (IAPH), and (at least partly) the World Association for Waterborne Transport Infrastructure (PIANC).
- **Single terminal operators,** such as Gdansk Container Terminal Co. (GTK), and many other single terminal operators worldwide.
- **National and/or regional terminal operators** or operators institutions/ associations, such as Patrick in Australia, Eurogate in parts of Europe, and

other operators; as well as institutions like the Federation of European Private Port Operators (FEPORT).

– **Global terminal operators associations:** this column is empty in Figure 15.1, because such an association or interest group on global level does not exist. This means that there is no comparable partner to IAPH. To demonstrate this, the column was deliberately listed with and released. But it should be stated very clearly: Global Terminal Operators such as HPH or PSA have very active marketing departments; but this is not what should be listed here. Associations or institutions of more than one company and so a lobbying group does not exist.

– **Local port marketing institutions**, such as the local active Seaports of Niedersachsen Association in northwest Germany, the "French Atlantic Ports of call" in France as marketing partnership of Atlantic ports, or the Amsterdam Cruise Port organization (ACP), a nonprofit organization aiming to promote Amsterdam as cruise destination.

– **National and/or regional port marketing institutions** such as the American Association of Port Authorities (AAPA), the alliance of ports in Canada, the Caribbean, Latin America and the United States of America that is (beside other activities) very active in port marketing; or the Port Management Association of Eastern & Southern Africa (PMAESA), or its pendants the North African Ports Association (UAPNA) and the Port Management Association of West and Central Africa (PMAWCA). All of these are very active in regional port marketing. Others are CMF the Cluster Maritime Francais as voice of the French Maritime Industry, or Cruise Europe for the European Cruise Industry (Ports and Shipping Lines). Via Donau–Danube Ports Online is a marketing and information platform of ports along the Danube.

– **Global port marketing institutions** also do not exist; this is worth mentioning, and therefore, the column in Figure 15.1 is listed, but empty.

– **Local Employers Associations**, such as the Long Beach Harbor Employers Association in the United States, the Unternehmensverband Bremische Häfen (UBH) in Germany, or the Halifax Employers Association (HEA) in Canada as designated bargaining representative for all the employers of labor in the longshoring industry in the Port of Halifax exist for most of the ports worldwide.

– **National and/or regional employers' associations**, such as the Maritime Employers Association (MEA) in Canada, or the Federation of German Seaport Operators (ZDS), or the Australian Maritime Employers Association (AMEA), or the Association Ports of Sweden as an industry and employers' association with focus on Swedish ports.

All institutions listed in the first row of Figure 15.1 are active on different geographical levels, that is, not all goals they intend to realize are relevant on same regional level. Some goals are only important to pursue in the direct neighborhood, whereas others need to be addressed on national or even international level. The regional dimension of the target group is important to consider; therefore, Figure 15.1 indicates the following four levels of activity:

- **L** = Activities concentrated on the *local* market/for the target group in adjacent neighborhood.
- **N** = Activities concentrated on *national* and/or *regional* level; for smaller countries it is sometimes necessary to consider the relevant region in the neighborhood which may cover an area beyond the national border; for huge countries, on the other hand, the national scope may be too large. Important here is the so-called relevant market.
- **I** = Activities concentrated on *international* markets. Several lobbying activities concentrate on huge international markets, like the European Union, the GCC states, South America, etc.
- **G** = Activities relevant for the *global* market. All activities that focus on this scale are indicated with the letter "G."

A few examples explain how to read and understand the geographical scope of Figure 15.1. The examples below will describe how an institution follows a specific goal within a defined relevant market. This is easy to understand, and it is correct to do so. But reality has shown that the institutions set priorities in their goals. They do not pursue all goals with the same intensity, because not all are of the same importance in daily business. Therefore, an additional level of importance is included in Figure 15.1. The most important goals per institution are highlighted by a gray backround color.

Example 1:
>**Institution:** Single port authority
>**Goal:** Advocacy
>**Attributed level:** L

Port lobbying of a single port authority, which is an authority that is—like most authorities—active in and for one port only; will influence port and transport related policies that strengthen and support its position inside the port community with a focus at the local level. To achieve its targets, the authority must concentrate on the most influential politicians, political institutions, and governmental bodies; and due to the nature of daily port business, they are concentrated on local - often municipality—level. Therefore, the goal "advocacy" for a single authority is marked with the letter "L" only. This also means that the "big policy" on the international level is not the focus of the authority. And due to the importance of this lobbying target group, the box is highlighted.

Example 2:
    Institution: Local Employers Association
    Goal: Public Awareness
    Attributed level: L, N

Local employers' associations represent the interests of one side of the local port market, and their interest is to create public awareness of the economic situation of the companies working inside the port. Political support on all levels is very important for these, and so creating public awareness is essential. On the local level (and because many regulations are installed on the national level also on this higher level) a better understanding of the important role and economic value of employers' interest is of huge important for this lobby group. Therefore, the box is marked with "L, N" and highlighted.

Example 3:
    Institution: Local Port Marketing
    Goal: Business Development
    Attributed level: L, N, I

Local port marketing in many ports of the world is organized as a set of marketing activities for a single local port. "Business Development" is often the major goal to encourage and stimulate trade and so traffic for the development of the port community. This is a key activity, so the box is highlighted in gray. The level of engagements is wide spread with "L, N, I." This means that starting from the local via the national and further on international level the marketing activities try to attract business wherever possible, and due to the nature of port business as partner in supply chains these are widespread activities for the marketing team.

Example 4:
    Institution: Local Port Marketing
    Goal: Public Awareness
    Attributed level: L, N

Creating public awareness is an additional goal for a local port marketing institution. It is helpful when the economic role and value of the port business on a local and national level is highlighted. Realistically, the influence of marketing should not be overrated. Marketing for public awareness might have some influence on the local level. On the international level, however, marketing regarding the goal of public awareness has generally no impact. Nevertheless, on both local and national levels, this is an important task for port marketing. Due to marketing's limited effect, this box is not highlighted.

Example 5:
   Institution: Global Port Authority Association
   Goal: Representation
   Attributed level: I, G

Representation and relationship building with key government and transport policy officials and valued private business partners is an important task of the International Association of Ports and Harbors (IAPH), as major global representative of port authorities. Due to the nature of the port business, their focus is on international and global relations, and IAPH has representation and relationship building to officials as a key goal; therefore, this box in Figure 15.1 is highlighted.

The few examples above should help to interpret the content of Figure 15.1. The other boxes for all institutions in the first row of Figure 15.1 can be interpreted in a similar way. What is finally missing to fully understand port lobbying is the list of target groups for the activities mentioned above? Behind the goals are individuals and institutions that together form the target group:

– Individual politicians on all level
– Political institutions on all level
– Embassies + consulates
– Port and transport related associations
– Customs institutions
– Im- and export associations
– Single companies in industry and trade
– Shipping lines
– Partner companies in port hinterland, like railways, forwarders, etc.
– Individual sales and procurement persons in companies
– Business associations
– Social partners/unions
– The own port community solicitors

When it comes assigning the objectives of port lobbying (as expressed in the mission statement) to the different target groups, it makes sense to cluster the groups according to the key content of the activities. One important goal of port lobbying is communicating the key messages and intentions of port policy, that is, to act as "advocates of port policy" (Chapter 15.3). The key direction of this goal goes from internal stakeholder (e.g., the supervisory board) to the outside world; i.e. this is primarily one-way outward information. A second goal is to start a real bilateral communication with (mainly) customers, that is, setting up "port marketing" (Chapter 15.4). Both goals are often conflated and packed together; this to mix important customer information (e.g., about port extension plans) with policy statements. However, in the following two chapters these shall be considered separately.

Finally, port lobbying needs organizations and people, and thus it is a cost intensive business. All institutions spending money for port lobbying must justify the expenses. Public institutions are often subject to local or municipal ordinance programs; i.e. they must make public why and for what they spend money. Especially in landlord models, this kind of transparency gets more and more important and will help to support the lobbyists in setting up a normal business. In the absence of official ordinance programs, several port institutions established their own codes of conduct to create the necessary transparency and trustworthiness.

15.3 Advocate of Port Policy

Lobbying structures were created to articulate and channel the interests of the port, the port operators, and port administrators. This is necessary because of the importance of ports as partners within a maritime supply chain, and the fact that port administration and operation is a cost intensive business that requires huge investments from the public as well as from the private side. Lobby institutions like specialized port marketing companies, business associations or economic interest groups were thus built both for very specialized interests (e.g., hydraulic engineering), others for more general interests (e.g., all port authorities, terminal operators or other groups).

Typical objectives of such lobby groups with interest in port policy are:
- To provide advocacy and intelligence on issues that will impact the competitiveness and business interests of the port industry
- To discuss, formulate and communicate common points of view regarding port policy and maritime trade matters

- To serve as an interlocutor for other lobby groups, political institutions and national or international organizations
- To share administrative, technical and operational know-how and professional development

The typical subjects of interest of these lobby groups as sub-groups of port policy can be categorized as follows:
- Transport policy
- Harbors and navigation
- Facilities engineering
- Maritime policy
- Maritime economic development
- Finance
- Security/defense
- Safety and environment
- Logistics
- Information technology
- Law Review
- Social Policy
- Public Relations
- Research and development

Not all subject matters are of similar interest for all lobby groups; therefore, specialization became necessary to focus the core topics and to concentrate on the key target groups. The relevant work domains are usually in line with the specific interests of the lobby group. For example, in the following, few of these domains are shortly mentioned (most of them are self-explanatory):

Transport Policy:
Legal security for investments, fair competition in and between ports, transparency of financial flows, predictable application of environmental rules, port labor, state aid guidelines, transparency of public funding, choice of new additional services (operators), including how and for how long concessions are granted as well as prolongation conditions of concessions, internalization of external costs, rail liberalization, revision of transport policy guidelines, development of inland navigation transparent rules, discussion of transport master plans, positioning of port interests in transport policy working groups, etc.

Logistics Policy:
Logistic action plans, common maritime space without barriers, measures intended to enhance the quality and performance of maritime logistics, key performance indicators of maritime supply chains, benchmarking, short sea shipping, logistics bottlenecks exercise, dissemination of best practices, advanced informatics and quality infrastructure connections for uni- and multimodal solutions, intermodal policy, etc.

Environmental Policy:
Marine climate change, water and habitat directives, thematic strategy for environmental development, air quality, climate change, sulfur content of marine fuel, ECA and SECA policy, sediment pollution, shore-side electricity/cold ironing, environmental electricity taxation, dredging conditions, ballast water pollution, soil protection, etc.

Security Policy:
ISPS code, minimum standards, container security initiative (CSI), port security directive, intermodal security, status of secure operator, protection of critical infrastructure, risk analysis and 100% scanning of cargo, phytosanitary border inspection protocols, etc.

Maritime Policy:
National and global maritime strategy, maritime safety, including double hull tankers, port state control, IMO policy, European Maritime Safety Agency, ISM code, MSP, etc.

Social Policy:
Social Dialogue at the national and international levels between employers and employees, access to profession and training, tariff policy, accidents statistics, etc.

The lobby institutions are usually financed and supported by their members. Very often they are organized as nonprofit organizations with the typical setup of a small company; i.e. a chairman, a secretary general and several specialists for the variety of tasks. Depending on the size and the financial power of the lobby group, the staff is partly or full-time employed by the lobby institution. In many groups, high-ranking officials from the port business have a lead, voluntary position at the lobby. For special subtasks, dedicated working groups or technical committees work diligently throughout the year on specific aspects of port administration and operation, participate in special programs, and guide the institutions staff in these specific matters. Voluntary staff is usually elected by lobby members.

The publication of political statements, resolutions, reports, studies, open letters or other white papers is another key task of each lobby group. With a tool kit of PR instruments, the lobby groups position themselves and their statements express the interest of the members regarding specific topics. Resolutions and statements are used to support the lobby group's declaration, and are cited in presentations, press releases, brochures, etc.

A key interest of the lobby group is to be identified and accepted as a leading institution for port policy issues. Much of the work undertaken by committees relate to compliance with existing legislation and regulations, development of new regulations, and ongoing monitoring of government activity impacting the members and the port community generally. Lobbyists work to: communicate regularly with their internal committees and their external target group, provide an "early warning" of issues, and provide relevant research and information of interest to members.

The ways of information are manifold, and the port policy officials often use port marketing tool kits to convey their messages. Very typical are annual general meetings where information is provided and messages are placed, but also conferences, working groups, chambers of industry and commerce meetings, seminars, publications, etc.; all this in parallel to the direct and bilateral communication with members of the target groups.

15.4 Port Marketing

Marketing can be defined as the process of identifying, anticipating (predicting), and satisfying customer needs profitably. To satisfy the needs of customers, an adequate and successful mix of marketing activities is necessary. Marketers must promote the right product (or service), sell it at the right price and in the right place using the best means promotion. This "4Ps strategy" and the resulting "marketing mix" are two famous marketing terms.[1] The marketing mix is the tactical or operational part of a marketing plan. The "services marketing mix" is often enlarged and labeled as "7Ps" (the original 4Ps, plus process, people and physical evidence). In a very condensed view, the port marketing mix is a set of

---

1 See: UNCTAD Monographs on Port Management 12: Marketing Promotion Tools.

controllable tactical marketing tools that port marketing officials blend to influence their target market.

In highly competitive markets, "marketing" is often understood as this holistic approach toward market-oriented corporate governance. This stems from the consumer goods industry, where in fast moving markets, adequate fast reactions are vital. However, the modern port industry is far from using the consumer goods approach. "Port marketing" is understood as an inherent part of port operation and administration. This can be seen when analyzing the organizational charts and the positions the marketing departments have in port operating companies and port administration. Many approaches of today's port marketing officials are still rooted in the "doctrine of selling products." Correspondingly, the influence of the marketing departments and/or specialized marketing organizations at the ports is small. Today there is still a strict distinction between marketing and sales. In an ideal world, both departments and/or organizations should complement and influence each other, but in reality a systematic or even targeted approach is rarely in existence.[2] Here there is much room for improvement.

Port marketing in practice refers almost exclusively to the function of "communication" (formerly and above in a narrower sense called promotion). Port marketing has a limited influence on the overall business and a limited acceptance by the customers because of a serious lack of competence. It is a vicious cycle in that port management in full realization that they cut themselves away from the vital contacts and essential signals of the market which should come from open minded marketing officials, they—within the same process—limit the influence and competence of marketing because they (the marketing officials) are not in close contacts with their customers. It is not wrong to suppose that several port officials created this "isolated environment" in full consciousness, because it is an easy living without too much disturbance from the outside market. And even worse is the fact that marketing officials in ports seem to feel very comfortable in this reduced role, too, and they (must) accept the limitation of influence as guideline from the management. That port marketing in such an environment is not very effective can be described as a self-fulfilling prophecy. Customer satisfaction or a "customer first"-attitude as overall goal will not be achieved in such an environment.

---

2 Especially in the economic crisis of 2009, it was clear that the warning functions of port marketing were ignored, and the early warnings were dismissed as misinterpretations of market reactions. For an analysis of the North European port range refer to: Sorgenfrei, Jürgen: Port Marketing. Eine Bestandsaufnahme, Internationales Verkehrswesen, Vol. 61, Nr. 12, Hamburg, Germany 2009, pages 473–479.

The key issues at the top of the port marketing agenda include issues related to the overall competitiveness of the port, infrastructure development, sustainable development, security, legislation and regulation as well as innovation and technology. Marketing of ports is composed of activities related to market research and marketing implementation—both parts of the communication function. The research activities—understood as process of systematic design, collection, analysis and reporting of data and findings—will allow port officials to have the market analyzed, objectives fixed, strategy built and targets identified. A regularly renewed SWOT-Analysis (an analysis that identifies the strong and weak points, threats, and opportunities of a port) is helpful in this process. Port marketing is responsible for implementing the specified guidelines that result after a SWOT-Analysis.

The ideal instrument for targeting the port marketing activities is the already mentioned "marketing plan." This plan should include at least the following five elements:

1. The "strategy": Here guidelines are outlines and the why, where, and what should be done are fixed. A definition of the relevant market is also noted.
2. "Aims": Here the long-term marketing objectives of port lobbying as fixed in cooperation with major stakeholders are formulated.
3. "Measures": Here it is explicitly outlined, what exactly should be done in which market niche.
4. "Budget plan": the planned costs of the measures are defined as multiannual totals (e.g., for a new rep. office) and broken down into annual budgets.
5. "Action plan": Following approval of measures and the budget plan, the individual activities are described and calculated accurately.

Individual stages of the marketing plan can be broken down even further, but the strategy and the aims remain and the activities must be formulated in line with these. All activities for market research and implementation are integrated parts of the marketing plan.

Because of the high costs and often tight public budgets, investments in marketing are considered sensitive. Often tax money will be spent, which increases the pressure for public scrutiny by institutions and other lobbyists. Many interest groups compete for scarce public resources; accordingly, the objectives of port marketing need to be highly transparent. One of the basic requirements for effective marketing must therefore be drawing up an approved transparent marketing plan.

All activities of port marketing should start with a thorough understanding of the relevant market (e.g., the two markets for cruise business and dry bulk cargo). Key objectives of market research in port marketing are:

– To monitor the trade development in all relevant markets
– To analyze trends in existing markets
– To analyze available forecasts
– To monitor the activities of existing and potential new competitors
– To support shareholders, stakeholders, local authorities, etc.
– To provide short-term port related analysis of trade and transportation flows
– To collect and analyze relevant hinterland transportation data
– To monitor the developments in the shipping markets
– To support customer negotiations by customer analysis
– To establish port and terminal knowledge for identifying communication goals
– To provide detailed statistics for publications
– To support studies about the port
– To monitor customer satisfaction
– To establish the feasibility of potential new markets or products/services
– To develop strategies for future port development (markets, services, . . .)

This long list of important tasks already implies that the importance of a substantiate market research can hardly be overrated. It is an essential task that forms the necessary foundation for solid and rational decision making in terminal and port management. Without this substantial task, decision making is guesswork.

Marketing tools for the implementation of the plan in the reduced sense of communication policy are those elements that will have an influence on the sales of port services. The influence of those tools will differ from one country to another. Therefore, it is necessary to find the appropriate mix of all those elements for a given market, so that the result matches the targets. Various tools can be complementary and interchangeable. The appropriate mix for a defined market will have some degree of individuality and reflect the image the port marketing individuals have of themselves. Typical means of marketing communication—often referred to as the communication mix—are:

– Advertising
– Sales promotion (e.g., events, fairs)
– Public relations (PR)
– Personal sales support = key account information
– Direct marketing

Ideally all actions of port marketing should be SMART: specific, measurable, achievable, relevant, and time-based. This can best be guaranteed by a transparent marketing plan that lists and explains in detail all implementation actions.

Part 4: **Subjects with a Major Impact on Port Business**

Ports are nodal points in a supply chain, and they must interact with partners along this chain. Immediate contacts are with vessels and vessel operators, shipping agents, railway companies, forwarders, etc. Problems that occur from incorrect declaration of cargoes or wrong stowage plans put them in contact with ports, agents, logistics providers, etc., in other countries. Every single influence on one link of the supply chain may have an escalating, de-escalating, or even reverse effect on the whole chain. The interaction within a chain is high, which can make a chain vulnerable; and therefore, the process needs to be managed to reduce unexpected impacts.

Several effects causing interruptions that may influence more than one partner along the chain are often relatively easy to manage just by adding a little more buffer time or improving the operations at the interface; if this is possible and can be financed. But on a higher level, there are trends that influence trade and transportation in a more general way via changing underlying patterns. Most of these effects do not occur "overnight", virtually with a big bang; they rather come in slowly, but with a huge impact. These effects are not easily manageable in daily business because they change the structure of trade and transportation. These effects are megatrends, or subjects with a major impact on trade, traffic, and ports; "mega" because their impact on the business is huge, and "trends" because they have the tendency to change the patterns of maritime trade. In the following chapter, we will briefly analyze some megatrends, see how the trends evolved, and what can be expected for the future.

Chapter 16
Increased Economic Efficiency

In economic theory, *economic efficiency* implies an economic state in which every resource is optimally allocated to serve each individual or entity in the best way while minimizing waste and inefficiency. When an economy is economically efficient, any changes made to assist one entity would harm another. In terms of production, goods are produced at their lowest possible cost, as are the variable inputs of production. This definition is appropriate for static theory, but in reality, we are far away from an ideal world where resources are optimally allocated, and second, we need to take into consideration the fact of time: inventions occur and technical progress has the power to change the pattern of optimal allocation.

Also, in port and maritime logistics, inventions changed the world dramatically, especially when looking back decades or centuries. We are aware that the theoretically optimal situation of economic efficiency is an ideal conception that will never be achieved. But it is worth it to try to be better: in the sense that we try to get closer to the optimal situation.

16.1 Economies of Scale for Ships and Ports

Container Vessel Size

The trend in the container shipping industry in recent decades has been toward the use of increasingly larger vessels to maximize cost-effectiveness of cargoes through major trade lanes. This trend is driven both by economies of scale and the availability of infrastructure to serve these vessels—such as the depth of fairways, the cranes at the terminals, or in a more global perspective, the size of canals like Panama and Suez as potential bottlenecks for global trade. Realizing substantial economies of scale with increasing container vessel size will now be analyzed.

Figure 16.1 illustrates the fast-growing volume of the container carrying fleet; measured in TEU per categorized vessel size. The large vessels with 8,000+ TEU capacity grew fastest, and—according to the order book—will grow fast in upcoming years. In early 2018, the largest ships on order reached a capacity of 22,000 TEU, and it is very likely that the maximum vessel size will grow even further. Some experts expect that it is very likely to see vessels with 25,000 TEU carrying capacity soon. Beyond 25,000 TEU it is—according to operational specialists—not very likely to see many vessels due to extended operational times in ports and increased inflexibility.

DOI 10.1515/9781547400874-016

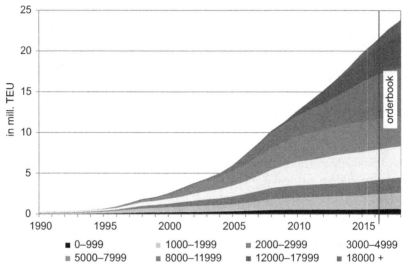

Figure 16.1: Development of container carrier fleet

In the mid-1990s, there was no container vessel on the market with more than 5,000 TEU carrying capacity. Less than 20 years later, the group of vessels with more than 5,000 TEU represent more than 50% of the market. Increasing competition and the need for the liner shipping companies to realize economies of scale pushed this trend. Economies of scale with larger vessels can mainly be realized via crewing costs and bunkering.

Typical key cost elements to operate container vessels are:
- Bunker (fuel):   35% up to 50%
- Port charges: 10% up to 21%
- Crewing: 10% up to 19%
- Insurance   2% up to 8%
- Repair & maintenance   6% up to 9%

Further cost components are: commissions, classification, procurement, financing, management, spare parts, lubricants, registration, etc. But all these components represent minor costs. The exact composition of the costs vary from vessel to vessel, depending on size, design, engine type, etc. But the fact is the first mentioned three components represent between 55% and approximately 75% of the total vessel operating costs: bunker, crewing, and port charges.

Fuel-efficient engines and a hydrodynamic optimized vessel design are key elements to reduce costs per unit (per TEU). It is true that total fuel consumption increases with vessel size, but it is a degressive increase, that is, relative fuel savings per unit are possible. A 4,000 TEU container vessel can be operated with a crew of twelve to fourteen members, and a vessel triple that size (12,000 TEU) also needs a crew of twelve to fourteen. Crewing is another key element to realize economies of scale. Table 16.1 shows a cost comparison for a 4,000 TEU Panamax vessel and a 12,000 TEU vessel that represents the New Panamax size after opening of the new Panama-Canal locks in 2014.

The data used for the calculations in Table 16.1 are based on real costs within Asia–U.S. East Coast (USEC) trade. Therefore, in this calculation the Panama Canal toll is included. The total cost for a 20 ft standard container on a 4,000 TEU vessel amounts to 1,481 USD, whereas the cost for the same container onboard a 12,000 TEU vessel is only 953 USD. The cost saving per TEU is 528 USD. Per round-trip (528 * (12,000 *0.8) * 2 = 528 * 19,200), the savings amount to approximately 10.1 mill USD. Bearing in mind the total cost per round-trip for the vessel, this is a real substantial savings. Also, this is the main reason why the liner shipping companies intend to realize these huge economies of scale.

The total cost for the two vessels amount to approximately 55 and 106 mill USD. If we, in a kind of sensitivity analysis, exclude the very special Panama Canal tolls and consider just the traveling cost, they will amount to 51.5 and 96 mill USD. For the cost per TEU, this leads to 1,390 and 863 USD per TEU. With a 527 dollar difference, the cost saving potential is the same; or in other words, bigger vessels have the potential to realize essential cost savings per TEU; regardless of destination.

In Table 16.1, we assume that both vessels will have a capacity utilization of 80%. For the 4,000 TEU vessel this results in 6,400 TEU moved per round-trip, and for the 12,000 TEU vessel 19,200 TEU per round-trip. The bigger vessel needs more volume. Therefore, these vessels concentrate on hub ports that can attract these large volumes. This is the negative implication of a bigger vessel: the dependency on bigger volumes.

A positive effect of bigger vessel size is the fuel efficiency per TEU, that—in times of increasing oil prices—leads to lower cost for energy per unit; but again, on a higher volume level. With less than 50% of cargo on board, a big vessel is inefficient, too.

The resulting question of this calculation is: what is the minimum quantity a 12,000 TEU vessel needs to realize "cost per TEU moved" compared with a 4,000 TEU vessel = approximately 1,481 USD? Calculations based on the cost components in Table 16.1 show that the bigger vessel must at least realize at minimum a utilization of 51% to be comparable, that is, approx. 6,120 TEU per trip. The dependency on volumes is still a matter of fact, although the big vessel only needs to be half laden to be competitive.

Table 16.1: Cost comparison 4,000 TEU vessel–12,000 TEU vessel, Asia–US East coast

	4,000 TEU	12,000 TEU
Annualized vessel capital costs (6% discount rate)		
– vessel purchase cost in mill. USD	60	120
– vessel lefe span (years)	30	30
– annual capital cost in USD	**4,358,935**	**8,717,869**
Fuel consumption		
– main engine load factor at sea	80%	80%
– average main engine power rating in kw	38,000	72,240
– hours of transit per day	24	24
– Energy per day (kw –hr)	729,600	1,387,008
– specific fuel content (g/kwh)	290	290
– Main Engine metric tons of fuel per day at sea	211.6	402.2
– auxiliary engine power usage at sea in kw	1,400	1,834
– auxiliary engine metric tons of fuel per day at sea	9.7	12.8
– **total fuel consumption per day at sea in metric tons**	**221**	**415**
– auxiliary engine power usage at berth (kw)	1,300	2,445
– auxiliary engine metric tons of fuel per day at berth	9.0	17.0
– boiler power at berth in kw	510	765
– boiler metric tons of fuel per day at berth	3.5	5.3
– **total fuel consumption per day at berth in metric tons**	**12.6**	**22.3**
Annual fuel cost		
– operating speed (knots)	20	20
– fuel unit cost per metric ton in USD	700	700
– fraction of time at sea (remainder at berth)	80%	80%
– days at sea per year	292	292
– days at berth per year	73	73
– **fuel cost per year in USD**	**45,883,000**	**85,967,000**
Panama Canal tolls		
– Asia – USEC round trip time (days)	63	63
– annual trips per vessel	5.8	5.8
– Panama Canal toll per TEU (containers on vessel) in USD	74	74
– Panama Canal toll per TEU (ballast) in USD	65.60	65.60
– average vessel capacity utilization	80%	80%
– Panama Canal toll per passage in USD	289,280	867,840
– **annual toll cost**	**3,351,975**	**10,055,924**
Annual crew cost		
– vessel crew size	12	12
– crew cost per person –day in USD	300	300
– Total vessel crew cost per day in USD	3,600	3600
– **total vessel crew cost per year in USD**	**1,314,000**	**1,314,000**
Total Annual cost per TEU		
– total vessel cost per year in USD	54,908,090	106,054,472
– TEU moved per round-trip voyage	6,400	19,200
– TEU moved per year	37,079	111,238
– **cost per TEU moved in USD**	**1,481**	**953**
– cost per TEU moved in USD / 4,000 TEU vessel = 100%	100%	64%

Source: AECOM 2012

Larger Terminals

The use of ever larger container vessels implies that fewer port calls are required, and that volumes are concentrated on hub ports. This move to larger vessels reduces shipping lines' dependence on particular ports, but intensifies competition among ports for the remaining calls (assuming each port can handle the larger vessels).

Second, the emergence of efficient intermodal rail, road, and barge corridors has extended the hub ports' geographical reach. The extension of each single ports hinterland leads to increasing overlap among all port hinterlands and hence to stronger competition. Third, the ports must be able to serve the bigger vessel: the fairways must be deep enough, that is, dredging is an important topic for many ports (and a topic where port authorities and terminals have only limited influence, because very often the assess fairways are under control of the central or regional government; a budgetary compromise is often required). The water in front of the quay walls needs to be deep enough to berth these vessels, the berths itself must be long enough, there must be a sufficient number of cranes available to serve these vessels within an adequate time, the terminal area must be large enough for all pre- and post-stowings, a larger number of reefer slots are needed, more dangerous cargo space is required, etc.

The list of infra- and superstructure investments that are needed to fulfill the hub port function that allow a single port to serve the big vessels is long. Huge investments for port authorities and terminal operators are necessary. Shipping lines drive this trend, but larger terminals can also realize economies of scale; provided no additional "extra-investments" are needed just to be a partner in this business. Here a consideration port-by-port and terminal-by-terminal is necessary. In the past, several approaches and models have been discussed[1] to optimize the ship-to-shore interface, and so to find the optimum size and best utilization of terminals. But, it seems to be the same case as above with the definition of "economic efficiency": a theoretical optimum seems to be possible, but the fast and frequent changing framework parameter led to something that is suboptimum at best.

---

1 See, for example, Musso, Enrico L., Claudio Ferrari, Marco Benacchio: "On the Global Optimum Size of Port Terminals," in: *International Journal of Transport Economics*/Rivista internazionale di economia dei trasporti, Vol. 26, No. 3 (October 1999), pp. 415–437; and: Kidson, Renee, Thomas Rutherford, Adam Malarz and Simon O'Mahony: Impact of increasing container ship size on container handling productivity at Australian ports, Australasian Transport Research Forum 2015 Proceedings, 30 September–2 October 2015, Sydney, Australia Publication website: http://www.atrf.info/papers/index.aspx

Deep Water

Bigger vessels are longer, wider, heavier, and need deeper water as Table 16.2 highlights. This is not such a problem for bulkers and tankers because they call dedicated facilities with specialized jetties or dry bulk loading and unloading facilities. The problem occurs mainly in the container business, and here due to the fast-increasing vessel size, and in universal ports with the intention to serve big tankers and bulker as well as container vessel.

Table 16.2: Selected categories of vessel

category	type	draught	width	length	dwt	TEU
Handysize	Bulker	10.0	27.0	180.0	15.000 – 35.000	–
Handymax	Bulker	12.0	30.0	190.0	50.000 – 60.000	–
Panamax	Container	12.5	32.3	294.3	60.000 – 65.000	max. 5.000
Panamax	Bulker	12.5	32.3	294.3	60.000 – 75.000	–
Post –Panamax	Container	14.5	43.0	318.0	65.000 – 100.000	4.500 – 8.000
Panamax new	Container	15.2	49.0	366.0	110.000	13.500
VLCS/ULCS	Container	17.0	65.0	420.0	120.000 – 220.000	26.000
VLCC	Tanker	20.0	60.0	470.0	200.000 – 350.000	–
ULCC	Tanker	30.0	63.0	415.0	350.000 – 550.000	–

* sorted by dwt; figures in meters

Many so-called very or ultra large container ships (VLCS/ULCS) with a size of up to 420 m and a draught of a maximum of 16.0 m are too large for many ports around the world. Existing draught restrictions do not allow that these vessels with a relevant number of containers on board enter the fairways and terminals. The problem here is the rapidly growing vessel size over the last two decades and thus the increased draught of these vessels. Not mentioned in Table 16.2 are container vessels that are designed for the next decade, and that will have maximum drafts of up to 17 to 18 m and a carrying capacity of more than 25,000 TEU. We do not know if we will ever see such vessels, but they are technically feasible. The opposing trend to ever bigger vessels will come from the economics, as discussed above. Many ports globally can only be called by already existing vessels when having fewer containers on board. But this destroys the economies of scale these vessels offer, that is, from an economic point of view it is no longer justified to call such ports. A reduced number of hub ports will be respectively the logical consequence of these restrictions.

It is obvious which maritime supply chain partner optimizes the cost structure by realizing economies of scale: big vessels are saving costs per unit for the shipping line, *not* for the port. The authorities must dredge the fairways and the basins in front of the quay walls, and they must build stronger (measured in maximum tons allowed per running meter) and deeper quay walls that allow heavier cranes with extended outreach to operate on top of them. The terminals must invest in quay and yard operating equipment. Critical voices name this trend a "privatization of profit" via realizing economies of scale in private shipping companies in combination with the necessary "socialization of costs" for upgrading the infra- and superstructure.

For many ports, the big container vessels have been and still are real game changers, because the "extra-investments" are tremendously high or even can not be realized due to natural conditions (e.g., due to insurmountable draught restrictions in the fairway). Ports that have been integrated in regular liner services before with vessels up to 8,000 TEU and fairway restrictions of 12 to 14 m maximum draught (approximately 40 to 46 ft) will now have to extend the port infra- and superstructure as well as deepen the access channels. If the necessary volumes realistically do not exist and can not be attracted in future, these ports will fall out of the liner service network and will lose their hub port function.

"Necessary volumes" in this case is identical with "minimum demand." If the market and the trading volumes adjacent to the port or in the hinterland are not large enough, or when the competition to others (eventually with better cost position due to less dredging costs) leads to low volumes, these ports may be excluded from the liner network of these trunk lines. The feeder lines will no longer call this port, because they are serving and following the big lines. For a single port, these changes in network design of liner shipping companies may cause serious consequences. Again, this underlines the necessity to consider ports as partners along the supply chain. The best positions in this game are with ports that have substantially high and regular trade volumes adjacent to the port, that is, a high loco potential. This reinforces huge importance of best possible cargo demand forecasting to predict realistic growth scenarios as a base for investment planning.

Dedicated Terminals; Vertical Integration; Concentration

From a liner shipping point of view, ports are ubiquity facilities, and the vessel operators are free to choose the one or the other port if competition allows. From a ports point of view, they are strong when having an exclusive position and are a "must port of call"; this because an economical alternative is not available, or because their loco potential and hinterland together provides attractive trade volumes. Shipping lines realize this, as do global terminal operators. The difference is that global terminal operators extend their business on a horizontal level, whereas the shipping lines realize a vertical integration along the supply chain. Both concepts are different, but both concentrate with routing concepts or for future investments on same ports and terminals. If there will be a winning concept in future is an open question today; most probably both concepts will find their own market niches.

In the last two decades, liner shipping companies have been more and more engaged in terminal business; the so-called dedicated terminals. Although these facilities are often declared as open facilities, most of trade at dedicated terminals often comes from one shipping group or alliance. The reason for this is that the competitors will not allow the dedicated terminal operators to get detailed customer information. For the shipping line, these terminals are part of their production chain, and the concept of dedicated terminals allows them to consider terminals as part of their internal cost calculation and to optimize the total supply chain cost via realizing economies of scale. In addition, dedicated terminals are better integrated in information flows. The main reasons for being engaged in terminal business are to secure sufficient terminal space, a more efficient network design, and an integrated cost calculation. Next step in this approach is to be engaged in trunk hinterland operation concepts; i.e. to compete with companies like DHL, Amazon or FedEx. Few of the big shipping lines realize this already for selected destinations.[2] These concepts will go beyond the already existing engagement in hinterland, road, and rail operations. The target is rather the so-called last mile, and with this the direct contact to final customers. This will lead to increased concentration, and many governments and intergovernmental institutions watch this closely.

Horizontal Integration

Horizontal integration is another argument to realize economies of scale to increase economic efficiency. Global terminal operators[3] like HPH, PSA, or DP World enlarge their business by integrating terminals within a selected region or globally into their business portfolio. Economies of scale can be realized mainly with all types

---

2 See, for example, a statement quoted by Maersk, in: Hellenic Shipping News Worldwide, Daily Newsletter February 22, 2018: World's Biggest Container Liner Looks for Deals Outside Shipping, Athens, Greece 2018: "Jakob Stausholm, A. P. Moller-Maersk A/S's chief financial officer and head of transformation and strategy, says the company needs to expand its land-based activities to meet a growing need from clients. 'We're currently very big in the ocean segment, and we'd rather grow in non-ocean, so it may be a good idea to look for M&A targets there,'"....
3 For more details on global terminal operator, see Chapter 11: "Port Operator."

of central staff functions and within the purchasing sector. It makes a real difference whether a single terminal places a one-time order of a small number of gantry cranes that may cost 20 mill USD per unit, or if a global terminal operator orders such a set of cranes two or three times each year. The same is true for most of the movable terminal equipment like van carriers, RTGs, RMGs, forklifts, chassis, tractors, trucks, etc. In this field, real economies of scale can be realized.

16.2 Performance Measurement

Technical Port and Terminal Indicator

Key performance indicators (KPI) assist the port and maritime industry in finding the most appropriate way of organizing the business to assess the performance of single measures and to increase efficiency. KPIs are quantifiable measurements, agreed to beforehand, that reflect the critical success factors of port or terminal operations. They will differ depending on the size and structure of operators. Once the port or terminal has analyzed its mission, identified all its stakeholders, and defined its goals, it needs a way to measure progress toward those goals. KPIs are these measurements.

A common way for choosing KPIs is to apply a management framework, such as the balanced scorecard, that is a semistandard structured report supported by design methods and automation tools. Managers can use this to keep track of the execution of activities. KPIs are also relevant for reaching targets. KPIs are most commonly defined in a way that is understandable, meaningful, and measurable.

The set of relevant KPIs varies from terminal to terminal, depending on the kind of cargo handled and structure of trade and/or passengers. Because of this, it is necessary to adjust the KPI to be sure it is measured correctly. A selected list of typical indicators is displayed in Table 16.3. These indicators need to be adjusted for each single port or terminal.

KPIs are helpful in creating transparency, but for less performing ports and terminals they may cause disadvantages in competition. Therefore, the correct definition is so important, because only accepted and comparable indicators create the necessary transparency and support efficiency.

Example: KPI 18 in Table 16.3: Dwell time per vessel
The important indicator "Dwell time per vessel" is sometimes also called vessel turnaround time (VTT). This means: it already starts with the correct naming to create a common understanding. VTT is understood as time between first line down and last line up, that is, the total time the vessel lays at the berth. Dwell

time is defined similarly by the Bureau of Transportation Statistics/U.S. Department of Transportation.[4]

Table 16.3: Selected key performance indicator

No.	description	unit
1	Number of vessel calls	vessels
2	Number of vessels per type	vessels
3	Share of import cargo	t or TEU
4	Import cargo per country	t or TEU
5	Share of export cargo	t or TEU
6	Export cargo per country	t or TEU
7	Transhipment cargo	t or TEU
8	Empty containers	TEU
9	Number of passenger	quantity
10	Maximum draught of vessels	m
11	Average draught of vessels; per type	m
12	Maximum beam of vessels	m
13	Maximum length of vessels	m
14	Physical length per berth / per quay	m
15	Berth productivity	t/m or TEU/m
16	Berth occupancy	% of hours
17	Availability + productivity of labor	no.; per hour
18	Dwell times per vessel / for cargo	days
19	Terminal area	sqm
20	Terminal productivity (Yard)	t/ sqm
21	Storage area	sqm
22	Number of cranes	cranes
23	Productivity per crane	t / crane / hour
24	Number of yard equipment	quantity
25	Productivity of equipment	t / device / hour
26	Age of equipment	years
27	Number of rail tracks / length	number / m
28	Rail capacity	t per hour / day
29	Road capacity / Interchange productivity	number / hour
30	Availability of inland nav. Facilities	share of total

"Vessel dwell time" according to the definition of Bureau of Transportation Statistics is a function of:

---

4 Please refer to the web site for general definitions: https://www.rita.dot.gov/bts/port_ performance

- The number of containers or tonnage to be loaded and unloaded
- Terminal resources available (e.g., cranes per berth and vessel)
- The efficiency with which those resources are employed

Vessel dwell time is not a linear function of cargo volume, since each vessel typically requires:
- 2–4 hours to be tied up and readied for cargo operations
- 2–4 hours to be readied for departure after cargo operations

Vessel dwell time also varies with the timing of arrival and departure.
- Late vessels may result in overlapping calls and delays
- A vessel that arrives in mid-shift my not be worked until the start of the next full shift[5]

Both definitions try to measure the time the vessel stays within the port, but it is not automatically clear that both indicators measure the same period. The time between "first line down—last line up" may be a few hours longer than the corresponding dwell time when the vessel, for example, arrives in mid-shift, is fixed alongside the berth, but work has not started. This example shall only make clear that indicators need to be defined precisely; otherwise KPI measurement may lead to erroneous results.

Trade Indicator

For global trade development, it is necessary to find indicators that show how developed an economy (or trading partner) is. This is not that relevant for bulk products because these are mostly preliminary industrial products, and few of them can (at least in parts and in the long run) be substituted by others. For example, coal power plants can be replaced by LNG power plants. This will then reduce coal imports and increase LNG imports.

Therefore, for container and consumer goods, the situation is different. Here it can be useful to build relations with demographic or economic indicators, like the popular indicator "TEU per 1,000 inhabitants" per country as shown in Table 16.4. The idea behind this is: the more developed a country is and the more it is integrated in the world economy, the higher the ratio is. Sometimes this indicator is described as an indicator for the welfare of the country, which is not true! It

---

5 See: https://www.rita.dot.gov/bts/port_performance/smith/slide24_text

does not describe how many consumer goods are available per inhabitant. This indicator just shows how many containers are handled in the ports of a specific country/per 1,000 inhabitants.

Table 16.4: Indicator: TEU per 1,000 inhabitants

	top 10			lowest 10	
1	Singapore	5218	1	Bangladesh	6
2	Malta	4775	2	India	6
3	China	3355	3	Pakistan	10
4	UAE	2072	4	Russia	21
5	Panama	1160	5	Iran	22
6	Belgium	983	6	Indonesia	25
7	Oman	931	7	Mexico	27
8	Canary Islands	929	8	Brazil	31
9	Jamaica	698	9	Peru	40
10	Netherlands	675	10	Philippines	42

Source: Own calculations. * moves = port throughput figures; base year 2007.

The top ten in the list describe this very precisely. Most of the top ten countries and their ports are typical hub ports/transhipment ports, that is, many containers enter and/or leave the ports via the quay walls; without any products entering or leaving the country. Ranked as no. 1, Singapore is one of the world largest ports, serving as hub in South East Asia. Malta is a hub port for the Mediterranean, UAE Dubai serves as hub port for the Middle East, Panama and Jamaica for the Caribbean, Belgium/Antwerp and Netherlands/Rotterdam for the European North Range. The Netherlands and Jamaica are on the same level in the top ten list; but nobody would realistically assume that the living standards in these two countries are similar, that is, this is just an indicator for trade, not to be interpreted as living standard.

The right side of the chart shows countries with the lowest shipments per inhabitant. This list helps us get a sense of how these countries have integrated into the world economy. If the ports of a country do not function as hub ports, then the indicator shows how good or poor the supply with consumer goods in the country is. Here the land connections (highways, railroads) must be considered as well. The extreme case: for landlocked countries like the Czech Republic in Europe, Bolivia in South America, or Mali in Africa, this indicator doesn't work.

What is valid for many indicators is true here as well: the interpretation of the data is only as good as the question itself. In other words: many indicators lead to misinterpretations because they are used incorrectly. But for measuring efficiency and for creating transparency, indicators can be helpful tools.

Weighting Rules

KPIs attempt to make the technical performance of terminals and ports more transparent and comparable. Weighting rules as indicators are being discussed in the port business as a way of finding a scale or benchmark for the value added of different port activities. "Value added" in this discussion according to Haezendonck and others[6] is usually calculated as a derivative of employment or surplus value. In other words, the weighting rules indicate via labor costs how many jobs are created from different port activities. Most of these rules are thumb rules and just describe the relation of statistical rows; but nevertheless, general indication is given.

> The first rule that put forward value added as a relevant concept for analyzing port competition was developed by the port of Hamburg in 1976.... This rule suggests that the value added created by one tone of conventional cargo corresponds to that of five tons of dry bulk and fifteen tones of liquid bulk.

The second rule was the Bremen Rule, which concluded that one ton of general cargo equals three tons of dry bulk and twelve tons of liquid bulk in terms of value added. In other words: twelve times more cargo is needed to create the same amount of work as one ton of general cargo. Therefore, general cargo is considered a labor-intensive job creator.

The Rotterdam Rule of 1985—based on a different approach, but with the same intention—elaborated more detailed results: one ton of conventional cargo equals 2.5 tons of oil products, 3 tons of containers, 4 tons of cereals, 7.5 tons of other bulk, 8 tons of RoRo traffic, 10 tons of coal, 12.7 tons of iron, and 15 tons of crude oil. Although more detailed, the general message is the same: the categories of cargoes that needs more attentiveness and care because of the nature of the products lead to more value-added and create more jobs.

---

6 For example, refer to: Haezendonck, Elvira, Chris Coeck, Alain Verbeke: "The Competitive Position of Seaports: Introduction of the Value-Added Concept," in: *International Journal of Maritime Economics*, Vol. 2, No. 2, pages 107–118, Basingstoke, UK, April 2000.

Other rules take the specific cargo structure of a selected port into consideration and arrive at only slightly different results. A generalized rule of thumb for added value or—simplified—for the creation of port jobs in daily port practice can be summarized as outlined in Table 16.5. This rule should be interpreted with great caution; it is only a rule of thumb. Because these rules in practice are often applicable, they should not be concealed here.

Table 16.5: Generalized value-added creator*

General Cargo	Container	Dry Bulk / Liquid Bulk	Crude Oil
1	3	6	15

* answers the question: how many units of cargo are necessary to create 1 unit of value (jobs)

We shall not discuss other indicators in detail, but regarding classical economic indicators it is necessary to mention that shipping analysts like Martin Stopford have analyzed long term shipping cycles (Stopford 2009), which are often the result of global business cycles. The same applies for the port business. Global economic trends and cycles also influence port development, but a port business usually can not react that fast to these trends. In most countries of the world, port development is a time consuming and long-lasting task. The reasons for this are different and span from inefficient bureaucracy to sprawling democracy with extremely broad discussions and studies about every detail. Here we shall not judge about this but realize that port planning has little to do with short-term economic cycles. A recession may delay a good project, that is, a modern container terminal, for a couple of months or even years, but in most cases the project will not be canceled.

16.3 Productivity of Container Terminals

Improving productivity at terminals is emerging as one of the major challenges for the container shipping industry in the mega-ship era. Container ship sizes are rapidly increasing as container lines seek to achieve competitive advantages in reducing vessel operating costs per TEU by deploying ever larger ships (Figure 16.1). As these ships have entered service, arrival delays have become more widespread, terminal dwell times have expanded, and service reliability has declined. Thus, while mega-ships allow carriers to reduce per-container operating costs, they pose a significant challenge for ports and terminals that have not expanded capacity at the same pace as the size of the ships. They are thus too small to accommodate the big ships, having been built for an earlier era of container ship sizes. Therefore, container terminal productivity has inevitably come into focus.

Container terminals must integrate and balance an increasing number of dynamic market-place processes—including globalization, containerization, hub-and-spoke concepts and modern logistics—as they work to define their competitive position within an increasingly competitive framework. These dynamic processes demand that terminals as well as their customers measure and benchmark performance correctly, and steadily improve operational and managerial efficiencies and overall productivity. As the demand for international trade and global logistic services continues to increase, substantial investments and improvements in both physical capacity and operational efficiencies are necessary to enhance terminal productivity.

If the pace of loading and unloading is too slow, the ships' time at port is extended and they fall behind schedule. Carriers are loathe to speed up and incur additional fuel costs, with the result that ships arrive late to subsequent ports which compounds delays because terminals schedule berthing windows and make cranes and other equipment available based on the assumption that ships will arrive on schedule. When they are delayed, the cargo is delayed to the customer, published on-time arrival performance is undermined, and ships are idled, which incurs costs and may require additional ships to maintain a fixed-day weekly schedule.

Pure physical expansion is often constrained by a limited supply of available land, especially for urban center ports, and amid escalating environmental concerns. In this context, expanding port capacity by improving the productivity of terminal facilities appears to be the only viable solution. How to improve productivity sufficiently to accommodate a large portion of the anticipated increase in container traffic, however, presents a challenge to terminal operators and port authorities.

In general, the productivity of a container terminal is influenced by a range of factors, only some of which can be controlled by terminal operators. Factors internal to the terminal and under the control of the operator include terminal configuration and layout, capital resources invested, and—to a certain extent— labor productivity. External factors beyond the control of operators include trade volumes, shipping patterns, and the ratio of import to export containers (which influences the number of empty containers). The size and type of ships accommodated by a terminal, as well as the landside capacities and performance of intermodal rail and highway systems, are additional external factors affecting the productivity of terminal operations.

Terminal operators are concerned with maximizing operational productivity as containers are handled at the berth and in the marshaling yards, and with efficiently utilizing available ground space. Container handling productivity is directly related to the transfer functions of a container terminal, including the number and movement rate of quayside container cranes, the use of yard equipment, and the productivity of workers employed in waterside, landside, and gate operations. The efficient use of available ground space relates to the number of containers stored in a given area of the terminal. Improving the utilization of ground space typically reduces the operational accessibility to containers; that is, ground space utilization and container accessibility are inversely related. For the terminal itself it is necessary to identify the bottlenecks of all logistics flow from berth to outgate, or vice versa from ingate to berth. Figure 16.2 illustrates the interdependent terminal flow stations; in this example, the demand is for 1000 boxes/hour, and the limiting constraints (encircled) result from the Gate productivity.

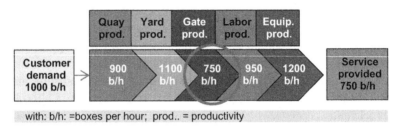

with: b/h: =boxes per hour; prod.. = productivity

Figure 16.2: Terminal constraints

For a customer, all these terminal details are nice to know, but what finally counts is what is in focus of customers' interest. For a shipping line, a key interest is what from a terminals perspective is called "berth or quay productivity," and what shipping lines often call "ship productivity," that is, the amount of container or TEU handled per hour.[7] From a terminals perspective, it is much more important to concentrate on moves at the berth, because this is what a crane performs: moves from ship to shore or vice versa.

---

7 A 20 ft container represents one TEU; a 40 ft container represents two TEUs. 45, 50, 53 ft or other container units are on the market as well, but will in most cases be subsumed as 40 ft; this because the corner fittings for the spreader still have 40 ft size. But it should not be forgotten that oversized boxes cause operational problems on the yard as well as on board of vessels.

From a terminal perspective, there are at least two categories of moves that need to be considered separately:
- Cargo moves
- Operational moves

Cargo move (CM): loading one or more containers from a quay onto a vessel or discharging one or more containers from a vessel onto a quay; as an operating metric, moves are calculated without controlling for container size (20 ft, 40 ft, 2*20 ft., twin lifts, double twin or quad lifts as illustrated in Figure 16.3) and shipping customers are invoiced by terminal operators for the number of moves performed, not the number of TEU moved. This means a move can represent the lift of: 1 TEU, 2 TEU (1 of 40 ft or 2 of 20 ft), 4 TEU (2 * 40 ft or 4 * 20 ft), etc. These are the moves that are of core interest for the shipping lines; but instead of counting moves, the line operators often count TEU. From their side, this is understandable because they earn revenue based on the number of TEUs transported.

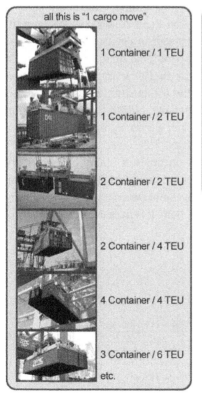

Figure 16.3: Cargo and operational moves

Operational move (OM): loading or unloading a lash box, shifting or re-organization on board without moving boxes over the quay wall (to get other containers out), Lilo or lift on-lift off operations or reorganization with moving containers over board and re-stowing them later (this represents two operational moves, but no cargo move, because it's just a reorganization of boxes), removal of hatch cover and later on replacement of hatch cover. All these moves are necessary operations to load/discharge a container, but they are not counted as cargo moves.

For terminal operators, operational moves are included in productivity counting; shipping lines often don't count them because they are not cargo moves. This just shows that the term "productivity" is not equally defined; it depends on the perspective. In some definitions of operational moves, all times necessary for these handlings are called "idle times," because no cargo moves happen.[8] But from a port's perspective this is not correct, because it is not possible to discharge boxes that are stowed below hatch covers without removing the hatch cover before. In this sense, the times are necessary operational times, although the respective moves are not cargo moves.

An additional term used in this context is "move time"; this is the time the crane needs to move from one bay to the next. And again, from a port's perspective these times are necessary operational times as well; as a consequence, terminals don't consider the sum of "move time" and "operational time" as idle times—the moves are operational moves. Ports also argue that they are not solely responsible for the vessel stow plans; this lies in the responsibility of shipping lines as well (even when the planning tasks are often outsourced to stevedores)—and therefore the number of operational moves is not a terminal operator's responsibility alone.

Ship productivity is not only dependent on times of operations at the terminal or while waiting for customs before operations could start. The total time spent in the port is relevant. Sometimes a vessel must wait in the port after arriving, e.g. for a free berth, or for a pilot. In some ports it is necessary to anchor, that is, there are a variety of reasons for waiting.

---

8 Idle times in this respect can be defined as: unproductive time on the part of port workers or cranes because of factors beyond their control. Idle time is the time associated with waiting, or when a piece of the crane is not being used but could be. Idle time could also be associated with computing/starting the crane.

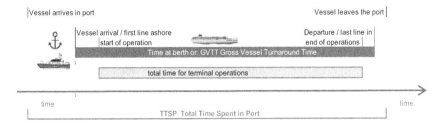

Figure 16.4: Vessel times spent in port

Figure 16.4—as well as 16.5 and 16.6 below—show the time from arrival at the port (leftmost position), the necessary travel and waiting times before the vessel arrives at the berth, the time between arrival at berth and start of operations (e.g., while waiting for customs), the total time of all terminal operations (the light gray bar), the time between end of operations, departure, and the time it takes to leave the port. The time between departure (last line in) and leaving the port can also include waiting times for pilot or for next tide window; like waiting times when arriving at the port.

The berth time or average vessel turnaround time (AVTT) is calculated in hours and spans the time between berth arrival, or "lines down" and berth departure, or "lines up. This is a clear and defined time span, but from the terminal operator's perspective, it is necessary to distinguish between:

Gross vessel turnaround time (GVTT): in the definition as described above: the time between first-line-ashore and last-line-in.

Net vessel turnaround time (NVTT): GVTT minus time elapsing between arrival (first-line-ashore) and start of operation, nor time elapsing between end of operations and departure from berth (last-line-in).

The distinction between gross and net time is easy to understand from a port or terminal point of view: When the first line is down and fixed, the gangway is down as well, and the vessel is fixed at the berth, it is often the case that it can take additional hours before the terminal operator can start working on the vessel. First customs go on board and check the vessel and documents (drug control, smuggling, identification papers, etc.). Also, port state control based on Paris MOU is an important topic and can take time. All this is completely out of the terminal operator's control. Ships also sometimes must wait for departure (or better, must wait to ride out on next tide). This is also out of the terminal operator's control. Therefore, NVTT is commonly used by stevedores, whereas shipping lines prefer to use GVTT.

Ship productivity from a terminal operator's perspective is commonly defined as the number of crane moves divided by the time between first and last move (total moves/hours per ship); hours per ship is here understood as NVTT:

$$\text{ship productivity} = \frac{\text{total moves}}{\text{hours per ship}}$$

The problems here are the breaks in between (the stoppages or idle times), as well as the number of operational moves (e.g., lash box operations or hatch cover movements). If it is force majeure it is commonly agreed to exclude idle times, but operational moves like change of crane driver are normally included. But here important differences occur: hot seat change or cold seat change? In the case of hot seat changes, the next driver will directly take over from the one who leaves the bridge; the operation will not stop. But in the case of a cold seat change (which is still common in many ports), the driver whose shift ended (normally after 4 hours) will put the crane on "stand by," leave the crane, and return to the terminal office. When the next shift started, the new driver will move to the gantry, climb up, and continue operation. This procedure can easily take 20 to 30 minutes; and this every 4 hours on every crane. This again shows why a clear definition of "idle times" is necessary; otherwise up to 2.5 hours or 150 minutes as calculated in Table 16.6 out of 24 hours per crane are not correctly counted. The following example shows the real case of an Asian port.

Table 16.6: Nonoperational times included in a 24-hour operation

Nonoperational Time	Time	Duration (minutes)
Morning Shift Change	0700–0720	20
Changing for Lunch	1215–1235	20
Evening Tea Break	1500–1520	20
Evening Shift Change	1800–1830	30
Changing for Dinner	0900–0910	10
Midnight Snack	2400–2420	20
Staff Change	0200–0210	10
Early Morning Snack	0400–0420	20
Total		150 minutes

When comparing ports or terminals, often the number of TEUs moved per vessel is considered a productivity indicator by shipping lines. This KPI excludes the fact that terminal operators need several moves to start or continue the loading/unloading process. The lashing boxes need to be moved onto or from the vessel, or the lashing boxes need to be replaced. Some vessels have hatch covers, and these covers need to be moved as well. But it is also often the case that vessels require a reasonable number of other operational moves as described above, and these re-stowages take time and are not included when just counting the TEUs from ship to shore or vice versa.

$$\text{Container productivity} = \frac{\text{TEU moves}}{\text{GVTT}}$$

In this sense, "container productivity" as "number of TEU moves/hours per ship or GVTT" only reflects a part of the terminal's performance and should therefore not be called "ship productivity." The units moved per hour are what count for the BCOs (containers with cargo) or the shipping lines (full container plus empty boxes), but it is not an indicator of the terminals performance alongside the ship. A bad stowage plan that required a larger number of operational moves is not a mis-performance of the terminal.

Example:
- A 10,000 TEU vessel
- At a berth with standard gantry cranes & standard 20/40 ft spreader, no twin lifts possible
- Unloads 2,000 TEU (1,000 20 ft container, 500 40 ft container)
- Loads 2,000 TEU (1,000 40 ft container)
- And requires for lash boxes, covers (20) and re-stowage (100) additional 120 moves
- Net vessel turnaround time = 22 hours

Total crane moves = 1,500 + 1,000 + 120 = 2,620
ship productivity = 1,500 + 1000 + 120 = 2.620 divided by 22 hours = 119
container productivity = 2,000 + 2,000 = 4,000 TEU divided by 22 = 182

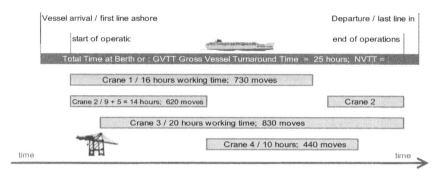

Figure 16.5: Vessel time and crane utilization

The adequate KPI calculation becomes a little more complicated when also including crane working times and a crane utilization indicator. Table 16.5 shows a situation with ineffective crane utilization during the 22 hours NVTT. Figure 16.6 indicates that the vessel can be served 7 hours faster with same number of moves; an ideal situation, but the example shows that performance increases are possible.

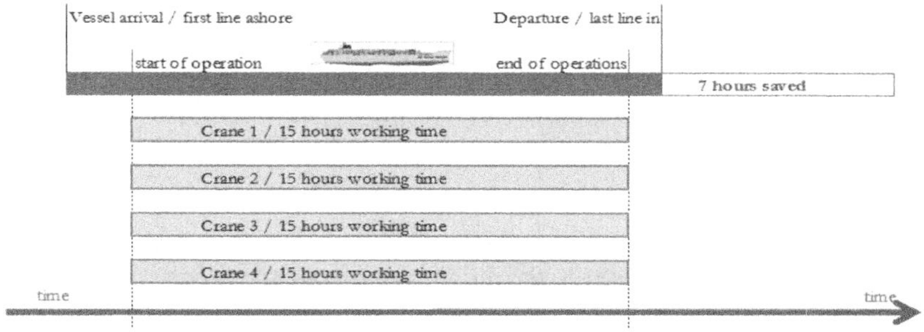

Figure 16.6: Vessel time and optimal crane utilization

It is crucial to have an exact definition for every KPI and to have this definition commonly accepted; otherwise a number of 119 moves per hour as calculated in the example above, or 182 TEU per hour is useless. The same is true for all other indicators, like berth productivity or crane density. Unfortunately, today there are many productivity indicators in the market that are used for various rankings and benchmarks, but rarely the exact base for calculation has been made transparent. Here there is much room for improvement.

16.4 Overcoming Market Imbalances

Market imbalances in shipping and port business are the results of: fluctuations in trade due to economic cycles or political disturbances, or a false estimation of shipping, port, and terminal institutions or companies. Market imbalances are temporary maladjustments of supply and demand. Normally these imbalances only last for relatively short periods, like several months or a few years. For the shipping industry, an imbalance means that either too much capacity is in the market (per type of vessel), the freight rates are low and many vessels are idle (all this can be indicators), or vice versa the market grows faster and not enough shipping capacity is available. Both situations have occurred in the past.

For ports and terminals, an imbalance means that either the capacity is under-utilized or parts (terminals resp. terminal areas) are even unemployed. Or, on the other hand, that the ports can not offer enough berth or terminal capacity to meet the requirements of the market. Extra shifts and costly measures need to be installed to overcome this situation. In fact, both situations are negative for economic efficiency and should be excluded by better forecasting and planning— as far as this is possible. In the case that this is not a temporary phenomenon, the situation is better called market disequilibrium. This may occur in parts of the global market or in contemplated regions. The situation in nearly all shipping markets in the aftermath of the 2008/2009 economic crisis has turned from a temporary imbalance to a substantial disequilibrium; with the result of several closures of shipping businesses over the last years.

Imbalances in the maritime industry, including ports, are far away from being a new phenomenon in container trade. Both the shipping and port markets experienced several ups and downs in economic activities and trade over the last decades, and as a result unexpected fluctuations in capacity utilization. Shipping, in addition, has seen a lot of cycles due to oversupply of capacity because of the long-time lags between ordering a vessel and bringing the new ships into operation. In combination with economic cycles, the shipping market has been very volatile (Stopford 2009).

Within this framework, it is necessary to bear in mind the realistic reaction speed of shipping lines compared with ports and terminals. Ports and terminals must deal with even longer time lags between planning and realization. Therefore, this market is more immune to short term seasonal and cyclical fluctuations. On the other hand, the market—at least in some parts of the world (like in Europe)—can be more inert and time consuming regarding decision making. Therefore, master planning and forecasting is so essential for ports and terminals.[9] It secures their competitive position in the market and increases economic efficiency.

16.5 Port Competition

Competition is a rivalry between two or more parties acting independently to secure the business of a third party by offering the most favorable terms. Port competition refers to competition between ports and/or terminals. The topic of port competition or port competitiveness has frequently been discussed in port literature,[10] and therefore it is not necessary to stress this topic in all its details, but instead to classify a few effects of port competition as it relates to economic efficiency.

The traditional monopolistic or oligopolistic power of (mostly public) ports has diminished since the 80s due to the need for effective cargo handling. Ports pursue efficiency through competition and privatization of terminals even within the same port or within the relevant range. Ports mainly aim to lower cost levels, raise productivity levels, and improve the quality of their services for users.

Usually two categories and in total four levels of port competition are referred to as:
– Internal port competition inside the port, that is, between terminals/terminal operators
– External competition:
    o between ports
    o between port clusters
    o between ranges
    o between countries

The distinction between levels and the main difference in competition is the geographical proximity; the competition factors differ geographically. In our understanding of ports as nodal points within a supply chain, port competition is more a competition of performance of supply chains, and these supply chains deter-

---

9 For details refer to Chapter 13: "Cargo Demand Forecasting."

10 See, for example, Huybrechts, Marc, Hilde Meersman, Eddy Van de Voorde, Eric Van Hooy donk, Alain Verbeke, Willy Winkelmans: *Port Competitiveness. An Economic and Legal Analysis of the Factors Determining the Competitiveness of Seaports*, Antwerp, Belgium 2002, as well as many additional articles published by Benelux universities.

mine the ports of call. The factors that created the competition and that lead customers to choose one port over another are the drivers of port business discussed in Chapter 2. Customers expect a professional, cost-effective, safe, and reliable service. This is only assured when the whole service is performed as offered and contracted. This is the positive prospect of port competition: keeping the whole set of variables and factors in mind that must act together to perform the supply chain service.

The negative prospect deals with the question of the single importance of each factor or driver when the performance is not secured. There is a big difference between an assured crane being unavailable due to technical problems, or if a dredging program that has been guaranteed is delayed for more than a decade or even not being realized. The sensitivity of competition factors or business drivers is diverging. Keeping an eye on this is one of port and terminal management's key tasks.

Port competition as an inherent part of supply chain competition is an important factor for economic efficiency, and therefore, port competition is often discussed and is a frequent topic in magazines and newspapers.

Chapter 17
Tendency to Oligopolize

In economic theory, a perfect market is characterized as a market that will reach an equilibrium in which the quantity supplied for every product or service, including labor, equals the quantity demanded at the current price. This equilibrium will be a Pareto optimum,[1] meaning that nobody can be made better off by exchange without making someone else worse off. For the maritime industry, this would mean that a huge number of shipping lines could choose between a huge number of ports for serving final customers. The opposite of such a market is a monopoly; a market situation where one producer (or a group of producers acting in concert) controls supply of a good or service, and where the entry of new producers is prevented or highly restricted (a supplier's monopoly).

The real world is far away from the optimum of a perfect market; this is also the case in maritime business. Fortunately, though, most markets are also not monopolies. The situation in-between these two systems is defined as an oligopoly: a market form wherein a market or industry is dominated by a small number of large sellers (a supplier's oligopoly), or—more rarely—where the market is dominated by a small number of large and influential buyers (a demand oligopoly). A typical supplier's oligopoly can be characterized as follows:

- **Few sellers:** Under the oligopoly market, the sellers are few, and the customers are many. Few firms dominating the market enjoy a considerable control over the price of the product.
- **Interdependence:** One of the most important features of an oligopoly market is that sellers must be aware of their competing firms. Since there are few sellers in the market, if any firm makes a change in their price or promotional scheme, all other firms in the industry must comply with it, to remain in the competition. Thus, every firm remains alert to the actions of others and plans their counterattack beforehand. Hence, there is a complete interdependence among the sellers with respect to their price-output policies.
- **Advertising:** Under an oligopoly market, every firm advertises their products on a frequent basis, with the intention to reach more and more customers and increase their customer base. Advertising makes the competition intense. If a firm does a lot of advertising while the others remain silent, then he will see more customers buying his product. Thus, to be in the race, each firm spends

---

1 For a definition of "Pareto optimum" as well as for further details of perfect markets please visit: http://www.businessdictionary.com/definition/Pareto-optimum.html

DOI 10.1515/9781547400874-017

a lot of money on advertising. Typical events for ports and shipping lines are conferences, workshops, and fairs.

- **Competition:** With a few players in the market, there will be an intense competition among the sellers. Any move taken by the firm will have a considerable impact on its rivals. Thus, every seller keeps an eye on its rivals and is prepared to counterattack.
- **Entry and exit barriers:** The firms can easily exit the industry whenever they want, but they face certain barriers to entering it. These barriers could be government licenses, high capital requirements, complex technology, etc. Also, sometimes the government regulations favor the existing large firms, thereby acting as a barrier for new entrants.
- **Lack of uniformity:** There is a lack of uniformity among the firms in terms of their size, some are big, and some are small. Since there is a small number of firms, any action taken by one firm has a considerable effect on the other. Thus, every firm must keep a close eye on its counterpart and plan the promotional activities accordingly.

The port and shipping industry today possesses most of these six typical oligopoly characteristics, and it seems to be true that the maritime industry shifts more and more into the direction of a market with less players and increased concentration. This tendency can be entitled best as a tendency to oligopolize. Competition tends into a more concentrated market within the so-called relevant market, and it is necessary to bear in mind how the relevant market is defined.[2] In the following, we will analyze a few trends that are obviously moving the market in a more concentrated oligopolistic direction.

17.1 "Big Is Beautiful"—Impact of Mega Vessels

One trend that already occurs in tanker business about three decades ago and that today is repeated in container shipping is the rapid increase in vessel size. Until 1956, tankers were designed to be able to navigate the Suez Canal. This size restriction became much less of a priority after the closing of the canal during the Suez Crisis of 1956. Forced to move oil around the Cape of Good Hope, ship owners realized that bigger tankers were the key to more efficient transport. While a typical T2 tanker of the World War II era was 532 ft (162 m) long and had a capacity of 16,500 dwt, the ultra-large crude oil carriers (ULCC) built in the

---

2 For details of the definition, refer to Chapter 6.2: "Port Hinterland."

1970s were over 1,300 ft (400 m) long and had a capacity of 500,000 dwt. Several factors encouraged this growth: hostilities in the Middle East, which interrupted traffic through the Suez Canal, the nationalization of Middle East oil refineries, and fierce competition among ship owners. Apart from these considerations, the realization of economies of scale and so the increased efficiency of ULCCs has been a major driver of this development.

The world's largest supertanker, Seawise Giant, was built in 1979 by a ship-yard in Kanagawa, Japan.[3] This ship was built with a capacity of 564,763 dwt, a length overall of 458.45 m (1,504.1 ft), and a draft of 24.611 m (80.74 ft). It had 46 tanks, 31,541 square meters (339,500 sq ft) of deck, and at her full load draft, could not navigate the English Channel. Seawise Giant was renamed Happy Giant in 1989, Jahre Viking in 1991, and Knock Nevis in 2004 (when she was converted into a permanently moored storage tanker). In 2009 she was sold for the last time, renamed Mont, and scrapped at an Indian shipyard in 2010. Since that time, no other tanker of that size has been built, although plans of tankers up to 750,000 dwt have been discussed. This again shows that economic drivers are of major importance. In other words: what is feasible from an engineering point of view is not automatically economically efficient. It is necessary to optimize the whole maritime supply chain—not just one link of the chain.

There are a few major reasons why the last four decades have seen tankers built in relatively small sizes: The reduced number of ports that big vessels are able to call, the problems big tankers have with draft restrictions, the need for large tankers to sometimes discharge at single buoy moorings (SBMs), the large tanker's increased risk of accidents like the Exxon Valdez oil spill in Alaska 1989, and the restrictions in navigation. For the ports serving these vessels, there is no indication that the tanker size will return to dimensions of the Seawise Giant or other mega vessels.

A similar development has been seen within the dry bulk-shipping sector, but with fewer large vessels. The big dry bulkers are employed for coal and iron ore transportation, for example, from Australia to China. The largest of them are the very large ore carriers (VLOC). The VLOC deadweight is more than 300,000 tons and they are specialized in iron ore transportation. Until 2011, the leader in this class was MS Berge Stahl, a Norwegian ore-carrier. She lost her position to vessels ordered by the Brazilian mining company Vale with the purpose of delivering iron ore from Brazil to Asia; mainly China. The first of these so-called Vale-max size vessels with a capacity ranging from 380,000 to 410,000 dwt had been ordered in 2009—three decades after the increase in tanker size. Chinese as well as Japanese

---

3 For more details of the vessel, visit: http://www.vesseltracking.net/article/seawise-giant

shipping companies followed Vale, and so it appears that this is the new standard for VLOCs.

In container shipping, a similar trend is visible, but it started one decade after the trend began in dry bulk shipping. Insurance company Allianz offered the free infographic below in Figure 17.1 that shows how big the vessels have grown in the past. And according to the order book we don't know at what point these vessels will stop growing.

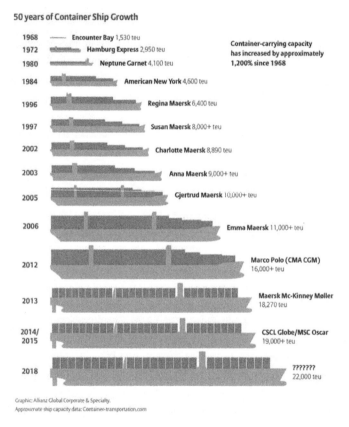

Source: Allianz Global Corporate & Specialty; inforgraphic download: http://www.agcs.allianz.com

Figure 17.1: Increase in container ship size

The largest container ship in service in early 2018 was the OOCL Hong Kong with a carrying capacity of 21,143 TEU. Constructed by the Samsung Heavy Industries (SHI) shipyard, the 197,317-DWT OOCL Hong Kong measures 58.8 m in breadth and 32.5 m in depth. According to OOCL, the OOCL Hong Kong will be serving the

Asia-Europe trade lane under the flag of Hong Kong. Vessels like Maersk Madrid, MOL Triumph or MSC Diana are all similar size with approximately 400 m in length and a maximum draught of 14.5 up to 16.0 m.

These vessels cause huge problems for many ports because they need larger berths, deeper water for the access channel, as well as higher cranes with extended outreach; all this as a reaction of increased vessel size by the ship owners. Ports and terminals can only react within this game of ever-growing vessels by ordering and installing new and bigger cranes that can serve the vessels.

Because the loading and unloading of containers out of and into a vessel is organized as top loading, upgrading (in most cases, replacing) cranes is a very cost intensive consequence of vessel size development. This has not been the case for the big dry bulker or the ultra large tanker. Unlike the pumps used for loading and unloading tankers, the gantry cranes for container vessel need to grow in parallel to the vessels they service. Table 17.1 shows how huge the cranes for the latest generation of containers vessels are. The outreach of the crane that is needed to serve all container rows within a bay has more than doubled, and serving up to twenty-five rows of container is what is required by the container shipping lines. Modern cranes are more than 80 m high, and when the cantilever beam is up, the crane is more than 100 m high. This is more than double the size of the first generation of cranes.

Table 17.1: Container gantry crane development

	Feeder	Panamax	Post-Panamax	Super Post Panamax	Malacca Max
Dimensions (m)					
Outreach	21–30	30–42	42–48	48–60	60–72
Height under spreader	15–25	20–30	30–35	35–42	42–54
Rail span	15–24	15.24–23	15.24–30.48	15.24-30.48	30.48
Speeds (m/min)					
Main hoist	60/120	60/120	75/150	90/180	90/180
Trolley travel	150	150/180	180/210	210/240	210/240
Gantry drive	45	45	45	45	45
Safe working load (t)					
Under spreader	30–40	30–45	40–60	50–70	60–70

Source: Paceco Espana web site: www.paceco.es

Ports and terminals are thus required to frequently update equipment that easily costs hundreds of millions of USD per terminal. Terminals that wish to stay in business feel that they must react and invest. This is a trend that maximizes the profit of the private shipping lines via realization of economies of scale, and that—at least via the extra costs of the authorities—needs to be financed by taxpayers' money.

17.2 Vertical Integration of Services

Vertical integration in port business is a strategy where a terminal operator or (theoretically possible, but uncommon) a port authority expands its business operations into different steps on the same production path. For example, a terminal operator might integrate hinterland operations via rail or forwarding activities, or expand into supporting shipping services like feeders. Vertical integration can help to reduce costs and improve efficiencies by optimized logistics, decreasing transportation expenses, and reducing turnaround time, among other advantages. However, sometimes it is more effective for an operator to rely on the established expertise and economies of scale of other vendors rather than trying to become vertically integrated.

In general, the motive to vertically integrate is expressed as follows:
- The market is too risky and unreliable—it "fails."
- Companies in adjacent stages of the industry chain have more market power than ports and terminals.
- Integration would create or exploit market power by raising barriers to entry or allowing price discrimination across customer segments.
- The relevant market is young (e.g., cruise) and the company must forward integrate to develop a market, or the market is declining and independents are pulling out of adjacent stages.

Some of these are better reasons than others. The first reason—vertical market failure—is the most important one. A vertical market "fails" when transactions within it are too risky and the contracts designed to overcome these risks are too costly (or not feasible). The typical features of a failed vertical market are (1) a small number of buyers and sellers, that is, an oligopolistic situation that exists in several of the relevant maritime markets; (2) high asset specificity, durability, and intensity; a situation that occurs in the shipping, port, and railway industry; and (3) frequent transactions, that is, alliances and mergers and acquisitions (M&As) that frequently happen in maritime business. Vertical market failure is a key driver for vertical integration within the maritime industry.

Overcoming the vertical market failure is supported by:
– Strengthening the company's competitive position via integration
– Achieving operational efficiencies
– Building barriers to entry
– Boosting profitability
– Commoditization and a unique selling proposition (USP)

Especially in container business, it is necessary to "create commoditization": a competitive environment in which differentiation of the product is difficult, customer loyalty is low, and competing offerings are virtually indistinguishable from customer perspective. This is combined with the intention to convert the market of such interchangeable commodities into an unrivaled commodity market/create a "brand." Containerization has gradually led to the commoditization of the container shipping service: all carriers have the same ships, sail at the same speeds, call at the same ports with the same frequency, carry the same type of container and charge similar tariffs. Creating a USP and—in an ideal situation—creating an inimitable product is a great windfall gain.

But there are also good arguments from ports and terminals against vertical integration that need to be analyzed:
– Cost disadvantages
– Demand unpredictability
– Loss of corporate identity
– Administrative burden
– Rapid technological change

In Chapter 6.1 we analyzed the position of ports in maritime supply chains, and Figure 6.1 showed where ports are allocated within this chain. Bearing this in mind, there are two key markets that are of interest for vertical integration:
– Inland transport
– Oceanic transportation

A very special kind of vertical integration that without considering the key supply chains can also be classified as horizontal integration is a strategy that port practitioners describe as "meet your customer twice." An example of this: A terminal in Europe invests in shares in a terminal in South America to serve a liner shipping company at both ends: when loading in Europe as well as for discharging in South America, or vice versa. It is a vertical integration when considering the flow of cargoes, but regarding the business itself, it is a terminal that invests in another terminal, that is, a classical horizontal integration. This happens, for example, with at that time independent company Hamburg Süd and terminals in Hamburg as well as in Brazil and Argentina. This strategy only works in niche markets, not in mass markets serving various countries.

Example: Terminal & Rail Integration
Dry bulk commodities like iron ore and coal are often transported by rail from the mines to the port, for example, in Brazil or Australia. But these railways only exist because of the mines, and so this is not a real vertical integration. It is a necessary cooperation, without which the business would not exist or would have higher production costs. Although sometimes cited as multimodal integration, this is not vertical integration. The pure existence of a rail is a necessary, but insufficient argument for vertical integration.

In the container business, there are several examples of terminal-rail integration concepts. Rail links between the terminal and a country in the hinterland exist before the business cooperation started. The port of Hamburg in Germany, for example, has been active in hinterland rail business for nearly thirty years. It was the terminal operator pushing this business. The first two rail companies that were integrated into the terminal operator HHLA[4] are services that link Poland[5] and the Czech Republic[6] to the port of Hamburg. With this, the terminal operator intended to secure a relevant market share of container business in the respective countries. And for the Czech Republic, the rail link Hamburg-Prague in some years carried more than 50% of total Czech maritime containers.

Example: Liner Service & Terminal Integration
Ports do not always have the sufficient terminal capacity needed for accessing interesting markets. Especially during the boom phase of container trade between 2002 and 2008, when terminals experienced double-digit growth rates for years, liner shipping companies realized that terminal capacity might be a limiting growth factor soon. This was a key argument for the company Hapag Lloyd becoming a shareholder of a container terminal in 2001. Their main intention was to secure priority at selected terminals, and so to secure sufficient capacity along the whole supply chain. In this type of integration, the liner service

---

4 For details of the intermodal network of HHLA, visit Annual Report 2016, pages 15 and 16: http://bericht.hhla.de/geschaeftsbericht-2016/serviceseiten/downloads/files/HHLA_ Geschäfts-bericht_2016.pdf
5 For more details, refer to: www.polzug.de. Web site will be integrated into HHLA
6 For more details, refer to: www.metrans.eu

company was the driver for vertical business enlargement. Many followed Hapag Lloyd's example: Maersk Line as part of the AP Moller Group cooperates with APM Terminals, the container terminal group of AP Moller. Others like CMA CGM, MSC, or the China COSCO Group found set ups for their own container terminals. Some of these terminals were integrated so closely to one liner service, that they were called "dedicated terminals"; although some of them offered services to others as well; mainly to partners within the same alliance. In the aftermath of the financial crisis and the years of overcapacity in container shipping, this strategy became less relevant.

Example: Terminal & Liner Service Integration

This third example may sound exactly like the one before—a terminal integrates liner services. But in this example the terminal is the driver behind the integration. This is rather uncommon, but does happen from time to time. In December 2017, the Chinese dry bulk port of Zhuhai, a major seaport in the Pearl River Delta that handled 80 mill tons of volume, announced their plans to invest in a fleet. This would include more than forty river multipurpose vessels plus four bulkers of 22,500 dwt, and 44,500 dwt, respectively. Zhuhai port believes that the fleet integration fits its strategy to transform into an integrated logistics solution provider and will meet the growing demand for coal, grain, and steel shipping. With this strategy, Zhuhai follows the port of Shanghai, which also invests in inland navigation vessels.

Example: Terminal & Forwarder Integration

The trucking business is normally not an oligopolistic or monopolistic business; this means that within the terminal hinterland there are various companies that offer general or specialized trucking services. And within such a market situation of well-functioning competition, it does not make much sense to invest in vertical integration. But for some specialized trucking, like container services between terminals, it occurs quite often that the terminals invest in such companies and integrate them. Later on it often happens that the trucking services are enlarged to the adjacent hinterland to widen the scope of the forwarder.

17.3 Horizontal Integration of Services

Horizontal integration is the acquisition of additional business activities that are at the same level on the value chain in similar or different industries, that is, a container terminal operator in port "A" expanded to another port "B" for similar terminal operations. It is an integration strategy pursued by a company to strengthen its position in the industry. This can be achieved by internal expansion through reinvestment of operating profits or by external expansion through a M&A. Since the different firms integrating are involved at the same stage of production, horizontal integration allows them to share resources at that level.

The purpose of horizontal integration is to grow the company in size, increase product differentiation/commoditization, achieve economies of scale, reduce competition, or access new markets. When many firms pursue this strategy in the same industry, it leads to industry consolidation (oligopoly or even monopoly within the relevant market). The intention of horizontal integration is to create port networks as described in Chapter 6.3/Port Networks. In the following, two examples shall demonstrate today's market.

In the container business there have been frequent changes in the list of the top global terminal operators as Tables 11.4–11.8 have shown. For APM Terminals/ Maersk Group, we will illustrate in Figure 17.2 the global network of terminals as it was in 2016 after years of successful horizontal expansion. Every dot is an engagement of APMT; in total seventy-seven port and terminal engagements.

Source: www.apmterinals.com; see also Figure 11.11 and explanations in Chapter 11.5: "Global Container Terminal Operator"

Figure 17.2: APM terminals global network 2016

The networks of other global container terminal operators look similar, but HPH clearly has a focus on Asia, while DP World is already strong in South Asia and concentrates more and more on Africa. However, all these horizontal engagements grew within the last few decades.

Horizontal cooperation can also be found in the bulk business, but the scope of engagement is less broad and often focused on one region. In Australia/ Queensland, for example, the mining and agriculture export ports of Hay Point, Abbot Point, Weipa and Maryborough merged in 2009 with Mackay to become part of the new port authority of North Queensland Bulk Ports (NQBP). In the financial year 2016/2017,[7] more than 50% of Queensland's trade by tonnage passed through NQBPs ports. NQBP clearly has strong market power and already achieved or intends to achieve the remaining targets of horizontal integration.

A similar situation happened in Western Australia when Port Hedland Port Authority and Dampier Port Authority merged to create the new Pilbara Port Authority. They are now stronger, with a bigger market share in their relevant markets, and they are more efficient due to concentrated overheads.

This finally leads to the question whether all types of regional or national port authorities should consider horizontal integration to gain market power? The answer is no. In most national port authorities, there is still a strong decision-making power at the single port level. National port authorities are government agencies that are normally not engaged in business operations.[8]

All the strategies discussed in this chapter are used to reduce competition and to gain market share for the big players, that is, to oligopolize markets. This trend needs to be observed carefully in order not to destroy the markets.

---

7 For details, refer to: www.nqbp.com.au/trade
8 For a detailed definition of what a national port authority should perform, see. for example, South Africa's National Port Act: www.portsregulator.org/images/documents/ national_ports_ act.pdf

Chapter 18
Affairs of Geostrategic Concern

Ports are immobile nodal points within highly flexible networks of other modes of transportation. For a shipping line, it is easy to switch from one port to another, and trucks, inland barges, or trains are free to call other ports—contingent on infrastructure. Therefore, new trends in the geospatial positioning of transport and logistics companies have an influence on ports, too; although ports themselves are immobile by nature. In the following, the key implications of major affairs of geostrategic concern like the Chinese "One Belt, One Road"—initiative or the possibility of Arctic Shipping on ports will be discussed.

18.1 Port Positioning in Global Container Trade

There are two major routes in global container trade: the Europe-East Asia route with a trade volume of 23.1 mill TEU in 2017, and the Transpacific route from Asia to North America (west coast mainly) with a trade volume of 26.1 mill TEU in 2017. These two routes dominate the global container trade since years. Beginning of the 2000s Transpacific has been the trade route with highest volume, and between 2008 and 2013 both trade routes have been on nearly similar volume, and since 2014 Transpacific again shows higher volumes. A third important global container trade lane connecting continents is the east-west-route: The Transatlantic trade connection between Europe and North America (east coast mainly). In 2017, the volume on this route amounted to 7.4 mill TEU; that is approximately one-third of the volume of the other routes. Figure 18.1 displays the three intercontinental routes.

With respect to trade volumes the most important area on the globe is the Intra-Asian trade, accounting for approximately 35.1 mill TEU in 2017 (substantially more than the Transpacific and Far East-Europe routes). Because huge parts of the Intra-Asian volumes are short sea trade and not long-haul intercontinental volumes, this trade is of a different nature than the three global routes mentioned above.

Figure 5.3 in Chapter 5.1 shows that global container trade in 2015 equaled 129.2 mill TEU. Only the three a.m. major routes generate a volume of 40% of global container trade. When including the Intra-Asian volumes, these four trade routes equal approximately 62% of global trade. Because they are so voluminous, they are so dominant in trade discussions.

DOI 10.1515/9781547400874-018

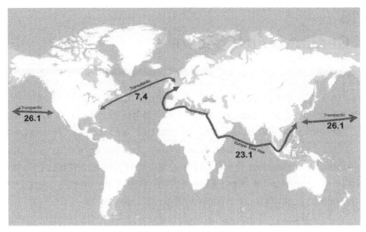

Figure 18.1: Major container trade routes; in TEU 2017

Table 18.1 shows that there is an unhealthy imbalance of trade amongst global trade routes. The so-called headhaul trades out of Asia to Europe and the United States account for approximately double the volume of the backhaul trade. The transatlantic route has similar problem, but it is less dramatic.

Table 18.1: Estimated containerized cargo flows on major trade routes, 1995–2017

year	Transpacific		Europe Asia		Transatlantic	
	Asia - NA	NA - Asia	Asia - Europe	Europe Asia	Europe - NA	NA - Europe
1995	4.0	3.5	2.4	2.0	1.7	1.7
2000	7.3	3.5	4.7	2.5	2.7	1.7
2005	11.9	4.5	9.3	4.4	3.7	2.0
2010	12.3	6.5	13.3	5.7	3.2	2.7
2011	12.4	6.6	14.1	6.2	3.4	2.8
2012	13.1	6.9	13.7	6.2	3.6	2.7
2013	13.9	7.4	14.1	6.4	3.8	2.8
2014	15.8	7.4	15.2	6.8	3.9	2.8
2015	16.8	7.2	14.9	6.8	4.1	2.7
2016	17.7	7.7	15.3	7.1	4.3	2.7
2017	17.9	8.2	15.5	7.6	4.5	2.9
	26.1		23.1		7.4	
2017 mbalance	68.6%	31.4%	67.1%	32.9%	60.8%	39.2%

Source: UNCTAD Review of Maritime Transport, multiple years + own calc.. NA = North America

Millions of containers transported laden out of East Asia (mainly China) generate a huge volume of empty boxes that needs be redispositioned, that is, carried back empty. This cost a lot of money for the ship owner, and it is a huge burden that needs to be debited to others, and that raises the price for the full container. This in turn makes shipping a less competitive mode of transportation due to increased prices, which again limits trade.

To increase trade volumes and to stay competitive, it is a permanent task of shipping lines to rethink the way they structure global routings. In the past there were round-the-world (rtw) services through the Suez and Panama Canal. These services were based on the idea that a combination of pendulum and rtw-services may reduce empty container positioning. But with increased vessel size and the limitation of the Panama Canal, these services stopped.

Economic efficiency leads to new network concepts from time to time. And these changes in shipping networks have a direct influence on ports. If an optimized network structure bypassed a port that previously had handled relevant transhipment volumes, then this port will lose substantial throughput and trade. And it is not only the all-water transhipment cargo that gets lost, but also relevant parts of the hinterland cargo volumes due to optimized rail, road, or inland navigation links. As a result, the simple effect of redesigned global routings has the potential to jeopardize the economic situation of a port; investments in infra- and superstructure may become underutilized, jobs may get loss, and revenues may drop.

This brings us to the old chicken-or-the-egg question: what was first, or what must be first? It is often the case that ports build infra- and superstructure without having signed contracts with a shipping line. Local politicians combine the wish to create local work places with the intention to stimulate port business. The problems in this scenario are the long-time frames between planning and the start of operations: several legislative periods may lie in between, and the—existing or potential—port calls in the home country are dependent on liner decisions in other parts of the world. Many inefficient and underutilized port projects around the world testify to this.

In this context, we must distinguish between strategic (re-)routing and adaptive (re-)routing, as well as between permanent and temporary (re-)routing. In an ideal world, decisions of network design and global routings would be based on the economic potential of countries and the best ports of call to install competitive supply chains. These networks are then based on strategic decisions that are permanent, because the economic potentials of countries do not change quickly. But the reality is different, and so we often see routings of shipping lines that are based on other factors—therefore, this should be called adaptive routing. And due to the underlying short-term factors, these routings are often temporary. An example will make this clearer.

But first it should be pointed out that shipping companies are often subject to fierce competition. Many of them are private entities without public subsidies, that is, they must be competitive and they must earn money. One tool that helps to operate efficiently and increase productivity is the purchase policy, that is, the adequate ordering of vessel; another one the vessel employment policy we are discussing here.

Adaptive routing: In shipping cycles there are periods when demand is low and there is enough shipping capacity in the market. In response to these periods, the shipping lines can take the vessels out of the market—but this is a very expensive alternative, because costs still occur. Adaptive routing is the alternative: shipping lines extend their networks and call additional ports. After the financial crisis in 2008, adaptive routing could be seen in the Baltic Sea. Liner vessels started calling smaller ports to stay in business. Volume and rates were lowered as needed, but at least part of the shipping line's fixed costs were covered. Often low demand is in parallel with very low order activities of new build vessel. After a period, the demand-supply situation hopefully balances, and vessels are employed on more economic routes. This redirection led to the temporary effect of these routings.

When bigger vessels call more ports during bad economic times, they edge out the smaller vessels that had called these ports before. The small and inefficient vessels are the final losers in this game. But how does this look from a port perspective? Even in bad times (e.g., after the financial crisis) the ports are being called—from even bigger vessels! This seems to be positive, and therefore, several port managers—now very proud of having more and larger vessels calling—are initiating port expansion projects.

When the market improves, shipping lines stop calling these secondary ports; big vessel calls get lost, sometimes cargo gets lost (transhipment volumes), and the big terminals with huge capacities are no longer efficient; all this is the consequence of a global market situation that is not judged comprehensively.

The situation gets more complex when including the order policy of the shipping lines and their finance policy. The prices for new build vessel are lowest in bad economic times. After a "waiting period" with less order activities, shipyards look for new jobs. Because shipyards are often public bodies or receive public subsidies, they offer attractive conditions. The question then is: what is the right time for placing new orders? And under what financial market conditions? We will not discuss this, but regularly repeating shipping crises taught us that the adaptive policies need to be judged in a holistic picture, and that not all positive signs due to a temporary imbalanced situation have a lasting effect. Serious forecasts can help to judge the global situation. Routing changes based on geostrategic repositioning's have implications for ports, and in some cases these implications cause essential effects—positive and negative.

18.2 Offshore Resourcing

The offshore industry is primarily comprised of two industries—the older and established offshore oil and gas industry and the relatively young offshore wind energy industry. The first oil and gas offshore platform was erected in 1947 in the Gulf of Mexico, and still today oil and gas production have a significant effect on the associated local onshore economies as well as the corresponding national economies. There are broadly three "phases" of development that contribute to state economic growth:

1. The initial exploration and development of offshore facilities
2. The extraction of oil and gas resources
3. Refining crude oil into finished petroleum products

Industries supporting those phases are most evident in ports that are currently open to offshore drilling. For example, the U.S. shipbuilding industry—based largely in the Gulf region—benefits significantly from initial offshore oil exploration efforts. Exploration and development also require specialized exploration and drilling vessels, floating drilling rigs, and miles and miles of steel pipe, as well as highly educated and specialized labor. The onshore support does not end with production; a wide variety of industries depend on offshore oil and gas production and the production supports onshore production with chemicals, platform fabrication, drilling services, transportation, and gas processing. Fleets of helicopters and specialized vessels also supply offshore facilities with a wide range of industrial and consumer goods, from industrial spare parts to groceries.

The economic effects in the refining phase (phase 3) are even more diffuse for ports than the effects for the two preceding phases. However, it is certain that several ports around the world positioned themselves as offshore hubs including the provision of dedicated areas for refineries. In addition, these specialized ports offer sufficient space for offshore development projects, both on land and out on the water, offering a wide range of repair and servicing facilities, sheltered inland berths with sufficient water depths, and a huge range of complementary maritime services.

Although often criticized, it is obvious that due to missing environmental friendly alternatives for the next decades, the oil and gas industry will remain a major energy supplier. Therefore, the situation for the ports supporting the traditional industry seems to be quite stable. New options may occur when it will be economically feasible to support the development of deep-water methane hydrate production, but this is a very young business that is still in testing phase; but worse to bear in mind.

The second large industry, offshore wind energy production, is already in the stage of an established industry in some parts of the world. Since the construction of the first offshore wind farm (i.e., a wind farm in the sea at some distance from the coast) off the coast of Denmark in 1991, the offshore wind energy sector has grown enormously—driven mainly by northern European countries, and particularly the UK, Germany, and Denmark. Wind is an important source of energy in today's world, with undeniable potential for the future. It is expected, for example, that in the European Union by 2030, 253 GW onshore and 70 GW offshore power supply capacity will be produced; a substantial part for the offshore industry. With this capacity, wind energy would produce 888 TWH of electricity, equivalent to 30% of the EU's power demand. The wind energy industry would invest €239 bn by 2030 and provide employment to 569,000 people, and offshore plays an increasingly important role.

Bearing in mind that offshore wind energy production is a fast-growing industry, several ports specialized themselves as supporting partners for the industrial supply chain or as production hubs for the energy industry.[1] To achieve the targets set by the industry, ports had a critical role to play within the supply chain. Depending on the installation strategy adopted, a port can be used as a base for assembly, a handling provider, or a manufacturer. In all cases it acts as the supply chain hub, through which all components, structures and turbines making up the wind farm must pass. This means that the first step in the construction of a wind farm must be the selection of one or more base ports.

Over the life cycle of a wind farm project, the manufacturing, preinstallation, installation, commissioning, operation and maintenance, and eventually decommissioning phases will require one or several terminals with specific facilities. The main companies in the supply chain will set up an operating base in the port, and the terminal will thus become a hub for first tier logistics, and as such, a key factor in the smooth running of the project. The port is therefore of critical strategic value for all stakeholders.

The installation strategy used by the project developer will have a direct impact on the properties and facilities that manufacture and assembly terminals must have, as well as on the type of port to be used. There are currently two dif

---

1 See, for example, the offshore promotion web site: www.4coffshore.com, that included a long list of ports supporting the wind energy industry.

ferent approaches based on the number and types of installation and transport vessels, and the level of assembly to be carried out in the port.

– Transiting strategy: Transport of components to the wind farm in installation vessels. Depending on the operations carried out in the port terminal, two methods of construction can be further differentiated: if manufacture and assembly of components is carried out in the port or only if they are preassembled.

– Feeding approach: Components are transported to the wind farm in transport or feeder vessels.

The most widely used strategy in the past was transporting components, which were preassembled at the terminals. Ports used during preinstallation and installation of a wind farm must have major components and facilities, and depending on the installation strategy to be used, can be of the following types; it is also possible in some ports to jack up installation ships alongside selected berths:

– Import/export ports: Ports receiving components from onshore manufacturers. Components are handled and stored for subsequent loading onto vessels which will transport them to manufacturing and assembly ports.

– Manufacturing ports: Due to the ever-larger size and weight of wind turbine components, road transportation is becoming less viable, and turbine and foundation manufacturers are increasingly establishing manufacturing facilities in suitable ports. This follows the example of cable manufacturers, where production at ports has been well established since the beginning of the offshore cable industry.

– Assembly ports: Preassembly of components received from manufacturing plants takes place here. Components are received either by road transport or, increasingly, by sea.

Using the same terminal for manufacturing and assembling wind turbines and nacelles will depend on the savings offered through optimization of the supply chain. The type of port used will depend on the installation strategy adopted, a cost analysis, the distance from the manufacturing centers to the wind farm, the distance from the coast to the wind farm, and future developments in the area. After the commissioning of the wind farm, an operating base within a port is also required, but with different and less exacting requirements. These ports provide the wind farm with support services for operation and maintenance. They must support a rapid response for contingencies in operation, and so must be located at a relatively short distance from the farm to reduce travel times for staff and parts, and optimize offshore on-site working times. These ports require no large-scale installations or specific properties; the short distance and fast accessibility is what counts.

All services together offered by terminal operators can be summarized as follows:
- Import and export hub for onshore wind turbines
- Base port for the installation of offshore wind farms
- Service port for large components
- Consulting, preparing and implementing customized transport, transhipment and storage solutions
- Extensive value-added services, such as equipping or preassembling components

The ports and terminals for wind energy construction and operation are of critical strategic value for all stakeholders, and thus selection of the most appropriate port and/or terminal is a critical and decisive investment decision for the smooth running of the wind energy project. Because an alternative energy supply is an important factor for future economic growth and the welfare of a country, it can be expected that the wind energy sector will remain an important industry for future port business.

18.3 OBOR/BRI/New Maritime Silk Road

China's Belt and Road Initiative (BRI) is an economic framework developed to increase connectivity between China and over 100 countries and international organizations, based on the ancient Silk Road land and maritime routes. The BRI aims to link different regions through infrastructure construction, transport and economic corridors, and by bridging China with the rest of the world both physically, financially, digitally, and socially. BRI is an ambitious program, with investments of as much as $1 trillion in new transport and trade infrastructure between China and the rest of the world. When initiated, the program was called "One Belt, One Road" or in short, OBOR, and in search machines OBOR is still a more popular search term than BRI, but the interpretation of OBOR has brought numerous misinterpretations, as the partners tend to focus too much on the word "one." OBOR might make one assume that there is to be only one maritime route and one single land belt. The BRI aims to connect Asia, Europe, and Africa along five routes with several supporting access routes ("antennas").

The BRI was labeled an "initiative" as it has few concrete goals or strategies and lacks institutional structure; it is not a treaty, but rather a road map for Chinese political vision. Chinese ministries, state-owned enterprises, and regional and ɔcal authorities seemingly develop their own linked proposals in response to road, overarching concepts. As a result, the BRI serves as an umbrella for sepaate, existing projects and investments as well as new initiatives.

In economic terms, the BRI aims to boost China's slowing economy by developing new markets and generating demand for the country's overcapacity in aluɪinum, steel, construction and other industries; the initiative thus has a major ɔcus on dry bulk and container trade. China wants to be the key trading and ɪvestment partner for states in Eurasia, Central and Western Europe, Middle East s well as Africa.

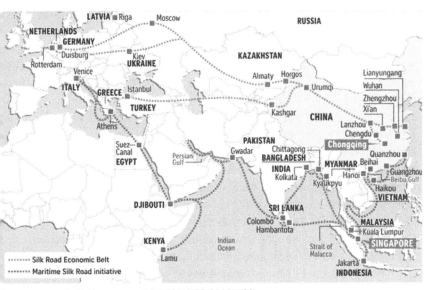

ʻource: www.straitstimes.com: STRAITS TIMES GRAPHICS

ɪgure 18.2: Corridors of China's Belt and Road Initiative

'here are two major strategic goals for BRI. First, to provide China with alternaɪve import/export and energy supply routes and lessen its dependence on straɪegic shipping lanes in South East Asia. Second, to produce a zone of stability on ɪoth sides of China's western border.

Geographically, the BRI includes two main routes as Figure 18.2 shows: the Silk Road Economic Belt" and the "21st-Century Maritime Silk Road." The ecoɪomic belt focuses on bringing together China, Central Asia, Russia, and Europe ɪhe Baltic), thereby linking China with the Persian Gulf and the Mediterranean ʻea through Central Asia and West Asia, and connecting China with Southeast ɪsia, South Asia and the Indian Ocean. It aims at building an international network for developing six main economic corridors (New Eurasian Land Bridge, China-Mongolia-Russia, China-Central Asia-West Asia, China-Pakistan, Bangladesh-China-India-Myanmar, and China-Indochina Peninsula), which rely on international transport routes, core cities, and key economic industrial parks as cooperation platforms.

The Maritime Road focuses on building efficient transport routes that connect major sea ports, and runs from China's coast to Europe, through the South China Sea and the Indian Ocean in one route, and to the South Pacific through the South China Sea in the other. The main objective is to realize closer cooperation and connection between the land and maritime routes.

The two main routes reflect China's global intention to act as a bridge builder. Expectations are high that the BRI will address cross-cutting international development cooperation issues. The BRI can contribute to global governance by placing inclusiveness at its core and by offering an effective implementation mechanism towards a more balanced, multi-polar and multilateral international architecture.

For ports like Gwadar in Pakistan, Lamu and Mombasa in Kenya, or Athens and Venice in Europe, the BRI maritime Silk Road projects have the potential to revitalize port business and act as a facilitator for trade. For the CPEC, China Pakistan Economic Corridor, this has already turned into reality. The multimodal corridor spans from western China's Xinjiang region (city of Kashgar) via Pakistan and the port of Gwadar via the short distance over the Arabian Sea to Saudi Arabia, or other GCC states. For supplying western China with oil, this corridor is a substantial shortcut compared with routings via an East China port and transportation via the Strait of Malacca. According to various sources, more than 1 bn USD have been spent by Chinese companies to develop the port of Gwadar.

Also impressive are the strategic investments of China in East Africa. Here China secures access to a variety of natural resources. Under critique is the way China pushes the projects; many journalists mark this as a new kind of colonization, but many details of China's engagements in Africa are not transparent. Therefore, it should just be mentioned, but can not be judged.

In Europe, China is already engaged in the port of Piraeus/Athens via the state-owned shipping line and their terminal branch. More critical are BRI's plans to invest in Venice. Although Venice is a very old port and was already part of the ancient Silk Road, it seems to be unrealistic to invest for larger amounts of cargoes in Venice Port. The port is not able to function as a hub port for a maritime trade link. Therefore "Venice" should better be read as, for example, "North Adriatic Port." However, by mentioning this link, it is obvious that BRI will extend China's connection to Central Europe.

Bearing all this in mind, the BRI has the potential to effectively stimulate economic growth and promote sustainable development. While trade and investment can create employment, raise incomes, and spread knowledge and technology throughout the regions of the BRI, it must be ensured that there is equal access to the BRI's projected benefits in economic growth and that barriers to inclusion are removed. While the enhancement of quality infrastructure investment implies considering all aspects of economic, social and environmental sustainability, such an approach is not only a technical matter, but is intrinsically linked to institutional set-ups and policy domains. The key challenge is to bring into alignment the goals of the BRI's projects and those of sustainable and inclusive development. The maritime silk roads ports will play major roles within this initiative.

18.4 Arctic Shipping

Due to global warming, the world is edging closer to an ice-free Arctic summer with conditions allowing a major increase in commercial shipping movements in the regions. Trans-Arctic shipping is most viable where it offers a significant shortcut in comparison to traditional trade routes. In the case of China, this applies only to its trade with Europe, especially Central and Northern Europe. Trade with all other regions, including Africa, the Americas, and the Middle East, will not be routed though the Arctic even if ice-free periods were to increase dramatically. For nearly all Far East-Europe trade of China, Japan, or South Korea, the Arctic Shipping routes are of interest.

As Figure 18.3 shows, there are four potential routes for commercial shipping crossing the Arctic. The first one that already today reports considerable increases year-to-year is the Northern Sea Routes (NSR); in Figure 18.3 displayed on the right side. This route passes the pole region close to the Russian coastline in mainly Russian waters. Therefore, it is no surprise that most of the vessels in recent years sported the Russian flag.[2]

---

[2] For statistics and further details, visit: www.arctic-lio.com, the web page of the Centre for High North Logistics (CHNL).

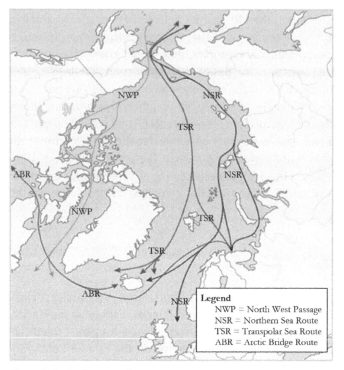

Figure 18.3: Arctic sea routes

The Transpolar Sea Route (TSR) won't be a real option in the coming years as it passes the center of the Arctic that is still covered with ice at this time. However, it may become an interesting connection in the future, especially for connecting North America's East Coast with North Asian countries. The same is true for the much more difficult North West Passage (NWP) that crosses the region in mainly Canadian waters. This route requires formidable navigation.

Recent studies calculated various routes for the NSR,[3] such as Yokohama-Rotterdam or Shanghai-Hamburg, and concluded that the distance for the trunk routes is on average 35% to 40% shorter via Arctic waters. This can result in sub-

---

3 See, for example: Bekkers, Eddy, Joseph F. Francois, Hugo Rojas-Romagosa: Melting Ice Caps and the Economic Impact of Opening the Northern Sea Route, CPB Netherlands Bureau for Economic Policy Analysis, Discussion Paper 307, The Hague, Netherlands 2015. Or: Smith, Laurence C., Scott R. Stephenson: New Trans-Arctic Shipping Routes Navigable by Midcentury, Proceedings of the National Academy of Sciences of the United States of America, published on pnas web page: www.pnas.org/cgi/doi/10.1073/pnas.1214212110, Columbus, OH, 2013.

stantial savings for the shipping line, but there are a few downsides to using the arctic route. Major argument against the obvious savings due to reduced sailing times is the topic that the NSR is open and navigable for only three to four months during summer time; this means that no all-year services via NSR are possible.

A second issue with the route is that only a few vessels can navigate in arctic waters, because they need to have ice-class and must be constructed to resist the ice. As a rule of thumb, such vessels are 30% more expensive. Out of the world container fleet of 5,502 vessels in 2013, only 765 were classified as ice capable to any extent, totaling around 1.2 m TEU, while the rest of the fleet of 4,258 vessels account for some 15.9 m TEU. Operators have not been in any hurry to improve their numbers of ice capable ships either, with only seven out of 479 ice capable container vessels on order at that time. These seven ships were mostly small classes with none possessing over 1,000 TEU capacity. In total they added 5,370 TEU to the fleet while the other 472 vessels were set to add around 3.6 m TEU. For the container vessels, these number indicate that at least for the near future the Artic route is not of relevance. But this may change in a few decades.

For Russian energy exports as well as for bulk transits, the picture looks slightly different. The a.m. statistics of the Centre for High North Logistics shows that the three to four-month period of Arctic navigation is of increasing interest. With Russian energy exploration in Yamal territory, it is very likely that also for equipment (conventional carrier) as well as for small tankers, the route appears more and more attractive. Due to the sensitive environment in the Arctic region, environmentalists around the globe are keeping an eye on these developments.

One of the several initiatives to protect the Arctic waters is the so-called Arctic Commitment, an ambitious campaign of more than eighty companies, organizations, politicians, NGOs and explorers that seek to ban heavy fuel oil in Artic waters. The Arctic Commitment aims to protect Arctic communities and eco-systems from the risks posed using heavy fuel oil, and calls on the International Maritime Organization (IMO) to ban its use and carriage as marine fuel by Arctic shipping. An HFO ban has already been in place in Antarctic waters since 2011. In July 2017, the Clean Arctic Alliance welcomed action being taken by IMO member states to start work to identify measures to mitigate the risks of HFO spills. This as campaign goes far beyond tanker business and shows how far-ranging initiatives can be.

Ports in Northern Europe such as Hamburg in Germany, Rotterdam in the Netherlands or Gothenburg in Sweden, as well as in the northern Pacific Rim, such as Busan in South Korea or Yokohama in Japan, are expressing great interest in the potential of the new Arctic routes; they consider themselves as winners of potential route changes. Also, the port of Churchill, Canada's main Arctic seaport s positioning itself as an access point for European mineral markets. The distance between Churchill and Rotterdam is just under fourteen sailing days, whereas rival Canadian port Thunder Bay is a further four days away from Rotterdam. In the long run, the Artic routes may become of increased importance and have the potential to reroute shipping with the consequence of substantial impact on ports engaged in Far East-Europe trade. Typical trans-shipment hubs further south like Singapore, Hong Kong or Malaysian ports may lose substantial amounts of cargo when the Artic Shipping route evolves into a reliable alternative. Ports should consider how these routes might mature.

Chapter 19
Global Maritime Bottlenecks

19.1 Major Oil Chokepoints

The free flow of oil is critical to world commerce and global economic prosperity. Oil trade requires the use of maritime trade routes, which can span from hundreds to thousands of miles, as well as unhindered access to jetties and other port facilities. Hence, oil tankers often travel through straits and canals to reduce transport costs. These passageways—referred to as chokepoints—are narrow channels along the most widely used global sea routes, some so narrow that restrictions are placed on the size of the vessel that can navigate through them.[1]

Chokepoints are a critical part of global energy security because of the high volume of petroleum and other liquids transported through their narrow straits. In 2015, total world petroleum and other liquid production summed up to 96.7 mill barrels per day (bbl/d). The U.S. Energy Information Agency (EIA) estimates that about 61% of this amount (58.9 mill bbl/d) traveled via seaborne trade. In 2016, oil tankers accounted for 28% of the world's shipping by deadweight tonnage, according to data from the United Nations Conference on Trade and Development (UNCTAD), having fallen steadily from 50% in 1980.

International energy markets depend on reliable transport routes. The inability of oil tankers to transit a major chokepoint, even temporarily, can lead to substantial supply delays and higher shipping costs, resulting in higher world energy prices. As maritime choke points are located at indispensable marine trade routes, in case of global security problems, avoiding these choke points has often been suggested as a workable solution. While most chokepoints can be circumvented by using other routes that add significant transit time, no practical alternatives are available in some cases. Chokepoints also leave oil tankers vulnerable to theft from pirates, terrorist attacks, shipping accidents that can result in disastrous oil spills, and political unrest in the form of wars or hostilities.

However, since avoiding these maritime chokepoints would drastically increase energy transportation costs, most of oil shipping operations are still carried out by navigating through these chokepoints.

---

1 Refer to: World Oil Transit Chokepoints, U.S. Energy Information Administration (EIA), last Updated: July 25, 2017, published on EIA BETA website: https://www.eia.gov/beta/ international/ regions-topics.cfm?RegionTopicID=WOTC, Washington, 2017.

DOI 10.1515/9781547400874-019

The famous maritime chokepoints around the world are (see Figure 19.1):
-   The Strait of Malacca linking the Indian Ocean with the Pacific
-   The Gulf of Hormuz in the Middle East linking the Arabian Gulf with the Indian Ocean
-   The Suez Canal linking the Mediterranean and the Red Sea
-   The Panama Canal linking the Atlantic with the Pacific Ocean
-   The Strait of Bosporus (Turkish Strait) linking the Mediterranean Sea to the Black Sea
-   The three Danish Straits linking the Baltic Sea with the North Sea
-   The Strait of Bab el-Mandeb forming a gateway for vessels to pass through the Suez Canal, through the east coast of Africa

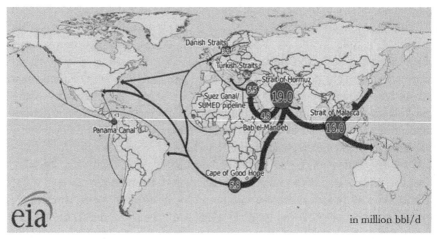

Source: World Oil Transit Chokepoints eia U.S. Energy Information Administration, last updated July 25, 2017; www.eia.gov.

Figure 19.1: Daily transit volumes through world maritime oil chokepoints

By volume of oil transit, the Strait of Hormuz, leading out of the Arabian Gulf with 19.0 mill bbl/d, and the Strait of Malacca with 16.0 mill bbl/d are the world's most important strategic chokepoints. Corresponding to these, daily shipping volumes are the throughput figures of major liquid bulk ports as described in Table 3.6 in Chapter 3. By far the largest crude oil and petroleum products port is Ras Tanura in Saudi Arabia with nearly 350 mill mt in 2015, located inside the Arabian Gulf. Singapore, at the entrance of the Strait of Malacca, ranks fourth with close to 200 mill mt per year. Also, Al Basrah in Iraq, Mina al Ahmadi in Kuwait, Jebel Dhanna in UAE and Yanbu in Saudi Arabia are ports inside the Arabian Gulf and are the key contributors for the high amount of cargo travelling via the Strait of Hormuz.

Table 19.1 indicates the relevance of the chokepoints for the global tanker business as well as for the ports serving these vessels.

Table 19.1: Daily transit volumes of crude oil and petroleum liquids through chokepoints, 2010–2016 in mill bbl/d

chokepoint/year	2010	2011	2012	2013	2014	2015	2016
Strait of Hormuz	15.9	17.0	16.8	16.6	16.9	17.0	19.0
Strait of Malacca	14.5	14.5	15.1	15.4	15.5	15.5	16.0
Suez Canal and SUMED Pipeline	3.1	3.8	4.5	4.6	5.2	5.4	5.5
Bab el-Mandeb	2.7	3.3	3.6	3.8	4.3	4.7	4.8
Danish Straits	3.2	3.0	3.3	3.1	3.0	3.2	3.2
Turkish Straits	2.8	2.9	2.7	2.6	2.6	2.4	2.4
Panama Canal	0.7	0.8	0.8	0.8	0.9	1.0	0.9
Cape of Good Hope	n/a	4.7	5.4	5.1	4.9	5.0	5.8
World maritime oil trade	55.5	55.5	56.4	56.5	56.4	58.9	n/a
World total oil supply	87.5	88.8	90.8	91.3	93.8	96.7	97.2

Source: U.S. Energy Information Administration; own calculations.

Most of these seven maritime chokepoints, plus the Cape of Good Hope, are considered as critical and dangerous shipping routes, especially because of the heavy geopolitical pressure surrounding them. The Strait of Hormuz is under a direct threat of closure by Iran. The Strait of Bab el-Mandeb and the Suez Canal as well as the Strait of Malacca are facing huge operational problems because of pirating attacks. To successfully stop these threats from continuing further, maritime bodies and leading maritime operators have tried to come up with alternate shipping routes. Alongside, it has also been proposed that key economic powers like the United States and other European countries try to use their naval supremacy to ensure the safety of tanker vessels using these chokepoints. This tactic has also been suggested to counter the hostile political tactics in certain chokepoints of the world.

Regarding vessel size, ships carrying crude oil and petroleum products are limited by size restrictions imposed by these maritime oil chokepoints. The global crude oil and refined product tanker fleet uses a classification system to standardize contract terms, to establish shipping costs, and to determine the ability of ships to travel into ports or through certain straits and channels. This system, known as the average freight rate assessment (AFRA) system, was established by Royal Dutch Shell six decades ago, and is overseen by the London Tanker Brokers' Panel (LTBP), an independent group of shipping brokers.

The seven chokepoints are described below.

Strait of Hormuz

Located between Oman (Musandam Peninsular) and Iran, the Strait of Hormuz connects the Arabian Gulf with the Gulf of Oman and the Arabian Sea. For the whole area of the Arabian Gulf, the Strait of Hormuz is the only sea passage to the open ocean and thus to global markets. At its narrowest point, the Strait of Hormuz is 21 miles wide, but the width of the shipping lane in either direction is only 2 miles wide, separated by a 2-mile buffer zone. The Strait of Hormuz is deep enough and wide enough to handle the world's largest crude oil tankers. The Strait of Hormuz is the world's most important oil chokepoint because its daily oil flow of about 19 mill bbl/d in 2016, accounted for approximately 30% of all seaborne-traded crude oil and other liquids. Analysts estimate that about 80% of the crude oil that moved through this chokepoint went to Asian markets, with China, Japan, India, South Korea, and Singapore as the largest destinations. Qatar, as the largest LNG producer globally, exported about 104.4 billion cubic meter or bcm per year of liquefied natural gas through the Strait of Hormuz in 2016.[2] This volume accounts for more than 30% of global LNG trade.

Strait of Malacca

This is the shortest passageway from the Indian Ocean to the South China Sea and the Pacific Ocean, located between Indonesia, Malaysia, and Singapore. The depth of the Strait of Malacca is restricted to 25 m or 82 ft. Bulk carriers and super-tankers have been built to this size, and the term "Malacca-max" is chosen for very large crude carriers, with a maximum length of 333 m (1,093 ft), beam of 60 m (197 ft), draught of 20.5 m (67.3 ft), and tonnage of 300,000 dwt. The latest generation of container vessels is also oriented at Malacca-max size. The Strait of Malacca route supplies oil to China and Indonesia, two of the fastest growing economies in the world, and is the primary chokepoint in Asia. Some 16 mill bbl/d flowed through here in 2016, making it the second most important energy passageway. The Strait of Malacca is among the narrowest chokepoints in the world, measuring only 1.7 miles in the narrow area named "Phillips Channel." In the Strait

---

2 For further details on LNG trade, refer to: BP Statistical Review of World Energy June 2017 issued by: BP plc, London, UK 2017, page 34.

of Malacca, maritime traffic will increase significantly as Asia's demand for oil grows. With the increased traffic, there will be more targets for pirates and terrorists. China holds a great interest in this chokepoint. Chinese former president Hu Jintao has stated that China faces a "Malacca Dilemma"—China's oil supply lines are vulnerable to disruption. The a.m. Belt-and-Road Initiative (BRI) or One Belt-One Road (OBOR) projects like the China-Pakistan Economic Corridor (CPEC) are an option to overcome the dependency of the Strait of Malacca. Visionary ideas like the Thailand Canal or the Arctic Route as alternatives to the Strait of Malacca are also motivated by the chance to overcome dependency on this chokepoint.

The Suez Canal
The Suez Canal is an artificial waterway in Egypt extending from Port Said to Suez and connecting the Mediterranean Sea with the Red Sea. The canal separates the African continent from Asia and provides the shortest maritime route between Europe and the lands lying around the Indian and western Pacific oceans. The passageway accounted for about 9% of the world's maritime oil trade in 2016 or 5.5 mill b/d. The canal was last expanded in 2015 to allow 60% of all tankers in the world to pass through, and a plan exists to upgrade the Canal by building an additional bypass to allow more two directional traffic and to speed up the time for a passage from 18 to 11 hours.[3] Although the region is subject to political unrest, shipping via the canal continues. Still, security remains an issue.

Bab el-Mandeb Strait
The Bab el-Mandeb Strait is located between Djibouti, Yemen, and Eritrea in the Horn of Africa. It connects the Red Sea to the Gulf of Aden and is a critical chokepoint for all Asian—Europe traffic. Bab el-Mandeb and the Suez Canal are both part of the Asian-Europe route. If the Bab el-Mandeb Strait was closed, it could keep tankers in the Persian Gulf from reaching the Suez Canal, diverting them around the Cape of Good Hope, another of the world's chokepoints. An estimated 4.8 mill bbl/d flowed through this strait en route to Europe, the United States, and Asia in 2016. The strait is another restricted passageway, only 18 miles wide at its narrowest point, which limits tanker traffic to two, 2-mile-wide channels.

---

[3] For further details of the "New Suez Canal," visit the Suez Canal Authority web site: www.suezcanal.gov.eg

The Danish Straits

The Danish Straits are international waterways between Denmark, Sweden and Germany connecting the Baltic Sea to the North Sea through the Kattegat and Skagerrak. Ships should note that the maximum obtainable depth in most parts of the straits is 17 m. However, in the area northeast of Gedser, the maximum obtainable depth is reduced to 16.4 m due to sand migration. Navigating Danish waters presents difficulties to large ships due to narrow waters, sharp bends, strong currents, and shallow depths. All this excludes the utilization of VLCCs. This passageway is a crucial one for Russian-based oil exports to Europe. An estimated 3.2 mill bbl/d of crude flowed through here in 2016.

Turkish Straits

The Turkish Straits are a series of internationally significant waterways in northwestern Turkey that connect the Aegean and Mediterranean seas to the Black Sea. They consist of the Dardanelles, the Sea of Marmara, and the Bosporus, all part of the sovereign sea territory of Turkey and subject to the regime of internal waters. The straits form the boundary between Europe and Asia. The Turkish Straits are important for shipping oil from the Caspian Sea region; however, the straits have seen declining volumes, falling to 2.4 mill bbl/d in 2016. Oil moving through these straits supplies Western and Southern Europe. The straits are only a half-mile wide at the narrowest point, making them among the most difficult waterways to navigate larger vessels.

The Panama Canal

The Panama Canal joins the Atlantic and Pacific oceans. It is an important global shipping canal, but with only marginal relevance for global oil trade; this not just because of the nature of the oil trade, but also due to the existing restrictions of the canal. Only about 0.9 mill bbl/d flowed through the canal in 2016. Since 2016, the new Panama Canal locks have allowed a maximum vessel size of 1,200 ft length (366 m), 161 ft width (49 m) and 49.9 ft draft (15.2 m), which means larger super-tankers, as well as huge bulker and container ships have to avoid the canal entirely.[4] The maximum size of a container ship of the so called Neo-Panamax class is in the range of nearly 15,000 TEU capacity. The CMA CGM vessel *Theodore Roosevelt* with a maximum capacity of 14,855 TEU is such a vessel; it measures 365.9 m in length and 48.2 m in beam and is one of the largest container vessels that already passed through.

---

4 Details can be found at the website of the Canal Authority: www.pancanal.com

Cape of Good Hope

The cape isn't technically a chokepoint, but its status as a major global trade route qualifies it as chokepoint as it's responsible for about 9%, or 5.8 mill bbl/d, of all maritime oil trade. The cape is also a standard alternate route for ships traveling westward wanting to bypass the Bab el-Mandeb Straits or the Suez Canal. However, diverting around the cape increases costs and shipping time—as much as fifteen added days in transit to Europe and ten days to the United States.

If all the seven chokepoints work and shipping can pass through, there is no disturbing impact on ports. But it is easy to understand that a closure of the Suez Canal or a conflict caused by Iran for the Strait of Hormuz will have tremendous impact on global oil trade. Huge consequences for the ports along the supply chain will be the result. Here it becomes very clear that ports and shipping companies are partners along the supply chain. The disruption one partner feels will result in consequences for the others. Therefore, it is necessary for ports to watch the impact of global policy on oil trade chokepoints.

19.2 Strategic Canals: Panama, Suez, etc.

A shipping canal is an artificial type of water canal specifically created along major seawater routes to aid the passage of ships. The major ones are specially designed or enlarged to accommodate the latest generation of cargo vessels; not just tankers as discussed above in section 19.1, but for all types of cargo. Such canals are of vital importance in the maritime world as they offer shorter, alternative transportation routes across major seawater networks and help to regulate maritime traffic internally within countries. Across the world there are many such shipping canals that aid the movement of ships on an everyday basis. Some of these canals are also the busiest traffic routes around the world. Below are mentioned a few of them:

- Suez Canal
- Panama Canal
- Kiel Canal
- Volga-Don-Canal
- Houston Ship Canal
- Rhine-Main-Danube Canal
- Beijing-Hangzhou Grand Canal

There are thousands of canals around the world, and a few of them like the Beijing-Hangzhou Grand Canal (or in short, the Grand Canal), reveal a history of more than 2,500 years of port and shipping business. The Grand Canal is not only one of the oldest canals in the world, it is also the longest one; the total length of the Grand Canal is 1,776 km (1,104 miles). Starting at Beijing, it passes through Tianjin and the provinces of Hebei, Shandong, Jiangsu, and Zhejiang to the city of Hangzhou, linking the Yellow and Yangtze rivers. This is impressive construction, but when analyzing the supraregional economic impact of canals it becomes clear that that the Grand Canal is only of local importance today. But beside this it is an impressive maritime tourist attraction.

In the following, we will analyze the impact the first three canals have on global trade; and here for all types of products. This does not mean that a local ship canal like in Houston is not important! Local access canals are necessary and of essential importance for many ports, but the effects are often regional effects only; this is different for the first three canals. When, for example, the German river Elbe Canal (and, this is a canal, although it is still named "river") will no longer be dredged, this will have a major impact on the local economy, just as the lack of dredge for larger vessels (overdue since 2001) has a negative effect. But the intensive competition within the Helgoland Bay port cluster[5] will easily take this over, and everybody beyond the local boundaries will probably not even realize that there are serious local problems. The same is true for many other ports around the globe. Therefore, we will concentrate on canals with supra-regional effects on many ports.

Suez Canal

The Suez Canal connects the Mediterranean with the Red Sea and the Indian Ocean. To take an example, the route via Suez Canal instead of travelling around South Africa and the Cape of Good Hope cuts a modern journey from Singapore to Rotterdam by nearly 3,500 nautical miles (6,480 km)—saving vessel owners lots of time and money. The Canal is of huge importance especially for the Far East-Europe trade lane.

---

5 See: Table 4.1: World Port Cluster.

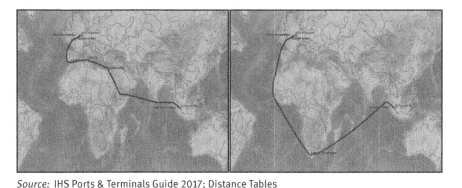

Source: IHS Ports & Terminals Guide 2017; Distance Tables

Figure 19.2: Suez Canal route versus Cape of Good Hope

A vessel from the huge Asian transhipment hub Singapore to Rotterdam can save approximately 30% of distance; the route via Strait of Malacca, south of Sri Lanka, Bab el-Mandeb, Red Sea, Suez Canal, Mediterranean Sea, Gibraltar, and finally the English Channel (left picture in Figure 19.2) is just 8,344 nm long, instead of 11,798 nm when sailing around the Cape of Good Hope in South Africa (right picture in Figure 19.2). At a speed of 14 kn, the vessel via Suez will need 24.8 days instead of 35.1 days when sailing via the Cape of Good Hope, that is, saving ten days when traveling via Suez Canal. This is a huge saving potential! However, the Suez Canal is an artificial canal, and this means that ship owners must pay for every passage. That this is okay and acceptable goes without any doubt, because construction and maintenance need to be paid by the Egyptian Canal Authority, and the user-pays-principle is the best way to refinance the investments.

Big vessels easily pay several hundred thousand USD for just one passage. But the alternative sailing around the Cape of Good Hope is normally not an alternative.[6] The costs per passage are calculated by taking the alternative costs as reference. When taking a second route from Singapore to the Mediterranean port of Athens (Piraeus; important facility for the Chinese BRI or OBOR strategy) as an example, the saving potential becomes more obvious:

- Distance via Suez Canal = 5,613 nm
- Distance via Cape of Good Hope = 12,184 nm
- Sailing time at 14 kt via Suez Canal = 16.7 days
- Sailing time via Cape of Good Hope = 36.3 days

---

6 In the aftermath of th Financial Crisis 2008/2009 there was an oversupply of vessel capacity in the market, caused by gaps in demand. In order not to lay up the vessels few, shipping line rerouted the traffic via Cape of Good Hope to supply the vessels. For an interim period, this was an acceptable solution to reduce the negative effect of capacity oversupply.

Taking the Suez Canal to the eastern Mediterranean instead of traveling via the Cape of Good Hope will cut the distance and time in half!

About one-third of all vessels are container vessels, as shown in Table 19.2. Tankers are the second largest group, followed by Bulk Carriers. The Suez Canal is of huge importance for all type of vessels, but the canal focuses on the most popular vessels: container ships.

Table 19.2: Suez Canal traffic—number of ships, 2017

Ship Type	Laden N/S	Laden S/N	Laden sum	Ballast N/S	Ballast S/N	Ballast sum	Total
Tanker	1,822	1,989	**3,811**	233	493	**726**	**4,537**
LNG Ship	104	232	**336**	160	71	**231**	**567**
Bulk Carrier	1,909	834	**2,743**	9	536	**545**	**3,288**
General Cargo	759	501	**1,260**	58	224	**282**	**1,542**
Container Ship	2,883	2,628	**5,511**	35	22	**57**	**5,568**
RoRo	180	172	**352**	7	11	**18**	**370**
Car Carrier	413	465	**878**	7	0	**7**	**885**
Passenger Ship	27	42	**69**	6	7	**13**	**82**
others	322	336	**658**	38	15	**53**	**711**
Total	8,419	7,199	**15,618**	553	1,379	**1,932**	**17,550**

Source: Suez Canal Authority, web page: www.suezcanal.gov.eg

This becomes clearer when considering the size and cargo-carrying capacity of the vessels, expressed in net tons as Table 19.3 illustrates. Here the steadily increasing size of container ships during the last decades, combined with the fact that these vessels are primarily engaged on the Asian-Europe trade routes, led to container ships equaling more than half of total trade. After the last widening of the canal in 2010, the maximum draft of a vessel allowed to pass is 24 m, maximum load 240,000 dwt. With this, the canal can handle about two-thirds of all tankers in service and nearly all bulker and container vessels. This means, there are only minor restrictions caused by infrastructure.

Table 19.3: Suez Canal traffic—net tons, 2017 (in 1000 mt)

Ship Type	Laden			Ballast			Total
	N/S	S/N	sum	N/S	S/N	sum	
Tanker	71,334	88,337	**159,671**	7,779	20,674	**28,453**	**188,124**
LNG Ship	10,491	24,932	**35,423**	17,407	7,120	**24,527**	**59,950**
Bulk Carrier	69,521	25,792	**95,313**	115	18,404	**18,519**	**113,832**
General Cargo	7,586	6,412	**13,998**	718	1,371	**2,089**	**16,087**
Container Ship	300,545	286,355	**586,900**	1,154	756	**1,910**	**588,810**
RoRo	4,353	4,379	**8,732**	86	98	**184**	**8,916**
Car Carrier	25,866	29,429	**55,295**	393	0	**393**	**55,688**
Passenger Ship	1,377	2,139	**3,516**	390	110	**500**	**4,016**
others	2,549	2,613	**5,162**	819	169	**988**	**6,150**
Total	493,622	470,388	**964,010**	28,861	48,702	**77,563**	**1,041,573**

Source: Suez Canal Authority, web page: www.suezcanal.gov.eg

Panama Canal

The Panama Canal, about 80 km (50 miles) in length, connects the Atlantic and Pacific oceans at one of the narrowest points of the American continent. Since its opening in 1914, more than a million vessels from around the world have transited the waterway. Every day, about 37 ships on average pass along the canal. Like the Suez Canal for the Egyptian economy, the Panama Canal contributes considerably to Panama's economy.

While the direct contribution to the government budget is about US$ 1.2 billion a year (8% of the budget; 2015 figures), considering all indirect effects, such as the maritime and logistics industry it supports, the canal influences about 25% of Panama's GDP. The canal is also key to global trade and plays a prominent role in many of the leading economies in the world. About 5% of total global cargo is transported through the canal, including 10% of U.S. exports and imports. The savings for taking the Panama Canal instead of the journey around Cape Horn are tremendous, as Figure 19.3 shows.

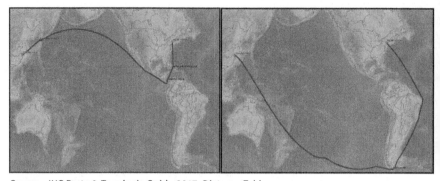

Figure 19.3: Panama Canal route versus Cape Horn

A vessel from China's Port of Shanghai to New York on the U.S. East Coast can cut its travel distance by 35%; the route from Shanghai via Tsugaru Strait (the strait between Honshu and Hokkaido in northern Japan connecting the Sea of Japan with the Pacific Ocean), further north bypassing Rat, Andreanof and Aleutian Islands, heading to US West coast and via Panama Canal to New York (Figure 19.3, picture left) is 10,583 nm long, compared with 16,767 nm when sailing southwards out of Shanghai across the South Pacific and via Cape Horn northwards along the South American East Coast (Figure 19.3, picture right).

At a speed of 14 kn, the vessel via Panama Canal will need 31.5 days instead of 49.8 days when sailing via Cape Horn; saving eighteen days when taking the Panama Canal. 49.8 days is a very long time, but the alternative route via Suez and Gibraltar across the Atlantic as an alternative option to the South Pacific route is not much shorter: 36.8 days; 5.5 days longer than Panama route and burdened with Suez Canal fees. Taking the Panama Canal has huge time saving potential! However, like the Suez Canal, the Panama Canal is an artificial canal, and this means that ship owners must pay for every passage. In 2017, exactly 9,998 ships traveled the Panama Canal with cargo, plus an additional 3,415 ships with ballast that is, with no cargo on board; a relation of 2.9 to 1 as Table 19.4 shows. For the Suez Canal, the figures are 15,618 ships with cargo, and only 1,932 ships with ballast; a relation of 8.1 to 1. This means that the Panama Canal saw much more empty vessels passing through. This occurs especially for tankers and is likely a fact of the oil and gas industry within the Gulf of Mexico and their business relations to the Pacific region. Chemical and LPG tankers frequently sail back empty

Table 19.4: Panama Canal traffic—number of ships, 2017

Ship Type	Laden			Ballast			Total
	N/S	S/N	sum	N/S	S/N	sum	
Tanker	1,756	373	2,129	27	1,307	1,334	3,463
LNG Ship	88	8	96	0	67	67	163
Bulk Carrier	1,388	1,066	2,454	10	451	461	2,915
General Cargo	283	328	611	11	32	43	654
Container Ship	1,095	1,380	2,475	11	7	18	2,493
RoRo	262	441	703	89	9	98	801
Reefer Vessel	279	433	712	152	4	156	868
Passenger Ship	154	91	245	3	2	5	250
others	172	401	573	883	350	1,233	1,806
Total	5,477	4,521	9,998	1,186	2,229	3,415	13,413

Source: Panama Canal Authority, web page: www.pancanal.com

As with the Suez Canal, most of the ships taking the Panama Canal are container ships. Tanker and dry bulkers are nearly employed at the same level. Only when taking the cargo carrying capacity in Table 19.5 into consideration, does it become clear how important the container ships are for the Panama Canal. 142,278 net tons out of a total of 336,314 net tons of all laden ships, and so about 40% of ships that pass through the canal, are container ships.

Table 19.5: Panama Canal traffic—net tons, 2017 (in 1000 mt)

Ship Type	Laden			Ballast			Total
	N/S	S/N	sum	N/S	S/N	sum	
Tanker	45,043	7,186	52,229	174	35,910	36,084	88,314
LNG Ship	9,359	838	10,197	0	6,894	6,894	17,092
Bulk Carrier	37,815	25,466	63,281	88	15,766	15,854	79,135
General Cargo	3,232	4,238	7,470	113	224	337	7,808
Container Ship	58,719	83,559	142,278	198	138	336	142,614
RoRo	15,539	25,908	41,447	4,954	404	5,358	46,806
Reefer Vessel	2,878	4,240	7,118	1,312	20	1,332	8,450
Passenger Ship	7,235	2,572	9,807	8	2	10	9,818
others	1,183	1,302	2,485	414	385	799	3,284
Total	181,004	155,310	336,314	7,262	59,745	67,007	403,321

Source: Panama Canal Authority, web page: www.pancanal.com

When comparing Suez and Panama, one sees that the Suez Canal (a total of 17,550 passages) is approximately 30% more busy than the Panama Canal (with 13,413 ships). Regarding the cargo carrying capacity of the vessels, the Suez Canal is used by much larger vessels than those seen in the Panama Canal. More than 1 bn net tons pass through the Suez compared with 400 mill net tons for the Panama Canal. This underlies the huge global importance of the Suez Canal as the most important artificial global chokepoint. This also results from the largest container ships always being employed on the Far East-Asia route. Panama Canal, with less traffic and less cargo, ranks at position two.

Kiel Canal

Compared with the two global shortcuts of the Suez and Panama Canal, both saving thousands of miles, the Kiel Canal in northern Germany offers minimal distance and time saving potential, as Figure 19.4 shows.

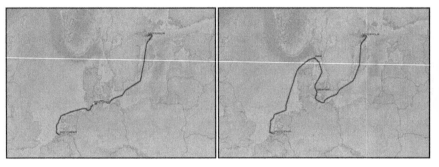

Source: IHS Ports & Terminals Guide, 2017; Distance Tables

Figure 19.4: Kiel Canal route versus Skagerrak

The Rotterdam-Stockholm route via the Kiel Canal is up to 340 nm shorter in distance, or approximately one day in sailing time, than the route via northern Denmark (Skagerrak). Vessels departing northern UK or coming via the North Atlantic will save much less miles and time. A few hundred miles (or up to one day) is not very much, and bearing in mind that the Kiel Canal is an artificial waterway like Suez and Panama and the ships must pay for the passage, there must be other arguments for using the Kiel Canal. In addition, the nautical restrictions show that the canal is navigable for small and medium vessels only.

Kiel Canal maximum ship dimensions:
- Length: 235.0 m
- Breadth: 32.5 m
- Draught: 9.5 m
- Air draught: 40.0 m

In history, one of the key arguments for using the Kiel Canal came from the military; German Emperor Wilhelm II pushed building the Canal prior to World War I.[7] So, building the canal was motivated by military arguments, but using the canal today stems from two different arguments:
1. **Nautical problems:** The route via the Belt and Sund-region between Denmark and Sweden is a nautical challenge still today. Although with modern navigational aids the passage has become much safer, the difficulty of sailing this route was and still is a reason to use the Kiel Canal.
2. **Service culture:** The Baltic Sea region is used for weekly and fortnightly services to and from the major hub ports in the Hamburg-Antwerp-Range. Baltic ports are served on a fixed schedule, and the days of call stay fixed in weekly or fortnightly schedules. And the more ports and terminals a vessel can call with such a schedule, the more efficient they are; and within such tight schedules every half day counts. This service culture combined with the goal to maximize revenues within a buyers' market led to the utilization of the Kiel Canal and results in extreme high traffic figures.

The Kiel Canal, with 30,269 transit passages in 2017, has nearly double the traffic the Suez Canal has. With this, the Kiel Canal is by far the busiest artificial waterway for commercial shipping globally; and this is the reason why the Kiel Canal is mentioned here. With 86,7 mill tons of cargo in 2017, the Canal is good for only a fraction of Suez or Panama volumes, but within its niche the canal functions quite well.

19.3 Backlash on Ports

Because of bottlenecks and chokepoints, caused by infrastructure somewhere in the world, it happened that ports that are thousands of kilometers away are influenced by each other. For example, an export from Shanghai to Chicago that

---

[7] At that time the Canal was named "Kaiser Wilhelm-Kanal"; later it was renamed to "Nord-Ost-ee-Kanal" in German, or "Kiel Canal" internationally.

in past sailed to a U.S. west coast port and further on with land-based transportation, may now travel as all water service to New York and further on to Chicago. The reason for the switchover of Chinese-U.S. trade is the extended Panama Canal, which causes rerouting and leads to traffic increases in the Port of New York. This shows that interdependencies in the port and shipping business are high and that huge infrastructure projects like the widening and deepening of canals and locks have an influence on ports as well; not directly, but indirectly. Let this be a positive one like for the Port of New York in the example, or a negative one for the west coast ports.

A port like the Port of Cuxhaven in northern Germany as another example, located near the entrance of the Kiel Canal, depends on the canal traffic the Kiel Canal brings. Cuxhaven is a typical way port or zero-deviation port: all vessels between the UK and Scandinavia that take the Kiel Canal directly bypass Cuxhaven. This is the reason why this port has been built and what founded the economic base for the business. This traffic represents most of Cuxhaven's cargo business, although additional market niches have been developed. Anything that happens with the canal (infrastructure changes like locks or vessel dimensions, pricing, traffic regulations, etc.) has a direct impact on such a port.

Supply chains may be reorganized because of problems occurring at major chokepoints (e.g., because of piracy) or because of economic arguments, for example, when it needs to be recalculated how much transit via an artificial canal costs compared with revenue gained. These are normal business decisions, but because ports are immobile assets, decisions made far away in another country may have an impact on the respective port. In this sense, ports are the weakest partners in such rerouting programs, and they must live with decisions caused by others. They are reduced to reacting. Proactive marketing and sales activities are the limited actions they can take. And with more and more global terminal operators—some in the hands of shipping lines—the room for maneuvering is rather limited. This is not new, but should always be considered when requirements occur. Ports are small partners within global supply chains—not less, but also not more.

Chapter 20
Port-City Interface

20.1 Historic Port-City Relations

Due to the lack of transport infrastructure in the past, shipping on rivers and along coast lines was a key element of trade and natural solution for transportation. Consequently, many ports started as small landings at prominent river and coastal locations. The link between rivers and ocean was an important knot already in ancient times, and so it is an obvious consequence that important ports and cities have been built in river estuaries.

The long search for the prominent city of Pi-Ramesses in ancient Egypt is a great example for the port-city relationship. Pi-Ramesses (meaning "House of Ramesses") was the new capital built by the 19th dynasty Pharaoh Ramesses II (1279–1213 BC; known as "The Great"). At that time, the city was located directly at the Pelusiac branch of the river Nile. The Pelusiac branch of the Nile began silting up around 1060 BC, leaving the city without water when the river established a new course to the west, called the Tanitic branch. The city dried out, the river could no longer be used for agricultural and transport purposes, and finally the city died and was relinquished.[1] This is a dramatic story about the close relationship that ports and cities have had since the beginning of human settlements.

An early example of a leading European port city is Venice, a city that is situated across a group of 118 small islands that are separated by canals and linked by bridges. The city is built in the Venetian Lagoon, an enclosed bay that lies between the mouth of the Po and the Piave rivers. From about 1000 to 1500 AD, Venice played a major role in developing trade within Europe and the Mediterranean and acted as a gateway for technology transfer from Asia, Greece, and Egypt to the West.

From the late 17th century onward, port cities such as Amsterdam, Genoa, Gothenburg, Hamburg, Liverpool, London, Marseilles, Portsmouth, and Rotterdam were the front-runners in urban development in Europe. By the 18th century, western Europe was an effectively integrated area, with port-cities functioning as key connecting links in terms of national and international trade and of capital and labor mobility. Port cities accounted for about 40% of the world's cities, with populations of more than 100,000 in 1850, and they dominated the European urban hierarchy until the 1950s, when they were finally overtaken by industrial

---

[1] For more details, refer to: Ancient History Encyclopedia, www.ancient.eu/Per-Ramesses

DOI 10.1515/9781547400874-020

cities.[2] Histories of other locations around the world show that many big cities trace their roots to the establishment of a port. They have long played a vital role in the international transport system, but have become increasingly important since the second half of the 20th century with the rapid globalization of the world economy and expansion of world trade.

The political structure of port cities was usually dominated by mercantile and shipping interests who, through their trading activities, had amassed wealth and prestige. Port cities typically enjoyed a cosmopolitan atmosphere as they were places in which various people, cultures, and ideas as well as goods from a variety of places jostle, mix, and enrich city life. This development attracted poor people living in rural areas and was a source of migration into cities, and so a large casual labor force originated. The need for large amounts of unskilled labor meant that port cities acted as magnets for migrants, one outcome of which was residential segregation based on ethnic group and socioeconomic status. Apart from direct employment in trade and shipping, ports were centers for many related industries such as fish processing, flour milling, soap making, sugar refining, and, from the 20th century, oil refining. Typical port work often was performed by unskilled labor.

Many cities began as ports, but as they have grown, port activities have gradually been overshadowed by manufacturing, financial, or service activities. Port-related activities, although usually still vital to the economy, have been relegated to a relatively "hidden" role. As the cities grew, ports "competed" for land with industry, housing, and other urban uses. After World War II, many ports escaped from their metropolitan straitjackets and developed new ports with access to deep water and adequate land areas. Sometimes the existing inner-city facilities were no longer required for commercial port operations and fell into decay. Container terminals, for example, required specially designed wharves, and made existing wharves, otherwise useable for many years, obsolete. The port and city authorities were also forced to either demolish or find alternative uses for old cranes, cargo sheds, warehouses, and other port facilities. Some imaginative uses for cargo sheds and warehouses included museums, art galleries, restaurants, and shopping arcades.

Port extension also moved away from the historic city center. Antwerp, Rotterdam and, as the latest example, London with the new Gateway Terminal

---

2 The AIVP "Association Internazionale des Villes Portes" is one of the associations that concentrates on the city-port relations and organized annual "World Conferences on Cities and Ports." In addition, they publish various background papers on port and city projects. For more details refer to www.aivp.org

are examples of ports that developed relatively close to the city centers. Over time, however, they shifted operations away from the center; this for a variety of reasons, like larger operational space required, deeper water in response to increasing ship sizes, or the competition between urban and port utilization for limited inner-city areas. Another reason contributing to the weakening of links between port and city centers is the rapid mechanization and specialization of port work and the accompanying increase in the operational scale and scope. These shifts led to increased storage space requirements and make ports very space-intensive.

The port city as a social phenomenon has largely ceased to exist: despite the huge space taken up by harbors and ancillary installations, port cities have in fact become general cities that also happen to contain ports. The development of new harbor areas away from the inner-city areas means that shipping activity is far less visible to the public. Ships are more sparsely crewed and spend less time in port, leading to the decline of "sailor towns"—the areas containing taverns and other service industries catering to itinerant sailors. The rapid growth in vessel size and volume of cargo transported over the past thirty years has led to ever-growing demands on port space, not only for new berths to accommodate bigger vessels, but also for cargo-handling and storage facilities, cargo-related industries, and the necessary transport infrastructure. Gradually, ports have moved out of city centers, leaving the port-city with fewer direct economic benefits, but having to cope with various negative local impacts, such as on air and water quality, noise, and traffic. It is no longer taken for granted that a well-functioning port automatically has a net positive impact on the city.

Today, ports and their host cities interact across many dimensions: economic, social, environmental, and cultural, and any kind of port development should consider the linkages between city objectives and the port objectives. The smooth transfer of cargo and equipment from land to waterborne systems does not take place in isolation. A seaport node within a multimodal transport system is frequently associated with the development of an urban center and generates substantial employment, industrial activity, and national and regional development. A city today can not continue to thrive and maintain its position as a preeminent international city without a vibrant and well-run port. The futures of both are inseparably entwined; if one withers, so will the other. Although the relationship between ports and cities has changed, their fortunes are still intertwined.

20.2 Regional & City Development Policies

In the last decades, urban waterfronts have been discovered for urban redevelopment. No longer used for port activities, many derelict port areas have been transformed into up and coming neighborhoods. Well-known examples of waterfront redevelopment can be found in the Port of Buenos Aires, where the Special Purpose Company "Corporación Antiguo Puerto Madero" ("Old Puerto Madero Corporation") redeveloped the old city docks for mixed commercial, residential, and recreational use. The Port of London is another example, where the London Docklands Development Corporation converted the old docks, stretching from Stepney to Woolwich, also for commercial industrial, residential, and recreational use.

In general, three approaches commonly have been used for the urban redevelopment of surplus port land:

12. **Retaining it within the port authority for redevelopment as in the case of the Port of Barcelona.**[3]

    This implies a widening of the port's function from that of a port into a property developer. Such a change may require modifications to the statutes of the public port authority, or of the trust port. The experience of Associated British Ports shows that when the port is in private hands, it is capable of effective development of surplus lands. The Port Authority of New York and New Jersey is an example of a public port authority with wide redevelopment powers.

13. **Transferring it to the local authority or municipality for redevelopment.**

    In practice this is not always effective because the municipality might lack the resources to realize the full value of the land in question. On the other hand, there are examples (such as Baltimore and Rotterdam) of successful regeneration by the municipality of port lands near the city center.

14. **Creating a special development corporation for the specific purpose of redeveloping an old dock area.**

    This is most appropriate when the area is very extensive, involves various municipalities, and involves high redevelopment costs. Probably the biggest and best-known special purpose corporation is the London Docklands Development Corporation (LDDC), created to redevelop the old docks of the Port of

---

[3] For details of the Barcelona development, refer to: Jauhiainen, Jussi S.: "Waterfront Redevelopment and Urban Policy: The Case of Barcelona, Cardiff and Genoa," in: *European Planning Studies*. March 1995, Vol. 3 Issue 1, page 3ff, UK 1995.

London. The LDDC was established in 1981 by the government and endowed with extensive planning powers because of the inability of six riparian municipalities to agree on a coherent and feasible plan for the docks' redevelopment. Efforts to redevelop the docks began almost as soon as they were closed, although it took a decade for most plans to move beyond the drawing board and another decade for redevelopment to take full effect. The situation was greatly complicated by the large number of landowners involved. However, the project started and many flats for comparatively high prices were built, as well as a huge amount of office space. The fact that the city has been developed too fast and too much space has been offered in short times results in the effect that many investment projects failed, and several of the investment companies went bankrupt.

Another example of a separate corporation established for this purpose is the already mentioned "Old Puerto Madera Corporation" in Argentina, which is a joint venture by the City of Buenos Aires and the national government for the redevelopment of old city docks. With the objective of urbanizing the area, the federal and city governments participated as egalitarian partners in the incorporated development company. The lesson learned from LDDC—that the project should not be developed too fast with the effect of reduced market prices for flats and office space—had been learned. Today, one of the trendiest boroughs in Buenos Aires, Puerto Madera has become the preferred address for growing numbers of young professionals and retirees, alike. Increasing property prices have also generated interest in the area as a destination for foreign buyers, particularly those in the market for premium investment properties.

Another example can be found in the city of Hamburg where the "Hafen-City GmbH" is responsible for the development of an urban city on the area of the old port. This project is still under way and will bring additional capacity step-by-step to the market.

Ports and cities are historically strongly linked, but the link between port and city growth has become weaker. Economic benefits often spill over to other regions, whereas negative impacts are localized in the port-city. Modern port business no longer takes place in city centers, but has been shifted to the outskirts for a variety of good reasons, like the need for larger terminals and deeper water, pollution including noise, security, and hinterland access. However, ports can become the drivers of urban economic growth and have the potential to support the regional and city development policy. Returning no longer used port areas to the city is one way of development policy; promoting industrial development that is closely linked with the port is another.

20.3 Port Industry

A port is primarily a point where goods are transferred from one mode of transport to another. Goods are stored temporarily within the port boundaries, waiting for onward transportation via open sea as outgoing maritime cargo or further on to hinterland destinations via rail or road as incoming products. It is this storage function that makes ports interesting especially for industries that need high volumes of low unit cost cargoes. These are typically bulk cargoes like liquid (crude oil, refined products) and dry (coal, ore) bulk products. Natural gas, biomass, steam, heat, wind, and solar energy are also products that are moved and stowed within the port area and so are of interest for industrial investors. A second group comprises a set of processing industries that transform imported material before their onward shipment/reexport, taking advantage of the intermodal, transhipment and break of bulk functions of ports. A third group of industries, located in port-industrial complexes, are those whose inputs comprise bulk commodities imported through the port.

Port areas are of interest for industrial settlements because they often built the centers of regional industrial development areas; they are focal points for economic activities and for associated industrial development. Alongside the direct attraction of port-related industries, two more general mechanisms also shape the development of port-industrial complexes. The first is the existence of external economies: the availability of shared infrastructures generates external economies that can attract other economic activities and encourage processes of agglomeration, although ports and their associated industrial areas also generate a series of negative externalities in the shape of noise, pollution and visual blight that can also deter further economic diversification and development. The second relates to the way in which the concentration of port-dependent economic activities can itself attract customers and suppliers. Indeed, the existence of backward and forward linkages was often seen in growth pole theories[4] as creating the possibility of cumulative processes of industrial development. In practice, the degree of downstream diversification achieved was quite limited,

---

4 The main author of growth poles theory, created in the 1950s, was Francois Perroux (1903–1987). The key and the most important theoretical foundation of the whole concept was Perroux's argument which explains the procedure of economic growth in the following way: It is a blunt and indisputable fact that growth is not uniform in different places, but growth has different degrees of intensity in different points, or poles, and then it spreads via channels and its result for the state economy is different in different regions. For further details, see: Komarovskiy, Viktor, Viktor Bondaruk: "The Role of the Concept of 'Growth Poles' for Regional Development, in *Journal of Public Administration, Finance and Law*, Issue 4/2013, pages 31–42, Iasi, Romania 2013

making employment in port-industrial complexes particularly dependent on the fortunes of a few industries.

The development of port-industrial complexes was a striking feature of economically advanced and rapidly industrializing economies, especially in the 1960s and 1970s. European examples include Rotterdam in The Netherlands, Antwerp in Belgium, Teeside in the UK, Fos-sur-Mer in France, and Brindisi and Gioia Tauro in Italy. Gioia Tauro shows an interesting story of the ups and downs of industrial development in port areas, and it is also a story of exaggerated expectations that ended in a disaster, and where finally the development of a South-European container business spurred a successful turnaround.

In the spring of 1970, Gioa Tauro in southern Italy (an area of rich citrus groves) was selected as a future port industrial development area, and more specifically, as the site for state-owned Italsider's fifth integrated shore-based steel plant. Italsider in the past was Italy's largest steelwork. By the late 1970s, 7,500 jobs were to be created in an area of high un- and under-employment and very limited industrialization. State regional development funds were devoted to port construction and site preparation, which started in 1975. Although the construction of a port capable of receiving the largest ore and coal carriers was complete, after several revised plans the steel project was quietly dropped. The reason why lay in the steel overproduction crises of the 1970s and their devastating financial consequences for Italsider. A subsequent electrical power station project designed to make use of Gioa Tauro's infrastructure was dropped for environmental reasons. In the mid-1990s, however, this large and still modern port finally found a use as a container port and as a pole for the transhipment of containers from ocean-going vessels (a classic hub and spoke network), not least due to its location in southern Italy with very little deviation from main Far East-Europe-Services.

Starting from 16,034 TEUs and docking facilities for fifty ships in 1995, its operations expanded at breathtaking speed to more than 3 million TEUs in 2004 and 3,060 ships, making it the largest container transhipment terminal in the Mediterranean. The German-Italian group Eurogate was the operator of the medcenter container terminal (MCT) in Gioia Tauro from the very beginning of container operations. Rail and road connections directly link MCT with the industrial and consumer centers of Italy and central Europe. Its large scale and extensive facilities, including super-post-Panamax quay cranes for up to twenty-two container rows, make MCT the unique container terminal in the Mediterranean that regularly operates three ocean carriers of more than 10,000 TEU simultaneously. With this, Gioia

Tauro is a success story of port development,[5] but the development of substantial industry within the area—as intended at the beginning—failed.

One of the most successful examples of port development (from a transhipment port to the city-hub of Pacific Asia) with agglomeration economies in its hinterland is Hong Kong. Because of its strategic location and its ice-free 12.5 meter deep harbor, Hong Kong has long been the leading gateway in East Asia, especially to the southern China.

Options available for port development being limited by the lack of available sites and strict environmental requirements, the struggle for space between the port and the city has sharpened. Some ports have been obliged to maintain their activities near, or return them to, urban areas as discussed above for the cases of London Docklands or Puerto Madera.

Port-industrial development creates linkages with the local economy. The circular economy can seize opportunities for ecological synergies offered by the proximity of industrial firms from different sectors (such as for heating or waste treatment). Also, renewable energy can be developed, offshore wind energy, which however, requires a competitive institutional framework set by the national government. Successful cases of interrelations between port and industry bear the term "maritime cluster," meaning that the coexistence of port, shipping, and industry creates spill-over and synergy effects. Both shipping and port industries depend heavily on subcontracting and require a specialized local workforce. As maritime clusters can generate high added value to the surrounding city and region, governments use a range of instruments to support them. However, as the success of these instruments depends on the local context, the cluster policy should respond to locally identified needs. Clusters typically bring together the port and logistics, shipping and maritime services, shipbuilding, and repair.

However, whether as part of a maritime cluster or as a stand-alone business, a port needs to be competitive if cities want to benefit from it. Port-related value added and employment is strongly related to urban wealth. Ports can be made more competitive by strengthening their maritime links, port operations, and hinterland connections. Local goodwill for port functions in cities is essential and can be earned. Environmental policies and incentive schemes have reduced a variety of environmental impacts, transport policies in and around ports have mitigated congestion and port relocations have freed up centrally located urban land for other functions.

---

5 For a more detailed review, see: Centre for Industrial Studies (CSIL): Ex post evaluation of investment projects co-financed by the European Regional Development Fund (ERDF) or Cohesion Fund (CF) during the period 1994–1999: The Port of Gioia Tauro, Milan, Italy 2012.

20.4 Cruise Shipping/Tourism

Within the first seventeen years of the 21st century, the cruise industry recorded admirable growth. The global growth rate of the cruise industry has been enduring and stable, despite the economic cycles of growth and recession. For 2018, total worldwide ocean cruise industry is estimated at \$45.6 billion (a 4.6% increase over 2017) with 26.0 mill annualized passengers carried (2017 = 25,165,425 passengers carried on ocean cruise vessels; a 3.3% increase over 2017). For 2020, the industry expects to reach 27.6 mill cruise passengers. Total worldwide ocean cruise capacity at the end of 2018 will be 537,000 passengers and 314 ships.[6] This pace of growth was faster than the one observed at the beginning of the 2000's, yet when examining the trend of the 2010s it seems that a specific development path, slower than the one that happened in 2000s, is in place.

Cruise industry observers like "cruise market watch" and others report that 5% of global tourists arrived at their destinations by water, cruise and ferry; the majority still comes via road and rail or by plane. Since 1990, over 280 million passengers have taken a two- or more day cruise, with each of them visiting more than one port. These trends confirm the remarkable dynamics of the cruise industry and its resilience in the face of the economic, social, political, or any other crises that regularly challenge the tourism sector. Cruise shipping as part of the tourist industry requires specific port operation that is capable of handling huge amounts of passengers in a short time—often including immigration services—to allow all passengers to enter or leave the vessel. Of key interest for this business are the tourist attractions around the port. With this, the close relationship between cruise shipping and cruise terminal operations with the city is more than obvious.

Cruise Lines International Association (CLIA), the world's largest cruise industry trade association, releases an annual Cruise Travel Report[7] a revealing look at the attitudes, behaviors, and travel preferences of cruisers and noncruisers, and highlighting trends and the new "cruise generation." For years CLIA has clustered cruise passengers into the following four groups (by dates of birth are as follows):

- 1982–1998 Gen Y/Millennial
- 1967–1981 Gen X
- 1948–1966 Boomers
- 1917–1947 Traditionalists

---

6 For more details, visit: www.cruisemarketwatch.com
7 See, for example, CLIA's Cruise Travel Report January 2018, Washington, 2018.

Preferences of these tourist groups are substantially different, and this results in different touristic offerings tailored to the travelers. For the tourist industry, this is of huge importance, but also for the port industry that finally needs to provide the infra- and superstructure at the berth. Cruise travel has become the most popular travel preference among younger generations, including Millennials, creating a new cruise generation. This generation rates cruise travel as the best type of vacation compared to land-based vacations, all-inclusive resorts, tours, vacation house rentals and camping, and 90% that have experienced cruise travel say they will continue to cruise.

The results of the CLIA's Cruise Travel Report also indicates that cruising is experiencing a rejuvenation as Millennials and Generation X are becoming enthusiastic cruisers and the cruise generation is adopting the cruising lifestyle.

The CLIA Report findings include:
1. **A New World:** 42% of both cruisers and non-cruisers alike seem to agree that they go on vacation to see or do new things, while many other travelers (33%) look to relax and disconnect from their daily stressors. Eighty-eight percent of cruisers say cruises are better for total relaxation over land-based vacations.
2. **Diversity at Sea:** Contrary to common perceptions, according to the study sample, people who take cruises are younger than those who take land-based vacations. The cruise generation is also more diverse than the noncruisers.
3. **Proper Planning:** The clear majority of cruisers plan a trip between four and eighteen months prior to departure, as opposed to half of non-cruisers who book land-based vacations less than three months before. Cruisers also dive deep into planning relying on numerous sources of information, including travel agents, multiple websites, word of mouth, travel guides and magazines, social media, and various travel apps.
4. **Kid-Friendly Cruising:** Families looking to travel together often look to the water for a vacation with 46% bringing children along, compared to 29% of land-based travelers. The typical cruise travel group has an average of more than two children, and 42% of cruise parties have children under the age of eighteen.
5. **Destined for Destinations:** In terms of vacation choices, the clear majority of cruisers (68%) and noncruisers (56%) alike identify the vacation destination as the most important factor. This is followed closely by cost and value, with more noncruisers (37%) citing it as the second most important factor versus cruisers (24%). For attractive tourist locations not too far away from ports, the collaboration may become a win-win situation, because cruise scouts are always looking for attractive new destinations.

6. **A Party of Planners:** When it comes to planning vacations, most report the planning is typically left to themselves and their spouses/partners. When children, other family members, and/or travel agents participate in the vacation planning process, the likeliness to take a cruise over a land-based getaway increases. When parents include children over the age of 18 in travel decisions, travelers report it has a positive impact on overall cruise enjoyment.

7. **Agent Allegiance:** Travel agents play a vital role in cruise vacation planning with 82% of cruisers stating they tend to work with a travel agent when booking a cruise compared to 40% of noncruisers.

8. **Cruise Loyalty:** Across all generations, an overwhelming number of those who cruise are loyal to cruise travel. More than six out of ten (63%) of Generation Y/Millennial cruisers will take another cruise, almost seven out of ten (69%) of Generation X cruisers will take a repeat cruise, and half of Boomers will go on to take another cruise trip.

9. **A Matter of Time:** It may only be a matter of time before noncruisers try out a cruise. When asked about the best type of vacation a substantial number (13%) of noncruisers named an ocean cruise as their vacation of choice.

The a.m. nine key arguments presented by cruise industry promoters all have a close link to port business. The touristic industry plays an important role for many cities, and cruise business strengthens the port-city relationship.

20.5 Port Hinterland Access

The interests of ports extend beyond local traffic and transport. Hinterland connections, nationally and internationally, rely on road, rail, and waterway links; plus pipelines for the liquid bulk and gas industry. Both the port authority and the port city should use their influence to establish needed intermodal infrastructure and should collaborate to efficiently accommodate traffic flows and limit transport costs (including external costs). Both, port authorities and terminal operators have a role to play in the integration of hinterland connections into the logistics chain, particularly where they have a public policy role to reduce the externalities of logistics-related activities. While this typically will involve improvements within the port area itself, or in the connections between the port and the hinterland networks, there may be arguments for involvement in hinterland connections more distant from the port. Driven by a desire to grow business, to create jobs, and to increase local revenues and taxes, an important objective is typically the intention to boost port throughput in the face of competition from other ports.

It has been asserted in many studies and consulting works that in door-to-door transport chains, the costs of hinterland transportations are higher than maritime transport costs (sea freight including all components) and port costs combined.[8] Various examples show that the share of land-based transportation is often less than 20% of total distance, but covers 80% + of all costs. Therefore, an efficient interface between port and hinterland transport mode—often referred to as "the last mile in" or "the first mile out"—is of huge importance and is an integral part of the ports competitive strategy. Efficient access from the national road, rail, or waterway network into the port—or out of the port—should be of key interest for the port authority, the operators and the port industry. Although they do not have a direct influence on transport and infrastructure policy, they depend on it.

Due to the frequent direct business contacts with BCOs or their agents, shipping lines are aware of the increasing importance of the quality of the land connections for their customers, given the potential that they must affect the overall door-to-door performance of the logistics chain. Given that ports' hinterland areas have typically been growing, from both the perspective of specific ports and of product supply chains, the importance of considering port hinterland connections including the last miles in and out of the terminals has increased. The increase of costly traffic jams caused by congested port access connections led to the availability and performance of inland connections becoming one of the key criteria applied by deep-sea container shipping lines when deciding on port calls. Inland transport costs are an important factor in port choice, with this being a function of the quality of the connections available.

Poorly performing ports, interfaces, or internal transport networks could significantly reduce the volume of international trade. Even with full internalization of environmental and social costs, further capacity will be required at ports and on the hinterland routes. It seems clear that an increasing strain will be placed on port hinterland connections if the current hub-based shipping model in container business continues to develop, since larger volumes of goods will need to be moved to/from the hinterland areas of the major ports. This may benefit the rail and inland waterway modes, which are better able than roads to move large volume efficiently. If there is a move towards more direct service provision, a different set o hinterland connections would be expected to develop. Pricing of the environmental and social costs is an important issue, too. If fully implemented into hinterlan

---

8 See, for example, Figure 6.10: Logistics Costs Analysis.

costs it will substantially alter the status quo of port hinterland flows in favor of alternative modes and, perhaps, different logistic chain structures.

The Sad Case of Koper

Along with efficient port operations, well-functioning hinterland connections are an important factor in maintaining the dominance of the established northern range ports of the Hamburg-Antwerp-Range in Europe. This makes it more difficult for ports in the Mediterranean to gain a larger share of the market, even from Asia where they would be expected to have an advantage in terms of distance and time. Therefore, all Mediterranean ports including the Port of Koper (see Figure 20.1) still largely serve hinterlands that are far more restricted than those of the large North-European ports such as Rotterdam, Antwerp, and Hamburg.

The port of Koper (in Slovene: Luka Koper) is the principal port in Slovenia and the most important container port in the North Adriatic. Luka Koper is some 2,000 nautical miles closer to destinations east of Suez than the ports of northern Europe, that is, it could be an attractive, efficient, and cost saving alternative nodal point for supply chains from East Asia to South and Central Europe. Hinterland transport by road and rail to the main industrial regions in Central Europe is substantially shorter than from North European ports; up to 500 km.

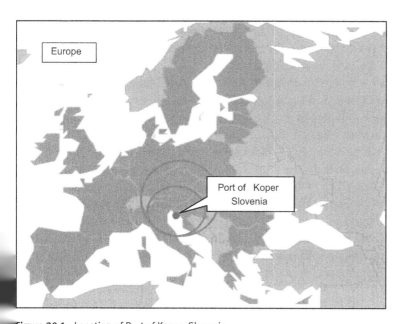

Figure 20.1: Location of Port of Koper, Slovenia

Around 60% of total traffic moves by rail over a steeply-graded single-line connection to the main network. Its continued growth is a function, to a greater or lesser extent, of three factors:

- The forecasted general growth in traffic, particularly containers
- The extent to which the port can increase its market share for central European traffic at the expense of the Dutch and German ports
- The extent to which Koper can maintain or increase its share of transit traffic in competition with other North Adriatic ports

The first factor is primarily influenced by the growth in GDP of the main trading regions whose traffic uses North Adriatic Ports. The second factor is heavily influenced by the strategies of major container lines and the extent to which they operate direct intercontinental hub port calls in the Mediterranean, and/or calls to North Adriatic ports, and Koper in particular. Finally, the share of the market which Koper can achieve is a function of port capacity, efficiency, charges, and hinterland connections compared to neighboring ports within the relevant hinterland.

Approximately 70% of the traffic the Port of Koper handled in the past was transit traffic from Central European countries (particularly Austria, Slovakia, Germany, and Hungary), which has increased substantially over the past decade. Forecasts of several studies[9] show that the largest cargo potential is in southern Germany, but it is also true that the port in southern Germany has not been able to get access to this potential for more than a decade; although it is obvious that substantial cost savings are achievable.

This sad story of failed market access originated from management failure. The port management was not willing to accept that they needed to team up with partners that could help them gain access to the main high-volume markets. The management over years has been self-centered, only saw the own success, but neglected that port business is part of supply chain business, and that partners are needed. And since the city is represented in the management board of the port as well, the port-city relationship deteriorated this process.

There is no doubt that a port like Koper with such a prominent location has the potential to change the transport geography and reroute a substantial amount of cargo; but only when bearing in mind that ports need to act as partners. Narcissistic and self-serving behavior in management is certainly not helpful in this process.

---

9 See, for example, OECD Koper 2015.

Chapter 21
Port Community Systems

21.1 Background of PCS

Fast, safe, reliable, and efficient communication between stakeholders of international cargo transport and all other transport and logistics providers is an important factor of success for a port. Or in other words: good communication is a key driver that has the power to influence (positively or negatively) the growth of a part of a port or the whole port. A port community system (PCS) is an electronic platform that facilitates communication via connection of the multiple systems operated by a variety of companies and organizations that make up a seaport community. Key drivers for the establishment of PCSs were, on the one hand, the need for a standardized and easy-to-use communication platform to improve individual systems in terms of punctuality, reliability or costs. On the other hand, the system arose out of the need to increase a port's competitive position. Simplification and reduction of procedures and documents made PCS necessary, especially in growing markets. An often-heard argument is that of a "single window" solution, as Figure 21.1 (which has already been used in Chapter 2/Figure 2.2) illustrates:

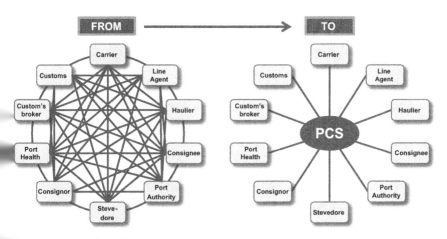

Figure 21.1: Idea of a port community system

Instead of having a communication infrastructure where everybody communicates with everyone else individually, as illustrated on the left side, the central

DOI 10.1515/9781547400874-021

PCS provides the infrastructure and tools in order to handle electronic communication in ports between the terminals, shipping lines, hinterland transport operators (pre- and on-carriage by road, rail and inland waterways), importers and exporters, port authorities, customs, other authorities like port health or veterinary control, as well as with other stakeholders. In this understanding, a PCS is a trade facilitation tool that links administrative and operational procedures electronically via the exchange of messages. Typical messages that are centrally connected:

- Electronic exchange of customs declarations and customs responses, and cargo releases between private parties and customs
- Electronic handling of all information regarding import and export of containerized, general and bulk cargo for the port community
- Status information and control, tracking and tracing goods through the whole logistics chain
- Processing declarations of dangerous goods with the responsible authorities

One of the most useful functions of a PCS is to automatically derive information needed by customs, such as the customs manifest. This information can then be sent to customs without further manual intervention. Most PCSs have their own internal standards but communicate with other PCSs or trade communities using international standards, in particular those developed by United Nations/ Electronic Data Interchange for Administration, Commerce and Transport (UN/ EDIFACT; ISO standard ISO 9735); further development of this standard is done through the United Nations Centre for Trade Facilitation and Electronic Business (UN/CEFACT). These standards allow:

- A set of syntax rules to structure data
- An interactive exchange protocol (I-EDI)
- Standard messages, which allow multicountry and multi-industry exchange

According to the web page of the International Port Community Systems Association (IPCSA)[1] PCSs in Europe have a long tradition. The first to be established in ports in Germany, France, and UK began to operate in the late 1970s or early 1980s. Countries such as the Netherlands and Spain started their PCSs in the 1990s or at the turn of the century.

A good collaboration with the key authorities, as well as with stakeholders, potential customers and local trade associations, was critical in the setting up of

---

1 Refer to: http://ipcsa.international

the respective PCS, which were—and still are—implemented by means of special training and workshops with the end users.

The installed IT infrastructure in ports varies a lot; from a situation where little or no automated processes are in place up to sophisticated solutions. The installation or upgrade of a PCS is widely an organizational task, and not that much a technical problem, because processes of, for example, communication lines, need to be restructured. Therefore, an ideal situation for the installment of a PCS is a situation where changes in port organization have been identified, and the necessity of reorganization is widely accepted.

The number of ports connected to a PCS varies from one to many. Smaller ports often join forces to set up a PCS or connect to an already existing PCS of a larger port or ports.

International PCS Association—Definitions

A PCS:
-   Is a neutral and open electronic platform enabling intelligent and secure exchange of information between public and private stakeholders to improve the competitive position of the sea and air ports' communities
-   Optimizes, manages, and automates port and logistics processes through a single submission of data and connecting transport and logistics chains

A PCS Operator:
-   Is an organization that is either public, private, or public/private that operates and maintains a PCS and where the PCS represents the core of that organization's business
-   Has a board, or some form of steering committee, made up of representatives from different internal and external groups within the port and logistics community
-   Has "service level agreements" with PCS users to manage the electronic exchange of information between different parties on their behalf

A Single Window Operator:
-   Is the organization that has the legal responsibility for implementation and operation of a single window within a country or region and that operates the single window within that remit, whereby the single window allows parties involved in trade and transport to lodge standardized information and documents

Typical PCS Services

A PCS is a modular system with functionality designed to provide all the various sectors and players within a port community environment with tools specific to them, thus delivering a tightly integrated system. Developed for port users by port users, a PCS encompasses exports, imports, transhipments, consolidations, hazardous cargo, and maritime statistics reporting.

PCSs in general provide a huge range of services and key features, which can be summarized as follows:
– Easy, fast, and efficient EDI information exchange, reuse and centralization, available 24/7/365
– Customs declarations
– Electronic handling of all information regarding import and export of containerized, general, and bulk cargo
– Status information and control, tracking and tracing through the whole logistics chain
– Processing of dangerous goods
– Processing of maritime and other statistics

With all these services come many advantages. The core benefits for all parties involved are higher efficiency and speed regarding port processes, particularly through automatization and the reduction of paperwork. In this way, PCSs contribute to sustainable transport logistics and support a port's ambitions to meet global carbon reduction requirements.

The functionality is aimed at eliminating unnecessary paperwork, which can slow down cargo handling. Using electronic data exchange, the PCS is an effective real-time information system; fast, focused, flexible, and multifaceted, it aims to improve efficiency at all stages of the process of manifesting, through vessel discharge and loading, Customs clearance, port health formalities and delivery in and out of the terminal.

As well as the above, the PCS offers improved security, cost reduction and potentially more competitiveness for each user. At the beginning of their development, PCSs were criticized as nothing more than a better "central mailbox system," but as the descriptions of IPCSA show: today such a system has the real potential to offer a variety of value-added services that are featured to strengthen a ports competitive edge.

21.2 Big Data in Port Business

Big data is the name given to the large volume of data—both structured and unstructured—that is generated in personal and professional lives. The analysis of this big data can be extremely useful as it allows businesses to uncover hidden patterns, unknown correlations, ambiguities, market trends, and other useful information. The term "Big Data" itself was defined in 2001 by Doug Laney of the information technology (IT) research and advisory firm Gartner under the three Vs of variety, velocity, and volume. Variety relates to the wide-ranging methods available for capturing data, velocity occurs in the rate of changes and the speed at which data is linked, and volume describes the amount of data that is collected and/or needed. This definition has since been enlarged, and today the dimensions of big data are often described by five Vs:

- Volume
- Velocity (speed retrieve and process)
- Variety (sources and methods)
- Veracity (reliability or quality of data)
- Value

Big data from ports and terminals mainly originates from three major sources, but a PCS with all its information collected might be a source in the future as well. Today's key sources are:

- The technical terminal operating system (TOS), that manages most of the terminal processes, from documentation to planning and from execution of vessel operations to billing. It is a treasure house of rich data, especially on inventory changes, work plans, and sequences for dispatching jobs.
- Data from the field, from sensors and programmable logic controllers that are integrated parts of cargo handling equipment.
- Commercial data from the administrative management and controlling systems, like SAP data.

Usually, such data mostly remains under-processed or under-analyzed. The pure existence of huge data volumes is not a target by itself; "Big data" is not a target, rather the insights that arise when that data is mined and analyzed are. Massive and detailed information without proper analytical tools are useless and are often a source of frustration, because the value inside is not visible. Adequate analytical tools are necessary to extract the value.

The use of big data analytics in ports and terminals goes beyond analyzing past operations to forecast future activities. With the help of detailed data collection and tracking, port operators can easily report real-time data to customers, improving their service offerings and minimizing complaints. This feature not only boosts overall customer service, it also frees up time for operators to focus on other matters. The following are some enhanced possibilities:

Optimizing Usage:

Unlocking big data from port operations makes it easier to optimize usage of resources and infrastructure. For example, a typical crane operator works only one-quarter of the time, remaining idle for three-quarters of the time, waiting to get a container ready to load or for an empty truck to unload a container. Increasing the number of trucks may not be a viable solution owing to the congestion it would cause. Rather, big data analysis could synchronize movements, so that the crane operator is enabled to a more continuous and efficient work flow. For instance, signals related to crane position, status, and GPS position signals could synchronize movement of trucks and containers, to reduce idle time. Also, cranes show different performance levels according to various factors such as skill of driver, workload, weather, container type, and yard density. Understanding such patterns makes it possible to either find solutions to overcome the roadblocks, or synchronize operations, ultimately enhancing productivity. All this information can potentially be shared via a PCS with relevant customers.

The application of statistical analytics to the data stream uncovers operational insights, such as underutilized equipment. Harvesting operational data from sensors placed inside machines also makes it possible to predict when a part might fail, paving the way for a more effective preventive or maintenance schedule as opposed to following the maintenance schedule recommended by the manufacturer. Such an approach allows for timely replacements, fixing problems before they happen, resulting in significant direct and indirect savings.

The primary goal of preventive maintenance based on data-analysis is to avoid or mitigate the consequences of equipment failure. This may be by preventing the failure before it occurs. It is designed to preserve and restore equipment reliability by replacing worn components before they fail. Maintenance activities include partial or complete overhauls at specified periods, oil changes, lubrication, minor adjustments, and so on. In addition, workers can record equipment deterioration, so they know to replace or repair worn parts before they cause system failure. The ideal big data-supported machine maintenance program would prevent any unnecessary and costly repairs.

The main promise of predictive maintenance is to allow convenient scheduling of corrective maintenance, and to prevent unexpected equipment failures. The key is the right information in the right time; here the analysis based on big data comes in. By knowing which equipment needs maintenance, the work can be better planned (spare parts, people, etc.) and what would have been "unplanned stops" are transformed to shorter and fewer "planned stops," thus increasing plant availability. Other potential advantages include increased equipment lifetime, increased terminal safety, fewer accidents with a negative environmental impact, and optimized spare parts handling.

Accurate Predictions:
Big data analytics unlocks data hitherto not visible, and consolidates information from various sources, including yard equipment, vessels, machinery, and terminal operating software. This leads to insights otherwise difficult or impossible to fathom. Unlocking relevant operational patterns allows decision makers to not just optimize operations, but also anticipate events.

Data from sensors placed in port equipment could help port operators design a predictive model for each type of machine, maximizing the efficiency of port equipment, leading to cost savings. Sensors and monitoring cameras could identify patterns of container stacking according to vessels, and such information could simulate future terminal operations and performance predictions, allowing for optimized plans for yard space and equipment, and making it possible to accurately predict the number of cranes, yard trucks, and other container handling equipment required.

Benefits to the Port Ecosystem:
The positive benefits of data analytics help not just the port operators, but extend to the complete port ecosystem as well. As shared information via a PCS, these benefits can also be used as input for other supply chain partners and stakeholders. This information is also of interest to partners not directly involved in the business but with interest in port and shipping activities, like several government institutions that are connected to the PCS. For instance, shipping companies with access to the port's big data insights can predict costs and turnaround times with accuracy. Logistics companies with access to the port's big data can anticipate the expected demand of trucks on any given day, and schedule accordingly.

Major international hubs like the Port of Rotterdam and the Port of Los Angeles are harnessing the power of data to gain insights and drive transparency across the industry, while reducing costs and improving overall productivity. As the industry continues to evolve, the way in which ports leverage the value of data will become an increasingly important competitive differentiator.

Challenges

The three essential basic parts of infrastructure required for the successful application of big data in any port environment are:

- Devices that can measure different conditions, such as GPS sensors and RFID tags.
- An environment that transmits measured data reliably and in real time, mostly Wi-Fi connection.
- A system that can store and manage the transmitted data and offer a platform to analyze it.

The success of big data interventions on the port site depends on reliability of the communication network, and its real-time responsiveness. Networks in port cannot rely on wired connections; they require high-speed Wi-Fi, with stability, or a means to bypass the network infrastructure into an alternative route if problems crop up. A key challenge specific to port environment is that radio waves that carry Wi-Fi connection bounce off instead of passing through iron equipment such as cranes and containers. Areas with such Wi-Fi shadows need to be identified and eliminated. Stories of straddle carrier drivers who only share with good friends the secret information about "invisible parking lots" e.g. behind a shed are stories of the past.

Big data in combination with applied analytics has the potential to transform the maritime industry. Through application and insights, big data has the power to create new opportunities and to drive innovation and deliver tangible operational efficiencies across the port and shipping world. But information alone, also when shared with interested PCS partners, is not enough. It is the analysis of this data and the actionable insights it provides that will move the industry forward and determine its future. An advanced PCS may take over additional functionalities in the future.

21.3 Maritime 4.0

Historically, the world has experienced three major growth periods where disruptive technology has brought about huge productivity improvements in manufacturing. More specifically, the invention and implementation of the steam engine in the 1800s (phase 1: mechanization), Ford's mass production model of the early 1900s (phase 2: mass production/assembly lines), and the first wave of automation with the birth of IT in the 1970s (phase 3: automation, computers & electronics). Industry 4.0 is the common name used to describe the overall current trend towards a fully connected and automated manufacturing system, or Smar

Factory. All production decisions are optimized based on real time information from a fully integrated and linked set of equipment and people (phase 4: cyber physical systems, internet of things and advanced networks). Maritime 4.0 in this context describes the process the maritime industry is currently undergoing: a transformation because of increasing digitalization in the areas of development, production, and services. Maritime 4.0 brings the fourth industrial revolution to the maritime sector and leads to the increased digitalization of this industry.

Maritime 4.0 will result in great opportunities for the maritime sector: it is anticipated that new processes in development, production, operation and port logistics will result in a substantial increase in efficiency. IT-based development, for instance, will lead to an increased innovation dynamic and faster implementation of ideas in products that are ready for market. Flexible and interlinked manufacturing systems enable small batch and custom-made production at competitive prices. 3D printing will also become more common, competing with traditional manufacturing processes in the maritime industry.

Existing digital industry technologies encompassed by Maritime 4.0 include:
- Internet of things
- Autonomous robots
- Cloud computing
- Big data/analytics
- Additive manufacturing
- System integration
- Augmented reality
- Simulation
- Cyber security

This merging of IT with operational maritime technology provides the potential for automation to facilitate process improvement and productivity optimization. The resulting innovation will eventually lead to the development of radical new business models and, eventually, alternate revenue sources, all of which have their foundations in information and services. PCSs in this context can act as a data provider and facilitator.

Targeted analysis, assessment, and management of data flows will transform processes used in merchant shipping and in the ports sector. The collection and collation of data—where applicable even in real time—(e.g., data on weather, navigation, shipping operations, loading, railway, and truck operations) are an important requirement for optimizing shipping operations and for ensuring that operations run smoothly at ports and in the logistics chain. Interlinking production and logistics using IT systems, or the so-called digital life cycle management, opens new business segments. The use of digital technologies, which are continuing to grow at a rapid pace, is becoming a decisive competitive factor for the whole maritime sector.

Given its international activity, it is of the utmost importance that the maritime industry pursues a common international approach for technical regulation. Digitalization in marine technology brings with it new safety and security requirements such as the approval and certification of ship components, systems, and digital networks on board. This too requires the amendment of international provisions. It is important to make experts views known early on in international agreement and standardization processes—and to voice these views to the International Maritime Organization (IMO), International Organization for Standardization (ISO), and the International Electro-Technical Commission (IEC). At the same time, the correct parameters must be set for data security, data protection, and the management of rights of disposal.

A key to success for Maritime 4.0, however, will remain the question of data security. The interconnected nature of Maritime 4.0-driven operations and the pace of digital transformation mean that cyber-attacks can have far more extensive effects than ever before, and terminal operators and their supply networks may not be prepared for the risks. For cyber risk to be adequately addressed in the age of Industry 4.0, cyber security strategies should be secure, vigilant, and resilient, as well as fully integrated into corporate strategy from the start. Developing a fully integrated strategic approach to cyber risk is fundamental for the success of all Maritime 4.0 initiatives, and exactly here the fire-wall-function of a PCS can be of help: PCS in the future may act as an outside fire-wall against cyber-attacks and will protect the data that is handled inside the PCS network. Today, this is still a vision, but due to the utmost importance of data security in networks, this topic may become the crux of the matter for Maritime 4.0.

Another important factor for success is the workforce. Education and needs geared training remains a crucial lever and must be adapted to meet the requirements of rapid digitalization.

21.4 Game Changer: Blockchain

A game changer changes the way that something is done, thought about or made and a key question that needs to be answered is whether the blockchain technology has the potential to re-define the business purpose of PCSs, or whether PCS can act as a facilitator by exploring the benefits of this new technology.

Blockchain is considered a groundbreaking innovation in IT. Known by most as the technology that enabled the rise of Bitcoin, blockchain has lately sparke a huge hype around its potential applications. It is known as the first native digital medium for value, just as the Internet was the first native digital medium for information. Although the technology is still in its early stages and has not reached enterprise adoption yet, blockchain applications advance far beyond digital currencies. Financial, health, energy and logistics sectors are just a few examples of industries that can profit from the disruptive technology. Sometimes blockchain is discussed as a logical enhancement of Maritime 4.0.

As blockchain technology becomes more established in different sectors, vendors, and developers are also looking at its potential use in the logistic sector. Supply chains and logistics, in particular, are considered as fertile ground for blockchain implementation due to the several parties involved in the logistic processes and the lack of trust that usually characterizes the industry. The disruptive technology is regarded as a potential means of establishing the integration of the different actors in the supply chain, enhancing the information flow among them, and ensuring security as well as cost effectiveness.

Frontrunners within the maritime industry have already taken an interest in blockchain technology. In January 2018, for example, IBM and Maersk announced their intention to establish a joint venture to provide more efficient and secure methods for conducting global trade using blockchain technology. The new company aims at bringing the industry together on an open global trade digitization platform that offers a suite of digital products and integration services.[2] The target is to create a blockchain platform that will benefit participants throughout shipping supply chains, including manufacturers, shipping lines, freight forwarders, port and terminal operators, shippers, and customs authorities. To do this, the joint venture will promote an open industry platform using IBM Blockchain technology that will benefit all the players in the ecosystem.

As an innovative player in port logistics, the Port of Rotterdam is interested in inspecting the potential advantages brought by the disruptive technology, particularly by the applications that are currently on the market. Commissioned by PCS "portbase," this project aims to provide a clearer overview of the technology capabilities in the environment of the port of Rotterdam as well as a starting point for future research.

Despite the several private projects and startups that are blossoming in the market, there is still great uncertainty concerning the implementations and benefits of blockchain solutions for the industry. Still, expectations are high, and the

---

2 For more details, visit IBM's website: https://www.ibm.com/blogs/blockchain/2018/01/digitizing-global-trade-maersk-ibm/

future will show to what extent the technology can support the need to ease maritime transport and to increase efficiency along the maritime supply chain. The role the existing PCS can play will be seen.

Chapter 22
Environmental Issues

International shipping is the most energy efficient mode of mass transport. However, because no progress in emissions reductions have been realized in years, shipping is an ever-growing contributor to overall carbon dioxide (CO_2) emissions, and ports as partners along the supply chains are also contributors. A global approach to further improve port and shipping energy efficiency, to reduce emissions and to install effective emission control is needed, as maritime transport will continue growing apace with world trade.

An important step toward emission reduction is the Kyoto Protocol to the United Nations Framework Convention on Climate Change (UNFCCC), an international treaty that sets binding obligations on industrialized countries; adopted in Kyoto, Japan, in 1997. It is an international agreement, binding targets for 37 industrialized countries and the European community for reducing greenhouse gas (GHG) emissions. The detailed rules for the implementation of the Protocol were adopted in Marrakesh in 2001, and are called the "Marrakesh Accords." The Kyoto Protocol entered into force on February 16, 2005. It contains provisions for reducing GHG emissions from international aviation and shipping and treats these sectors in a different way to other sources due to their global activities. The International Maritime Organization (IMO), as the United Nations' specialized agency for shipping, is responsible for enforcing this for the shipping sector.

In 2007, the so-called Bali Roadmap was agreed to: a framework for climate change mitigation beyond 2012. Regular meetings, workshops as well as national and international conferences took place since then, including the 2009 United Nations Climate Change Conference, commonly known as the Copenhagen Summit. Close to 115 world leaders attended the high-level summit, making it one of the largest gatherings of world leaders ever outside UN headquarters in New York. More than 40,000 people, representing governments, nongovernmental organizations, intergovernmental organizations, faith-based organizations, media, and UN agencies applied for accreditation. The Copenhagen Conference marked the culmination of a two-year negotiating process to enhance international climate change cooperation under the Bali Roadmap. But unfortunately, the conference resulted in a weak and non-binding political agreement entitled the "Copenhagen Accord," which was not based on the texts developed by either of the official working groups preparing the conference input.

After the conference, many recognized the historical significance of the Copenhagen Conference, highlighting its unprecedented success in bringing together most of the world's leaders to consider climate change and listing miti-

DOI 10.1515/9781547400874-022

gation actions pledged by developed and developing countries, as well as provisions on finance and technology. Most delegates, however, left Copenhagen disappointed at what they saw as a "weak agreement," and questioning its practical implications given that the Copenhagen Accord had not been formally adopted as the outcome of the negotiations. Almost everyone participating in the negotiations openly admitted that the Copenhagen Summit and the Accord is "far from a perfect agreement" and not a step forward on the Bali Roadmap. For the port and logistics industry, key questions for emission reduction and control are still not answered.

From a technical and operational point of view, it is obvious that GHG emissions from international shipping can not be attributed to any national economy due to its global activities and complex operation. Therefore, IMO has been energetically pursuing the limitation and reduction of GHG emissions from international shipping, in recognition of the magnitude of the climate change challenge and the intense focus on this topic. Because of these activities within the shipping sector, and as reaction of increasing pressure out of the producing industry, ports must follow these developments.

According to the Second IMO GHG Study in 2009, which is the most comprehensive and authoritative assessment of the level of GHG emitted by ships, total shipping was estimated to have emitted 1,046 million tons, or about 3.3% of the global man-made emissions of carbon dioxide in 2007. Exhaust gases are the primary source of GHG emissions from ships and CO_2 is the most important GHG, both in terms of quantity and of global warming potential. Mid-range scenarios of the Second IMO GHG Study 2009 show that, by 2050, those emissions could grow by a factor of 2 to 3 if no regulations to stem them are enacted. The Study identifies a significant potential for reduction of GHG emissions through technical and operational measures. The Study estimates that, if implemented, these measures could increase efficiency and reduce the emissions rate by 25% to 75% below the current level. This has a huge influence on shipping networks and consequently on ports, terminals, and hinterland operation.

In 1973, the "International Convention for the Prevention of Pollution from Ships" was adopted. This worldwide convention for the protection of the marine environment is commonly known as MARPOL or, more formally, MARPOL 73/7 (as in MARitime POLlution). The Articles of the Convention contain general provisions such as applicable definitions and scope. The Convention additionally contains two Protocols and six Annexes, each dealing with oil pollution or other noxious or harmful liquids or substances carried by ship, and the pollution caused by ships, as opposed to their cargo, such as ship garbage, sewage and air pollution. The annexes I to VI of the Convention deal with different types of marine pollution attributable to shipping.

MARPOL replaced and enhanced a 1954 treaty called OILPOL, short for International Convention for the Prevention of Pollution of the Sea by Oil. The treaty had not yet come into force when, in 1978, some high-profile oil tanker environmental disasters motivated the international law community, acting through the IMO, to amend the 1973 version so that by the time it was formally released for acceptance by individual states, it included both the original 1973 version and the 1978 amendments; hence, "MARPOL 73/78." The Annexes I to VI of the Convention deal with different types of marine pollution attributable to shipping:

Annex I: Prevention of Pollution by Oil
Annex II: Control of Pollution by Noxious Liquid Substances in Bulk
Annex III: Prevention of Pollution by Harmful Substances carried by Sea in Packaged Form
Annex IV: Prevention of Pollution by Sewage from Ship
Annex V: Prevention of Pollution by Garbage from Ships
Annex VI: Prevention of Air Pollution from Ships

22.1 Emission Control Areas

Emission control areas (ECAs) are sea areas in which stricter controls were established to minimize airborne emissions from ships as defined by Annex VI of the 1997 MARPOL Protocol. Two sets of emission and fuel quality requirements are defined by MARPOL Annex VI:

1. Global requirements
2. More stringent requirements applicable to ships in ECAs. An ECA can be designated for Sulfur (SOx) and particulate matter (PM), or oxides of nitrogen (NOx), or all three types of emissions from ships.

Existing ECAs as displayed in Figure 22.1 include:

- Baltic Sea (SOx, adopted: 1997/entered into force: 2005)
- North Sea (SOx, 2005/2006)
- North American ECA, including most of the U.S. and Canadian coast (NOx & SOx, 2010/2012)
- U.S. Caribbean ECA, including Puerto Rico and the U.S. Virgin Islands (NOx & SOx, 2011/2014).

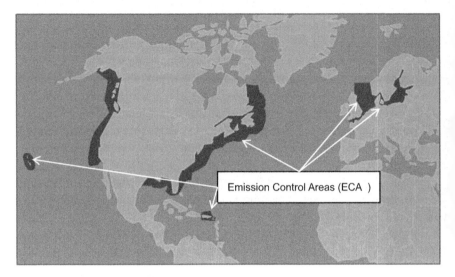

Figure 22.1: Emission control areas

Additional areas may be added to Annex VI in the future. Potential future ECAs (already under discussion for a few years) are:
- Gulf of Mexico/Caribbean
- English Channel/Bay of Biscay/Celtic Sea
- South European Atlantic coast/France, Spain, Portugal
- Mediterranean Sea
- Black Sea
- Gulf of Thailand/Street of Malacca/Andaman Sea
- East China Sea
- Sea of Japan/Japan East coast

Sulfur (SOx) and particulate matter (PM) emission controls for ships apply to all fuel oil, combustion equipment, and devices onboard and therefore include both main and all auxiliary engines together with items such as boilers and inert gas generators. These controls differentiate between those applicable inside Emission Control Areas established to limit the emission of SOx and particulate matter, and those applicable outside such areas. The controls are primarily achieved by limiting the maximum sulfur content of the fuel oils as loaded, bunkered, and subsequently used onboard. These fuel oil sulfur limits (expressed in terms of % m/m—that is, by weight) are subject to a series of step changes over the years. The actual IMO MARPOL regulations 14.1 and 14.4 of Annex VI are defining the roadmap (see Table 22.1).

Table 22.1: IMO Regulations 14.1 and 14.4 (inside an ECA and outside)

Outside an ECA established to limit SOx and particulate matter emissions	Inside an ECA established to limit SOx and particulate matter emissions
4.50% m/m prior to 1 January 2012	1.50% m/m prior to 1 July 2010
3.50% m/m on and after 1 January 2012	1.00% m/m on and after 1 July 2010
0.50% m/m on and after 1 Jan. 2020*	0.10% m/m on and after 1 Jan. 2015

* depending on the outcome of a review, to be concluded in 2018, as to the availability of the required fuel oil, this date could be deferred to 1 January 2025.

Unlike nitric oxide emissions, sulfur oxides can not be reduced by modifying the combustion process inside an engine. All the sulfur contained in the fuel is released in the exhaust gas. A substantial reduction in sulfur emissions can be achieved by switching from heavy fuel oil to fuels with lower sulfur content—such as marine diesel oil or natural gas. This solution could initially be used in coastal ECAs or in harbors, while ships on the high seas can continue to be powered by conventional fuel. The dual tank arrangement required for this, however, is costly and space-consuming. The fuels mentioned above are also significantly more expensive than conventional heavy fuel oil. It must be kept in mind that the operating costs of a vessel are largely made up of fuel costs.

Ships trading in designated emission control areas must use fuel oil on board with a sulfur content of no more than 0.10% from January 1, 2015, against the limit of 1.00% in years before. These sulfur emission control areas (SECAs) are sea areas where there are stricter requirements to use bunker fuel compared to other sea areas. Actual SECAs include the North Sea, Baltic Sea, and within 24 miles of the California coast. Several states over the last few years added special areas for oil, sewage, garbage and air pollution, so that it became complicated for the shipping industry to oversee all regulations that exist.

In 2017 the IMO provided an overview about all relevant areas for shipping. In circulation 778-REV2, dated 6. April 2017 the IMO published this overview about "Special Areas, Emission Control Areas and Particularly Sensitive Sea Areas."[1] Regarding air pollution, the ECAs are still the most important areas that ships need to observe. The stricter rules and the implementation dates are displayed in Figure 22.2. In this figure we assume that the regulation will not be postponed. A review that will be concluded in 2018 may propose at the next IMO MEPC meeting

---

International Maritime Organization (IMO): List of Special Areas, Emission Control Areas and Particularly Sensitive Sea Areas, MEPC.1/Circ.778/Rev.2, London, UK 2017.

that the date could be deferred to 2025, the latest possible day. Although the initiative to postpone is heavily supported by shipping industry lobbyists; the outcome of the review according to political statements will likely be to keep January 2020 as the implementation date.

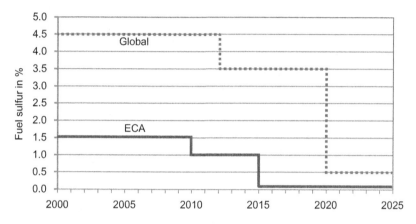

Figure 22.2: Fuel sulfur limits and implementation dates

A ship normally is equipped with a heavy fuel oil system with a one-day tank system or two-day tanks. If the ship has two-day tanks, then one day tank can be filled with high sulfur heavy fuel oil and the other with low sulfur fuel oil. The level of filling in the low sulfur tank must be sufficiently high before changing from one to the other tank to avoid a shortage of fuel in case of separator or fuel problems. Before entering the ECA, the fuel supply must be changed from the high sulfur to the low sulfur tank and must be completed in advance before entering the ECA. The necessary records of the fuel change shall be made in the log book or into a separate "fuel change over bunker record book."

In the case of a one-fuel system with one day tank, the preparation of low sulfur heavy fuel oil must start well in advance before entering the ECA. The preparation time for the mixing of low and high sulfur fuel must be precalculated to ensure that the sulfur limit of 0.1% is reached before entering the area. For this calculation, computer files (e.g., EXCEL files from fuel oil suppliers) or approved change over manuals (e.g., from classification societies) can be used. Depending on the sulfur content of the fuels and the tank capacities the mixing time can be up to 40 hours or even longer. Changing back to high sulfur fuel oil (HSFO) is allowed only after leaving the ECA; the relevant records shall be made into the appropriate ship's logbook.

CO_2, Sox, and PM have been in environmental discussions for years, and most people are aware of and accept environmental protection activities; although the exact limits of regulations and their dates of implementation aren't widely agreed upon. In coming years, NOx emissions will be a main feature of environmental debate. This is because they are more than twenty times more harmful to the environment compared with CO_2, and also because the supposed fuel of the future liquefied natural gas (LNG) has substantial problems in combustion engines with the so-called methane-slip, that is, the emission of unburned gas. LNG has the advantage of burning with less CO_2 and very limited PM; but critics wonder if this is a real solution. However, many ports in Europe have already invested huge amounts of money to build LNG bunkering stations. The bottom line: NOx emissions needed to be investigated seriously.

Figure 22.3 indicates clearly that NOx emissions caused by shipping are already a serious problem. Data from the Dutch and Finnish-built ozone monitoring instrument (OMI) on NASA's Aura satellite show long tracks of elevated nitrogen dioxide (NO_2) levels along certain shipping routes. NO_2 is among a group of highly-reactive NOx, that can lead to the production of fine particles and ozone that damage the human cardiovascular and respiratory system. Combustion engines, such as those that propel ships and motor vehicles, are a major source of NO_2 pollution.

Tropospheric NO$_2$ Column Density (x 10^{15} molecules/cm^2)

| 0.0 | 0.1 | 0.2 | 0.5 | 1.0 | 2.0 |

Source: http://earthobservatory.nasa.gov/IOTD/view.php?id=80375

Figure 22.3: Tropospheric NOx density caused by shipping

This map is based on OMI measurements acquired between 2005 and 2012. The NO2 signal is most prominent in an Indian Ocean shipping lane between Sri Lanka and Singapore, appearing as a distinct line against (lighter) background levels of NO_2. Other shipping lanes that run through the Gulf of Aden, the Red Sea, and the Mediterranean Sea also show elevated NO_2 levels, as do routes from Singapore to points in China. These aren't the only busy shipping lanes in the world, but they are the most apparent because ship traffic is concentrated along narrow, well-established lanes.

The IMO MARPOL regulations deal with shipping and not with ports; at least not directly. But this does not mean that they have no influence on ports. The interrelations along the supply chain are high, and (beginning in 2020) when a port is located inside a stricter ECA, then this will impact more than just bunkering activities. Shipping lines might re-route trades to other ports outside this area. This can easily be the case for intra-European landlocked markets like Austria or Hungary that have alternatives in going north to the Baltic Sea, or routing the cargo southwards into the Mediterranean Sea, but also directly for countries with sea ports like Poland or the Baltic States. Also, the a.m. OBOR or BRI activities and the promotion of land-based "New Silk Roads" show an option to bypass stricter IMO regulations. The advantages for the shipping lines are obvious: they can use their existing fleet with "more dirty" emissions for a longer time. This saves money. For ports this may lead to (temporary?) losses of ship calls due to reroutings.

New bunker fuel is another topic combined with the ECAs. Ports need to invest to provide bunkers for vessels. This can provide opportunities but might also cause additional costs to stay competitive. However, the emission control areas affect ports in different ways, and it is recommended that ports act proactively.

22.2 Bunker Fuel

The term "bunkering" is commonly used for the replenishment of fuel (or "bunkers") for use by ships. The term originated in the days of steamships, when the fuel (at that time: coal) was stored in special storage containers, called "bunkers." Nowadays the term bunker is generally applied to the storage of petroleum products (fuel oil like HSFO) in tanks, and the practice and business of refueling ships. The process of refilling gas-driven vessels that are powered by LNG is also called "bunkering."

Bunkering operations are located at seaports, and they include the storage of bunker (ship) fuels and the provision of the fuel to vessels.

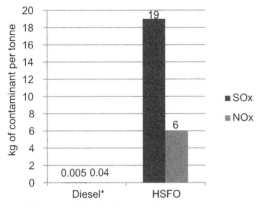

Figure 22.4: Harmful substances in diesel versus bunker fuel oil

All industries are looking to becoming cleaner, greener and more energy efficient—and shipping is no exception. Improved energy efficiency means less fuel is used, and that means fewer harmful emissions. But the most commonly used bunker fuel HSFO compared with the typical automotive gas oil (AGO) or "diesel" at a standard that now common in Europe, Canada, the United States, Russia, Australia, or New Zealand contains much more harmful substances as Figure 22.4 illustrates:

–   SOx 3800 times higher than diesel
–   NOx 150 times higher than diesel
–   Plus, much higher PM pollution

The reason for the huge discrepancy between diesel and bunker fuel lies in the refinery process. Marine distillates historically come from poorer-quality distillate recycle streams that are unsuitable for upgrading to diesel fuel or other low-sulfur products. Thus, the supply chain for the marine fuels industry begins with integrated petroleum refineries, where "bottoms" from atmospheric and vacuum distillation unit operations are combined to form the bulk of residual fuel stocks.

Marine fuel characteristics are determined in part by the quality of the crude oil used to create them and by the refining process. The refining processes used to produce petroleum products, including marine fuels, involve the physical, thermal, and chemical separation of crude oil into its major distillation fractions, followed by further processing into finished petroleum products that can be grouped into three major categories:

Fuels: Motor gasoline, diesel and distillate fuel oil, liquefied petroleum gas, jet fuel, residual fuel oil, kerosene, and coke

- **Finished nonfuel products:** Solvents, lubricating oils, greases, petroleum wax, petroleum jelly, asphalt, and coke
- **Chemical industry feedstocks:** Naphtha, ethane, propane, butane, ethylene, propylene, butylenes, butadiene, benzene, toluene, and xylene

There are three major types of marine fuel: distillate fuel, residual fuel, and a combination of the two to create a fuel type known as "intermediate" fuel oil (IFO). Distillate and residual fuels are blended into various combinations to derive different grades of marine fuel oil. In terms of cost, distillates are more expensive than intermediates, and residual fuels are the least expensive.

Because bunker fuel often represents the highest single cost component in vessel operation, the dirtiest residual fuels are the most commonly used ship fuels. These kinds of bunker fuels are a big threat to the environment, which is why the IMO has pressed the industry for years to substantially reduce harmful pollutants. Studies from J.J. Corbitt[2] and others about mortality from CO, SOx, NOx, and PM generated by shipping calculated that annual mortalities in the EU will increase from 49,500 in 2000 up to 53,400 in 2020. This in addition to 50.000+ premature deaths annually in the EU and health costs that will increase from 58.4 bn Euros/year (2000) to an estimated 64.1 bn Euros/year (2020).

These are inacceptable figures that support the IMO initiatives to reduce the harmful substances in ship fuels, for example, with pollution abatement technologies/exhaust gas cleaning technologies like the so-called "scrubber technologies," or via initiatives to introduce alternative ship fuels, like LNG or methanol. The implication for ports in this process will be that typical bunker ports like Singapore, Rotterdam, and Houston will have to follow the developments and will need to invest in technology; either in new or additional tanks and supportive equipment, or in completely new bunkering facilities for LNG.

Figure 22.5 shows that this will be a long-term process; data for the forecast is taken by various sources, and they all expect the share of residual fuel oil (that is mainly used for bunkering) to decrease very slowly. Only globally active institutions like the IMO will have the power via regulations to speed up the process of replacing the dirty bunker fuel by more environmental friendly ones.

---

2 See, Corbitt 2007: *Mortality from Ship Emissions.*

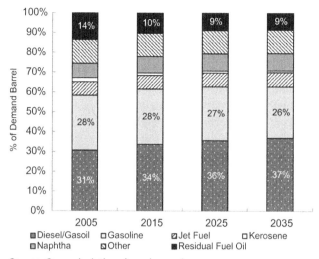

Source: Own calculations based on various sources

Figure 22.5: Long-term oil demand as expected by the oil industry

Even in the long run until 2035 the share of residual fuel oil will be stable at a 9% share; this is only slightly less than what has been burned in 2015. Whether this will materialize, or how fast alternative fuels will come up will be seen. But fact is that the environmental friendliness of ocean transport is a key factor of future sustainability.

Alternatives—LNG, Methanol, and Scrubbers

Alternatives to low sulfur fuel are being sought, and the main alternatives are LNG, methanol, or by the addition of flue gas scrubbing technology.

The proposals for *LNG* are well advanced and several ports are gearing up to supply LNG bunkers. The use of LNG is particularly suited to point-to-point business, such as ferry routes and in river transportation. This is a very fertile field for oil companies, as they have advanced technology and investment capabilities. Should the price of crude oil rise out of line with LNG, it might be worthwhile to ship owners in retrofitting their fleet. This will not happen soon but work on ferries and coasters could be relatively easy to justify.

Methanol is in its infancy and a lot of safety issues are involved that may not be easy to overcome. However, it is a liquid, it is easy to produce from methane, and is sourced from the same fields as the LNG currently being extracted. Methanol is a liquid at room temperature and requires neither cryogenic nor pressure tanks for storage. It can be stored onboard and ashore in similar tanks as oil products. Bunker barges will be small chemical carriers for methanol compared to small gas carriers for LNG. Conversion kits from diesel engines to dual fuel engines (HFO/MGO—methanol) are already on the market, and conversion to methanol will be considerably less expensive than conversion to LNG. Companies like Stena operate several methanol powered ferries already today.

Scrubbing: Exhaust gas cleaning technology installed on board of a vessel causes several problems and requires several years of pay-back, depending on the type and size of the vessel. In addition, enough space on board must be available and the sailors need to be trained. Another big question concerning scrubbing technology is what to do with the liquid that will have scrubbed out the pollutants extracted by the scrubbers? There is no coordinated view on this and unless this issue is solved, many ports could end up with this material.

22.3 Green Ships

According to the Second IMO GHG Study in 2009, only a fraction of the fuel energy going into the ship's main engines ends up generating propulsion thrust. Calculations based on real figures identified that only 43% of the fuel energy is converted into shaft power while the remaining energy is lost in the exhaust or as heat. Due to further losses in the propeller and transmission, only 28% of the energy from the fuel that is fed to the main engine generates propulsion thrust for the vessel investigated. The rest of the energy ends up as heat, as exhaust, and as transmission and propeller losses. The majority of this 28% are spent overcoming hull friction, while the remaining energy is spent in overcoming weather resistance and air resistance, as residual losses and for generating waves.

Ships other than the ones investigated in the IMO GHG Study will have the same types of losses; however, the relative sizes will differ. But what remains is the fact that a lot of smaller and bigger energy saving potentials are available for shipping. The IMO Study provides a long list, where energy savings potentials are realistically available:
- Power transmission
- Power generation
- Design improvements
- Optimization of the superstructure (wind resistance)
- Recovery of propeller energy
- After-body flow-control systems
- Engine energy recovery
- Operational improvements (fleet composition/speed reduction/network design)

- Hull coatings
- Derating of engines
- Engine upgrades
- Propeller maintenance and upgrades
- Other upgrades
- Alternative fuels and energy/LNG/wind power/solar power
- Emission-reduction options for other relevant substances

The challenge and objective of a "green ship" is—according to MARPOL regulations—to be more energy efficient and to reduce CO_2 emissions by around 30% and nitric and sulfuric oxides as well as particulate matters by 90%. Initiatives following this direction are using both familiar and new technologies. Some initiatives already promote the "Zero-emission vessel"[3]; a research project that identifies and tests new technologies like advanced exhaust gas scrubber, exhaust gas recirculation, or—in close combination with ports—the so-called cold ironing; the electric power supply from terminals to ships.[4] Especially when it comes to ports and terminals that are located close or directly inside city centers, like cruise terminals, it is of huge importance to reduce emissions, noise, and vibrations. For this, electricity is an attractive energy alternative. However, due to low standards of electric systems on board as well as at berth, this energy source often fails because of wrong connection plugs with land-based stations or missing converters. Here there is room for improvement for ports.

As already explained in Chapter 22.1, there are a lot of interrelations between vessel, terminals, and ports when installing green technologies to protect the environment, reduce GHG emissions and—if possible—save money. Initiatives to increase energy efficiencies offer cost saving potential.

---

3 With a dream to achieve a Zero Emission Ship by 2030, the Japanese Shipping Line NYK has designed the futuristic "Eco-Ship 2030." The green ship concept has a variety of unique features such as weight reducing structure, optimized hull form for propulsion efficiency, solar and wind power harnessing equipment, and fuel cell utilization to reduce the emission of carbon dioxide by staggering 69%. The ship concept also utilizes new materials such as extra high tensile steel and alloys, and composites, and carries lighter containers and less fuel for a total reduction of 0% weight and 9% carbon dioxide. Further details can be found on NYK web pages: http://www.nyk.com/english/csr/envi/ecoship/

The name "cold ironing" was one of the first names on the market for electric power supply to vessels while at berth; alternatives are: shore connection, shore-to-ship power (SSP) or alternative maritime power (AMP). The Port of Los Angeles was one of the front runner in AMP; refer to: https://www.portoflosangeles.org/environment/amp.asp

22.4 Green Ports

Ports and terminals as well as shipping lines are often not innovators and front-runners when it comes to environmental protection. However, the joint customers within producing industries as well as consumer markets are pushing these topics and asking for a port's carbon footprint and other environmental quality indicators. This means that from the external side there is increasing pressure on ports to offer and produce environmentally friendly services. This, in combination with the pressure coming from local municipalities, is driving the port business to engage more and more in environmental friendly operation. A key question in this process always is "where to be engaged" in protecting the environment and becoming a Green Port.

In 1996 the European Ports Organization (ESPO) sent out a questionnaire with an environmental survey to their member ports, asking about priorities. Two hundred eighty-one ports from fifteen different European countries provided an answer. The process of interviewing a big sample of ports has been repeated in 2004, 2009, 2013 and 2016, and the results are published in the ESPO Green Ports Guide as well as in the EcoPorts Review 2016. Table 22.2 provides an overview of the varying priorities over time; within the twenty-year period (1996 to 2016) the ranking of priorities changed substantially. This has to do with the effect that environmental protection is a relatively young field, and port authorities as public entities must follow the political mainstreams and need to address political pain points.

Table 22.2: ESPO top ten environmental priorities, 1996–2016

	1996	2004	2016
1	Port Development (water)	Garbage / Port waste	Air quality
2	Water quality	Dredging: operations	Energy consumption
3	Dredging disposal	Dredging disposal	Noise
4	Dredging: operations	Dust	Relationship local community
5	Dust	Noise	Garbage/Port waste
6	Port development (land)	Air quality	Ship waste
7	Contaminated land	Hazardous cargo	Port development (land)
8	Habitat loss/degradation	Bunkering	Water quality
9	Traffic volume	Port development (land)	Dust
10	Industrial effluent	Ship discharge (bilge)	Dredging: operations

Source: ESPO/EcoPorts Port Environmental Review 2016, Brussels, Belgium 2016, page 7 + 8.

Six of the top ten topics of 1996 disappeared over time and are no longer on the top ten list in 2016, including the no. 1 priority of 1996: port development (water). At that time, the race began for ever-growing ships, especially in container shipping. The fear of no longer being able to serve bigger vessels made port development a top priority in 1996. In direct relation to this is priority no. 3 in 1996: Dredging disposal. On the other hand, there are also environmental priorities in 2016 on top of the list that were not identified as important issues 20 years before, like air quality, energy consumption, and noise. The different shades in Table 22.2 make it easier to follow up the priorities over time.

Making ports more environmentally friendly, operating them with better energy efficiency, and reducing greenhouse gases where possible is a permanent task that needs to be implemented at the highest level. Port authorities and terminal operators must include environmental targets in their goals, and they should be obligated to follow them. Personal targets of the port and terminal management staff should be linked to the degree of how successful the management has fulfilled these targets. Only this implementation on the highest-level guarantees success. The biggest mistake in the first years of implementing green port targets was made by just creating a new department "environmental protection," providing managers with important titles (like "sustainability manager") and continuing operation in the same way as before. The era of "green-washing" is gone, and today green port targets must be implemented seriously with frequently follow-up.

There is no task in the list of activities of port authorities and terminal operators that can be excluded from an environmental control. For example, as all investment activities of ports and terminals are checked and controlled against KPIs or internal financial criteria, so must activities be checked against their environmental friendliness (measured by reduction of emissions, reduced energy consumption, or other indicators). The list of KPIs needs to be adjusted and indicators for sustainability implemented.

In addition, ports and terminals must be open to new technologies to protect the environment. The use of eco-energy, new fuels like LNG, cold ironing for vessel, investments in technologies that produce less pollution, electric cars and vehicles (Forklifts, AGVs, etc.), advanced management practices, silent operations, waste reduction, and recycling of materials are only a few of the topics that need to be considered and that are discussed in the ESPO Green Port Guide. Sustainability is a permanent task on all levels of port and terminal activity.

22.5 Marine Environment

The world's oceans are mistakenly believed to be an inexhaustible supply of resources with an unlimited capacity for regeneration. The consequences of this false mindset are high ecological risks and considerable negative impacts on the marine environment. Even though the United Nations declared 1998 the "year of the ocean" to highlight the major importance of the oceans for a global balance, oceans often only become the focus of attention when there is yet another accident, or when packing for a holiday by the sea.

Threats are posed by inputs of persistent pollutants (i.e., substances that are nondegradable or not readily degradable in water) and excessive nutrient inputs via rivers, as well as the widespread transport of pollutants via the atmosphere. As a result, organic pollutants such as polychlorinated biphenyls (PCBs), which were formerly used for insulation, or as hydraulic or cooling fluids, can be detected in remote polar regions. Other hazards to the marine environment are caused by shipping (e.g., illegal disposal of wastes, accidents, problems caused by antifouling paints) and inputs of oil and pollutants from the offshore oil and gas industry. Marine ecosystems are also endangered by overfishing and other negative effects of fishing on marine species and habitats. A further threat is that of climate change, which causes sea levels to rise and causes changes in ocean flora and fauna.

As pollution of and processes in the oceans do not stop at political borders, successful marine environmental protection can only be achieved through international cooperation at the regional and global levels. Tackling climate change globally is a priority issue because climate change affects water cycle processes in all regions of our planet. Reckless deforestation and its consequences—erosion, droughts and flooding—affect water resources as well. Due to urbanization, intensive agriculture, and population growth, the pollution of water resources through nitrates and pesticides is still on the rise in many countries around the world.

The IMO's original mandate was principally concerned with maritime safety. However, as the custodian of the 1954 International Convention for the prevention of pollution of the sea by oil (OILPOL Convention), the Organization, soon after it began functioning in 1959, assumed responsibility for pollution issues and subsequently has adopted a wide range of measures to prevent and control pollution caused by ships and to mitigate the damage caused by maritime operations and accidents.

The International Association of Ports and Harbors (IAPH), like the IMO, also focuses more and more on environmental protection and safety of marine life. In 2018 IAPH officially launched the World Ports Sustainability Program (WPSP). The Program aims to demonstrate global leadership of ports in contributing to th

Sustainable Development Goals of the United Nations. It seeks to empower port community actors worldwide to engage with businesses, as well as governmental and societal stakeholders in creating sustainable added value for local port communities and regions.

IMO's Marine Environment Protection Committee (MEPC) in the meantime has evolved from a simple committee to IMO's senior technical body on marine pollution related matters. It is aided in its work by several IMO Sub-Committees, in particular, the Sub-Committee on Pollution Prevention and Response (PPR). This is a great sign that marine environment protection work is a growing cause. It is widely accepted that huge environmental problems exist and oceans need to be cleaned and no longer used as garbage dumps. With at least 8 million tons of plastic waste entering our oceans every year, this issue isn't going away anytime soon. The fact that one in three species of marine mammals have been found entangled in marine litter, and that over 90% of all seabirds have plastic pieces in their stomachs is unacceptable and inhumane.

The marine ecosystem is the largest aquatic system on the planet. Its size and complexity make it difficult to deal with. As a result, it is convenient to divide it into more manageable arbitrary subdivisions, and ports and terminals are part of these subdivisions. To address the complexity of marine environment management regimes, it is essential to develop a methodology and collect the information required for the systematic valuation of ocean assets and services. A lot of these initiatives are already underway, and from a port perspective it is essential not to forget that the port business is part of global life. Ports need to bring their business into the right perspective—not more; but also: not less!

Appendices

Appendix A
Abbreviations

ABS: The American Bureau of Shipping is a U.S. classification society that certifies if a ship follows standard rules of construction and maintenance.

bbl/d: barrels per day; the second "b" in "bbl" can be explained when looking into history: "In the early 1860s, when oil production began, there was no standard container for oil, so oil and petroleum products were stored and transported in barrels of all different shapes and sizes (beer barrels, fish barrels, molasses barrels, turpentine barrels, etc.). By the early 1870s, the 42-gallon barrel had been adopted as the standard for oil trade. This was 2 gallons per barrel more than the 40-gallon standard used by many other industries at the time. The extra 2 gallons was to allow for evaporation and leaking during transport (most barrels were made of wood). Standard Oil began manufacturing 42 gallon barrels that were blue to be used for transporting petroleum. The use of a blue barrel, abbreviated "bbl," guaranteed a buyer that this was a 42-gallon barrel (Source: EIA).

bcm: Billion cubic meter; for conversion into alternative units please refer to: IGU International Gas Union: Natural Gas Conversion Pocket Book.

B/L: Bill of lading; a document that establishes the terms of contract between a shipper and a shipping line. It serves as a document of title, a contract of carriage, and a receipt for goods.

BOT—build-operate-transfer: A form of concession wherein a private party or consortium agrees to finance, construct, operate, and maintain a facility for a specified period and then transfer the facility to a government or other public authority. The concessionaire bears the commercial risk of operating the facility.

BOO—build-own-operate: A form of project wherein a private party or consortium agrees to finance, construct, operate, and maintain a facility previously owned and/or operated by a public authority. The concessionaire retains ownership of the facility. The concessionaire bears the commercial risk of operating the facility.

CFS: Container freight station; a location on terminal grounds where cargo is loaded ("stuffed") into or unloaded ("stripped") from containers.

DOI 10.1515/9781547400874-023

CT: Container terminal.

CTPAT: Customs Trade Partnership Against Terrorism.

DWT: Dead weight tonnage; maximum weight of a vessel including the vessel, cargo and ballast.

e.g.: From Latin "exempli gratia" = "for the sake of example."

EDI or EDIFACT: Electronic data interchange for administration, commerce and trade, the standards being sponsored by the United Nations.

EIA: U.S. Energy Information Administration

FCL: Full container load.

FEU: Forty-foot equivalent unit.

FIO: Free in and out means that the cost of loading and unloading a vessel is borne by the charterer.

GT: Gross tonnage; the sum of container, breakbulk and bulk tonnage.

HNS: Hazardous and noxious substances.

HS: Harmonized system, or, harmonized commodity description and coding system is an internationally standardized system of names and numbers to classify traded products.

IAPH: International association of ports and harbors.

i.e.: From Latin "id est" = "that is."

IMDG: International maritime dangerous goods.

IMO: International Maritime Organization, established through the United Nations to coordinate international maritime safety and related practices.

IPCC: Intergovernmental panel on climate change.

ISO: International Organization for Standardization. Worldwide organization formed to promote development of standards to facilitate the international carriage and exchange of goods and services. Governs construction specifications for ISO containers.

ISPS: International ship and port facilities security code.

JIT: The abbreviation for "just in time," which is a way to minimize warehousing costs by having cargo shipped to arrive just in time for its use. This inventory control method depends on extremely reliable transportation.

LCL: The acronym for "less than container load." It refers to a partial container load that is usually consolidated with other goods to fill a container.

LDO: Lease-develop-operate: A form of concession wherein, under a long-term lease, a private terminal operator upgrades and expands an existing facility and manages its cash flows. The public authority holds title to the facility throughout the concession period and receives lease payments on the assets.

LOA: Length overall: Linear measurement of a vessel from bow to stern.

L/C: Letter of credit: a document issued by a bank per instructions by a buyer of goods authorizing the seller to draw a specified sum of money under specified terms.

LoLo: Lift on-lift off (LO/LO or lolo): Cargo handling technique involving transfer of commodities to and from the ship using shoreside cranes or ship's gear.

LTL: Means a shipment that is "less than truckload." Cargoes from different sources are usually consolidated to save costs.

LT: long ton; a long ton equals 2240 pounds or 1016.047 kg.

MARPOL: International Convention for the Prevention of Pollution from Ships.

MEPC: Marine Environment Protection Committee.

MLW: Mean low water: Lowest average level water reaches on an outgoing tide.

MHW: Mean high water: Highest average level water reaches on an outgoing tide.

MS: Motor ship.

MV: Motor vessel.

NAFTA: North American Free Trade Agreement.

NOx: Nitrogen oxide.

NVOCC: Nonvessel operating common carrier.

OPRC: Convention on Oil Pollution Preparedness, Response, and Cooperation.

pb: Per barrel.

PPP: Public–private partnership.

RMG: Rail-mounted gantry.

Ro/Ro or ro/ro: Roll on/roll/off. A ro/ro ship is designed with ramps that can be lowered to the dock, so cars, buses, trucks, or other vehicles can drive into the belly of the ship, rather than be lifted aboard. A ro/ro ship, like a container ship, has a quick turnaround time of about twelve hours.

RTG: Rubber-tired gantry; a traveling crane used for the movement and positioning of containers in a container field. RTGs may also be used for loading and unloading containers from rail cars.

SOLAS: International Convention for the Safety of Life at Sea.

SOx: Sulfur oxide.

ST: Short ton: A short ton equals 2000 pounds or 907.185 kg.

TEU: A twenty-foot equivalent unit. A standard linear measurement used in quantifying container traffic flows and for describing container ship or terminal capacity. A standard 40 ft container equals 2 TEUs.

THC: Terminal handling charge; a charge made by the shipping line to the shipper reflecting the terminal handling costs.

ULCC: Ultra-large crude carrier.

ULCS: Ultra-large container ship.

UNCLOS: United Nations Convention on the Law of the Sea.

UNFCCC: United Nations Framework Convention on Climate Change.

VLCC: Very large crude carrier.

VLOC: Very large ore carrier.

Appendix B
Glossary[1]

Anchorage: Port charge relating to a vessel moored at approved anchorage site in a harbor.

Apron: The area immediately in front of or behind a wharf shed where cargo is lifted. On the "front apron," cargo is unloaded from or loaded onto a ship. Behind the shed, cargo moves over the "rear apron" into and out of railroad cars.

Backhaul: To haul a shipment back over part of a route where it has already traveled; a marine transportation carrier's return movement of cargo, usually opposite from the direction of its primary cargo distribution.

Barge: Flat-bottomed vessel designed to carry cargo on inland waterways. Barges have no locomotion and are pushed by towboats. A single, standard barge can hold 1,500 tons of cargo or as much as either fifteen railroad cars or sixty trucks can carry. A barge typical is 200 ft long, 35 ft wide and has a draft of 9 ft. Barges carry dry bulk (grain, coal, lumber, gravel, etc.) and liquid bulk (petroleum, vegetable oils, molasses, etc.).

Berth: (verb) To bring a ship to a berth. (noun) The wharf space where a ship docks. A wharf may have two or three berths, depending on the length of incoming ships.

Board of commissioners: The members of the governing board of a port authority in the United States are called commissioners. Members of a board of commissioners can be elected or appointed and usually serve for several years.

Bonded warehouse: A building designated by customs authorities for storage of goods without payment of duties to customs until goods are removed.

Box: Slang term for a container.

---

[1] The Glossary contains definitions taken from various sources; the definitions are taken directly from the sources, have been modified, shortened, or specified. Major sources for the Glossary are: Glossary EU 2003; Glossary OECD 2007; UN Transport Glossary; AAPA website (for details of source, see Bibliography).

DOI 10.1515/9781547400874-024

Breakbulk cargo: Conventional cargo that is shipped as a unit (e.g., palletized cargo, boxed cargo, iron, steel, large machinery, trucks, woodpulp, and preslung cargo).

Bulk cargo: Loose cargo (dry or liquid) that is loaded (shoveled, scooped, forked, mechanically conveyed, or pumped) in volume directly into a ship's hold; e.g., grain, coal and oil.

Bulkhead: A structure used to protect against shifting cargo and/or to separate the load.

Buoys: Floats that warn of hazards such as rocks or shallow ground, to help ships maneuver through unfamiliar harbors.

Cabotage: Shipment of cargo between a nation's ports; also called coastwise trade. The United States and some other countries require such trade to be carried on domestic ships only.

Cargo: The freight (goods, products) carried by a ship, barge, train, truck or plane.

Carrier: An individual, partnership or corporation engaged in the business of transporting goods or passengers.

Chandlers: Originally, chandlers (candle makers) provided illumination to ships. Over time they expanded the variety of products they could provide to ships: groceries, paper products, engine parts, electronics, hardware, etc. A chandler sells these supplies to the ship's agent.

Common carrier: Trucking, railroad, or barge lines that are licensed to transport goods or people nationwide are called common carriers.

Concession: Arrangement whereby a private party (concessionaire) leases assets from a public authority for an extended period and has responsibility for financing specified new fixed investments during the period and for providing specified services associated with the assets; in return, the concessionaire receives specified revenues from the operation of the assets; the assets revert to the public sector at expiration of the contract.

Consignment: A shipment of goods. The buyer of this shipment is called the consignee; the seller of the goods is called the consignor.

Conference: An affiliation of shipping lines operating over the same route(s) who agree to charge uniform rates and/or other terms of carriage.

Consignee: The receiver of freight shipped by the shipper (consignor).

Consolidator: The person or firm that consolidates (combines) cargo from several shippers into a container that will deliver the goods to several buyers.

Container: A box made of aluminum, steel or fiberglass used to transport cargo by ship, rail, truck or barge. Common dimensions are 20' x 8' x 8' (called a TEU or twenty-foot equivalent unit) or 40' x 8' x 8', called an FEU. Variations are collapsible containers, tank containers (for liquids) and "rag tops" (open-topped containers covered by a tarpaulin for cargo that sticks above the top of a closed box). In the container industry, containers are usually simply called boxes.

Container freight station: The facility for stuffing and stripping a container of its cargo, especially for movement by railroad.

Container chassis: A piece of equipment specifically designed for the movement of containers by highway to and from container terminals.

Container crane: Usually, a rail-mounted gantry crane located on a wharf for loading and unloading containers on vessels.

Container terminal: A specialized facility where ocean container vessels dock to discharge and load containers, equipped with cranes with a safe lifting capacity of up to 50 tons, with booms having an outreach of up to 58m to reach the outside cells of vessels. Most such cranes operate on rail tracks and have articulating rail trucks on each of their four legs, enabling them to traverse along the terminal and work various bays on the vessel and for more than one crane to work a single vessel simultaneously. Most terminals have direct rail access and container storage areas, and are served by highway carriers.

Containerization: The technique of using a container to store, protect and handle cargo while it is in transit. This shipping method has both greatly expedited the speed where cargo is moved from origin to destination and lowered shipping costs.

Customs: A duty or tax on imported goods. These fees can make a major bonus to the economy. The department of customs also works to prevent the importation of illegal items.

Cut-off time (closing time): The latest time a container may be delivered to a terminal for loading to a vessel.

Demurrage: A penalty fee assessed when cargo is not moved off a terminal before the free time allowance ends

Detention: A charge from the shipping line to the cargo for using the container beyond the agreed free time.

Dockage: A charge by a port authority for the length of water frontage used by a vessel tied up at a berth.

Draft: The depth of a loaded vessel in the water taken from the level of the water line to the lowest point of the hull of the vessel; or distance between the bottom of the ship and waterline.

Drayage: Transport by truck for short distances; e.g. from berth or terminal to warehouse.

Dry bulk: Minerals or grains stored in loose piles moving without mark or count for example, potash, coal, industrial sand, ore, wheat.

Duty: A government tax on imported merchandise.

Dwell time: The length of time a container remains at the terminal before being loaded onto a vessel or picked-up for inland transportation.

Elevator: A complex including storage facilities, computerized loading; inspection rooms and docks to load and unload dry bulk cargo such as grain or green coffee.

Feeder vessel: A vessel that connects with deep-sea line vessel to service region ports not directly served by the deep-sea vessel.

Forwarder: A company that arranges for the carriage of goods and associated formalities on behalf of a shipper. The duties of a forwarder include booking space on a ship, providing all the necessary documentation and arranging customs clearance.

Free port: A port that is a Foreign Trade Zone open to all traders on equal terms, or more specifically a port where merchandise may be stored duty-free pending re-export or sale within that country.

Freight: Merchandise hauled by transportation lines.

Freight forwarder: An individual or company that prepares the documentation and coordinates the movement and storage of export cargoes.

Freight rate: The charge made for the transportation of freight.

Gantry crane: Track-mounted, shoreside crane utilized in the loading and unloading of breakbulk cargo, containers and heavy lift cargo.

General cargo: Two definitions exist: consists of both containerized and break-bulk goods, or breakbulk goods only (see Chapter 3.3); in contrast to bulk cargo.

Grain elevator: Facility where bulk grain is unloaded, weighed, cleaned, blended and exported.

Groupage: The grouping together of several consignments into a full container load. Also referred to as consolidation.

Heavy lift: Very heavy cargoes that require specialized equipment to move the products to and from ship/truck/rail/barge and terminals. This "heavy lift" machinery may be installed aboard a ship designed just for such transport. Shore cranes, floating cranes and lift trucks may also be adapted for such heavy lifts.

Hinterland: A loan word of German language (literally "the land behind"). Hinterland is the area where traffic demand originates. The term Port Hinterland is applied to the inland region lying behind a port. The Port Hinterland is connected to a port by lines of communication or transport routes: roads, railways, pipelines and rivers/canals.

Home port: Port where a cruise ship loads passengers and begins its itinerary, and where it returns to disembark passengers upon conclusion of voyage. Sometimes referred to as "embarkation port" and "turn around port."

Hopper car: A freight car used for handling dry bulks, with an openable top and one or more opening on the bottom where the cargo is dumped.

Hub: A central location where traffic from several ports is directed and where traffic is fed to other areas. Refers to the practice where shipping lines call at one port in a country or region, rather than at several ports.

Inland carrier: Transportation company that hauls export or import traffic between ports and inland points.

Interchange: Point of entry/exit for trucks delivering and picking up containerized cargo. Point where pickups and deposits of containers in storage area or yard are assigned.

Intermodal: Transport by more than one transportation mode, usually truck and rail.

Landlord port: At a landlord port, the port authority builds the quay walls and the terminal area up to the pavement, which it then rents or leases to a terminal operator (usually a stevedoring company). The operator invests in cargo-handling equipment (forklifts, cranes, etc.), hires port laborers to operate such lift machinery and negotiates contracts with ocean carriers (steamship services) to handle the unloading and loading of ship cargoes.

Lashing: Containers stacked on the deck of a ship are secured (lashed) at all four corners by wires or rods.

Liner vessel service: A service for cargo carried in vessels according to a fixed scheduled of routes and port calls. Most containerized, as well as some break-bulk cargo, falls in this category.

Longshoremen: In the United States, stevedores or dock workers are called longshoremen. Workers who load and unload ships, or perform administrative tasks associated with the loading or unloading of cargo. They may or may not be members of labor unions.

Management contract: An arrangement whereby the operation and management of a terminal is contracted by the public authority to a container terminal operator for a specified period and under specified conditions relating to performance criteria, economic incentives, maintenance and infrastructure commi ments, etc. The public authority retains ownership of the facility and the commercial risk associated with its operation.

Manifest: A declaration document containing a full list of the ship's cargo, extracted from the bills of lading.

Marine surveyor: Person who inspects a ship hull or its cargo for damage or quality.

Master or captain: The officer in charge of the ship.

Maritime: (adjective) Located on or near the sea. Commerce or navigation by sea. The maritime industry includes people working for transportation (ship, rail, truck and towboat/barge) companies, freight forwarders and customs brokers; stevedoring companies; labor unions; chandlers; warehouses; ship building and repair firms; importers/exporters; pilot associations, etc.

Motor ship (MS) or motor vessel (MV): A ship propelled by internal-combustion engines.

NVOCC—nonvessel operating common carrier: A cargo consolidator in ocean trades who buys space from a carrier and re-sells it to smaller shippers. The NVOCC issues bills of lading, publishes tariffs, and otherwise conducts itself as a shipping line, except that it does not provide the actual ocean or intermodal service.

Neo-bulk cargo: Uniformly packaged goods, such as wood pulp bales, which stow as solidly as bulk, but are handled as general cargoes.

Ocean carrier: Vessels with combustion engines that have replaced the old steamships of the past, although many people still refer to modern vessels as steamships. Likewise, the person who represents the ship in port is still often called a steamship agent.

On-dock rail: Direct shipside rail service. Includes the ability to load and unload containers/breakbulk directly from rail car to vessel.

On-terminal rail: Rail service and trackage provided by a railroad within a designated terminal area.

Pallet: A short wooden, metal, or plastic platform where package cargo is placed, then handled by a forklift truck.

Pier: A structure just out into a waterway from the shore, for mooring vessels and cargo handling. Sometimes called a finger pier.

Piggyback: A rail transport mode where a loaded truck trailer is shipped on a rail flatcar.

Pilot: A licensed navigational guide with thorough knowledge of a section of a waterway whose occupation is to steep ships along a coast or into and out of a harbor. Local pilots board the ship to advise the captain and navigator of local navigation conditions (difficult currents; hidden wrecks, etc.).

Port: This term is used both for the harbor area where ships are docked and for the agency (port authority), which administers use of public wharves and port properties.

Port-of-call: Port where ships make a stop along its itinerary.

Project cargo: The materials and equipment to assemble a special project overseas, such as a factory or highway.

Quay or quay wall: A wharf, which parallels the waterline.

Railhead: End of the railroad line or point in operations where cargo is loaded and unloaded.

Railyard: A rail terminal where traditional railroad activities occur for sorting and redistribution of railcars and cargo.

Reach stacker: Heavy hoist machine that stacks containers.

Receipt and delivery: Export cargo is received into the port and import cargo delivered to truck, barge or rail.

Reefer: Controlled temperature container suitable for chilled or frozen cargoes.

Reloading: Changing the position of a container on a vessel via the quay.

Seal: A device fastened to the doors of a container used to secure the cargo and to insure the integrity of a shipment.

Shipper: Company that purchases transportation services.

Spreader: Device used to lift containers by their corner castings with a locking mechanism at each corner.

Steamship agent: The local representative who acts as a liaison among ship owners, local port authorities, terminals and supply/service companies. An agent handles all details for getting the ship into port; having it unloaded and loaded; inspected and out to sea quickly. An agent arranges for pilots, tug services, stevedores, inspections, etc., as well as, seeing that a ship is supplied with food, water, mail, medical services, etc. A steamship agency does not own the ship (see: ocean carrier).

Stevedores: Labor management companies that provide equipment and hire workers to transfer cargo between ships and docks. Stevedore companies may also serve as terminal operators. The laborers hired by the stevedoring firms are called stevedores, dock workers or longshoremen.

Straddle carrier: Container terminal equipment, which is motorized and runs on rubber tires. It can straddle a single row of containers and is primarily used to move containers around the terminal, but also to transport containers to and from the transtainer and load/unload containers from truck chassis.

Stowage: The placing of containers in a vessel in such a manner as to provide the utmost safety, stability and efficiency for the ship and the goods it carries, as well as to create a minimum number of shifters and reloaders.

Stripping: The process of removing cargo from a container.

Stuffing: The process of packing a container with loose cargo prior to inland or ocean shipment.

Tanker: Vessels carrying bulk liquid cargo, such as crude oil or oil products.

Tariff: Schedule, system of duties imposed by a government on the import/export of goods; also, the charges, rates and rules of a transportation company as listed in published industry tables.

Terminal: The place where cargo is handled is called a terminal.

Terminal operator: The company that operates cargo handling activities on a terminal. A terminal operator oversees unloading cargo from ship to dock, checking the quantity of cargoes versus the ship's manifest (list of goods), transferring of the cargo into the shed, checking documents authorizing a trucker to pick up cargo, overseeing the loading/unloading of railroad cars, etc.

Tons: A short (or "net") ton = 2000 pounds. A long tong = 2240 pounds. A metric ton = 2205 pounds. The symbol "t" is recommended for the metric ton or tonne (see Chapter 7.2.3).

Toplift: A piece of equipment like a forklift that lifts from above rather than below. Used to handle containers in the storage yard to and from storage stacks, trucks and railcars.

Tramp: A ship operating with no fixed route or published schedule.

Tramp vessel service: A service for dry cargo carried on chartered vessels. Includes mainly dry bulks such as coal, grain, and fertilizers, as well as steel and, in some cases, autos.

Transit port: When most cargo moving through a port are not coming from or destined for the local market, the port is called a transit (or through) port.

Transit shed: The shed on a terminal is designed to protect cargoes from weather damage and is used only for short-term storage. Warehouses operated by private firm's house goods for longer periods.

Transshipment: The unloading of cargo at a port or point where it is ther reloaded, sometimes into another mode of transportation, for transfer to a des tination.

Transtainer: A type of crane used in the handling of containers, which is motor ized, mounted on rubber tires and can straddle at least four railway tracks, some up to six, with a lifting capacity of approximately 40 tons for loading and unload ing containers to and from railway cars.

Turnaround time: The time it takes between the arrival of a vessel, truck or trai and its departure from the terminal.

Vessel: A ship or large boat.

Vessel operator: A firm that charters vessels for its service requirements, which are handled by their own offices or appointed agents at ports of call. Vessel operators also handle the operation of vessels on behalf of owners.

Warehouse: A place for the reception, delivery, consolidation, distribution, and storage of goods and cargo.

Way bill: The document used to identify the shipper and consignee, present the routing, describe the goods, present the applicable rate, show the weight of the shipment, and make other useful information notations.

Wharf or quay or quay area: The place where ships tie up to unload and load cargo. The wharf typically has front and rear loading docks (aprons), a transit shed, open (unshedded) storage areas, truck bays, and rail tracks.

Wharfage: A charge against the cargo or a shipping line for use of the pier or dock.

Yard: A system of tracks within a certain area used for making up trains, storing cars, placing cars to be loaded or unloaded, etc.

Appendix C
Bibliography

Articles and Working Papers

AAPA American Association of Port Authorities, U.S. Department of Transportation, Maritime Administration: Port Planning and Investment Toolkit, 2017 (AAPA Planning and Investment Toolkit 2017).

Bekkers, Eddy, Joseph F. Francois, Hugo Rojas-Romagosa: Melting Ice Caps and the Economic Impact of Opening the Northern Sea Route, CPB Netherlands Bureau for Economic Policy Analysis, Discussion Paper 307, The Hague, Netherlands 2015.

Coia, Anthony and Christopher Ludwig, 2015 European ports survey: Rising volume and risky conditions, article published on: www.automotivelogistics.media 30. March 2016, UK 2016 (European ports survey 2015).

Corbett, James J., James J. Winebrake, Erin H. Green, Prasad Kasibhatla, Veronika Eyring, Axel Lauer: Mortality from Ship Emissions: A Global Assessment, in: *Environmental Science & Technology*, 2007, 41 (24), page 8512–8518, Washington, 2007 (Corbett 2007).

Drewry Maritime Research, Global Container Terminal Operators 2011: Annual Review and Forecast, Addendum, published 1. August 2011, UK/London 2011 (Drewry 2011).

ESPO European Sea Ports Organisation: ESPO/EcoPorts Port Environmental Review 2016, Brussels, Belgium April 2016.

Haezendonck, Elvira, Chris Coeck, Alain Verbeke: The Competitive Position of Seaports: Introduction of the Value-Added Concept, in: *International Journal of Maritime Economics*, Volume 2, Issue 2, pages 107–118, Basingstoke, UK, April 2000.

Hellenic Shipping News Worldwide, Daily Newsletter February 22, 2018: World's Biggest Container Liner Looks for Deals Outside Shipping, Athens, Greece 2018.

ISL Institut für Seeverkehrswirtschaft und Logistik, Tonnage Measurement Study, MTCP Work Package 2.1 Quality and Efficiency, Final Report, Germany/Bremen and Belgium/Brussels 2006 (ISL Tonnage Measurement Study 2006).

Jauhiainen, Jussi S.: Waterfront redevelopment and urban policy: The case of Barcelona, Cardiff and Genoa, in: *European Planning Studies*. March 1995, Vol. 3 Issue 1, page 3ff, UK 1995.

KMI Korean Maritime Institute in cooperation with ESCAP United Nations Economic and Social Commission for Asia and the Pacific: Comparative Analysis of Port Tariffs in the ESCAP Region, New York, 2002.

Komarovskiy, Viktor, Viktor Bondaruk: The role of the concept of "Growth Poles" for regional development, in: *Journal of Public Administration, Finance and Law*, Issue 4/2013, page 31-42, Iasi, Romania 2013.

Langen, Peter W. De, Time to move beyond competition, in: *Ports & Harbors*, March 2008, pages 34–35, London 2008.

Langen, Peter W. De and Athanasios A. Pallis, Analysis of the benefits of intra-port competition, paper presented at the IAME International Association of Maritime Economists Cyprus 2005 Conference, Cyprus 2005 (De Langen Intra-port competition).

DOI 10.1515/9781547400874-025

Musso, Enrico L., Claudio Ferrari, Marco Benacchio: On the global optimum size of port terminals, in: *International Journal of Transport Economics/Rivista internazionale di economia dei trasporti*, Vol. 26, No. 3 (October 1999), pages 415–437.

Notteboom, Theo, Jean-Paul Rodrigues, The Corporate Geography of Global Container Terminal Operators, Maritime Policy & Management, 39(3), 249-279. Document was uploaded from www.porteconomics.eu on December 27th, 2012 (Notteboom + Rodrigues, Corporate Geography of GCTO 2012).

Pantouvakis, Angelos M, C.I. Chlomoudis, Athanasios G. Dimas: Marketing Strategies in Port Industry: An Exploratory Study and Research Agenda, American Journal of Economics and Business Administration 2 (1), pages 64–72, 2010.

Park, Yong-An and Francesca Medda, Classification of Container Ports on the Basis of Networks, 12th WCTR July 11–15, Lisbon, Portugal 2010 (Park Medda 2010).

Portopia, EC 7th Framework Programme: Deliverable 1.3 Port Traffic Forecasting Tool, Document ID Portopia/D/1.3/DT/201506.15, Brussels, Belgium 2015 (Portopia Port Traffic Forecasting Tool).

Rodrigue, Jean-Paul, Theo Notteboom: Challenges in the Maritime-Land Interface: Port Hinterlands and Regionalization, in: The master development plan for port logistics parks in Korea, Korea, Seoul 2006, pages 333–363; copy available on the internet site of the Universiteit Antwerpen, http://snet.ua.ac.be; visited on August 8, 2012 (Rodrigue Notteboom Hinterlands 2006).

Smith, Laurence C., Scott R. Stephenson: New Trans-Arctic shipping routes navigable by midcentury, Proceedings of the National Academy of Sciences of the United States of America, published pnas web page: www.pnas.org/cgi/doi/10.1073/ pnas.1214212110, Columbus (OH), 2013.

Sorgenfrei, Jürgen: Hong-Mi-Sing-Sha, in: *The Journal of Commerce*, April 18, 2005, page 49, New Jersey, 2005 (Sorgenfrei Hong-Mi-Sing-Sha).

Sorgenfrei, Jürgen: Port Marketing. Eine Bestandsaufnahme, in: *Internationales Verkehrswesen*, Vol. 61, Nr. 12, page 473–479, Hamburg, Germany 2009.

Sorgenfrei, Jürgen: What is Port Marketing? in: *ITJ International Transport Journal*, October 23, 2009, pages 8–9, Basel, Switzerland 2009 (Sorgenfrei Port Marketing).

Tallet, Pierre and Gregory Marouard: The Harbor of Khufu on the Red Sea Coast at Wadi al-Jarf, Egypt, in: *Near Eastern Archaeology*, American School of Oriental Research, Vol. 77/1, pages 4–14, Boston 2014.

U.S. Department of Transportation: 2010 National Census of Ferry Operators, presentation held from: RITA Research and Innovative Technology Administration, Bureau of Transportation Statistics, Washington, 2010.

Voorde, Eddy van de, Thierry Vanelslander: Market Power and Vertical and Horizontal Integration in the Maritime Shipping and Port Industry, OECD/ITF Discussion Paper No 2009-2, Antwerp, Belgium, 2009.

World Oil Transit Chokepoints, EIA U.S. Energy Information Administration, last Updated: July 25, 2017, published on EIA beta website: https://www.eia.gov/beta/international/ regions-topics.cfm?Region TopicID=WOTC, Washington, 2017.

Books

Bernstein, William J.: *A Splendid Exchange; How Trade Shaped the World*, Grove/Atlantic, First Edition, New York, 2008.

Brandt, Arno: *Maritime Wirtschaft in Deutschland*, Murmann Verlag, Hamburg, Germany 2011 (Brandt 2011).

Bund der Steuerzahler: *Das Schwarzbuch*. Die öffentliche Verschwendung 2016/17, Berlin, Germany 2016.

Dollinger, Philippe: *Die Hanse*, 5th edition, Kröner-Verlag, Stuttgart, Germany 1998 (Dollinger 1998).

Donovan, Arthur, Joseph Bonney: *The box that changed the world*, East Windsor, New Jersey, 2006 (Donovan 2006).

Eggebrecht, Arno: *Das alte Ägypten, 3000 Jahre Geschichte und Kultur des Pharaonenreiches*, C. Bertelsmann Verlag, Munich 1984 (Eggebrecht 1984).

Heyerdahl, Thor: *Kon-Tiki: Across the Pacific by Raft*, Rand McNally & Company, 1950 (Heyerdahl 1950).

Huybrechts, Marc, Hilde Meersman, Eddy Van de Voorde, Eric Van Hooydonk, Alain Verbeke, Willy Winkelmans: *Port Competitiveness. An economic and legal analysis of the factors determining the competitiveness of seaports*, Antwerp, Belgium 2002 (Huybrechts et al 2002).

Illig, Herbert, Franz Löhner: *Der Bau der Cheopspyramide: nach der Rampenzeit*, 4. Auflage, Gräfeling, Germany 1999 (Illig 1999).

Lehmann-Hartleben, Karl: *Die antiken Hafenanlagen des Mittelmeeres*. Beiträge zur Geschichte des Städtebaus im Altertum. 1923. Neudruck: Scientia-Verlag, Aalen, Germany 1963.

Levinson, Marc: *The Box. How the Shipping Container Made the World Smaller and the World Economy Bigger*, Princeton, 2006 (Levinson 2006).

Lun, Y.H. Venus, Olli-Pekka Hilmola, Alexander M. Goulielmos, Kee.hung Lai, T:C: Edwin Cheng: *Oil Transport Management*, Springer-Verlag London, UK 2013.

Maddison, Angus: *Contours of the World Economy, 1–2030 AD. Essays in Macro-Economic History*, Oxford University Press, New York, 2007 (Maddison 2007).

Masseron, Jean: *Petroleum Economics*, 4th edition, updated and expanded, Editions Technip, Paris, France, 1990.

McEachern, William A.: *Economics: A Contemporary Introduction*, Eighth Edition, Mason, 2009 (McEachern 2009).

Menzies, Gavin: *1421. The Year China discovered the World*, Bantam Books, Reading, UK 2003 (Menzies 2003).

Muller, Gerhardt: *Intermodal Freight Transportation*, Fourth Edition, Washington, DC, 1999 (Muller 1999).

Needham, Joseph; Lu Gwei-djen: *Science and Civilisation in China*, Volume 4, Section 3: Civil Engineering and Nautics, Cambridge University Press, Cambridge, England 1971 (Needham 1971).

Petrie, Sir W. Flinders: *The Pyramids and Temple of Gise*, London, UK 1883 (Petrie 1883).

Reiss, Peter C. and Frank A. Wolak (Stanford University): *Structural Econometric Modeling: rationales and examples from industrial organization, Handbook of Econometrics*, Volume 6A, Elsevier, 2007, pages 4280–4412.

Ricardo, David: *Über die Grundsätze der politischen Ökonomie und der Besteuerung*, 3. Auflage, John Murray, London 1821, übersetzt und mit einer Einleitung versehen von

Gerhard Bondi, Ökonomische Studientexte, Band 1, 2., durchgesehene Auflage, Akademie-Verlag, Berlin 1979 (Ricardo 1979).

Rodrigue, Jean-Paul, Claude Comtois, Brian Slack: *The Geography of Transport Systems*, Second edition, London and New York 2009.

Samuelson, Paul A., William D. Nordhaus: *Economics*, Fourteenth Edition, New York, 1992 (Samelson 1992).

Selbourne, David: *The City of Light*/Jacob d`Ancona; translated and edited by David Selbourne, first trade paperback March 2003, New York NY 10022, 2003 (Selbourne 2003).

Stopford, Martin: *Maritime Economics*, 3rd edition, Milton Park, Abingdon, Oxon, UK 2009 (Stopford 2009).

Stroob, Heinz: *Die Hanse*, Styria-Verlag Graz Wien Köln, Austria 1995 (Stroob 1995).

Verhoeven, Patrick: *European Port Governance. Report of an enquiry into the current governance of European Seaports*; The ESPO Fact-Finding Report, revised and enlarged in 2010, prepared by Patrick Verhoeven, Brussels, Belgium 2011 (Verhoeven 2011).

Voigt, Fritz: Verkehr, Erster Band. Erste Hälfte, *Die Theorie der Verkehrswirtschaft*, Berlin, Germany 1973 (Voigt 1973).

Voigt, Fritz: Verkehr, Zweiter Band. Erste Hälfte, *Die Entwicklung des Verkehrssystems*, Berlin, Germany 1965 (Voigt 1965).

Dissertations and Theses

Douvier, Stefan Wendelin: MARPOL Technische Möglichkeiten, rechtliche und politische Grenzen eines internationalen Übereinkommens, Dissertation at the University at Bremen, Germany, Fachbereich 7: Wirtschaftswissenschaft, Bremen, Germany 2004.

Gaur, Prakash: Port Planning as a Strategic Tool: A Typology, Thesis submitted in partial fulfilment of the requirements for the degree Master of Science in Transport and Maritime Economics, Institute of Transport and Maritime Management Antwerp, University of Antwerp, Antwerp, Belgium 2005.

Höltgen, Daniel: Terminals, intermodal logistics centres and European infrastructure policy, Dissertation submitted for the degree of Doctor of Philosophy at the University of Cambridge, Gesellschaft für Verkehrsbetriebswirtschaft und Logistik (GVB), Nürnberg, Germany 1996 (Höltgen 1996).

Schönknecht, Axel: Entwicklung eines Modells zur Kosten- und Leistungsbewertung von Containerschiffen in intermodalen Transportketten, Dissertation submitted for the degree of Doctor of Engineering at the Technical University of Hamburg-Harburg, Hamburg, Germany 2007.

Government and International Agency Documents

Bureau International des Containers et du Transport Intermodal (BIC), Containers 2011; BIC-Code Register. Official Register of Internationally protected ISO ALPHA CODES for identification of container owners. Yearly publication, France/Paris 2011.

Commission of the European Communities. Report on "The main seaports of the Community." Prepared by the Working Group on Ports, No. VII/9/87, FR. Brussels, Belgium, 1986 (EC 1986).

Connecting to Compete 2010, Trade Logistics in the Global Economy, The Logistics Performance Index and Its Indicators, The International Bank for Reconstruction and Development/The World Bank, Washington, 2010 (WB 2010)

DBRS (originally known as Dominion Bond Rating Service), Rating Container Terminal Operators. Methodology, August 2017, DBRS, Ontario, Canada 2017.

ESPO Green Guide. Towards excellence in port environmental management and sustainability, published in October 2012 by the European Sea Ports Organisation, Brussels, Belgium 2012 (ESPO Green Guide 2012).

European Communities, United Nations Economic Commission for Europe, European Conference of Ministers of Transport: Glossary for transport statistics. Document prepared by the Intersecretariat Working Group on Transport Statistics, Third edition, Luxemburg 2003 (Glossary EU 2003).

European Parliament, Directorate General for Internal Policies, Policy Department B: Structural and Cohesion Policies, Transport and Tourism, State Aids to EU Seaports, Brussels, Belgium 2011. Document is available on the Internet at: www.europarl.europa.eu/studies (EU State Aids).

Global Port Development Report (2016), Shanghai International Shipping Institute (SISI), Shanghai 2017, China (SISI 2016).

International Chamber of Shipping: ISGOTT International Safety Guide for Oil Tankers and Terminals, fifth edition, Witherby & Co., London, UK 2006.

IMO International Maritime Organization, International Maritime Dangerous Goods Code (IMDG code), Resolution MSC.328(90)—Adoption of amendments to the International Maritime Dangerous Goods (IMDG) Code (Amendment 36-12), London, UK 2016.

IMO International Maritime Organization, Second IMO GHG Study 2009, London 2009 (Second GHG Study 2009).

Lloyd's Register-Fairplay: OPTIMAR _ Benchmarking strategic options for European shipping and for the European maritime transport system in the horizon 2008-2018, Final Report, Gothenburg, Sweden 2008 (Lloyds 2008).

National Institute of Standards and Technology: Specifications, Tolerances, and Other Technical Requirements for Weighing and Measuring Devices; National Institute of Standards and Technology Handbook 44, 2017 Edition, Editors: Tina Butcher, Linda Crown, Rick Harshman, U.S. Department of Commerce, Washington, November 2017 (NIST Handbook 2017).

Notteboom, Theo: Economic analysis of the European seaport system. Report serving as input for the discussion on the TEN-T policy, Report commissioned by: European Sea Ports Organization (ESPO); Report prepared by ITMMA—University of Antwerp, Belgium 2009 (Nottebom 2009).

OECD Organisation for Economic Co-operation and Development: The Competitiveness of Global Port-Cities, OECD, Paris, France 2014 (OECD 2014).

OECD Organisation for Economic Co-operation and Development, Glossary of Statistical Terms, Paris/France December 2007 (Glossary OECD 2007).

OECD/ITF Organisation for Economic Co-operation and Development, International Transport Forum: A new hinterland rail link for the Port of Koper, Review of Risks and Delivery Options, Paris/France 2015 (OECD Koper 2015).

Port Reform Toolkit, Second Edition, The World Bank, Washington, 2007 (Port Reform Toolkit 2007).

Ships Visiting European Ports, 2011-07-31, IHS Fairplay, Gothenburg, Sweden 2011. Report can be downloaded from this address (visited May 23, 2012): http://ec.europa.eu/clima/policies/transport/shipping/docs/ships_visiting_en.pdf (Fairplay 2011).

TT Club, World Shipping Council, ICHCA International Limited, Global Shippers' Forum: Verified Gross Mass; Industry FAQS, London, UK December 2015 (TT Club 2015).

UNESCAP—Korean Maritime Institute, Free Trade Zone and Port Hinterland Development, Thailand 2005.

United Nations, Glossary for Transport Statistics, 3rd Edition, Document prepared by the Intersecretariat Working Group on Transport Statistics, Office for Official Publications of the European Communities, Luxemburg 2003 (UN Transport Glossary).

United Nations Conference on Trade and Development (UNCTAD), Gustaaf DeMonie: Guidelines for Port Authorities and Governments on privatization of port facilities, GE.98-51748, Belgium, Antwerp 1998.

United Nations Conference on Trade and Development (UNCTAD), Marketing Promotion Tools for Ports. UNCTAD Monographs on Port Management 12, New York and Geneva, 1995 (UNCTAD Monographs on Port Management 12: Marketing Promotion Tools).

United Nations Conference on Trade and Development (UNCTAD), Port development; A handbook for planners in developing countries, Second edition, New York 1985 (UNCTAD Handbook for Port Planners).

United Nations Conference on Trade and Development (UNCTAD), Review of Maritime Transport, Switzerland/Geneva, multiple years.

United Nations Economic and Social Council, Economic Commission for Europe, Inland Transport Committee, Working Paper on Transport Statistics: Report of the working party on transport statistics on its fifty-ninth session (28-30 May 2008); Addendum Classification system for transport statistics (NST 2007), ECE/TRANS/WP.6/155/Add.1, 2008 (NST 2007).

United Nations Economic Commission for Europe, Hinterland Connections of Seaports, New York and Geneva 2010 (UN Hinterland 2010).

Magazines, Newspapers, and Periodicals

Cargo Systems & International Freighting (weekly)
cm Container Management (monthly)
Containerisation International (monthly)
Fairplay (weekly)
International Bulk Journal (monthly)
Lloyd's List (daily newspaper)
Lloyd's Shipping Economist (monthly)
Maritime Policy and Management (quarterly)
Port Technology (quarterly journal & website)
Seatrade (monthly)
UNCTAD Review of Maritime Transport (annual)
World Cargo News (monthly)

Maritime Statistics

Alphaliner Fleet Statistics
BP Statistical Review of World Energy, issued by: BP plc, London, UK.
China Statistical Yearbook, National Bureau of Statistics of China
Containerisation International Yearbook (National Magazine Company, London)
Cruise Travel Report; issued by CLIA Cruise Lines International Association
ESPO Port Statistics
Eurostat; Eurostat statistics explained; Official statistics of European Union
IHS Maritime, Ports & Terminals Guide; Sea-Web
ISL Shipping Statistics and Market Review
IAPH Statistics, Tokyo
United Nations, Monthly Bulletin of Statistics (New York: UN)

Private Reports and Documents

AECOM in association with URS: North Carolina Maritime Strategy. NC Maritime Strategy. Vessel Size vs. Cost. Prepared for the North Carolina Department of Transportation/Raleigh/NC, May 2012 (AECOM2012).
A.P. Møller-Maersk A/S Group Annual Report 2011, Copenhagen, Denmark 2012.
Copenhagen Malmö Port, Copenhagen Kommune, City of Copenhagen: Options for Establishing shore power for Cruise Ships in Port of Copenhagen Nordhavn, Copenhagen, Denmark 2015 (Cruise Ships Copenhagen 2015).
Dublin Port Company: Port Charges on Vessels (Tonnage Dues), Dublin, Ireland April 2017.
Germanischer Lloyd: Container Terminal Quality-Indicator Standard. The concept for increasing container terminal efficiency, version 1.0, Germany/Hamburg 2008 (GL CT Quality-Indicator).
Gidson, Renee, Thomas Rutherford, Adam Malarz and Simon O'Mahony: Impact of increasing container ship size on container handling productivity at Australian ports, Australasian Transport Research Forum 2015 Proceedings, 30 September - 2 October 2015, Sydney, Australia Publication website: http://www.atrf.info/papers/index. aspx.
Lloyd's Register Fairplay, Emission study of One week Shipping activity: Ship's emissions in River Schelde Ports and fairways with focus on Port of Antwerp, UK/London 2009 (LR Emissions Study 2009).
Lloyd's Register Fairplay, Ship dimensions 2030. Study of trends in vessel dimensions in a 2030 perspective, UK/London 2009 (LR ship dimensions 2030).
Ocean Shipping Consultants Limited, Remco Stenvert and Andrew Penfold: Marketing of container terminals, UK 2004.
Ships Visiting European Ports, 2011-07-31, IHS Fairplay, Gothenburg, Sweden 2011 (Fairplay 2011). Report can be downloaded from this address (visited May 23, 2012): http://ec.europa.eu/clima/policies/transport/shipping/docs/ships_visiting_en.pdf

Public Internet Websites (plus date when visited)

http:// http://www.businessdictionary.com/definition/Pareto-optimum.html Website
"Business Dictionary" of Web Finance Inc., Austin/Texas. Visited February 27, 2018.

http://cscmp.org/digital/glossary/glossary.asp, Supply Chain Management Terms and
Glossary, Updated February 2010, Council of Supply Chain Management Professionals
(CSCMP), Lombard. Visited on June 13, 2012.

http://en.wikipedia.org/wiki/Abraham_Maslow. Wikipedia website about Abraham Maslow and
his Hierarchy of Needs. Visited on June 11, 2012.

http://en.wikipedia.org/wiki/File:Extent_of_the_Hansa.jpg#globalusage Wikipedia website
showing the extent of the Hanseatic League about AD 1400. Visited on February 29, 2012.

http://en.wikipedia.org/wiki/Grand_Canal_(China) Wikipedia website about the Beijing-
Hangzhou Grand Canal in China. Visited on February 28, 2012.

http://en.wikipedia.org/wiki/ISO_6346 Wikipedia website about ICO 6346 and the classification of container. Visited on June 5, 2012.

http://en.wikipedia.org/wiki/List_of_oil_spills Wikipedia website with a long list of oil spills.
Visited on March 6, 2013.

http://en.wikipedia.org/wiki/Port_of_Tianjin Wikipedia website about the Port of Tianjin in
China; containing the Port of Tianjin Planning Map 2030; visited on December 1, 2017.

http://en.wikipedia.org/wiki/Srivijaya Wikipedia website about the long time forgotten
Kingdom of Srivijaya in Sout-East Asia. Visited on July 28, 2012.

http://www.globeinst.org/Conferences/ctqi_master_powerpoint.pdf Website of the Global
Institute of Logistics; providing a PowerPoint information about the "Container Terminal
Quality Indicator (CTQI). A benchmarking certification scheme for auditing global container
terminal operation. A joint project of Global Institute of Logistics and Germanischer Lloyd
Certification; New York & Hamburg 2008. Visited on February 19, 2013 (GIL/GLC Container
Terminal Quality Indicator).

http://www.iaphworldports.org/AboutIAPH/TechnicalCommitttee.aspx Official website of
the IAPH International Association of Ports and Harbors website and their technical
committees; visited on January 11, 2013.

http://www.2wglobal.com/www/Images/productsServices/routeMaps Website of Wallenius
Wilhelmsen shipping line. Visited on August 12, 2012.

http://www.aapa-ports.org Website of American Association of Port Authorities. Alliance of the
Ports of Canada, the Caribbean, Latin America and the United States. Visited on July 25,
2012 (AAPA website).

http://www.apmterminals.com Website of A.P. Moller Maersk Terminals, the terminal group of
Maersk. Visited on August 14, 2012.

http://www.bremenports.de/standort/statistiken/automobilumschlag.html Website of Brem-
Ports Authority "bremenports." Visited on May 29, 2012.

http://www.britannica.com/EBchecked/topic/113260/George-G-Chisholm. Article about the
author of the Handbook of Commercial Geography, who first used the word "hinterland"
English language. Visited on August 1, 2012.

http://www.changingthewaywethinkaboutshipping.com is a web page of Maersk Line, the
Danish Shipping Company. Target of the web page is to initiate new ways of thinking about
the shipping industry. Visited on June 19, 2012.

http://www.cma-cgm.com/eBusiness/Schedules/LineServices Website of French Shipping L
CMA CGM with all services offered. Visited on August 12, 2012.

http://www.cbp.gov The Container Security Initiative (CSI) is a program intended to help increase security for maritime containerized cargo. A list of CSI ports as well as additional CSI information can be found on this website. Visited December 1, 2017.

http://www.dailymaersk.com Website about the new concept of Maersk Line in Copenhagen, Denmark, about a new way of delivering containers in time. Visited on June 19, 2012.

http://www.drewry.co.uk/news.php Website of London based Drewry Maritime Research. Article "Drewry 'Industry Bible' Tracks Many Changes Over the Last Decade," published in London on August 21, 2012, UK/London 2012 (Drewry website 2012).

http://www.ect.nl Website of Rotterdam Terminal operator Europe container terminals (ECT). Visited on November 30, 2017.

http://www.ihs.com/products/maritime-information/port/ports-terminals-guide.aspx Website of IHSMarkit with information about the IHS Ports & Terminals Guide. Visited on December 1, 2017.

http://www.ilo.org/global/standards/subjects-covered-by-international-labour-standards/dock-workers/lang--en/index.htm. Website of the International Labor Organization. Visited on November 13, 2017

http://www.inttra.com. INTTRA is a multicarrier e-commerce platform for the ocean shipping industry. It enables shippers, freight forwarders, third-party logistics providers, brokers and importers to electronically plan, process and manage their shipments fast and efficiently, replacing the traditional use of faxes and phone calls. Visited on June 19, 2012.

http://www.livius.org/cn-cs/constantinople/constantinople01.html LIVIUS: Articles on Ancient History; website with short story about Constantinople. Visited on February 19, 2012.

http://www.maerskline.com/link/?page=brochure&path=/routemaps Website of Maersk Line, showing all Liner Services of Maersk. Visited on August 12, 2012.

http://www.pma.gov.sg Website of the Maritime and Port Authority of Singapore. Visited December 27, 2012.

http://www.portoflosangeles.org Website of the Port of Los Angeles. Visited December 27, 2012.

https://www.portofrotterdam.com Website of the Port of Rotterdam Authority. Visited on November 30, 2017.

https://www.rita.dot.gov/bts/port_performance Website of the U.S. Bureau of Transportation Statistics. Visited February 22, 2018.

https://www.seattletimes.com/business/local-business/seattle-tacoma-dockworkers-earn-less-than-reported-average/ Visited on November 13, 2017.

http://www.straitstimes.com/sites/default/files/attachments/2017/07/14/st_20170714_vnmap3_3274005.pdf ; Vital to keep Malacca, S'pore straits open and safe: DPM Teo," in: The Straits Times, July 14, 2017, Singapore 2017 (www.straitstimes.com). Website visited March 6, 2018.

http://www.zeebruggeport.be/en/node/679 Website of Zeebrugge Port Authority "Port of Zeebrugge." Visited on May 29, 2012.

http://ngm.nationalgeographic.com/ngm/0507/feature2/map.html National Geographic website, showing details of Admiral Zheng He's voyages.

ttp://www.saudiaramcoworld.com/issue/200901/uncovering.yenikapi.htm Saudi Aramco, the oil company born as an international enterprise seventy-five years ago, distributes Saudi Aramco World to increase cross-cultural understanding. The bimonthly magazine's goal is to broaden knowledge of the cultures, history and geography of the Arab and Muslim worlds and their connections with the West. Saudi Aramco World is distributed without charge, upon request, to interested readers worldwide (original text from the website). Visited on February 27, 2012.

http://www2.nykline.com/liner/service_network Website of NYK Shipping Line. Visited to get information about the NYK service network. Visited on August 12, 2012.

http://www2.rgzm.de/Navis2/Home/Frames.htm Website of the Römisch-Germanisches Zentralmuseum in Mainz, Germany. Procet: "The NAVIS II project." Visited on February 19, 2012.

https://ppp.worldbank.org/public-private-partnership/node/335/ Website of The World Bank Group's PPPIRC Public-Private-Partnership in Infrastructure Resource Center. Visited on February 14, 2017 (World Bank, PPP 2017).

Appendix D
Definition: "Container"

According to the "Glossary for transport statistics" (Glossary EU 2003, page 85) an *ISO freight container* is a unit of transport equipment, which is:

i. Of a permanent character and accordingly strong enough to be suitable for repeated use
ii. Specially designed to facilitate the carriage of goods, by one or more mode of transport, without intermediate reloading
iii. Fitted with devices permitting its ready handling, particularly its transfer from one mode of transport to another
iv. Designed as to be easy to fill and empty
v. Having a length of 20 ft or more

> "In addition, containers should be stackable and have an internal volume of 1 m3 or more. Swap bodies are excluded. Although without internal volume, and therefore with no internal volume, flats used in maritime transport should be considered to be a special type of container and therefore are included here. For a fuller description, reference should be made to ISO 668 and 1496."

In addition, ISO 6346 gives size and type for containers. According to this regulation, containers can be classified as follows[1]:

When displayed on the container, the size and type codes shall be used. The codes are compiled of the following elements:
First character, representing the length (coded)
Second character, representing the width and height (coded)
Third and fourth character indicating the type of the container

---

Refer to: http://en.wikipedia.org/wiki/ISO_6346 Wikipedia website about the classification of container; visited on June 5, 2012.

10.1515/9781547400874-026

The following is an overview of the most common codes:

ISO Type Group		ISO Size Type	
Code	Description	Code	Description
20GP	GENERAL PURPOSE CONT.	20G0	GENERAL PURPOSE CONT.
		20G1	GENERAL PURPOSE CONT.
20HR	INSULATED CONTAINER	20H0	INSULATED CONTAINER
20PF	FLAT (FIXED ENDS)	20P1	FLAT (FIXED ENDS)
20TD	TANK CONTAINER	20T3	TANK CONTAINER
		20T4	TANK CONTAINER
		20T5	TANK CONTAINER
		20T6	TANK CONTAINER
20TG	TANK CONTAINER	20T7	TANK CONTAINER
		20T8	TANK CONTAINER
20TN	TANK CONTAINER	20T0	TANK CONTAINER
		20T1	TANK CONTAINER
		20T2	TANK CONTAINER
22BU	BULK CONTAINER	22B0	BULK CONTAINER
22GP	GENERAL PURPOSE CONT.	22G0	GENERAL PURPOSE CONT.
		22G1	GENERAL PURPOSE CONT.
22HR	INSULATED CONTAINER	22H0	INSULATED CONTAINER
22PC	FLAT (COLLAPSIBLE)	22P3	FLAT (COLLAPSIBLE)
		22P8	FLAT (COLL.FLUSH FOLDING)
		22P9	FLAT (COLLAPSIBLE)
22PF	FLAT (FIXED ENDS)	22P1	FLAT (FIXED ENDS)
		22P7	FLAT (GENSET CARRIER)
22RC	REEFER CONT.(NO FOOD)	22R9	REEFER CONT.(NO FOOD)
22RS	BUILT-IN GEN. F. POWER SPLY OF REEF	22R7	BUILT-IN GEN. F. POWER SPLY OF REE
22RT	REEFER CONTAINER	22R1	REEFER CONTAINER
22SN	NAMED CARGO CONTAINER	22S1	NAMED CARGO CONTAINER
22TD	TANK CONTAINER	22T3	TANK CONTAINER
		22T4	TANK CONTAINER
		22T5	TANK CONTAINER
		22T6	TANK CONTAINER
22TG	TANK CONTAINER	22T7	TANK CONTAINER
		22T8	TANK CONTAINER
22TN	TANK CONTAINER	22T0	TANK CONTAINER
		22T1	TANK CONTAINER
		22T2	TANK CONTAINER
22UP	HARDTOP CONTAINER	22U6	HARDTOP CONTAINER
22UT	OPEN TOP CONTAINER	22U1	OPEN TOP CONTAINER
22VH	VENTILATED CONTAINER	22V0	VENTILATED CONTAINER
		22V2	VENTILATED CONTAINER
		22V3	VENTILATED CONTAINER
25GP	GP-CONTAINER OVER-HEIGHT	25G0	GP-CONTAINER OVER-HEIGHT

ISO Type Group		ISO Size Type	
Code	Description	Code	Description
26GP	GP-CONTAINER OVER-HEIGHT	26G0	GP-CONTAINER OVER-HEIGHT
26HR	INSULATED CONTAINER	26H0	INSULATED CONTAINER
28TG	TANK FOR GAS	28T8	TANK FOR GAS
28UT	OPEN TOP (HALF HEIGHT)	28U1	OPEN TOP (HALF HEIGHT)
28VH	VE-HALF-HEIGHT =1448 MM HEIGHT	28V0	VE-HALF-HEIGHT =1448 MM HEIGHT
29PL	PLATFORM	29P0	PLATFORM
2EGP	GEN. PURP. WITHOUT VENT WIDTH 2.5M	2EG0	HIGH CUBE CONT. (WIDTH 2.5M)
42GP	GENERAL PURPOSE CONT.	42G0	GENERAL PURPOSE CONT.
		42G1	GENERAL PURPOSE CONT.
42HR	INSULATED CONTAINER	42H0	INSULATED CONTAINER
42PC	FLAT (COLLAPSIBLE)	42P3	FLAT (COLLAPSIBLE)
		42P8	FLAT (COLL.FLUSH FOLDING)
		42P9	FLAT (COLLAPSIBLE)
42PF	FLAT (FIXED ENDS)	42P1	FLAT (FIXED ENDS)
42PS	FLAT (SPACE SAVER)	42P6	FLAT SPACE SAVER
42RC	REEFER CONT.(NO FOOD)	42R9	REEFER CONT.(NO FOOD)
42RS	REEFER CONT.(DIESEL GEN.)	42R3	REEFER CONT.(DIESEL GEN.)
42RT	REEFER CONTAINER	42R1	REEFER CONTAINER
42SN	NAMED CARGO CONTAINER	42S1	NAMED CARGO CONTAINER
42TD	TANK CONTAINER	42T5	TANK CONTAINER
		42T6	TANK CONTAINER
42TG	TANK CONTAINER	42T8	TANK CONTAINER
42TN	TANK CONTAINER	42T2	TANK CONTAINER
42UP	HARDTOP CONTAINER	42U6	HARDTOP CONTAINER
42UT	OPEN TOP CONTAINER	42U1	OPEN TOP CONTAINER
45BK	BULK CONTAINER	45B3	BULK CONTAINER
45GP	HIGH CUBE CONT.	45G0	HIGH CUBE CONT.
		45G1	HIGH CUBE CONT.
45PC	FLAT (COLLAPSIBLE)	45P3	FLAT (COLLAPSIBLE)
		45P8	FLAT (COLL.FLUSH FOLDING)
45RC	REEFER CONT.(NO FOOD)	45R9	REEFER CONT.(NO FOOD)
45RT	REEFER HIGHCUBE CONTAINER	45R1	REEFER HIGHCUBE CONTAINER
45UT	OPEN TOP CONTAINER	45U1	OPEN TOP CONTAINER
45UP	HIGH CUBE HARDTOP CONT.	45U6	HIGH CUBE HARDTOP CONT.
46HR	INSULATED CONTAINER	46H0	INSULATED CONTAINER
48TG	TANK FOR GAS	48T8	TANK FOR GAS
49PL	PLATFORM	49P0	PLATFORM
4CGP	GP CONTAINER	4CG0	GP CONTAINER (WIDTH 2.5 M)
L0GP	HIGH CUBE CONT.	L0G1	HIGH CUBE CONT.
L2GP	HIGH CUBE CONT.	L2G1	HIGH CUBE CONT.
L5GP	HIGH CUBE CONT.	L5G1	HIGH CUBE CONT.

Use the below to calculate Length/Height/Type of less commonly used ISO 6346 container:

ISO Length Codes		ISO Height Codes	
Code	**Description**	**Code**	**Description**
1	10'	0	8'
2	20'	2	8'6"
3	30'	4	9'
4	40'	5	9'6"
B	24'	6	9'6"
C	24'6"	8	4'3"
G	41'	9	4'3"
H	43'	C	8'6" × 8'3"
L	45'	D	9' × 8'3"
M	48'	E	9'6" × 8'3"
N	49'	9	9'6" × 8'3"

ISO Type Codes

Code	Description
G0	General - Openings at one or both ends
G1	General - Passive vents at upper part of cargo space
G2	General - Openings at one or both ends + full openings on one or both sides
G3	General - Openings at one or both ends + partial openings on one or both sides
V0	Fantainer - Non-mechanical, vents at lower and upper parts of cargo space
V2	Fantainer - Mechanical ventilation system located internally
V4	Fantainer - Mechanical ventilation system located externally
R0	Integral Reefer - Mechanically refrigerated
R1	Integral Reefer - Mechanically refrigerated and heated
R2	Integral Reefer - Self powered mechanically refrigirated
R3	Integral Reefer - Self powered mechanically refrigirated and heated
H0	Refrigerated or heated with removable equipment located externally; heat transfer coefficient K=0.4W/M2.K
H1	Refrigerated or heated with removable equipment located internally
H2	Refrigerated or heated with removable equipment located externally; heat transfer coefficient K=0.7W/M2.K
H5	Insulated - Heat transfer coefficient K=0.4W/M2.K
H6	Insulated - Heat transfer coefficient K=0.7W/M2.K
U0	Open Top - Openings at one or both ends
U1	Open Top - Idem + removable top members in end frames
U2	Open Top - Openings at one or both ends + openings at one or both sides

Code	Description
U3	Open Top - Idem + removable top members in end frames
U4	Open Top - Openings at one or both ends + partial on one and full at other side
U5	Open Top - Complete, fixed side and end walls (no doors)
T0	Tank - Non dangerous liquids, minimum pressure 0.45 bar
T1	Tank - Non dangerous liquids, minimum pressure 1.50 bar
T2	Tank - Non dangerous liquids, minimum pressure 2.65 bar
T3	Tank - Dangerous liquids, minimum pressure 1.50 bar
T4	Tank - Dangerous liquids, minimum pressure 2.65 bar
T5	Tank - Dangerous liquids, minimum pressure 4.00 bar
T6	Tank - Dangerous liquids, minimum pressure 6.00 bar
T7	Tank - Gases, minimum pressure 9.10 bar
T8	Tank - Gases, minimum pressure 22.00 bar
T9	Tank - Gases, minimum pressure to be decided
B0	Bulk - Closed
B1	Bulk - Airtight
B3	Bulk - Horizontal discharge, test pressure 1.50 bar
B4	Bulk - Horizontal discharge, test pressure 2.65 bar
B5	Bulk - Tipping discharge, test pressure 1.50 bar
B6	Bulk - Tipping discharge, test pressure 2.65 bar
P0	Flat or Bolter - Plain platform
P1	Flat or Bolter - Two complete and fixed ends
P2	Flat or Bolter - Fixed posts, either free-standing or with removable top member
P3	Flat or Bolter - Folding complete end structure
P4	Flat or Bolter - Folding posts, either free-standing or with removable top member
P5	Flat or Bolter - Open top, open ends (skeletal)
S0	Livestock carrier
S1	Automobile carrier
S2	Live fish carrier

Index

DOI 10.1515/9781547400874-027

Made in the USA
Coppell, TX
19 May 2021